Windows Server 2012 R2 Inside Out: Services, Security, & Infrastructure

William R. Stanek

PUBLISHED BY
Microsoft Press
A Division of Microsoft Corporation
One Microsoft Way
Redmond, Washington 98052-6399

Library of Congress Control Number: 2013955708
ISBN: 978-0-7356-8255-9

Printed and bound in the United States of America.

First Printing

Microsoft Press books are available through booksellers and distributors worldwide. If you need support related to this book, email Microsoft Press Book Support at mspinput@microsoft.com. Please tell us what you think of this book at http://aka.ms/tellpress.

Acquisitions Editor: Anne Hamilton
Developmental Editor: Karen Szall
Project Editor: Rosemary Caperton
Editorial Production: nSight, Inc.
Technical Reviewer: Charlie Russel; Technical Review services provided by Content Master, a member of CM Group, Ltd.
Copyeditor: Joseph Gustaitis
Indexer: Lucie Haskins
Cover: Twist Creative • Seattle

To my readers—Windows Server 2012 R2 Inside Out: Services, Security, & Infrastructure *is my 49th book for Microsoft Press. Thank you for being there with me through many books and many years. It's been an honor and a privilege.*

To my wife—for many years, through many books, many millions of words, and many thousands of pages she's been there, providing support and encouragement and making every place we've lived a home.

To my kids—for helping me see the world in new ways, for having exceptional patience and boundless love, and for making every day an adventure.

To Anne, Karen, Martin, Lucinda, Juliana, and many others who've helped out in ways both large and small.

Special thanks to my son Will for not only installing and managing my extensive dev lab for all my books since Windows 8 Pocket Consultant *but for also performing check reads of all those books as well.*

—WILLIAM R. STANEK

Contents at a glance

Table of contents

What do you think of this book? We want to hear from you!

Microsoft is interested in hearing your feedback so we can improve our books and learning resources
for you. To participate in a brief survey, please visit:

http://aka.ms/tellpress

What do you think of this book? We want to hear from you!

Microsoft is interested in hearing your feedback so we can improve our books and learning resources for you. To participate in a brief survey, please visit:

http://aka.ms/tellpress

Introduction

Welcome to *Windows Server 2012 R2 Inside Out: Services, Security, & Infrastructure*. As the author of many popular technology books, I've been writing professionally about Microsoft Windows and Windows Server since 1994. Over the years I've gained a unique perspective—the kind of perspective you can gain only after working with technologies for a long time. The advantage for you, the reader, is that my solid understanding of these technologies allowed me to dig into Windows Server 2012 R2 architecture, internals, and configuration to see how things really work under the hood and then pass this information on to you throughout this book.

Anyone transitioning to Windows Server 2012 R2 from Windows Server 2012 might be surprised at just how much has been updated as changes both subtle and substantial have been made throughout the operating system. For anyone transitioning to Windows Server 2012 R2 from Windows Server 2008 R2 or an earlier release of Windows Server, I'll let you know right up front that Windows Server 2012 and Windows Server 2012 R2 are substantially different from earlier versions of Windows Server. Not only are there major changes throughout the operating system, but also this just might be the first version of Windows Server that you manage using a touch-based user interface. If you do end up managing it this way, mastering the touch-based UI and the revised interface options will be essential for your success. For this reason, I discuss both the touch UI and the traditional mouse and keyboard techniques throughout this book.

When you are working with touch UI–enabled computers, you can manipulate onscreen elements in ways that weren't previously possible. You can enter text using the onscreen keyboard and manipulate onscreen elements in the following ways:

- **Tap.** Tap an item by touching it with your finger. A tap or double-tap of elements on the screen is generally the equivalent of a mouse click or double-click.

- **Press and hold.** Press your finger down and leave it there for a few seconds. Pressing and holding elements on the screen is generally the equivalent of a right-click.

- **Swipe to select.** Slide an item a short distance in the opposite direction from how the page scrolls. This selects the items and also might bring up related commands. If pressing and holding doesn't display commands and options for an item, try swiping to select instead.

- **Swipe from edge (slide in from edge).** Starting from the edge of the screen, swipe or slide in. Sliding in from the right edge opens the Charms panel. Sliding in from the left edge shows open apps and allows you to easily switch between them. Sliding in from the top or bottom edge shows commands for the active element.

- **Pinch.** Touch an item with two or more fingers and then move those fingers toward each other. Pinching zooms out.

- **Stretch.** Touch an item with two or more fingers and then move those fingers away from each other. Stretching zooms in.

In this book I teach you how server roles, role services, and features work; why they work the way they do; and how to customize them to meet your needs. Regardless of your job title, if you're deploying, configuring, managing, or maintaining Windows Server 2012 R2, this book is for you. To pack in as much information as possible, I had to assume that you have basic networking skills and a basic understanding of Windows Server and that you are familiar with Windows commands and procedures. With this in mind, I don't devote entire chapters to basic skills or to why you want to use Windows Server. Instead, I focus on essential services, infrastructure servers, and security.

Conventions

The following conventions are used in this book:

- **Abbreviated menu commands.** For your convenience, this book uses abbreviated menu commands. For example, "Tap or click Tools, Track Changes, Highlight Changes" means that you should tap or click the Tools menu, select Track Changes, and then tap or click the Highlight Changes command.

- **Boldface type.** **Boldface** type is used to indicate text that you enter or type.

- **Initial Capital Letters.** The first letters of the names of menus, dialog boxes, dialog box elements, and commands are capitalized. Example: the Save As dialog box.

- **Italicized type.** *Italicized* type is used to indicate new terms.

- **Plus sign (+) in text.** Keyboard shortcuts are indicated by a plus sign (+) separating two key names. For example, Ctrl+Alt+Delete means that you press the Ctrl, Alt, and Delete keys at the same time.

How to reach the author

Email: williamstanek@aol.com

Web: *http://www.williamrstanek.com/*

Facebook: *https://www.facebook.com/William.Stanek.Author*

Twitter: *http://twitter.com/williamstanek*

Errata and book support

We've made every effort to ensure the accuracy of this book and its companion content. You can access updates to this book—in the form of a list of submitted errata and their related corrections—at:

http://aka.ms/WSIO_R2_SSI

If you discover an error that is not already listed, please submit it to us at the same page.

If you need additional support, email Microsoft Press Book Support at *mspinput@microsoft.com*.

Please note that product support for Microsoft software and hardware is not offered through the previous addresses. For help with Microsoft software or hardware, go to *http://support.microsoft.com*.

We want to hear from you

At Microsoft Press your satisfaction is our top priority and your feedback our most valuable asset. Please tell us what you think of this book at:

http://aka.ms/tellpress

We know you're busy, so we've kept it short with just a few questions. Your answers go directly to the editors at Microsoft Press. (No personal information will be requested.) Thanks in advance for your input!

Stay in touch

Let's keep the conversation going! We're on Twitter: *http://twitter.com/MicrosoftPress*.

CHAPTER 1

Using Remote Desktop for Management

Systems that run Microsoft Windows Server 2012 R2 are the heart of any Windows network. These are the systems that provide the essential services and applications for users and the network as a whole. As an administrator, your job is to keep these systems running, and to do this you must be able to connect to them no matter where they are located and no matter where you might be. Your front-line defenses in managing systems running Windows Server 2012 R2 are the administration and the support tools, many of which have built-in features for working remotely.

To run most of the administration tools, you must have Administrator privileges. If these aren't included with your current account, you need to provide the credentials for the administrator account when you see the User Account Control prompt.

The one tool you'll use the most for system administration tasks is Server Manager. Server Manager provides setup and configuration options for the local server and options for managing roles, features, and related settings on any remotely manageable server in the enterprise. On servers, Server Manager is pinned to Start and the desktop taskbar by default. This means that you can open Server Manager by tapping or clicking the related Start tile or by tapping or clicking the related taskbar button.

Many other utilities are available for administering Windows Server 2012 R2 systems. The tools you'll use the most include the following:

- **Control Panel.** A collection of tools for managing system configuration. You can organize Control Panel in different ways according to the view you're using. A view is simply a way of organizing and presenting options. Category view is the default view, and it provides access to tools by category, tool, and key tasks. Icons view is an alternative view that lists each tool separately by name.

- **Graphical administrative tools.** The key tools for managing network computers and their resources. You can access these tools by choosing them individually from the Tools menu in Server Manager.

- **Administrative wizards.** Tools designed to automate key administrative tasks. You can access many administrative wizards in Server Manager—the central administration console for Windows Server 2012 R2.

- **Command-line utilities.** You can launch most administrative utilities from the command line. In addition to these utilities, Windows Server 2012 R2 provides others that are useful for working with Windows Server 2012 R2 systems.

- **Windows PowerShell cmdlets.** Windows PowerShell is a full-featured command shell that can use built-in commands called *cmdlets*, built-in programming features, and standard command-line utilities. Use Windows PowerShell for additional flexibility in your command-line scripting.

Remote support also is an important part of administration. Although Server Manager and related Microsoft Management Consoles (MMCs) enable you to perform remote management, you might prefer to connect and work with remote systems as if you were logged on locally, and Remote Desktop enables you to do this. Remote Desktop has traditionally been the administrator's primary method of remote support, and the technology is the subject of this chapter.

Remote Desktop essentials

Using Remote Desktop, you can use a local area network (LAN), a wide area network (WAN), or an Internet connection to manage computers remotely with the Windows graphical interface. Because all the application processing is performed on the remote system, only the data from devices such as the display, keyboard, and mouse are transmitted over the network.

Remote Desktop is part of Remote Desktop Services. Microsoft has separated Remote Desktop Services into two operating modes:

- Remote Desktop mode

- Remote Desktop Server mode

You enable and configure Remote Desktop using the System utility in Control Panel. You set up a Remote Desktop Server by installing and configuring the appropriate role services for the Remote Desktop Services role.

To be operational, the Remote Desktop and Remote Desktop Server modes both depend on the Remote Desktop Services service being installed and running on the server. By default, the Remote Desktop Services service is installed and configured to run automatically. Both features use the same client, Remote Desktop Connection (RDC), for connecting to remote systems.

NOTE

Remote Desktop isn't designed for application serving. Most productivity applications, such as Microsoft Office Word, Outlook, and Excel, require specific environment settings that are not available through this feature. If you want to work with these types of applications (rather than with server applications), you should install and use the Remote Desktop Services role.

No Remote Desktop Client Access License (RD CAL) is required to use Remote Desktop. Windows Server 2012 R2 allows two active administration sessions:

- One administrator can be logged on locally, and another administrator can be logged on remotely.

- Two administrators can be logged on remotely.

Most remote sessions run in admin mode. The reason for this is that the admin session provides full functionality for administration. Standard Remote Desktop Services connections are created as virtual sessions.

Why is this important? Using admin mode, you can interact with the server just as if you were sitting at the keyboard. This means that all notification area messages directed to the console are visible remotely. For security, only two sessions are allowed. If a third administrator tries to log on, the administrator will be prompted to end an existing session so that the administrator can log on.

Although it's recommended that administrators use admin sessions, you can use virtual sessions—hey, that's what they're there for! When working with a virtual session, you can perform most administration tasks and your key limitation is in your ability to interact with the console session itself. This means that users logged on using a virtual session don't see console messages or notifications, can't install some programs, and can't perform tasks that require console access.

You'll want to formalize a general policy on how Remote Desktop should be used in your organization. You don't want multiple administrators trying to perform administration tasks on a system because this could cause serious problems. For example, if two administrators are both working with Disk Management, this could cause serious problems with the volumes on the remote system. Because of this, you'll want to coordinate administration tasks with other administrators.

Additionally, it's important to point out that you can't change display settings remotely. The reason for this is that you are working in a virtual display session whether you are running Remote Desktop in admin mode or virtual session mode, and in a virtual display session the display settings are locked.

Configuring Remote Desktop

The two components of Remote Desktop you need to support and configure are Remote Desktop Services for the server portion and the Remote Desktop Connection (RDC) for the client portion.

Enabling Remote Desktop on servers

Enabling the Remote Desktop mode on all servers on your network is recommended, especially for servers in remote sites that have no local administrators. To view the current status of Remote Desktop on the server, select Local Server in Server Manager and then check the enabled or disabled status for the Remote Desktop entry. Just because Remote Desktop is enabled doesn't mean that the feature is fully configured. With that in mind, tap or click the Enabled or Disabled link for the Remote Desktop entry. This opens the System Properties dialog box to the Remote tab, as shown in Figure 1-1.

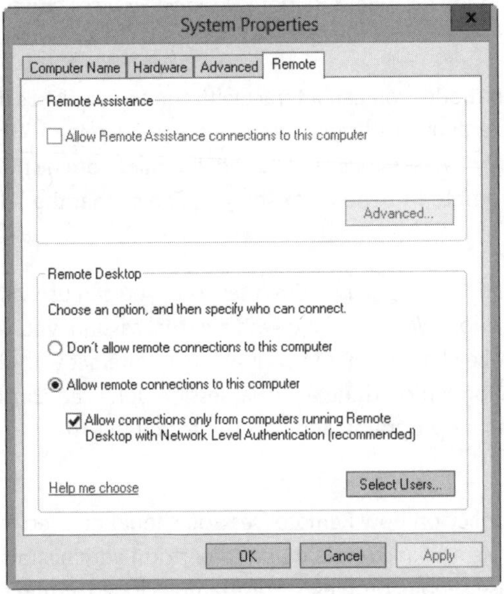

Figure 1-1 Enable Remote Desktop.

You have two configuration options for enabling Remote Desktop. You can do either of the following:

- Select Allow Remote Connections To This Computer, which allows connections from any version of Windows.

- Select Allow Remote Connections To This Computer and also select the Allow Connections Only From Computers Running Remote Desktop With Network Level Authentication check box to allow connections only from Windows Vista or later and from other computers with secure network authentication.

Keep in mind the following details about using Remote Desktop:

- All remote connections must be established using accounts that have passwords. If a local account on the system doesn't have a password, you can't use the account to connect to the system remotely.

- If the computer is running Windows Firewall, the operating system automatically creates an exception that allows Remote Desktop Protocol (RDP) connections to be established. The default port used is TCP port 3389. The registry value HKEY_LOCAL_MACHINE \System\CurrentControlSet\Control\TerminalServer\WinStations\RDP-Tcp\PortNumber controls the actual setting.

- If you are running a different firewall on the computer, you must open a port on the firewall to allow incoming RDP connections to be established. Again, the default port used is TCP port 3389.

Inside OUT
Authentication certificate validation

Before establishing an RDP connection, your computer validates the remote computer's identify by default. If the remote computer's authentication certificate is invalid or has expired, you won't be allowed to connect and will see a warning prompt stating, "The authentication certificate received from the remote computer has expired or is not valid." Because a date/time disparity between the two computers can make it appear that the authentication certificate is invalid, you should check the current date and time on both computers.

If you don't want your computer to authenticate the remote computer's identity, you can disable this feature by setting the Server Authentication option to Connect And Don't Warn Me. To set the Server Authentication option, tap or click Options to display the additional configuration tabs, tap or click the Advanced tab, and then use the selection list on the Server Authentication panel to set the option as desired. However, disabling authentication is significantly less secure because you can no longer be certain that you are actually connecting to the server you think you are. A DNS exploit, for example, could retarget your RDP session. Although session retargeting isn't a big risk when you are working on a LAN, it could be a more significant concern when you are connecting to a server over a WAN or an Internet connection.

Permitting and restricting remote logon

By default, all members of the Administrators group can log on remotely. The Remote Desktop Users group has been added to Active Directory to ease managing Remote Desktop Services users. Members of this group are allowed to log on remotely.

If you want to add a member to this group, select Local Server in Server Manager and then tap or click the Enabled or Disabled link for the Remote Desktop entry. This opens the System Properties dialog box to the Remote tab. In the Remote tab, tap or click Select Users. As shown in Figure 1-2, any current members of the Remote Desktop Users group are listed in the Remote Desktop Users dialog box. To add users or groups to the list, tap or click Add. This opens the Select Users Or Groups dialog box.

Figure 1-2 Configure Remote Desktop users.

In the Select Users Or Groups dialog box, type the name of a user in the selected or default domain and then tap or click Check Names. If multiple matches are found, select the name or names you want to use and then tap or click OK. If no matches are found, either you entered an incorrect name part or you're working with an incorrect location. Modify the name and try again or tap or click Locations to select a new location. To add users or groups, type a semi-colon (;) and then repeat this procedure. When you tap or click OK, the users and groups are added to the list in the Remote Desktop Users dialog box.

In Group Policy, members of the Administrators and Remote Desktop Users groups have the user right Allow Log On Through Remote Desktop Services by default. If you modified Group Policy, you might need to double-check to ensure that this user right is still granted to these groups. Typically, you will want to do this through local policy on a per-machine basis. You can also do this through site, domain, and organizational policy. Access the appropriate Group Policy Object and select Computer Configuration, Windows Settings, Security Settings, Local

Policies, and User Rights Assignments. To see a list of users and groups currently granted this right, double-tap or double-click Allow Log On Through Remote Desktop Services.

Inside OUT

Restrict remote logon through Group Policy

If you want to restrict users or groups from remotely administering a server, access the appropriate Group Policy Object and expand Computer Configuration\Windows Settings\Security Settings\Local Policies\User Rights Assignments. Double-tap or double-click Deny Log On Through Remote Desktop Services. In the policy Properties dialog box, select Define These Policy Settings and then tap or click Add User Or Group. In the Add User Or Group dialog box, tap or click Browse. This displays the Select Users, Computers, Or Groups dialog box. Type the name of the user or group for which you want to deny logon through Remote Desktop Services and then tap or click OK. You can also change the default permissions for groups in the Remote Desktop Services Configuration tool. For instance, you could remove Administrators from having Full Control of the Remote Desktop Services objects.

Configuring Remote Desktop through Group Policy

Remote Desktop is part of Remote Desktop Services, and you can use Group Policy to configure Remote Desktop Services. Microsoft recommends using Group Policy as the first choice when you are configuring Remote Desktop Services for use with Remote Desktop. The precedence hierarchy for Remote Desktop Services configuration is as follows:

- Computer-level Group Policy

- User-level Group Policy

- Local computer policy using the Remote Desktop Services Configuration tool

- User policy on the Local User And Group level

- Local client settings

You can configure local policy on individual computers or on an organizational unit (OU) in a domain. You can use Group Policy to configure Remote Desktop Services settings per connection, per user, per computer, or for groups of computers in an OU of a domain. You modify the Group Policy settings for Remote Desktop Services by using the Group Policy Object Editor. These settings are located in Computer Configuration\Administrative Templates\Windows Components\Remote Desktop Services and in User Configuration\Administrative Templates \Windows Components\Remote Desktop Services.

Create a separate OU for Remote Desktop Services

Typically, Remote Desktop is used throughout an organization, but Remote Desktop Services servers are isolated to a particular group of servers operating in a separate OU. So if you plan to also use Remote Desktop Services servers in the organization, you should consider creating a separate OU for the Remote Desktop Services servers. This way you can manage Remote Desktop Services servers separately from Remote Desktop.

Tracking who's logged on

When you deploy Remote Desktop Services, you can use the Remote Desktop Services Manager to view and manage logon sessions. With Remote Desktop, you can use this as well, but you typically don't need all the additional options and details. A more basic way to keep track of who is logged on to a server is to use the QUSER command. Type **quser** to see who is logged on to the system on which you are running the command prompt, or type **quser /server:ServerName** to see who is logged on to a remote server. Consider the following example:

```
USERNAME      SESSIONNAME      ID    STATE     IDLE TIME    LOGON TIME
tedg          rdp-tcp#1        1     Active    .            5/04/2014 11:42 AM
Wrstanek      console          2     Active    2:27         5/04/2014 09:43 AM
```

Here, there are two active sessions:

- TEDG is logged on to an active RDP session. The session ID is 1, meaning it is Session 1.

- WRSTANEK is logged on locally to the console. The session ID is 2, meaning it is Session 2.

You can also use Task Manager to view user sessions. If you want to examine user sessions on a computer to which you are logged on locally, press Ctrl+Alt+Delete and then tap or click Task Manager. If you want to examine user sessions on a computer to which you are logged on remotely, press and hold or right-click the Windows button in the lower-left corner of the desktop or Start screen and then select Task Manager.

In the Task Manager dialog box, if details are not displayed, select More Details and then tap or click the Users tab. Here, each user connection is listed by default with user name, status, CPU utilization, and memory usage. You can add other columns by pressing and holding or right-clicking any column header and then tapping or clicking the columns to add. If you double-tap or double-click a user's name, there's an entry for each running process. Processes are listed by name, CPU usage, and memory usage.

You can also use Task Manager to manage remote user sessions:

- To disconnect a user session, select the user entry, tap or click Disconnect, and then, when prompted to confirm the action, tap or click Disconnect User.

- To log off a user, select the user entry, tap or click Logoff, and then, when prompted to confirm the action, tap or click Log Off User.

The difference between disconnecting a session and logging off a session is important. When you disconnect a session, the session goes into a disconnected state and continues executing current processes. If you log off a user, you end that user's session, closing any applications the user was running and ending any foreground processes the user was running as well. A foreground process is a process being run by an active application as opposed to a background or batch process being run independently from the user session.

When you are working remotely, you can use the Shutdown Or Sign Out options to disconnect a remote session or shut down a remote server. To do this, press and hold or right-click the Windows button in the lower-left corner of the desktop or Start screen. On the shortcut menu, select Shutdown Or Sign Out and then select either Disconnect or Shutdown as appropriate.

Although you can't use the Shutdown Or Sign Out options to shut down a remote desktop computer running Windows 8 or later, you can use the Shutdown utility to shut down a remote desktop computer. At a prompt, enter **shutdown /s** to shut down the computer or **shutdown /r** to shut down and restart the computer.

Supporting Remote Desktop Connection clients

The Remote Desktop Connection client is the Remote Desktop Services client. It uses the Microsoft Remote Desktop Protocol (RDP) version 6.0 or later. Clients can use the Remote Desktop Connection client to connect to a remote server or workstation that has been set up to be administered remotely.

Remote Desktop Connection client

Most current versions of Windows include the Remote Desktop Connection client. The features you should be aware of when supporting RDC are the following:

- Custom display resolutions allow for high-color and full-screen viewing. Resolutions of 1680 × 1920, 1920 × 1200, and higher are fully supported. To set the resolution from a command prompt or from the Search box, add the /w and /h options, such as **mstsc /w:1920 /h:1200**. In an RDP file, you can set the screen size using desktopwidth and desktopheight, such as **desktopwidth:i:1920** or **desktopheight:i:1200**.

- Monitor spanning settings enable you to display remote sessions across multiple monitors. All monitors must be horizontally aligned and use the same resolution. The maximum resolution across all monitors shouldn't exceed 4096 × 2048. To enable monitor spanning from a command prompt or from the Search box, add the /span option, such as **mstsc /span**. In an RDP file, you can enable spanning by typing **Use Span:i:1**.

- As an alternative to monitor spanning, you can enable multiple monitor support to expand a remote session across all the monitors on your local computer regardless of the monitor configuration. To enable multiple monitor support from a command prompt or from the Search box, add the /multimon option, such as **mstsc /multimon**. In an RDP file you can enable spanning by typing **Use Multimon:i:1**. You also can just select the Use All Monitors For The Remote Session check box in the Display tab.

- By default, data sent between the client and the server is encrypted at the maximum key strength supported by the client. If you configure RDP on your Remote Desktop Services server to require high encryption, a client can make a connection only if it supports 128-bit or higher encryption.

- If a connection is interrupted or lost while you are performing a task, the client software attempts to reconnect to the session and, in the interim, processing continues on the server so that any running processes can be finished without interruption. If for some reason you are unable to log on remotely after you are disconnected, you can access your logon session by logging on locally.

Enhanced experience settings include font smoothing and display data prioritization. Font smoothing ensures that computer fonts appear clear and smooth (as long as the desktop has ClearType enabled). Display data prioritization gives priority to display, keyboard, and mouse data over other types of data, such as printing or file transfers. The default bandwidth ratio is 70:30. This means that display and input data is allocated 70 percent of the bandwidth and all other traffic, such as file transfers or print jobs, is allocated 30 percent of the bandwidth.

You can adjust the data prioritization settings by making changes to the registry of the Remote Desktop Services server. Change the value of the following entries under the HKEY_LOCAL_MACHINE\SYSTEM\CurrentControlSet\Services\TermDD subkey:

- FlowControlDisable

- FlowControlDisplayBandwidth

- FlowControlChannelBandwidth

- FlowControlChargePostCompression

When working with flow control, keep the following in mind:

- If these entries don't appear, you can create them. To do this, press and hold or right-click TermDD, point to New, and then tap or click DWORD (32-bit) Value.

- You can disable display data prioritization completely by setting the value of FlowControlDisable to 1. If you do this, all requests are handled on a first-in-first-out basis and other registry settings are ignored.

- You can set the relative bandwidth priority for display and input data by setting the FlowControlDisplayBandwidth value. The default value is 70. The maximum allowed value is 255.

- You can set the relative bandwidth priority for other data, such as file transfers or print jobs, by setting the FlowControlChannelBandwidth value. The default value is 30. The maximum allowed value is 255.

- The bandwidth ratio for display data prioritization is based on the values you set. For example, if you set FlowControlDisplayBandwidth to 200 and FlowControlChannelBandwidth to 50, the ratio is 200:50 (or 4:1), so display and input data is allocated 80 percent of the bandwidth.

- The FlowControlChargePostCompression value determines whether the bandwidth allocation is based on the precompression or postcompression data size. The default value is 0, which means that the calculation is based on the size of the data before it's compressed. This is the value you'll usually want to use. This setting ensures that the client doesn't have to wait or perform compression calculations prior to sending data.

- If you make any changes to the registry values, you need to restart the Remote Desktop Services for the changes to take effect.

Resource redirection enables the client computer to handle audio, mapped drives, ports, printers, and certain key combinations. If an application generates audio feedback, such as an error notification, this can be redirected to the client. Key combinations that perform application functions are passed to the remote server, except for Ctrl+Alt+Delete, which is handled by the client computer. Local devices such as drives, printers, and serial ports are also available. Because both local and network drives are available on the client, users can easily access local drives and transfer files between the client and the server.

Plug and Play device redirection extends the resource redirection features to enable locally connected and supported Plug and Play devices to be installed on and used with a remote computer. You can now redirect media players that support Media Transfer Protocol (MTP) and digital cameras that support Picture Transfer Protocol (PTP). Plug and Play notifications will appear in the taskbar on the remote computer. When you start a remote session for the first time after connecting a supported device locally, you should see the device become installed automatically on the remote computer. After the redirected device is installed on the remote computer, the device is available for use in your session with the remote computer. For example, if you are redirecting a Windows Portable Device (WPD), such as a digital camera, you can access the device directly from a remote application.

You can control Plug and Play device redirection in the Client Settings tab in the Remote Desktop Services Configuration tool (tsconfig.msc). Use the Supported Plug And Play Devices options. You can also control Plug and Play device redirection by using Group Policy. To do this, you can use the Do Not Allow Supported Plug And Play Device Redirection policy setting in the Administrative Templates for Computer Configuration under Windows Components \Remote Desktop Services\Remote Desktop Session Host\Device and Resource Redirection. You can find several related policy settings under Computer Configuration\Administrative Templates\System\Device Installation\Device Installation Restrictions.

Running the Remote Desktop Connection client

As discussed previously, you now can open two administrator sessions on computers that run Windows Server 2012 R2 without needing an RD CAL. The use of an admin or console session greatly enhances your capabilities as an administrator to successfully execute programs, applications, and processes that will not run in a virtual session.

There are several ways to start the Remote Desktop Connection client:

- **Run in admin mode.** Admin mode is used by administrators to enable full interaction with the console of the remote system. To run the client in admin mode, type **mstsc /admin** at the command prompt or in the Apps Search box.

- **Run in virtual session mode.** Virtual session mode is used by administrators and users to start a virtual session on a remote system. To run the client in virtual session mode, type **mstsc** at the command prompt or in the Apps Search box.

After the client is started, enter the name or Internet Protocol (IP) address of the computer to which you want to connect, as shown in Figure 1-3. If you don't know the name of the computer, you may be able to use the drop-down list. This list displays computers to which you've previously connected.

By default, Windows uses your current user name and domain to log on to the remote computer. If you want to use different account information, tap or click Options and then enter your user name in the field provided. (See Figure 1-4.) To set the domain, you can enter your user name in the DOMAIN\USERNAME format, such as ADATUM\WILLIAMS. Select the Allow Me To Save Credentials check box to enable automatic logon if desired.

Figure 1-3 Specify the remote computer with which to establish a connection.

NOTE
Even if you select the Allow Me To Save Credentials check box, you might be prompted to enter your password during the logon process. This depends on your network's policies and the configuration of the Remote Desktop Services server.

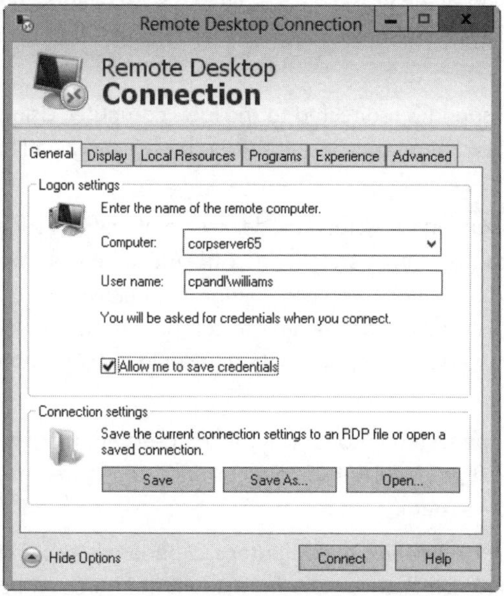

Figure 1-4 Set RDC options.

CHAPTER 1

There are six tabs you can use to change the client settings:

- **General.** You might want to use these options to save keystrokes by adding logon information. Rather than typing in your settings each time, you can save the connection settings and load them when you want to make a connection.

  To save the current connection settings, tap or click Save As and then use the Save As dialog box to save the .rdp file for the connection.

  To load previously saved connection settings, tap or click Open and then use the Open dialog box to find and open the previously saved connection settings.

- **Display.** The default settings for RDC are full-screen and high-color. You can modify these settings here.

  Use the Display Configuration option to set the screen size. The size options available depend on the display size on the local computer.

  Use the Colors option to choose the preferred color depth. The default is 32-bit highest-quality color, but settings on the remote computer might override this setting.

- **Local Resources.** You can modify the way the resource and device redirection work, including audio redirection, keystroke combination redirection, and local device and resource redirection.

  By default, remote computer sound is redirected to the local computer. Using the Remote Audio option, you can change the default setting by selecting Do Not Play or Play On Remote Computer.

  By default, when you are working in full-screen mode, key combinations such as Alt+Tab and Ctrl+Esc are redirected to the remote system and Ctrl+Alt+Delete is handled locally. Using Apply Windows Key Combinations, you can change this behavior so that key combinations are sent to the local computer or the remote computer only. However, if you send key combinations to the remote computer only, you could get into a situation in which you can't log on locally.

  By default, local printers are connected automatically when users are logged on to the remote computer. This makes it easy to print to your currently configured printers when you are working with a remote system.

  By default, anything you copy to the remote computer's Clipboard is copied to the local computer's Clipboard. This makes it easy to copy from a remote source and paste into a local source.

  To see additional options, tap or click More on the Local Devices And Resource panel. By default, the additional options ensure that smart cards connected to a remote computer are available for use in your remote session. You can also connect serial ports, local disk drives, and supported Plug and Play devices to make them available for use. Drives and supported devices can be selected by name, or you can just select the Drives and Supported Plug And Play Devices options to make all drives and devices available for use. Selecting drives allows you to easily transfer files between the local computer and the remote computer. Selecting Plug and Play devices allows you to work with supported devices, including media players and digital cameras.

- **Programs.** From this dialog box, you can configure the execution of programs when a session starts. Select the Start The Following Program On Connection check box and then set the program path or file name and the start folder for the program.

- **Experience.** You can select the connection speed and other network performance settings. For optimal performance, choose the connection speed you are using, such as Modem (56 Kbps) or LAN (10 Mbps or higher), and allow only bitmap caching.

  Other options you can allow include Desktop Background, Font Smoothing, Desktop Composition, Show Window Contents While Dragging, Menu And Window Animation, and Visual Styles. If you select these additional check boxes, you cause additional processing on the remote system and additional network traffic, which can slow down performance. Desktop composition creates an enhanced desktop as long as you installed the Desktop Experience feature on the Remote Desktop Services servers and clients that are using Windows Vista or later. Font Smoothing allows the client to pass through ClearType fonts as long as Clear Type is enabled (which is the default setting).

  By default, Reconnect If Connection Is Dropped is selected. If the session is interrupted, the RDC will try to reconnect it automatically. Getting disconnected from a connection doesn't stop processing. The session will go into a disconnected state and continue executing whatever processes the session was running.

- **Advanced.** You can select these options to control the use of server authentication and the Remote Desktop Gateway feature. By default, the RDP client is configured to warn you if the authentication protocols fail and automatically detect RD Gateway settings.

When you tap or click Connect, you are connected to the remote system. Enter your account password if prompted and then tap or click OK. If the connection is successful, you'll see the Remote Desktop window on the selected computer and you'll be able to work with resources on the computer. In the case of a failed connection, check the information you provided and then try to connect again.

When you are working in full-screen mode, a connection bar is displayed at the top of the screen. On the left side of the connection bar is a push pin. If you tap or click the push pin, it unpins the connection bar so that the bar disappears when you move the mouse away. To make the bar reappear, you need to point the mouse to the top part of the screen. On the right side of the connection bar are several other buttons. The first button switches you to the local desktop. The second button switches between full mode and tile display mode. The third button disconnects the remote session.

Disconnecting from a session does not end a session. The session continues to run on the server, and this uses resources and can prevent other users from connecting because only one console session and two virtual sessions are allowed. The proper way to end a session is to sign off the remote computer just as you would a local computer. In the Remote Desktop Connection window, press and hold or right-click the Windows button in the lower-left corner of the desktop or Start screen. On the shortcut menu, select Shutdown Or Sign Out and then select Sign Out.

CAUTION

Don't try to log off the remote session by pressing Ctrl+Alt+Delete and tapping or clicking Logoff. Doing this will log you off the console session on your local client but still leave the remote session running on the Remote Desktop Server.

Connecting to a virtual machine in Windows Azure

For a virtual machine that is running the Windows Server operating system in a Windows Azure environment, you use the Connect button in the Windows Azure Management Portal to start a Remote Desktop Connection. When you set up a new virtual machine using the Windows Azure Management Portal, you specify the TCP port for Remote Desktop connections and the TCP port for remote Windows PowerShell connections.

By default, TCP port 3389 is used for Remote Desktop connections to virtual machines and TCP port 5986 is used for remote Windows PowerShell connections to virtual machines. Although these ports may be open on your company's firewall, any nonstandard ports that you configure as alternatives will need to be accessible through your company's firewall to access external virtual machines.

You can establish a Remote Desktop connection to a virtual machine in a Windows Azure environment by completing the following steps:

1. In a web browser, enter **https://manage.windowsazure.com** in the Address box.

2. Sign in to Windows Azure by entering the email address and password of an authorized Microsoft account and then selecting Sign In.

3. In the Windows Azure Management Portal, click Virtual Machines and then select the virtual machine you want to work with.

4. The main pane provides options for working with the selected virtual machine. Choose Dashboard.

5. On the command bar, click Connect. When prompted by the web browser, click Open to open the remote desktop protocol file for the virtual machine in Remote Desktop Connection (mstsc.exe).

6. You'll see a warning prompt that the publisher of the remote connection can't be identified. Click Connect to proceed.

7. In the Windows Security dialog box, enter the credentials for an account authorized to log on to the virtual machine. For your first logon, enter the user name and password of the administrator account that was created when you deployed the new virtual machine.

8. You'll see a warning prompt that the identity of the remote connection can't be verified. Click Yes to proceed.

9. Use Remote Desktop Connection to work with the virtual machine just as you would any other remote server.

Networking with TCP/IP

TCP/IP is a protocol suite consisting of Transmission Control Protocol (TCP) and Internet Protocol (IP). TCP is a connection-oriented protocol designed for reliable end-to-end communications. IP is an internetworking protocol that is used to route packets of data called *datagrams* over a network. An IP datagram consists of an IP header and an IP payload. The IP header contains information about routing the datagram, including source and destination IP addresses. The IP payload contains the actual data being sent over the network.

TCP/IP is the backbone for Microsoft Windows networks. It is required for internetwork communications and for accessing the Internet. Before you can implement TCP/IP networking, you should understand IP addressing conventions, subnetting options, and name-resolution techniques—all of which are covered in this chapter.

Navigating networking in Windows Server 2012 R2

The networking features in Windows Server 2012 R2 are different from those in early releases of Windows. Windows Server 2012 R2 has a suite of networking tools, including the following:

- **Network Explorer.** Provides a central console for browsing computers and devices on the network

- **Network And Sharing Center.** Provides a central console for viewing and managing a computer's networking and sharing configuration

- **Windows Network Diagnostics.** Provides automated diagnostics to help diagnose and resolve networking problems

Before discussing how these networking tools are used, we must first look at the features on which these tools rely:

- **Network Discovery.** Controls the ability to see other computers and devices

- **Network Location Awareness.** Reports changes in network connectivity and configuration

IMPORTANT

Network Location Awareness also enables a computer with multiple network interfaces to select the best route for a particular data transfer. As part of selecting the best route, Windows chooses the best interface (either wired or wireless) for the transfer. This mechanism improves the selection of wireless over wired networks when both interfaces are present.

The network discovery settings of the computer you are working with determine the computers and devices you can browse or view in networking tools. Discovery settings work in conjunction with a computer's Windows Firewall to either block or allow the following:

- Discovery of network computers and devices

- Discovery of your computer by others

Network discovery settings are meant to provide the appropriate level of security for each of the various categories of networks to which a computer can connect. Three categories of networks are defined for servers:

- **Domain Network.** Intended as a designation for a network in which computers are connected to the corporate domain to which they are joined

- **Private Network.** Intended as a designation for a network in which computers are configured as members of a homegroup or workgroup and are not connected directly to the public Internet

- **Public Network.** Intended as a designation for a guest network in a public place, such as a coffee shop or airport, rather than for an internal network

In domains, you can enable discovery on domain controllers to view member computers. On member computers, you can enable discovery to see other member computers. With computers running nonserver versions of Windows, both homegroups and workgroups are available on private networks. Homegroups have special sharing settings that are not available in workgroups.

TROUBLESHOOTING

Correcting the network category

If Windows detects the wrong type of network, you should check the TCP/IP configuration settings for the related network adapter. If the public category is incorrectly assigned and the TCP/IP settings are correct, you can change the network category to private (or domain, if appropriate) using Network Explorer. Open Network Explorer, tap or click the warning message in the notification area, and then tap or click Turn On

Network Discovery And File Sharing. In the dialog box provided, tap or click No, Make The Network That I Am Connected To A Private Network. This sets the network category as private while leaving network discovery disabled.

Another way to change the network category is to use Windows PowerShell. Enter **Get-NetConnectionProfile** to list information about the networks to which the computer is currently connected, including the name and interface alias for these networks. At an elevated Windows PowerShell prompt, use Set-NetConnectionProfile to change the category for a specific network adapter. The basic syntax is

```
Set-NetConnectionProfile -Name NetworkName -NetworkCategory Category
```

where *NetworkName* is the network name and *Category* is Private for a private network or Public for a public network, such as

```
Set-NetConnectionProfile -Name Network -NetworkCategory Private
```

After you use Network Explorer or Set-NetConnectionProfile to change the network category to private, computers on domain networks should eventually be listed as such. If the network type doesn't change automatically, you can disable and then enable the related network connection to force Windows to reevaluate the network category. One way to disable and then enable a network adapter is to use Disable-NetAdapter and Enable-NetAdapter. The basic syntax for each is

```
Disable-NetAdapter -Name NetworkName
Enable-NetAdapter -Name NetworkName
```

where *NetworkName* is the network name, such as

```
Disable-NetAdapter -Name Network
Enable-NetAdapter -Name Network
```

Because a computer saves settings separately for each category of network, you can use different block and allow settings for each network category. When you connect to a network for the first time, Windows automatically sets the network category based on the computer's network settings. If the computer has multiple network adapters, the adapters can be connected to different networks and, therefore, can be assigned different network categories.

Based on the network category, Windows Server 2012 R2 automatically configures settings that turn discovery either on or off. You can manage these settings as well. Regardless of whether network discovery was managed automatically and configured manually, the On (Enabled) state means the following:

- The computer can discover other computers and devices on the network.

- Other computers on the network can discover the computer.

The Off (Disabled) state means the following:

- The computer can't discover other computers and devices on the network.

- Other computers on the network can't discover the computer.

Network Explorer, shown in Figure 2-1, displays a list of discovered computers and devices on the network. In any File Explorer view, you can access Network Explorer by tapping or clicking the leftmost option button in the address list and then tapping or clicking Network. The computers and devices listed in Network Explorer depend on the network discovery settings of the computer.

If discovery is blocked, you'll see a note about this. When you tap or click the warning message, you can enable network discovery by selecting Turn On Network Discovery And File Sharing. This opens the appropriate Windows Firewall ports so that network discovery is allowed. If no other changes have been made with regard to network discovery, the computer will be in the discovery-only state. You need to manually configure the sharing of printers, files, and media, as discussed in Chapter 18, "Managing file sharing," in *Windows Server 2012 R2 Inside Out: Configuration, Storage, & Essentials* (Microsoft Press, 2014).

When you attempt to enable network discovery for a network identified as public, you'll see an additional prompt with options for making the network a private network or turning on network discovery and file sharing for all public networks. Generally, you don't want to turn on network discovery and file sharing on public networks because this can open the computer to attack. Therefore, if the computer is actually connected to a public (open) network, click Cancel and do not turn on network discovery. Otherwise, if the computer is connected to an unidentified private network, select the option for making the network a private network.

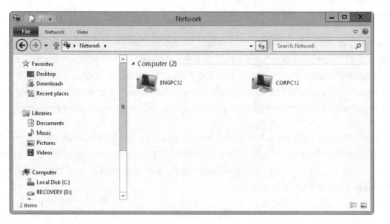

Figure 2-1 Use Network Explorer to browse network resources.

Network And Sharing Center, shown in Figure 2-2, provides the current network status and an overview of the current network configuration. In Control Panel you can access Network And Sharing Center by tapping or clicking View Network Status And Tasks under the Network And Internet heading. In Network Explorer, tap or click Network on the toolbar and then tap or click Network And Sharing Center.

Network And Sharing Center lists the current network by name and provides an overview of the network, including the category of the current network as Domain Network, Private Network, or Public Network. The Access Type field specifies whether and how the computer is connected to its current network as No Internet Access or Internet Access. The Connections field shows the name of the Local Area Connection being used to connect to the current network. If you tap or click the connection, you can view the connection status in the related Status dialog box.

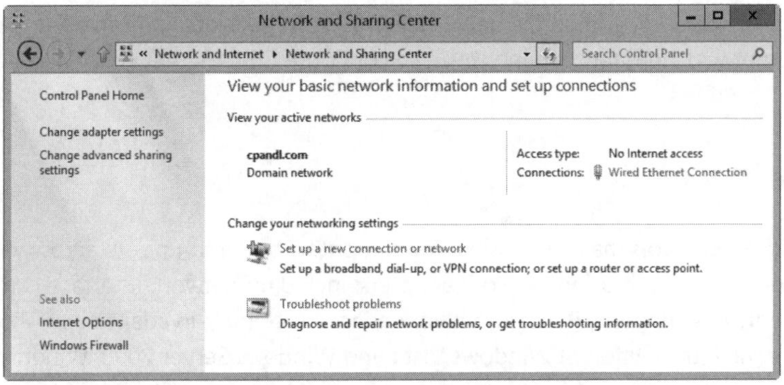

Figure 2-2 View and manage network settings with Network And Sharing Center.

Windows assigns the public category to any unidentified network, even on domain-joined computers. In Network And Sharing Center, the network adapter used to connect to the domain should identify the domain and show the network category as Domain Network. However, if a computer's TCP/IP settings aren't set correctly, Windows might misidentify a network as public or private rather than as a domain network. To resolve this, change the network adapter's TCP/IP settings. When you enter the correct TCP/IP settings, Windows attempts to identify the network again and should set the network category correctly.

Windows might occasionally identify multiple networks on a computer with only one network adapter. Often the quickest solution for this mixed-state problem is to disable and then enable the network adapter. In Network And Sharing Center, tap or click Change Adapter Settings. Next, tap or click the network adapter and then tap or click Disable This Network Device. Finally, tap or click Enable This Network Device.

NOTE
You also can use Windows PowerShell to work with network adapters. Use Get-NetAdapter to list details for network adapters, including the network name. Next, use Disable-NetAdapter to disable the network adapter and then use Enable-NetAdapter to reenable the network adapter.

If a computer has multiple network adapters connected to different networks, Windows Server might incorrectly identify the connected networks as either public or private instead of domain as well. Often the quickest solution for this mixed-state problem is to disable the network adapter that isn't connected to the corporate network. For example, during development testing, I often run Windows Server on laptops with both wired and wireless connections. To get Windows Server to correctly identify the domain-connected adapter, I disable the wireless adapter.

Windows Server does allow multiple network adapters to be used. You can aggregate bandwidth using network adapter teaming. You can configure up to 32 network adapters to work together.

Using TCP/IP

The TCP and IP protocols make it possible for computers to communicate across various networks and the Internet using network adapters, including network-interface cards, USB-attachable network adapters, PC Card network adapters, or built-in adapters on the motherboard. Since the introduction of Windows Vista and Windows Server 2008, Windows has had a dual IP layer architecture in which both Internet Protocol version 4 (IPv4) and Internet Protocol version 6 (IPv6) are implemented and share common Transport and Frame layers.

IPv4 and IPv6 are used in very different ways. IPv4 has 32-bit addresses and is the primary version of IP used on most networks, including the Internet. IPv6 has 128-bit addresses and is the next-generation version of IP.

When networking hardware is detected during installation of the operating system, both IPv4 and IPv6 are enabled by default in Windows Vista and later and you don't need to install a separate component to enable support for IPv6. The modified IP architecture is referred to as the Next Generation TCP/IP stack. Table 2-1 summarizes the key TCP/IP enhancements implemented in the Next Generation TCP/IP stack. Table 2-2 summarizes the key TCP/IP enhancements that are specific to IPv6.

Table 2-1 Key TCP/IP enhancements in the Next Generation TCP/IP stack

Feature Supported	Description
Automatic Black Hole Router Detection	Prevents TCP connections from terminating due to intermediate routers silently discarding large TCP segments, retransmissions, or error messages.
Automatic Dead Gateway Retry	Ensures that an unreachable gateway is checked periodically to determine whether it has become available.
Compound TCP	Optimizes TCP transfers for the sending host by increasing the amount of data sent in a connection while ensuring that other TCP connections are not affected.
Extended Selective Acknowledgments	Extends the way Selective Acknowledgments (SACKs) are used, enabling a receiver to indicate up to four noncontiguous blocks of received data and to acknowledge duplicate packets. This helps the receiver determine when it has retransmitted a segment unnecessarily and adjust its behavior to prevent future retransmissions.
Modified Fast Recovery Algorithm	Provides faster throughput by altering the way that a sender can increase the sending rate if multiple segments in a window of data are lost and the sender receives an acknowledgment stating that only part of the data has been received.
Neighbor Unreachability Detection for IPv4	Determines when neighboring nodes and routers are no longer reachable and reports the condition.
Network Diagnostics Framework	Provides an extensible framework that helps users recover from and troubleshoot problems with network connections.
Receive Window Auto Tuning	Optimizes TCP transfers for the host receiving data by automatically managing the size of the memory buffer (the receive windows) to use for storing incoming data based on the current network conditions.
Routing Compartments	Prevents unwanted forwarding of traffic between interfaces by associating an interface or a set of interfaces with a login session that has its own routing tables.
SACK-Based Loss Recovery	Makes it possible to use SACK information to perform loss recovery when duplicate acknowledgments have been received and to more quickly recover when multiple segments are not received at the destination.
Spurious Retransmission Timeout Detection	Provides correction for sudden, temporary increases in retransmission timeouts and prevents unnecessary retransmission of segments.
TCP Extended Statistics	Helps determine whether a performance bottleneck for a connection is the sending application, the receiving application, or the network.
Windows Filtering Platform	Provides application programming interfaces (APIs) for extending the TCP/IP filtering architecture so that it can support additional features.

CHAPTER 2

Table 2-2 Key TCP/IP enhancements for IPv6

Feature Supported	Description
DHCPv6-Capable DHCP client	Extends the Dynamic Host Configuration Protocol (DHCP) client to support IPv6 and allows stateful address autoconfiguration with a DHCPv6 server.
IP Security	Allows use of Internet Key Exchange (IKE) and data encryption for IPv6.
IPv6 over Point-to-Point Protocol (PPPv6)	Allows native IPv6 traffic to be sent over PPP-based connections, which in turn allows remote-access clients to connect with an IPv6-based Internet service provider (ISP) through dial-up or PPP over Ethernet (PPPoE)–based connections.
Link-Local Multicast Name Resolution (LLMNR)	Allows IPv6 hosts on a single subnet without a Domain Name System (DNS) server to resolve each other's names.
Multicast Listener Discovery version 2 (MLDv2)	Provides support for source-specific multicast traffic and is equivalent to Internet Group Management Protocol version 3 (IGMPv3) for IPv4.
Random Interface IDs	Prevents address scanning of IPv6 addresses based on the known company IDs of network-adapter manufacturers. By default, Windows Vista and later generate random interface IDs for nontemporary autoconfigured IPv6 addresses, including public and link-local addresses.
Symmetric Network Address Translators	Maps the internal (private) address and port number to different external (public) addresses and ports, depending on the external destination address.

Windows 8.1 and Windows Server 2012 R2 have several enhancements in their built-in DNS clients that improve name resolution on IPv4 and IPv6 networks, including the following:

- **Adaptive query timeout.** With adaptive query timeout, the DNS client adapts the timeout interval based on the time required for previous queries. Thus, instead of waiting 1000 milliseconds (ms) before timing out a query, the timeout is adjusted based on past performance for the network, resulting in timeouts between 25 ms and 1000 ms.

- **Query coalescing.** With query coalescing, the DNS client combines multiple DNS queries for the same name. This results in only one query and optimizes performance.

- **Parallel queries.** With parallel queries, the DNS client issues IPv4 and IPv6 queries for A and AAAA records in parallel when both IP interfaces are enabled, which streamlines the query process and improves performance. Link-local multicast name resolution (LLMNR) and NetBIOS queries also are issued in parallel for IPv4 and IPv6.

- **Persistent caching.** With a persistent cache, the DNS client maintains the DNS cache across changes that occur on the same network. For example, the DNS client now persists the cache after address change notifications and when the computer is resuming from the sleep or standby state.

Windows PowerShell 3.0 includes the NetTCPIP module for working with TCP/IP from the command line and in scripts. This module is imported automatically when you open a Windows PowerShell prompt. Cmdlets you might want to use for TCP/IP troubleshooting include the following:

- **Get-NetIPAddress.** Lists information about IP address configuration

- **Get-NetIPInterface.** Provides summary information about IP interface properties

- **Get-NetIPv4Protocol.** Provides summary information about the IPv4 protocol configuration

- **Get-NetIPv6Protocol.** Provides summary information about the IPv6 protocol configuration

- **Get-NetNeighbor.** Displays information about the neighbor cache for IPv4 and IPv6

- **Get-NetOffloadGlobalSetting.** Lists the status of the global TCP/IP offload settings, including receive-side scaling, receive-segment coalescing, and TCP/IP chimney

- **Get-NetRoute.** Lists the IP routing table

- **Get-NetTCPConnection.** Lists details about current TCP connection statistics

- **Get-NetTCPSetting.** Displays TCP settings and configuration

To list all of the available NetTCPIP cmdlets, type **Get-Command –Module NetTCPIP** at a Windows PowerShell prompt. Alternatively, you can get a sorted list of commands by entering the following:

```
Get-Command -Module Net-TCPIP | Sort Noun,Verb | ft -auto Verb,Noun
```

Understanding IPv4 addressing

The most important thing IPv4 gives you is the IPv4 address. It's the existence of IPv4 addresses that enables information to be routed from point A to point B over a network. An IPv4 address is a 32-bit logical address that has two components: a network address and a node address. Typically, IPv4 addresses are divided into four 8-bit values called *octets* and are written as four separate decimal values delimited by a period (referred to as a *dot*). The binary values are converted to decimal equivalents by adding the numbers represented by the bit positions that are set to 1. The general way to write this value is in the form *w.x.y.z*, where each letter represents one of the four octets.

IPv4 addresses can be used in three ways:

- **Unicast.** Unicast IPv4 addresses are assigned to individual network interfaces that are attached to an IPv4 network and are used in one-to-one communications.

- **Multicast.** Multicast IPv4 addresses are addresses for which one or multiple IPv4 nodes can listen on the same or different network segments and are used in one-to-many communications.

- **Broadcast.** Broadcast IPv4 addresses are designed to be used by every IPv4 node on a particular network segment and are used in one-to-everyone communications.

Each of these IPv4 addressing techniques is discussed in the sections that follow.

Unicast IPv4 addresses

Unicast IPv4 addresses are the ones you'll work with the most. These are the IPv4 addresses that are assigned to individual network interfaces. In fact, each network interface that uses TCP/IPv4 must have a unique unicast IPv4 address. A unicast IPv4 address consists of two components:

- **A network ID.** The network ID or address identifies a specific logical network and must be unique within its boundaries. Typically, IPv4 routers set the boundaries for a logical network and this boundary is the same as the physical network defined by the routers. All nodes that are on the same logical network must share the same network ID. If they don't, routing or delivery problems occur.

- **A host ID.** The host ID or address identifies a specific node on a network, such as a router interface or server. As with a network ID, it must be unique within a particular network segment.

Address classes are used to create subdivisions of the IPv4 address space. With unicast IPv4 addresses, the classes A, B, and C can be applied. Each describes a different way of dividing a subset of the 32-bit IPv4 address space into network addresses and host addresses.

NOTE

Classes D and E are defined as well. Class D addresses are used for multicast, as discussed in the next section of this chapter. Class E addresses are reserved for experimental use. Class D addresses begin with a number between 224 and 239 for the first octet. Class E addresses begin with a number between 240 and 255 for the first octet. Although Windows Server 2012 R2 supports the use of Class D addresses, it does not support Class E addresses.

Class A networks

Class A networks are designed for when you need a large number of hosts but only a few network segments, and they have addresses that begin with a number between 1 and 127 for the first octet. As shown in Figure 2-3, the first octet (the first 8 bits of the address) defines the network ID, and the last three octets (the last 24 bits of the address) define the host ID. As you'll learn shortly, the Class A address 127 has a special meaning and isn't available for your use. This means that there are 126 possible Class A networks and each network can have 16,277,214 nodes. For example, a Class A network with the network address 100 contains all IPv4 addresses from 100.0.0.0 to 100.255.255.255.

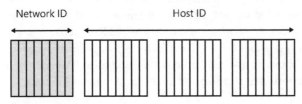

Figure 2-3 IPv4 addressing on Class A networks.

Class B networks

Class B networks are designed for when you need a moderate number of networks and hosts, and they have addresses that begin with a number between 128 and 191 for the first octet. As shown in Figure 2-4, the first two octets (the first 16 bits of the address) define the network ID, and the last two octets (the last 16 bits of the address) define the host ID. This means that there are 16,384 Class B networks and each network can have 65,534 nodes.

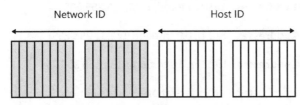

Figure 2-4 IPv4 addressing on Class B networks.

Class C networks

Class C networks are designed for when you need a large number of networks and relatively few hosts, and they have addresses that begin with a number between 192 and 223 for the first octet. As shown in Figure 2-5, the first three octets (the first 24 bits of the address) define the network ID and the last octet (the last 8 bits of the address) defines the host ID. This means that there are 2,097,152 Class C networks and each network can have 254 nodes.

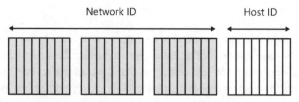

Network ID   Host ID

Figure 2-5 IPv4 addressing on Class C networks.

Loopback, public, and private addresses

When using any of the IPv4 address classifications, you need to follow certain rules. The network ID can't begin with 127 as the first octet. All IPv4 addresses that begin with 127 are reserved as loopback addresses. Any packets sent to an IPv4 address beginning with 127 are handled as if they've already been routed and have reached their destination, which is the local network interface. This means that any packets addressed to an IPv4 address of 127.0.0.0 to 127.255.255.255 are addressed to and received by the local network interface.

In addition, some addresses in the ranges are defined as public and others are defined as private. Public IPv4 addresses are assigned by Internet service providers (ISPs). ISPs obtain allocations of IPv4 addresses from a local Internet registry (LIR), from a national Internet registry (NIR), or from their appropriate regional Internet registry (RIR). Private addresses are addresses reserved for organizations to use on internal networks. Because they are nonroutable, which means they are not reachable on the Internet, they do not affect the public Internet and do not have to be assigned by an addressing authority.

The private IPv4 addresses defined are as follows:

- **Class A private IPv4 addresses.** 10.0.0.0 through 10.255.255.255

- **Class B private IPv4 addresses.** 172.16.0.0 through 172.31.255.255

- **Class C private IPv4 addresses.** 192.168.0.0 through 192.168.255.255

Because you shouldn't connect hosts on an organization's private network directly to the Internet, you should indirectly connect them using the Network Address Translation (NAT) protocol or a gateway program such as a proxy. When NAT is configured on the organization's network, a device, such as a router, is responsible for translating private addresses to public addresses, allowing the nodes on the internal network to communicate with the nodes on the public Internet. When proxies are configured on the organization's network, the proxy acts as the go-between. It receives requests from nodes on the internal network and sends the requests to the public Internet. When the response is returned, the proxy sends the response to the node that made the original request. In both cases the device providing NAT or proxy services has a private IP address on its internal network interface and a public address on its Internet interface.

Multicast IPv4 addresses

Multicast IPv4 addresses are used only as destination IPv4 addresses and allow multiple nodes to listen for packets sent by a single originating node. In this way, a single packet can be delivered to and received by many hosts. Here's how it works: a sending node addresses a packet using a multicast IPv4 address. If the packet is addressed to the sending node's network, nodes on the network that are listening for multicast traffic receive and process the packet. If the packet is addressed to another network, a router on the sending node's network forwards the packet as it would any other packet. When it's received on the destination network, any nodes on the network that are listening for multicast traffic receive and process the packet.

The nodes listening for multicast packets on a particular IPv4 address are referred to as the *host group*. Members of the host group can be located anywhere—as long as the organization's routers know where members of the host group are located so that the routers can forward packets as appropriate.

One address class is reserved for multicast: Class D. Class D addresses begin with a number between 224 and 239 for the first octet.

Multicast IPv4 addresses in the range of 224.0.0.0 through 224.0.0.255 are reserved for local subnet traffic. For example, the address 224.0.0.1 is an all-hosts multicast address and is designed for multicasting to all hosts on a subnet. The address 224.0.0.2 is an all-routers multicast address and is designed for multicasting to all routers on a subnet. Other addresses in this range are used as specified by the Internet Assigned Numbers Authority (IANA), which is a function of the Internet Corporation for Assigned Names and Numbers (ICANN). For details, see the IANA website at *http://www.iana.org/assignments/multicast-addresses/multicast-addresses.xml*.

Broadcast IPv4 addresses

Broadcast IPv4 addresses are used only as destination IPv4 addresses, and they allow a single node to direct packets to every node on the local network segment. When a sending node addresses a packet using a broadcast IPv4 address, every node on that network segment receives and processes the packet.

To understand how broadcasts are used, you must understand the difference between classful networks and nonclassful networks. A *classful network* is a network that follows the class rules as defined, meaning a Class A, B, or C network is configured with network addresses and host addresses as described previously. A *nonclassful network* is a network that doesn't strictly follow the class rules. Nonclassful networks might have subnets that don't follow the normal rules for network and host IDs. You'll learn more about subnets later in this chapter in the section entitled "Using subnets and subnet masks."

NOTE

A nonclassful network can also be referred to as a *classless network*. However, classless inter-domain routing (CIDR) and all it implies are specifically spelled out in Request For Comments (RFCs), such as RFC 1812. RFC 1812 provides rules that supersede those of some previous RFCs, such as RFC 950, which prohibited the use of all-zeros subnets.

All nodes listen for and process broadcasts. Because IPv4 routers usually do not forward broadcast packets, broadcasts are generally limited by router boundaries. The broadcast address is obtained by setting all the host bits in the IPv4 address to 1 as appropriate for the broadcast type. Three types of broadcasts are used:

- **Network broadcasts.** Network broadcasts are used to send packets to all nodes on a classful network. For network broadcasts, the host ID bits are set to 1. For a nonclassful network, there is no network broadcast address, only a subnet broadcast address.

- **Subnet broadcasts.** Subnet broadcasts are used to send packets to all nodes on a nonclassful network. For subnet broadcasts, the host ID bits are set to 1. For a classful network, there is no subnet broadcast address, only a network broadcast address.

- **Limited broadcasts.** Limited broadcasts are used to send packets to all nodes when the network ID is unknown. For a limited broadcast, all network ID and host ID bits are set to 1.

DHCP uses limited broadcasts

Limited broadcasts are sent by nodes that have their IPv4 address automatically configured, as is the case with Dynamic Host Configuration Protocol (DHCP). With DHCP, clients use a limited broadcast to advertise that they need to obtain an IPv4 address. A DHCP server on the network acknowledges the request by assigning the node an IPv4 address, which the client then uses for normal network communications.

NOTE

Previously, a fourth type of broadcast was available, called an *all-subnets-directed broadcast*. This broadcast type was used to send packets to all nodes on all the subnets of a nonclassful network. Because of the changes specified in RFC 1812, all-subnets-directed broadcasts have been deprecated, meaning they are no longer going to be supported.

Special IPv4 addressing rules

As you've seen, certain IPv4 addresses and address ranges have special uses:

- The addresses 127.0.0.0 through 127.255.255.255 are reserved for local loopback.

- The addresses 10.0.0.0 through 10.255.255.255, 172.16.0.0 through 172.31.255.255, and 192.168.0.0 through 192.168.255.255 are designated as private and, as such, are nonroutable.

- On classful networks, the Class A addresses w.255.255.255, the Class B addresses w.x.255.255, and the Class C addresses w.x.y.255 are reserved for broadcasts.

- On nonclassful networks, the broadcast address is the last IPv4 address in the range of IPv4 addresses for the associated subnet.

NOTE

Certain IPv4 addresses are also reserved for other purposes. For example, the IPv4 addresses 169.254.0.1 to 169.254.255.254 are used for Automatic Private IPv4 Addressing (APIPA) as discussed in the section entitled "Configuring TCP/IP networking" in Chapter 3, "Managing TCP/IP networking."

On classful networks, all the bits in the network ID can't be set to 0 because this expression is reserved to indicate a host on a local network. Similarly, on a classful network all the bits in the host ID can't be set to 0 because this is reserved to indicate the IPv4 network number.

Table 2-3 lists the ranges of network numbers based on address classes. You can't assign the network number to a network interface. The network number is common to all network interfaces attached to the same logical network. On a nonclassful network, the network number is the first IPv4 address in the range of IPv4 addresses for the associated subnet—as specified in RFC 1812.

Table 2-3 Network IDs for classful networks

Address Class	First Network Number	Last Network Number
Class A	1.0.0.0	126.0.0.0
Class B	128.0.0.0	191.255.0.0
Class C	192.0.0.0	223.255.255.0

When you apply all the rules for IPv4 addresses, you find that hosts on a network can't use many IPv4 addresses. This means that the first available host ID and last available host ID are different from the range of available IPv4 addresses. Table 2-4 shows how these rules apply to

CHAPTER 2

classful networks. On a nonclassful network, the same rules apply—you lose the first and last available host IDs from the range of available IPv4 addresses.

Table 2-4 Available host IDs on classful networks

Address Class	First Host ID	Last Host ID
Class A	w.0.0.1	w.255.255.254
Class B	w.x.0.1	w.x.255.254
Class C	w.x.y.1	w.x.y.254

Inside OUT

Routers, gateways, and bridges connect networks

A router is needed for hosts on a network to communicate with hosts on other networks. It is standard convention for the network router to be assigned the first available host ID. On Windows systems, you identify the address for the router as the gateway IPv4 address for the network. Although the terms "gateways" and "routers" are often used interchangeably, technically the two are different. A *router* is a device that sends packets between network segments. A *gateway* is a device that performs the necessary translation so that communication between networks with different architectures is possible. When working with networks, you might also hear the term "bridge." A *bridge* is a device that directs traffic between two network segments using physical machine addresses (Media Access Control, or MAC, addresses). Routers, gateways, and bridges can be implemented in hardware as separate devices or in software so that a system on the network can handle the role as a network router, gateway, or bridge as necessary.

Using subnets and subnet masks

Anyone who works with computers should learn about subnetting and what it means. A *subnet* is a portion of a network that operates as a separate network. Logically, it exists separately from other networks, even if hosts on those other networks share the same network ID. Typically, such networks are also physically separated by a router. This ensures that the subnet is isolated and doesn't affect other subnets.

Subnetting is designed to make more efficient use of the IPv4 address space. Thus, rather than having networks with hundreds, thousands, or millions of nodes, you have a subnet that is sized appropriately for the number of nodes you use. This is important, especially for the crowded public IPv4 address space, where it doesn't make sense to assign the complete IPv4 address range for a network to an individual organization. Thus, instead of getting a complete network address for the public Internet, your organization is more likely to get a block of consecutive IPv4 addresses to use.

Subnet masks

You use a 32-bit value known as a subnet mask to configure nodes in a subnet to communicate only with other nodes on the same subnet. The mask works by blocking areas outside the subnet so that they aren't visible from within the subnet. Because they are 32-bit values, subnet masks can be expressed as an address for which each 8-bit value (octet) is written as four separate decimal values delimited by a period (dot). As with IPv4 addresses, the basic form is *w.x.y.z.*

The subnet mask identifies which bits of the IPv4 address belong to the network ID and which bits belong to the host ID. Nodes can see only the portions of the IPv4 address space that aren't masked by a bit with a value of 1. If a bit is set to 1, it corresponds to a bit in the network ID. If a bit is set to 0, it corresponds to a bit in the host ID.

Because a subnet mask must be configured for each IPv4 address, nodes on both classful and nonclassful networks have subnet masks. On a classful network, all the bits in the network ID portion of the IPv4 address are set to 1 and can be presented in dotted decimal, as shown in Table 2-5.

Table 2-5 Standard subnet masks for classful networks

Address Class	Bits for Subnet Mask	Subnet Mask
Class A	11111111 00000000 00000000 00000000	255.0.0.0
Class B	11111111 11111111 00000000 00000000	255.255.0.0
Class C	11111111 11111111 11111111 00000000	255.255.255.0

Inside OUT

Blocks of IPv4 addresses on the public Internet

For internal networks that use private IPv4 addresses, you'll often be able to use the standard subnet masks. This isn't true, however, when you need public IPv4 addresses. Most of the time you'll be assigned a small block of public IPv4 addresses to work with. For example, you might be assigned a block of eight (six usable) addresses. In this case you must create a subnet that uses the subnet mask to isolate your nodes as appropriate for the number of nodes you've been assigned. I say there are six usable addresses out of eight because the lowest address is reserved as the network number and the highest address is reserved as the broadcast address for the network. This is always the case, as any good Cisco Certified Network Associate (CCNA) will tell you.

CHAPTER 2

Network prefix notation

With subnetting, an IPv4 address alone doesn't help you understand how the address can be used. To be sure, you must know the number of bits in the network ID. As discussed, the subnet mask provides one way to determine which bits in the IPv4 address belong to the network ID and which bits belong to the host ID. If you have a block of IPv4 addresses, writing out each IPv4 address and the subnet mask is rather tedious. A shorthand way to do this is to use network prefix notation, which is also referred to as the classless inter-domain routing (CIDR) notation.

In network prefix notation, the network ID is seen as the prefix of an IPv4 address and the host ID is seen as the suffix. To write a block of IPv4 addresses and specify which bits are used for the network ID, you write the network number followed by a forward slash and the number of bits in the network ID, as in the following:

```
NetworkNumber/# of bits in the network ID
```

The slash and the number of bits in the network ID are referred to as the *network prefix*. Following this, you could rewrite Table 2-5 in the way shown in Table 2-6.

Table 2-6 Standard network prefixes for classful networks

Address Class	Bits for Subnet Mask	Network Prefix
Class A	11111111 00000000 00000000 00000000	/8
Class B	11111111 11111111 00000000 00000000	/16
Class C	11111111 11111111 11111111 00000000	/24

You now have two ways of detailing which bits are used for the network ID and which bits are used for the host ID. With the network number 192.168.1.0, you could use either of the following to specify that the first 24 bits identify the network ID:

- 192.168.1.0, 255.255.255.0

- 192.168.1.0/24

With either entry, you know that the first 24 bits identify the network ID and the last 8 bits identify the host ID. This, in turn, means that the usable IPv4 addresses are 192.168.1.1 through 192.168.1.254.

Subnetting

When you use subnetting, nodes no longer follow the class rules for determining which bits in the IPv4 address are used for the network ID and which bits are used for the host ID. Instead, you set the 32 bits of the IPv4 address as appropriate to be either network ID bits or host ID bits based on the number of subnets you need and then number nodes for each subnet. There is an inverse relationship between the number of subnets and the number of nodes per subnet that can be supported. As the number of subnets goes up by a factor of two, the number of hosts per subnet goes down by a factor of two.

Because Class A, B, and C networks have a different number of host ID bits to start with, borrowing bits from the host ID yields different numbers of subnets and hosts. The technique is the same, however. Each bit represented as a 1 in the subnet mask corresponds to a bit that belongs to the network ID. This means the value of each bit can be represented as shown in Figure 2-6.

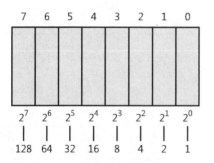

Figure 2-6 Represents the value of each bit when it's set to 1.

You start with the high-order bits and work your way to the low-order bits. When you borrow 1 bit of the host ID, you increase the number of possible subnets by a factor of two and reduce the number of possible hosts by a factor of two.

Subnetting Class A networks

The network entry mask for a standard Class A network can be defined as follows:

Address Class	Bits for Subnet Mask	Network Prefix	Decimal
Class A	11111111 00000000 00000000 00000000	/8	255.0.0.0

If you want to divide a Class A network into two separate subnets, you can borrow the high-order bit from the host ID in the second octet and add this bit to the network ID. Because the value of this bit taken from the host ID is 128, the corresponding subnet mask is 255.128.0.0. Thus, the network entry for the subnetted Class A network can be defined as follows:

Address Class	Bits for Subnet Mask	Network Prefix	Decimal
Class A	11111111 10000000 00000000 00000000	/9	255.128.0.0

CHAPTER 2

NOTE

Each time you borrow a bit from the host ID, the network prefix bits go up by one.

If you take an additional bit from the host ID bits, you allow the Class A network to be divided into up to four subnets. The value of this bit taken from the host ID is 64. When you add this value to the value of the previous bit taken from the host ID, the sum is 192 (128 + 64) and the corresponding subnet mask is 255.192.0.0. This means that the network entry for a subnetted Class A network that can be divided into up to four subnets can be defined as follows:

Address Class	Bits for Subnet Mask	Network Prefix	Decimal
Class A	11111111 11000000 00000000 00000000	/10	255.192.0.0

Table 2-7 shows how Class A networks can be subnetted and how this affects the number of possible subnets and hosts per subnet.

Table 2-7 Subnetting Class A networks

Maximum Subnets	Bits for Subnet Mask	Network Prefix	Decimal	Maximum Nodes
1	11111111 00000000 00000000 00000000	/8	255.0.0.0	16,777,214
2	11111111 10000000 00000000 00000000	/9	255.128.0.0	8,388,606
4	11111111 11000000 00000000 00000000	/10	255.192.0.0	4,194,302
8	11111111 11100000 00000000 00000000	/11	255.224.0.0	2,097,150
16	11111111 11110000 00000000 00000000	/12	255.240.0.0	1,048,574
32	11111111 11111000 00000000 00000000	/13	255.248.0.0	524,286
64	11111111 11111100 00000000 00000000	/14	255.252.0.0	262,142
128	11111111 11111110 00000000 00000000	/15	255.254.0.0	131,070
256	11111111 11111111 00000000 00000000	/16	255.255.0.0	65,534
512	11111111 11111111 10000000 00000000	/17	255.255.128.0	32,766
1024	11111111 11111111 11000000 00000000	/18	255.255.192.0	16,382
2048	11111111 11111111 11100000 00000000	/19	255.255.224.0	8190
4096	11111111 11111111 11110000 00000000	/20	255.255.240.0	4094
8192	11111111 11111111 11111000 00000000	/21	255.255.248.0	2046
16,384	11111111 11111111 11111100 00000000	/22	255.255.252.0	1022
32,768	11111111 11111111 11111110 00000000	/23	255.255.254.0	510
65,536	11111111 11111111 11111111 00000000	/24	255.255.255.0	254

Maximum Subnets	Bits for Subnet Mask	Network Prefix	Decimal	Maximum Nodes
131,072	11111111 11111111 11111111 10000000	/25	255.255.255.128	126
262,144	11111111 11111111 11111111 11000000	/26	255.255.255.192	62
524,288	11111111 11111111 11111111 11100000	/27	255.255.255.224	30
1,048,576	11111111 11111111 11111111 11110000	/28	255.255.255.240	14
2,097,152	11111111 11111111 11111111 11111000	/29	255.255.255.248	6
4,194,304	11111111 11111111 11111111 11111100	/30	255.255.255.252	2

Subnetting Class B networks

The network entry mask for a standard Class B network can be defined as follows:

Address Class	Bits for Subnet Mask	Network Prefix	Decimal
Class B	11111111 11111111 00000000 00000000	/16	255.255.0.0

A standard Class B network can have up to 65,534 hosts. If you want to divide a Class B network into two separate subnets, you can borrow the high-order bit from the host ID in the third octet and add this bit to the network ID. Because the value of this bit taken from the host ID is 128, the corresponding subnet mask is 255.255.128.0. Thus, the network entry for the subnetted Class B network can be defined as follows:

Address Class	Bits for Subnet Mask	Network Prefix	Decimal
Class B	11111111 11111111 10000000 00000000	/17	255.255.128. 0

If you take an additional bit from the host ID bits, you allow the Class B network to be divided into up to four subnets. The value of this bit taken from the host ID is 64. When you add this value to the value of the previous bit taken from the host ID, the sum is 192 (128 + 64) and the corresponding subnet mask is 255.255.192.0. This means that the network entry for a subnetted Class B network that can be divided into up to four subnets can be defined as follows:

Address Class	Bits for Subnet Mask	Network Prefix	Decimal
Class B	11111111 11111111 11000000 00000000	/18	255.255.192.0

Table 2-8 shows how Class B networks can be subnetted and how this affects the number of possible subnets and hosts per subnet.

CHAPTER 2

Table 2-8 Subnetting Class B networks

Maximum Subnets	Bits for Subnet Mask	Network Prefix	Decimal	Maximum Nodes
1	11111111 11111111 00000000 00000000	/16	255.255.0.0	65,534
2	11111111 11111111 10000000 00000000	/17	255.255.128.0	32,766
4	11111111 11111111 11000000 00000000	/18	255.255.192.0	16,382
8	11111111 11111111 11100000 00000000	/19	255.255.224.0	8190
16	11111111 11111111 11110000 00000000	/20	255.255.240.0	4094
32	11111111 11111111 11111000 00000000	/21	255.255.248.0	2046
64	11111111 11111111 11111100 00000000	/22	255.255.252.0	1,022
128	11111111 11111111 11111110 00000000	/23	255.255.254.0	510
256	11111111 11111111 11111111 00000000	/24	255.255.255.0	254
512	11111111 11111111 11111111 10000000	/25	255.255.255.128	126
1024	11111111 11111111 11111111 11000000	/26	255.255.255.192	62
2048	11111111 11111111 11111111 11100000	/27	255.255.255.224	30
4096	11111111 11111111 11111111 11110000	/28	255.255.255.240	14
8192	11111111 11111111 11111111 11111000	/29	255.255.255.248	6
16,384	11111111 11111111 11111111 11111100	/30	255.255.255.252	2

Subnetting Class C networks

The network entry mask for a standard Class C network can be defined as follows:

Address Class	Bits for Subnet Mask	Network Prefix	Decimal
Class C	11111111 11111111 11111111 00000000	/24	255.255.255.0

A standard Class C network can have up to 254 hosts. If you want to divide a Class C network into two separate subnets, you can borrow the high-order bit from the host ID in the fourth octet and add this bit to the network ID. Because the value of this bit taken from the host ID is 128, the corresponding subnet mask is 255.255.255.128. Thus, the network entry for the subnetted Class C network can be defined as follows:

Address Class	Bits for Subnet Mask	Network Prefix	Decimal
Class C	11111111 11111111 11111111 10000000	/25	255.255.255.128

If you take an additional bit from the host ID bits, you allow the Class C network to be divided into up to four subnets. The value of this bit taken from the host ID is 64. When you add this value to the value of the previous bit taken from the host ID, the sum is 192 (128 + 64) and the corresponding subnet mask is 255.255.255.192. This means that the network entry for a sub-netted Class C network that can be divided into up to four subnets can be defined as follows:

Address Class	Bits for Subnet Mask	Network Prefix	Decimal
Class C	11111111 11111111 11111111 11000000	/26	255.255.255.192

Table 2-9 shows how Class C networks can be subnetted and how this affects the number of possible subnets and hosts per subnet.

Table 2-9 Subnetting Class C networks

Maximum Subnets	Bits for Subnet Mask	Network Prefix	Decimal	Maximum Nodes
1	11111111 11111111 11111111 00000000	/24	255.255.255.0	254
2	11111111 11111111 11111111 10000000	/25	255.255.255.128	126
4	11111111 11111111 11111111 11000000	/26	255.255.255.192	62
8	11111111 11111111 11111111 11100000	/27	255.255.255.224	30
16	11111111 11111111 11111111 11110000	/28	255.255.255.240	14
32	11111111 11111111 11111111 11111000	/29	255.255.255.248	6
64	11111111 11111111 11111111 11111100	/30	255.255.255.252	2

Understanding IP data packets

With IPv4, computers send data in discrete packets of information with a header and a pay-load. IPv4 headers are variable in size, between 20 and 60 bytes, in 4-byte increments. Each bit range is broken into different sections, and each section corresponds to the range of a related field in a packet. Header bit ranges consist of 0–3, 4–7, 8–15, 16–18, and 15–31. These corre-spond to the values 0, 32, 64, 96, 128, 160, and 160/152+ for data.

For examples of the ranges and their use, see Table 2-10. The IP payload is of variable size as well, ranging from 8 bytes to 65,515 bytes. Although most people will never use this infor-mation on a regular basis, it's very useful for understanding how to troubleshoot network problems.

CHAPTER 2

Table 2-10 IPv4 packets

+	Bits 0–3	4–7	8–15	16–18	15–31
0	Version	Header length	Type of service	Total length	
32	Identification			Flags	Fragment offset
64	Time to Live (TTL)		Protocol	Header checksum	
96	Source address information				
128	Destination address information				
160	Optional information				
160/152+	Data transmitted				

Getting and using IPv4 addresses

As discussed previously, there are two categories of IPv4 addresses:

- **Public.** Public addresses are assigned by Network Solutions (formerly this was InterNIC) and can also be purchased from the IANA/ICANN. Most organizations don't need to purchase their IPv4 addresses directly, however. Instead, they get the IPv4 addresses they need from their Internet service provider (ISP).

- **Private.** Private addresses are reserved for Class A, B, and C networks and can be used without specific assignment. Most organizations follow the private addressing scheme determined by their Information Technology (IT) department; in this case they request IPv4 addresses from the IT department.

IMPORTANT

Technically, if your organization doesn't plan to connect to the Internet, you can use any IPv4 address. However, I still recommend using private IPv4 addresses in this case and taking the time to plan out the IPv4 address space carefully. If you do this and you later must connect the organization to the Internet, you won't have to change the IPv4 address of every node on the network. Instead, you'll need to reconfigure only the network's Internet-facing nodes, such as a proxy server or NAT router, to connect your organization to the Internet.

Inside OUT

Public IPv4 address space

The public IPv4 address space is running out of new addresses that can be assigned to public devices (and might have run out completely by the time you read this). Whether public IPv4 addresses are exhausted for you depends on where your company is located, what regional Internet registry (RIR) is responsible for allocating IP addresses in your area of the world, and whether your Internet service provider (ISP) has any IPv4 addresses left from those it obtained from an RIR. In February 2011 the IANA/ICANN, the global authority coordinating IP addresses, ran out of new IPv4 address blocks to allocate to RIRs. Now, the RIRs themselves are running out (or have already run out) of new IPv4 addresses to assign. Because of this, if your company needs public IPv4 addresses, you might not be able to get them. In this case you need to use IPv6 for your company's public Internet communications.

If you are planning your organization's network infrastructure, you must determine how you want to structure the network. In many cases you'll want to isolate the internal systems from the public Internet and place them on their own private network. An example of this is shown in Figure 2-7.

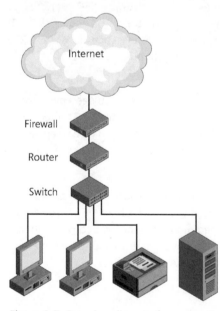

Figure 2-7 Overview diagram for connecting a private network to the Internet.

In this example hosts on the internal network connect to a switch. The switch, in turn, connects to a router, which performs the necessary internal-to-external IPv4 address translation using NAT. The NAT router, in turn, is connected to a firewall, and the firewall connects to the Internet. If the internal network ID is 192.168.1.0/24, the internal IPv4 addresses range from 192.168.1.1 to 192.168.1.254 and all hosts use the network mask 255.255.255.0. After this occurs, the hosts might include the following:

- A router with IPv4 address 192.168.1.1 on the interface facing the internal network

- A manageable switch with IPv4 address 192.168.1.2

- Computers with IPv4 addresses 192.168.1.20 to 192.168.149

- Servers with IPv4 addresses 192.168.1.150 to 192.168.199

- A network printer with the IPv4 address 192.168.1.200

Follow an IPv4 addressing plan

Notice how the IPv4 addresses are assigned. I generally recommend reserving blocks of IPv4 addresses for the various types of hosts you'll have on a network. On an internal network with the ID 192.168.1.0/24, you might designate that IPv4 addresses 192.168.1.1 to 192.168.1.19 are reserved for network hardware, IPv4 addresses 192.168.1.20 to 192.168.1.149 are reserved for workstations, IPv4 addresses 192.168.1.150 to 192.168.1.199 are reserved for servers, and IPv4 addresses above 192.168.1.200 are reserved for other types of network hardware, such as printers.

You can then determine the number of public IPv4 addresses you need by assessing the number of public Internet-facing nodes you need. In this example the NAT router needs a public IPv4 address, as does the external firewall. To be able to send and receive email, you'll need an IPv4 address for the organization's email server. To set up a public website, you'll need an IPv4 address for the organization's web server.

That's a total of four IPv4 addresses (six, including the network ID address and the broadcast address). In this case your ISP might assign you a /29 subnet, giving you a total of six usable addresses. If you think you might need more than this, you could ask for a /28 subnet. However, keep in mind that you might have to pay a per–IPv4 address leasing fee.

Understanding IPv6

As with IPv4, the most important thing IPv6 gives you is the IPv6 address. Although IPv4 allows for more than 4 billion networked devices, the world is running out of available IPv4 addresses. To resolve this problem, IPv6 uses 128-bit addresses, and this allows for 340,282,237,000,000 ,000,000,000,000,000,000,000,000 addresses—give or take a few hundred million quadrillion addresses. Put another way, IPv6 makes available enough IP addresses so that every person on 100 billion worlds of 100 billion people could have 34 quadrillion IP addresses (and there would still be 2.8236 x 10^33 IP addresses left over).

> **NOTE**
>
> Okay, so 128 bits might seem like overkill. However, the abundance of IPv6 addresses makes it possible to allocate addresses in large blocks. Not only does this help simplify administration, it also avoids fragmentation of the address space, which in turn leads to smaller routing tables. One reason for selecting 128 bits for the address length is the increasing prevalence of 64-bit processors over 32-bit processors. 64-bit processors can efficiently work with 128-bit addresses. As we look to the future, the next logical step is 128-bit computing, and 128-bit addresses will already be in place by that time. A key advantage of the larger address space in IPv6 is that it makes scanning certain IP blocks for vulnerabilities significantly more difficult than in IPv4, which makes IPv6 more resistant to malicious attacks by hackers looking for vulnerable computers.

Keeping track of so many IPv6 addresses using the numbering scheme used with IPv4 is impractical. This is why IPv6 uses hexadecimal numbers rather than decimal numbers to define the address space. This means that instead of allowing only the numbers 0 through 9 for each position in the IP address, IPv6 allows the values 0 through 9 and A through F, with A representing 10, B representing 11, and so on, up to F representing 15. Therefore, the values 0 through 15 can be represented using the values 0 through F.

IPv6's 128-bit addresses are divided into eight 16-bit blocks delimited by colons. Each 16-bit block is expressed in hexadecimal form. With standard unicast IPv6 addresses, the first 64 bits represent the network ID and the last 64 bits represent the network interface. An example of an IPv6 address follows:

```
FE80:0:0:02BC:00FF:BECB:FE4F:961D
```

Because many IPv6 address blocks are set to 0, a contiguous set of 0 blocks can be expressed as ":", a notation referred to as the *double-colon notation*. Using double-colon notation, the two 0 blocks in the previous address are compressed as follows:

```
FE80::02BC:00FF:BECB:FE4F:961D
```

Three or more 0 blocks would be compressed in the same way. For example, FFE8:0:0:0:0:0:0:1 becomes FFE8::1. However, more than one double-colon abbreviation in an address is invalid because it makes the notation ambiguous. Also, leading zeros in a group can be omitted. Thus, FE80::02BC:00FF:BECB:FE4F:961D can be shortened to FE80::2BC:FF:BECB:FE4F:961D. Following this, the following addresses are all valid and equivalent:

- FE80:0000:0000:02BC:00FF:BECB:FE4F:961D

- FE80:0:0:02BC:00FF:BECB:FE4F:961D

- FE80::02BC:00FF:BECB:FE4F:961D

- FE80::2BC:FF:BECB:FE4F:961D

Finally, you can write a sequence of 4 bytes at the end of an IPv6 address in decimal, using dots as separators. You can use this notation with IPv4 compatibility addresses, such as FE80::192.168.10.52.

As with IPv4 addresses, there are different types of IPv6 addresses. As Table 2-11 shows, the type of an IPv6 address is identified by the high-order bits of the address. Link-local unicast IPv6 addresses are the equivalent of IPv4 private addresses because they are not globally reachable on the Internet. Global unicast IPv6 addresses are the equivalent of IPv4 public addresses because they are globally reachable on the Internet and must be assigned by an IP address authority.

Table 2-11 IPv6 address types

Address Type	Binary Prefix	IPv6 Notation	Description
Unspecified	000000	::/128	The IPv6 address 0:0:0:0:0:0:0:0 is an unspecified address and should be used only in software.
Loopback	0000000001	::1/128	The IPv6 address 0:0:0:0:0:0:0:1 is used for local loopback. If an application sends packets to this address, the IPv6 stack will loop these packets back to the same host (corresponding to 127.0.0.1 in IPv4).
Multicast	1111111100	FF00::/8	IPv6 addresses beginning with FF00 are used for multicast transmissions (both link local and across routers). There are no address ranges reserved for broadcast in IPv6—the same effect can be achieved by multicasting to the all-hosts group with a hop count of one.

Address Type	Binary Prefix	IPv6 Notation	Description
Link-local unicast	1111111010	FE80::/10	IPv6 addresses beginning with FE80 are used for link-local unicast transmissions and are valid only in the local physical link (similar to the autoconfiguration IP address 169.254.x.x in IPv4).
Global unicast	All other addresses		All other IP addresses are used for global unicast transmissions and are valid on the public Internet.

IPv6 doesn't use subnet masks to identify which bits belong to the network ID and which bits belong to the host ID. Instead, each IPv6 address is assigned a subnet prefix length that specifies how the bits in the network ID are used. The subnet prefix length is represented in decimal form. Therefore, if 48 bits in the network ID are used, the subnet prefix length is written as shown in the following example:

FE01:1234:5678::/48   FE01:1234:5678:: through address FE01:1234:5678::FFFF:FFFF:FFFF:FFFF

Like IPv4, IPv6 packets are composed of two parts: a header and a payload. Unlike IPv4, IPv6 allows for sending jumbograms. A *jumbogram* is an IP datagram containing a payload larger than 64 KBs. IPv4 does not support this type of transmission, and it has a 64-KB payload limit.

Jumbograms greatly increase the throughput of high-performance networks. The first 40 octets of an IPv6 packet contain the header (composed of the source and destination addresses, including an IPv4 version where necessary), a traffic class section, a flow label (for packet priority information), the payload length, the next header addressing section, and the hop limit. The payload section consists of the actual data sent during transmission. The payload section can contain either 64 KBs of information, as with IPv4 packets, or a jumbogram for true IPv6 networking architectures.

Another major difference between IPv4 and IPv6 is that IP security (IPsec) is implemented within the IPv6 protocol. IPsec lies within the IP network layer and encrypts and authenticates as an integrated part of the protocol by default. This eliminates additional overhead in encoding and decoding packets using separate IPsec functionality.

Understanding name resolution

Although IP addressing works well for computer-to-computer communications, it doesn't work so well when you want to access resources. Could you imagine having to remember the IP address of every computer you work with? That would be difficult, and it would make working with computers on networks a chore. This is why computers are assigned names. Names are easier to remember than numbers—at least for most people.

CHAPTER 2

When a computer has a name, to access it you can type that name rather than its IP address. This name resolution doesn't happen automatically. In the background, a computer process translates the computer name you type into an IP address that computers can understand. Windows Vista and later versions natively support three name-resolution systems:

- Domain Name System (DNS)

- Windows Internet Naming Service (WINS)

- Link-Local Multicast Name Resolution (LLMNR)

The sections that follow examine these services.

Domain Name System

DNS provides a distributed database that enables computer names to be resolved to their corresponding IP addresses. When working with DNS, you need to understand what is meant by the terms "host name," "domain name," "fully qualified domain name," and "name resolution."

Host names

A *host name* identifies an individual host in DNS. Ordinarily, you might call this a computer name. The difference, however, is that there is an actual record in the DNS database called a *host record* that corresponds to the computer name and details how the computer name is used on the network. Host names can be assigned by administrators and other members of the organization.

Domain names

A *domain name* is the logical identity of a network in DNS. Domain names follow a specific naming scheme that is organized in a tree-like structure. Periods (dots) are used to separate the name components or levels within the domain name.

The first level of the tree is where you find the top-level domains. *Top-level domains* describe the kinds of networks that are within their domain. For example, the .edu top-level domain is for educational domains, the .gov top-level domain is for U.S. government domains, and the .com top-level domain is for commercial domains. As you can see, top-level domains generally are organized by category. There are also top-level domains organized geographically, such as .ca for Canada and .uk for United Kingdom.

The second level of the tree is where you find parent domains. *Parent domains* are the primary domain names of organizations. For example, City Power & Light's domain name is cpandl .com. The domain name cpandl.com identifies a specific network in the .com domain. No parent domain can be used on the public Internet without being reserved and registered. Name registrars, such as Network Solutions, charge a fee for this service.

Additional levels of the tree belong to individual hosts or subsequent levels in the organiza-tion's domain structure. These subsequent levels are referred to as *child domains*. For example, City Power & Light might have Tech, Support, and Sales child domains, which are named tech .cpandl.com, support.cpandl.com, and sales.cpandl.com, respectively.

Inside OUT
Connect the network to the Internet

If your organization's network must be connected to the Internet, you should obtain a public domain name from a name registrar or use a similar service provided by an ISP. Because many domain names have already been taken, you should have several previ-ously agreed-upon alternative names in mind when you go to register. After you obtain a domain name, you must configure DNS hosting for that domain. You do this by speci-fying the addresses of two or more DNS servers that will handle DNS services for this domain. Typically, these DNS servers belong to your ISP.

Inside OUT
Additional top-level domains

Although top-level domains generally are organized by category and country/region, new top-level domains are introduced periodically after approval by the ICANN. Additional top-level domains that have been approved include .aero for the air-trans-port industry, .asia for the Asia-Pacific region, .biz for businesses, .info for information, .jobs for companies with jobs to advertise, .mobi for mobile-compatible sites, .museum for museums, and .travel for the travel and tourism industry.

Fully qualified domain names

All hosts on a TCP/IP network have what is called a *fully qualified domain name (FQDN)*. The FQDN combines the host name and the domain name and serves to uniquely identify the host. For a host named CPL05 in the cpandl.com domain, the FQDN would be cpl05.cpandl .com. For a host named CORPSVR17 in the tech.cpandl.com domain, the FQDN would be corpsvr17.tech.cpandl.com.

Name resolution

Name resolution is the process by which host names are resolved to IP addresses and vice versa. When a TCP/IP application wants to communicate with another host on a network, it needs the IP address of that host. Typically, the application knows only the name of the host it is looking for, so it has to resolve that name to an IP address.

To do this, the application first looks in its local DNS cache of names that it has previously looked up. If the name is in this cache, the IP address is found without having to look elsewhere and the application can connect to the remote host. If the name isn't in the cache, the application must ask the network's DNS server or servers to help resolve the name. These servers perform a similar lookup. If the name is in their database or cache, the IP address for the name is returned. Otherwise, the DNS server has to request this information from another DNS server.

That's the way it works—the simplified version at least. Most of the time, a TCP/IP application has the host name and needs to find the corresponding IP address. Occasionally, a TCP/IP application has the IP address and needs to find the corresponding host name. To do this, the application must perform a reverse lookup, so instead of requesting an IP address, the application requests a host name using the IP address.

The application first looks in its local cache of information that it has previously looked up. If the IP address is in this cache, the name is found without having to look elsewhere and the application can perform whichever tasks are necessary. If the IP address isn't in the cache, the application must ask the network's DNS server or servers to help resolve the IP address. These servers perform a similar lookup. If the IP address is in their reverse lookup database or cache, the name for the IP address is returned. Otherwise, the DNS server has to request this information from another DNS server.

Windows Internet Naming Service

Windows Internet Naming Service (WINS) is a name-resolution service that resolves computer names to IP addresses. For example, using WINS, the computer name COMPUTER84 could be resolved to an IP address that enables computers on a Microsoft network to find one another and transfer information. WINS is needed to support applications that use Network Basic Input/Output System (NetBIOS) over TCP/IP, such as Exchange Server 2003, the .NET command-line utilities, and network browsing for users in pre–Windows Server 2008 environments. If you don't have NetBIOS applications on the network or pre–Windows Server 2008 infrastructure, you don't need to use WINS.

WINS is designed for client/server environments in which WINS clients send queries to WINS servers for name resolution and WINS servers resolve the queries and respond. To transmit WINS queries and other information, computers use NetBIOS. NetBIOS is an interface developed to allow applications to perform basic network operations, such as sending data, connecting to remote hosts, and accessing network resources.

NetBIOS computer names can be up to 15 characters long. They must be unique on the network and can be looked up on a server called a WINS server. WINS supports both forward lookups (NetBIOS computer name to IP address) and reverse lookups (IP address to NetBIOS computer name).

NetBIOS applications rely on WINS or the local LMHOSTS file to resolve computer names to IP addresses. On early Windows networks, WINS was the primary name-resolution service available. On current Windows networks, DNS is the primary name-resolution service and WINS has a different function. This function is to allow applications written to the NetBIOS interface to browse lists of resources on the network and to allow systems to locate NetBIOS resources. To enable WINS name resolution on a network, you need to configure WINS clients and servers. When you configure WINS clients, you tell the clients the IP addresses of WINS servers on the network. Using the IP address, clients can communicate with WINS servers anywhere on the network, even if the servers are on different subnets. WINS clients can also communicate using a broadcast method in which clients broadcast messages to other computers on the local network segment requesting their IP addresses. Because messages are broadcast, the WINS server isn't used. Any non-WINS clients that support this type of message broadcasting can also use this method to resolve computer names to IP addresses.

If you are using applications that rely on NetBIOS over TCP/IP, your organization must set up WINS. If you are currently using WINS and don't have applications that rely on NetBIOS over TCP/IP, you can eliminate the need for this service by moving workstations and servers to currently supported versions of Windows.

IMPORTANT

Where legacy systems have been upgraded to current Windows Server versions, WINS might be needed to establish or reestablish trust relationships in Active Directory. The only way to be sure WINS is not needed for trusts is to ensure that there are no legacy references within Active Directory, and that means performing a bare-metal install of Windows Server with forest and domain operations in Windows Server 2003 Native Mode or higher. NetBIOS names are still used under the hood for trust relationships in Active Directory with current Windows Server operating systems.

Link-Local Multicast Name Resolution

Link-Local Multicast Name Resolution (LLMNR) fills a need for peer-to-peer name-resolution services for devices with IPv4, IPv6, or both addresses, enabling IPv4 and IPv6 devices on a single subnet without a WINS or DNS server to resolve each other's names—a service that neither WINS nor DNS can fully provide. Although WINS can provide NetBIOS name-resolution services for IPv4, it does not support IPv6 addresses. Although DNS supports IPv4 and IPv6 addresses, it depends on designated servers to provide name-resolution services.

Windows Vista and later support LLMNR. LLMNR is designed for both IPv4 and IPv6 clients when other name-resolution systems are not available, such as on a small-office or ad hoc network. LLMNR can also be used on corporate networks where DNS services are not available.

LLMNR is designed to complement DNS by enabling name resolution in scenarios in which conventional DNS name resolution is not possible. Although LLMNR can replace the need for WINS in cases in which NetBIOS is not required, LLMNR is not a substitute for DNS because it operates only on the local subnet. Because LLMNR traffic is prevented from propagating across routers, it can't accidentally flood the network.

As with WINS, you use LLMNR to resolve a host name, such as COMPUTER84, to an IP address. By default, LLMNR is enabled on all computers running Windows Vista and later, and these computers use LLMNR only when all attempts to look up a host name through DNS fail. As a result, name resolution works like this for Windows Vista and later:

1. A host computer looks up the name in its internal name cache. If the name is not found in the cache, the host sends a query to its configured primary DNS server. If the host computer does not receive a response or receives an error, it tries each configured alternate DNS server in turn. If the host has no configured DNS servers or fails to connect to a DNS server without errors, name resolution fails over to LLMNR.

2. The host computer sends a multicast query over User Datagram Protocol (UDP) requesting the IP address for the name being looked up. This query is restricted to the local subnet (also referred to as the *local link*).

3. Each computer on the local link that supports LLMNR and is configured to respond to incoming queries receives the query and compares the name to its own host name. If the host name is not a match, the computer discards the query. If the host name is a match, the computer transmits a unicast message containing its IP address to the originating host.

You can also use LLMNR for reverse mapping. With reverse mapping, a computer sends a unicast query to a specific IP address, requesting the host name of the target computer. An LLMNR-enabled computer that receives the request sends a unicast reply containing its host name to the originating host.

LLMNR-enabled computers are required to ensure that their names are unique on the local subnet. In most cases a computer checks for uniqueness when it starts, when it resumes from a suspended state, and when you change its network-interface settings. If a computer has not yet determined that its name is unique, it must indicate this condition when responding to a name query.

By default, LLMNR is automatically enabled on computers running Windows Vista and later. You can disable LLMNR through registry settings. To disable LLMNR for all network interfaces, create and set the following DWORD value to 0 (zero): HKLM/SYSTEM/CurrentControlSet /Services/Dnscache/Parameters/EnableMulticast. To disable LLMNR for a specific network interface, create and set the following DWORD value to 0 (zero): HKLM/SYSTEM /CurrentControlSet/Services/Tcpip/Parameters/Interfaces/AdapterGUID/EnableMulticast, where *AdapterGUID* is the globally unique identifier (GUID) of the network interface adapter for which you want to disable LLMNR.

You can reenable LLMNR at any time by setting these DWORD values to 1. You also can manage LLMNR through Group Policy.

CHAPTER 2

Managing TCP/IP networking

As an administrator, you enable networked computers to communicate by using the basic networking protocols built into Microsoft Windows Server 2012 R2. The key protocol you'll use is Transmission Control Protocol/Internet Protocol (TCP/IP). TCP/IP is actually a collection of protocols and services used for communicating over a network. It's the primary protocol used for internetwork communications. Compared to configuring other networking protocols, configuring TCP/IP communications is fairly complicated, but TCP/IP is the most versatile protocol available.

NOTE

Group Policy settings can affect your ability to install and manage TCP/IP networking. The key policies you'll want to examine are in User Configuration\Administrative Templates\Network\Network Connections and Computer Configuration\Administrative Templates\System\Group Policy. Group Policy is discussed in Chapter 17, "Managing Group Policy."

Installing TCP/IP networking

If you want to install networking on a computer, you must install TCP/IP networking and a network adapter. Windows Server 2012 R2 uses TCP/IP as its networking protocol. Normally, networking is installed during setup of the operating system. You can also install TCP/IP networking through network connection properties. Although name resolution can be performed using Domain Name System (DNS), Windows Internet Naming Service (WINS), or Link-Local Multicast Name Resolution (LLNMR), the preferred technique on Windows Server domains is DNS.

Preparing for installation of TCP/IP networking

Before you can configure TCP/IP networking on individual computers, you need the following information:

- **Domain name.** The name of the domain in which the computer will be located. This can be a parent or child domain.

- **IP address type, value, or both.** The IP address information to assign to the computer, which can include both Internet Protocol version 4 (IPv4) and Internet Protocol version 6 (IPv6) addressing details.

- **Subnet mask.** The subnet mask for the IPv4 network to which the computer is attached.

- **Subnet prefix length.** The subnet prefix length for the IPv6 network to which the computer is attached.

- **Default gateway address.** The address of the router or routers that will function as the computer's gateway.

- **DNS server address.** The address of the DNS server or servers that provide DNS name-resolution services on the network.

- **WINS server address.** The address of the WINS server or servers that provide WINS name-resolution services on the network.

If you are unsure of any of this information, you should ask the IT staff. In many cases, even if you are an administrator, there is a specific person you must ask for the IP address setup that should be used. Typically, this is your organization's network administrator, and it is that person's job to maintain the spreadsheet or database that shows how IP addresses are assigned within the organization.

If no one in your organization has this role yet, this role should be assigned to someone or jointly managed to ensure that IP addresses are assigned following a specific plan. The plan should detail the following information:

- The address ranges that are reserved for network equipment and hardware and which individual IP addresses in this range are currently in use

- The address ranges that are reserved for DHCP and, as such, can't be assigned using a static IP address

- The address ranges that are for static IP addresses and which individual IP addresses in this range are currently in use

Installing network adapters

Network adapters are hardware devices that are used to communicate on networks. You can install and configure network adapters by following these steps:

1. Configure the network adapter following the manufacturer's instructions. For example, you might need to use the software provided by the manufacturer to modify the Interrupt setting or the Port setting of the adapter.

2. If you're installing an internal network interface card, shut down the computer, unplug it, and install the adapter card in the appropriate slot on the computer. When you're finished, plug in the computer and start it.

3. Windows Server should detect the new adapter during startup. If you have a separate driver disk for the adapter, insert it now. Otherwise, you might be prompted to insert a driver disk.

4. If Windows Server doesn't detect the adapter automatically, the most common reason is a missing driver, especially for motherboards with an embedded network adapter that isn't from Intel. If the driver wasn't found and you don't have a driver disk, you can obtain the required driver by visiting the manufacturer's website. For other issues, you'll need to try to diagnose and resolve the problem.

    ■ The built-in hardware diagnostics can detect many types of problems with hardware devices. If a problem is detected, you might see a Problem Reporting balloon telling you there is a problem. Tapping or clicking this balloon opens Action Center. You can also access Action Center in Control Panel by tapping or clicking the System And Security link and then selecting Action Center. To open Action Center, tap or click the Action Center icon in the notification area of the taskbar and then select Open Action Center.

    ■ Events related to malfunctioning hardware often will be written to the system logs. You can quickly find events related to a specific device by using Device Manager. In Device Manager, press and hold or right-click the device that you want to troubleshoot and then select Properties. If there's a problem with a device, there will be an error status and a related error code in the General tab. In the Events tab, you'll see the most recent events related to the device.

5. If networking services aren't installed on the system, install them as described in the next section.

Installing networking services (TCP/IP)

If you're installing TCP/IP after installing Windows Server 2012 R2, log on to the computer using an account with Administrator privileges and then follow these steps:

1. In Control Panel, under the Network And Internet heading, tap or click View Network Status And Tasks.

2. In Network And Sharing Center, tap or click Change Adapter Settings.

3. In Network Connections, press and hold or right-click the connection you want to work with and then select Properties.

CHAPTER 3

4. This displays the Properties dialog box for the connection, shown in Figure 3-1.

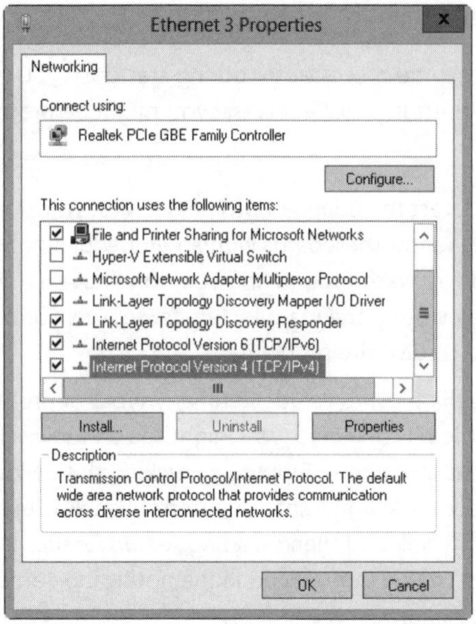

Figure 3-1 Install and configure TCP/IP in the Properties dialog box for the connection.

5. If Internet Protocol Version 6 (TCP/IPv6), Internet Protocol Version 4 (TCP/IPv4), or both aren't shown in the list of installed components, you need to install them. Tap or click Install. Select Protocol and then tap or click Add. In the Select Network Protocol dialog box, select the protocol to install and then tap or click OK. If you are installing both TCP/IPv6 and TCP/IPv4, perform this procedure for each protocol.

6. In the Properties dialog box for the connection, make sure that the following are selected as appropriate: Internet Protocol Version 6 (TCP/IPv6), Internet Protocol Version 4 (TCP/IPv4), or both. Then tap or click OK.

7. As necessary, follow the instructions in the next section for configuring network connections for the computer.

Configuring TCP/IP networking

A network connection is created automatically if a computer has a network adapter and is connected to a network. If a computer has multiple network adapters and is connected to a network, you'll have one network connection for each adapter. If no network connection is available, you should connect the computer to the network or create a different type of connection, as explained later in this chapter in the section entitled "Managing network connections."

Computers use IP addresses to communicate over TCP/IP. Windows Server provides the following ways to configure IP addressing:

- **Manually.** IP addresses that are assigned manually are called *static IP addresses*. Static IP addresses are fixed and don't change unless you change them. You'll usually assign static IP addresses to Windows servers, and when you do this, you'll need to configure additional information to help the server navigate the network.

- **Dynamically.** A Dynamic Host Configuration Protocol (DHCP) server (if one is installed on the network) assigns dynamic IP addresses at startup, and the addresses might change over time. Dynamic IP addressing is the default configuration.

- **Alternatively (IPv4 only).** When a computer is configured to use DHCPv4 and no DHCPv4 server is available, Windows Server assigns an alternate private IP address automatically. By default, the alternate IPv4 address is in the range from 169.254.0.1 to 169.254.255.254 with a subnet mask of 255.255.0.0. You can also specify a user-configured alternate IPv4 address, which is particularly useful for laptop users.

IMPORTANT
Unless an IP address is specifically reserved, DHCP servers assign IP addresses for a specific period of time, known as an *IP address lease*. If this lease expires and can't be renewed, the client assigns itself an automatic private IP address.

Configuring static IP addresses

When you assign a static IP address, you need to tell the computer the IP address you want to use, the subnet mask for this IP address, and, if necessary, the default gateway to use for internetwork communications. An IP address is a numeric identifier for a computer. IP addressing schemes vary according to how your network is configured, but they're normally assigned based on a particular network segment.

IPv6 addresses and IPv4 addresses are very different. With IPv6, the first 64 bits represent the network ID and the remaining 64 bits represent the network interface. With IPv4, a variable number of the initial bits represents the network ID and the rest of the bits represent the host ID. For example, if you're working with IPv4 and a computer on the network segment 192.168.10.0 with a subnet mask of 255.255.255.0, the first 24 bits represent the network ID and the address range you have available for computer hosts is from 192.168.10.1 to 192.168.10.254. In this range, the address 192.168.10.255 is reserved for network broadcasts.

CHAPTER 3

If you're on a private network that is indirectly connected to the Internet, you should use private IPv6 addresses. Link-local unicast addresses are private IPv6 addresses. All link-local unicast addresses begin with FE80.

If you're on a private network that is indirectly connected to the Internet, you should use private IPv4 addresses. Table 3-1 summarizes private network IPv4 addresses.

Table 3-1 Private IPv4 network addressing

Private Network ID	Subnet Mask	Network Address Range
10.0.0.0	255.0.0.0	10.0.0.0–10.255.255.255
172.16.0.0	255.240.0.0	172.16.0.0–172.31.255.255
192.168.0.0	255.255.0.0	192.168.0.0–192.168.255.255

All other IPv4 network addresses are public and must be leased or purchased. If the network is connected directly to the Internet and you've obtained a range of IPv4 addresses from your Internet service provider, you can use the IPv4 addresses you've been assigned.

Testing an IP address

Before you assign a static IP address, you should make sure that the address isn't already in use or reserved for use with DHCP. You can do this with the PING command and with the Test-Connection cmdlet.

TROUBLESHOOTING

Blocked pings

Windows Firewall (and other firewalls) can be configured to block pings. If a firewall is configured in this way, ping tests will fail, as will connection tests using Test-Connection. The reason Test-Connection fails if pings are blocked is because the cmdlet uses Get-WMIObject Win32_PingStatus to test connections.

With the PING command, you can check to see whether an address is in use. Open a command prompt and enter **ping**, followed by the IP address you want to check.

To test the IPv4 address 10.0.10.12, you would use the following command:

```
ping 10.0.10.12
```

To test the IPv6 address FEC0::02BC:FF:BECB:FE4F:961D, you would use the following command:

```
ping FEC0::02BC:FF:BECB:FE4F:961D
```

If you receive a successful reply from the PING test, the IP address is in use and you should try another one. If no current host on the network uses this IP address, the PING command output should be similar to the following:

```
Pinging 192.168.1.100 with 32 bytes of data:

Request timed out.
Request timed out.
Request timed out.
Request timed out.

Ping statistics for 192.168.1.100:
Packets: Sent = 4, Received = 0, Lost = 4 (100% loss)
```

You can then use the IP address.

IMPORTANT

Pinging an IP address will work as long as all the hosts are active and reachable on the network at the time you ping the address. However, a firewall could be blocking your PING request. It's more important to plan the assignment of static addresses to machines on your network carefully.

You also can use the Test-Connection cmdlet to check whether an IP address is in use. The cmdlet's basic syntax is this:

```
test-connection [-count Count] IPAddressOrServerName
```

Here, you can optionally use the *–Count* parameter to specify the number of times to test a connection and *IPAddressOrServerName* is the IP address or server name you want to check. If you don't specify a count, Windows PowerShell tries to connect to a server or IP address only once. In the following example, you try to connect five times to 192.168.10.42:

```
test-connection -count 5 192.168.10.42
```

If the IP address is in use, the test results will look similar to the following:

Source	Destination	IPV4Address	IPV6Address	Bytes	Time(ms)
CORPSERVER64	192.168.10.42	192.168.10.42		32	0
CORPSERVER64	192.168.10.42	192.168.10.42		32	0
CORPSERVER64	192.168.10.42	192.168.10.42		32	0
CORPSERVER64	192.168.10.42	192.168.10.42		32	0
CORPSERVER64	192.168.10.42	192.168.10.42		32	0

CHAPTER 3

As with PING, a successful reply from the test means the IP address is in use and you should try another one. If no current host on the network uses this IP address, the output should be similar to the following:

```
test-connection : Testing connection to computer '192.168.10.42' failed:
A non-recoverable error occurred
At line:1 char:1
+ test-connection -count 5 192.168.10.42
+ ~~~~~~~~~~~~~~~~~~~~~~~~~~~~~~~~~~~~~~~~
    + CategoryInfo          : ResourceUnavailable: (192.168.10.42:String)
[Test-Connection], PingException
```

Configuring a static IPv4 or IPv6 address

One local area network (LAN) connection is available for each network adapter installed. These connections are created automatically. To configure static IP addresses for a particular connection, follow these steps:

1. In Control Panel, tap or click View Network Status And Tasks under the Network And Internet heading.

2. In Network And Sharing Center, tap or click Change Adapter Settings. In Network Connections, press and hold or right-click the connection you want to work with and then select Properties.

3. Double-tap or double-click Internet Protocol Version 6 (TCP/IPv6) or Internet Protocol Version 4 (TCP/IPv4) as appropriate for the type of IP address you are configuring.

4. For an IPv6 address, do the following:

    ■ Select Use The Following IPv6 Address and then enter the IPv6 address in the IPv6 Address text box. The IPv6 address you assign to the computer must not be used anywhere else on the network.

    ■ Press the Tab key. The Subnet Prefix Length field ensures that the computer communicates over the network properly. Windows Server should insert a default value for the subnet prefix into the Subnet Prefix Length text box. If the network doesn't use variable-length subnetting, the default value should suffice. If your network does use variable-length subnets, you need to change this value as appropriate for your network.

5. For an IPv4 address, do the following:

    ■ Select Use The Following IP Address and then enter the IPv4 address in the IP Address text box. The IPv4 address you assign to the computer must not be used anywhere else on the network.

    ■ Press the Tab key. The Subnet Mask field ensures that the computer communicates over the network properly. Windows Server should insert a default value for the subnet prefix into the Subnet Mask text box. If the network doesn't use variable-length subnetting, the default value should suffice. If your network does use variable-length subnets, you need to change this value as appropriate for your network.

6. If the computer needs to access other TCP/IP networks, the Internet, or other subnets, you must specify a default gateway. Enter the IP address of the network's default router in the Default Gateway text box.

7. DNS is needed for domain-name resolution. Select Use The Following DNS Server Addresses and then enter a preferred address and an alternate DNS server address in the text boxes provided.

8. When you're finished, tap or click OK three times to save your changes. Repeat this process for other network adapters and IP protocols you want to configure.

9. With IPv4 addressing, configure WINS as necessary, following the technique outlined later in this chapter in the section entitled "Configuring WINS resolution."

Configuring dynamic IP addresses and alternate IP addressing

Many organizations use DHCP servers to dynamically assign IPv4 and IPv6 addresses. To receive an IPv4 or IPv6 address, client computers use a limited broadcast to advertise that they need to obtain an IP address. DHCP servers on the network acknowledge the request by offering the client an IP address. The client acknowledges the first offer it receives, and the DHCP server in turn tells the client that it has succeeded in leasing the IP address for a specified amount of time.

The message from the DHCP server can, and typically does, include the IP addresses of the default gateway, the preferred and alternate DNS servers, and the preferred and alternate WINS servers. This means these settings don't need to be manually configured on the client computer.

Inside OUT

DHCP is primarily for clients

Dynamic IP addresses aren't for all hosts on the network, however. Typically, you'll want to assign dynamic IP addresses to workstations and, in some instances, to member servers that perform noncritical roles on the network. But if you use dynamic IP addressing for member servers, these servers should have reservations for their IP addresses. For any server that has a critical network role or provides a key service, you definitely want to use static IP addresses. Finally, with DNS and DHCP servers you must use static IP addresses, so don't try to assign dynamic IP addresses to these servers.

CHAPTER 3

Although you can use static IP addresses with workstations, most workstations use dynamic addressing, alternative IP addressing, or both. You configure dynamic and alternative addressing by following these steps:

1. In Control Panel, under the Network And Internet heading tap or click View Network Status And Tasks.

2. In Network And Sharing Center, tap or click Change Adapter Settings. In Network Connections, one LAN connection is shown for each network adapter installed. These connections are created automatically. If you don't see a LAN connection for an installed adapter, check the driver for the adapter. It might be installed incorrectly. Press and hold or right-click the connection you want to work with and then select Properties.

3. Double-tap or double-click Internet Protocol Version 6 (TCP/IPv6) or Internet Protocol Version 4 (TCP/IPv4) as appropriate for the type of IP address you are configuring.

4. Select Obtain An IPv6 Address Automatically or Obtain An IP Address Automatically, whichever is appropriate for the type of IP address you are configuring. If desired, select Obtain DNS Server Address Automatically. Or select Use The Following DNS Server Addresses and then enter preferred and alternate DNS server addresses in the text boxes provided.

5. When you use dynamic IPv4 addressing with desktop computers, you should configure an automatic alternative address. To use this configuration, in the Alternate Configuration tab select Automatic Private IP Address. Tap or click OK, tap or click Close, and then skip the remaining steps.

6. When you use dynamic IPv4 addressing with mobile computers, you'll usually want to configure the alternative address manually. To use this configuration, in the Alternate Configuration tab select User Configured and then enter the IP address you want to use in the IP Address text box. The IP address you assign to the computer should be a private IP address, as shown in Table 3-1, and it must not be in use anywhere else when the settings are applied.

7. With dynamic IPv4 addressing, complete the alternate configuration by entering a subnet mask, a default gateway, DNS, and WINS settings. When you're finished, tap or click OK and then tap or click OK again.

CHAPTER 3

Inside OUT

Disabling APIPA

Whenever DHCP is used, Automatic Private IP Addressing (APIPA) is enabled by default. If you don't want a computer to use APIPA, you can either assign a static TCP/IP address or disable APIPA. For example, if your network uses routers or your network is connected to the Internet without a Network Address Translation (NAT) or proxy server, you might not want to use APIPA. You can disable APIPA in the registry.

You can disable APIPA by creating *IPAutoconfigurationEnabled* as a DWORD value in the registry under HKEY_LOCAL_MACHINE\SYSTEM\CurrentControlSet\Services\Tcpip \Parameters\Interfaces*AdapterGUID*, where *AdapterGUID* is the globally unique identifier (GUID) for the computer's network adapter. Set the value to 0×0.

If you create *IPAutoconfigurationEnabled* as a DWORD value entry, you can enable APIPA at any time by changing the value to 0×1.

For more information about disabling APIPA, see Microsoft Knowledge Base article 220874 at *http://support.microsoft.com/kb/220874*.

CHAPTER 3

Configuring multiple IP addresses and gateways

Using advanced TCP/IP settings, you can configure a single network interface on a computer to use multiple IP addresses and multiple gateways. This allows a computer to appear to be several computers and to access multiple logical subnets to route information or to provide internetworking services.

To provide fault tolerance in case of a router outage, you can choose to configure Windows servers so that they use multiple default gateways. When you assign multiple gateways, Windows Server uses the gateway metric to determine which gateway is used and at what time. The gateway metric indicates the routing cost of using a gateway. The gateway with the lowest routing cost, or metric, is used first. If the computer can't communicate with this gateway, Windows Server tries to use the gateway with the next lowest metric.

The best way to configure multiple gateways depends on the configuration of your network. If your organization's computers use DHCP, you'll probably want to configure the additional gateways through settings on the DHCP server. If computers use static IP addresses or you want to set gateways specifically, assign them by following these steps:

1. In Control Panel, tap or click View Network Status And Tasks under the Network And Internet heading.

2. In Network And Sharing Center, tap or click Change Adapter Settings. In Network Connections, press and hold or right-click the connection you want to work with and then select Properties.

3. Double-tap or double-click Internet Protocol Version 6 (TCP/IPv6) or Internet Protocol Version 4 (TCP/IPv4) as appropriate for the type of IP address you are configuring.

4. Tap or click Advanced to open the Advanced TCP/IP Settings dialog box. Figure 3-2 shows advanced settings for IPv4. The dialog box for IPv6 is similar.

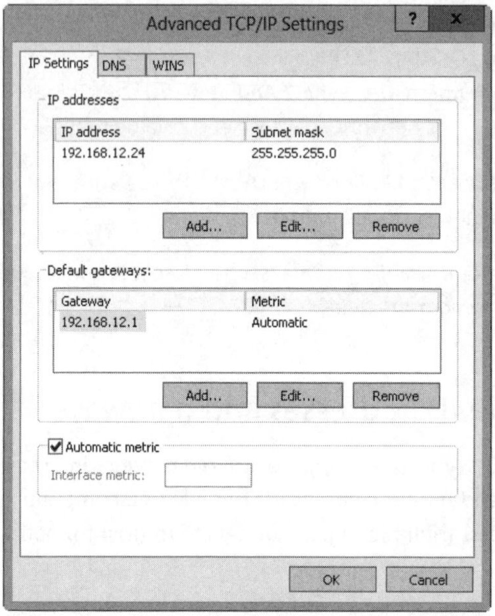

Figure 3-2 Configure multiple IP addresses and gateways in the Advanced TCP/IP Settings dialog box.

5. To add an IP address, tap or click Add below IP Address to display the TCP/IP Address dialog box. After you enter the IP address in the IP Address field, enter the subnet mask in the Subnet Mask field for IPv4 addresses or the subnet prefix length in the Subnet Prefix Length field for IPv6 addresses. Tap or click Add to return to the Advanced TCP/IP Settings dialog box. Repeat this step for each IP address you want to add.

6. The Default Gateways panel shows the gateways that are currently manually configured (if any). To add a default gateway, tap or click Add below Default Gateways to display the TCP/IP Gateway Address dialog box. Enter the gateway address in the Gateway field. By default, Windows Server automatically assigns a metric to the gateway, which determines the order in which the gateway is used. To assign the metric manually, clear

the Automatic Metric check box and then enter a metric in the field provided. Tap or click Add. Repeat this step for each gateway you want to add.

7. Tap or click OK three times to close the open dialog boxes.

Configuring DNS resolution

DNS is a host-name resolution service that you can use to determine the IP address of a computer from its host name. This lets users work with host names, such as fileserver18.cpandl.com or www.microsoft.com, rather than IP addresses, such as 192.168.5.102 or 192.168.12.68. DNS is the primary name service for Windows Server and the Internet.

As with gateways, the best way to configure DNS depends on the configuration of your network. If computers use DHCP, you'll probably want to configure DNS through settings on the DHCP server. If computers use static IP addresses or you want to configure DNS specifically for a particular computer, you'll want to configure DNS manually.

Configuring Basic DNS settings

You can configure basic DNS settings by following these steps:

1. In Control Panel, under the Network And Internet heading tap or click View Network Status And Tasks.

2. In Network And Sharing Center, tap or click Change Adapter Settings. In Network Connections, press and hold or right-click the connection you want to work with and then select Properties.

3. Double-tap or double-click Internet Protocol Version 6 (TCP/IPv6) or Internet Protocol Version 4 (TCP/IPv4) as appropriate for the type of IP address you are configuring.

4. If the computer is using DHCP and you want DHCP to specify the DNS server address, select Obtain DNS Server Address Automatically. Otherwise, select Use The Following DNS Server Addresses and then enter primary and alternate DNS server addresses in the text boxes provided.

5. Tap or click OK three times to save your changes.

Configuring Advanced DNS settings

You configure advanced DNS settings in the DNS tab of the Advanced TCP/IP Settings dialog box, shown in Figure 3-3. You use the fields of the DNS tab as follows:

- **DNS Server Addresses, In Order Of Use.** Use this area to specify the IP address of each DNS server that is used for domain-name resolution. Tap or click Add if you want to add a server IP address to the list. Tap or click Remove to remove a selected server

CHAPTER 3

address from the list. Tap or click Edit to edit the selected entry. You can specify multiple servers for DNS resolution. Their priority is determined by the order. If the first server isn't available to respond to a host-name resolution request, the next DNS server on the list is accessed, and so on. To change the position of a server in the list box, select it and then tap or click the Up or Down arrow button.

- **Append Primary And Connection Specific DNS Suffixes.** Normally, this option is selected by default. Select this option to resolve unqualified computer names in the primary domain. For example, if the computer name Gandolf is used and the parent domain is microsoft.com, the computer name resolves to gandolf.microsoft.com. If the fully qualified computer name doesn't exist in the parent domain, the query fails. The parent domain used is the one set in the System Properties dialog box in the Computer Name tab. (Tap or click System And Security\System in Control Panel and then tap or click Change Settings and view the Computer Name tab to check the settings.)

- **Append Parent Suffixes Of The Primary DNS Suffix.** This option is selected by default. Select this check box to resolve unqualified computer names using the parent/child domain hierarchy. If a query fails in the immediate parent domain, the suffix for the parent of the parent domain is used to try to resolve the query. This process continues until the top of the DNS domain hierarchy is reached. For example, if the computer name Gandolf is used in the dev.microsoft.com domain, DNS attempts to resolve the computer name to gandolf.dev.microsoft.com. If this doesn't work, DNS attempts to resolve the computer name to gandolf.microsoft.com.

- **Append These DNS Suffixes (In Order).** Select this option to set specific DNS suffixes to use rather than resolving through the parent domain. Tap or click Add if you want to add a domain suffix to the list. Tap or click Remove to remove a selected domain suffix from the list. Tap or click Edit to edit the selected entry. You can specify multiple domain suffixes, which are used in order. If the first suffix doesn't resolve properly, DNS attempts to use the next suffix in the list. If this fails, the next suffix is used, and so on. To change the order of the domain suffixes, select the suffix and then tap or click the Up or Down arrow button to change its position.

- **DNS Suffix For This Connection.** This option sets a specific DNS suffix for the connection that overrides DNS names already configured for use on this connection. You'll usually set the DNS domain name through the System Properties dialog box in the Computer Name tab.

- **Register This Connection's Addresses In DNS.** Select this option if you want all IP addresses for this connection to be registered in DNS under the computer's fully qualified domain name (FQDN). This option is selected by default.

NOTE

Dynamic DNS updates are used in conjunction with DHCP to enable a client to update its A (Host Address) record if its IP address changes and to enable the DHCP server to update the PTR (Pointer) record for the client on the DNS server. You can also configure DHCP servers to update both the A and PTR records on the client's behalf. Dynamic DNS updates are supported only by BIND 8.2.1 or higher DNS servers and by server editions of Microsoft Windows.

- **Use This Connection's DNS Suffix In DNS Registration.** Select this check box if you want all IP addresses for this connection to be registered in DNS under the parent domain.

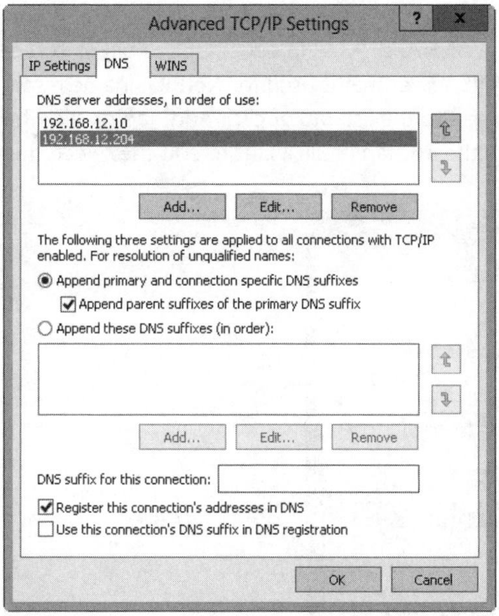

Figure 3-3 Configure advanced DNS settings in the DNS tab of the Advanced TCP/IP Settings dialog box.

Configuring WINS resolution

You use WINS to resolve Network Basic Input/Output System (NetBIOS) computer names to IPv4 addresses. You can use WINS to help computers on a network determine the address of other computers on the network. If a WINS server is installed on the network, you can use the server to resolve computer names. Although WINS is supported on all versions of Windows, Windows Server 2012 R2 primarily uses WINS for backward compatibility.

CHAPTER 3

You can also configure Windows Server 2012 R2 computers to use the local file LMHOSTS to resolve NetBIOS computer names. However, LMHOSTS is consulted only if normal name resolution methods fail. In a properly configured network, these files are rarely used. Thus, the preferred method of NetBIOS computer name resolution is WINS in conjunction with a WINS server.

As with gateways and DNS, the best way to configure WINS depends on the configuration of your network. If computers use DHCP, you'll probably want to configure WINS through settings on the DHCP server. If computers use static IPv4 addresses or you want to configure WINS specifically for a particular computer, you'll want to configure WINS manually.

You can manually configure WINS by following these steps:

1. Access the Advanced TCP/IP Settings dialog box for IPv4 and tap or click the WINS tab, as shown in Figure 3-4. In the WINS Addresses, In Order Of Use panel, you can specify the IPv4 addresses of each WINS server that is used for NetBIOS name resolution. If you want to add a server IPv4 address to the list, tap or click Add. Tap or click Remove to remove a selected server from the list. Tap or click Edit to edit the selected entry.

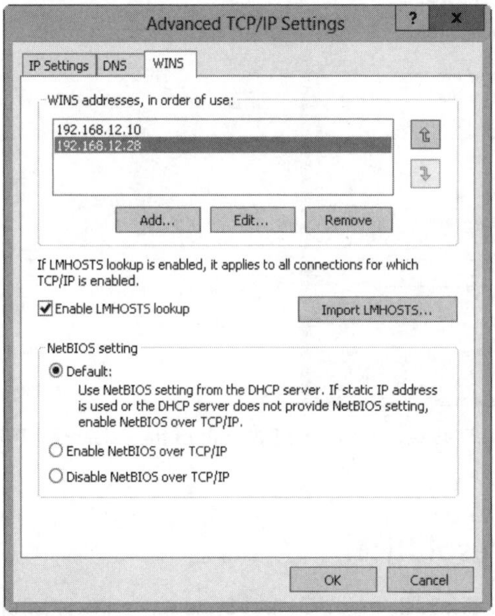

Figure 3-4 Configure WINS resolution for NetBIOS computer names in the WINS tab of the Advanced TCP/IP Settings dialog box.

2. You can specify multiple servers, which are used in order, for WINS resolution. If the first server isn't available to respond to a NetBIOS name-resolution request, the next WINS

server on the list is accessed, and so on. To change the position of a server in the list box, select it and then tap or click the Up or Down arrow button.

3. To enable LMHOSTS lookups, select the Enable LMHOSTS Lookup check box. If you want the computer to use an existing LMHOSTS file defined somewhere on the network, retrieve this file by tapping or clicking Import LMHOSTS. You generally will use LMHOSTS only when other name-resolution methods fail.

4. WINS name resolution requires NetBIOS Over TCP/IP services. To configure WINS name resolution using NetBIOS, select one of the following options:

   - If you use DHCP and dynamic addressing, you can get the NetBIOS setting from the DHCP server. Select Default: Use NetBIOS Setting From The DHCP Server.

   - If you use a static IP address or if the DHCP server does not provide NetBIOS settings, select Enable NetBIOS Over TCP/IP.

   - If WINS and NetBIOS are not used on the network, select Disable NetBIOS Over TCP/IP. This eliminates the NetBIOS broadcasts that would otherwise be sent by the computer.

5. Tap or click OK two times and then tap or click OK. As necessary, repeat this process for other network adapters.

NOTE
LMHOSTS files are maintained locally on a computer-by-computer basis, which can eventually make them unreliable. Rather than relying on LMHOSTS, ensure that your DNS and WINS servers are configured properly and are accessible to the network for centralized administration of name-resolution services.

Managing network connections

Local area connections make it possible for computers to access resources on the network and the Internet. One network connection is created automatically for each network adapter installed on a computer. This section examines techniques you can use to manage these connections.

Checking the status, speed, and activity for network connections

To check the status of a network connection, follow these steps:

1. In Control Panel, under the Network And Internet heading tap or click View Network Status And Tasks.

CHAPTER 3

2.   In Network And Sharing Center, tap or click Change Adapter Settings. In Network Connections, press and hold or right-click the connection you want to work with and then tap or click Status.

3.   The Status dialog box for the connection is displayed. If the connection is disabled or the media is unplugged, you won't be able to access this dialog box. Enable the connection or connect the network cable to resolve the problem and then try to display the Status dialog box again.

The General tab of this dialog box, shown in Figure 3-5, provides useful information regarding the following:

- **IPv4 Connectivity.**   The current IPv4 connection state and type. You'll typically see the status as No Internet Access when connected to an internal network or as Not Connected when not connected to a network.

- **IPv6 Connectivity.**   The current IPv6 connection state and type. You'll typically see the status as No Internet Access when connected to an internal network or as Not Connected when not connected to a network.

- **Media State.**   The state of the media. Because the Status dialog box is available only when the connection is enabled, you'll typically see this as Enabled.

- **Duration.**   The amount of time the connection has been established. If the duration is fairly short, the user either recently connected to the network or the connection was recently reset.

- **Speed.**   The speed of the connection. This should read 100.0 megabits per second (Mbps) for 100 Mbps connections, 1 gigabit per second (Gbps) for 1-gigabit connections, and 10 Gbps for 10-gigabyte connections. An incorrect setting can affect the computer's performance.

- **Bytes.**   The number of bytes sent and the number received by the connection.

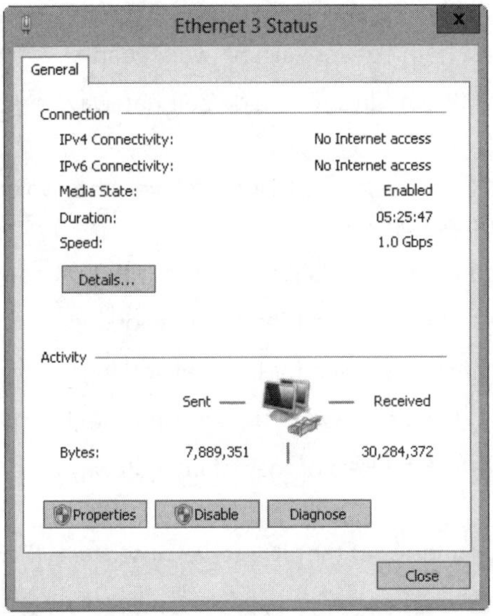

Figure 3-5 The General tab of the Status dialog box for the connection provides access to summary information regarding connections, properties, and support.

Viewing network configuration information

You can view the current configuration for network adapters in several ways. To view configuration settings using the Status dialog box for the connection, follow these steps:

1. In Control Panel, under the Network And Internet heading tap or click View Network Status And Tasks.

2. In Network And Sharing Center, tap or click Change Adapter Settings. In Network Connections, press and hold or right-click the connection you want to work with and then tap or click Status. This displays the Status dialog box for the connection. If the connection is disabled or the media is unplugged, you won't be able to access this dialog box. Enable the connection or connect the network cable to resolve the problem and then try to display the status dialog box again.

3. Tap or click Details to view the following detailed information about the IP address configuration:

    - **Connection-Specific DNS Suffix.** The DNS suffix used to resolve unqualified computer names (if any) for this connection.

    - **Description.** Normally shows the descriptive name of the network adapter.

CHAPTER 3

- **Physical Address.** The machine or Media Access Control (MAC) address of the network adapter. This address is unique for each network adapter.

- **IPv4 Default Gateway.** The IPv4 address of the default gateway used for IPv4 networking.

- **IPv4 DHCP Server.** The IPv4 address of the DHCPv4 server from which the current lease was obtained (DHCPv4 only).

- **IPv4 DNS Servers.** IPv4 addresses for DNS servers used with IPv4 networking.

- **IPv4 IP Address.** The IPv4 address assigned for IPv4 networking.

- **IPv4 Subnet Mask.** The subnet mask used for IPv4 networking.

- **IPv4 WINS Servers.** IPv4 addresses for WINS servers used with IPv4 networking.

- **IPv6 Default Gateway.** The IPv6 address of the default gateway used for IPv6 networking.

- **IPv6 DNS Servers.** The IPv6 address of the DNS servers used with IPv6 networking.

- **Lease Expires.** A date and time stamp for when the DHCPv4 lease expires (DHCPv4 only, when enabled).

- **Lease Obtained.** A date and time stamp for when the DHCPv4 lease was obtained (DHCPv4 only, when enabled).

- **Link-Local IPv6 Address.** Shows the computer's link-local IPv6 address.

- **NetBIOS Over Tcpip Enabled.** Shows whether NetBIOS over TCP/IP is enabled.

You can also use the IPCONFIG command to view advanced configuration settings. To do so, follow these steps:

1. Enter **cmd** in the Apps Search field and press Enter.

2. At the command line, enter **ipconfig /all** to see detailed configuration information for all network adapters configured on the computer.

NOTE

The command prompt is started in standard user mode. You also can enter the command at the Windows PowerShell prompt.

> ## Inside OUT
> *Getting IP configuration in Windows PowerShell*
>
> Although you can use Windows PowerShell to obtain similar information, there really is no single-command substitute for **ipconfig /all**. That said, you can enter **Get-NetIPAddress –AddressState Preferred** to view information about all the valid and active IP addresses that a computer is using. You also can enter **Get-NetIPInterface –ConnectionState Connected | FL –Property *** to get detailed information about each active and connected interface.

Enabling and disabling network connections

Local area connections are created and connected automatically. If you want to disable a connection so that it can't be used, follow these steps:

1. In Control Panel, under the Network And Internet heading, tap or click View Network Status And Tasks.

2. In Network And Sharing Center, tap or click Change Adapter Settings. In Network Connections, press and hold or right-click the connection and select Disable to deactivate the connection and disable it.

3. If you want to enable the connection later, press and hold or right-click the connection in Network Connections and select Enable.

Another way to disable a network adapter is to use Disable-NetAdapter. The basic syntax for each is

```
Disable-NetAdapter -Name NetworkName
```

Where *NetworkName* is the network name, such as

```
Disable-NetAdapter –Name Network
```

If you want to disconnect from a network or start another connection, follow these steps:

1. In Control Panel, under the Network And Internet heading tap or click View Network Status And Tasks.

2. In Network And Sharing Center, tap or click Change Adapter Settings. In Network Connections, press and hold or right-click the connection and select Disconnect. Typically, only remote access or wireless connections have a Disconnect option.

3. If you want to activate the connection later, press and hold or right-click the connection in Network Connections and select Connect.

Renaming network connections

Windows Server 2012 R2 initially assigns default names for network connections. In Network Connections, you can rename the connections at any time by pressing and holding or right-clicking the connection, selecting Rename, and then typing a new connection name. If a computer has multiple network connections, proper naming can help you and others better understand the uses of a particular connection.

Troubleshooting and testing network settings

Windows Server 2012 R2 includes many tools for troubleshooting and testing TCP/IP connectivity. This section looks at automated diagnostics, basic tests that you should perform whenever you install or modify a computer's network settings, and techniques for resolving difficult networking problems involving DHCP and DNS. The final section shows you how to perform detailed network diagnostics testing.

Diagnosing and resolving network connection problems

Occasionally, network cables can get unplugged or the network adapter might experience a problem that temporarily prevents it from working. After you plug the cable back in or solve the adapter problem, the connection should automatically reconnect. To diagnose network connection problems, follow these steps:

1. In Control Panel, under the Network And Internet heading tap or click View Network Status And Tasks.

2. In Network And Sharing Center, tap or click Change Adapter Settings.

3. Press and hold or right-click the connection you want to work with and select Diagnose.

Windows Network Diagnostics will then try to identify the problem. A list of possible solutions is provided for identifiable configuration problems. Some solutions provide automated fixes you can make by tapping or clicking the solution. Other solutions require manual fixes, such as might be required if you need to reset a network router or broadband modem. If your actions don't fix the problem, refer to other appropriate parts of this troubleshooting section.

Diagnosing and resolving Internet connection problems

Because of the many interdependencies among services, protocols, and configuration settings, troubleshooting network problems can be difficult. Fortunately, Windows Server 2012

R2 includes a powerful network diagnostics tool for pinpointing problems that relate to the following:

- General network connectivity

- Internet service settings for email, newsgroups, and proxies

- Settings for modems, network clients, and network adapters

- DNS, DHCP, and WINS configuration

- Default gateways and IP addresses

To diagnose Internet connection problems, follow these steps:

1. In Control Panel, under the Network And Internet heading tap or click View Network Status And Tasks.

2. Tap or click Troubleshoot Problems and then tap or click a troubleshooter to run, such as Incoming Connections or Network Adapter.

3. When the troubleshooter starts, tap or click Next.

Windows Network Diagnostics will then try to identify the problem. If identifiable configuration problems exist, a list of possible solutions is provided. Some solutions provide automated fixes you can make by tapping or clicking the solution. Other solutions require manual fixes, such as might be required if you need to reset a network router or broadband modem. If your actions don't fix the problem, refer to other appropriate parts of this troubleshooting section.

Performing basic network tests

Whenever you install a new computer or make configuration changes to the computer's network settings, you should test the configuration. The most basic TCP/IP test is to use the PING command or the Test-Connection cmdlet to test the computer's connection to the network. PING is a command-line command. To use it, enter **ping <*host*>** at the command prompt or **Test-Connection <*host*>** at a Windows PowerShell prompt, where <*host*> is either the computer name or the IP address of the host computer you're trying to reach. Keep in mind that Test-Connection is a wrapper for Get-WMIObject Win32_PingStatus, so whether you enter **Ping** at a command prompt or Test-Connection at a Windows PowerShell prompt, you are using PING.

You can use the following methods to test the configuration using PING:

- **Try to PING IP addresses.** If the computer is configured correctly and the host you're trying to reach is accessible to the network, PING should receive a reply—as long as the computer's firewall allows pinging. If ping can't reach the host or is blocked by a firewall, PING times out.

- **On domains that use WINS, try to PING NetBIOS computer names.** If PING correctly resolves NetBIOS computer names, the NetBIOS facilities, such as WINS, are correctly configured for the computer.

- **On domains that use DNS, try to PING DNS host names.** If PING correctly resolves fully qualified DNS host names, DNS name resolution is configured properly.

You might also want to test network browsing for the computer. If the computer is a member of a domain and computer browsing is enabled throughout the domain, log on to the computer and then use File Explorer or Network Explorer to browse other computers in the domain. Afterward, log on to a different computer in the domain and try to browse the computer you just configured. These tests tell you if the DNS resolution is being handled properly in the local environment. If you can't browse, check the configuration of the DNS services and protocols.

In some cases, discovering and sharing might be set to block discovery. You'll need to allow discovery to resolve this by following these steps:

1. In Control Panel, under the Network And Internet heading tap or click View Network Status And Tasks.

2. In Network And Sharing Center, in the left pane tap or click Change Advanced Sharing Settings.

3. You'll then see options for configuring the computer's sharing and discovery settings for each network profile. Manage the settings for each profile as appropriate. For example, if network discovery is disabled for a profile and should be enabled, tap or click the related Turn On Network Discovery option.

4. Tap or click Save Changes.

Diagnosing and resolving IP addressing problems

You can obtain the current IP address settings of a computer as discussed earlier in this chapter in the section entitled "Viewing network configuration information." If a computer is having problems accessing network resources or communicating with other computers, there might be an IP addressing problem. Take a close look at the IP address currently assigned and other IP address settings and use the following tips to help in your troubleshooting:

- If the IPv4 address currently assigned to the computer is in the range 169.254.0.1 to 169.254.255.254, the computer is using Automatic Private IP Addressing (APIPA). An automatic private IP address is assigned to a computer when it is configured to use

DHCP and its DHCP client can't reach a DHCP server. When using APIPA, Windows Server will automatically periodically check for a DHCP server to become available. If a computer doesn't eventually obtain a dynamic IP address, the network connection usually has a problem. Check the network cable and if necessary trace the cable back to the switch or hub into which it connects.

- If the IPv4 address and the subnet mask of the computer are currently set as 0.0.0.0, either the network is disconnected or someone has attempted to use a static IP address that duplicated another IP address already in use on the network. In this case you should access Network Connections and determine the state of the connection. If the connection is disabled or disconnected, this should be shown. Press and hold or right-click the connection and select Enable or Diagnose as appropriate. If the connection is already enabled, you need to modify the IP address settings for the connection.

- If the IP address is dynamically assigned, make sure that another computer on the network isn't using the same IP address. You can do this by disconnecting the network cable for the computer you are working with and pinging the IP address in question. If you receive a response from the PING test, you know that another computer is using the IP address. This computer probably has an improper static IP address or a reservation that isn't set up properly.

- If the IP address appears to be set correctly, check the subnet mask, gateway, DNS, and WINS settings by comparing the network settings of the computer you are troubleshooting with those of a computer that is known to have a good network configuration. One of the biggest problem areas is the subnet mask. When subnetting is used, the subnet mask used in one area of the network might look very similar to the subnet mask in another area of the network. For example, the subnet mask in one IPv4 area might be 255.255.255.240, and it might be 255.255.255.248 in another IPv4 area.

When you are using static IP addressing, you can check the current IPv4 or IPv6 settings by entering **ipconfig /all** at a command prompt. The display of the **ipconfig /all** command includes IPv4/IPv6 addresses, default routers, and DNS servers for all interfaces. You can also check IPv4 and IPv6 addressing separately. To check the IPv4 addressing configuration, enter **netsh interface ipv4 show address**. To check IPv6 addressing, enter **netsh interface ipv6 show address**. To use Netsh to show the configuration of a remote computer, use the **–r** *RemoteComputerName* command-line option. For example, to display the configuration of the remote computer named CORPSERVER26, you would enter **netsh –r corpserver26 interface ipv4 show address**.

To make changes to the configuration of IP interfaces, use the **netsh interface ipv4 set interface** and **netsh interface ipv6 set interface** commands. To add the IP addresses of DNS servers, use the **netsh interface ipv4 add dns** and **netsh interface ipv6 add dns** commands.

CHAPTER 3

Diagnosing and resolving routing problems

As part of troubleshooting, you can verify the reachability of local and remote destinations. You can ping your default router by its IPv4 or IPv6 address. You can obtain the local IPv4 address of your default router by entering **netsh interface ipv4 show route** at a command prompt or **get-netroute –addressfamily ipv4** at a Windows PowerShell prompt. You can obtain the link-local IPv6 address of your default router by entering **netsh interface ipv6 show route** at a command prompt or **get-netroute –addressfamily ipv6** at a Windows PowerShell prompt. Pinging the default router tests whether you can reach local nodes and whether you can reach the default router, which forwards IP packets to remote nodes.

When you ping the default IPv6 router, you must specify the zone identifier (ID) for the interface on which you want the ICMPv6 Echo Request messages to be sent. The zone ID for the default router is listed when you enter the **ipconfig /all** command.

If you are able to ping your default router, ping a remote destination by its IPv4 or IPv6 address. If you are unable to ping a remote destination by its IP address, there might be a routing problem between your node and the destination node. Enter **tracert –d *IPAddress*** to trace the routing path to the remote destination. You use the **–d** command-line option to speed up the response by preventing Tracert from performing a reverse DNS query on every near-side router interface in the routing path.

Being unable to reach a local or remote destination might be due to incorrect or missing routes in the local IP routing table. To view the local IP routing table, enter the **netsh interface ipv4 show route** command or the **netsh interface ipv6 show route** command. Use the command output to verify that you have a route corresponding to your local subnet. The route with the lowest metric is used first. If you have multiple default routes with the same lowest metric, you might need to modify your IP router configuration so that the default route with the lowest metric uses the interface that connects to the correct network.

You can add a route to the IP routing table by using the **netsh interface ipv4 add route** command or the **netsh interface ipv6 add route** command. To modify an existing route, use the **netsh interface ipv4 set route** command or the **netsh interface ipv6 set route** command. To remove an existing route, use the **netsh interface ipv6 delete route** command or the **netsh interface ipv6 delete route** command.

If you suspect a problem with router performance, use the **pathping –n *IPAddress*** command to trace the path to a destination and display information on packet losses for each router in the path. You use the **–n** command-line option to speed up the response by preventing Pathping from performing a reverse DNS query on every near-side router interface in the routing path.

Inside OUT

Checking IPsec policies and Windows Firewall

A problem reaching a destination node might be due to the configuration of Internet Protocol security (IPsec) or packet filtering. Check for IPsec policies that have been configured on the computer having the problem, on intermediate IPv6 routers, and on the destination computer. On computers running Windows Vista or later, connection security rules are configured using Windows Firewall With Advanced Security and IPsec policies are configured using the IP Security Policy Management snap-in for MMC.

Packet filtering is often configured to allow specific types of traffic and discard all others or to discard specific types of traffic and allow all others. Because of this, you might be able to view webpages on a web server but not ping the web server by its host name or IP address.

Each network connection configured on a computer can be enabled or disabled in Windows Firewall. When enabled, IPv4 and IPv6 drop incoming requests. During troubleshooting, you can disable Windows Firewall for a specific IPv4 or IPv6 interface with the **netsh interface ipv4 set interface interface=NameOrIndex firewall=disabled** and **netsh interface ipv6 set interface interface=NameOrIndex firewall=disabled** commands. You can also completely turn off Windows Firewall with the **netsh firewall set opmode disable** command. Don't forget to reenable the firewall when you are done troubleshooting.

CHAPTER 3

Releasing and renewing DHCP settings

DHCP servers can assign many network configuration settings automatically, including IP addresses, default gateways, primary and secondary DNS servers, primary and secondary WINS servers, and more. When computers use dynamic addressing, they are assigned a lease on a specific IP address. This lease is good for a specific time period and must be renewed periodically. When the lease needs to be renewed, the computer contacts the DHCP server that provided the lease. If the server is available, the lease is renewed and a new lease period is granted. You can also renew leases manually as necessary on individual computers or by using the DHCP server itself.

Problems that prevent network communications can occur during the lease assignment and renewal process. If the server isn't available and can't be reached before a lease expires, the IP address can become invalid. If this happens, the computer might use the alternate IP address configuration to set an alternate address, which usually has settings that are inappropriate and prevent proper communications. To resolve this problem, you need to release and then renew the DHCP lease.

Another type of problem occurs when users move around to various offices and subnets within the organization. While users are moving from location to location, their laptop or tablet might obtain DHCP settings from the wrong server. When the users return to their offices, the laptop or tablet might seem sluggish or perform incorrectly because of the settings assigned by the DHCP server at another location. If this happens, you need to release and then renew the DHCP lease. (Alternatively, because computers don't retain their dynamically assigned settings, you can just restart the computer.)

You can use the graphical interface to release and renew DHCP leases by following these steps:

1. In Control Panel, under the Network And Internet heading tap or click View Network Status And Tasks.

2. In Network And Sharing Center, tap or click Change Adapter Settings. In Network Connections, press and hold or right-click the connection you want to work with and then select Diagnose.

3. After Windows Network Diagnostics tries to identify the problem, a list of possible solutions is provided. If the computer has one or more dynamically assigned IP addresses, one of the solutions should be Automatically Get New IP Settings. Tap or click this option.

You can also follow these steps to use the IPCONFIG command to renew and release settings:

1. Open an elevated command prompt.

2. To release the current settings for all network adapters, enter **ipconfig /release** at the command line. Then renew the lease by entering **ipconfig /renew**.

3. To renew a DHCP lease for all network adapters, enter **ipconfig /renew** at the command line.

4. You can check the updated settings by entering **ipconfig /all** at the command line.

TROUBLESHOOTING

Identifying a specific interface

If a computer has multiple network adapters and you want to work with only one or a subset of the adapters, specify all or part of the connection name after the **ipconfig /renew** or **ipconfig /release** command. Use the asterisk as a wildcard to match any characters in a connection's name. For example, if you want to renew the lease for all connections with names starting with *Loc*, enter the command **ipconfig /renew Loc***. If you want to release the settings for all connections containing the word *Network*, enter the command **ipconfig /release *Network***.

Diagnosing and fixing name-resolution issues

When you can reach a destination using an IP address but you can't reach a host using a host name, you might have a problem with host-name resolution. Typically, name-resolution problems have to do with improper configuration of the DNS client or problems with DNS registration. You can use the following tasks to troubleshoot problems with DNS name resolution:

- Display and flush the DNS client resolver cache.

- Verify DNS configuration.

- Test DNS name resolution with the Ping tool.

- Use the Nslookup tool to view DNS server responses.

  ### NOTE

  Problems with the DNS cache will give misleading results for the other tests you do. If you flush the cache first using ipconfig /flushdns, then you know you're getting the correct answer and not a cached error. Typically, you'll want to flush the cache on the DNS client and on the DNS server.

On the computer having DNS name-resolution problems, verify the following information:

- Host name

- Primary DNS suffix

- DNS suffix search list

- Connection-specific DNS suffixes

- DNS servers

You can obtain this information by entering **ipconfig /all** at a command prompt. To obtain information about which DNS names should be registered in DNS, enter **netsh interface ip show dns**.

Computers running Windows Vista and later support DNS traffic over IPv6. By default, IPv6 configures the well-known, site-local addresses of DNS servers at FEC0:0:0:FFFF::1, FEC0:0:0:FFFF::2, and FEC0:0:0:FFFF::3. To add the IPv6 addresses of your DNS servers, use the properties of the Internet Protocol Version 6 (TCP/IPv6) component in Network Connections or the **netsh interface ipv6 add dns** command. To register the appropriate DNS names as IP address resource records with DNS dynamic update, use the **ipconfig /registerdns** command. Computers running Windows XP or Windows Server 2003 do not support DNS traffic over IPv6.

TCP/IP checks the DNS client resolver cache before sending DNS name queries. The DNS resolver cache maintains a history of DNS lookups that have been performed when a user accesses network resources using TCP/IP. This cache contains forward lookups, which provide host name–to–IP address resolution, and reverse lookups, which provide IP address–to–host name resolution. After a DNS entry is stored in the resolver cache for a particular DNS host, the local computer no longer has to query external servers for DNS information on that host. This enables the computer to resolve DNS requests locally, providing a quicker response.

How long entries are stored in the resolver cache depends on the Time to Live (TTL) value assigned to the record by the originating server. To view current records and see the remaining TTL value for each record, enter **ipconfig /displaydns** at an elevated command prompt. These values are given as the number of seconds that a particular record can remain in the cache before it expires. These values are continually being counted down by the local computer. When the TTL value reaches zero, the record expires and is removed from the resolver cache.

Occasionally, you'll find that you need to clear out the resolver cache to remove old entries and enable computers to check for updated DNS entries before the normal expiration and purging process takes place. This typically happens because server IP addresses have changed and the current entries in the resolver cache point to the old addresses rather than the new ones. Sometimes the resolver cache itself can get out of sync, particularly when DHCP has been misconfigured.

Inside OUT

Decreasing TTLs for important DNS records

Skilled administrators know that several weeks in advance of the actual change, they should start to decrease the TTL values for important DNS records that are going to be changed. Typically, this means reducing the TTL from a number of days (or weeks) to a number of hours, which allows for quicker propagation of the changes to computers that have cached the related DNS records. After the change is completed, administrators should restore the original TTL value to reduce renewal requests.

You can usually resolve problems with the DNS resolver cache by either flushing the cache or reregistering DNS. When you flush the resolver cache, all DNS entries are cleared out of the cache and new entries are not created until the next time the computer performs a DNS lookup on a particular host or IP address. When you reregister DNS, Windows Server attempts to refresh all current DHCP leases and then performs a lookup on each DNS entry in the resolver cache. By looking up each host or IP address again, the entries are renewed and reregistered in the resolver cache. You'll generally want to flush the cache completely and allow the computer to perform lookups as needed. Reregister DNS only when you suspect problems with DHCP and the DNS resolver cache.

You can test DNS name resolution by pinging a destination using its host name or its fully qualified domain name (FQDN). If an incorrect IP address is shown, you can flush the DNS resolver cache and use the Nslookup tool to determine the set of addresses returned in the DNS Name Query Response message.

You can use the IPCONFIG command to flush and reregister entries in the DNS resolver cache by following these steps:

1. Start an elevated command prompt.

2. To clear out the resolver cache, enter **ipconfig /flushdns** at the command line.

3. To renew DHCP leases and reregister DNS entries, enter **ipconfig /registerdns** at the command line.

4. When the tasks are complete, you can check your work by entering **ipconfig /displaydns** at the command line.

To start Nslookup, enter **Nslookup** at a command prompt. At the *Nslookup* > prompt, use the **set d2** command to get detailed information about DNS response messages. Then use Nslookup to look up the desired FQDN. Look for A and AAAA records in the detailed display of the DNS response messages.

With IPv6, the DNS client maintains a neighbor's cache of recently resolved link-layer addresses and a standard resolver cache. To display the current contents of the neighbor's cache, enter **netsh interface ipv6 show neighbors**. To flush the neighbor's cache, enter **netsh interface ipv6 delete neighbors**.

With IPv6, the DNS client also maintains a destination cache. The destination cache stores next-hop IPv6 addresses for destinations. To display the current contents of the destination cache, enter **netsh interface ipv6 show destinationcache**. To flush the destination cache, enter **netsh interface ipv6 delete destinationcache**.

CHAPTER 3

Deploying DHCP Services

Most Microsoft Windows networks should be configured to use Dynamic Host Configuration Protocol (DHCP). DHCP simplifies administration and makes it easier for users to get their devices on the organization's network. How does DHCP do this? DHCP is a protocol that allows client devices to start up and automatically receive an Internet Protocol (IP) address and other related Transmission Control Protocol/Internet Protocol (TCP/IP) settings, such as the subnet mask, default gateway, Domain Name System (DNS) server addresses, and Windows Internet Naming Service (WINS) server addresses. DHCP servers can assign a dynamic IP version 4 (IPv4), IP version 6 (IPv6), or both addresses to any of the network interface cards (NICs) on a device.

DHCP essentials

DHCP is a standards-based protocol that was originally defined by the Internet Engineering Task Force (IETF) and based on the Bootstrap Protocol (BOOTP). It has been implemented on a variety of operating systems, including UNIX and Windows. Because DHCP is a client/server protocol, a server component and a client component are necessary to implement the protocol on a network. To make it easier to deploy DHCP in the enterprise, all server editions of Windows Server 2012 R2 include the DHCP Server service, which can be installed to support DHCP, and all current versions of the Windows operating system automatically install the DHCP Client service as part of TCP/IP.

A device that uses dynamic IP addressing and configuration is called a *DHCP client*. When you boot a DHCP client, a 32-bit IPv4 address, a 128-bit IPv6 address, or both can be retrieved from a pool of IP addresses defined for the network's DHCP server. It's the job of the DHCP server to maintain a database about the IP addresses that are available and the related configuration information. When an IP address is given out to a client, the client is said to have a *lease* on the IP address. The term "lease" is used because the assignment generally is not permanent. The DHCP server sets the duration of the lease when the lease is granted and can also change it later as necessary, such as when the lease is renewed.

DHCP also provides a way to assign a lease on an address permanently. To do this, you can create a reservation by specifying the IP address to reserve and the unique identifier of the device that will hold the IP address. The reservation thereafter ensures that the client device with the specified device address always gets the designated IP address. With IPv4, you specify the necessary unique identifier by using the Media Access Control (MAC) address of the network card. With IPv6, you specify the DHCP unique identifier for the DHCPv6 client and the identity association identifier (IAID) being used by the DHCPv6 client.

NOTE

MAC addresses are tied to the network interface card (NIC) of a device. If you remove a NIC or install an additional NIC on a device, the MAC address of the new or additional card will be different from the address of the original NIC.

Consider DHCP for non-DHCP member servers

You'll find that configuring member servers to use DHCP and then assigning them a reservation is an easy way to ensure that member servers have a fixed IP address while maintaining the flexibility provided by DHCP. After the member servers are configured for DHCP, they get all their TCP/IP options from DHCP, including their IP addresses. If you ever need to change their addressing, you can do this from within DHCP rather than on each member server—and changing IP addressing and other TCP/IP options in one location is much easier than doing it in multiple locations. Keep in mind that some server applications or roles might require a static IP address to work properly.

Microsoft recommends that a single DHCP server service no more than 10,000 clients. You define a set of IP addresses that can be assigned to clients by using a *scope*. A scope is a pool of IPv4 or IPv6 addresses and related configuration options. The IP addresses set in a scope are contiguous and are associated with a specific subnet mask or network prefix length. To define a subset of IP addresses within a scope that should not be used, you can specify an *exclusion*. An exclusion defines a range of IP addresses that you can exclude so that it isn't assigned to client devices.

All current releases of Windows Server support integration of DHCP with dynamic DNS. When configured, this ensures that the client's DNS record is updated when it receives a new IP address. To ensure that client names can be resolved to IP addresses, you should configure the integration of DHCP and DNS.

DHCP can be integrated with the Routing and Remote Access Service (RRAS). When configured, dial-up networking clients or virtual private network (VPN) clients can log on to the network remotely and use DHCP to configure their IP address and TCP/IP options. The server managing their connection to the network is called a *remote access server*, and it's the responsibility of this server to obtain blocks of IP addresses from a DHCP server for use by remote clients. If a DHCP server is not available when the remote access server requests IP addresses, the remote clients are configured with Automatic Private IP Addressing (APIPA). APIPA works differently for IPv4 and IPv6.

DHCPv4 and autoconfiguration

The availability of a DHCP server doesn't affect startup or logon (in most cases). DHCP clients can start and users can log on to the local machine even if a DHCP server isn't available. During startup, the DHCP client looks for a DHCP server. If a DHCP server is available, the client gets its configuration information from the server. If a DHCP server isn't available and the client's previous lease is still valid, the client pings the default gateway listed in the lease.

A successful ping tells the client that it's probably on the same network it was on when it was issued the lease, and the client will continue to use the lease as described previously. A failed ping tells the client that it might be on a different network. In this case, the client uses IP autoconfiguration. The client also uses IP autoconfiguration if a DHCP server isn't available and the previous lease has expired.

IPv4 autoconfiguration works like this:

1. The client device selects an IP address from the Microsoft-reserved Class B subnet 169.254.0.0 and uses the subnet mask 255.255.0.0. Before using the IPv4 address, the client performs an Address Resolution Protocol (ARP) test to make sure that no other client is using this IPv4 address.

2. If the IPv4 address is in use, the client repeats step 1, testing up to 10 IPv4 addresses before reporting failure. When a client is disconnected from the network, the ARP test always succeeds. As a result, the client uses the first IPv4 address it selects.

3. If the IPv4 address is available, the client configures the NIC with this address. The client then attempts to contact a DHCP server, sending out a broadcast every five minutes to the network. When the client successfully contacts a server, the client obtains a lease and reconfigures the network interface.

DHCPv6 and autoconfiguration

You can use DHCP to configure IPv6 addressing in two key ways: DHCPv6 stateful mode and DHCPv6 stateless mode. In DHCPv6 stateful mode, clients acquire their IPv6 address and their network-configuration parameters through DHCPv6. In DHCPv6 stateless mode, clients use autoconfiguration to acquire their IP address and acquire their network-configuration parameters through DHCPv6. You also can use a combination of stateful and stateless address autoconfiguration.

CHAPTER 4

A device that uses dynamic IPv6 addressing, configuration, or both is called a *DHCPv6 client*. Windows Vista and later include a DHCPv6 client. Like DHCPv4, the components of a DHCPv6 infrastructure consist of DHCPv6 clients that request configuration, DHCPv6 servers that provide configuration, and DHCPv6 relay agents that convey messages between clients and servers when clients are on subnets that don't have a DHCPv6 server.

Unlike DHCPv4, you must also configure your IPv6 routers to support DHCPv6. A DHCPv6 client performs autoconfiguration based on the M and O flags in the Router Advertisement message sent by a neighboring router. When the Managed Address Configuration, or M, flag is set to 1, the client uses a configuration protocol to obtain stateful addresses. When the Other Stateful Configuration, or O, flag is set to 1, the client uses a configuration protocol to obtain other configuration settings.

Windows Vista and later obtain dynamic IPv6 addresses by using a process similar to that used for dynamic IPv4 addresses. Typically, IPv6 autoconfiguration for DHCPv6 clients in stateful mode works like this:

1. The client device selects a link-local unicast IPv6 address. Before using the IPv6 address, the client performs an ARP test to make sure that no other client is using this IPv6 address.

2. If the IPv6 address is in use, the client repeats step 1. Note that when a client is disconnected from the network, the ARP test always succeeds. As a result, the client uses the first IPv6 address it selects.

3. If the IPv6 address is available, the client configures the NIC with this address. The client then attempts to contact a DHCP server, sending out a broadcast every five minutes to the network. When the client successfully contacts a server, the client obtains a lease and reconfigures the network interface.

This is not how IPv6 autoconfiguration works for DHCPv6 clients in stateless mode. In stateless mode, DHCPv6 clients configure link-local addresses and additional non-link-local addresses by exchanging Router Solicitation and Router Advertisement messages with neighboring routers. Although stateless address autoconfiguration is convenient, one reason for deploying a DHCPv6 server on an IPv6 network is that Windows does not support stateless address autoconfiguration of DNS server settings using Router Advertisement messages. Because of this, a DHCPv6 server is required if your Windows devices need to be able to perform DNS name resolution using IPv6. Also, keep in mind that link-local IPv6 addresses are always autoconfigured, regardless of whether DHCPv6 is being used.

DHCP security considerations

DHCP is inherently insecure. Anyone with access to the network can perform malicious actions that could cause problems for other clients trying to obtain IP addresses. A user could take the following actions:

- Initiate a denial of service (DoS) attack by requesting all available IP addresses or by using large numbers of IP addresses, either of which could make it impossible for other users to obtain IP addresses.

- Initiate an attack on DNS by performing a large number of dynamic updates through DHCP.

- Use the information provided by DHCP to set up rogue services on the network, such as using a non-Microsoft DHCP server to provide incorrect IP address information.

To reduce the risk of attacks, you should limit physical access to the network. Don't make it easy for unauthorized users to connect to the network. If you use wireless technologies, configure the network so that it doesn't broadcast the service set identifier (SSID) or use protected-access encryption, which prohibits wireless users from obtaining a DHCP lease until they provide an appropriate encryption key using strong data encryption. Wi-Fi Protected Access (WPA) and Wi-Fi Protected Access Version 2 (WPA2) are the preferred strong-data-encryption techniques.

To reduce the risk of a rogue DHCP server, configure Active Directory Domain Services (AD DS) on the network and use it to determine which DHCP servers are authorized to provide services and which aren't. By using Active Directory, any device running a current Windows operating system must be authorized to provide DHCP services. After a server is authorized, it's available for clients to use. This, unfortunately, doesn't restrict the use of unauthorized servers running DHCP, but it's a start.

Unauthorized DHCP servers are detected by the DHCP Server service running on authorized DHCP servers, and they are tracked in the event logs with the event source Microsoft-Windows-DHCP-Server and the event ID 1042. Look also for event IDs 1098, 1100, 1101, 1103, 1105, 1107, 1109, 1110, and 1111. Tracking these events can help you prevent most of the accidental damage caused by either misconfigured DHCP servers or correctly configured DHCP servers running on the wrong network.

In addition, the DHCP Server service should not be placed on an Active Directory domain controller if you can avoid it. The reason for this is that this changes security related to service locator (SRV) records, which domain controllers are responsible for publishing. SRV records detail the location of domain controllers, Kerberos servers, and other servers, and the changes to the security of these records when you install DHCP means that any client on the network could alter the records.

CHAPTER 4

The reason this happens is that DHCP servers must be able to update client records dynamically if a client's IP address changes. Because of this, they are made members of the DNSUpdateProxy group, and members of this group don't have any security applied to objects they create in the DNS database. If you can't avoid placing DHCP on a domain controller, it's recommended that you remove the DHCP server from the DNSUpdateProxy group. This should help you avoid the security problem outlined here, but it will also prevent the DHCP server from dynamically updating client records in DNS when the client IP addresses change.

DHCP and IPAM

When you want to manage your IP address space and track IP address usage trends, you can deploy IP Address Management (IPAM) servers. You can use IPAM to automatically discover DHCP and DNS servers, and then you can manage these servers using IPAM. Because auditing, reporting, and monitoring capabilities are key components of IPAM, you can more easily maintain the IP address space across the enterprise.

You deploy IPAM servers by using a distributed approach, with an IPAM server deployed at every site in an enterprise, or by using a centralized model, with only a central IPAM server in an enterprise. Each IPAM server can have a secondary configured as a backup. Because there is no communication or database sharing between IPAM servers, you must customize the scope of discovery for each distributed IPAM server or filter the list of managed servers for each location.

IPAM Server is a feature that you can add using the Add Roles And Features Wizard. Several security groups are created when you install IPAM:

- **IPAM Users.** Members can view all information in server discovery, IP address space, operational events, and server management, but they can't view IP address tracking information.

- **IPAM MSM Administrators.** IPAM Multi-Server Management (MSM) administrators have the privileges of IPAM Users and can also perform most IPAM management tasks.

- **IPAM ASM Administrators.** IPAM Address Space Management (ASM) administrators have the privileges of IPAM Users, can perform IPAM common management tasks, and can manage the IP address space.

- **IPAM IP Audit Administrators.** Members of this group have the privileges of IPAM Users, can perform IPAM common management tasks, and can view IP address-tracking information.

- **IPAM Administrators.** IPAM Administrators view all IPAM information and perform all IPAM tasks.

CHAPTER 4

Each IPAM server periodically attempts to locate other servers within its scope of management. When new servers are discovered, you must choose whether IPAM manages and monitors these servers. With DHCP servers, IPAM allows you to monitor DHCP and configure certain server and scope properties. With DNS servers, IPAM allows you to monitor zone status and configure some properties. In addition to detecting DHCP and DNS servers, IPAM discovers domain controllers for monitoring purposes and Network Policy servers for IP address tracking purposes.

These discovery tasks run daily as a scheduled task called DiscoveryTask, which is under Microsoft\Windows\IPAM in Task Scheduler. Other scheduled tasks for IPAM are the following:

- **AddressUtilizationCollectionTask.** Runs every two hours and collects address space utilization data from the DHCP servers

- **AuditTask.** Runs daily and collects auditing information from DHCP and IPAM servers and IP Lease Audit logs from domain controllers and Network Policy servers

- **ConfigurationTask.** Runs every six hours and collects configuration information from DHCP and DNS servers for ASM and MSM

- **ServerAvailabilityTask.** Runs every 15 minutes and collects the service availability status for DHCP and DNS servers

After you install IPAM Server, you must provision IPAM to set its scope of management. When you add the IPAM server as a managed server or log on locally to the IPAM server, you can select the IPAM node in Server Manager and then tap or click Provision The IPAM Server to start the Provision IPAM Wizard. By default, IPAM is provisioned using Group Policy, which will be applied to managed servers by linking Group Policy Objects (GPOs) at the appropriate levels in Active Directory. One GPO is created for DHCP servers, another for DNS servers, and a third for domain controllers and Network Policy servers. Follow the wizard steps, wait for provisioning to complete, and then, on the Completion page, verify that IPAM provisioning was successful. If it was, tap or click Close.

In Server Manager, with the IPAM node selected, you can then do the following:

- Configure discovery settings.

- Start server discovery.

- Select or add servers to manage and verify IPAM access to those servers.

- Use the Invoke-IpamGpoProvisioning cmdlet to create and link the GPOs.

CHAPTER 4

Planning DHCPv4 and DHCPv6 implementations

Planning a new DHCP implementation or revamping your existing DHCP implementation requires a good understanding of how DHCP works. You need to know the following information:

- How DHCP messages are sent and received

- How DHCP relay agents are used

- How multiple servers should be configured

These processes are essentially the same whether you are working with IPv4 or IPv6.

DHCPv4 messages and relay agents

When a DHCP client is started, it uses network broadcasts to obtain or renew a lease from a DHCP server. These broadcasts are in the form of DHCP messages. A client obtains its initial lease as shown in Figure 4-1. Here, the client broadcasts a DHCP DISCOVER message. All DHCP servers on the network respond to the broadcast with a DHCP OFFER message, which offers the client an IP lease. The client accepts the first offer received by sending a DHCP Request message back to the server. The server accepts the request by sending the client a DHCP Acknowledgment message.

DHCP clients must renew their leases periodically, either at each restart or when 50 percent of the lease time has passed. If the renewal process fails, the client tries to renew the lease again when 87.5 percent of the lease time has passed. Renewing the lease involves the client sending the DHCP server a DHCP Request and the server accepting the request by sending a DHCP Acknowledgment. This streamlined communication process is shown in Figure 4-2.

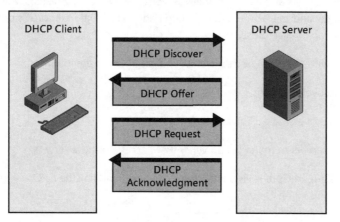

Figure 4-1 Obtaining an initial lease.

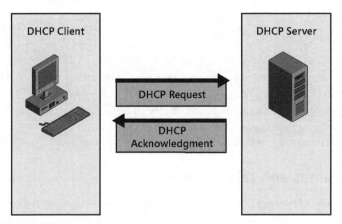

Figure 4-2 Renewing a lease.

If a DHCP client is unable to reach a DHCP server at startup or to renew its lease, it pings the default gateway that was previously assigned. If the default gateway responds, the client assumes that it's on the subnet from which the lease was originally obtained and continues to use the lease. If the default gateway doesn't respond, the client assumes that it has been moved to a new subnet and that no DHCP server is on this subnet. It then autoconfigures itself. The client will continue to check for a DHCP server when it's autoconfigured. By default, it does this by sending a DHCP DISCOVER message every five minutes. If the client gets back a DHCP Offer message from a DHCP server, it sends a DHCP Request to the server. When it gets back a DHCP Acknowledgment, it abandons its autoconfiguration and uses the address and other configuration settings sent by the DHCP server.

Typically, the messages sent by DHCP clients and servers are limited by the physical boundaries of the network. As a result, DHCP client broadcasts aren't routed and stay on only the originating network. In this configuration you need at least one DHCP server per subnet.

To reduce the number of DHCP servers needed for your organization, you can configure a DHCP relay agent on any subnet that has no DHCP server. This relay agent is a router or a device on the network that is configured to listen for DHCP broadcasts from clients on the local subnet and forward them as appropriate to a DHCP server on a different subnet. A router that supports BOOTP can be configured as a relay agent. You can also configure Windows servers on the network to act as DHCP relay agents.

CHAPTER 4

CHAPTER 4

Relay agents are best for LANs

Relay agents work best in local area network (LAN) environments, in which subnets are all in the same geographic location. In a wide area network (WAN) environment, in which you are forwarding broadcasts across links, you might not want to use relay agents. If a WAN link goes down, clients won't be able to obtain or renew leases, and this could cause the clients to autoconfigure themselves.

DHCPv6 messages and relay agents

The way a DHCPv6 client attempts DHCPv6-based configuration depends on the values of the M and O flags in received Router Advertisement messages. If there are multiple advertising routers for a given subnet, they should be configured to advertise the same stateless address prefixes and values of the M and O flags. All current Windows desktop and server operating systems include DHCPv6 clients and therefore accept the values of the M and O flags in received router advertisements.

You can configure an IPv6 router that is running Windows to set the M flag to 1 in router advertisements by using either of the following commands:

- netsh interface ipv6 set interface InterfaceName managedaddress=enabled

- Set-NetIPInterface –addressfamily ipv6 –interfacealias InterfaceName –advertising

Similarly, you can set the O flag to 1 in router advertisements by using either of the following commands:

- netsh interface ipv6 set interface InterfaceName otherstateful=enabled

- Set-NetIPInterface –addressfamily ipv6 –interfacealias InterfaceName –otherstatefulconfiguration

When you are working with the M and O flags, keep the following in mind:

- If both the M and O flags are set to 0, the network is considered not to have DHCPv6 infrastructure. Clients use router advertisements for non-link-local addresses and manual configuration to configure other settings.

- If both the M and O flags are set to 1, DHCPv6 is used for both IP addressing and other configuration settings. This combination is known as *DHCPv6 stateful mode*, in which DHCPv6 is assigning stateful addresses to IPv6 clients.

- If the M flag is set to 0 and the O flag is set to 1, DHCPv6 is used only to assign other configuration settings. Neighboring routers are configured to advertise non-link-local address prefixes from which IPv6 clients derive stateless addresses. This combination is known as *DHCPv6 stateless mode*.

- If the M flag is set to 1 and the O flag is set to 0, DHCPv6 is used for IP address configuration but not for other settings. Because IPv6 clients typically need to be configured with other settings, such as the IPv6 addresses of DNS servers, this combination typically is not used.

As with DHCPv4, DHCPv6 uses User Datagram Protocol (UDP) messages. DHCPv6 clients listen for DHCP messages on UDP port 546. DHCPv6 servers and relay agents listen for DHCPv6 messages on UDP port 547. The structure for DHCPv6 messages is much simpler than for DHCPv4, which had its origins in the BOOTP protocol to support diskless workstations.

DHCPv6 messages start with a 1-byte Msg-Type field that indicates the type of DHCPv6 message. This is followed by a 3-byte Transaction-ID field that is determined by a client and used to group together the messages of a DHCPv6 message exchange. Following the Transaction-ID field, DHCPv6 options are used to indicate client and server identification, addresses, and other configuration settings. Three fields are associated with each DHCPv6 option:

- A 2-byte Option-Code field indicates a specific option.

- A 2-byte Option-Len field indicates the length of the Option-Data field in bytes.

- An Option-Data field contains the data for the option.

Messages exchanged between relay agents and servers use a different message structure to transfer additional information. A 1-byte Hop-Count field indicates the number of relay agents that have received the message. A receiving relay agent can discard the message if it exceeds a configured maximum hop count. A 16-byte Link-Address field contains a non-link-local address that is assigned to an interface connected to the subnet on which the client is located. Based on the Link-Address field, the server can determine the correct address scope from which to assign an address. A 16-byte Peer-Address field contains the IPv6 address of the client that originally sent the message or the previous relay agent that relayed the message. Following the Peer-Address field are DHCPv6 options. A key option is the Relay Message option. This option provides an encapsulation of the messages being exchanged between the client and the server.

IPv6 does not have broadcast addresses. Because of this, the limited broadcast address for some DHCPv4 messages has been replaced with the All_DHCP_Relay_Agents_And_Servers address of FF02::1:2 for DHCPv6. A DHCPv6 client attempting to discover the location of the DHCPv6 server on the network sends a Solicit message from its link-local address to FF02::1:2. If there is a DHCPv6 server on the client's subnet, it receives the Solicit message and sends an appropriate reply. If the client and server are on different subnets, a DHCPv6 relay agent on the client's subnet receiving the Solicit message will forward it to a DHCPv6 server.

DHCP availability and fault tolerance

As part of planning, you must consider how many DHCP servers should be made available on the network. In most cases you'll want to configure at least two DHCP servers. If they are configured properly, having multiple DHCP servers increases reliability and allows for load balancing and fault tolerance.

In a large enterprise, a server cluster can be your primary technique for ensuring DHCP availability and providing for fault tolerance. Here, if a DHCP server fails, the DHCP Server service can be failed over to another server in the cluster, allowing for the seamless transition of DHCP services. Clustering uses a shared storage and is fairly complex to set up.

Although you can configure the DHCP Server service for failover on a cluster, much simpler fault-tolerance implementations are now available natively in the DHCP Server service on Windows Server 2012 R2, and these implementations work with large networks in addition to small and medium networks. The implementations use failover scopes that are shared between two DHCP servers to increase fault tolerance, provide redundancy over using a single DHCP server, and enable load balancing.

The way scopes are shared depends on the failover-scope configuration settings. You can optimize the shared scope for either load sharing (using the Load Balancing setting) or fault tolerance (using the Hot Standby setting). Whether you optimize a failover scope for load balancing or fault tolerance, the DHCP servers involved replicate lease information between them to maintain the scope state. The key difference lies in how the member servers are used.

In a load-balancing configuration, the two servers simultaneously serve IP addresses and options to clients in the scope. The client requests are load balanced and shared between the two servers. More specifically, a failover scope optimized for load balancing has little or no time delay configured in its scope properties. With no time delay, both the primary and the secondary servers can respond to DHCP DISCOVER requests from DHCP clients. This allows the fastest server to respond to and accept a DHCP OFFER first. Fault tolerance continues to be a part of the scope. If one of the servers becomes unavailable or overloaded and is unable to respond to requests, the other server handles requests and continues distributing addresses until the normal process is restored.

In a fault-tolerance configuration, there is an active partner and a standby partner for the scope. The active server is responsible for leasing IP addresses and options to all clients in the scope. The standby server, also referred to as the *passive server*, assumes this responsibility if the active server becomes unavailable or doesn't respond in a timely manner. More specifically, a failover scope optimized for fault tolerance can have an extended time delay configured in its scope properties. This time delay causes the standby server to respond with a delay to DHCP DISCOVER requests from DHCP clients. The delay on the standby server allows the active server to respond to and accept the DHCP OFFER first. However, if the active server becomes unavailable or overloaded and is unable to respond to requests, the standby server handles requests and continues distributing addresses until the active server is available to service clients again. Because failover scopes are a server-side enhancement, no additional configuration is required for DHCP clients. Because scope state and lease information are automatically replicated between the active and passive servers, the state of the scope is always maintained.

IMPORTANT

For failover scopes to work properly, time must be kept synchronized between the two servers in the failover relationship. If the time difference between the servers is greater than 60 seconds, you won't be able to complete the failover setup process. If the time doesn't remain synchronized, workloads might not be properly balanced between servers in failover scopes. Replication and other errors might also occur.

Inside OUT

IPv6 doesn't use or require failover scopes

Failover scopes apply only to IPv4 addresses. IPv6 clients typically determine their own IPv6 address using stateless IP autoconfiguration. In this mode, DHCP servers deliver only the DHCP option configuration and don't maintain lease state information. Further, you can ensure high availability for stateless DHCPv6 just by setting up two servers with identical DHCPv6 option configurations.

CHAPTER 4

Failover scope: Load sharing

Whether you are configuring a failover scope for load sharing or fault tolerance, the scope you are configuring is shared between two servers, with each server having a relative weighting preference assigned as a load-balancing percentage. For load balancing, you'll typically want to use a weighting between 50/50 and 60/40. When you configure load sharing in this way, each DHCP server has an equal or nearly equal workload. To see how this would be implemented, consider the following example. The organization has two DHCP servers. Scope 1 is configured to use the IPv4 address range 192.168.10.1 to 192.168.10.254 and is 60/40 load balanced between Server A and Server B.

Here, 254 IP addresses are available, which could be used to service 200 or more clients. When a client starts up on the network, both DHCP servers respond. The client accepts the first IP address offered, which could be on either Server A or Server B and which is often the server that is closest to the client. Because both servers are configured to use the same IP address range, both servers can service clients on that subnet.

The way the workload is load balanced is through a small time delay configured in the scope properties for Server B. This small time delay ensures that Server A has a 60/40 preference over Server B for responding to DHCP DISCOVER requests from DHCP clients and accepting DHCP OFFER requests.

Keep in mind that the length of the time delay is relative to the weighting for load balancing. The higher percentage of workload that one server has over the other, the stronger the preference for one server over the other. If one of the servers fails, lease information is maintained, because lease information was replicated between both DHCP servers, and the remaining server has all the lease information.

As you can see, the load-sharing approach is designed to provide load balancing and also has some redundancy and fault tolerance built in. Because the lease information is replicated between the servers, the DHCP servers share a common pool of IP addresses and it doesn't matter whether one of the servers actually assigns more IP addresses than the other. The common IP address pool ensures that as long as there are available addresses, the addresses are available to be assigned by either server. Keep in mind that once all IP addresses in the pool have been allocated, no IP addresses are available to clients seeking new leases and they are configured to use automatic private IP addressing.

Failover scope: Fault tolerance

As stated previously, whether you are configuring a failover scope for load sharing or fault tolerance, the scope you are configuring is shared between two servers, with each server having a relative weighting preference assigned as a load-balancing percentage. For fault tolerance, you'll typically want to use a weighting between 80/20 and 90/10. By configuring fault tolerance in this way, you ensure that one server handles most of the workload. Here, you have a primary DHCP server that assigns most of the IP addresses to clients and a backup DHCP server that assigns few or no IP addresses to clients. This situation is ideal when the DHCP servers are separated from each other, such as when the primary DHCP server is on the primary subnet and the backup DHCP server is on a centralized site.

To see how this would be implemented, consider the following example. The organization has two DHCP servers. Scope 1 is configured to use the IPv4 address range 192.168.10.1 to 192.168.10.254 and is 90/10 load balanced between Server A and Server B. Here, 254 IP addresses are again available, which could be used to service 200 or more clients—most of which are located on the primary subnet. You are using a DHCP server in a central site as a backup for this scope. If the primary server goes down, the backup can respond to client requests and handle their leases. When the primary comes back online, it handles the majority of client leases because it's located on the primary subnet closer to most of the client devices. Again, you achieve basic fault tolerance and availability.

The workload is load balanced through an extended time delay configured in the scope properties for Server B. This extended time delay ensures that Server A has a 90/10 preference over Server B for responding to DHCP DISCOVER requests from DHCP clients and accepting DHCP OFFER requests. As you can see, the fault-tolerance approach is designed to provide redundancy and ensure availability. Because the lease information is replicated between the servers, the DHCP servers share a common pool of IP addresses and it doesn't matter which server actually assigns the IP address to a client. The common IP address pool ensures that as long as there are available addresses, the addresses are available to be assigned by either server. Keep in mind that once all IP addresses in the pool have been allocated, no IP addresses are available to clients seeking new leases and they are configured to use automatic private IP addressing.

Traditional split scopes

In addition to failover scopes, which are managed automatically by the DHCP Server service and share their entire pool of leasable addresses, you can continue to use existing split scopes, which don't share their pool of leasable addresses and generally require closer monitoring to ensure proper operations. You won't, however, be able to create new split scopes once you create a failover scope on a server, because failover scopes are designed to replace split scopes.

With split scopes, you use two DHCP servers to make a specific percentage of a scope's IP addresses available on one server and the rest of the IP addresses available on another server. Here, each DHCP server is configured with an identical scope range but with different exclusions within that range. The first server gets the first portion of the scope's IP address range and excludes the rest. The second server gets the rest of the scope's IP address range and excludes the first portion.

As with failover scopes, you split scopes between two servers with one of two goals:

- Load balancing

- Fault tolerance

For load balancing, you split the scope equally—or nearly so—between the two servers. For fault tolerance, you assign most of the available IP addresses to the primary server and few IP addresses to the backup server. To see how split scopes could be implemented, consider the following example. The organization has two DHCP servers configured as follows:

- Server A's primary scope is configured to use the IPv4 address range 192.168.10.1 to 192.168.10.254 and has an exclusion range of 192.168.10.203 to 192.168.10.254.

- Server B's primary scope is configured to use the IPv4 address range 192.168.10.1 to 192.168.10.254 and has an exclusion range of 192.168.10.1 to 192.168.10.202.

CHAPTER 4

Here, 254 IP addresses are available, which could be used to service 200 or more clients—most which are located on the primary subnet. You are using a DHCP server on a central site as a backup. If the primary server goes down, the backup can respond to client requests and handle their leases. When the primary comes back online, it handles the majority of client leases because it's located on the primary subnet closer to the bulk of the client devices. Thus you achieve basic fault tolerance and availability.

Although this approach is designed to provide some redundancy and fault tolerance, it's possible that the primary would be offline too long and the backup DHCP server would run out of available IP addresses. If this were to happen, no IP addresses would be available to clients seeking new leases and they would be configured to use APIPA.

Keep in mind that split scopes don't share their lease information. As a result, each server can assign only a subset of the available IP addresses. In this example, the primary server has 80 percent of the assignable IP addresses and the backup server has only 20 percent. As a result, if the primary is offline too long, the backup could run out of assignable IP addresses much more quickly than it would if the entire pool of IP addresses were shared.

Because split scopes don't share their address pool, you might want to use a 100/100 failover technique. Here, you make twice as many IP addresses available than are needed. Thus, if you must provide DHCP services for 200 clients, you make at least 400 IP addresses available to those clients. As before, each DHCP server is configured with an identical scope range, but with different exclusions within that range. The first server gets the first half of the scope's IP address range and excludes the second half. The second server gets the second half of the scope's IP address range and excludes the first half.

To make twice as many IP addresses available than are needed, you must think carefully about the IP address class you use and would most likely want to use a Class A or Class B network. With this in mind, the organization's two DHCP servers might be configured as follows:

- Server A's primary scope is configured to use the IPv4 address range 10.0.1.1 to 10.0.10.254 and has an exclusion range of 10.0.6.1 to 10.0.10.254. You also must block the potential broadcast addresses in the nonexcluded range, so you also exclude 10.0.1.255, 10.0.2.255, 10.0.3.255, 10.0.4.255, and 10.0.5.255.

- Server B's primary scope is configured to use the IPv4 address range 10.0.1.1 to 10.0.10.254 and has an exclusion range of 10.0.1.1 to 10.0.5.254. You also must block the potential broadcast addresses in the nonexcluded range, so you also exclude 10.0.6.255, 10.0.7.255, 10.0.8.255, 10.0.9.255, and 10.0.10.255.

Here, more than 2,500 IP addresses are available, which is more than twice the number needed to service the network's 1,000 clients. When a client starts up on the network, both DHCP servers respond. The client accepts the first IP address offered, which could be on either Server A or Server B and which is often the server that is closest to the client. Because both servers are configured to use the same IP address range, both servers can service clients on that subnet. If one of the servers fails, a client using an IP address in the excluded range of the remaining server would be allowed to obtain a new lease.

Because more than twice as many IP addresses are available, every client on the network can obtain a lease even if one of the DHCP servers goes offline. This approach not only offers availability and fault tolerance but also gives you flexibility. You are able to take one of the DHCP servers offline and perform maintenance or upgrades without worrying about running out of available IP addresses. That said, split scopes are not as dynamic as failover scopes, and failover scopes are the preferred technique to use for availability and fault tolerance.

NOTE

Split scopes apply only to IPv4 addresses. You can't split a superscope or a scope that is part of a superscope. You create a split scope on the DHCP server that you want to act as the primary server by splitting an existing scope. During the split-scope creation process, you need to specify the DHCP server with which you want to split the primary server's scope. This additional server acts as the secondary server for the scope. Because split scopes are a server-side enhancement, no additional configuration is required for DHCP clients.

Setting up DHCP servers

The approach you use to set up DHCP servers depends on many factors, including the number of clients on the network, the network configuration, and the Windows domain implementation you are using. From a physical-server perspective, the DHCP Server service doesn't use a lot of system resources and can run on just about any system configured with Windows Server 2012 R2. The DHCP Server service is, in fact, often installed as an additional service on an existing infrastructure server or on an older server that isn't robust enough to offer other types of services. Either approach is fine as long as you remember the security precaution discussed previously about not installing DHCP on a domain controller if possible. However, I prefer to install the DHCP Server service on hardware that I know and trust. Rather than installing it on an older system that might fail, I install it on either a workstation-class system running Windows Server 2012 R2 or an existing infrastructure server that can handle the additional load.

Speaking of server load, a single DHCP server can handle about 10,000 clients and about 1,000 scopes. This is, of course, if the system is a dedicated DHCP server with adequate processing power and memory. Because DHCP is so important for client startup and network access, I don't trust the service to a single server, and you shouldn't either. In most cases you'll want to have at least two DHCP servers on the network. If you have multiple subnets, you might want two DHCP servers per subnet. However, configuring routers to forward DHCP broadcasts or having DHCP relay agents reduces the need for additional servers.

Many organizations also have standby DHCP servers available. A standby DHCP server is a server that has the DHCP Server service fully configured but has its scopes deactivated. Then, if a primary DHCP server fails and can't be recovered immediately, the scopes can be activated to service clients on the network as necessary.

After you select the server hardware, you should plan the IP address ranges and exclusions you want to use. The "Planning DHCPv4 and DHCPv6 implementations" section earlier in this chapter should have given you some good ideas on how to configure IP address ranges and exclusions for availability and fault tolerance. At the implementation stage, don't forget about IP addresses that might have been assigned (or will be assigned) to devices using static IP addresses. You should either specifically exclude these IP address ranges or just not include them in the scopes you configure.

The way you set up DHCP services depends on whether the network in which the DHCP server will be placed is using Active Directory domains or workgroups. With Active Directory domains, you set up DHCP services by completing the following steps:

1. Installing the DHCP Server service

2. Authorizing the DHCP server in Active Directory

3. Configuring the DHCP server with the appropriate scopes, exclusions, reservations, and options

4. Activating the DHCP server's scopes

With workgroups, you don't need to authorize the DHCP server in Active Directory. This means the steps for setting up DHCP services look like this:

1. Installing the DHCP Server service

2. Configuring the DHCP server with the appropriate scopes, exclusions, reservations, and options

3. Activating the DHCP server's scopes

The sections that follow examine the related procedures in detail.

Installing the DHCP Server service

You install the DHCP Server service as a server role. To install the DHCP Server service using the Add Roles And Features Wizard, follow these steps:

1. DHCP servers should be assigned a static IPv4 and IPv6 address on each subnet they will service and to which they are connected. Ensure that the server has static IPv4 and IPv6 addresses.

2. In Server Manager, tap or click Manage and then tap or click Add Roles And Features, or select Add Roles And Features in the Quick Start pane. This starts the Add Roles And Features Wizard. If the wizard displays the Before You Begin page, read the Welcome text and then tap or click Next.

3. On the Installation Type page, Role-Based Or Feature-Based Installation is selected by default. Tap or click Next.

4. On the Server Selection page, you can choose to install roles and features on running servers or virtual hard disks (VHDs). Only servers that are running Windows Server 2012 R2 and that have been added for management in Server Manager are listed. Either select a server from the server pool or select a server from the server pool on which to mount a VHD. If you are adding roles and features to a VHD, tap or click Browse and then use the Browse For Virtual Hard Disks dialog box to locate the VHD. When you are ready to continue, tap or click Next.

5. On the Select Roles page, select DHCP Server. If additional features are required to install a role, you'll see an additional dialog box. Tap or click Add Features to close the dialog box, and add the required features to the server installation. When you are ready to continue, tap or click Next three times.

6. If the server on which you want to install the DHCP Server role doesn't have all the required binary source files, the server gets the files through Windows Update by default or from a location specified in Group Policy. To specify an alternate path for the required source files, click the Specify An Alternate Source Path link, type that alternate path in the box provided, and then tap or click OK. For network shares, type the Universal Naming Convention (UNC) path to the share, such as **\\CorpServer65 \WinServer2012**. For mounted Windows images, type the WIM path prefixed with *WIM:* and including the index of the image to use, such as **WIM:\\CorpServer65 \WinServer2012\install.wim:4**.

7. After you review the installation options and save them as necessary, tap or click Install to begin the installation process. The Installation Progress page tracks the progress of the installation. If you close the wizard, tap or click the Notifications icon in Server Manager and then tap or click the link provided to reopen the wizard. When Setup finishes installing the DHCP Server role, the Installation Progress page will be updated to reflect this. Review the installation details to ensure that all phases of the installation were completed successfully.

8. As stated in the Post-Deployment Configuration task panel, additional configuration is required for DHCP servers. Tap or click the Complete DHCP Configuration link. This starts the DHCP Post-Install Configuration Wizard.

CHAPTER 4

9. The Description page states that DHCP Administrators and DHCP Users groups will be created in the domain for delegation of DHCP server administration. In addition, if the DHCP server is joined to a domain, the server will be authorized in Active Directory. Tap or click Next.

10. On the Authorization page, do one of the following to specify the credentials to use to authorize the DHCP server in Active Directory:

    - Your current user name is shown in the User Name box. If you have administrator privileges in the domain of which the DHCP server is a member and you want to use your current credentials, tap or click Commit to attempt to authorize the server using these credentials.

    - If you want to use alternate credentials or if you are unable to authorize the server using your current credentials, select Use Alternate Credentials and then tap or click Specify. In the Windows Security dialog box, enter the user name and password for the authorized account and then tap or click OK. Tap or click Commit to attempt to authorize the server using these credentials.

    - If you want to authorize the DHCP server later, select Skip AD Authorization and then tap or click Commit. Keep in mind that in domains only authorized DHCP servers can provide dynamic IP addresses to clients.

11. When the wizard finishes the post-install configuration, review the installation details to ensure that tasks were completed successfully and then tap or click Close. Next, you need to restart the DHCP Server service on the DHCP server so that the DHCP Administrators and DHCP Users groups can be used. To do this, tap or click DHCP in the left pane of Server Manager. Next, in the main pane, on the Servers panel, select the DHCP server. Finally, on the Services panel, press and hold or right-click the entry for the DHCP server and then tap or click Restart Service.

12. To complete the installation, you need to do the following:

    - If the server has multiple network cards, review the server bindings and specify the connections that the DHCP server supports for servicing clients. See the section entitled "Binding the DHCP Server service to a network interface" in Chapter 5, "Configuring DHCP Services."

    - Configure server or scope options to assign common configuration settings for DHCP clients, including 003 Router, 006 DNS Servers, 015 DNS Domain Name, and 044 WINS/NBNS Servers. See the section entitled "Configuring TCP/IP options" in Chapter 5.

    - Create and activate any DHCP scopes that the server will use, as discussed later in this chapter in the section entitled "Creating and configuring scopes."

After you install the DHCP Server service, the DHCP console is available. In Server Manager, tap or click Tools and then tap or click DHCP to open the DHCP console, shown in Figure 4-3. The main window is divided into two panes. The left pane lists the DHCP servers in the domain according to their fully qualified domain name (FQDN). You can expand a server listing to show subnodes for IPv4 and IPv6. If you expand the IP nodes, you'll see the scopes and options defined for the related IP version. The right pane shows the expanded view of the current selection.

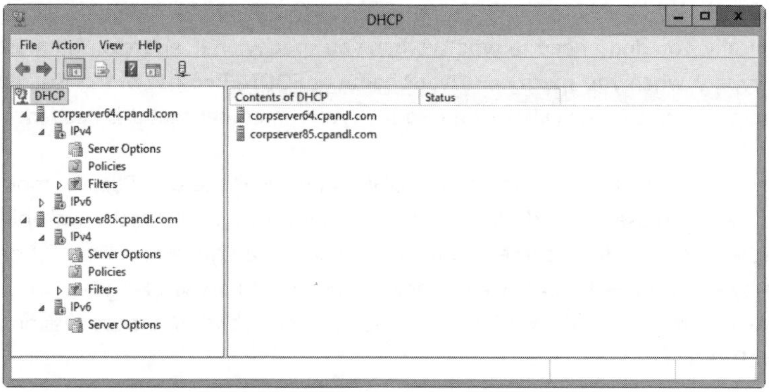

Figure 4-3 The DHCP console.

When you start the DHCP console, you are connected directly to a local DHCP server, but you won't see entries for remote DHCP servers. You can connect to remote servers by pressing and holding or right-clicking DHCP in the console tree and then tapping or clicking Add Server. In the Add Server dialog box, select This Server, type the IP address or device name of the DHCP server you want to manage, and then tap or click OK. An entry for the DHCP server is added to the console tree.

The command-line counterpart to the DHCP console is the Netsh DHCP command. From the command prompt on a device running Windows Server 2012 R2, you can use Netsh DHCP to perform all the tasks available in the DHCP console and to perform some additional tasks that can't be performed in the DHCP console. To start Netsh DHCP and access a particular DHCP server, follow these steps:

1.   Start an elevated, administrator command prompt, and then enter **netsh** to start Netsh. The command prompt changes to netsh>.

2.   Access the DHCP context within Netsh by entering **dhcp**. The command prompt changes to netsh dhcp>.

3.   Enter **server** followed by the UNC name or IP address of the DHCP server, such as **\\corpsvr02** or **\\192.168.1.50**. If the DHCP server is in a different domain from your

CHAPTER 4

logon domain, you should type the FQDN of the server, such as **\\corpsvr02 .cpandl.com**.

4. The command prompt changes to netsh dhcp server>. You can now work with the selected server. If you later want to work with a different server, you can do this without having to start over. Just enter **server** followed by the UNC name or IP address of that server.

NOTE

Technically, you don't need to type \\ when you specify an IP address. You must, however, type \\ when you specify a server's name or FQDN. Because of this discrepancy, you might want to use \\ all the time so that you remember that it is needed.

The Windows PowerShell counterpart to the DHCP console is the DHCPServer module. As with Netsh DHCP, you can use the DHCPServer module to perform all the tasks available in the DHCP console and to perform some additional tasks. You can get a complete list of all related commands by entering **Get-Help *DHCPServer***. When you are working remotely, you can either invoke commands on the remote DHCP server or establish a remote session with the remote DHCP server.

The following command entered as a single line invokes the Get-DHCPServerv4Scope and Get-DHCPServerv6Scope commands on the named servers:

```
invoke-command -computername DhcpServer12, DhcpServer27, DhcpServer34
-scriptblock {get-dhcpserver4scope; get-dhcpserver6scope}
```

The following command establishes a remote session with the named computers:

```
$s = new-PSSession -computername DhcpServer12, DhcpServer27, DhcpServer34
-Credential Cpandl\WilliamS
```

After you establish the session, you can use the $s session with Invoke-Command to return commands on all remote computers to which you are connected. This example looks for stopped Exchange services on each computer:

```
invoke-command -session $s
-scriptblock {get-service dhcp* | where { $_.status -eq "stopped"}}
```

In this example you pipe the output of Get-Service to the Where-Object cmdlet and filter based on the Status property. Because the $_ automatic variable operates on the current object in the pipeline, Windows PowerShell examines the status of the DHCP Client service and the DHCP Server service in turn and displays output only if one or both of the services are stopped.

You can connect and disconnect remote sessions using Connect-PSSession and Disconnect-PSSession. If you close a Windows PowerShell window and there is an active session, the session continues in a disconnected state. To end a remote session and free the resources the session is using, you must end your session using Exit-PSSession.

NOTE

You need to use an elevated, administrator Windows PowerShell prompt to complete most administrative tasks. When you work with a server remotely, you establish connections through the Windows Remote Management (WinRM) service. On a server running Windows Server 2012 R2, WinRM and related services are set up automatically. On your management computer, you need to install the Remote Server Administration Tools and other required components. You also need to configure WinRM.

Authorizing DHCP servers in Active Directory

Before you can use a DHCP server in an Active Directory domain, you must authorize the server in Active Directory. In the DHCP console, any unauthorized DHCP server to which you connect will have an icon showing a red down arrow. Authorized DHCP servers have an icon showing a green up arrow.

New DHCP servers are not authorized automatically. In the DHCP console, you can authorize a DHCP server by pressing and holding or right-clicking the server entry in the console tree and selecting Authorize. To remove the authorization later, press and hold or right-click the server entry in the console tree and select Unauthorize.

In Netsh, you can authorize a server by typing the following command:

```
netsh dhcp server ServerID initiate auth
```

Here, *ServerID* is the UNC name or IP address of the DHCP server on which you want to create the scope, such as \\CORPSVR03 or \\192.168.1.1. Keep in mind that if you are already at the netsh dhcp server prompt, you only need to type **initiate auth**.

In Windows PowerShell, you can authorize a server using Add-DhcpServerInDC. Use the –DnsName parameter to specify the name of the server to authorize or the –IpAddress to specify the IP address of the server to authorize, such as:

```
Add-DhcpServerInDC –DnsName CorpSvr03.cpand1.com
Add-DhcpServerInDC –IpAddress 192.168.1.1
```

CHAPTER 4

Creating and configuring scopes

After you install the DHCP Server service, the next thing you must do is create the scopes that will provide the range of IP addresses and TCP/IP options for clients. With IPv4, the DHCP Server service supports four types of scopes:

- **Normal scope.** A normal scope is used to assign IPv4 address pools for Class A, B, and C networks. Normal scopes have an IP address range assignment that includes the subnet mask and can also have exclusions and reservations and TCP/IP options that are specific to the scope. When you create normal scopes, each scope must be in its own subnet. This means that if you add a normal scope, it must be on a different subnet from any of the existing scopes configured on the server.

- **Multicast scope.** A multicast scope is used to assign IP address pools for IPv4 Class D networks. Multicast scopes are created in the same way as normal scopes except that they do not have an associated subnet mask, reservations, or related TCP/IP options. This means that there is no specific subnet association for multicast scopes. Instead of a subnet mask, you assign the scope a Time to Live (TTL) value that specifies the maximum number of routers through which messages sent to devices over multicast can go. The default TTL is 32. Also, because multicast IP addresses are used for destination addresses only, they have a longer lease duration than unicast IP addresses—typically from 30 to 60 days.

- **Superscope.** A superscope is a container for IPv4 scopes and also can be used to distribute IP addresses from multiple logical IP networks to the same physical network segment. If you configure multiple scopes on a server and want to be able to activate or deactivate them as a unit or view the usage statistics for all the scopes at once, you can use a superscope to do this. Create the superscope and then add to it the scopes you want to manage as a group.

- **Failover scope.** A failover scope is a scope split between two DHCP servers to increase fault tolerance, to provide redundancy, and to enable load balancing.

Before you create a normal scope, you should plan the IP address range you want to use and any necessary exclusions and reservations. You must know the IP address of the default gateway and any DNS or WINS servers that should be used. You must also configure DHCPv4 and DHCPv6 relays to relay DHCPv4 and DHCPv6 broadcast requests between network segments.

NOTE

You can configure relay agents with the RRAS and the DHCP Relay Agent Service. You can configure some routers as relay agents, too.

Creating normal scopes for IPv4 addresses

In the DHCP console, you can create a normal scope for IPv4 addresses by expanding the node for the server you want to work with, selecting the IPv4 node, and then pressing and holding or right-clicking the IPv4 node. Next, from the shortcut menu, select New Scope.

In the New Scope Wizard, tap or click Next to display the Scope Name page, as shown in Figure 4-4. Type a descriptive name for the scope and a description that will be used as a comment.

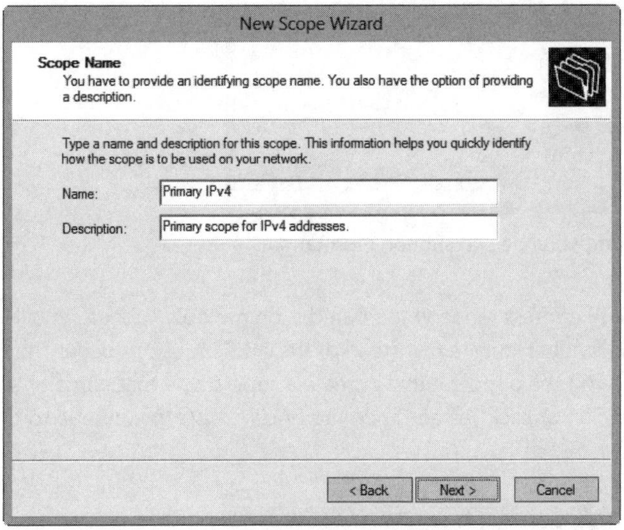

Figure 4-4 Set the scope name and description.

Tap or click Next to display the IP Address Range page, as shown in Figure 4-5. Enter the start and end IP addresses to use for the scope in the Start IP Address box and the End IP Address box. Be sure to specify the first and last usable IP address only, which means you shouldn't include the x.x.x.0 and x.x.x.255 addresses. When you enter an IP address range, the bit length and subnet mask are filled in automatically for you. If you use subnets, change the default values.

CHAPTER 4

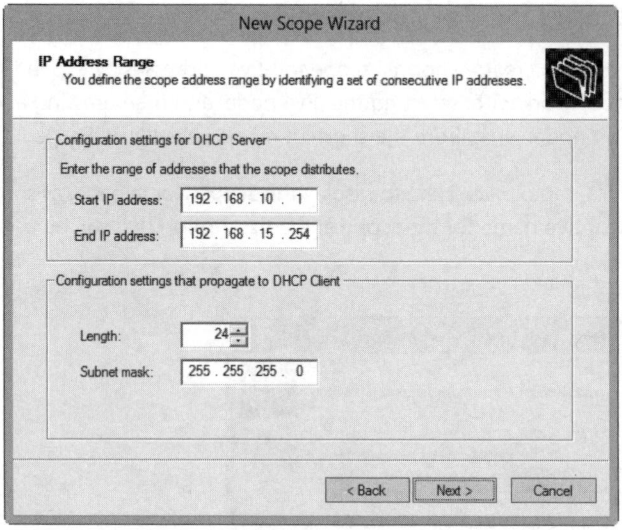

Figure 4-5 Set the IP address range and subnet information.

Tap or click Next. If the IP address range you entered is on multiple subnets, you'll see a Create Superscope page, as shown in Figure 4-6, instead of the Add Exclusions page. The Create Superscope page gives you the opportunity to create a superscope that contains separate scopes for each subnet. Tap or click Yes and then tap or click Next to continue to the Lease Duration page.

Figure 4-6 The New Scope Wizard knows when you cross subnet boundaries and lets you create a superscope with multiple scopes automatically.

Inside OUT

Multiple subnets on the same physical network

If you're wondering how it would work to have multiple subnets on the same network segment, it should work just fine, and it generally won't matter to which subnet a client connects as long as you've set up DHCP to give clients the appropriate TCP/IP options. The physical network provides the boundaries for these subnets unless you've configured routers or DHCP relay agents to forward DHCP broadcasts. Incidentally, if you want to be sure that clients use a specific subnet, there is a way to do that using reservations. However, you don't want to create reservations for a lot of clients. Instead, you might want to create a user-defined or vendor-defined class and allow clients to connect to any subnet to get their class-specific TCP/IP options. Policy-based assignment also is available, and it can be configured per scope, per server, or both.

If all the IP addresses you entered are on the same subnet, you'll have the opportunity to specify an exclusion range, as shown in Figure 4-7. Use the Start IP Address box and the End IP Address box to define IP address ranges that are to be excluded from the scope, such as servers that have static IP addresses assigned to them. After you enter the Start IP Address and End IP Address for the exclusion range, tap or click Add. You can then add exclusion ranges as necessary.

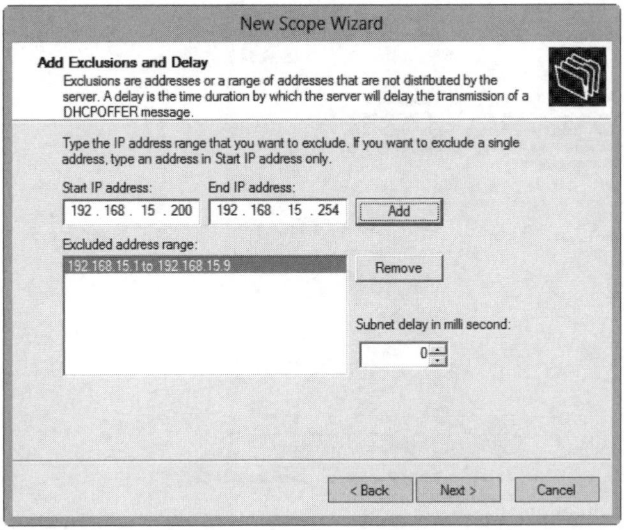

Figure 4-7 Set exclusion ranges.

CHAPTER 4

Tap or click Next to display the Lease Duration page, as shown in Figure 4-8. Specify the duration of leases for the scope. The default lease duration is eight days, but don't accept the default without first giving some thought to how leases will be used. A lease duration that's too long or too short can reduce the effectiveness of DHCP. If a lease is too long, you could run out of IP addresses because the DHCP server is holding IP addresses for devices that are no longer on the network, such as when there are a lot of mobile users who connect and disconnect their portable devices. If a lease is too short, this could generate a lot of unnecessary broadcast traffic on the network as clients attempt to renew leases.

By default, clients try to renew leases when 50 percent of the lease time has passed and then, if the first attempt fails, when 87.5 percent of the lease time has passed. With this in mind, you generally want to find a balance in the lease time that serves the types of clients on the subnet. If there are only fixed desktops and servers, you could use a longer lease duration of 14 to 21 days. If there are only mobile users with portable devices, you could shorten the lease duration to two to three days. If there's a mix of fixed systems and mobile systems, a lease duration of five to seven days might be most appropriate.

Tap or click Next to display the Configure DHCP Options page. If you want to set TCP/IP options now, select Yes and then tap or click Next to continue to the Router (Default Gateway) page, as shown in Figure 4-9. If you don't want to set TCP/IP options now, select No, tap or click Next, and then tap or click Finish to create the scope and exit the wizard.

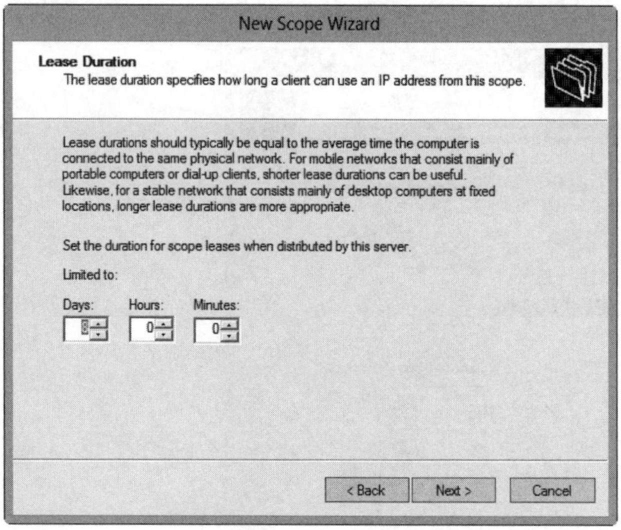

Figure 4-8 Set the lease duration.

On the Router (Default Gateway) page, in the IP Address box enter the IP address of the primary default gateway, and then tap or click Add. You can repeat this process to specify other default gateways. Keep in mind clients try to use gateways in the order in which they are listed, and you can use the Up and Down buttons to change the order of the gateways as necessary.

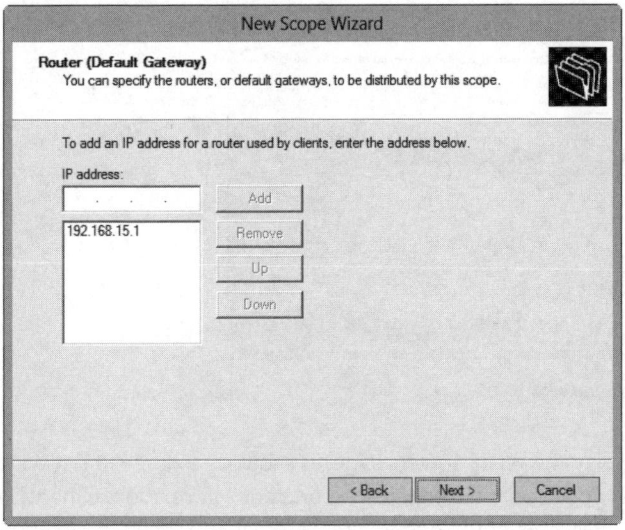

Figure 4-9 Set the default gateways.

Tap or click Next to display the Domain Name And DNS Servers page, as shown in Figure 4-10. Although the parent domain and DNS server IP addresses typically are filled in for you, make sure this information is correct for the subnet for which you are configuring the scope. If the default values are incorrect, replace them.

In the Parent Domain box, enter the name of the parent domain to use for DNS resolution of device names that aren't fully qualified. In the IP Address box, remove any invalid entries. Next, as necessary, type the IP address of the primary DNS server, and then tap or click Add. As necessary, repeat this process to specify the IP addresses of additional DNS servers. As with gateways, the order of the entries determines which DNS server is used first, and you can change the order as necessary by using the Up and Down buttons.

CHAPTER 4

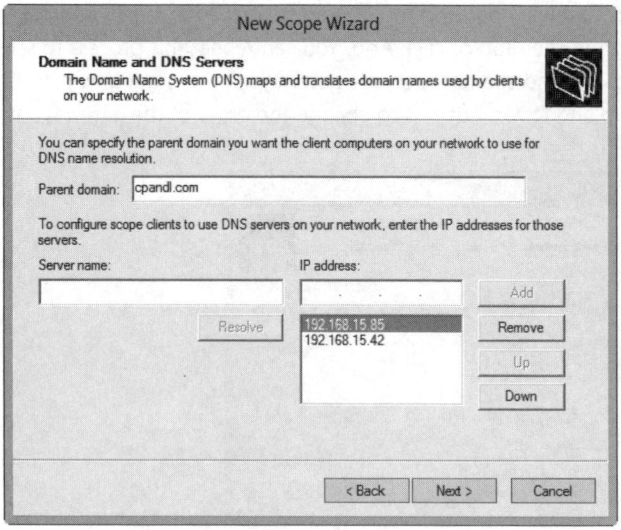

Figure 4-10 Set the DNS servers to use.

Tap or click Next to display the WINS Servers page, as shown in Figure 4-11. If WINS servers aren't used on your network, continue without entering any information. Otherwise, in the IP Address box, type the IP address of the primary WINS server and then tap or click Add. You can repeat this process to specify additional WINS servers. As with gateways, the order of the entries determines which WINS server is used first, and you can change the order as necessary by using the Up and Down buttons.

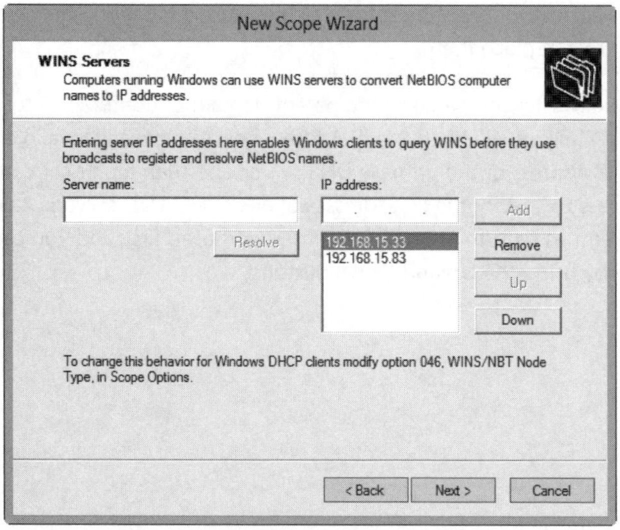

Figure 4-11 Set the WINS servers to use.

Tap or click Next to display the Activate Scope page. If you want to activate the scope, select Yes, I Want To Activate This Scope Now. Otherwise, select No, I Will Activate This Scope Later. Tap or click Next, and then tap or click Finish to create the scope and exit the wizard.

Creating normal scopes for IPv6 addresses

With IPv4 addresses, normal scopes, multicast scopes, and superscopes are all available. With IPv6 addresses, only normal scopes are available. Your IPv6 scopes will use either link-local unicast addresses beginning with FE80 or multicast IPv6 addresses beginning with FF00.

You create normal scopes for IPv6 addresses by using the New Scope Wizard. When you are configuring DHCP for IPv6 addresses, you must enter the network ID and a preference value. Typically, the first 64 bits of an IPv6 address identify the network, and a 64-bit value is what the New Scope Wizard expects you to enter. The preference value sets the priority of the scope relative to other scopes. The scope with the lowest preference value will be used first, the scope with the second lowest preference will be used second, and so on.

In the DHCP console, you create a normal scope for IPv6 addresses by expanding the node for the server you want to work with, selecting the IPv6 node, and then pressing and holding or right-clicking the IPv6 node. Next, from the shortcut menu, select New Scope.

In the New Scope Wizard, tap or click Next to display the Scope Name page. Type a name and description for the scope that will be used as a comment. Tap or click Next to display the Scope Prefix page, shown in Figure 4-12. Enter the 64-bit network prefix and then set a preference value. Tap or click Next.

CHAPTER 4

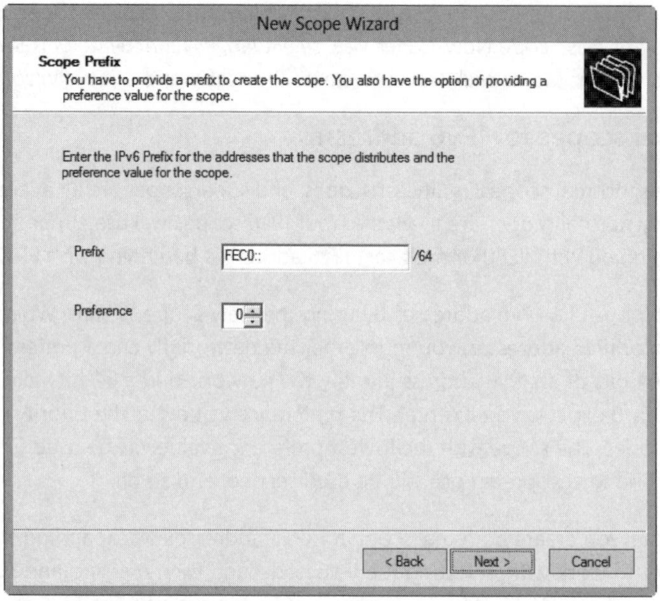

Figure 4-12 In the New Scope Wizard, enter the network prefix and preference value.

On the Add Exclusions page, shown in Figure 4-13, use the Start IPv6 Address and End IPv6 Address fields to define IPv6 address ranges that are to be excluded from the scope. You can exclude addresses as follows:

- To define an exclusion range, type a start address and an end address in the Start IPv6 Address and End IPv6 Address fields, respectively, and then tap or click Add.

- To exclude a single IPv6 address, use that address as the start IPv6 address and then tap or click Add.

- To track which address ranges are excluded, use the Excluded Address Range list box.

- To delete an exclusion range, select the range in the Excluded Address Range list box and tap or click Remove.

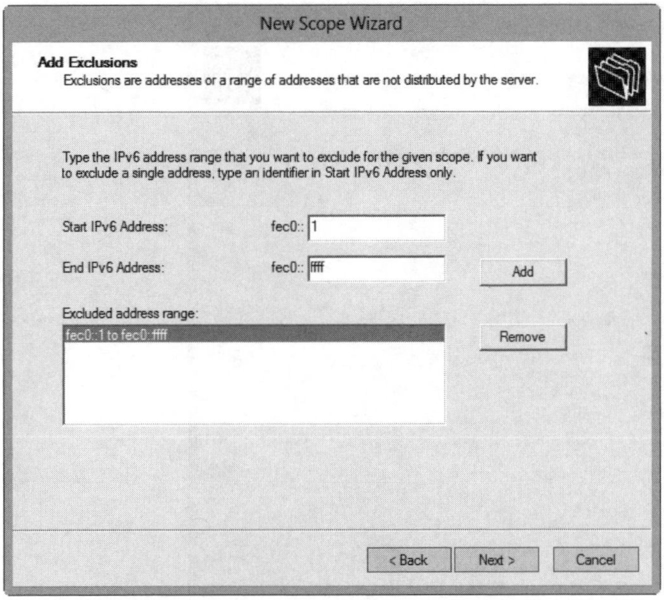

New Scope Wizard

Add Exclusions
Exclusions are addresses or a range of addresses that are not distributed by the server.

Type the IPv6 address range that you want to exclude for the given scope. If you want to exclude a single address, type an identifier in Start IPv6 Address only.

Start IPv6 Address: fec0:: 1

End IPv6 Address: fec0:: ffff   Add

Excluded address range:
fec0::1 to fec0::ffff   Remove

< Back   Next >   Cancel

Figure 4-13 Set the exclusions for IPv6 addresses.

Tap or click Next to display the Scope Lease page, shown in Figure 4-14. Dynamic IPv6 addresses can be temporary or nontemporary. A nontemporary address is similar to a reservation. Specify the duration of leases for temporary and nontemporary addresses using the Day(s), Hour(s), and Minutes fields under Preferred Life Time and Valid Life Time. The preferred lifetime is the preferred amount of time the lease should be valid. The valid lifetime is the maximum amount of time the lease is valid. Tap or click Next.

CHAPTER 4

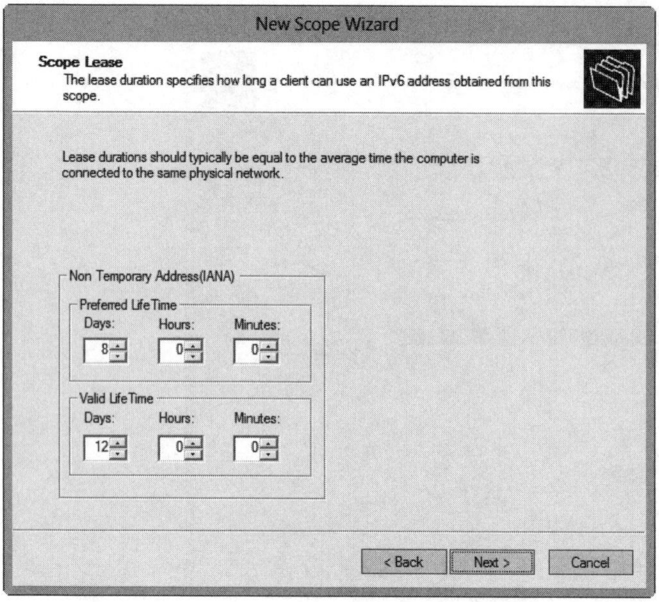

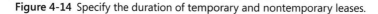

Figure 4-14 Specify the duration of temporary and nontemporary leases.

NOTE

Take a few minutes to plan the lease lifetime you want to use. A lease lifetime that's too long can reduce the effectiveness of DHCP and might eventually cause you to run out of available IP addresses, especially on networks with mobile users or other types of devices that aren't fixed members of the network. A good lease duration for temporary leases is from one to three days. A good lease duration for nontemporary leases is from 8 to 30 days.

If you want to activate the scope, select Yes under Activate Scope Now and then tap or click Finish. Otherwise, select No under Activate Scope Now and then tap or click Finish.

Creating normal scopes using Netsh

Using Netsh, you can create an IPv4 scope by typing the following command at an elevated command prompt:

```
netsh dhcp server ServerID add scope NetworkID SubnetMask ScopeName
```

Here, the following is true:

- *ServerID* is the UNC name or IP address of the DHCP server on which you want to create the scope, such as \\CORPSVR03 or \\192.168.1.1.

- *NetworkID* is the network ID of the scope, such as 192.168.1.0.

- *SubnetMask* is the subnet mask of the scope, such as 255.255.255.0.

- *ScopeName* is the name of the scope, such as Primary IPv4.

Using Netsh, you can create an IPv6 scope by typing the following command:

```
netsh dhcp server ServerID add scope NetworkPrefix PrefValue ScopeName
```

Here, the following is true:

- *ServerID* is the UNC name or IP address of the DHCP server on which you want to create the scope, such as \\CORPSVR03 or \\192.168.1.1.

- *NetworkPrefix* is the network prefix of the scope, such as FE80:0:0:0.

- *PrefValue* is the preference value of the scope, such as 1.

- *ScopeName* is the name of the scope, such as Primary IPv6.

After you create the scope, you must use separate commands to set the scope's IP address, exclusions, reservations/lease permanence, and options. You can add an IP range to the scope using the add iprange command for the NETSH DHCP SERVER SCOPE context. Type the following:

```
netsh dhcp server ServerID scope NetworkID add iprange StartIP EndIP
```

Here, the following is true:

- *ServerID* is the UNC name or IP address of the DHCP server on which the scope resides, such as \\CORPSVR03 or \\192.168.1.1.

- *NetworkID* is the network ID of the scope, such as 192.168.1.0.

- *StartIP* is the first IP address in the range, such as 192.168.1.1.

- *EndIP* is the last IP address in the range, such as 192.168.1.254.

Other commands available when you are working with the Netsh DHCP server scope context include the following:

- **add excluderange *StartIP EndIP*.** Adds a range of excluded IP addresses to the scope

- **delete iprange *StartIP EndIP*.** Deletes an IP address range from the scope

- **delete excluderange *StartIP EndIP*.** Deletes an exclusion range from the scope

CHAPTER 4

- **show iprange.** Shows currently configured IP address ranges for the scope

- **show excluderange.** Shows currently configured exclusion ranges for the scope

- **show clients.** Lists clients using the scope

- **show state**. Shows the state of the scope as active or inactive

Creating normal scopes using Windows PowerShell

Using Windows PowerShell, you can create an IPv4 scope by typing the following command at an elevated shell prompt:

```
Add-DhcpServerv4Scope -ComputerName ServerID -Name "ScopeName"
-StartRange StartIP -EndRange EndIP -SubnetMask SubnetMask
```

Here, the following is true:

- *ServerID* is the DNS name or IP address of the DHCP server on which you want to create the scope, such as CORPSVR03.cpandl.com or 192.168.1.1.

- *ScopeName* is the name of the scope, such as "Primary IPv4".

- *StartIP* is the first IP address in a range of IP addresses for the scope, such as 192.168.1.0.

- *EndIP* is the last IP address in a range of IP addresses for the scope, such as 192.168.1.255.

- *SubnetMask* is the subnet mask of the scope, such as 255.255.255.0.

The default lease duration is eight days. You can set the lease duration using the –LeaseDuration parameter. Specify the time interval using the following format:

```
Days.Hours:Minutes:Seconds
```

The following example sets the lease duration to 12 hours:

```
-LeaseDuration 0.12:00:00
```

Enter Get-DhcpServerv4Scope to list all the available IPv4 scopes and confirm that the new scope was created as expected. The network ID of the scope is set automatically, based on the IP address range, and is shown as the scope ID. As necessary, you can use Set-DhcpServerv4Scope to change scope settings. To specify the scope you want to work with, you use the scope ID, such as:

```
Set-DhcpServerv4Scope -ComputerName corpserver03.cpandl.com -ScopeId 192.168.1.0
-LeaseDuration 0.24:00:00
```

Using Windows PowerShell, you can create an IPv6 scope by typing the following command:

```
Add-DhcpServerv6Scope -ComputerName ServerID -Name "ScopeName"
-Prefix NetworkPrefix -Preference PrefValue -SubnetMask SubnetMask
```

Here, the following is true:

- *ServerID* is the DNS name or IP address of the DHCP server on which you want to create the scope, such as CORPSVR03.cpandl.com or 192.168.1.1.

- *ScopeName* is the name of the scope, such as "Primary IPv6".

- *NetworkPrefix* is the network prefix of the IPv6 scope, such as FE80:0:0:0.

- *PrefValue* is the preference value of the scope, such as 1.

The default lease renewal time is four days. If the renewal attempt fails, the client attempts to rebind the lease according to the lease rebind time, which by default is 6.4 days. You can set the lease renewal time and lease rebind time using the –T1 and –T2 parameters respectively. Specify the time interval using the following format:

```
Days.Hours:Minutes:Seconds
```

The following example sets the lease renewal time to 2.5 days and the lease rebind time to four days:

```
-T1 2.12:00:00 -T2 4.00:00:00
```

Enter Get-DhcpServerv6Scope to list all the available IPv6 scopes and confirm that the new scope was created as expected. As necessary, you can use Set-DhcpServerv6Scope to change scope settings. To specify the scope you want to work with, you use the network prefix, such as:

```
Set-DhcpServerv6Scope -ComputerName corpserver03.cpandl.com -Prefix FE80:0:0:0
-T1 3.00:00:00 -T2 4.12:00:00
```

After you create the scope, you must use separate commands to set the scope's exclusions, reservations, and options. Commands you can use include the following:

- **Add-DhcpServerv4ExclusionRange.** Adds a range of excluded IPv4 addresses to the scope. The basic syntax is:

  ```
  Add-DhcpServerv4ExclusionRange -ComputerName ServerID -ScopeID NetworkID
  -StartRange StartIP -EndRange EndIP
  ```

CHAPTER 4

- **Add-DhcpServerv6ExclusionRange.** Adds a range of excluded IPv6 addresses to the scope. The basic syntax is:

  ```
  Add-DhcpServerv6ExclusionRange –ComputerName ServerID –Prefix NetworkPrefix
  –StartRange StartIP –EndRange EndIP
  ```

- **Get-DhcpServerv4ExclusionRange.** Lists a range of excluded IPv4 addresses for a specified scope. The basic syntax is:

  ```
  Get-DhcpServerv4ExclusionRange –ComputerName ServerID –ScopeID NetworkID
  ```

- **Get-DhcpServerv6ExclusionRange.** Lists a range of excluded IPv6 addresses for a specified scope. The basic syntax is:

  ```
  Get-DhcpServerv6ExclusionRange –ComputerName ServerID –Prefix NetworkPrefix
  ```

- **Remove-DhcpServerv4ExclusionRange.** Removes a range of excluded IPv4 addresses from the scope. The basic syntax is:

  ```
  Remove-DhcpServerv4ExclusionRange –ComputerName ServerID –ScopeID NetworkID
  –StartRange StartIP –EndRange LastIPAddress
  ```

- **Remove-DhcpServerv6ExclusionRange.** Removes a range of excluded IPv6 addresses from the scope. The basic syntax is:

  ```
  Remove-DhcpServerv6ExclusionRange –ComputerName ServerID –Prefix NetworkPrefix
  –StartRange StartIP –EndRange EndIP
  ```

Activating scopes

Scopes are available only when they are activated. If you want to make a scope available to clients, you must press and hold or right-click it in the DHCP console and then select Activate. Activating a scope won't make clients switch to that scope. If you want to force clients to switch to a different scope or to use a different DHCP server, you can terminate the client leases in the DHCP console and then deactivate the scope that the clients are currently using.

To terminate a lease, you expand the scope you want to work with in the DHCP console and then select Address Leases. You will then see a list of current leases, and you can terminate a lease by pressing and holding or right-clicking it and selecting Delete. The next time the client goes to renew its lease, the DHCP server will tell the client that the lease is no longer valid and that a new one must be obtained.

To prevent clients from reusing the original scope, you can deactivate that scope by pressing and holding or right-clicking it in the DHCP console and then selecting Deactivate.

You can perform these same actions using Netsh. To terminate a lease, use the following command:

```
netsh dhcp server ServerID scope NetworkID delete lease IPAddress
```

Here, the following is true:

- *ServerID* is the UNC name or IP address of the DHCP server on which the scope resides, such as \\CORPSVR03 or \\192.168.1.1.

- *NetworkID* is the network ID of the scope, such as 192.168.1.0.

- *IPAddress* is the IP address for the lease you want to remove, such as 192.168.1.8.

To activate or deactivate a scope, type the following:

```
netsh dhcp server ServerID scope NetworkID state StateVal
```

Here, the following is true:

- *ServerID* is the UNC name or IP address of the DHCP server on which the scope resides, such as \\CORPSVR03 or \\192.168.1.1.

- *NetworkID* is the network ID of the scope, such as 192.168.1.0.

- *StateVal* is set to 0 to deactivate the scope and 1 to activate it. If you are using a switched network on which multiple logical networks are hosted on a single physical network, use 2 to deactivate the scope and 3 to activate the scope.

In Windows PowerShell you can terminate a lease using the following commands:

```
Remove-DhcpServerv4Lease –ComputerName ServerID -IPAddress IPAddress
Remove-DhcpServerv6Lease –ComputerName ServerID -IPAddress IPAddress
```

Here, the following is true:

- *ServerID* is the DNS name or IP address of the DHCP server on which the scope resides, such as CORPSVR03.cpandl.com or 192.168.1.1.

- *IPAddress* is the IP address for the lease you want to remove, such as 192.168.1.8.

You can activate or deactivate a scope using the following commands:

```
Set-DhcpServerv4Scope –ComputerName ServerID -ScopeID NetworkID -State StateVal
Set-DhcpServerv6Scope –ComputerName ServerID -Prefix NetworkPrefix -State StateVal
```

Here, the following is true:

- *ServerID* is the DNS name or IP address of the DHCP server on which the scope resides, such as CORPSVR03.cpandl.com or 192.168.1.1.

- *NetworkID* is the network ID of an IPv4 scope, such as 192.168.1.0.

CHAPTER 4

- *NetworkPrefix* is the network prefix of an IPv6 scope, such as FE80:0:0:0.

- *StateVal* is set to Inactive to deactivate the scope and Active to activate it.

Scope exclusions

To exclude IPv4 or IPv6 addresses from a scope, you can define an exclusion range. Typically, you exclude IP addresses from a scope when they are otherwise assigned. For example, if you assign static IP addresses to certain devices on the network and they are within the range of addresses used by a particular scope, you should define exclusions for those IP addresses to ensure that DHCP doesn't try to use them.

In the DHCP console, any existing exclusions for a scope can be displayed by expanding the scope and selecting Address Pool, as shown in Figure 4-15. To list exclusions at the command line, enter the following:

```
netsh dhcp server ServerID scope NetworkID show excluderange
```

Here, *ServerID* is the UNC name or IP address of the DHCP server on which the scope resides, such as \\CORPSVR03 or \\192.168.1.1, and *NetworkID* is the network ID of the scope, such as 192.168.1.0.

To list exclusions at the shell prompt, use the following commands:

```
Get-DhcpServerv4ExclusionRange –ComputerName ServerID –ScopeID NetworkID
Get-DhcpServerv6ExclusionRange –ComputerName ServerID –Prefix NetworkPrefix
```

Here, *ServerID* is the DNS name or IP address of the DHCP server on which the scope resides, such as CorpServer03.cpandl.com or 192.168.1.1. *NetworkID* is the network ID of an IPv4 scope, such as 192.168.1.0. *NetworkPrefix* is the network prefix of an IPv6 scope, such as FE80:0:0:0.

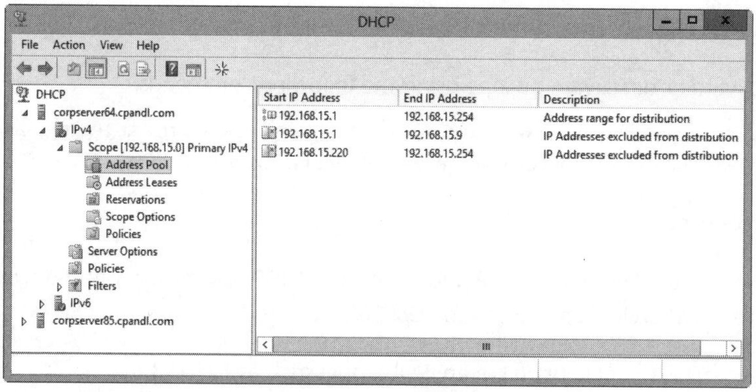

Figure 4-15 Exclusions listed under the Address Pool node.

In the DHCP console, you can define an exclusion range by pressing and holding or right-clicking Address Pool within the scope you want to work with and choosing New Exclusion Range. In the Add Exclusion dialog box, enter a start address and an end address for the exclusion range, as shown in Figure 4-16, and then tap or click Add. Keep in mind that the range excluded must be a subset of the scope's range and must not currently be in use by DHCP clients.

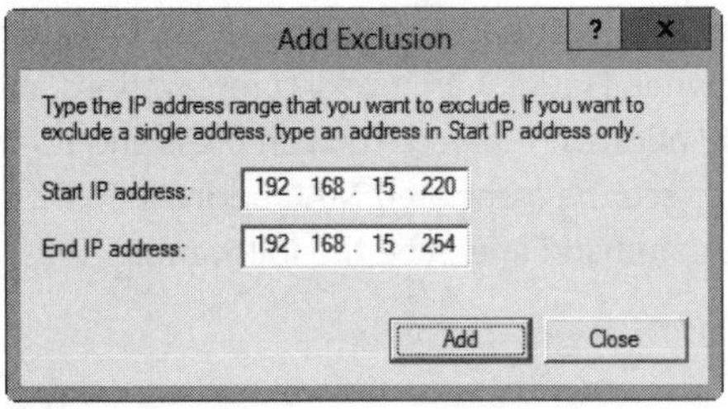

Figure 4-16 Set the exclusion range.

Using Netsh, you can add an exclusion range in much the same way. Type the following:

```
netsh dhcp server ServerID scope NetworkID add excluderange StartIP EndIP
```

Here, the following is true:

- *ServerID* is the UNC name or IP address of the DHCP server on which the scope resides, such as \\CORPSVR03 or \\192.168.1.1.

- *NetworkID* is the network ID of the scope, such as 192.168.1.0.

- *StartIP* is the first IP address in the exclusion range, such as 192.168.1.200.

- *EndIP* is the last IP address in the exclusion range, such as 192.168.1.219.

With Windows PowerShell, you can add an exclusion range using the following command:

```
Add-DhcpServerv4ExclusionRange –ComputerName ServerID –ScopeID NetworkID
–StartRange StartIP –EndRange EndIP
```

Here, *ServerID* is the DNS name or IP address of the DHCP server on which the scope resides, such as CORPSVR03.cpandl.com or 192.168.1.1, and the other parameter values are used as discussed previously.

Scope reservations

Reservations provide a way to assign a permanent lease on an IPv4 address to a client. In this way, the client has a fixed IP address but you retain flexibility because you could change the IPv4 address at any time if necessary through DHCP rather than having to do it on the client.

Reservations also are used to show clients with static IP addresses. Here, you create reservations to display these clients, not to assign IP addresses to them.

IMPORTANT

Reserved IP addresses are not static IP addresses. Reserved IP addresses can be leased from DHCP. Static IP addresses must be manually assigned on the client.

In the DHCP console, you can display any existing reservations for a scope by expanding the scope and selecting Reservations. As shown in Figure 4-17, existing reservations are shown according to the reservation name and IP address reserved. You can press and hold or right-click a reservation and select Properties to see the associated MAC address. To list reservations by IPv4 address and MAC address at the command line, type the following:

```
netsh dhcp server ServerID scope NetworkID show reservedip
```

Here, *ServerID* is the UNC name or IP address of the DHCP server on which you want to create the scope, such as \\CORPSVR03 or \\192.168.1.1, and *NetworkID* is the network ID of the scope, such as 192.168.1.0.

With Windows PowerShell, you can list reservations using the following command:

Get-DhcpServerv4Reservation –ComputerName *ServerID* **–ScopeID** *NetworkID*

Here, *ServerID* is the DNS name or IP address of the DHCP server on which the scope resides, such as CORPSVR03.cpandl.com or 192.168.1.1, and *NetworkID* is the network ID of the scope.

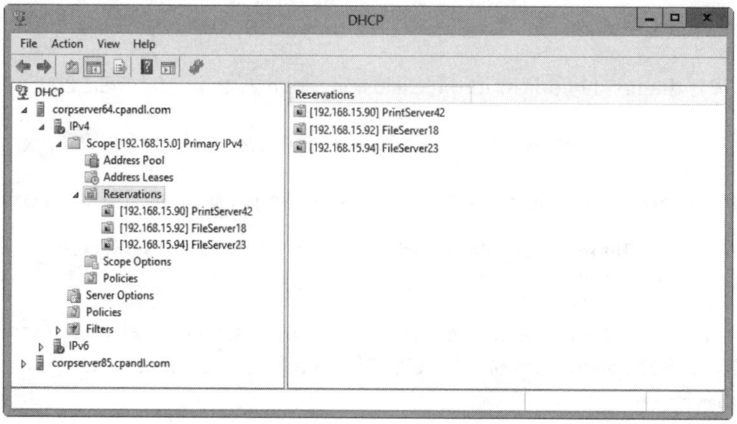

Figure 4-17 Current reservations listed by reservation name and IP address.

To create a reservation, you need to know the MAC or device unique identifier (DUID) address of the device that will hold the IP address. MAC and DUID addresses are specific to an individual network interface configured on the client. You can view the MAC address of an interface by typing **ipconfig /all** at the command prompt. The output will list the MAC address as the physical address of the network interface, as it does under Physical Address in the following example:

```
Windows IP Configuration
Host Name . . . . . . . . . . . : corpserver64
Primary Dns Suffix . . . . . . : cpandl.com
Node Type . . . . . . . . . . . : Hybrid
IP Routing Enabled. . . . . . . : No
WINS Proxy Enabled. . . . . . . : No
DNS Suffix Search List. . . . . : cpandl.com

Ethernet adapter Local Area Connection:
Connection-specific DNS Suffix  . : cpandl.com
Description . . . . . . . . . . : Intel(R) PRO/1000 PM Network Connection
Physical Address. . . . . . . . : 23-24-AE-67-B4-E8
DHCP Enabled. . . . . . . . . . : Yes
Autoconfiguration Enabled . . . . : Yes
IPv4 Address. . . . . . . . . . : 192.168.15.124(Preferred)
Subnet Mask . . . . . . . . . . : 255.255.255.0
Lease Obtained. . . . . . . . . : Sunday, Feb 21, 2014 5:25:14 AM
Lease Expires . . . . . . . . . : Sunday, Feb 28, 2014 3:28:56 PM
Default Gateway . . . . . . . . : 192.168.15.1
DHCP Server . . . . . . . . . . : 192.168.15.1
DNS Servers . . . . . . . . . . : 192.168.15.1
NetBIOS over Tcpip. . . . . . . : Enabled

Tunnel adapter Local Area Connection* 6:
Connection-specific DNS Suffix  . :
Description . . . . . . . . . . : Teredo Tunneling Pseudo-Interface
Physical Address. . . . . . . . : 23-24-AE-67-B4-E8
DHCP Enabled. . . . . . . . . . : No
Autoconfiguration Enabled . . . . : Yes
IPv6 Address. . . . . . . . . . : fe80::fd1b:2778:f7e1:67d2%10(Preferred)
Link-local IPv6 Address . . . . . : fe80::2beb:f99:fe57:f87b%10(Preferred)
Default Gateway . . . . . . . . : ::
NetBIOS over Tcpip. . . . . . . : Disabled
```

NOTE

You create IPv6 reservations in much the same way that you create IPv4 reservations. When you create the reservation, you enter the DUID and the IAID for the DHCPv6 client instead of a MAC address.

In the DHCP console, you can reserve a DHCPv4 address for a client as follows:

1. After you expand the scope you want to work with, press and hold or right-click the Reservations folder and choose New Reservation. This opens the New Reservation dialog box, as shown in Figure 4-18.

2. In the Reservation Name box, type a descriptive name for the reservation. This doesn't have to be the name of the device to which the reservation belongs, but that does help simplify administration.

3. In the IP Address box, enter the IP address you want to reserve for the client. This IP address must be valid for the currently selected scope and can't be in an excluded range.

4. In the MAC Address box, type the MAC address in the text box provided and as previously obtained using the **ipconfig /all** command.

5. If desired, enter an optional comment in the Description box.

6. By default, the reservation is configured to accept both DHCP and BOOTP clients. Change the default only if you want to exclude a particular type of client. DHCP clients include devices running the standard version of the DHCP client, like most Windows operating systems. BOOTP clients are clients running other operating systems and could also include devices such as printers that can use dynamic IP addressing.

7. Tap or click Add to create the address reservation.

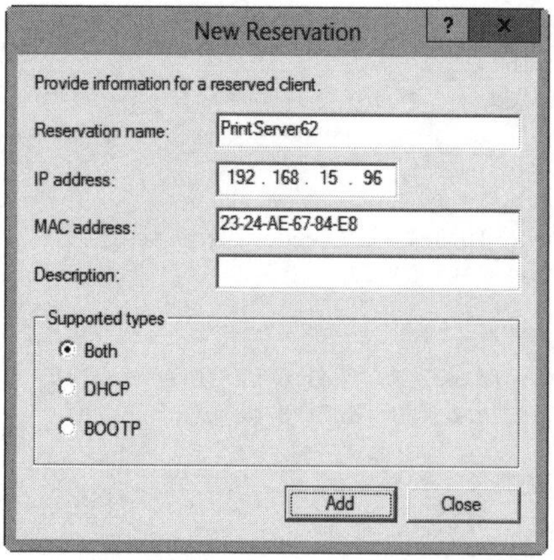

Figure 4-18 Create a reservation for an IP address using the MAC address of the client.

In Netsh, you can create a reservation by typing the following command:

```
netsh dhcp server ServerID scope NetworkID add reservedip ReservedIP MacAddress Name
Comment
```

Here, the following is true:

- *ServerID* is the UNC name or IP address of the DHCP server on which the scope resides, such as \\CORPSVR03 or \\192.168.1.1.

- *NetworkID* is the network ID of the scope, such as 192.168.1.0.

- *ReservedIP* is the IP address you are reserving, such as 192.168.1.20.

- *MacAddress* is the MAC address of the client (excluding the dashes), such as 2324AE67B4E8.

- *Name* is the descriptive name of the reservation.

- *Comment* is the optional comment describing the reservation.

When you assign reservations, keep in mind that a client with an existing lease won't automatically use the reservation. If a client has a current lease, you must force the client to release that lease and request a new one. If a client has an existing address and you want to force it to start using DHCP, you must force the client to stop using its current IP address and request a new IP address from DHCP.

To force a client to release an existing lease or drop its current IP address, log on to the client and type **ipconfig /release** at an elevated, administrator command prompt. Next, if the client isn't already configured to use DHCP, you must configure the client to use DHCP as discussed in the section entitled "Configuring dynamic IP addresses and alternate IP addressing" in Chapter 3, "Managing TCP/IP networking."

To get a client to request a new IP address from DHCP, log on to the client and type **ipconfig /renew** at the command prompt.

Creating and using failover scopes

Failover scopes apply only to IPv4 addresses. You create a failover scope on the DHCP server that you want to act as the primary server by splitting an existing scope or a superscope that contains multiple scopes. The scope or superscope you want to work with must already be defined.

During the failover-scope creation process, you need to specify the partner server with which you want to split the primary server's scope. This additional server acts as the secondary server for the scope. Because failover scopes are a server-side enhancement, no additional configuration is required for DHCP clients.

Time synchronization is essential for failover scopes to function correctly. Partner servers must have their time synchronized. You can synchronize time on servers using Network Time Protocol (NTP) or other techniques. When you are creating failover scopes, the time difference between the servers can't be significant (usually this means greater than one minute). If it is significant, setup will fail and you see an error telling you to synchronize the time on the partner servers.

CHAPTER 4

To create a failover scope, complete the following steps:

1. In the DHCP console, connect to the primary DHCP server for the failover scope. Expand the entry for the primary server and then expand its IPv4 folder in the tree view.

2. Press and hold or right-click the scope or superscope that you want to configure for failover, and then tap or click Configure Failover to open the Configure Failover Wizard. The wizard shows the scope or scopes that will be included. Tap or click Next to continue.

NOTE

With superscopes, child scopes that are already configured for availability are not listed and all other child scopes are shown and selected by default. If you'd rather select the child scopes to include individually, clear Select All and then select the individual scopes to include.

IMPORTANT

The scope you are configuring for failover can't already exist on the partner server. If the scope is already on the partner server, you need to delete it before configuring failover. But don't delete scopes on partner servers without first determining how the scopes are being used. For example, if a scope has been split between two servers, you might be deleting part of a split scope.

3. As shown in Figure 4-19, you can now specify the partner server to use for failover. You can select from a list of servers that were previously or are currently used as failover partners, or you can select other authorized DHCP servers. Tap or click Add Server to browse a list of authorized servers. In the Add Server dialog box, select the partner server for the failover scope and then tap or click OK.

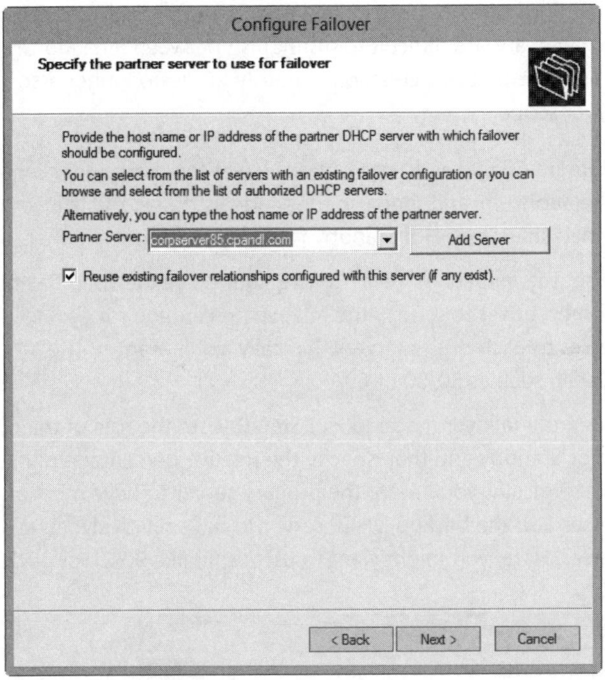

Figure 4-19 Select the partner server.

Inside OUT

Reusing failover relationships

By default, if you configured failover previously, the wizard will reuse the configuration. Because you can't edit the failover settings after creating a failover scope, you'll usually want to clear the Reuse Existing Failover Relationships Configured With This Server check box and manually configure the failover scope to ensure that you can optimize each failover scope as appropriate. That said, if you don't clear this check box and decide to reuse settings, the next page will display the settings that will be used. When there are multiple existing failover relationships, you'll be able to select the failover relationship to use and the settings for the selected relationship will be displayed. When you are ready to continue, tap or click Next and then skip ahead to step 8.

4. On the Create A New Failover Relationship page, shown in Figure 4-20, a default relationship name is set based on the names of the partner servers. Rather than use the default value, I recommend entering a relationship name that helps you uniquely identify each failover relationship. The reason for this is that you can't edit the active

relationship settings directly. Instead, you edit them indirectly according to the relationship name, and it's difficult to distinguish between a relationship that's actively being used and one that was created previously but is no longer associated with a specific failover scope.

5. Use the Maximum Client Lead Time options to set the maximum client lead time for the failover relationship, and then use the Mode list to set the failover mode to Load Balance for load sharing or Hot Standby for fault tolerance.

  ■ If you set the failover mode to Load Balance, use the Load Balance Percentage combo boxes to specify the relative percentage for how to allocate the IP addresses to each of the servers. Typically, you'll want to use an equal or nearly equal split, such as 50/50 or 60/40.

  ■ If you set the failover mode to Hot Standby, set the role of the partner as either Active or Standby and then specify the relative percentage of IP addresses to reserve. Typically, you'll want the primary server to have most of the available IP addresses and the backup DHCP server to have relatively few of the available IP addresses. Here, you might want to use a split like 90/10 or 80/20.

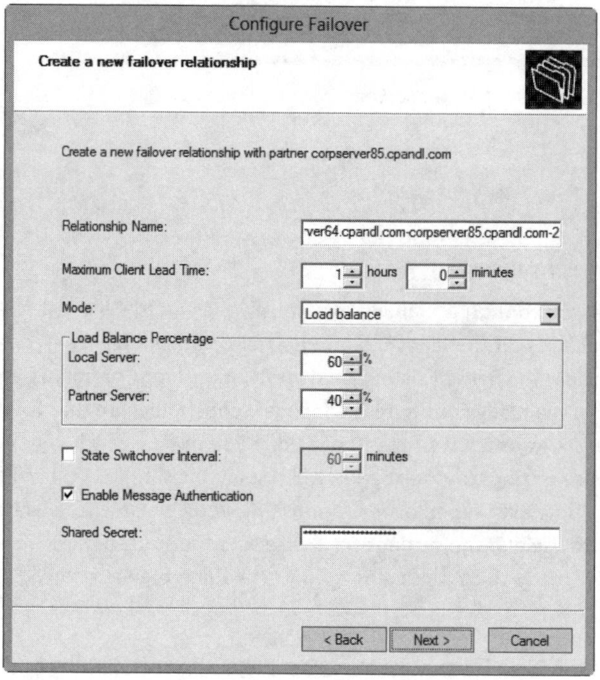

Figure 4-20 Set the mode and address space split.

6. By default, the switchover interval is disabled, which allows for an immediate switchover to the Partner Down state. Any other value sets the timer for automatic state transition.

IMPORTANT

When you enable failover scopes, the member servers track their own state and the state of their partner. The state switchover interval sets the time interval for which the DHCP Server service should continue operating in the Communication Interrupted state before transitioning to the Partner Down state. When the Partner Down state is reached, the partner takes over responsibility for the scope.

7. Type a shared secret for the partners. The shared secret is a password that the partners use when synchronizing the DHCP database and performing other tasks related to maintaining the DHCP failover partnership. When you are ready to continue, tap or click Next.

8. Tap or click Finish. Review the summary of the failover scope configuration. If any errors were encountered, you might need to take corrective action. Tap or click Close.

Failover scopes are not identified as such in the DHCP console. You can identify a failover scope by its network ID and IP address pool. Generally, you'll find a scope with the same network ID on two DHCP servers, and the scope properties will include information about the failover partnership. You'll find this information on the Failover tab in the Properties dialog box.

You can manage the partnership in several ways. If you suspect that the configuration details related to the partnership are out of sync, press and hold or right-click the scope and then select Replicate Relationship. If you suspect that the DHCP database that the partners share is out of sync, press and hold or right-click the scope and then select Replicate Scope.

You can't directly modify the failover settings once the partnership is established. However, you can deconfigure failover and then reconfigure failover. Alternatively, you use the IPv4 Properties dialog box to edit relationships. To do this, press and hold or right-click the IPv4 node and then select Properties. On the Failover tab, you'll see a list of every failover relationship created and applicable to the server. To modify a relationship, select, tap, or click Edit, and then use the options provided to change the failover settings.

However, because the relationships listed aren't necessarily active, it's not easy to differentiate between a live, active relationship and a previously created but no longer active relationship. If you have many active and inactive relationships, one way to specifically identify an active relationship, meaning one associated with a scope, is to try to delete a relationship. When you select a relationship and then tap or click Delete, the Delete Failover Relationship dialog box is displayed. If the relationship is active, the actual scope or scopes with which it is associated are listed on the Scopes panel. Otherwise, the Scopes panel will be blank.

If you no longer want the scope to fail over, you access the scope on the server on which the original scope should be maintained. Next, you press and hold or right-click the scope and then select Deconfigure Failover. This removes the scope from the partner while leaving the scope on the server you are working with.

Configuring DHCP Services

Dynamic Host Configuration Protocol (DHCP) is a client/server protocol. All server editions of Microsoft Windows Server 2012 R2 include the DHCP Server service, which can be installed to support DHCP, as discussed in Chapter 4, "Deploying DHCP Services." All current versions of the Windows operating system automatically install the DHCP Client service as part of TCP/IP, and you configure TCP/IP options for DHCP clients as discussed in this chapter.

Configuring TCP/IP options

The messages that clients and servers broadcast to each other allow you to set TCP/IP options that clients can obtain by default when they obtain a lease or can request if they need additional information. Note, however, that the types of information you can add to DHCP messages are limited in several ways:

- DHCP messages are transmitted using User Datagram Protocol (UDP), and the entire DHCP message must fit into the UDP datagram. On Ethernet with 1,500-byte datagrams, this leaves 1,236 bytes for the body of the message (which contains the TCP/IP options).

- Bootstrap Protocol (BOOTP) messages have a fixed size of 300 bytes as set by the original BOOTP standard. Any clients using BOOTP are likely to have their TCP/IP options truncated.

- Although you can set many options, clients understand only certain TCP/IP options. Thus, the set of options available to you is dependent on the client's implementation of DHCP.

With that in mind, let's look at the levels at which options can be assigned and the options that Windows clients understand.

Levels of options and their uses

Each individual TCP/IP option, such as a default gateway, is configured separately. There are different scope options for IPv4 and IPv6. DHCP administrators can manage options at five levels within the DHCP server configuration:

CHAPTER 5

- **Predefined options.** DHCP administrators can use these options to specify the way in which options are used and to create new option types for use on a server. In the DHCP console, you can view and set predefined options by pressing and holding or right-clicking the IPv4 or IPv6 node in the console tree and selecting Set Predefined Options.

- **Server options.** DHCP administrators can use these options to configure options that are assigned to all scopes created on the DHCP server. Think of server options as global options that are assigned to all clients. Server options can be overridden by scope, class, and client-assigned options. In the DHCP console, you can view and set server options by expanding the entry for the server you want to work with, pressing and holding or right-clicking Server Options, and then choosing Configure Options.

- **Scope options.** DHCP administrators can use these options to configure options that are assigned to all clients that use a particular scope. Scope options are assigned only to normal scopes and can be overridden by class and client-assigned options. In the DHCP console, you can view and set scope options by expanding the scope you want to work with, pressing and holding or right-clicking Scope Options, and then choosing Configure Options.

- **Class options.** DHCP administrators can use these options to configure options that are assigned to all clients of a particular class. Client classes can be user defined or vendor defined. Class options can be overridden by client-assigned options. You define new user and vendor classes by pressing and holding or right-clicking the IPv4 or IPv6 entry and selecting either Define User Classes or Define Vendor Classes as appropriate. When defined, class options can be configured in the Advanced tab of the Server Options, Scope Options, and Reservation Options dialog boxes.

- **Reservation options.** Administrators can use these options to set options for an individual client that uses a reservation. These options are also referred to as *client-specific options*. After you create a reservation for a client, you can configure reservation options by expanding the scope, expanding Reservations, pressing and holding or right-clicking the reservation, and selecting Configure Options. Only TCP/IP options manually configured on a client can override client-assigned options.

Policy-based assignment

To the complex maze of option levels, Windows Server 2012 R2 adds a policy-based assignment of options. Here, IP addresses and options are assigned based on fields contained in the DHCP client request packet, allowing for the targeted application of options.

Policy-based options can be configured at the server level and at the scope level. Server-level policies specify options that you want to assign. Scope-level policies specify IP addresses and options that you want to assign. Policies applicable for a particular scope can be inherited from the server level, assigned at the scope level, or both, with the DHCP server processing all matching policies sequentially according to a defined processing order.

At the server level and at the scope level, each policy has a defined precedence order, as shown in Figure 5-1. If you create policies at both the server and scope levels, the server applies both sets of policies and evaluates the scope policies before the server policies.

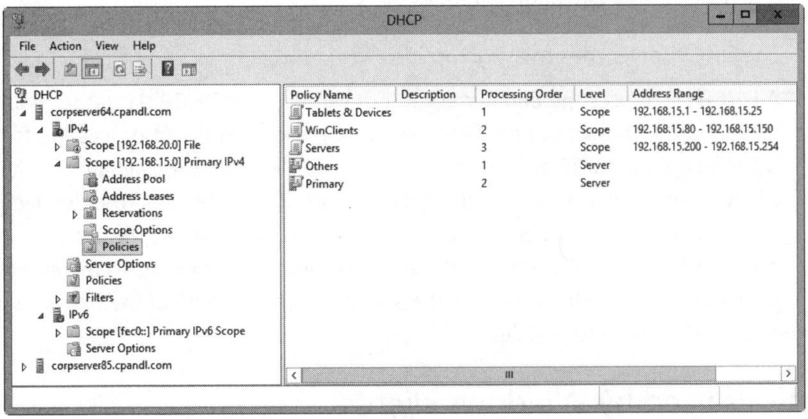

Figure 5-1 Each policy has a defined precedence order.

The DHCP server determines the scope to which a DHCP client belongs based on the gateway IP address of the relay agent or the interface of the DHCP server on which it receives the DHCP client packet. Once the server determines the client scope, the server evaluates the DHCP packet against the policies applicable for the scope according to the processing order. The policies applicable for a scope are those configured at the scope and those inherited from the server.

A single client request can match the targeting parameters of multiple policies. These policy matches determine how the server assigns IP addresses and options. DHCP servers process policies in two phases:

1. The DHCP server tries to assign an IP address.

   The DHCP server evaluates the fields in the client request against each policy applicable for the scope using the defined processing order. If a client request matches the conditions of a policy with an IP address range, the server assigns the first free IP address from the range. If a policy is associated with multiple address ranges, the server attempts to assign an IP address from the lowest address range.

   If no IP addresses are available in this address range, the server looks for a free IP address from the next higher address range, and so on. If no IP addresses are free in any of the address ranges associated with the policy, the server attempts to assign an IP address from the next matched policy, as determined by the processing order. If none of the matched policies has a free IP address, the server drops the client packet and logs an event.

If a DHCP client packet does not match any of the policies applicable for the scope, or none of the matched policies is associated with an IP address range, the server leases the client an IP address from the IP address range configured for the scope, exclusive of any policy-specific IP address ranges.

2.   The DHCP server tries to assign options.

A DHCP client uses the parameter request list field in a DHCP packet to request a list of standard options from the DHCP server. Option assignment processing for a client is similar to that for IP address assignment. The DHCP server evaluates the fields in the client request against each policy applicable for the scope using the defined processing order. If the client request matches the conditions of an applicable policy, and the policy includes specific options, the server returns these options to the client. If multiple policies match the client request, the server returns the sum of the options specified for each of the matched policies.

Options used by Windows clients

RFC 3442 defines many TCP/IP options that you can set in DHCP messages. Although you can set all of these options on a DHCP server, the set of options available depends on the client's implementation of DHCP.

Table 5-1 shows the options that administrators can configure and Windows computers running the DHCP Client service can use. Each option has an associated option code, which is used to identify it in a DHCP message, and a data entry, which contains the value setting of the option. Clients request these options to set their TCP/IP configuration.

Table 5-1 Standard TCP/IP options that administrators can configure

Option Name	Option Code	Description
Router	003	Sets a list of IP addresses for the default gateways that the client should use. IP addresses are listed in order of preference.
DNS Servers	006	Sets a list of IP addresses for the DNS servers that the client should use. IP addresses are listed in order of preference.
DNS Domain Name	015	Sets the DNS domain name that clients should use when resolving host names using DNS.

Option Name	Option Code	Description
WINS/NBNS Servers	044	Sets a list of IP addresses for the WINS servers that the client should use. IP addresses are listed in order of preference.
WINS/NBT Node Type	046	Sets the method to use when resolving NetBIOS names. The acceptable values are the following: 0x1 for B-node (broadcast), 0x2 for P-node (peer-to-peer), 0x4 for M-node (mixed), and 0x8 for H-node (hybrid). See the section entitled "NetBIOS node types" in Chapter 9, "Implementing and maintaining WINS."
NetBIOS Scope ID	047	Sets the NetBIOS scope for the client.

Using user-specific and vendor-specific TCP/IP options

DHCP uses classes to determine which options are sent to clients. The user classes let you assign TCP/IP options according to the type of user the client represents on the network. The default user classes include the following:

- **Default User Class.** An all-inclusive class that includes clients that don't fit into the other user classes. Any computer on the network is in this class, regardless of whether it is directly connected, subject to Network Access Protection (NAP), or remotely connected.

- **Default BOOTP Class.** Any computer directly connected to the local network has this class. Any settings applied to this class are used by directly connected clients.

- **Default Routing And Remote Access Class.** Any computer that connects to the network using Routing and Remote Access Service (RRAS) has this class. Any settings applied to this class are used by dial-in and VPN users, which allows you to set different TCP/IP options for these users.

- **Default Network Access Protection Class.** Any computer that connects to the network and is subject to the Network Access Protection (NAP) policy has this class. Any settings applied to this class are used by restricted-access clients, which allows you to set different TCP/IP options for these users.

Clients can be members of multiple user classes, and you can view the user class memberships for each network interface by typing **ipconfig /showclassid *** at the command prompt. (The asterisk tells the command that you want to see all the network interfaces.) The output you see on a computer running Windows will be similar to the following:

```
Windows IP Configuration
DHCP Classes for Adapter "Local Area Connection":

    DHCP ClassID Name           :    Default Routing and Remote Access Class
    DHCP ClassID Description     :    User class for remote access clients

    DHCP ClassID Name           :    Default BOOTP Class
    DHCP ClassID Description     :    User class for BOOTP Clients
```

Here, the client is a member of the Default Routing And Remote Access Class and the Default BOOTP Class. The client, however, doesn't get its options from both classes. Instead, the class from which the client gets its options depends on its connection state. If the client is connected directly to the network, it uses the Default BOOTP Class. If the client is connected by Routing and Remote Access, it uses the Default Routing And Remote Access Class.

Vendor classes work a bit differently because they define the set of options available to and used by the various user classes. The default vendor class, DHCP Standard Options, is used to set the standard TCP/IP options, and the various user classes all have access to these options so that they can be implemented in a user-specific way. Additional vendor classes beyond the default define extensions or additional options that can be implemented in a user-specific way. This means that the vendor class defines the options and makes them available, and the user class settings determine which of these additional options (if any) the clients use.

The default vendor classes that you'll likely use are as follows:

- **Microsoft Options.** Add-on options available to any client running any version of Windows

- **Microsoft Windows 2000 Options.** Add-on options available to any client running Windows 2000 or later

When it comes to these classes, a client applies the options from the most specific add-on vendor class. Thus, if both Microsoft Options and Microsoft Windows 2000 Options are configured, a Windows 2000 or later client would apply the Microsoft Windows 2000 Options vendor class. Again, these options are in addition to the standard options provided through the DHCP Standard Options vendor class and can be implemented in a manner specific to a user class. This means you can have one set of add-on options for directly connected clients (Default BOOTP Class) and one set for remotely connected clients (Default Routing And Remote Access Class).

The add-on options that can be set are listed in Table 5-2.

Table 5-2 Additional TCP/IP options that administrators can configure

Option Name	Option Code	Description
Microsoft Disable NetBIOS Option	001	Disables NetBIOS if selected as an option with a value of 0x1.
Microsoft Release DHCP Lease On Shut-down Option	002	Specifies that a client should release its DHCP lease on shutdown if selected as an option with a value of 0x1.
Microsoft Default Router Metric Base	003	Specifies that the default router metric base should be used if selected as an option with a value of 0x1.

Setting options for all clients

On the DHCP server, you can set IPv4 and IPv6 options at several levels. You can set standard options for the following components:

- **All scopes on a server.** In the DHCP console, expand the entry for the server and IP protocol you want to work with, press and hold or right-click Server Options, and then choose Configure Options.

- **A specific scope.** In the DHCP console, expand the scope you want to work with, press and hold or right-click Scope Options, and then choose Configure Options.

- **A single reserved IP address.** In the DHCP console, expand the scope you want to work with, expand Reservations, press and hold or right-click the reservation you want to work with, and select Configure Options.

Regardless of the level at which you are setting IPv4 and IPv6 options, the dialog box displayed has the same set of choices as that shown in Figure 5-2. You can now select each standard TCP/IP option you want to use in turn—such as Router, DNS Servers, DNS Domain Name, WINS/NBNS Servers, and WINS/NBT Node Type—and configure the appropriate values. Tap or click OK when you are finished.

CHAPTER 5

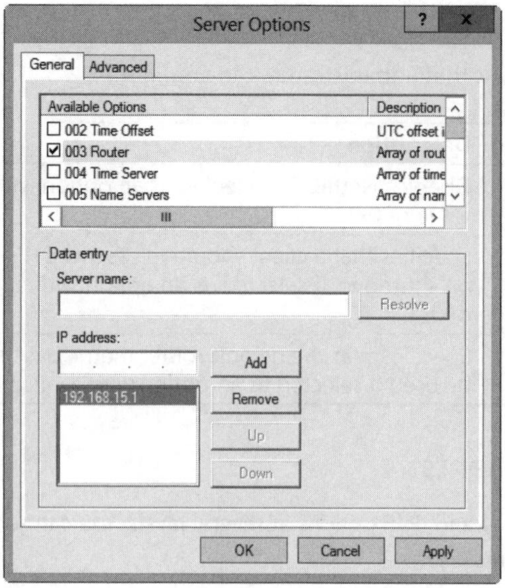

Figure 5-2 Set class-specific options using the General tab.

Instead of, or in addition to, standard options, you can set policy-based options that will be applied to clients matching specific criteria, which can include the following:

- User and vendor classes

- The MAC addresses of a client's primary network adapter

- Custom Client Identifiers defined in the registry of client machines

- Relay agent information

InsideOUT

Setting custom client identifiers

You set a client identifier by adding the DhcpClientIdentifier key to the HKEY_LOCAL_ MACHINE\SYSTEM\CurrentControlSet\Services*AdapterName*\Parameters\Tcpip key, where *AdapterName* is the actual name of the client's primary network adapter. The DhcpClientIdentifier key must be set as a REG_DWORD with a value range of 0x0 to 0xFFFFFFFF.

You can create policies for the following components:

- **All scopes on a server.** In the DHCP console, expand the entry for the server and the IPv4 protocol, press and hold or right-click Policies, and then choose New Policy.

- **A specific scope.** In the DHCP console, expand the scope you want to work with, press and hold or right-click Policies, and then choose New Policy.

When the DHCP Policy Configuration Wizard starts, do the following to configure the policy:

1. Type a policy name and description, and then tap or click Next.

2. On the Configure Conditions For The Policy page, shown in Figure 5-3, use the options provided to add conditions to the policy. The default operator is Equals. You use the Equals operator to match specifically. If you use the Not Equals operator, any value other than what you specified results in a match.

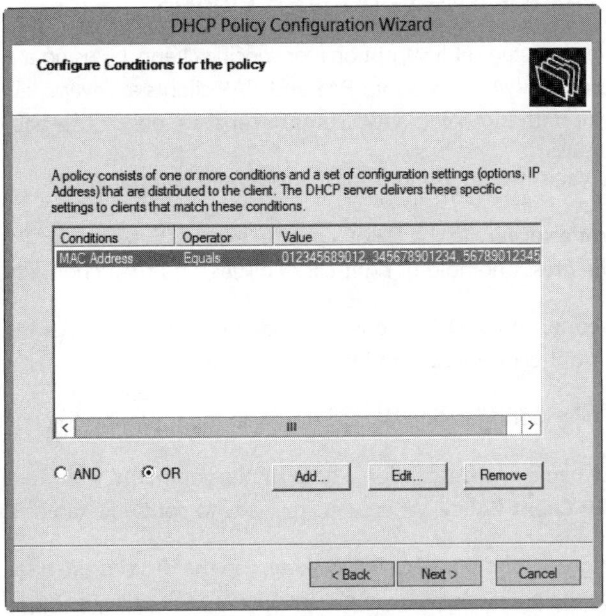

Figure 5-3 Define the conditions for the policy.

3. Conditions can be joined with AND clauses or OR clauses. Use AND clauses when a client must match each condition. Use OR clauses when a client can match either condition. Select AND or OR as appropriate.

CHAPTER 5

4. When you are ready to continue, tap or click Next. If you are assigning the policy at the scope level, you can next define the IP ranges that should be associated with this policy. You divide a scope into multiple IP address ranges for easier management. For example, you could have a specific range for printers, a different range for clients, and yet another range for servers.

5. Tap or click Next, and then select the check box for each standard TCP/IP option you want to use in turn—such as Router, DNS Servers, DNS Domain Name, WINS/NBNS Servers, and WINS/NBT Node Type—and configure the appropriate values.

6. Select each add-on TCP/IP option you want to use in turn—such as Microsoft Disable NetBIOS Option and Microsoft Release DHCP Lease On Shutdown Option—and accept the default value (0x1) to turn on the option.

7. Tap or click OK.

Setting options for RRAS and NAP clients

On the DHCP server, you can set IPv4 options for specific clients by using a policy-based assignment. You can set IPv4 options for RRAS and NAP clients at several levels, and you can create one policy for both RRAS and NAP clients or separate policies for each.

With DHCPv4, you can set client options for the following components:

- **All scopes on a server.** In the DHCP console, expand the entry for the server and the IPv4 protocol, press and hold or right-click Policies, and then choose New Policy.

- **A specific scope.** In the DHCP console, expand the scope you want to work with, press and hold or right-click Policies, and then choose New Policy.

When the DHCP Policy Configuration Wizard starts, do the following to configure the policy:

1. Type a policy name and description. For example, you might want to name the policy **RRAS** or **NAP Client Policy**. When you are ready to continue, tap or click Next.

2. On the Configure Conditions For Policy page, use the options provided to add conditions to the policy. As an example, if you want the policy to apply to both RRAS and NAP clients, you do the following:

   a. Add the RRAS client condition by tapping or clicking Add. Next, in the Add/Edit Condition dialog box, select User Class as the Criteria and then select Default Routing And Remote Access Class as the Value. Tap or click Add, and then tap or click OK. The default operator is Equals. You use the Equals operator to match the class specifically. If you use the Not Equals operator, any class other than the Default Routing And Remote Access Class results in a match.

    b. Conditions can be joined with AND clauses or OR clauses. Use AND clauses when a client must match each condition. Use OR clauses when a client can match either condition. Select AND or OR as appropriate.

    c. Add the NAP client condition by tapping or clicking Add. Next, in the Add/Edit Condition dialog box, select User Class as the Criteria and then select Default Network Access Protection Class as the Value. Tap or click Add and then tap or click OK. Again, the default operator is Equals because you want to match the NAP class specifically.

3. When you are ready to continue, tap or click Next. If you are assigning policy at the scope level, you can next define the IP ranges that should be associated with this policy. You divide a scope into multiple IP address ranges for easier management. For example, you could have a specific range for printers, a different range for clients, and yet another range for servers.

4. Tap or click Next, and then select the check box for each standard TCP/IP option you want to use in turn—such as Router, DNS Servers, DNS Domain Name, WINS/NBNS Servers, and WINS/NBT Node Type—and configure the appropriate values.

5. Select each add-on TCP/IP option you want to use in turn—such as Microsoft Disable NetBIOS Option and Microsoft Release DHCP Lease On Shutdown Option—and accept the default value (0x1) to turn on the option.

6. Tap or click OK.

Setting add-on options for directly connected clients

You can set add-on options for directly connected clients that are different from those of RRAS and NAP clients. For policy-based assignment, start the DHCP Policy Configuration Wizard at the appropriate level and then do the following to configure the policy:

1. Type a policy name and description. For example, you might want to name the policy **Directly Connected Client Policy**. When you are ready to continue, tap or click Next.

2. On the Configure Conditions For Policy page, use the options provided to add conditions to the policy. As you are configuring options for directly connected clients, tap or click Add. Then, in the Add/Edit Condition dialog box, select Vendor Class as the Criteria. Select Microsoft Windows 2000 Options as the vendor class. Tap or click Add, and then tap or click OK. The default operator is Equals. You use the Equals operator to match the class specifically.

3. Add the Default BOOTP Class as the user class. Add this client condition by tapping or clicking Add. Next, in the Add/Edit Condition dialog box, select User Class as the Criteria, and then select Default BOOTP Class as the Value. Tap or click Add, and then tap or click

CHAPTER 5

OK. Again, the default operator is Equals because you want to match the Default BOOTP class specifically.

4. When you are ready to continue, tap or click Next. If you are assigning policy at the scope level, you can next define the IP ranges that should be associated with this policy. You divide a scope into multiple IP address ranges for easier management. For example, you could have a specific range for printers, a different range for clients, and yet another range for servers.

5. Tap or click Next, and then select the check box for each standard TCP/IP option you want to use in turn—such as Router, DNS Servers, DNS Domain Name, WINS/NBNS Servers, and WINS/NBT Node Type—and configure the appropriate values.

6. Select each add-on TCP/IP option you want to use in turn—such as Microsoft Disable NetBIOS Option and Microsoft Release DHCP Lease On Shutdown Option—and accept the default value (0x1) to turn on the option.

7. Tap or click OK.

Defining classes to get different option sets

If you want a group of DHCP clients to use a set of options different from other computers, you can use classes to do this. It is a two-part process. First, create your own user-defined class on each DHCP server to which the clients might connect. Then configure the network interfaces on the clients to use the new class.

Creating the class

In the DHCP console, you can define the new user class by pressing and holding or right-clicking the IP protocol you want to work with and selecting Define User Classes. In the DHCP User Classes dialog box, shown in Figure 5-4, the existing classes are listed, except for the Default User Class because it's the base user class.

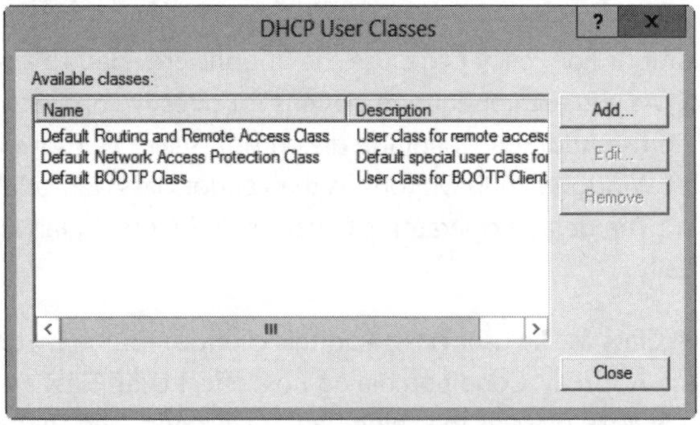

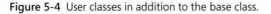

Figure 5-4 User classes in addition to the base class.

Tap or click Add to display the New Class dialog box shown in Figure 5-5. In the Display Name box, type the name of the class you are defining. The name is arbitrary, and it should be short but descriptive enough so that you know what that class is used for by seeing its name. You can also type a description in the Description box. Afterward, tap or click in the empty area below the term ASCII. In this space, type the class identifier, which DHCP uses to identify the class. The class identifier can't have spaces. Tap or click OK to close the New Class dialog box, and then tap or click Close to return to the DHCP console.

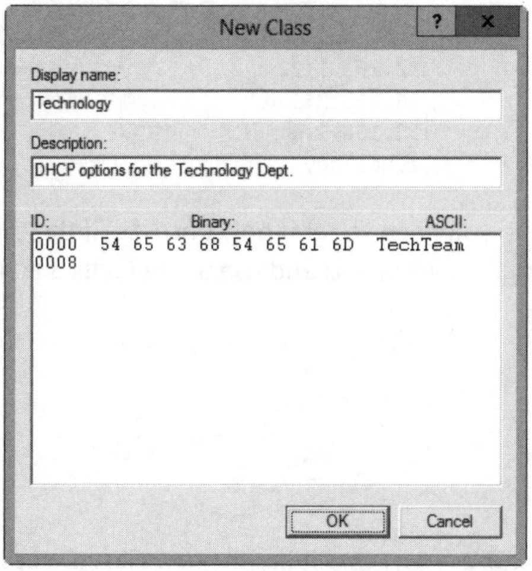

Figure 5-5 Set the class name, description, and class ID.

Next, you must configure the TCP/IP options that should be used by this class by using policy-based assignment.

Configuring clients to use the class

Now you must configure the network interfaces on the clients to use the new class. Assuming "Local Area Connection" is the name of the network interface on the client, you would type the following command to do this:

```
ipconfig /setclassid "Ethernet" ClassID
```

Here, *ClassID* is the ID of the user class to use. For example, if the class ID is Engineering, you would type

```
ipconfig /setclassid "Ethernet" Engineering
```

In these examples I use "Ethernet" as the network interface name because that is the default connection created by Windows. If a client has multiple network interfaces or a user has changed the name of the default network interface, you must use the name of the appropriate interface. You can get a list of all the network interfaces on a client by typing **ipconfig /all** at the command prompt.

After you set the class ID, type **ipconfig /renew** at the command prompt. This tells the client to renew the lease, and because the client has a new class ID, it also forces the client to request new TCP/IP options. The output should be similar to the following:

```
Windows IP Configuration
Ethernet adapter Ethernet:

    Connection-specific DNS Suffix    :
    IP Address                        :    192.168.1.22
    Subnet Mask                       :    255.255.255.0
    Default Gateway                   :    192.168.1.1
    DHCP Class ID                     :    Technology
```

That's it. Because the class ID is persistent, you need to set it only once. So, if the client is restarted, the class ID will remain. To remove the class ID and use the defaults again, type the following command:

```
ipconfig /setclassid "Ethernet"
```

TROUBLESHOOTING

Class ID problems

Sometimes the network interface won't report that it has the new class ID. If this happens, try releasing the DHCP lease first by typing **ipconfig /release** and then obtaining a new lease by typing **ipconfig /renew**.

Advanced DHCP configuration and maintenance

You manage DHCP servers through the DHCP Server service. As with any other service, you can start, stop, pause, and resume the DHCP Server service in the Services node of Computer Management or from the command line. You can also manage the DHCP Server service in the DHCP console. Press and hold or right-click the server you want to manage in the DHCP console, point to All Tasks, and then tap or click Start, Stop, Pause, Resume, or Restart, as appropriate.

NOTE

You also can use Server Manager to start and stop a DHCP server. Tap or click DHCP in the left pane of Server Manager. Next, in the main pane, on the Servers panel, select the DHCP server. Finally, on the Services panel, press and hold or right-click the entry for the DHCP server and then tap or click Start Services, Stop Services, Pause Services, Resume Services, or Restart Services, as appropriate.

When you install the DHCP Server service, many advanced features are configured for you automatically, including audit logging, network bindings, integration with DNS, integration with NAP, and DHCP database backups. You can fine-tune all of these features to optimize performance, and many of these features—such as auditing, logging, and backups—should be periodically monitored.

Monitoring DHCP audit logging

Audit logging is enabled by default for the DHCP Server service and is used to track DHCP processes and requests in log files. Although you can enable and configure logging separately for IPv4 and IPv6, by default the two protocols use the same log files. The DHCP logs are stored in the %SystemRoot%\System32\DHCP folder by default. In this folder you'll find a different log file for each day of the week. For example, the log file for Monday is named DhcpSrvLog-Mon.log. When you start the DHCP Server service or a new day arrives, a header message is written to the log file. As shown in Listing 5-1, the header provides a summary of DHCP events and their meanings. The header is followed by the actual events logged by the DHCP Server service. The event IDs and descriptions are entered because different versions of the DHCP Server service can have different events.

Listing 5-1 DHCP server log file

```
Microsoft DHCP Service Activity Log
Event ID  Meaning
00  The log was started.
01  The log was stopped.
02  The log was temporarily paused due to low disk space.
10  A new IP address was leased to a client.
11  A lease was renewed by a client.
12  A lease was released by a client.
13  An IP address was found to be in use on the network.
14  A lease request could not be satisfied because address pool was exhausted.
15  A lease was denied.
16  A lease was deleted.
17  A lease was expired and DNS records for an expired leases have not been deleted.
18  A lease was expired and DNS records were deleted.
20  A BOOTP address was leased to a client.
21  A dynamic BOOTP address was leased to a client.
22  A BOOTP request could not be satisfied, the address pool for BOOTP was exhausted.
23  A BOOTP IP address was deleted after checking to see it was not in use.
24  IP address cleanup operation has begun.
25  IP address cleanup statistics.
30  DNS update request to the named DNS server.
31  DNS update failed.
32  DNS update successful.
33  Packet dropped due to NAP policy.
34  DNS update request failed as the DNS update request queue limit exceeded.
35  DNS update request failed.
50+ Codes above 50 are used for Rogue Server Detection information.
```

```
QResult: 0: NoQuarantine, 1:Quarantine, 2:Drop Packet, 3:Probation,6:No Quarantine
Information ProbationTime:Year-Month-Day Hour:Minute:Second:MilliSecond.

ID,Date,Time,Description,IP Address,Host Name,MAC Address,User Name, TransactionID,
QResult,Probationtime, CorrelationID,Dhcid,VendorClass(Hex),VendorClass(ASCII),
UserClass(Hex),UserClass(ASCII),RelayAgentInformation.
00,10/02/14,09:18:27,Started,,,,,0,6,,,,,,,,
50,10/02/14,09:19:27,Unreachable Domain,,cpandl.com,,,0,6,,,,,,,,
56,10/02/14,09:19:27,Authorization failure, stopped servicing,,cpandl.com,,,0,6,,,,,,,,,
24,10/02/14,10:18:27,Database Cleanup Begin,,,,,0,6,,,,,,,,
25,10/02/14,10:18:27,0 leases expired and 0 leases deleted,,,,,0,6,,,,,,,,,
25,10/02/14,10:18:27,0 leases expired and 0 leases deleted,,,,,0,6,,,,,,,,,
24,10/02/14,11:18:27,Database Cleanup Begin,,,,,0,6,,,,,,,,
```

The events in the audit logs can help you troubleshoot problems with a DHCP server. As you examine Listing 5-1, you can see that the first event entry with ID 00 tells you that the DHCP Server service was started. The second event entry with ID 50 tells you there's a problem reaching the cpandl.com domain. The third event entry with ID 56 tells you the DHCP Server hasn't been properly authorized to service the cpandl.com domain. Resolving this problem is fairly easy but not as straightforward as you might think.

As stated earlier, in a domain each DHCP server must be authorized in Active Directory, and you can authorize a server in the DHCP console just by pressing and holding or right-clicking the server entry and then selecting Authorize. However, if the post-installation setup tasks in steps 7 through 11 in the section entitled "Installing the DHCP Server service" in Chapter 4 haven't been performed, authorization will fail. The reason for this is that you must specify the credentials to use to authorize the DHCP server in Active Directory as part of the deployment. Resolve the problem by completing the post-installation tasks as discussed previously. Display notifications by tapping the Notifications icon in Server Manager or the warning link in the main pane when you select the DHCP node in the left pane.

Every hour that the service is running, it performs cleanup operations. Database cleanup is used to check for expired leases and leases that no longer apply.

The audit logs also serve as a record of all DHCP connection requests by clients on the network. Events related to lease assignment, renewal, and release are recorded according to the IP address assigned, the client's fully qualified domain name (FQDN), the client's MAC address, vendor class, user class, and more.

Quarantine results, shown in the QResult column, apply when you've configured Network Access Protection. The QResult can be 0 for no quarantine, 1 for quarantine, 2 for drop packet, 3 for probation, or 6 for no quarantine information.

Declined leases are listed with the event ID 13, and the description of the event is DECLINE. A DHCP client can decline a lease if it detects that the IP address is already in use. The primary reason this happens is that a system somewhere on the network is using a static IP address in the DHCP range or has leased it from another DHCP server during a network glitch. When the server receives the decline, it marks the address as bad in the DHCP database. For details on how IP address conflicts can be avoided, see the section entitled "Enabling conflict detection on DHCP servers" later in this chapter.

Denied leases are listed with the event ID 15, and the description of the event is NACK. DHCP can deny a lease to a client that is requesting an address that can't be provided. This could happen if an administrator terminated the lease or if the client moved to a different subnet on which the original IP address held is no longer valid. When a client receives a NACK, the client releases the denied IP address and requests a new one.

As discussed previously, audit logging is enabled by default. If you want to check or change the logging setting, you can do this in the DHCP console. Expand the node for the server you want to work with, press and hold or right-click IPv4 or IPv6 as appropriate for the type of binding you want to work with, and then select Properties. This displays the dialog box shown in Figure 5-6.

In the General tab, select or clear the Enable DHCP Audit Logging check box as necessary. Afterward, select the Advanced tab. The Audit Log File Path box shows the current folder location for log files. Enter a new folder location or tap or click Browse to find a new location. Tap or click OK. If you change the audit log location, Windows Server will need to restart the DHCP Server service. When prompted to confirm that this is OK, tap or click Yes.

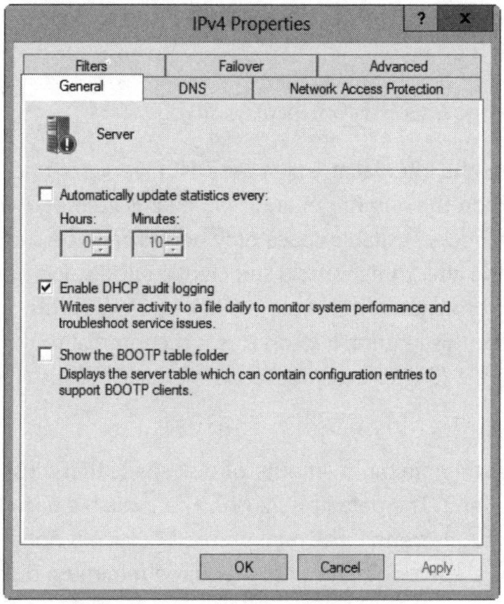

Figure 5-6 Audit logging enabled by default.

By default, the DHCP Server service allows audit logs to grow to a maximum of 70 MB and requires that there be at least 20 MB of free space to write events to the logs. The available disk space is checked at a specific interval, which is controlled according to the number of audit log events recorded. Specifically, by default the DHCP Server service checks the available disk space every 50 audit events.

You can check the auditing configuration by typing the following command at the shell prompt:

```
Get-DhcpServerAuditLog -ComputerName ServerID
```

Here, *ServerID* is the DNS name or IP address of the DHCP server, such as:

```
Get-DhcpServerAuditLog -ComputerName 192.168.1.50
```

The output of the following command shows you the current database properties for the DHCP server:

```
Path              : C:\Windows\system32\dhcp
Enable            : True
MaxMBFileSize     : 70
DiskCheckInterval : 50
MinMBDiskSpace    : 20
```

You can use the following parameters of Set-DhcpServerAuditLog to configure database properties:

- **–Enable.** Controls whether audit logging is enabled. Set to $True to enable audit logging or $False to disable audit logging.

- **–Path.** Sets the path for audit logs, such as D:\Dhcp\AuditLogs.

- **–DiskCheckInterval.** Specifies the interval at which the DHCP Server service checks the available disk space based on the number of audit log events recorded. To ensure that the DHCP Server service checks available space only periodically, be sure that you set a check interval and that the check interval is a sufficiently large value. For example, on a busy server you may want to check after every 5,000 audit log events. Setting the interval to 0 doesn't disable this feature. Instead it sets the interval to the smallest check interval possible, which is 2 (this value is not recommended because it's much too frequent).

- **–MinMBDiskSpace.** Specifies the minimum amount of disk space that must be available on the drive used for auditing. The default is 20 MB. The available disk space is checked only after every Nth audit event. If the minimum disk space is not available, the DHCP Server service stops audit logging until the required minimum disk space is available.

- **–MaxMBDiskSpace.** Specifies the maximum size of the audit log. If the log reaches the maximum size, a new audit log is created for that day.

If you modify the audit settings, you must stop the DHCP server and then start it again for the changes to take effect. To do this, type **stop-service "dhcp server"** to stop the server and then type **start-service "dhcp server"** to start the server again. If you forget to use an elevated, administrator shell prompt, you won't be able to work with the DHCP Server service and will get an error stating the service can't be found. The reason for this is you must have administrator privileges to work with the DHCP Server service.

Binding the DHCP Server service to a network interface

The DHCP Server service should bind automatically to the first network interface card (NIC) on the server. This means that the DHCP Server service should use the IP address and TCP/IP configuration of this network interface to communicate with clients. In some instances, the DHCP Server service might not bind to any available network interface or it might bind to a network interface that you don't want it to use. To resolve this problem, you must bind the DHCP Server service to a specific network interface by following these steps:

1. In the DHCP console, expand the node for the server you want to work with, press and hold or right-click IPv4 or IPv6 as appropriate for the type of binding you want to work with, and then select Properties.

2. In the Advanced tab of the IPv4 or IPv6 Properties dialog box, tap or click Bindings to display the Bindings dialog box. This dialog box displays a list of available network connections for the DHCP server.

3. If you want the DHCP Server service to use a connection to service clients, select the option for the connection. If you don't want the service to use a connection, clear the related option.

4. Tap or click OK twice when you are finished.

You can use Get-NetIPInterface to list all the IPv4 and IPv6 interfaces on a server. If you want the DHCP Server service to use an IPv4 connection to service clients, you can bind the service to the related interface using Set-DhcpServerv4Binding. The basic syntax is:

```
Set-DhcpServerv4Binding -ComputerName ServerID -BindingState $True
-InterfaceAlias "InterfaceName"
```

Here, ServerID is the DNS name or IP address of the server to work with and *InterfaceName* is the alias of the IPv4 interface to bind. If you omit the name of the server to work with, the local server is used. Here is an example working with the local server:

```
Set-DhcpServerv4Binding -BindingState $True -InterfaceAlias "Ethernet"
```

To bind the DHCP Server service to an IPv6 interface, use Set-DhcpServerv6Binding. The basic syntax is:

```
Set-DhcpServerv6Binding —ComputerName ServerID -BindingState $True
-InterfaceAlias "InterfaceName"
```

Here is an example working with the local server:

```
Set-DhcpServerv6Binding -BindingState $True -InterfaceAlias "Ethernet"
```

You can remove the binding by setting —BindingState to $False.

Integrating DHCP and DNS

Using the DNS Dynamic Update protocol, DHCP clients can automatically update their forward (A) and reverse lookup (PTR) records in DNS or request that the DHCP server do this for them. Clients running early versions of Windows can't dynamically update any of their records, so DHCP must do this for them. In either case, when the DHCP server is required to update DNS records, integration between DHCP and DNS is necessary.

In the default configuration of DHCP, a DHCP server will update DNS records for clients only if requested, but it will not update records for clients running early versions of Windows. You can modify this behavior globally for each DHCP server or on a per-scope basis.

To change the global DNS integration settings, start the DHCP console, expand the node for the server you want to work with, press and hold or right-click IPv4, and then select Properties. Tap or click the DNS tab, which is shown in Figure 5-7, and then select the Dynamically Update DNS A And PTR Records For DHCP Clients That Do Not Request Updates check box.

When you enable dynamic updates, the DHCP server updates both A and PTR records by default, which assumes that you've configured reverse lookup zones for your organization. If you haven't configured reverse lookups, attempts to update PTR records will fail. You can prevent repeated failed attempts to update PTR records by disabling dynamic updates for PTR records. If you select the Disable Dynamic Updates For DNS PTR Records check box in the IPv4 Properties dialog box, you disable PTR updates for all IPv4 scopes. Alternatively, you can use scope properties to disable PTR updates on a per-scope basis.

If you are using secure dynamic updates and have enabled DNSSEC, you can enable name protection. Name protection secures names so that other clients can't use them. Tap or click Configure on the Name Protection panel, select Enable Name Protection, and then tap or click OK.

Don't change the other settings. These settings are configured by default, and you usually don't need to modify the configuration.

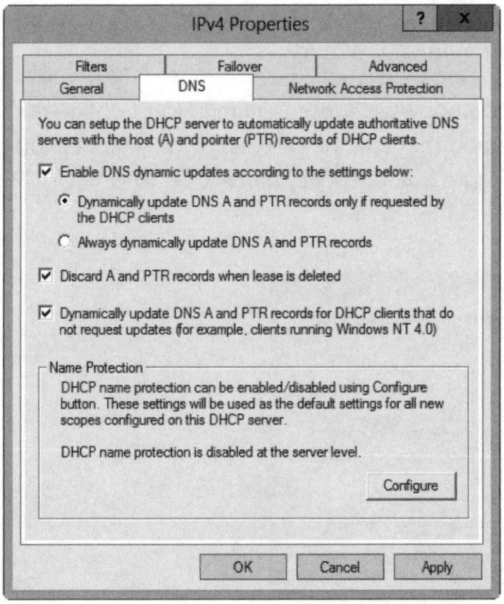

Figure 5-7 DHCP and DNS integration.

To change scope-specific settings, expand the node for the server you want to work with and then expand IPv4. Press and hold or right-click the scope you want to work with and then select Properties. Tap or click the DNS tab. The options available are the same as those shown in Figure 5-7. Because these settings are configured by default, you usually don't need to modify the configuration.

Integrating DHCP and NAP

Network Access Protection (NAP) is designed to protect the network from clients that do not have the appropriate security measures in place. The easiest way to enable NAP with DHCP is to set up the DHCP server as a Network Policy Server (NPS). To do this, you need to install the Network Policy console, configure a compliant policy for NAP and DHCP integration on the server, and then enable NAP for DHCP. This process enables NAP for network computers that use DHCP; it does not fully configure NAP for use.

You can create an NAP and DHCP integration policy by completing the following steps:

1. On the server that you want to act as the Network Policy Server, install the Network Policy And Access Services role using the Add Roles And Features Wizard. During setup, choose Network Policy Server as a role service.

2. After you install Network Policy Server, the Network Policy console will be available in Server Manager as an option on the Tools menu. In the Network Policy console, select

the NPS (Local) node in the console tree and then tap or click Configure NAP in the main pane. This starts the Configure NAP Wizard.

3. On the Network Connection Method list, choose Dynamic Host Configuration Protocol (DHCP) as the connection method that you want to deploy on your network for NAP-capable clients. As shown in Figure 5-8, the policy name is set to NAP DHCP by default. Tap or click Next.

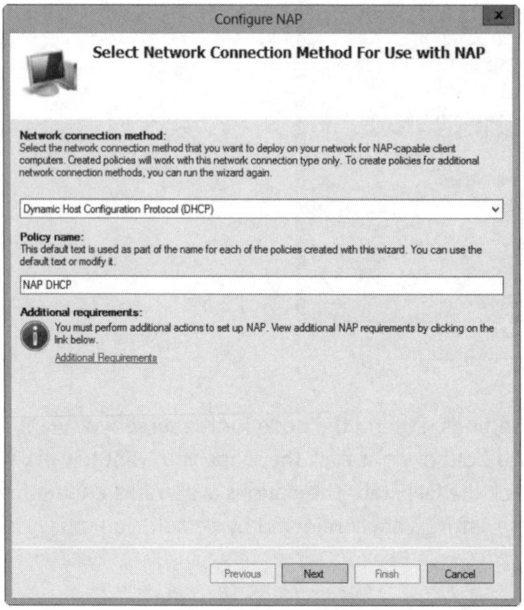

Figure 5-8 Configure the Network Access Protection policy for the local DHCP server.

4. On the Specify NAP Enforcement Servers Running DHCP Server page, you need to identify all remote DHCP servers on your network by doing the following and then tapping or clicking Next:

   - Tap or click Add. In the Add RADIUS Client dialog box, type a friendly name for the remote server in the Friendly Name text box. Then type the DNS name of the remote DHCP server in the Address text box. To validate the name and resolve it to its IP address, tap or click Verify. In the Verify dialog box, tap or click Resolve, and then tap or click OK.

   - On the Shared Secret panel, select Generate and then tap or click Generate to create a long shared-secret keyphrase. You need to enter this keyphrase in the NAP DHCP policy on all remote DHCP servers. Be sure to write down this keyphrase.

Alternatively, copy the keyphrase to Notepad and then save it in a file stored in a secure location. Tap or click OK.

5. On the Specify DHCP Scopes page, you can identify the DHCP scopes to which this policy should apply. If you do not specify any scopes, the policy applies to all NAP-enabled scopes on the selected DHCP servers. Tap or click Next twice to skip the Configure Machine Groups page.

6. On the Specify A NAP Remediation Server Group And URL page, select a remediation server or tap or click New Group to define a remediation group and specify servers to handle remediation. Remediation servers store software updates for NAP clients that need them. In the text box provided, type a URL to a webpage that provides users with instructions on how to bring their computers into compliance with the NAP health policy. Ensure that all DHCP clients can access this URL. Tap or click Next.

7. On the Define NAP Health Policy page, use the options provided to determine how NAP health policy works. In most cases the default settings work fine. With the default settings, NAP-ineligible clients are denied access to the network; NAP-capable clients are checked for compliance and automatically remediated, which allows them to get needed software updates that you've made available. Tap or click Next, and then tap or click Finish.

You can modify NAP settings globally for each DHCP server or on a per-scope basis. To view or change the global NAP settings, complete the following steps:

1. In the DHCP console, expand the node for the server you want to work with, press and hold or right-click IPv4, and then select Properties.

2. In the Network Access Protection tab, shown in Figure 5-9, tap or click Enable On All Scopes or Disable On All Scopes to enable or disable NAP for all scopes on the server.

NOTE

When the local DHCP server is also a Network Policy Server, the Network Policy Server should always be reachable. If you haven't configured the server as a Network Policy Server or the DHCP server is unable to contact the designated Network Policy Server, you'll see an error stating this in the Network Access Protection tab.

CHAPTER 5

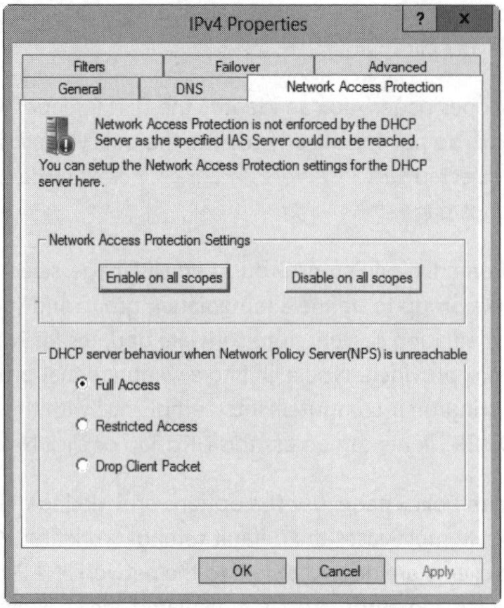

Figure 5-9 The Network Access Protection tab controls the protection options for DHCP.

3. Choose one of the following options to specify how the DHCP server behaves if the Network Policy Server is unreachable, and then tap or click OK to save your settings:

- **Full Access.** Gives DHCP clients full (unrestricted) access to the network. This means clients can perform any permitted actions.

- **Restricted Access.** Gives DHCP clients restricted access to the network. This means clients can work with access only on the server to which they are connected.

- **Drop Client Packet.** Blocks client requests and prevents the clients from accessing the network. This means clients have no access to resources on the network.

You can view and change the NAP settings for individual scopes by completing the following steps:

1. In the DHCP console, expand the node for the server you want to work with, and then expand IPv4.

2. Press and hold or right-click the scope you want to work with, and then select Properties.

3. In the Network Access Protection tab, tap or click Enable For This Scope or Disable For This Scope to enable or disable NAP for this scope.

4. If you're enabling NAP and want to use an NAP profile other than the default, tap or click Use Custom Profile and then type the name of the profile, such as **Alternate NAP DHCP**.

5. Tap or click OK to save your settings.

Enabling conflict detection on DHCP servers

No two computers on the network can have the same unicast IP address. If one computer is assigned the same unicast IP address as another, one of the computers will be disconnected from the network. Generally, the computer that caused the conflict (meaning the second or later computer to use the IP address) is the one that is disconnected.

To prevent IP address conflicts, DHCP has built-in conflict detection that enables clients to check the IP address they've been assigned by pinging the address on the network. If a client detects that an IP address that it has been assigned is in use, it sends the DHCP server a Decline message telling the server that it is declining the lease because the IP address is in use. When this happens, the server marks the IP address as bad in the DHCP database and then the client requests a new lease. This process works fairly well, but it requires additional time because the client is responsible for checking the IP address, declining a lease, and requesting a new one.

To speed up the process, you can configure DHCP servers to check for conflicts before assigning an IP address to a client. When conflict detection is enabled, the process works in much the same way as when it is not, except the server checks the IP address to see if it's in use. If the address is in use, the server marks it as bad without interaction with the client. You can configure conflict detection on a DHCP server by specifying the number of conflict-detection attempts that the DHCP server will make before it leases an IP address to a client. The DHCP server checks IP addresses by sending a ping request over the network.

You can configure conflict detection in the DHCP console by expanding the node for the server you want to work with, pressing and holding or right-clicking IPv4, and then selecting Properties. In the Advanced tab, set Conflict Detection Attempts to a value other than zero. At the command line, type the following command:

```
netsh dhcp server ServerID set detectconflictretry Attempts
```

Here, *ServerID* is the name or IP address of the DHCP server and *Attempts* is the number of conflict-detection attempts the server should use. If you omit the name of the server to work with, the local server is used.

You can confirm the setting by typing the following:

```
netsh dhcp server ServerID show detectconflictretry
```

CHAPTER 5

Again, if you omit the name of the server to work with, the local server is used.

With Windows PowerShell, you can use Set-DHCPServerSetting to configure conflict detection attempts. The basic syntax is the following:

```
Set-DHCPServerSetting –ComputerName ServerID –ConflictDetectionAttempts NumAttempts
```

Here, ServerID is the DNS name or IP address of the DHCP server and NumAttempts is the number of conflict-detection attempts the server should use. If you omit the name of the server to work with, the local server is used. Here is an example:

```
Set-DHCPServerSetting –ComputerName CorpServer14.cpandl.com
–ConflictDetectionAttempts 5
```

Saving and restoring the DHCP configuration

After you finish configuring a DHCP server, you should save the configuration settings so that you can easily restore the server to a known state or use the same settings on another server. To do this, type the following command at the command prompt:

```
netsh dhcp server dump ServerID > SavePath
```

Here, *ServerID* is the name or IP address of the DHCP server and *SavePath* is the path and name of the file in which you want to store the configuration settings. If you omit the name of the server to work with, the local server is used. If you omit the path, the save file is created in the current working directory. Here is an example:

```
netsh dhcp server dump > c:\data\dhcpconfig.dmp
```

If you examine the file Netsh creates, you'll find that it's a Netsh configuration script. To restore the configuration, run the script on the server you want to configure by typing the following command:

```
netsh exec SavePath
```

Here, *SavePath* is the path and name of the file in which you stored the configuration settings, such as:

```
netsh exec c:\data\dhcpconfig.dmp
```

Copy to a new DHCP server

You can run the script on a different DHCP server to configure it in the same way as the original DHCP server whose configuration you saved. Copy the configuration script to a folder on the destination computer, and then run it. The DHCP server will be configured like the original server.

With Windows PowerShell, the process is similar. You use Export-DhcpServer to save the configuration settings. The basic syntax is the following:

```
Export-DhcpServer -ComputerName ServerID -File SavePath
```

Here, *ServerID* is the DNS name or IP address of the DHCP server and *SavePath* is the path and name of the file in which you want to store the configuration settings. If you omit the name of the server to work with, the local server is used. If you don't specify a save path along with the file name, the configuration file is created in the current working directory. Here is an example:

```
Export-DhcpServer-File c:\data\dhcpconfig.dmp
```

You use Import-DhcpServer to restore the configuration. The basic syntax is the following:

```
Import-DhcpServer -ComputerName ServerID -File SavePath -BackupPath
CurrentConfiigSavePath
```

Here, *ServerID* is the DNS name or IP address of the DHCP server, *SavePath* is the path and name of the file in which you stored the configuration settings, and CurrentConfigSavePath specifies the path where the current configuration should be saved prior to importing and overwriting existing settings. Here is an example:

```
Import-DhcpServer -File c:\data\dhcpconfig.dmp -BackupPath c:\backup\origconfig.dmp
```

Managing and maintaining the DHCP database

Information about leases and reservations used by clients is stored in database files on the DHCP server. Like any other data set, the DHCP database has properties that you can set and techniques that you can use to maintain it.

Setting DHCP database properties

In the default configuration, these files are stored in the %SystemRoot%\System32 \Dhcp folder, and automatically created backups of the files are stored in %SystemRoot% \System32\Dhcp\Backup. The DHCP Server service performs two routine actions to maintain the database:

- Database cleanup, during which the DHCP Server service checks for expired leases and leases that no longer apply

- Database backup, during which the DHCP Server service backs up the database files

By default, both maintenance tasks are performed every 60 minutes, and you can confirm this and confirm the current DHCP folders being used by typing the following command at the shell prompt:

```
Get-DhcpServerDatabase -ComputerName ServerID
```

Here, *ServerID* is the DNS name or IP address of the DHCP server, such as:

```
Get-DhcpServerDatabase -ComputerName 192.168.1.50
```

The output of the following command shows you the current database properties for the DHCP server:

```
FileName             : C:\Windows\system32\dhcp\dhcp.mdb
BackupPath           : C:\Windows\system32\dhcp\backup
BackupInterval(m)    : 60
CleanupInterval(m)   : 60
LoggingEnabled       : True
RestoreFromBackup    : False
```

Note the *LoggingEnabled* and *RestoreFromBackup* properties. *LoggingEnabled* tracks whether audit logging is enabled. If the property is set to False, audit logging is disabled. If the property is set to True, audit logging is enabled. *RestoreFromBackup* is a special flag that tracks whether the DHCP Server service should restore the DHCP database from backup the next time it starts. If the property is set to False, the main database is used. If the property is set to True, the DHCP Server service restores the database from backup, overwriting the existing database.

You can use the following parameters of Set-DhcpServerDatabase to configure database properties:

- **–FileName.** Sets the path and name for the database backup file, such as D:\Dhcp\Dhcp1.mdb.

- **–BackupPath.** Sets the backup path for the database files, such as D:\Dhcp\Dbbackup.

- **–BackupInterval.** Sets the database backup interval in minutes, such as 120.

- **–RestoreFromBackup.** Forces DHCP to restore the database from backup when it's started. Set this to $True to restore.

- **–CleanupInterval.** Sets the database cleanup interval in minutes, such as 120.

NOTE

If you change the database name or folder locations, you must stop the DHCP server and then start it again for the changes to take effect. To do this, type **stop-service "dhcp server"** to stop the server and then type **start-service "dhcp server"** to start the server again. If you forget to use an elevated, administrator shell prompt, you won't be able to work with the DHCP Server service and will get an error stating the service can't be found. The reason for this is you must have administrator privileges to work with the DHCP Server service.

Backing up and restoring the database

The DHCP database is backed up automatically. You can also manually back it up at any time. In the DHCP console, press and hold or right-click the server you want to back up and then choose Backup. In the Browse For Folder dialog box, select the backup folder and then tap or click OK.

If a server crash corrupts the database, you might need to restore and then reconcile the database. Start by restoring a good copy of the contents of the backup folder from tape or other archive source. Afterward, start the DHCP console, press and hold or right-click the server you want to restore, and then choose Restore. In the Browse For Folder dialog box, select the folder that contains the backup you want to restore and then tap or click OK. During restoration of the database, the DHCP Server service is stopped and then started automatically.

Inside OUT

Moving the DHCP database to a new server

You can use the backup and restore procedure to move the DHCP database to a new server. For example, before upgrading a DHCP server or decommissioning it, you could configure a new DHCP server and move the current DHCP database from the old server to the new server. Start by installing the DHCP Server service on the destination server, and then restart the server. When the server restarts, log on, and at the command prompt type **net stop "dhcp server"** to stop the DHCP Server service. Remove the contents of the %SystemRoot%\System32\Dhcp folder on this server.

Afterward, log on to the original (source) server, and at the command prompt type **net stop "dhcp server"** to stop the DHCP Server service. In the Services node of Computer Management, disable the DHCP Server service so that it can no longer be started, and then copy the entire contents of the %SystemRoot%\System32\Dhcp folder to the %SystemRoot%\System32\Dhcp folder on the destination server. When all the necessary files are on the destination server, type **net start "dhcp server"** to start the DHCP Server service on the destination server, which completes the migration.

Setting up DHCP relay agents

In an ideal configuration, you have multiple DHCP servers on each subnet. However, because this isn't always possible, you can configure your routers to forward DHCP broadcasts or configure a computer on the network to act as a relay agent. Any computer running Windows Server 2012 R2 can act as a relay agent. Doing so requires that you configure and enable

Routing And Remote Access on the computer first, and then you can configure the computer as a relay agent using the Routing And Remote Access console.

Configuring and enabling Routing And Remote Access

You can install Routing And Remote Access Services as part of the Remote Access role. On a server with no other policy and access role services configured, you can install the Remote Access role using the Add Roles And Features Wizard. During setup, choose Direct Access And VPN and Routing as the role services to install.

You'll then be able to work with Routing And Remote Access Services in Computer Management. Under Services And Applications, press and hold or right-click the Routing And Remote Access node in the left pane and then Configure And Enable Routing And Remote Access. This starts the Routing And Remote Access Setup Wizard. Tap or click Next. Choose Custom Configuration, as shown in Figure 5-10, and then tap or click Next again. On the Custom Configuration page, select LAN Routing. Tap or click Next, and then tap or click Finish.

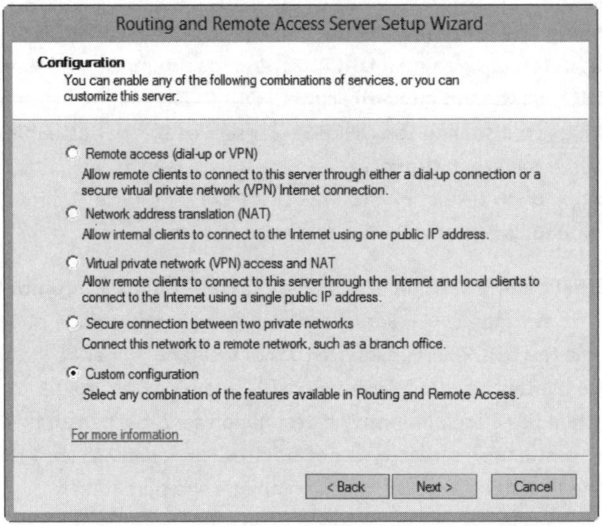

Figure 5-10 Configure and enable Routing And Remote Access.

The wizard then creates a default Network Policy Server connection request policy on your organization's Network Access Policy server. You need to review this policy in the Network Policy console to ensure that it's configured properly and does not conflict with existing policies. Tap or click OK. Finally, when prompted to start the Routing And Remote Access Service, tap or click Start Service.

Adding and configuring the DHCP relay agent

You can configure DHCP relay agents for IPv4 and IPv6. To configure a relay agent for IPv4, follow these steps:

1. In Computer Management, expand the Routing And Remote Access node and then expand IPv4.

2. Press and hold or right-click the General node, and then choose New Routing Protocol.

3. In the New Routing Protocol dialog box, select DHCP Relay Agent and then tap or click OK. This adds an entry under IPv4 labeled DHCP Relay Agent.

4. Press and hold or right-click the DHCP Relay Agent entry, and choose New Interface.

5. The New Interface For DHCP Relay Agent dialog box is displayed, as shown in Figure 5-11, showing the currently configured network interfaces on the computer. Select the network interface that is connected to the same network as the DHCP clients whose DHCP broadcasts need forwarding, and then tap or click OK.

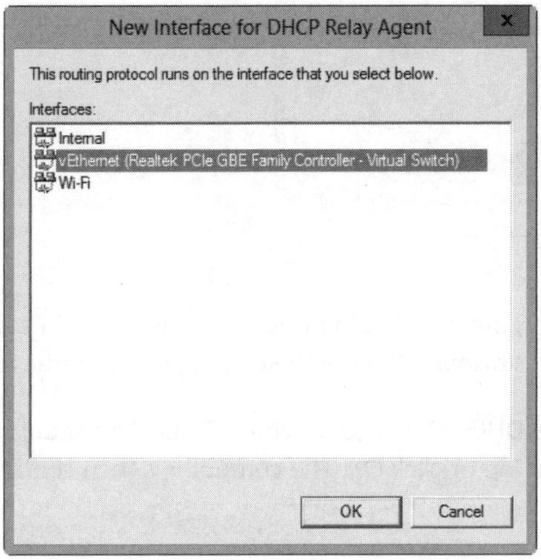

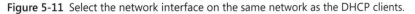

Figure 5-11 Select the network interface on the same network as the DHCP clients.

6. The DHCP Relay Properties dialog box is displayed automatically, as shown in Figure 5-12. After you set the following relay options, tap or click OK:

   - **Relay DHCP Packets.** When selected, this option ensures that DHCP packets are relayed.

- **Hop-Count Threshold.** Determines the maximum number of relay agents through which a DHCP request can pass. The default is 4. The maximum is 16.
- **Boot Threshold (Seconds).** Determines the number of seconds the relay agent waits before forwarding DHCP packets. The delay is designed so that local DHCP servers will be the first to respond if they are available. The default delay is four seconds.

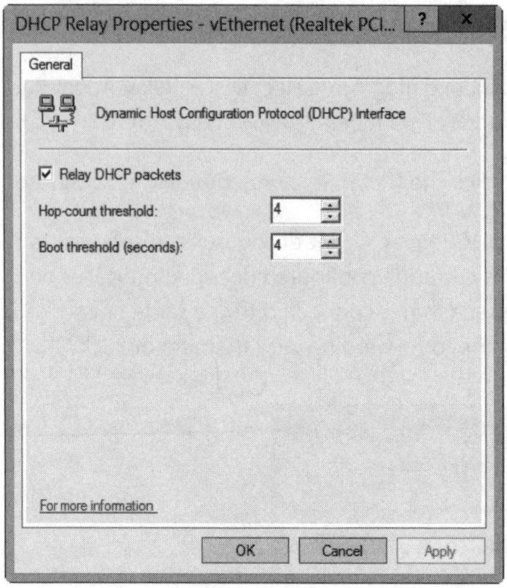

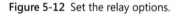

Figure 5-12 Set the relay options.

7. In Computer Management, press and hold or right-click the DHCP Relay Agent entry and choose Properties. This displays the DHCP Relay Agent Properties dialog box.

8. Type the IP address of the DHCP server to which DHCP packets should be forwarded, and then tap or click Add. Tap or click OK. The computer is then configured as a DHCPv4 relay agent.

To configure a relay agent for IPv6, follow these steps:

1. In Computer Management, expand the Routing And Remote Access node and then expand IPv6.

2. Press and hold or right-click the General node, and then choose New Routing Protocol.

3. In the New Routing Protocol dialog box, select DHCPv6 Relay Agent and then tap or click OK. This adds an entry under IPv6 labeled DHCPv6 Relay Agent.

4. In Computer Management, press and hold or right-click the DHCPv6 Relay Agent entry and choose New Interface.

5. The New Interface For DHCPv6 Relay Agent dialog box is displayed. Select the network interface that is connected to the same network as the DHCPv6 clients whose DHCPv6 broadcasts need forwarding, and then tap or click OK.

6. The DHCP Relay Properties dialog box is displayed automatically. After you set the following relay options, tap or click OK:

    - **Relay DHCP Packets.** When selected, this option ensures that DHCPv6 packets are relayed.

    - **Hop-Count Threshold.** Determines the maximum number of relay agents through which a DHCPv6 request can pass. The default is 4. The maximum is 16.

    - **Elapsed-Time Threshold (Centi-Seconds).** Determines the number of seconds the relay agent waits before forwarding DHCPv6 packets. The delay is designed so that local DHCPv6 servers will be the first to respond if they are available. The default delay is 32 seconds (3,200 centi-seconds).

7. In Computer Management, press and hold or right-click the DHCP Relay Agent entry and choose Properties. This displays the DHCP Relay Agent Properties dialog box.

8. In the Servers tab, type the IPv6 address of the DHCPv6 server to which DHCPv6 packets should be forwarded and then tap or click Add. Tap or click OK. The computer is then configured as a DHCPv6 relay agent.

CHAPTER 6

Architecting DNS infrastructure

The Domain Name System (DNS) is an Internet Engineering Task Force (IETF) standard name service. Its basic design is described in Requests for Comments (RFCs) 1034 and 1035, and it has been implemented on many operating systems, including UNIX and Microsoft Windows. All versions of Windows automatically install a DNS client as part of Transmission Control Protocol/Internet Protocol (TCP/IP). To get the server component, you must install the DNS Server service. All editions of Microsoft Windows Server 2012 R2 include the DNS Server service. Because DNS is the name-resolution service for Active Directory Domain Services (AD DS), DNS is installed automatically when you make a server a domain controller.

DNS essentials

Like Dynamic Host Configuration Protocol (DHCP), DNS is a client/server protocol. This means a client component and a server component are necessary to successfully implement DNS. Because of the client/server model, any computer seeking DNS information is referred to as a *DNS client*, and the computer that provides the information to the client is referred to as a *DNS server*. It's the job of a DNS server to store a database containing DNS information, to respond to DNS queries from clients, and to replicate DNS information to other DNS servers as necessary.

DNS provides for several types of queries, including forward-lookup queries and reverse-lookup queries. Forward-lookup queries enable a client to resolve a host name to an Internet Protocol (IP) address. A DNS client makes a forward lookup using a name query message that asks the DNS server for the host address record of a specific host. The response to this query is sent as a name query response message. If there's a host address record for the specified host, the name server returns this. If the host name is an alias, the name server returns the record for the alias (CNAME) and the host address record to which the alias points.

Reverse-lookup queries enable a client to resolve an IP address to a host name, as Figure 6-1 shows. The DNS Server service supports IPv4 and IPv6 for reverse lookups.

Computers use reverse lookups primarily to verify the identity of a remote computer. A DNS client makes a reverse lookup using a reverse name query message. The response to the query is sent as a reverse name query response message. This message contains the reverse address record (PTR) for the specified host.

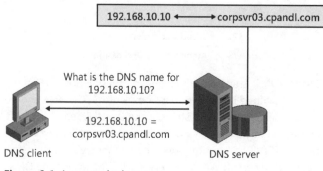

Figure 6-1 A reverse lookup query.

DNS also provides a way to cache DNS information to reduce the number of queries that are required. So, instead of having to send a query to a name server each time the host wants to resolve a particular name, the DNS client checks its local cache for the information first. All queries into the DNS cache are asynchronous and, as such, are processed one at a time in sequence.

DNS information in the cache is held for a set amount of time, referred to as the Time to Live (TTL) value of a record. When a record exists in cache and its TTL has not expired, it's used to answer subsequent queries. Not only does this reduce traffic on the network, but also it speeds up the name-resolution process. A record's TTL is set in the query response from a name server.

When a recursive DNS server responds to a query, the server caches the results obtained so that it can respond quickly if it receives another query requesting the same information. The TTL determines how long the DNS server will cache a resource record. During this time, the cache might be overwritten if updated information about a cached record is received. However, Windows Server 2008 R2 and later use DNS cache locking to ensure that cached records can't be overwritten until their TTL expires.

Inside OUT

DNS cache locking

Although cache locking is designed to enhance security and prevent cache poisoning attacks, sometimes you might want to allow cached records to be updated sooner. The registry key CacheLockingPercent under HKEY_LOCAL_MACHINE\SYSTEM \CurrentControlSet\services\DNS\Parameters controls how cache locking works. This key sets the percentage of the TTL duration that must be reached before a cached record can be overwritten.

By default, CacheLockingPercent is set to 100, meaning the TTL has to fully expire before a cached record can be overwritten. If you want to allow cached records to be overwritten after 50 percent or more of their TTL duration has been reached, you set CacheLockingPercent to 50.

You can configure cache locking in several ways. You can enter **dnscmd /config /cachelockingpercent Percent** at an elevated command prompt, where *Percent* is the percentage of the TTL duration that must be reached for a cached record to be overwritten. Or you can enter **Set-DNSServerCache –LockingPercent Percent** at an elevated Windows PowerShell prompt, where *Percent* is the percentage of the TTL duration that must be reached for a cached record to be overwritten. You can display information about the DNS server cache by entering **Get-DNSServerCache** at a Windows PowerShell prompt.

Planning DNS implementations

Creating a new DNS implementation or revamping your existing DNS implementation requires good planning. You need a solid understanding of how DNS works, and the areas you should know about include the following:

- How DNS namespaces are assigned and used

- How DNS name resolution works and can be modified

- How DNS devolution works and can be configured

- What resource records are available and how they are used

- How DNS zones and zone transfers can be used

- How internal and external servers can be used

- How DNS is integrated with other technologies

Public and private namespaces

The DNS domain namespace is a hierarchical tree in which each node and leaf in the tree represents a named domain. Each level of the domain namespace tree is separated by a period (called a "dot"). As discussed in the section entitled "Understanding name resolution" in Chapter 2, "Networking with TCP/IP," the first level of the tree is where you find the top-level domains, and these top-level domains form the base of the DNS namespace. The second level of the tree is for second-level or parent domains, and subsequent levels of the tree are for sub-domains. For example, cpandl.com is the parent domain of the child domains sales.cpandl.com and tech.cpandl.com.

> **NOTE**
> Although the actual root of the DNS namespace is represented by "." and doesn't have a name, each level in the tree has a name, which is referred to as its label. The fully quali-fied domain name (FQDN) of a node in the DNS namespace is the list of all the labels in the path from the node to the root of the namespace. For example, the FQDN for the host named CORPSVR02 in the cpandl.com domain is corpsvr02.cpandl.com.

To divide public and private namespaces, designated organizations establish and maintain the top-level domains. The top authority, Internet Corporation for Assigned Names and Numbers (ICANN), is responsible for defining and delegating control over the top-level domains to individual organizations. Top-level domains are organized functionally and geographically. Table 6-1 lists the functions of key generic top-level domains; the list can be extended to include other generic top-level domains. (See *http://www.iana.org/domains/root/db/* for the most current list.) The geographically organized top-level domains are identified by two-level country/region codes. These country/region codes are based on the International Organization for Standardization (ISO) country/region name and are used primarily by organi-zations outside the United States.

> **NOTE**
> The United Kingdom is the exception to the ISO naming rule. Although the ISO coun-try/region code for the United Kingdom is GB (Great Britain), its two-letter designator is UK.

Table 6-1 Top-level domain names for the Internet

Domain	Purpose
.aero	For aerospace firms, including airlines
.asia	For the Asia-Pacific region
.biz	For businesses; extends the .com area
.com	For commercial organizations
.coop	For business cooperatives
.edu	For educational institutions
.gov	For U.S. government agencies
.info	For information sources
.int	For organizations established by international treaties
.mil	For U.S. military departments and agencies
.mobi	For mobile-compatible sites
.museum	For museums
.name	For use by individuals
.net	For use by network providers
.org	For use by organizations, such as those that are nongovernmental or nonprofit
.pro	For professional groups, such as doctors and lawyers
.travel	For the travel and tourism industry

After ICANN delegates control over a top-level domain, it is the responsibility of the designated organization to maintain the domain and handle registrations. After an organization registers a domain name with one of these authorities, the organization controls the domain and can create subdomains within this domain without having to make a formal request. For example, if you register the domain cpandl.com, you can create the subdomains seattle.cpandl.com, portland.cpandl.com, and sf.cpandl.com without having to ask the registration authority for permission.

ICANN doesn't control private namespaces. You can create your own private namespace for use within your company. For example, you could use .local for your top-level domain. This keeps your internal network separate from the public Internet. You would then need to rely on Network Address Translation (NAT) or proxy servers to access the public Internet.

Name resolution using DNS

In DNS, name resolution is made possible using a distributed database. The resource records in this database detail host name and IP address information relating to domains. It is the job of DNS name servers to store the DNS database and respond to queries from clients about the information the database contains. A portion of the DNS namespace that is controlled by a DNS name server or a group of name servers is referred to as a *zone*.

Zones establish the boundaries within which a particular name server can resolve requests. On clients, it is the job of DNS resolvers to contact name servers and perform queries about resource records. Thus, the three main components of DNS are as follows:

- Resource records stored in a distributed database

- DNS name servers responsible for maintaining specific zones

- DNS resolvers running on clients

These key components are used to perform DNS operations, which can consist of query operations, query replies, and DNS update operations. A basic query and reply work as shown in Figure 6-2. Here, a DNS client wants information from a DNS name server, so it sends a DNS query. The DNS server to which the query is sent checks its local database and forwards the request to an authoritative server. The authoritative server sends back a response to the local DNS server, and that response is forwarded to the client.

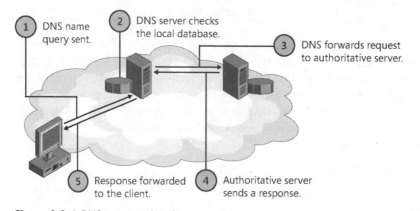

Figure 6-2 A DNS query and reply.

As Figure 6-3 shows, things get a bit more complicated when a client requests the name of an external resource, such as a website. If you were on an internal domain and requested a resource on the public Internet, such as the IP address for the www.cpandl.com server, the DNS client on your computer queries the local name server as specified in its TCP/IP configuration.

The local name server forwards the request to the root server for the external resource domain. This domain contacts the name server for the related top-level domain, which in turn contacts the name server for the cpandl.com domain. This authoritative server sends a response, which is forwarded to the client device, which can then access the external resource.

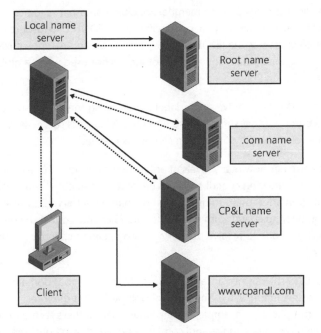

Figure 6-3 Name resolution using the DNS tree.

As you can see, in a normal DNS configuration, if your DNS name server can't resolve a request, it simply forwards the request to another name server for resolution. This allows your organization's name servers to get internal DNS information and external DNS information on the public Internet. However, what if the domain you were trying to reach was a resource in another of your own internal domains? In this case you wouldn't want requests to be forwarded to a public DNS name server for resolution. The public DNS server would have no idea how to resolve the request.

There are several ways to resolve this problem, one of which is to use conditional forwarding. By using conditional forwarding, you can tell your DNS name servers that if you see a request for domain XYZ, don't forward it to the public DNS name server for resolution. Instead, forward the request directly to the XYZ name server—which is the authoritative name server for the domain being looked up. This name server will then be able to reply to the query, and the DNS lookup will be resolved. For more information on resolving name-resolution problems and conditional forwarding, see the section entitled "Secondary zones, stub zones, and conditional forwarding" later in this chapter.

Understanding DNS devolution

DNS devolution allows client devices that are members of child namespaces to access resources in parent namespaces without explicitly specifying the FQDN of a resource. With devolution, the DNS resolver creates the FQDN of a resource by adding parent suffixes to single-label, unqualified domain names. However, devolution is not used when a global suffix search list is configured in Group Policy.

With devolution, DNS clients try to resolve single-label names using the parent suffix of the primary DNS suffix, the parent of that suffix, and so on until the name is successfully resolved or until the devolution level allowed by devolution settings is reached.

The devolution level determines how many levels of antecedents are used. For example, if the primary DNS suffix is engineering.cpandl.com and devolution is enabled with a devolution level of 2, an application attempting to query the host name mailserver23 will attempt to resolve mailserver23.engineering.cpandl.com and mailserver23.cpandl.com. If the devolution level is 3, an attempt will be made to resolve mailserver23.engineering.cpandl.com, but not mailserver23.cpandl.com.

However, if the primary DNS suffix is not a trailing subset of the forest root domain, the DNS resolver doesn't perform devolution. Why? The primary DNS suffix and the forest root domain don't share the same namespace. For example, if the primary DNS suffix is tech.cpandl.com but the forest root domain is engineering.cpandl.com, the resolver doesn't perform devolution. This is because tech.cpandl.com is not a trailing subset of engineering.cpandl.com.

More specifically, the DNS resolver first determines the primary DNS suffix and forest root domain of the client. If the number of labels for the primary DNS suffix is 1, the DNS resolver doesn't perform devolution. Otherwise, if the primary DNS suffix is a trailing subset of the forest root domain, the devolution level is set to the number of labels in the forest root domain. Here are some examples:

- If the primary DNS suffix is cpandl.com and the forest root domain is cpandl, no devolution is performed. Why? The forest root domain is single-labeled.

- If the primary DNS suffix is cpandl.com and the forest root domain is cpandl.com, the devolution level is 2. Why? The forest root domain has two labels, and the primary DNS suffix is a trailing subset of the forest root domain.

- If the primary DNS suffix is tech.cpandl.com and the forest root domain is cpandl.com, the devolution level is 2. Why? The forest root domain has two labels.

- If the primary DNS suffix is tech.cpandl.com and the forest root domain is tech.cpandl.com, the devolution level is 3. Why? The forest root domain has three labels.

- If the primary DNS suffix is tech.cpandl.com and the forest root domain is eng.cpandl.com, no devolution is performed. Why? The primary DNS suffix is not a trailing subset of the forest root domain.

DNS devolution is enabled by default. Prior to Windows 7 and Windows Server 2008 R2, the effective devolution level was 2. With current and updated DNS clients and servers, however, the devolution level is used to precisely control how clients resolve resource names within a domain.

NOTE

You can control devolution using Group Policy. If you don't want DNS clients to resolve names using devolution, disable the Primary DNS Suffix setting in the Administrative Templates for Computer Configuration under Network\DNS Client. To set a specific devolution level, enable and configure the Primary DNS Suffix Devolution Level policy in the Administrative Templates for Computer Configuration under Network\DNS Client.

DNS resource records

Resource records are used to store domain information. DNS name servers contain resource records for those portions of the DNS namespace for which they are authoritative. It is the job of administrators who maintain an authoritative DNS name server to maintain the resource records and ensure that they are accurate. DNS name servers can also cache resource records for those areas for which they can answer queries sent by hosts. This means that DNS name servers can cache resource records relating to any part of the domain tree.

Although DNS servers define and support many types of resource records, only a few record types are actually used on a Windows Server network. With that in mind, take a look at Table 6-2, which provides an overview of the resource records that you'll use.

Table 6-2 Common resource records used on Windows Server networks

Record Type	Common Name	Description
A	Host address	Contains the name of a host and its Internet Protocol version 4 (IPv4) address. Any computer that has multiple network interfaces or IP addresses should have multiple address records.
AAAA	IPv6 host address	Contains the name of a host and its Internet Protocol version 6 (IPv6) address.

Record Type	Common Name	Description
CNAME	Canonical name	Creates an alias for a host name. This allows a host to be referred to by multiple names in DNS. The most common use is when a host provides a common service, such as World Wide Web (WWW) or File Transfer Protocol (FTP), and you want it to have a friendly name rather than a complex name. For example, you might want www.cpandl.com to be an alias for the host dc06 .cpandl.com.
MX	Mail exchanger	Indicates a mail exchange server for the domain, which allows mail to be delivered to the correct mail servers in the domain. For example, if an MX record is set for the domain cpandl.com, all mail sent to username@cpandl.com will be directed to the server specified in the MX record.
NS	Name server	Provides a list of authoritative servers for a domain, which allows DNS lookups within various zones. Each primary and secondary name server in a domain should be declared through this record.
PTR	Pointer	Enables reverse lookups by creating a pointer that maps an IP address to a host name.
SOA	Start of authority	Indicates the authoritative name server for a particular zone. The authoritative server is the best source of DNS information for a zone. Because each zone must have an SOA record, the record is created automatically when you add a zone. The SOA record also contains information about how resource records in the zone should be used and cached. This includes refresh, retry, and expiration intervals and the maximum time that a record is considered valid.
SRV	Service location	Makes it possible to find a server providing a specific service. Active Directory Domain Services uses SRV records to locate domain controllers, global catalog servers, Lightweight Directory Access Protocol (LDAP) servers, and Kerberos servers. SRV records are created automatically. For example, Active Directory creates an SRV record when you set a domain controller as a global catalog. LDAP servers can add an SRV to indicate they are available to handle LDAP requests in a particular zone. All domains have SRV records associated with them. SRV records are created in the forest root zone, domain zones, and tree zones, as discussed in the section entitled "Using DNS with Active Directory" in Chapter 7, "Implementing and managing DNS."

DNS zones and zone transfers

DNS name servers that have complete information for a part of the DNS namespace are said to be *authoritative*. As mentioned earlier, a portion of the namespace over which an authoritative name server has control is referred to as a zone. Zones establish the boundaries within which a particular name server can resolve requests and are the main replication units in DNS. Zones can contain resource records for one or more related DNS domains.

Windows Server 2012 R2 supports four types of zones:

- **Standard primary.** Stores a writable master copy of a zone as a text file. All changes to a zone are made in the primary zone. The information in, and changes to, a primary zone can be replicated to secondary zones.

- **Standard secondary.** Stores a read-only copy of a zone as a text file. It's used to provide redundancy and load balancing for a primary zone. The information in, and changes to, a primary zone are replicated to a secondary zone using zone transfers.

- **Active Directory–integrated.** Integrates zone information in Active Directory Domain Services and uses Active Directory Domain Services to replicate zone information. This is a proprietary zone type that is possible only when you deploy Active Directory Domain Services on the network. Windows Server can selectively replicate DNS information.

Active Directory–integrated zones are only on domain controllers

Designating a zone as Active Directory–integrated means that only domain controllers can be primary name servers for the zone. These domain controllers can accept dynamic updates, and Active Directory security is used automatically to restrict dynamic updates to domain members. Any DNS servers in the zone that aren't domain controllers can act only as secondary name servers. These secondary name servers can't accept dynamic updates.

- **Stub.** Stores a partial zone that can be used to identify the authoritative DNS servers for a zone. A stub zone has no information about the hosts in a zone. Instead, it has information only about the authoritative name servers in a zone so that queries can be forwarded directly to those name servers.

Each of these four DNS zone types can be created for forward or reverse lookups. A forward-lookup zone is used to resolve DNS names to IP addresses and provide information about available network services. A reverse-lookup zone is used to resolve IP addresses to DNS names.

Zones that aren't integrated with Active Directory

With standard zones that aren't integrated with Active Directory, a master copy of the zone is stored in a primary zone on a single DNS server, called a *primary DNS server*. This server's SOA record indicates that it is the primary zone for the related domain. Secondary zones are used to improve performance and provide redundancy. A server storing a copy of a secondary zone is referred to as a *secondary DNS server*.

A primary DNS server automatically replicates a copy of the primary zone to any designated secondary servers. The transfer of zone information is handled by a zone-replication process and is referred to as a *zone transfer*. Although the initial zone transfer after configuring a new secondary server represents a full transfer of the zone information, subsequent transfers are made incrementally as changes occur. Here's how it works: when changes are made to a primary zone, the changes are made first to the primary zone and then transferred to the secondary zone on the secondary servers. Because only changes, rather than a complete copy of the zone, are transferred, the amount of traffic required to keep a secondary zone current is significantly reduced.

You can implement DNS zones in many ways. One way to do this is to mimic your organization's domain structure. Figure 6-4 shows an example of how zones and zone transfers could be configured for child domains of a parent domain. Here, you have separate zones that handle name services for the cpandl.com, tech.cpandl.com, and sales.cpandl.com domains. Zone transfers are configured so that copies of the primary zone on cpandl.com are transferred to the name servers for the tech.cpandl.com and sales.cpandl.com domains. The reason for this is that users in these zones routinely work with servers in the cpandl.com zone. This makes lookups faster and also reduces the amount of DNS traffic.

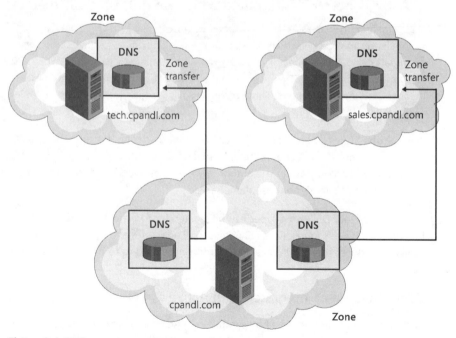

Figure 6-4 DNS zones on separate servers.

Although you can configure DNS services in this way, your organization's domain structure is separate from its zone configuration. If you create subdomains of a parent domain, they can either be part of the same zone or belong to another zone, and these zones can be on separate DNS servers or on the same DNS servers.

The example in Figure 6-5 shows a wide area network (WAN) configuration. The branch offices in Seattle and New York are separate from the company headquarters, and key zones are organized geographically. At company headquarters there's an additional zone running on the same DNS name server as the zone for the cpandl.com domain. This zone handles services. cpandl.com, tech.cpandl.com, and sales.cpandl.com.

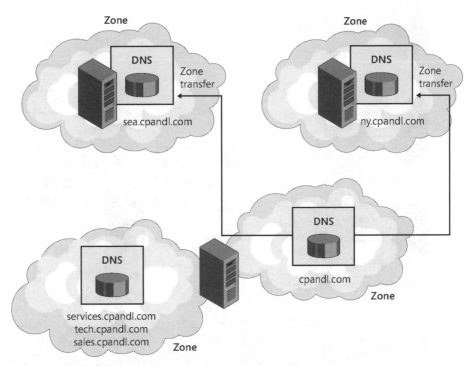

Figure 6-5 Zones that are separate from the domain structure.

Zones that are integrated with Active Directory

Using Active Directory–integrated zones, you can store DNS zone information within Active Directory. This gives you several advantages. Any primary zone or stub zone integrated with Active Directory is automatically replicated to other domain controllers using Active Directory replication. Because Active Directory can compress replication data between sites, you can more efficiently replicate DNS information, which is especially important over slow WAN links.

Figure 6-6 shows an example of Active Directory–integrated zones and replication. Here, zone information for cpandl.com, seattle.cpandl.com, portland.cpandl.com, and sf.cpandl.com has been integrated with Active Directory. This allows any DNS changes made at branch offices or at company headquarters to be replicated throughout the organization to all the available name servers. Because the decision to integrate zones with Active Directory isn't an all-or-nothing approach, there are also standard primary and secondary zones, and standard DNS zone transfers are used to maintain these zones.

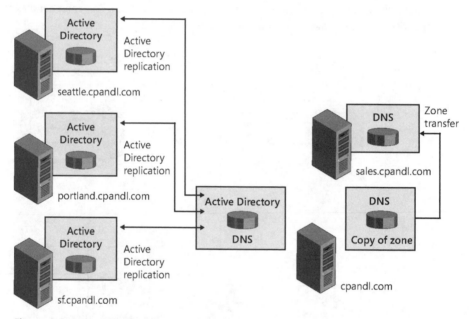

Figure 6-6 Active Directory–integrated zones.

Inside OUT

Multimaster replication for DNS changes

When you use Active Directory integration, copies of zone information are maintained on all domain controllers that are also configured as DNS servers. This is different from standard DNS zones. When you use standard zones, there's a single authoritative DNS server for a zone and it maintains a master copy of the zone. All updates to the primary zone must be made on the primary server. With Active Directory–integrated zones, each domain controller configured as a DNS server in a domain is an authoritative server for that domain. This means clients can make updates to DNS records on any of these servers and the changes will be automatically replicated.

With Active Directory–integrated zones, default application partitions are used to ensure that DNS information is replicated only to domain controllers that are also configured as DNS servers. Here's how it works: for every domain in an Active Directory forest, a separate application partition is created and used to store all records in each Active Directory–integrated zone configured for that domain. Because the application partition context is outside that of other Active Directory information, DNS information is not replicated with other Active Directory information. There's also a default application partition that stores DNS information and replicates that information to all DNS servers in an Active Directory forest. This simplifies DNS replication for organizations with multiple domains.

Another benefit of Active Directory integration is the ability to perform conditional forwarding. By using conditional forwarding, you can eliminate the split-brain syndrome that occurs when internal requests are incorrectly forwarded to external DNS servers. Finally, with dynamic updates using DHCP, clients become able to use secure dynamic updates. Secure dynamic updates ensure that only clients that created a record can subsequently update the record. You'll find more on secure dynamic updates in the section entitled "Security considerations" later in this chapter.

When you are working with early releases of a DNS server for Windows Server, restarting a DNS server could take a long time in very large organizations with extremely large Active Directory Domain Services–integrated zones. The reason is that the zone data was loaded in the foreground while the server was starting the DNS service. To ensure that DNS servers can be responsive after a restart, current releases of Windows Server load zone data from Active Directory Domain Services in the background while it restarts. This ensures that the DNS server is responsive and can handle requests for data from other zones.

DNS servers perform the following tasks at startup:

- Enumerate all zones to be loaded.

- Load root hints from files or Active Directory Domain Services storage.

- Load all zones that are stored in files rather than in Active Directory Domain Services.

- Begin responding to queries and remote procedure calls (RPCs).

- Create one or more threads to load the zones that are stored in Active Directory Domain Services.

Because separate threads load zone data, the DNS server is able to respond to queries while zone loading is in progress. If a DNS client performs a query for a host in a zone that has already been loaded, the DNS server responds appropriately. If the query is for a host that has not yet been loaded into memory, the DNS server reads the host's data from Active Directory Domain Services and updates its record list accordingly.

CHAPTER 6

Secondary zones, stub zones, and conditional forwarding

Secondary zones, stub zones, and conditional forwarding can all be used to resolve name-resolution problems—chiefly the split-brain scenario in which internal DNS servers blindly forward any requests that they can't resolve to external servers. Rather than blindly forwarding requests, you can configure internal servers so that they know about certain DNS domains. This ensures that name resolution works for domains that aren't known on the public Internet, and you can also use it to speed up name resolution for known domains, which makes users much happier than if name resolution fails or if they have to wait all the time for name requests to be resolved.

By using a secondary zone, you create a complete copy of a zone on a DNS server that can be used to resolve DNS queries without having to go to the authoritative name server for that domain. Not only can this be used for subdomains of a parent domain that exists in different zones, but also it can be used for different parent domains. For example, on the name servers for cpandl.com you could create secondary zones for a partner company, such as The Phone Company, whose domain is thephone-company.com. In this way, DNS clients in the cpandl .com domain can perform fast lookups for hosts in thephone-company.com domain.

The downside is that you must replicate DNS information between the domains. If this replication takes place over the public Internet, the administrators at The Phone Company would need to configure firewalls on their network to allow this and to make other security changes, which might not be acceptable. Because you are maintaining a full copy of the zone, any change generates replication traffic.

With a stub zone, you create a partial copy of a zone that has information about only the authoritative name servers in a zone. As Figure 6-7 shows, this allows a DNS server to forward queries directly to a name server for a particular domain and bypass the normal name-server hierarchy. This speeds up the lookup because you don't have to go through multiple name servers to find the authoritative name server for a domain.

Stub zones work like this: when you set up a stub zone for a domain, only the resource records needed to identify the authoritative name servers for the related domain are transferred to the name server. These records include the SOA and NS records and the related A records for these servers (referred to as *glue records*). You can maintain these records in one of two ways. If you use Active Directory integration, the normal Active Directory replication process can be used to maintain the stub zone. If you use a standard stub zone, standard zone transfers are used to maintain the stub zone. Both techniques require access to the domain specified in the stub zone, which can be a security issue. Replication traffic isn't an issue, however, because you are maintaining a very small amount of data.

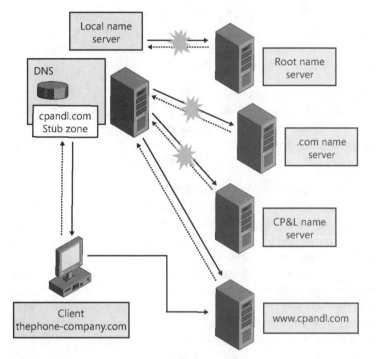

Figure 6-7 Using stub zones for lookups.

Conditional forwarding is very similar to stub zones except that you don't need to transfer any information from the domain to which you want to forward requests. Instead, you configure name servers in domain A so that they know the IP address of the authoritative name servers in domain B, allowing these name servers to be used as forwarders. There's no access requirement, so you don't need permission to do this, and there's no bandwidth requirement, so you don't need to worry about extra replication traffic.

When you use conditional forwarding, however, there are some trade-offs to be made. If the authoritative name servers change, the IP addresses aren't updated automatically as they are with stub zones or secondary zones. This means you would have to reconfigure name servers manually in domain A with the new IP addresses of the authoritative name servers in domain B. When you configure conditional forwarders on a name server, the name server has to check the forwarders list each time it resolves a name. As the list grows, it requires more and more time to work through the list of potential forwarders.

Integration with other technologies

The DNS client built into computers running Windows Vista and later supports DNS traffic over IPv4 and IPv6. By default, IPv6 configures the well-known site-local addresses of DNS servers at FEC0:0:0:FFFF::1, FEC0:0:0:FFFF::2, and FEC0:0:0:FFFF::3. To add the IPv6 addresses of your DNS servers, use the properties of the Internet Protocol Version 6 (TCP/IPv6) component in Network Connections. Alternatively, use the **netsh interface ipv6 set dns** command or the Set-DnsClientServerAddress cmdlet.

When the network uses DHCP, you should configure DHCP to work with DNS. DHCP clients can register IPv4 and IPv6 addresses. To ensure proper integration of DHCP and DNS, you need to set the appropriate DHCP scope options. For IPv4, you should set the 006 DNS Servers and 015 DNS Domain Name scope options. For IPv6, you should set the 00023 DNS Recursive Name Server IPV6 Address and 00024 Domain Search List scope options.

When a DNS server isn't available, DNS client computers running Windows Vista and later can use Link-Local Multicast Name Resolution (LLMNR) to resolve names on a local network segment. They also periodically search for a domain controller in the domain to which they belong and can be configured to locate the nearest domain controller instead of searching randomly. This functionality helps avoid performance problems that might occur if a DNS client creates an association with a distant domain controller located on a slow link rather than a local domain controller because of a network or server failure. Previously, this association continued until the client was forced to seek a new domain controller, such as when the client computer was disconnected from the network for a long time. By periodically renewing its association with a domain controller, a DNS client can reduce the probability that it will be associated with an inappropriate domain controller.

DNS clients for Windows 8.1 and Windows Server 2012 R2 have significant changes. You can control the way these changes work using Group Policy settings found in the Administrative Templates for Computer Configuration under Network\DNS Client.

By default, these clients do not send outbound LLMNR queries to mobile broadband or virtual private network (VPN) interfaces, and they do not send outbound NetBIOS queries to mobile broadband interfaces. These clients issue LLMNR and NetBIOS queries in parallel with DNS queries, optimized for IPv4 and IPv6 with a binding order preference. Interfaces are divided into networks to send parallel queries, and responses are preferred in binding order, too.

You can control whether queries are optimized and issued in parallel using the Turn Off Smart Multi-Home Name Resolution setting. When you enable this setting, parallel queries are not used. Instead, DNS queries are issued first across all networks. If DNS queries fail, LLMNR queries are issued. If LLMNR queries fail, NetBIOS queries are used.

By default, LLMNR and NetBIOS responses are preferred over DNS responses if the LLMNR and NetBIOS responses are from a network with a higher binding order. You can control the way binding order preference works using the Prefer Link Local Responses Over DNS setting. When you enable this setting, LLMNR and NetBIOS responses are preferred over DNS responses if the LLMNR and NetBIOS responses are from a network with a higher binding order.

To resolve a problem with computers in power-saving mode, the LLMNR query timeout has been increased to 410 milliseconds (ms) for the first retry and 410 ms for the second retry, giving a total timeout value of 820 ms instead of 300 ms. Additionally, if a specific interface is hijacking DNS names, these clients send LLMNR and NetBIOS queries in parallel with DNS queries on those networks and the LLMNR or NetBIOS response is preferred.

You can control LLMNR in several ways. To disable LLMNR, enable the Turn Off Multicast Name Resolution setting. To ensure that DNS clients on nondomain networks always prefer DNS responses, enable the Turn Off Smart Protocol Reordering setting. When this setting is enabled, DNS clients on nondomain networks prefer DNS responses to LLMNR responses and LLMNR responses to NetBIOS responses.

Security considerations

DNS security is an important issue, and this discussion focuses on three areas:

- DNS queries from clients

- DNS dynamic updates

- External DNS name resolution

DNS queries and security

A client that makes a query trusts that an authoritative DNS name server gives it the right information. In most environments this works fine. Users or administrators specify the initial DNS name servers to which DNS queries should be forwarded in a computer's TCP/IP configuration. In some environments in which security is a major concern, administrators might be worried about DNS clients getting invalid information from DNS name servers. Here, administrators might want to look at the DNS Security (DNSSEC) protocol. DNSSEC is especially useful for companies that have many branch locations and in which DNS information is transferred over the public Internet using zone transfers.

DNSSEC provides authentication of DNS information. Using DNSSEC, you can digitally sign zone files so that they can be authenticated. These digital signatures can be sent to DNS clients as resource records from DNS servers hosting signed zones. The client can then verify that the DNS information sent from the DNS server is authentic.

When you use DNS Server for Windows Server 2012 R2, there are some added benefits:

- Active Directory–integrated zones support dynamic updates in DNSSEC signed zones.

- DNS Server supports automated trust anchor distribution through Active Directory and automated trust anchor rollover.

CHAPTER 6

- DNS Server supports the validation of records with updated DNSSEC standards, including NSEC3 and RSA/SHA-2.

With Windows Server 2012 R2, an authoritative DNS server also can act as the Key Master for DNSSEC. The Key Master generates and manages signing keys for both Active Directory–integrated zones protected by DNSSEC and standard (file-backed) zones protected by DNSSEC. When a zone has a designated Key Master, the Key Master is responsible for the entire key signing process from key generation to storage, rollover, retirement, and deletion. Although key signing and management tasks can be initiated only from the Key Master, other primary DNS servers can continue to use zone signing—they just do so through the Key Master.

DNSSEC digital signatures are encrypted using private key encryption on a per-zone basis. In private key encryption, there is a public key and a private key. A zone's public key is used to validate a digital signature. Like the digital signature itself, the public key is stored in a signed zone in the form of a resource record. A zone's private key is not stored in the zone; it is private and used only by the name server to sign the related zone or parts of the zone. The records used with DNSSEC are summarized in Table 6-3.

Table 6-3 DNSSEC resource records

Record Type	Common Name	Description
KEY	Public Key	Contains the public key that is related to a DNS domain name. The public key can be for a zone, host, or other entity. KEY records are authenticated by SIG records.
NXT	Next	Indicates the next record in a digitally signed zone and states which records exist in a zone. It can be used to validate that a particular record doesn't exist in the zone. For example, if there's a record for corpsvr07.cpandl.com and the NXT record points to corpsvr09.cpandl.com, there isn't a record for corpsvr08.cpandl.com, so that server doesn't exist in the zone.
SIG	Signature	Contains the digital signature for a zone or part of a zone and is used to authenticate a resource record set of a particular type.

DNS dynamic updates and security

All current Windows desktop and server operating systems fully support DNS dynamic updates. Dynamic updates are defined in RFC 2136 and are used in conjunction with DHCP to allow a client to update its A record if its IP address changes and to allow the DHCP server to update the PTR record for the client on the DNS server. DHCP servers can also be configured to update both the A and PTR records on the client's behalf. Dynamic DNS is also supported for IPv6 AAAA records, which allows for dynamic updating of host addresses on systems that use IPv6 and DHCP.

If dynamic updates are enabled, the DNS name server trusts the client to update its own DNS record and trusts the DHCP server to make updates on behalf of the client. There are two types of dynamic updates:

- **Secure dynamic updates.** You can use secure dynamic updates to put security mechanisms in place to ensure that only a client that created a record can update a record.

- **Nonsecure dynamic updates.** When you use nonsecure dynamic updates, there is no way to ensure that only a client that created a record can update a record.

Secure dynamic updates are the default setting for Active Directory–integrated zones. By using secure updates, known clients that have DNS records in Active Directory can update their records dynamically and unknown clients are prevented from adding their records to a zone.

Any client capable of using secure dynamic updates can update its records. This means clients running any current version of Windows can update their own records. DHCP servers can be configured to make updates on behalf of these clients. For more information on this, see the section entitled "Integrating DHCP and DNS" in Chapter 5, "Configuring DHCP Services."

With standard zones, the default setting is to allow both secure and nonsecure dynamic updates. The reason standard zones are configured for both secure and nonsecure dynamic updates is that this allows clients running current Windows operating systems and clients running early Windows operating systems to update records dynamically. Although it seems to imply that security is involved, in fact it is not. Here, allowing secure updates simply means that the dynamic update process won't break when a secure update is made. By default, DNS doesn't validate updates, and this means dynamic updates are accepted from any client. This creates a significant security vulnerability because updates can be accepted from untrusted sources.

You can eliminate this security vulnerability using name protection. With name protection, which is a feature that you can enable on DHCP servers running Windows Server 2012 R2, the DHCP server registers records on behalf of the client only if no other client with this DNS information is already registered. On a DHCP server, you can configure name protection for IPv4 and IPv6 at the protocol level or at the scope level. Name protection settings configured at the scope level take precedence over the setting at the IPv4 or IPv6 level.

Name protection is designed to prevent name squatting. Name squatting occurs when a non-Windows-based computer registers a name in DNS that is already registered to a computer running a Windows operating system. By enabling name protection, you can prevent name squatting by non-Windows-based computers. Although name squatting generally does not present a problem when you use Active Directory to reserve a name for a single user or computer, it usually is a good idea to enable name protection on all Windows networks.

Name protection is based on the Dynamic Host Configuration Identifier (DHCID) and support for the DHCID RR (resource record) in DNS. DHCID is a resource record stored in DNS that maps names to prevent duplicate registration. DHCP uses the DHCID resource record to store an identifier for a computer along with related information for the name, such as the A and AAAA records of the computer. The DHCP server can request a DHCID record match and then refuse the registration of a computer with a different address attempting to register a name with an existing DHCID record.

External DNS name resolution and security

Typically, as part of a standard DNS configuration, you'll configure DNS servers on your internal network to forward queries that they can't resolve to DNS servers outside the organization. Normally, these servers are the name servers for the Internet service provider (ISP) that provides your organization's Internet connection. In this configuration, you know that internal servers forward to designated external servers. However, if those servers don't respond, the internal servers typically forward requests directly to the root name servers, and this is where security problems can be introduced.

By default, DNS servers include a list of root servers that can be used for name resolution to the top-level domains. This list is maintained in what is called a *root hints file*. If this file is not updated regularly, your organization's internal name servers could point to invalid root servers, and this leaves a hole in your security that could be exploited. To prevent this, periodically update the root hints file.

On a DNS server that doesn't use Active Directory, the root hints are read from the %SystemRoot%\System32\DNS\Cache.dns file. You can obtain an update for this file from *http://www.internic.net/zones/named.root*. To determine whether an update is needed, compare the version information in your current root hints file with that of the published version. Within the root hints file, you'll find a section of comments like this:

```
;    This file holds the information on root name servers needed to
;        initialize cache of Internet domain name servers
;        (e.g. reference this file in the "cache  .  <file>"
;        configuration file of BIND domain name servers).
;
;    This file is made available by InterNIC
;    under anonymous FTP as
;        file                        /domain/named.root
;        on server                   FTP.INTERNIC.NET
;
;        last update:                May 5, 2014
;        related version of root zone:   2014050500
```

Here, the version information is in the last two lines of the comments. If you changed the root hints file, you must stop and then start the DNS Server service so that the root hints file is reloaded. In the DNS console, you can do this by pressing and holding or right-clicking the server entry, pointing to All Tasks, and selecting Restart.

On a DNS server that uses Active Directory Domain Services–integrated zones, the root hints are read from Active Directory and the registry at startup. You can view and modify the root hints in the DNS console. To do this, press and hold or right-click the DNS server entry and then select Properties. In the Properties dialog box, tap or click the Root Hints tab. You can then manage each of the individual root hint entries using Add, Edit, or Remove as necessary. To update the entire root hints file using a known good DNS server, tap or click Copy From Server, type the IP address of the DNS server, and then tap or click OK. If you suspect the root hints file is corrupted, you might need to reload the file into Active Directory using the %SystemRoot%\System32\DNS\Cache.dns file. To do this, follow these steps:

1. At an elevated command prompt, type **net stop dns** to stop the DNS Server service. When the DNS Server service stops, type **copy %systemroot%\system32\dns \samples\cache.dns %systemroot%\system32\dns**. If you are prompted to overwrite the existing file, type **Y** for yes.

2. In Active Directory Users And Computers, make sure Advanced Features is selected from the View menu, and then expand System MicrosoftDNS. Next, press and hold or right-click RootDNSServers and then tap or click Delete.

3. When you are prompted to delete this object, tap or click Yes. When you are prompted to delete this object as well as the objects it contains, tap or click Yes.

4. At the elevated command prompt, type **net start dns** to start the DNS Server service.

5. In the DNS console, press and hold or right-click the server entry and then select Properties. In the Properties dialog box, verify that the root servers appear in the Root Hints tab.

6. In Active Directory Users And Computers, verify that the RootDNSServers container has been re-created and contains the root servers. The new root hints are automatically replicated as necessary.

CHAPTER 6

Inside OUT

Consider whether external root servers should be used

In some instances you might not want to use a root hints file or you might want to bypass using root servers. Here are two scenarios to consider:

- If your organization isn't connected to the Internet, your name servers don't need pointers to the public root servers. Instead, you should remove the entries in the Cache.dns file and replace them with NS and A records for the DNS server authoritative for the root domain at your site. For example, if you use a private top-level domain, such as .local, you must set up a root name server for the .local domain, and the Cache.dns file should point to these root name servers. You must then restart the DNS Server service so that the root hints file is reloaded. In the DNS console, you can do this by pressing and holding or right-clicking the server entry, pointing to All Tasks, and selecting Restart.

- Making a connection to the root name servers exposes your internal name servers. The internal name server must connect through your organization's firewall to the root name server. While this connection is open and your name server is waiting for a response, there is a potential vulnerability that could be exploited. Here, someone could have set up a fake name server that is waiting for such connections and then could use this server to conduct malicious activity on your DNS servers. To prevent this, you can configure forwarding to specific external name servers and tell your name servers not to use the root name servers. You do this by configuring the Do Not Use Recursion For This Domain option when you set up forwarding.

For more information, see the section entitled "Configuring forwarders and conditional forwarding" in Chapter 7.

Architecting a DNS design

After you complete your initial planning, you should consider an overall design architecture. Two primary DNS designs are used:

- Split-brain design

- Separate-name design

Although the split-brain design is less common these days, both are valid approaches.

Split-brain design: Same internal and external names

What a split-brain design means is that your organization uses the same domain name internally as it does externally and DNS is designed so that the name services for your organization's internal network are separate from that used for the organization's external network. Put another way, an organization's private network should be private and separate from its presence on the public Internet, so your internal name servers should be separate from your external name servers. You don't want a situation in which you have one set of name servers that is used both for users within the organization and users outside the organization. That's a security no-no that could open your internal network to attack.

The concern with this design—and this is why it's called split-brain—is that if your internal network uses the same domain namespace as your public Internet presence does, you can get in a situation in which users within the organization can't look up information related to the organization's public Internet presence and users outside the organization can't look up information for the organization's private network.

From an internal user perspective, it's a bad thing that users can't access the organization's public Internet resources. There's an easy fix, however. You just create records on the authoritative name server for the internal network that specify the IP address for the organization's public Internet resources. For example, to allow users on the internal cpandl.com domain to access www.cpandl.com on the public Internet, you create a host record on the internal DNS server for www in the cpandl.com domain that specifies its IP address.

From a security perspective, it's a good thing that outside users can't look up information for the organization's private network—you don't want them to be able to do this. If you have business partners at other locations that need access to the internal network, you should set up a secure link between your organizations or make other arrangements, such as using an extranet.

To implement split-brain design, do the following:

- **Complete your planning.** Complete your planning, and decide how many DNS servers you are going to use on the internal network. Decide on the host names and IP addresses these servers will use. In most cases you need only two DNS servers for a domain. It's a standard convention to set the host names of DNS servers as Primary and Secondary if there are two servers and, if there are more than two servers, as NS01, NS02, and so on. You can use this naming convention or adopt a different one.

- **Install and configure the DNS Server service.** Install the DNS Server service on each of the designated DNS servers. If you are using Active Directory, DNS is already implemented on some servers because it's required. With Active Directory Domain Services–integrated zones, every DNS server in a domain that is also configured as a domain controller is a primary name server; any DNS server not configured as a domain controller can be only a secondary in that zone. With standard primary and secondary zones, you can have only one primary server for a zone; every other DNS server in that zone must be a secondary.

- **Create records on internal name servers for your public resources.** For each of the organization's public Internet resources to which internal users need access, you must create records on the internal name servers. This allows the internal users to access and work with these resources. This includes the organization's WWW, FTP, and mail servers.

- **Configure forwarding to your ISP's name servers.** The ISP that provides your connection to the Internet should provide you with the host names and IP addresses of name servers to which internal users can forward DNS queries. Configure your internal name servers so that they forward to your ISP's name servers DNS queries that they can't resolve. As necessary, configure secondary zones, stub zones, or conditional forwarding to any domains for which you desire direct lookups.

- **Configure internal systems to use your internal DNS servers.** Every workstation and server on your internal network should be configured with the IP address of your primary and secondary DNS name servers. If you have more than two name servers, set the name servers that should be used as appropriate. Normally, you point a system to only one or two internal name servers. Don't point internal systems to external name servers—you don't want internal systems trying to resolve requests on these name servers.

- **Configure external name servers for internal resources as necessary.** Consider whether you need to create resource records on your ISP's external name servers for servers on your internal network that need to be resolvable from the Internet—by mobile users, for example. If you do, provide the necessary information to your ISP to set up these resource records.

Separate-name design: Different internal and external names

Another approach to DNS design is to use separate-name design. In separate-name design, your internal network uses different domain names than your organization's public Internet presence does. This creates actual separation between your organization's internal and external namespaces by placing them in different parent domains. For example, your organization could use cohovineyard.com for its internal network and cohowinery.com for its external network. Now you have a situation in which completely different namespaces are used to create separation.

As with split-brain design, you have different internal name servers and different external name servers. Unlike split-brain design, internal users should be able to look up information related to the organization's public Internet presence and you won't need to create additional records to do this. Here, it's only a matter of ensuring that the internal name servers forward to external name servers, which can perform the necessary lookups.

If you use different names that are in the public domain hierarchy, you should register all the internal and external domain names you use. In the previous example, you would register cohovineyard.com and cohowinery.com. This ensures that someone else can't register one of the domain names you use internally, which could mess up name resolution in some instances. You wouldn't need to register a domain name, such as cohowinery.local, however, because .local is not a public top-level domain.

Rather than using two completely different names, a more common separate-name design is to register a domain name for the company's public Internet presence and then use a child domain of that domain for the internal domain. For example, you could register cpandl. com for the company's external domain name and then use corp.cpandl.com as the internal domain name.

To implement separate-name design, do the following:

- **Complete your planning.** Complete your planning, and decide how many DNS servers you are going to use on the internal network. Decide on the host names and IP addresses these servers will use. In most cases you need only two DNS servers for a domain. It's a standard convention to set the host names of DNS servers as Primary and Secondary if there are two servers and, if there are more than two servers, as NS01, NS02, and so on. You can use this naming convention or adopt a different one.

- **Install and configure the DNS Server service.** Install the DNS Server service on each of the designated DNS servers. If you are using Active Directory, DNS is already implemented on some servers because it's required. With Active Directory Domain Services–integrated zones, every DNS server in a domain that is also configured as a domain controller is a primary name server; any DNS server not configured as a domain controller can be only a secondary in that zone. With standard primary and secondary zones, you can have only one primary server for a zone; every other DNS server in that zone must be a secondary.

- **Configure forwarding to your ISP's name servers.** The ISP that provides your connection to the Internet should provide you with the host names and IP addresses of name servers to which internal users can forward DNS queries. Configure your internal name servers so that they forward DNS queries that they can't resolve to your ISP's name servers. As necessary, configure secondary zones, stub zones, or conditional forwarding to any domains for which you desire direct lookups.

- **Configure internal systems to use your internal DNS servers.** Every workstation and server on your internal network should be configured with the IP addresses of your primary and secondary DNS name servers. If you have more than two name servers, set the name servers that should be used as appropriate. Normally, you point a system to only one or two internal name servers. Don't point internal systems to external name servers—you don't want internal systems trying to resolve requests on these name servers.

- **Configure external name servers for internal resources as necessary.** Consider whether you need to create resource records on your ISP's external name servers for servers on your internal network that need to be resolvable from the Internet—by mobile users, for example. If you do, provide the necessary information to your ISP to set up these resource records.

Securing DNS from attacks

When you are planning your DNS infrastructure, you should be aware of the common security threats and how those threats are commonly mitigated. Attackers can threaten DNS infrastructure in many ways. Often DNS domain names and computer names indicate the function or location of a domain or computer to help users identify domains and computers more easily. If so, an attacker can try to diagram your network by using his or her knowledge of your naming scheme to try to learn about other domains and computers on your network.

Once an attacker has a footprint of your network, the attacker can use this knowledge to generate IP packets containing valid IP addresses. This approach, called *IP spoofing*, makes it seem as if the packets are coming from a valid IP address in your network and allows the attacker to gain access to the network.

Attackers might attempt to redirect queries. One way of doing this is to pollute the DNS cache of a DNS server with DNS data that directs future queries to servers that are under the control of the attackers. This type of redirection attack can occur whenever attackers have writable access to DNS data. For example, if your network uses dynamic updates that are not secure, the attackers might be able to insert bad data during a dynamic update.

Attackers also might attempt to deny the availability of network services by flooding your DNS servers with recursive queries. The goal is to overwhelm your DNS servers until the DNS Server service becomes unavailable. When that happens, network services that use DNS will be unavailable to network users.

The way you mitigate DNS security threats is to increase the DNS security on your network as much as possible. You can implement three basic security configurations for DNS:

- **Low.** A DNS deployment without any security precautions. Deploy this level of DNS security only in a private network in which there is no threat from external sources or when you have no concern about the integrity of your DNS data. With this security level, the DNS infrastructure is fully exposed to the Internet.

- **Medium.** A DNS deployment with standard security precautions. Your DNS servers use available DNS security features. You might or might not run DNS servers on domain controllers and you might or might not store DNS zones in Active Directory. With this security level, the DNS infrastructure has limited exposure to the Internet.

- **High.** A DNS deployment with standard and additional security precautions. Your DNS servers use available DNS security features. You run DNS servers on domain controllers and store DNS zones in Active Directory. Your DNS infrastructure has no Internet communication by means of internal DNS servers. With this security level, the DNS infrastructure has no direct exposure to the Internet.

Table 6-4 compares the configuration settings for low-security, medium-security, and high-security DNS deployments. To help safeguard the network, most organizations will want to implement at least a medium security environment for DNS.

Table 6-4 Comparing low-security, medium-security, and high-security configurations for DNS servers

Low Security	Medium Security	High Security
DNS resolution is performed by all DNS servers in your network. DNS servers use root hints pointing to Internet root servers.	DNS servers that are configured with forwarders point to specific internal DNS servers when they can't resolve names locally.	Same as medium. Also, root hints point to internal DNS servers that host the root zone for your internal namespace.
DNS servers permit zone transfers to any server.	DNS servers limit zone transfers to servers that are listed in (NS) records in their zones.	DNS servers limit zone transfers to specific IP addresses.
DNS servers listen on all of their IP addresses.	DNS servers listen on specific IP addresses.	DNS servers listen on specific IP addresses.
Cache pollution prevention is disabled.	Cache pollution prevention is enabled.	Cache pollution prevention is enabled.
Dynamic update is allowed for all DNS zones.	Only secure dynamic updates are allowed.	Uses secure dynamic updates, except for top-level and root zones, which disable dynamic updates.
UDP and TCP port 53 is open on the network firewall for both source and destination addresses.	Firewalls use the allowed source and destination address list. Perimeter network DNS servers are configured with root hints that point to Internet root servers. Proxy servers and gateways perform Internet name resolution.	Permissions restrict who can configure DNS servers and who can create, modify, or delete DNS zones and resource records.

Implementing and managing DNS

Name services are essential for communications for Transmission Control Protocol/Internet Protocol (TCP/IP) networking. Windows Server uses the Domain Name System (DNS) as its primary method of name resolution. DNS enables computers to register and resolve DNS domain names. DNS defines the rules under which computers are named and how names are resolved to IP addresses.

Installing the DNS Server service

The way you install the DNS Server service depends on whether you plan to use DNS with Active Directory or without Active Directory. After you make that decision, you can install DNS as necessary.

Using DNS with Active Directory

On a domain with Active Directory, DNS is required. You can install DNS as part of the setup of the first domain controller in a domain or you can install DNS after installing the first domain controller. Active Directory doesn't require Windows DNS, however. Active Directory is designed to work with any DNS server that supports dynamic updates and service locator (SRV) records. This means Active Directory can work with any DNS server running Berkeley Internet Name Domain (BIND) version 8.1.2 or later. If you have DNS servers that use BIND version 8.1.2 or later, you can use those servers. If you don't already have BIND servers, you probably won't want to set these up because there are many benefits to using the Microsoft DNS Server service. It's also important to point out that only Microsoft DNS servers can automatically create the delegation records required by Active Directory.

When you install the DNS Server service as part of the Active Directory installation process, you can use Active Directory–integrated zones and take advantage of the many replication and security benefits of Active Directory. Here, any server configured as a domain controller with DNS and using Active Directory–integrated zones is an Active Directory primary name server.

Here's how installation of DNS on the first domain controller in a forest works:

1. You use the Active Directory Domain Services Configuration Wizard to install the first domain controller. During the installation process, you specify that you are installing a new forest and then specify the Active Directory domain name, as shown in Figure 7-1. This also sets the DNS name for the domain.

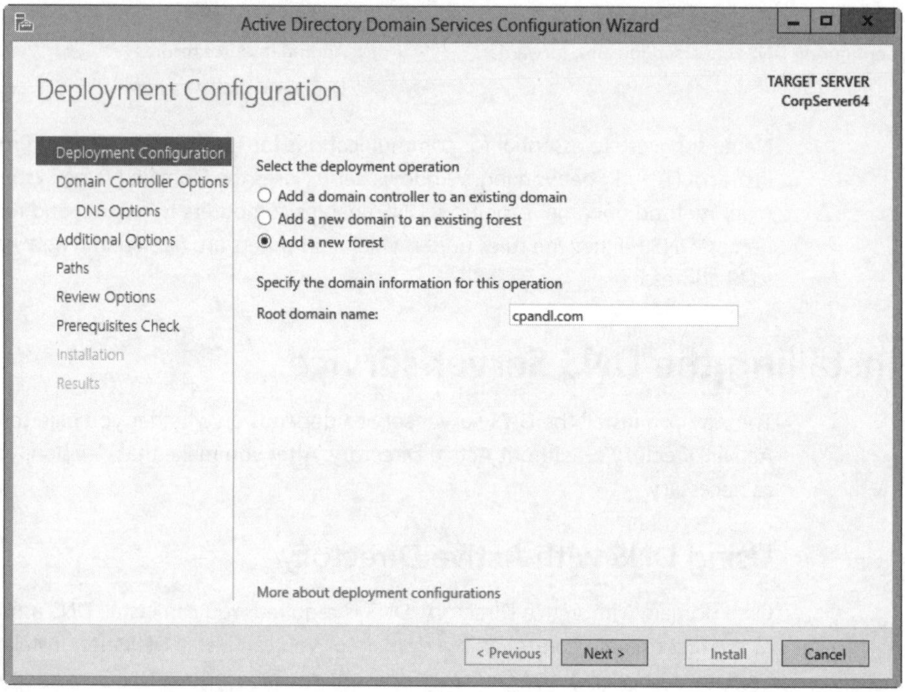

Figure 7-1 Specifying the Active Directory domain name.

NOTE

For more information about promoting domain controllers, see the section entitled "Installing Active Directory Domain Services" in Chapter 14, "Implementing Active Directory Domain Services."

2. When the Active Directory installation process begins, the Active Directory Domain Services Configuration Wizard checks the current DNS configuration. If no authoritative DNS servers are available for the domain, the wizard selects Domain Name System DNS Server as an additional installation option, as shown in Figure 7-2.

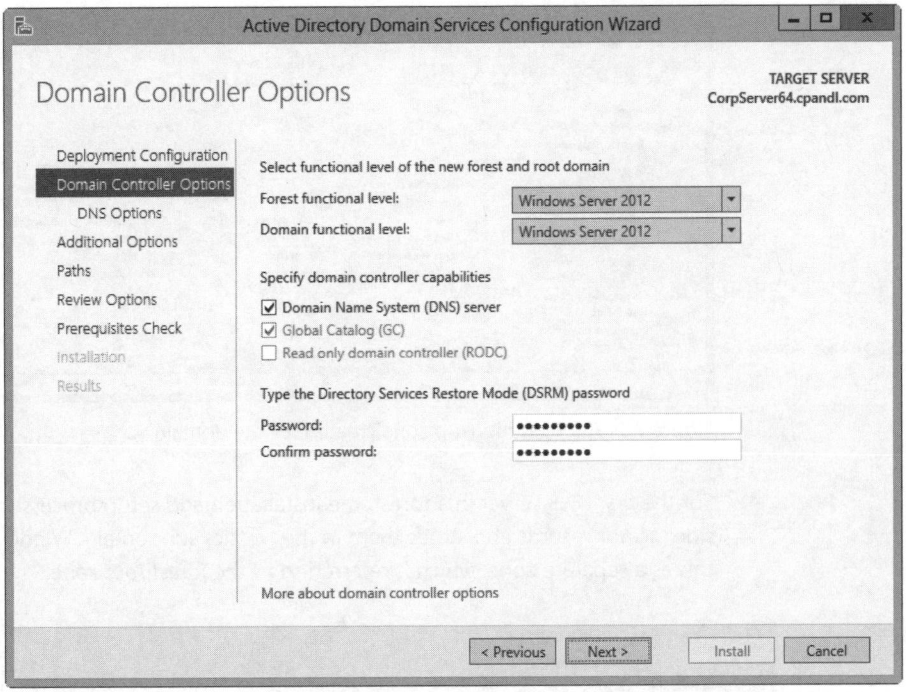

Figure 7-2 The wizard selecting the DNS server when no authoritative DNS servers are available.

3. In most cases you'll want to install DNS. If you install DNS, the Active Directory Domain Services Configuration Wizard installs DNS, and then you can use the Configure A DNS Server Wizard to complete the initial setup. As Figure 7-3 shows, this typically means that a forward lookup zone will be created for the domain. The forward lookup zone will have the Start of Authority (SOA), Name Server (NS), and Host Address (A) records for the server you are working with. This designates it as the authoritative name server for the domain. If you want to, you can also create reverse lookup zones to allow for IP-address-to-host-name lookups. DNS servers support IPv4 and IPv6 for reverse lookups.

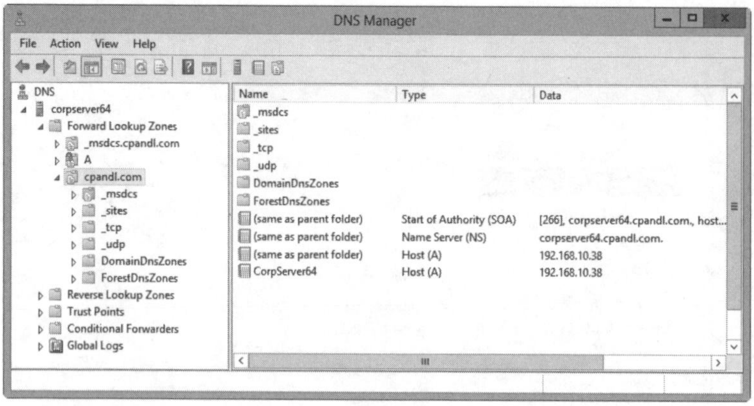

Figure 7-3 A forward lookup zone created for the domain.

4. For the first DNS server in a forest, the installation and setup process creates the forest-side locator records and stores them in the _msdcs subdomain. Windows Server creates this as a separate zone, which is referred to as the *forest root zone*.

Inside OUT

Forest root zones

The forest root zone is an important part of Active Directory. It is in this zone that Active Directory creates SRV resource records that are used when clients are looking for a particular resource, such as global catalog servers, Lightweight Directory Access Protocol (LDAP) servers, and Kerberos servers. The _msdcs subdomain is created as its own zone to improve performance with remote sites. With early implementations, remote sites had to replicate the entire DNS database to access forest root records, which meant increased replication and bandwidth usage. As a separate zone, only the zone will be replicated to the DNS servers in remote sites as long as Active Directory application partitions are used. You can enable application partitions for use with DNS as discussed in the section entitled "Configuring default partitions and replication scope" in Chapter 8, "Maintaining and troubleshooting DNS."

When you install additional domain controllers in a domain, the DNS Server service will be selected for installation by default. If you want the domain controller to also act as a DNS server, you should keep this selection.

In an Active Directory domain, secondary zones and stub zones can also be useful, as discussed in the section entitled "DNS zones and zone transfers" in Chapter 6, "Architecting DNS infrastructure." In fact, in certain situations you might have to use a secondary zone or stub zone for name resolution to work properly. Consider the case in which you have multiple trees in a forest, each in its own namespace. For instance, City Power & Light and The Phone Company are both part of one company and use the domains cpandl.com and thephone-company.com, respectively. If the namespaces for these domains are set up as separate trees of the same forest, your organization would have two namespaces. In the cpandl.com domain, you might want users to be able to access resources in thephone-company.com domain and vice versa. To do this, you would configure DNS as shown in Figure 7-4.

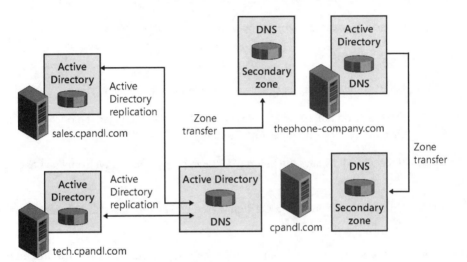

Figure 7-4 Using secondary zones with Active Directory.

The implementation steps for this example are as follows:

1. Set up a secondary zone or stub zone for thephone-company.com on the authoritative name server for cpandl.com.

2. Set up a secondary zone or stub zone for cpandl.com on the authoritative name server for thephone-company.com.

3. Configure zone transfers between cpandl.com and thephone-company.com.

4. Configure zone transfers between thephone-company.com and cpandl.com.

Using DNS without Active Directory

On a domain without Active Directory, DNS servers act as standard primary or standard secondary name servers. You must install the DNS Server service on each primary or secondary server. You do this using the Add Roles And Features Wizard, as explained in the next section, "DNS setup."

On primary name servers, you configure primary zones for forward lookups and as necessary for reverse lookups. The forward lookup zone will have SOA, NS, and A records for the server you are working with. This designates it as the authoritative name server for the domain. You can also create reverse lookup zones to allow for IP-address-to-host-name lookups.

On secondary name servers, you configure secondary zones to store copies of the records on the primary name server. You can create secondary zones for the forward lookup zones and for the reverse lookup zones configured on the primary.

Stub zones and forwarders are also options for these DNS servers.

DNS setup

You can install the DNS Server service by completing the following steps:

1. Start the Add Roles And Features Wizard. In Server Manager, tap or click Manage and then tap or click Add Roles And Features.

2. If the wizard displays the Before You Begin page, read the Welcome text and then tap or click Next.

3. On the Installation Type page, Role-Based Or Feature-Based Installation is selected by default. Tap or click Next.

4. On the Server Selection page, you can choose to install roles and features on running servers or virtual hard disks (VHDs). Only servers running Microsoft Windows Server 2012 R2 that have been added for management in Server Manager are listed. Either select a server from the server pool or select a server from the server pool on which to mount a VHD. If you are adding roles and features to a VHD, tap or click Browse and then use the Browse For Virtual Hard Disks dialog box to locate the VHD. When you are ready to continue, tap or click Next.

5. On the Select Server Roles page, select DNS Server. If additional features are required to install a role, you'll see an additional dialog box. Tap or click Add Features to close the dialog box, and add the required features to the server installation. When you are ready to continue, tap or click Next three times.

6. If the server on which you want to install the DNS Server role doesn't have all the required binary source files, the server gets the files through Windows Update by default or from a location specified in Group Policy. To specify an alternate path for the required source files, click the Specify An Alternate Source Path link, type that alternate path in the box provided, and then tap or click OK. For network shares, enter the UNC path to the share, such as **\\CorpServer24\WinServer2012**. For mounted Windows images, enter the WIM path prefixed with *WIM:* and including the index of the image to use, such as **WIM:\\CorpServer24\WinServer2012\install.wim:4**.

NOTE

Alternatively, you can use the DISM command to add the required binaries. To do this, enter **DISM /Online /Enable-Feature /FeatureName:DNS /All /LimitAccess /Source:E:\Sources\SxS** at an elevated, administrator prompt, where E: is the mounted ISO or DVD.

7. Tap or click Install to begin the installation process. The Installation Progress page tracks the progress of the installation. If you close the wizard, tap or click the Notifications icon in Server Manager and then tap or click the link provided to reopen the wizard.

8. When Setup finishes installing the DNS Server role, the Installation Progress page is updated to reflect this. Review the installation details to ensure that the installation was successful.

After you install the DNS Server service, DNS Manager is available. The DNS Server service should start automatically each time you reboot the server. If it doesn't start, you need to start it manually.

In Server Manager, tap or click Tools and then tap or click DNS to open DNS Manager, shown in Figure 7-5. Alternatively, you can enter **Dnsmgmt.msc** at the Everywhere prompt.

When you start DNS Manager, you are connected directly to a local DNS server but you won't see entries for remote DNS servers. You can connect to remote servers by pressing and holding or right-clicking DNS in the console tree and then selecting Connect To DNS Server. In the Connect To DNS Server dialog box, select The Following Computer, type the name or IP address of the DNS server, and then tap or click OK. In DNS Manager, host addresses are displayed as IPv4 or IPv6 addresses as appropriate.

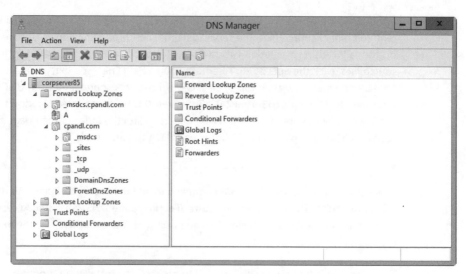

Figure 7-5 DNS Manager.

The command-line counterpart to DNS Manager is Dnscmd. The Dnscmd command-line tool accepts addresses in IPv4 and IPv6 formats. At an elevated, administrator command prompt, you can use Dnscmd to perform most of the tasks available in DNS Manager and to perform many troubleshooting tasks that are specific to Dnscmd. Unlike Netsh, Dnscmd doesn't offer internal command prompts. You can specify only the server you want to work with followed by the command and the command-line options to use for that command. Thus, the syntax is as follows:

```
dnscmd ServerName Command CommandOptions
```

Here:

- *ServerName* is the name or IP address of the DNS server you want to work with, such as CORPSVR03 or 192.168.10.15.

- *Command* is the command to use.

- *CommandOptions* are the options for the command.

   NOTE
   If you are working on the server you want to configure, you don't have to type the server name or IP address.

You also can use the DnsServer module in Windows PowerShell to manage DNS servers. To list all the cmdlets available with this module, type the following at the Windows PowerShell prompt: **Get-Command –Module DnsServer**.

After you set up a DNS server, the setup process should configure the server's TCP/IP settings so that the server attempts to resolve its own DNS queries. Setup does this by setting the server's primary DNS server address to its own address for both IPv4 and IPv6. You can confirm this by entering **ipconfig /all** at a command prompt. In the output of the command, you should see that the DNS servers are set as follows:

- ::1

- 127.0.0.1

Here, ::1 is the local loopback address for IPv6 and 127.0.0.1 is the local loopback address for IPv4. If necessary, you can modify the DNS server entries as discussed in Chapter 3, "Managing TCP/IP networking." For Preferred DNS Server, type the computer's own IP address. Set an alternate DNS server as necessary.

You also can set the preferred DNS server IP address from the command line. Type the following command:

```
netsh interface ip set dns ConnectionName static ServerIPAddress
```

Here, *ConnectionName* is the name of the local area connection and *ServerIPAddress* is the IP address of the server.

Consider the following example:

```
netsh interface ip set dns "Local Area Connection" static 192.168.1.100
```

Here, you set the preferred DNS server address for the network connection named Local Area Connection to 192.168.1.100. The Static option says that you want to use the local setting for DNS rather than the Dynamic Host Configuration Protocol (DHCP) setting when applicable.

You can confirm the new setting by typing **ipconfig /all** at the command prompt and checking for the DNS server entry. The server should have the same setting for the IP address and primary DNS server.

With Windows PowerShell, you can use Set-DNSClientServerAddress to set preferred DNS server IP addresses. The basic syntax is:

```
Set-DNSClientServerAddress –InterfaceAlias ConnectionName
–ServerAddresses ("ServerIPAddress1, ServerIPAddress2, … ServerIPAddressN")
```

Such as:

```
Set-DNSClientServerAddress -InterfaceAlias "Local Area Connection"
-ServerAddresses ("192.168.1.100, 192.168.1.101")
```

You can add the –Validate parameter to confirm that the DNS servers are responsive before the IP addresses are added to the specified interface.

Inside OUT

Dynamic port ranges for IPv4 and IPv6 with TCP and UDP

To enhance security and guard against some types of cache-poisoning attacks, the DNS Server service uses the socket pool to randomize the source port when issuing DNS queries. Randomization ensures that the server randomly picks a source point from a pool of available sockets that it opens when the DNS Server service starts. This makes it more difficult for an attacker to poison the DNS cache because the attacker would need to correctly guess the source port of a query and the query's random transaction ID. By default, the dynamic port range is 49152 to 65535. Some server applications, such as Exchange Server, might change this range. You also can modify the port range used by a server. One way to do this is to use Netsh. You configure the port range separately for TCP and UDP with regard to either IPv4 or IPv6.

The basic syntax for viewing the dynamic port range for either the IPv4 or IPv6 stack and either the TCP or UDP protocol is as follows:

```
netsh int [ipv4|ipv6] show dynamicport [tcp|udp]
```

Here, you specify that you want to work with either the IPv4 or IPv6 stack and either the TCP or UDP protocol.

When working with Netsh at an elevated command prompt, the basic syntax for changing the port range is:

```
netsh int [ipv4|ipv6] set dynamic [tcp|udp] start=StartPort num=NumPorts
```

Here, you specify that you want to work with either the IPv4 or IPv6 stack and either the TCP or UDP protocol. Then you set the start port of the range (*StartPort*) and the number of ports in the range (*NumPorts*). The minimum starting port is 1025. The maximum end port is 65535. The minimum number of ports is 255.

Configuring DNS using the wizard

From DNS Manager, you can start the Configure A DNS Server Wizard and use it to help you set up a DNS server. This wizard is useful for helping you configure small networks that work with Internet service providers (ISPs) and large networks that use forwarding.

Inside OUT

Are reverse lookups needed?

For small networks, the Configure A DNS Server Wizard creates only a forward lookup zone. For large networks, the Configure A DNS Server Wizard creates a forward lookup zone and a reverse lookup zone. This might get you to thinking about whether reverse lookup zones are needed on your network. Computers use reverse lookups to find out who is contacting them. Often this is so that they can display a host name to users rather than an IP address. So, although the Configure A DNS Server Wizard doesn't create a reverse lookup zone for small networks, you might still want to create one. If so, follow the procedure discussed in the section entitled "Creating reverse lookup zones" later in this chapter.

Configuring a small network using the Configure A DNS Server Wizard

For a small network, you can use the wizard to set up your forward lookup zone and query forwarding to your ISP or other DNS servers. You also can choose to configure this zone as a primary zone or secondary zone. If your organization maintains its own zone, you use the primary zone option. If your ISP maintains your zone, you use the secondary zone option. This gives you a read-only copy of the zone that can be used by internal clients. Because small networks don't usually need reverse lookup zones, these are not created. You can, of course, create these zones later if needed.

To configure a small network using the Configure A DNS Server Wizard, follow these steps:

1. Press and hold or right-click the server entry in DNS Manager, and select Configure A DNS Server. Then, when the wizard starts, tap or click Next.

   NOTE

   If the server you want to work with isn't shown, press and hold or right-click the DNS node in the left pane and select Connect To DNS Server. In the Connect To DNS Server dialog box, select The Following Computer, type the name or IP address of the DNS server, and then tap or click OK.

2. Choose Create A Forward Lookup Zone (Recommended For Small Networks), as shown in Figure 7-6, and then tap or click Next.

NOTE

If Active Directory is installed on the network, this zone will be automatically integrated with Active Directory. To avoid this, you can choose the second option, Create Forward And Reverse Lookup Zones (Recommended For Large Networks), and then proceed as discussed in the section entitled "Configuring a large network using the Configure A DNS Server Wizard" later in this chapter. When the wizard gets to the reverse lookup zone configuration part, you can skip this if you don't want to create a reverse lookup zone.

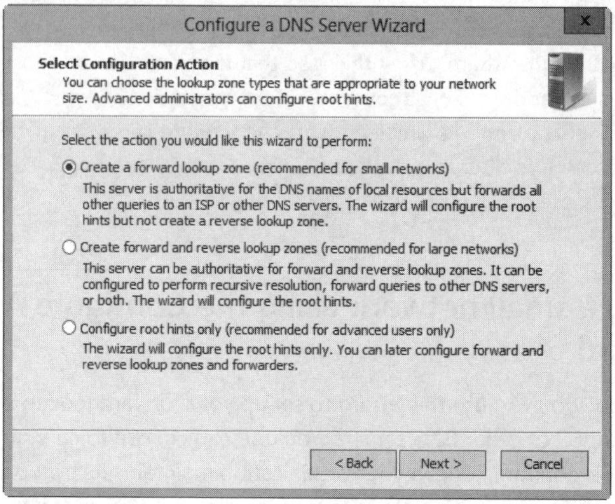

Figure 7-6 Selecting the first option to configure DNS for a small network.

3. As shown in Figure 7-7, you now can choose whether the DNS server or your ISP maintains the zone and then tap or click Next. Keep the following in mind:

- If the DNS server maintains the zone, the wizard configures a primary zone that you control. This allows you to create and manage the DNS records for the organization.

- If your ISP maintains the zone, the wizard configures a secondary zone that will get its information from your ISP. This means the staff at the ISP will need to create and manage the DNS records for the organization—and you will need to pay them to do so.

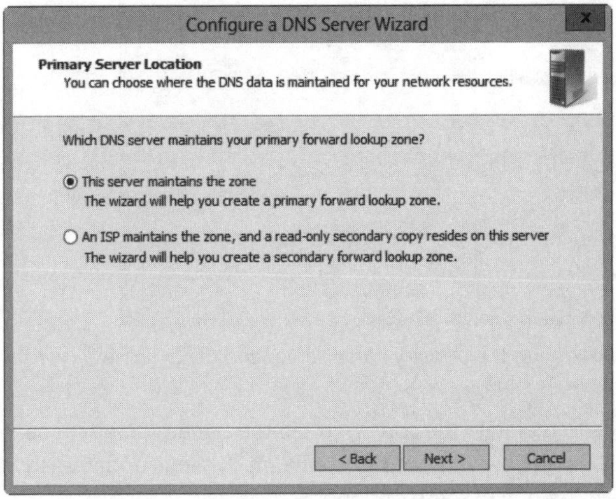

Figure 7-7 Specifying whether the server or your ISP will maintain the zone.

4. On the Zone Name page, type the full DNS name for the zone. The zone name should help determine how the zone fits into the DNS domain hierarchy. For example, if you're creating the primary server for the cpandl.com domain, you should type **cpandl.com** as the zone name. Tap or click Next.

5. If your ISP maintains the zone, you see the Master DNS Servers page, as shown in Figure 7-8. Type the IP address of the primary DNS server that's maintaining the zone for you and then press Enter. Repeat this step to specify additional name servers at your ISP. The wizard automatically validates the IP address or addresses you enter. Zone transfers will be configured to copy the zone information from these DNS servers.

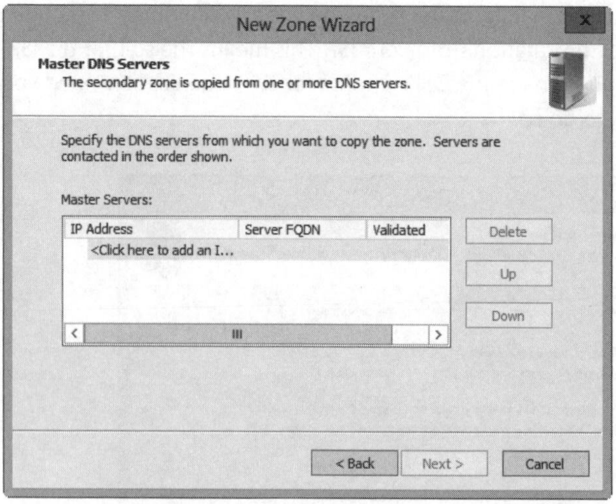

Figure 7-8 Specifying the primary name server and other name servers at the ISP.

6. If you choose to maintain the zone, you see the Dynamic Update page, as shown in Figure 7-9. Choose how you want to configure dynamic updates, and then tap or click Next. You can use one of these options:

- **Allow Only Secure Dynamic Updates.** This option is available only on domain controllers and when Active Directory is deployed. It provides for the best security possible by restricting which clients can perform dynamic updates.

- **Allow Both Nonsecure And Secure Dynamic Updates.** This option allows any client to update resource records in DNS. Although it allows both secure and nonsecure updates, it doesn't validate updates, which means dynamic updates are accepted from any client.

- **Do Not Allow Dynamic Updates.** This option disables dynamic updates in DNS. You should use this option only when the zone isn't integrated with Active Directory.

7. You can use the Forwarders page to configure the forwarding of DNS queries. If you want internal DNS servers to forward queries that they can't resolve to another server, type the IP address for that server. You can optionally include the IP address for a second forwarder, too. If you don't want to use forwarders, select No, It Should Not Forward Queries.

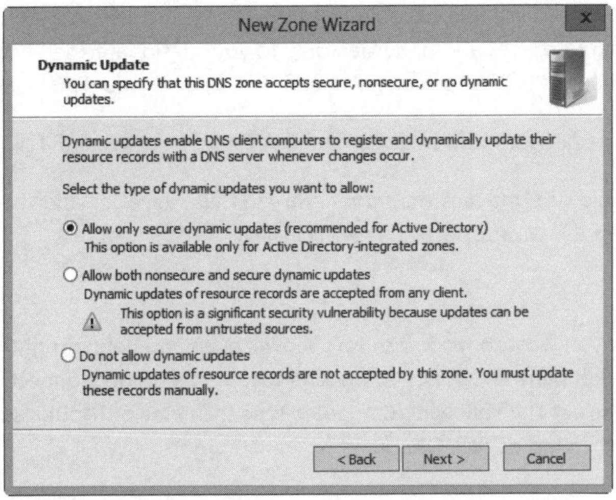

Figure 7-9 Setting the dynamic updates options.

IMPORTANT

Selecting the No, It Should Not Forward Queries option won't prevent internal name servers from forwarding queries altogether. A root hints file will still be created, which lists the root name servers on the public Internet. Thus, if you don't designate forwarders, such as the primary and secondary name servers of your ISP, the internal name servers will still forward queries. To prevent this, you must modify the root hints file as discussed in the section entitled "Security considerations" in Chapter 6.

8. When you tap or click Next, the wizard searches for and retrieves the current root hints. Tap or click Finish to complete the configuration and exit the wizard. If there's a problem configuring the root hints, you need to configure the root hints manually or copy them from another server. For more information, see the section entitled "External DNS name resolution and security" in Chapter 6. Keep in mind that a default set of root hints is included with the DNS Server service and that these root hints should be added automatically. To confirm, press and hold or right-click the server entry in DNS Manager and then select Properties. In the Properties dialog box, the currently configured root hints are shown in the Root Hints tab.

Configuring a large network using the Configure A DNS Server Wizard

For a large network, you can use the wizard to set up your forward and reverse lookup zones and to set up forwarding with or without recursion. With recursion, queries for external resources are first forwarded to your designated servers. If, however, those servers are unavailable, the DNS server forwards queries to the root name servers. Without recursion, queries for external resources are forwarded only to your designated servers. The DNS Server service can send queries to IPv4 servers, IPv4 and IPv6 servers, and IPv6-only servers.

To configure a large network using the Configure A DNS Server Wizard, follow these steps:

1. Press and hold or right-click the server entry in DNS Manager, and select Configure A Server. When the wizard starts, tap or click Next.

    NOTE

    If the server you want to work with isn't shown, press and hold or right-click the DNS node in the left pane and select Connect To DNS Server. In the Connect To DNS Server dialog box, select The Following Computer, type the name or IP address of the DNS server, and then tap or click OK.

2. Choose Create Forward And Reverse Lookup Zones (Recommended For Large Networks), as shown in Figure 7-10, and then tap or click Next.

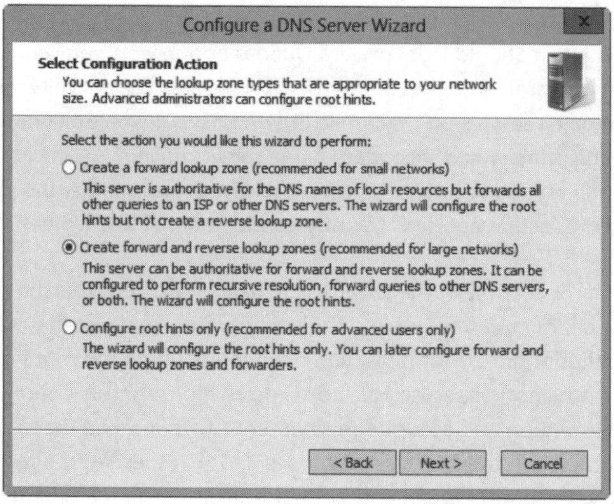

Figure 7-10 Selecting the second option to configure DNS for a large network.

3. To create a forward lookup zone, accept the default option on the Forward Lookup Zone page and then tap or click Next. Otherwise, tap or click No and skip to step 10.

4. As Figure 7-11 shows, you can now select the zone type. Choose one of the following options, and then tap or click Next:

    -   **Primary Zone.** Use this option to create a primary zone and designate this server to be authoritative for the zone. If you want to integrate DNS with Active

Directory, make sure that the Store The Zone In Active Directory check box is selected. Otherwise, clear this check box so that a standard primary zone is created.

- **Secondary Zone.** Use this option to create a secondary zone. This means the server will have a read-only copy of the zone and must use zone transfers to get updates.

- **Stub Zone.** Use this option to create a stub zone. This creates only the necessary glue records for the zone. Optionally, specify that this zone should be integrated with Active Directory. This means the zone will be stored in Active Directory and updated using Active Directory replication.

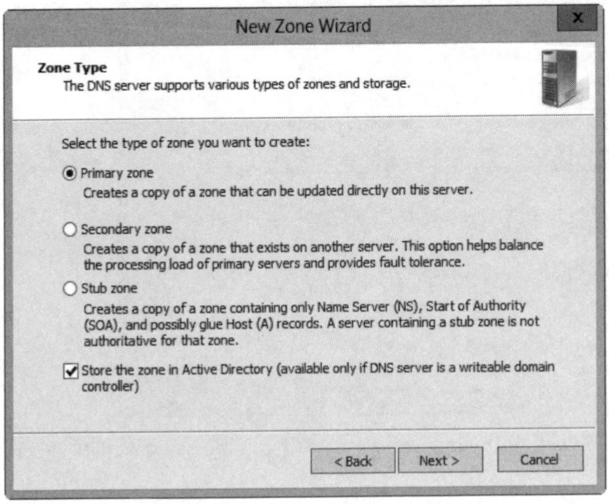

Figure 7-11 Selecting the zone type.

5. If you created an Active Directory–integrated zone, specify the replication scope and then tap or click Next. As Figure 7-12 shows, you have the following options:

- **To All DNS Servers Running On Domain Controllers In This Forest.** Enables replication of the zone information to all domains in the Active Directory forest. Each DNS server in the forest will receive a copy of the zone information and get updates through replication.

- **To All DNS Servers Running On Domain Controllers In This Domain.** Enables replication of the zone information in the current domain. Each DNS server in the domain will receive a copy of the zone information and get updates through replication.

- **To All Domain Controllers In This Domain.** Replicates zone information to all domain controllers in the Active Directory domain. All domain controllers will get a copy of the zone information and get updates through replication regardless of whether they are also running the DNS Server service.

- **To All Domain Controllers Specified In The Scope Of This Directory Partition.** If you configured application partitions other than the default partitions, you can limit the scope of replication to a designated application partition. Any domain controllers configured with the application partition will get a copy of the zone information and get updates through replication regardless of whether they are also running the DNS Server service.

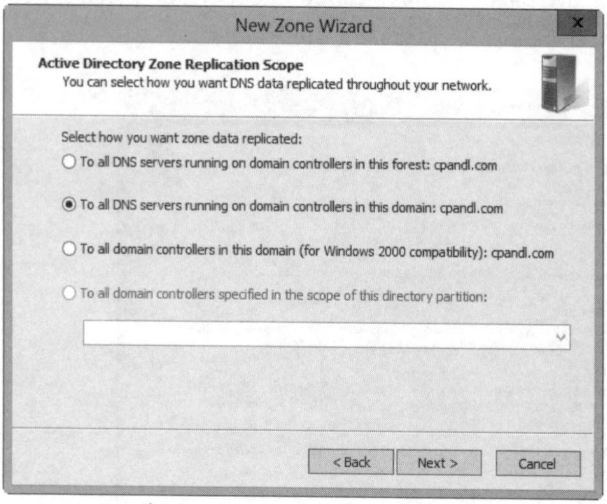

Figure 7-12 Selecting the replication scope if you are using Active Directory integration.

6. On the Zone Name page, type the full DNS name for the zone. The zone name should help determine how the zone fits into the DNS domain hierarchy. For example, if you're creating the primary server for the cpandl.com domain, you should type **cpandl.com** as the zone name. Tap or click Next.

7. If you're creating a standard primary zone, you see the Zone File page. This page allows you to create a new zone file or use an existing zone file. In most cases you'll just accept the default name and allow the wizard to create the file for you in the %SystemRoot%\System32\Dns folder. If you are migrating from a BIND DNS server or have a preexisting zone file, you can select Use This Existing File and then type the name of the file that you copied to the %SystemRoot%\System32\Dns folder. When you are ready to continue, tap or click Next.

8. If you're creating a secondary zone, you see the Master DNS Servers page. Type the IP address of the primary DNS server that's maintaining the zone, and then tap or

click Add. Repeat this step to specify additional name servers. Zone transfers will be configured to copy the zone information from these DNS servers.

9. On the Dynamic Update page, choose how you want to configure dynamic updates and then tap or click Next. You can use one of the following options:

   - **Allow Only Secure Dynamic Updates.** This option is available only on domain controllers and when Active Directory is deployed. It provides for the best security possible by restricting which clients can perform dynamic updates.

   - **Allow Both Nonsecure And Secure Dynamic Updates.** This option allows any client to update resource records in DNS. Although it allows both secure and nonsecure updates, it doesn't validate updates, which means dynamic updates are accepted from any client.

   - **Do Not Allow Dynamic Updates.** This option disables dynamic updates in DNS. You should use this option only when the zone isn't integrated with Active Directory.

10. To create a reverse lookup zone, accept the default option on the Reverse Lookup Zone page and then tap or click Next. Otherwise, tap or click No, and skip to step 16.

11. On the Zone Type page, you can select the zone type. The options available are the same as when creating a forward lookup zone. After making a selection, tap or click Next.

12. If you created an Active Directory–integrated zone, specify the replication scope and then tap or click Next.

13. Specify whether you are creating an IPv4 reverse lookup zone or an IPv6 reverse lookup zone, and then tap or click Next. Do one of the following:

    - If you are configuring a reverse lookup zone for IPv4, type the network ID for the reverse lookup zone, as shown in Figure 7-13, and then tap or click Next. The values you enter set the default name for the reverse lookup zone. If you have multiple subnets on the same network—such as 192.168.1, 192.168.2, and 192.168.3—you should enter only the network portion for the zone name, such as **192.168**, rather than the complete network ID. The DNS Server service will then fill in the necessary subnet zones as you use IP addresses on a particular subnet.

    - If you are configuring a reverse lookup zone for IPv6, type the network prefix for the reverse lookup zone and then tap or click Next. The values you enter are used to automatically generate the related zone names. Depending on the prefix you enter, up to eight zones might be created.

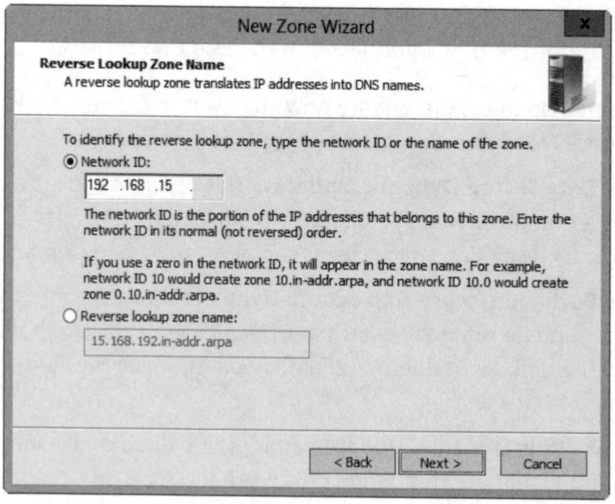

Figure 7-13 Setting the network ID for the reverse lookup zone.

14. If you're creating a standard secondary zone, you see the Zone File page. This page allows you to create a new zone file or use an existing zone file.

15. On the Dynamic Update page, choose how you want to configure dynamic updates and then tap or click Next.

16. You can use the Forwarders page to configure forwarding of DNS queries. If you want internal DNS servers to forward queries that they can't resolve to another server, type the IP address of that server. You can optionally include the IP address for a second forwarder. If you don't want to use forwarders, select No, It Should Not Forward Queries.

IMPORTANT

Selecting the No, It Should Not Forward Queries option won't prevent internal name servers from forwarding queries altogether. A root hints file will still be created, which lists the root name servers on the public Internet. Thus, if you don't designate forwarders, such as the primary and secondary name servers of your ISP, the internal name servers will still forward queries. To prevent this, you must modify the root hints file as discussed in the section entitled "Security considerations" in Chapter 6.

17. When you tap or click Next, the wizard searches for and retrieves the current root hints. Tap or click Finish to complete the configuration and exit the wizard. If there is a problem configuring the root hints, you need to configure the root hints manually or copy them from another server. For more information, see the section entitled "External

DNS name resolution and security" in Chapter 6. Keep in mind that a default set of root hints is included with the DNS Server service and that these root hints should be added automatically. To confirm, press and hold or right-click the server entry in DNS Manager and then select Properties. In the Properties dialog box, the currently configured root hints are shown in the Root Hints tab.

Configuring DNS zones, subdomains, forwarders, and zone transfers

Windows Server 2012 R2 supports primary, secondary, Active Directory–integrated, and stub zones, each of which can be created to support either forward lookups or reverse lookups. Forward lookup queries allow a client to resolve a host name to an IP address. Reverse lookups allow a client to resolve an IP address to a host name. At times you also might need to configure subdomains, forwarders, and zone transfers. All of these topics are discussed in this section.

Creating forward lookup zones

To create the initial forward lookup zone or additional forward lookup zones on a server, follow these steps:

1. In DNS Manager, expand the node for the server you want to work with. Press and hold or right-click the Forward Lookup Zones entry, and then choose New Zone. Afterward, in the New Zone Wizard, tap or click Next.

2. Select the zone type. Choose one of the following options, and then tap or click Next:

   - **Primary Zone.** Use this option to create a primary zone and designate this server to be authoritative for the zone. If you want to integrate DNS with Active Directory, make sure that the Store The Zone In Active Directory check box is selected. Otherwise, clear this check box so that a standard primary zone is created.

   - **Secondary Zone.** Use this option to create a secondary zone. This means the server will have a read-only copy of the zone and will need to use zone transfers to get updates.

   - **Stub Zone.** Use this option to create a stub zone. This creates only the necessary glue records for the zone. Optionally, specify that this zone should be integrated with Active Directory. This means the zone will be stored in Active Directory and updated using Active Directory replication.

3. If you created an Active Directory–integrated zone, specify the replication scope and then tap or click Next. You have the following options:

    - **To All DNS Servers In This Forest.** Enables replication of the zone information to all domains in the Active Directory forest. Each DNS server in the forest will receive a copy of the zone information and get updates through replication.

    - **To All DNS Servers In This Domain.** Enables replication of the zone information in the current domain. Each DNS server in the domain will receive a copy of the zone information and get updates through replication.

    - **To All Domain Controllers In This Domain.** Replicates zone information to all domain controllers in the Active Directory domain. All domain controllers will get a copy of the zone information and get updates through replication regardless of whether they are also running the DNS Server service.

    - **To All Domain Controllers Specified In The Scope Of This Directory Partition.** If you configured application partitions, you can limit the scope of replication to a designated application partition. Any domain controllers configured with the application partition will get a copy of the zone information and get updates through replication regardless of whether they are also running the DNS Server service.

4. On the Zone Name page, type the full DNS name for the zone. The zone name should help determine how the zone fits into the DNS domain hierarchy. For example, if you're creating the primary server for the cpandl.com domain, you should type cpandl.com as the zone name. Tap or click Next.

5. If you're creating a standard primary zone, you see the Zone File page. This page allows you to create a new zone file or use an existing zone file. In most cases, you'll just accept the default name and allow the wizard to create the file for you in the %SystemRoot%\System32\Dns folder. If you are migrating from a BIND DNS server or have a preexisting zone file, you can select Use This Existing File and then type the name of the file that you copied to the %SystemRoot%\System32\Dns folder. When you are ready to continue, tap or click Next.

6. If you're creating a secondary zone, you see the Master DNS Servers page. Type the IP address of the primary DNS server that's maintaining the zone, and then tap or click Add. Repeat this step to specify additional name servers. Zone transfers will be configured to copy the zone information from these DNS servers.

7. On the Dynamic Update page, choose how you want to configure dynamic updates, and then tap or click Next. You can use one of these options:

   - **Allow Only Secure Dynamic Updates.** This option is available only on domain controllers and when Active Directory is deployed. It provides for the best security possible by restricting which clients can perform dynamic updates.

   - **Allow Both Nonsecure And Secure Dynamic Updates.** This option allows any client to update resource records in DNS. Although it allows both secure and nonsecure updates, it doesn't validate updates, which means dynamic updates are accepted from any client.

   - **Do Not Allow Dynamic Updates.** This option disables dynamic updates in DNS. You should use this option only when the zone isn't integrated with Active Directory.

8. Tap or click Next, and then tap or click Finish to complete the configuration and exit the wizard.

Creating reverse lookup zones

To create the initial reverse lookup zone or additional reverse lookup zones on a server, follow these steps:

1. In DNS Manager, expand the node for the server you want to work with. Press and hold or right-click the Reverse Lookup Zones entry and choose New Zone. Afterward, in the New Zone Wizard, tap or click Next.

2. On the Zone Type page, you can select the zone type. The options available are the same as for forward lookup zones. After making a selection, tap or click Next.

3. If you created an Active Directory–integrated zone, specify the replication scope and then tap or click Next.

4. Specify whether you are creating an IPv4 reverse lookup zone or an IPv6 reverse lookup zone and then tap or click Next. Do one of the following:

   - If you are configuring a reverse lookup zone for IPv4, type the network ID for the reverse lookup zone and then tap or click Next. The values you enter set the default name for the reverse lookup zone. If you have multiple subnets on the same network—such as 192.168.1, 192.168.2, and 192.168.3—you should enter only the network portion for the zone name, such as **192.168**, rather than the complete network ID. The DNS Server service will then fill in the necessary subnet zones as you use IP addresses on a particular subnet.

- If you are configuring a reverse lookup zone for IPv6, type the network prefix for the reverse lookup zone and then tap or click Next. The values you enter are used to automatically generate the related zone names. Depending on the prefix you enter, up to eight zones might be created.

5. If you're creating a standard secondary zone, you see the Zone File page. This page allows you to create a new zone file or use an existing zone file.

6. On the Dynamic Update page, choose how you want to configure dynamic updates, and then tap or click Next.

7. Tap or click Next, and then tap or click Finish to complete the configuration and exit the wizard.

Configuring forwarders and conditional forwarding

In a normal configuration, if a DNS name server can't resolve a request, it forwards the request for resolution. A server to which DNS queries are forwarded is referred to as a *forwarder*. You can specifically designate forwarders that your internal DNS servers should use. For example, if you designate your ISP's primary and secondary name servers as forwarders, queries that your internal name servers can't resolve will be forwarded to those servers. Forwarding can still take place, however, even if you don't specifically designate forwarders. The reason for this is that the root hints file specifies the root name servers for the public Internet, and these servers can be used as forwarders.

Any time forwarders are not specified or available, requests can be forwarded to the root name servers. The root name servers then forward the requests to the appropriate top-level domain name server, which forwards them to the next level domain server, and so on. This process is referred to as *recursion*, and, as you can see, this involves a number of forwarding actions. DNS servers can send recursive queries to IPv4 servers, IPv4 and IPv6 servers, and IPv6-only servers.

Another forwarding option is to configure what is called a *conditional forwarder*. When using conditional forwarding, you can tell your DNS name servers that if they see a request for domain XYZ, they should not forward it to the public DNS name servers for resolution. Instead, the name servers should forward the request directly to the authoritative name server for the XYZ domain.

You can configure forwarding options by following these steps:

1. In DNS Manager, press and hold or right-click the server you want to work with and select Properties. In the Properties dialog box, tap or click the Forwarders tab, as shown in Figure 7-14.

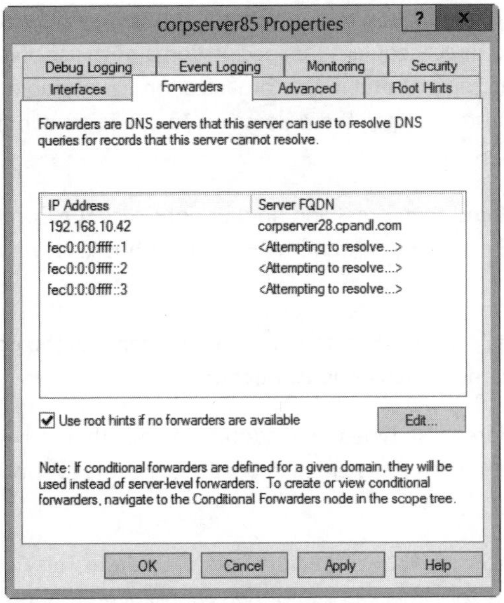

Figure 7-14 The Forwarders tab.

2. To allow forwarding to root name servers when configured forwarders are not available, select the Use Root Hints If No Forwarders Are Available check box.

3. Display the Edit Forwarders dialog box by tapping or clicking Edit. To forward queries that internal servers can't resolve to another server, type the IP address or DNS name for the other server and then press Enter. Repeat this process to add other forwarders. You can organize the forwarders in priority order by selecting each in turn and tapping or clicking the Up or Down buttons as appropriate.

4. Use Number Of Seconds Before Forward Queries Time Out to set the query timeout in seconds. By default, a DNS server will continue to attempt to contact and use a listed forwarder for three seconds. When the timeout expires, the server moves to the next forwarder on the list and does the same. When there are no additional forwarders, the server uses the root hints to locate a root server to which the query can be forwarded.

5. Tap or click OK to close the Edit Forwarders dialog box.

6. In the Properties dialog box, tap or click the Advanced tab. Ensure that the Disable Recursion check box is cleared, and then tap or click OK to close the Properties dialog box.

If you have multiple internal domains, you might want to consider configuring conditional forwarding. This allows you to direct requests for specific domains to specific DNS servers for resolution. Conditional forwarding is useful if your organization has multiple internal domains and you need to resolve requests between these domains. To configure conditional forwarding, follow these steps:

1. In DNS Manager, select and then press and hold or right-click the Conditional Forwarders folder for the server you want to work with. Choose New Conditional Forwarder from the shortcut menu.

2. In the New Conditional Forwarder dialog box, enter the name of the domain to which queries should be forwarded, such as **adatum.com**.

3. Tap or click in the IP address list, type the IP address of an authoritative DNS server in the specified domain, and then press Enter. Repeat this process to specify additional IP addresses.

4. If you're integrating DNS with Active Directory, select the Store This Conditional Forwarder In Active Directory check box and then choose a replication strategy:

    - **All DNS Servers In This Forest.** Choose this strategy if you want the widest replication strategy. Remember, the Active Directory forest includes all domain trees that share the directory data with the current domain.

    - **All DNS Servers In This Domain.** Choose this strategy if you want to replicate forwarder information within the current domain and child domains of the current domain.

    - **All Domain Controllers In This Domain.** Choose this strategy if you want to replicate forwarder information to all domain controllers within the current domain and child domains of the current domain. Although this strategy gives wider replication for forwarder information within the domain, not every domain controller is a DNS server (and you don't need to configure every domain controller as a DNS server either).

5. Set the Number Of Seconds Before Forward Queries Time Out value. This value controls how long the server tries to query the forwarder if it gets no response. When the Number Of Seconds Before Forward Queries Time Out interval passes, the server tries the next authoritative server on the list. The default is five seconds. Tap or click OK.

6. Repeat this procedure to configure conditional forwarding for other domains.

You can disable recursion and forwarders using DNS Manager. In DNS Manager, press and hold or right-click the server you want to work with and select Properties. In the Properties dialog box, tap or click the Advanced tab. Disable recursion and forwarders by selecting the Disable Recursion check box and tapping or clicking OK.

Configuring subdomains and delegating authority

Your organization's domain structure is separate from its zone configuration. If you create sub-domains of a parent domain, you can add these subdomains to the parent domain's zone or create separate zones for the subdomains. When you create separate zones, you must tell DNS about the other servers that have authority over a particular subdomain. You do this by telling the primary name server for the parent domain that you delegated authority for a subdomain.

When you add subdomains of a parent domain to the same zone as the parent domain, you have a single large namespace hosted by primary servers. This gives you a single unit to man-age, which is good when you want centralized control over DNS in the domain. The disad-vantage is that as the number of subdomains in the zone grows, there's more and more to manage and at some point you might want to partition the management of the DNS system—especially if dynamic updates are allowed and there are thousands of host records.

When you create a separate zone for a subdomain, you have an additional unit of manage-ment that you can place on the same DNS server or on a different DNS server. This means that you can delegate control over the zone to someone else, which would allow branch offices or other departments within the organization to manage their own DNS services. If the zone is on another DNS server, you shift the load associated with that zone to another server. The dis-advantage is that you lose centralized control over DNS.

> NOTE
> It isn't possible to combine domains from different branches of the namespace and place them in a single zone. As a result, domains that are part of the same Active Directory forest but on different trees must be in separate zones. For example, you would need separate zones for cohowinery.com and cohovineyards.com.

To create subdomains in separate zones on the same server as the parent domain, complete the following steps:

1. Create the necessary forward and reverse lookup zones for the subdomains as described earlier in this chapter in the sections entitled "Creating forward lookup zones" and "Creating reverse lookup zones."

2. You don't need to delegate authority because these subdomains are on the primary name server for the parent domain. This server automatically has control over the zones.

To create subdomains in separate zones and on separate servers, complete the following steps:

1. Install a DNS server in each subdomain, and then create the necessary forward and reverse lookup zones for the subdomains as described earlier in this chapter in the sections entitled "Creating forward lookup zones" and "Creating reverse lookup zones."

2. On the primary DNS server for the parent domain, you must delegate authority to each subdomain. In DNS Manager, expand the node for the server on which the parent domain is located and then expand the related Forward Lookup Zones folder.

3. Press and hold or right-click the parent domain entry and then select New Delegation. This starts the New Delegation Wizard. Tap or click Next.

4. As shown in Figure 7-15, type the name of the subdomain, such as **services**. Check the fully qualified domain name (FQDN) to ensure that it's correct and then tap or click Next.

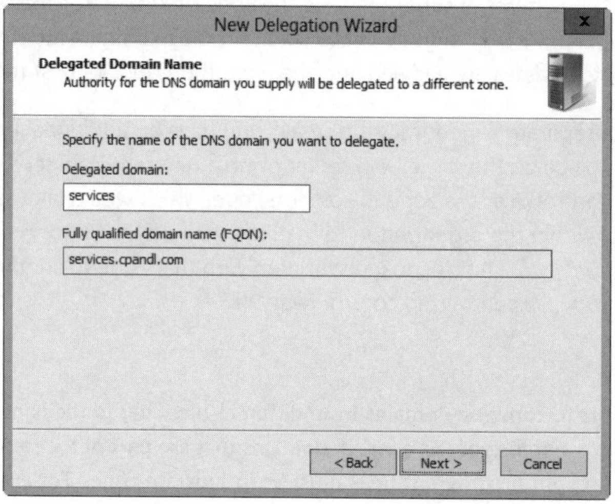

Figure 7-15 Specifying the subdomain name.

5. On the Name Servers page, tap or click Add. As shown in Figure 7-16, the New Name Server Record dialog box is displayed.

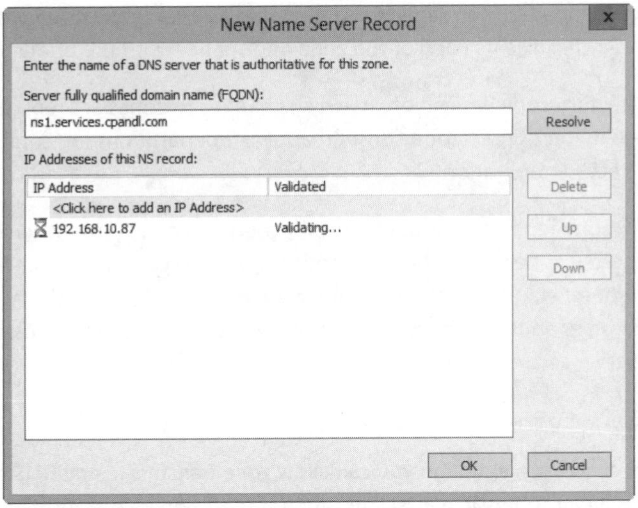

Figure 7-16 Specifying the server name and IP address.

6. In the Server Fully Qualified Domain Name (FQDN) box, type the fully qualified host name of a DNS server for the subdomain, such as **ns1.services.cpandl.com**, and then tap or click Resolve. The wizard then validates the name server and fills in its IP address. You can add IP addresses for the name server by tapping or clicking in the IP Address list, typing the IP address, and pressing Enter.

NOTE

You must specify the server name and at least one IP address. The order of the entries determines which IP address is used first. You can change the order as necessary by using the Up and Down buttons.

7. Tap or click OK to close the New Name Server Record dialog box. Repeat steps 5 and 6 to specify other authoritative DNS servers for the subdomain.

8. Tap or click Next, and then tap or click Finish.

Configuring zone transfers

Zone transfers are used to send a read-only copy of zone information to secondary DNS servers, which can be located in the same domain or in other domains. Windows Server supports three zone transfer methods:

- Standard zone transfers, in which a secondary server requests a full copy of a zone from a primary server

- Incremental zone transfers, in which a secondary server requests only the changes that it needs to synchronize its copy of the zone information with the primary server's copy

- Active Directory zone replication, in which changes to zones are replicated to all domain controllers in the domain (or a subset if application partitions are configured) using Active Directory replication

Active Directory zone replication is automatically used and configured when you use Active Directory–integrated zones. If you have secondary name servers, these name servers can't automatically request standard or incremental zone transfers. To allow this, you must first enable zone transfers on the primary name server. Zone transfers are disabled by default to enhance DNS server security.

SECURITY ALERT

Speaking of security, although you can allow zone transfers to any DNS server, this opens the server to possible attack. It is better to designate specific name servers that are permitted to request zone transfers.

Zone transfers can be enabled for domains and subdomains in forward lookup zones and for subnets in reverse lookup zones. You enable zone transfers on primary name servers. If a server is a secondary name server, it is already configured to perform zone transfers with the primary name server in the zone.

Inside OUT

Incremental zone transfers

To manage incremental zone transfers, DNS servers track changes that have been made to a zone between each increment of a zone's serial number. Secondary servers use the zone's serial number to determine whether changes have been made to the zone. If the serial number matches what the secondary server has for the zone, no changes have been made and an incremental transfer isn't necessary. If the serial number doesn't match, the secondary server's copy of the zone isn't current and the secondary server then requests only the changes that have occurred since the last time the secondary zone was updated.

Using DNS Manager, you can enable zone transfers on a primary name server and restrict the secondary name servers that can request zone transfers. In DNS Manager, expand the node for the primary name server and then expand the related Forward Lookup Zones or Reverse Lookup Zones folder as appropriate. Press and hold or right-click the domain or subnet you want to configure and then choose Properties. In the Properties dialog box, tap or click the Zone Transfers tab, as shown in Figure 7-17.

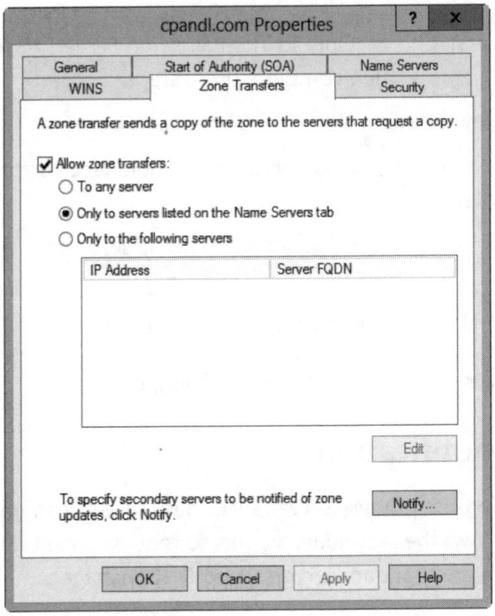

Figure 7-17 Configuring zone transfers for a domain or subnet.

Select the Allow Zone Transfers check box. You have three zone transfer options:

- **To Any Server.** Choose To Any Server to allow any DNS server to request zone transfers.

- **Only To Servers Listed On The Name Servers Tab.** Choose Only To Servers Listed On The Name Servers Tab to restrict transfers to name servers listed in the Name Servers tab, and then tap or click the Name Servers tab. Then complete the following steps:

    1. The Name Servers list shows the DNS servers currently configured to be authoritative for the zone and includes DNS servers that host secondary zones. If a secondary server isn't listed and you want to authorize the server to request zone transfers, tap or click Add. This displays the New Name Server Record dialog box.

        a. In the Server Fully Qualified Domain Name (FQDN) field, type the fully qualified host name of a secondary server for the domain and then tap or click Resolve. The wizard then validates the name server and fills in its IP address. You can add IP addresses for the name server by tapping or clicking in the IP Address list, typing the IP address, and pressing Enter.

    b.   Tap or click OK to close the New Name Server Record dialog box. Repeat this process to specify other secondary DNS servers for the domain or subnet.

- **Only To The Following Servers.** Choose Only To The Following Servers to restrict transfers to a list of approved servers. Then complete these steps:

    1.   Tap or click Edit to display the Allow Zone Transfers dialog box.

        a.   Type the IP address of a secondary server that should receive zone transfers and then press Enter.

        b.   Repeat this process to specify other secondary DNS servers for the domain or subnet.

        c.   Tap or click OK to close the Allow Zone Transfers dialog box.

When you are finished, tap or click OK to close the Properties dialog box.

Configuring secondary notification

When changes are made to a zone on the primary server, secondary servers can be automatically notified of the changes. This allows the secondary servers to request zone transfers. You can configure automatic notification of secondary servers using DNS Manager.

In DNS Manager, expand the node for the primary name server and then expand the related Forward Lookup Zones or Reverse Lookup Zones folder as appropriate. Press and hold or right-click the domain or subnet you want to configure and then choose Properties. In the Properties dialog box, tap or click the Zone Transfers tab. Tap or click Notify in the lower-right corner of the Zone Transfers tab. This displays the Notify dialog box, as shown in Figure 7-18.

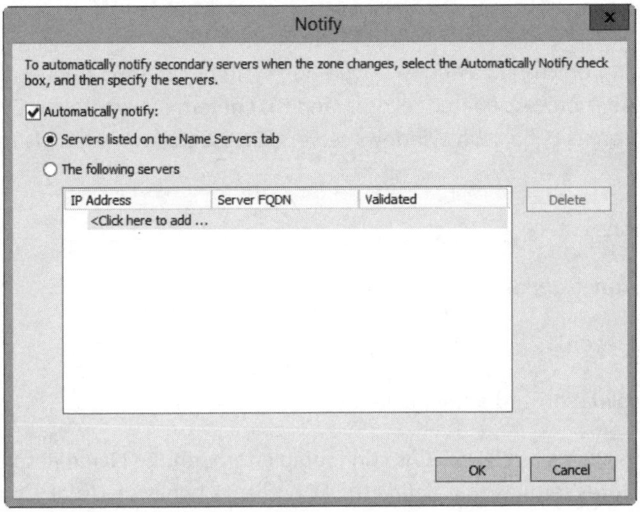

Figure 7-18 Configuring secondary notification.

Select the Automatically Notify check box. You have two notification options:

- **Servers Listed On The Name Servers Tab.** Choose this option to notify only the name servers listed in the Name Servers tab.

- **The Following Servers.** Choose this option to specify the name servers that should be notified. Then complete these steps:

  1. Type the IP address of a secondary server that should receive notification and then press Enter.

     a. Repeat this process to notify other secondary DNS servers for the domain or subnet.

     b. When you are finished, tap or click OK twice.

Deploying DNSSEC

You sign zones using DNS Security Extensions (DNSSEC). DNSSEC is supported by Windows 7 or later and by Windows Server 2008 R2 or later, and is defined in several Request For Comments (RFCs), including RFCs 4033, 4034, and 4035. These RFCs add origin authority, data integrity, and authenticated denial of existence to DNS.

DNSSEC essentials

The DNS clients running on current Windows operating systems can send queries that indicate support for DNSSEC, that process related records, and that determine whether a DNS server has validated records on its behalf. On Windows servers, DNSSEC allows your DNS servers to do the following:

- Securely sign zones

- Host DNSSEC-signed zones

- Process related records

- Perform both validation and authentication

The way in which DNS clients use DNSSEC is configurable through the Name Resolution Policy Table (NRPT), which stores settings that define the DNS client's behavior. Usually, you manage the NRPT through Group Policy. When a DNS server hosting a signed zone receives a query, the server returns the digital signatures in addition to the requested records. A resolver or another server configured with a trust anchor for a signed zone or for a parent of a signed zone can obtain the public key of the public/private key pair and validate that the responses are authentic and have not been tampered with.

Before you deploy DNSSEC, you need to identify the DNS zones that you want to secure with digital signatures. Zones signed with DNSSEC have several additional resource records. These include the following:

- DNSKEY (Domain Name System Key)

- RRSIG (Resource Record Signature)

- NSEC (NextSECure)

- DS (Domain Services)

When you install DNS Server service on Windows Server 2012 R2, support for DNSSEC is enabled by default. In DNS Manager you can confirm whether DNSSEC support is enabled or disabled by pressing and holding or right-clicking the server entry and then selecting Properties. In the Properties dialog box, click the Advanced tab. If you want to use DNSSEC, the Enable DNSSEC Validation For Remote Responses setting should be enabled.

DNS Server for Windows Server 2012 R2 has several significant enhancements for DNSSEC. Windows Server 2012 R2 supports secure dynamic updates in Active Directory–integrated zones. Previously, if an Active Directory domain zone was signed, you needed to manually update all SRV records and other resource records. This is no longer required because DNS Server now does this automatically.

Windows Server 2012 R2 also supports online signing, automated key management, and automated trust anchor distribution. Previously, you needed to configure and manage signings, keys, and trust anchors. This is no longer required because DNS Server now does this automatically.

Finally, Windows Server 2012 R2 supports validations of records signed with updated DNSSEC standards (NSEC3 and RSA/SHA-2 standards). Previously, you couldn't sign records with NSEC3 and RSA/SHA-2.

Securing zones with digital signatures

To secure DNS zones with digital signatures, you need to designate a key master. Any authoritative server that hosts a primary copy of a zone can act as the key master. Next, you need to generate a key signing key (KSK) and a zone signing key (ZSK). A KSK that is an authentication key has a private key and a public key associated with it. The private key is used for signing all of the DNSKEY records at the root of the zone. The public key is used as a trust anchor for validating DNS responses. A ZSK is used for signing zone records.

After you generate keys, you create resource records for authenticated denial of existence using either the more secure NSEC3 standard or the less secure NSEC standard. Because trust anchors are used to validate DNS responses, you also need to specify how trust anchors are updated and distributed. Typically, you'll want to automatically update and distribute trust anchors. By default, records are signed with SHA-1 and SHA-256 encryption. You can select other encryption algorithms, too.

You don't need to go through the configuration process each time you sign a zone. The signing keys and other signing parameters are available for reuse. Additionally, keep the following in mind:

- For file-backed zones, the primary server and all secondary servers hosting the zone must be a Windows Server 2008 R2 or later DNS server or a DNSSEC-aware server that is running an operating system other than Windows.

- For Active Directory–integrated zones, every domain controller that is a DNS server in the domain must be running Windows Server 2008 R2 or later if the signed zone is set to replicate to all DNS servers in the domain. Every domain controller that is a DNS server in the forest must be running Windows Server 2008 R2 or later if the signed zone is set to replicate to all DNS servers in the forest.

- For mixed environments, all servers that are authoritative for a DNSSEC-signed zone must be DNSSEC-aware servers. DNSSEC-aware Windows clients that request DNSSEC data and validation must be configured to issue DNS queries to a DNSSEC-aware server. Non-DNSSEC-aware Windows clients can be configured to issue DNS queries to DNSSEC-aware servers. DNSSEC-aware servers can be configured to recursively send queries to a non-DNSSEC-aware DNS server.

Signing a zone

In DNS Manager, press and hold or right-click the zone you want to secure. From the shortcut menu, choose DNSSEC and then select Sign The Zone. This starts the Zone Signing Wizard. If the wizard displays a welcome page, read the Welcome text and then tap or click Next. On the Signing Options page, choose how to sign the zone. Here, you can do the following:

- Use the default settings

- Use settings of an existing signed zone

- Use custom settings

If you want to use the default signing settings, choose Use Default Settings To Sign The Zone as the signing option. (See Figure 7-19.) When you use the default settings, the wizard sets the options for the KSK, ZSK, trusted anchors, polling, and authenticated denial of existence. KSK and ZSK rollover will be enabled, and trust anchors will update automatically on key rollover in accordance with RFC 5011. Click Next twice and then click Finish.

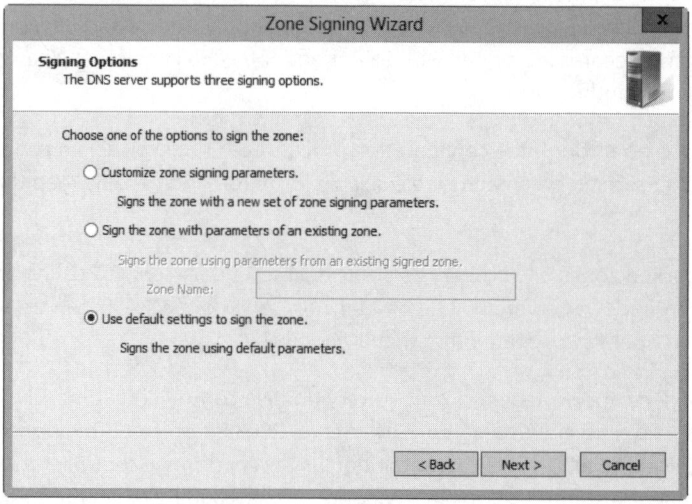

Figure 7-19 Using the default signing options to configure signing automatically.

If you signed other zones previously, you can use the settings of one of the signed zones. To do this, choose Sign The Zone With Parameters Of An Existing Zone as the signing option and then type the name of the zone. (See Figure 7-20.) When you tap or click Next, you can elect to use the same key master as the existing zone or you can select another primary server as the key master. When you are ready to continue, tap or click Next twice and then click Finish.

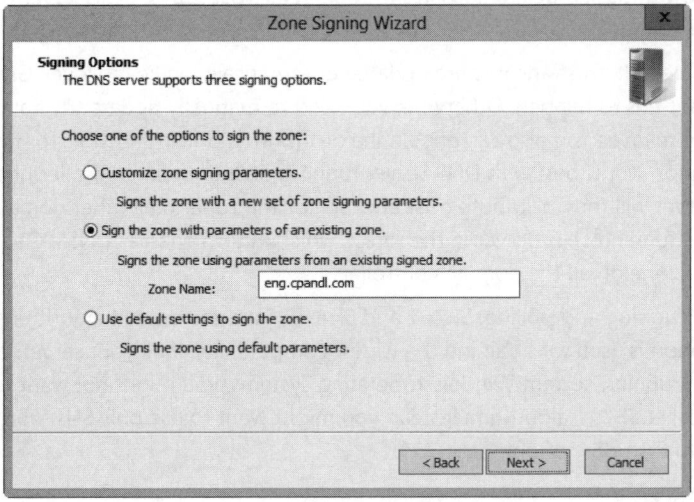

Figure 7-20 Using the settings of another signed zone to quickly set up a new zone.

If you want to use custom settings, sign the zone by completing the following steps:

1. Select Customize Zone Signing Parameters as the signing option and then tap or click Next.

2. Select a key master for the zone. Any authoritative server that hosts a primary copy of a zone can act as the key master. When you are ready to continue, tap or click Next until you see the Key Signing Key page that allows you to configure a KSK.

3. Configure a KSK by tapping or clicking Add, accepting or changing the default values for key properties and the key rollover frequency, and then tapping or clicking OK. When you are ready to continue, tap or click Next until you see the Zone Signing Key page that allows you to configure a ZSK.

4. Configure a ZSK by tapping or clicking Add, accepting or changing the default values for key properties and the key rollover frequency, and then tapping or clicking OK.

5. When you are ready, continue through the remaining pages, which allow you to configure the secure resource records, trust anchors, signing, and polling parameters. Keep the following in mind:

   - Typically, you'll want to use the more current NSEC3 resource record rather than the older NSEC resource record for authenticated denial of existence. If you allow unsigned delegations in the zone, select Use Opt-Out To Cover Unsigned Delegations.

   - By default, trust anchors are updated automatically on key rollover. Generally, you want this to happen. Otherwise, you need to manually update trust anchors on key rollover. You also can enable the distribution of trust anchors for the zone. This option works best with DNS Server running on a domain controller because DNS Server will then distribute trust anchors for the zone to all other domain controllers running DNS Server in the forest, which in turn enables DNSSEC validation for the zone on all the domain controllers.

   - For signing and polling, SHA-1 and SHA-256 are the default algorithms used. This option is used for attaining the widest compatibility. If all your servers and clients are running current Windows operating systems, you might not want to use the weaker SHA-1 algorithm; instead you might want to use only SHA-256, SHA-256 with SHA-384, or only SHA-384.

6. Tap or click Next twice. After the wizard signs the zone, click Finish.

After you sign a zone, you can manage the signing properties by pressing and holding or right-clicking the zone, selecting DNSSEC, and then selecting Properties. To remove zone signing, press and hold or right-click a signed zone, select DNSSEC, and then select Unsign The Zone. In the Unsign Zone Wizard, tap or click Next and then tap or click Finish.

Adding resource records

When you create a zone in Windows Server, several records are created automatically:

- For a forward lookup zone, these records include an SOA record, an NS record, and an A record. The SOA record contains information about how resource records in the zone should be used and cached. The NS record contains the name of the authoritative name server, which is the server on which the zone was configured. The A record is the Host Address record for the name server.

- For a reverse lookup zone, these records include an SOA record, an NS record, and a PTR record. The SOA record contains information about how resource records in the zone should be used and cached. The NS record contains the name of the authoritative name server, which is the server on which the zone was configured. The PTR record is the Pointer record for the name server that allows reverse lookups on the server's IP address.

- When you use Active Directory, SRV records are also automatically created for domain controllers, global catalog servers, and PDC emulators.

- When you allow dynamic updates, A, AAAA, and PTR records for clients are automatically created for any computer using DHCP.

Any other records that you need must be created manually. The technique you use to create additional records depends on the type of record.

Create and change records on primary servers

When you create records or make changes to records, you should do so on a primary server. For Active Directory–integrated zones, this means any domain controller running the DNS Server service. For standard zones, this means the primary name server only. After you make changes to standard zones, press and hold or right-click the server entry in DNS Manager and select Update Server Data Files. This increments the serial number for zones as necessary to ensure that secondary name servers know that changes have been made. You do not need to do this for Active Directory–integrated zones because Active Directory replicates changes automatically.

Host Address (A and AAAA) and Pointer (PTR) records

Host Address (A) records contain the name of a host and its IPv4 address. Host Address (AAAA) records contain the name of a host and its IPv6 address. Any computer that has multiple network interfaces or IP addresses should have multiple address records. Pointer (PTR) records enable reverse lookups by creating a pointer that maps an IP address to a host name.

You do not need to create A, AAAA, and PTR records for hosts that use dynamic DNS. These records are created automatically. For hosts that don't use dynamic DNS, you can create a new host entry with A and PTR records by completing the following steps:

1. In DNS Manager, expand the node for the primary name server and then expand the related Forward Lookup Zones folder. Press and hold or right-click the domain to which you want to add the records and then choose New Host (A or AAAA). This displays the dialog box shown in Figure 7-21.

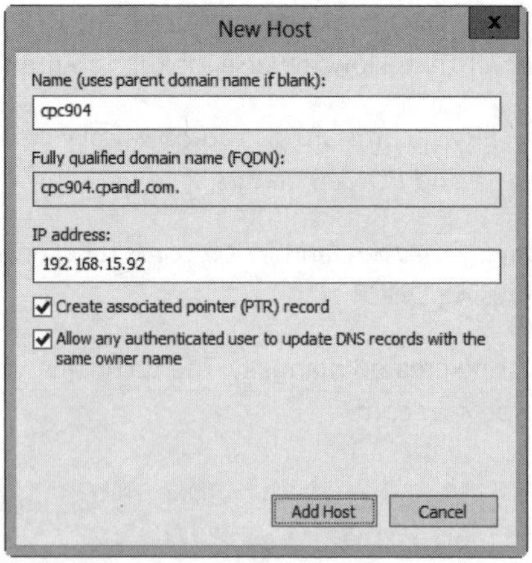

Figure 7-21 Creating a host record.

2. Type the host name, such as **cpc904**, and then type the IP address, such as **192.168.15.92**.

3. If a reverse lookup zone has been created for the domain and you want to create a PTR record for this host, select the Create Associated Pointer (PTR) Record check box.

NOTE

If you are working with an Active Directory–integrated zone, you have the option of allowing any authenticated client with the designated host name to update the record. To enable this, select the Allow Any Authenticated User To Update DNS Records With The Same Owner Name check box. This is a nonsecure dynamic update in which only the client host name is checked.

4. Tap or click Add Host. Repeat this process as necessary to add other hosts.

5. Tap or click Done when you're finished.

If you opt not to create a PTR record when you create an A record, you can create the PTR later as necessary. In DNS Manager, expand the node for the primary name server and then expand the related Reverse Lookup Zones folder. Press and hold or right-click the subnet to which you want to add the record and then choose New Pointer (PTR). This displays the dialog box shown in Figure 7-22. Type the Host ID part of the IP address, such as **43**, and then type the host name, such as **fileserver19**. Tap or click OK.

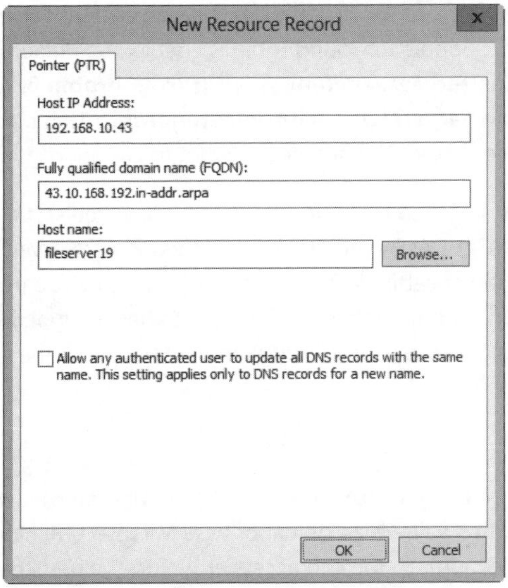

Figure 7-22 Creating a PTR record.

If a host name has multiple A records associated with it, the DNS Server service uses round robin for load balancing. With round robin, the DNS server cycles between the A records so that queries are routed proportionally to the various IP addresses that are configured. Here's how round robin works: say that your organization's web server gets a ton of hits—so many that the single web server you set up can't handle the load anymore.

To spread the workload, you configure three machines: one with the IP address 192.168.12.18, one with the IP address 192.168.12.19, and one with the IP address 192.168.12.20. On the DNS server, you configure a separate A record for each IP address, but you use the same host name: www.cpandl.com. This tells the DNS server to use round robin to balance the incoming requests proportionally. As requests come in, DNS will respond in a fixed circular fashion with the IP addresses. Although the DNS server gives clients all three IP addresses for the web server, the IP addresses are given in a changing order. For a series of requests, the first user might be directed to 192.168.12.18 (because this is the first IP address given to this client), the next user to 192.168.12.19 (because this is the first IP address given to this client), and the next user to 192.168.12.20 (because this is the first IP address given to this client). The next time around, the order will be the same, so the fourth user is directed to 192.168.12.18, the next user to 192.168.12.19, and the next user to 192.168.12.20. As you can see, with three servers, each server will get approximately one-third of the incoming requests and, ideally, about one-third of the workload.

Round robin isn't meant to be a replacement for clustering technologies, but it is an easy and fast way to get basic load balancing. Support for round robin is enabled by default. If you have to disable round robin, type **dnscmd *ServerName* /config /roundrobin 0**. To enable round robin again later, type **dnscmd *ServerName* /config /roundrobin 1**. In both cases, *ServerName* is the name or IP address of the DNS server you want to configure.

With Windows PowerShell, configuring round robin and any other advanced setting requires some additional work. First, you use Get-DnsServerSetting –All to work with server settings and return a list of all configurable server settings. By storing the returned value from this command in a variable, you can work with the related object (which has the type Microsoft. Management.Infrastructure.CimInstance#DnsServerSetting) and access any of the stored values. Consider the following example:

```
$Settings = "Get-DnsServerSetting –ComputerName CorpServer34 –All"
```

Here, you get all the DNS Server settings for CorpServer34 and store the returned value in a variable called $Settings. The returned value is an object of type Microsoft.Management .Infrastructure.CimInstance#DnsServerSetting. You can access any of the values stored in the object using the following syntax:

```
$Settings.PropertyName
```

Here, *PropertyName* is the name of the property you want to work with. Knowing this, you can display the current value of any property, such as RoundRobin:

```
$Settings.RoundRobin
```

If the property is configurable, you also can set the value of the property. Because RoundRobin is a configurable Boolean value, you can set the property to $True or $False as shown in this example:

```
$Settings = "Get-DnsServerSetting –ComputerName CorpServer34 –All"
$Settings.RoundRobin = $True
```

At this point your changes are stored in the object you are working with and you can make other changes to this object. When you are finished making changes, you check your changes by entering:

```
$Settings
```

To write your changes, use Set-DnsServerSetting and the following syntax:

```
Set-DnsServerSetting –ComputerName ServerName –InputObject ObjectName
```

Such as:

```
Set-DnsServerSetting –ComputerName CorpServer34 –InputObject $Settings
```

Canonical Name (CNAME) records

Canonical Name (CNAME) records create aliases for host names. This allows a host to be referred to by multiple names in DNS. The most common use is when a host provides a common service, such as World Wide Web (WWW) or File Transfer Protocol (FTP) service, and you want it to have a friendly name rather than a complex name. For example, you might want www.cpandl.com to be an alias for the host dc06.cpandl.com.

To create an alias for a host name in DNS Manager, expand the node for the primary name server and then expand the related Forward Lookup Zones folder. Press and hold or right-click the domain to which you want to add the record and then choose New Alias (CNAME). This displays the dialog box shown in Figure 7-23. Type the alias for the host name, such as **www**, and then type the FQDN for the host, such as **webserver73.cpandl.com**. Tap or click OK.

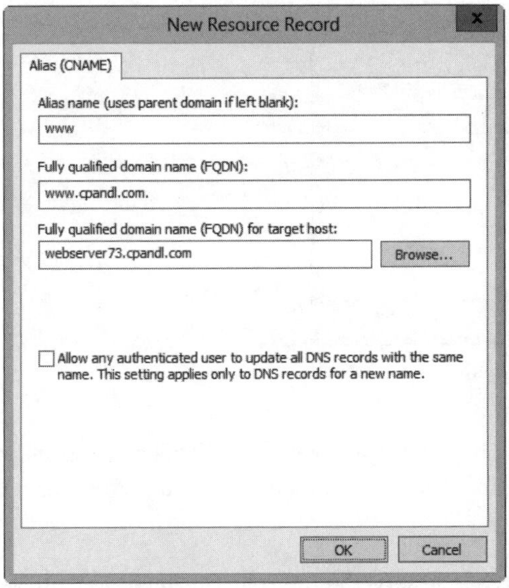

Figure 7-23 Creating a new alias.

Mail Exchanger (MX) records

Mail Exchanger (MX) records designate a mail exchange server for the domain, which allows mail to be delivered to the correct mail servers in the domain. For example, if an MX record is set for the domain cpandl.com, all mail sent to Username@cpandl.com will be directed to the server specified in the MX record.

You can create an MX record by completing the following steps:

1. In DNS Manager, expand the node for the primary name server and then expand the related Forward Lookup Zones folder. Press and hold or right-click the domain to which you want to add the record and then choose New Mail Exchanger (MX). This displays the dialog box shown in Figure 7-24.

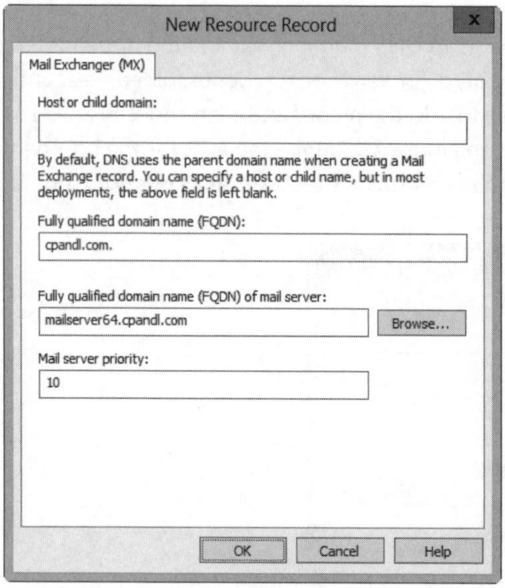

Figure 7-24 Creating an MX record.

2. Consider leaving the Host Or Child Domain box blank. A blank entry specifies that the mail exchanger is responsible for the parent domain, not for a child domain under the parent domain.

3. Type the FQDN of the mail exchange server in the Fully Qualified Domain Name (FQDN) Of Mail Server box, such as **mailserver64.cpandl.com**. This is the name used to route mail for delivery.

4. Specify the priority of the mail server relative to other mail servers in the domain. The mail server with the lowest priority is the mail server that is tried first when mail must be routed to a mail server in the domain.

5. Tap or click OK.

Name Server (NS) records

Name Server (NS) records provide a list of authoritative servers for a domain, which allows DNS lookups within various zones. Each primary and secondary name server in a domain should be declared through these records. These records are created automatically when Active Directory–integrated zones are used. For standard zones, you can create an NS record by doing the following:

1. In DNS Manager, expand the node for the primary name server and then expand the related Forward Lookup Zones or Reverse Lookup Zones folder as appropriate.

2. Press and hold or right-click the domain of the subnet for which you want to create name servers and then select Properties. In the Properties dialog box, tap or click the Name Servers tab, as shown in Figure 7-25.

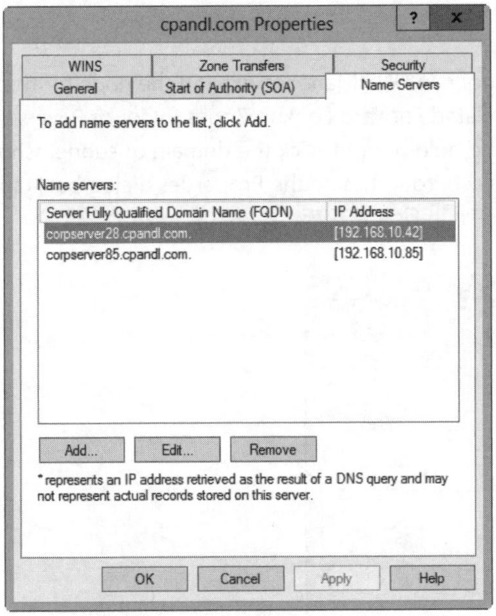

Figure 7-25 The Name Servers tab listing current name servers for the domain or subnet.

3. The Name Servers list shows the DNS servers currently configured to be authoritative for the zone and includes DNS servers that host secondary zones. If a name server isn't listed and you want to add it, tap or click Add. This displays the New Name Server Record dialog box.

4. In the Server Fully Qualified Domain Name (FQDN) field, type the fully qualified host name of a secondary server for the domain and then tap or click Resolve. If the IP address of the name server is filled in for you, tap or click Add, and then add other IP addresses for this name server as necessary.

5. Tap or click OK to close the New Name Server Record dialog box. Repeat this process to specify other name servers for the domain.

Start of Authority (SOA) records

Start of Authority (SOA) records indicate the authoritative name server for a particular zone. The authoritative server is the best source of DNS information for a zone. Because each zone must have an SOA record, the record is created automatically when you add a zone. The SOA record also contains information about how resource records in the zone should be used and cached. This includes refresh, retry, and expiration intervals and the maximum time that a record is considered valid.

To view the SOA record for a zone in DNS Manager, expand the node for the primary name server and then expand the related Forward Lookup Zones folder or Reverse Lookup Zones folder as appropriate. Press and hold or right-click the domain or subnet whose SOA record you want to view and then select Properties. In the Properties dialog box, tap or click the Start Of Authority (SOA) tab, as shown in Figure 7-26.

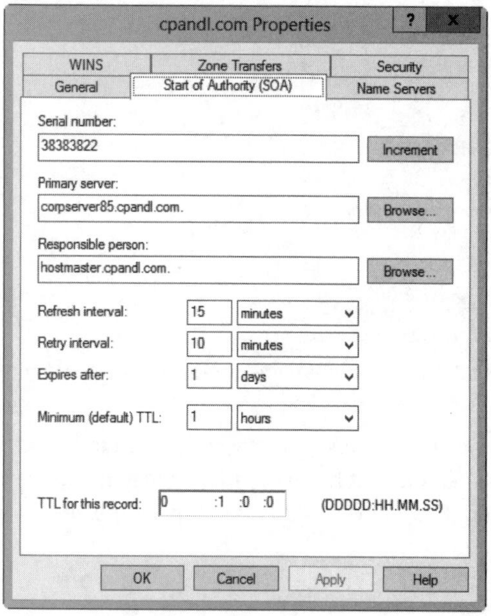

Figure 7-26 The Start Of Authority (SOA) tab for a domain or subnet.

Service Location (SRV) records

Service Location (SRV) records make it possible to find a server providing a specific service. Active Directory uses SRV records to locate domain controllers, global catalog servers, LDAP servers, and Kerberos servers. SRV records are created automatically. For example, Active Directory creates an SRV record when you promote a domain controller. LDAP servers can add an SRV record to indicate they are available to handle LDAP requests in a particular zone.

In the forest root zone, SOA, NS, CNAME, and SRV records are created. The SOA record contains information about the forest root zone. The NS records indicate the primary DNS servers for the forest root zone. The CNAME records are used to designate aliases that allow Active Directory to use the globally unique identifier (GUID) of a domain to find the forest root name servers for that domain. The SRV records used to locate Active Directory resources are organized by function as follows:

- **DC.** Contains SRV records for domain controllers. These records are organized according to the Active Directory site in which domain controllers are located.

- **Domains.** Contains SRV records for domain controllers listed by domain. Folders for each domain in the forest are organized by the domain's GUID.

- **GC.** Contains SRV records for global catalog servers in the forest. These records are primarily organized according to the Active Directory site in which domain controllers are located.

- **PDC.** Contains SRV records for PDC emulators in the forest.

In the forward lookup zone for a domain, you'll find similar SRV records used to locate Active Directory resources. These records are organized by the following criteria:

- Active Directory site

- The Internet protocol used by the resource, either TCP or User Datagram Protocol (UDP)

- Zone, either DomainDnsZones or ForestDnsZones

As Figure 7-27 shows, each record entry identifies a server that provides a particular service according to the following:

- **Domain.** The DNS domain in which the record is stored.

- **Service.** The service being made available. LDAP is for directory services on a domain controller. Kerberos indicates a Kerberos server that enables Kerberos authentication. GC indicates a global catalog server. KPasswd indicates Kerberos password service.

- **Protocol.** The protocol the service uses, either TCP or UDP.

- **Priority.** The priority or level of preference given to the server providing the service. The highest priority is 0. If multiple servers have the same priority, clients can use the weight to load balance between available servers.

- **Weight.** The relative weight given to the server for load balancing when multiple servers have the same priority level.

- **Port Number.** The TCP/IP port used by the server to provide the service.

- **Host Offering This Service.** The FQDN of the host providing the service.

Figure 7-27 An SRV record.

Deploying global names

The GlobalNames zone is a specially named forward lookup zone that is available when all the DNS servers for your zones are running Windows Server 2008 or later. Deploying a GlobalNames zone creates static, global records with single-label names without relying on Windows Internet Naming Service (WINS). This allows users to access hosts using single-label names rather than FQDNs.

You'll want to use the GlobalNames zone when name resolution depends on DNS, such as when your organization is no longer using WINS and you are planning to deploy only IPv6.

When you are using global names, an authoritative DNS server will try to resolve queries in the following order:

1. Using local zone data

2. Using the GlobalNames zone

3. Using DNS suffixes

4. Using WINS

The GlobalNames zone should be created as an Active Directory–integrated zone. Because dynamic updates can't be used to register updates in the GlobalNames zone, you should configure single-label name resolution only for your primary servers. An authoritative DNS server will check the GlobalNames zone before checking the local zone data. If you want DNS clients in another forest to use the GlobalNames zone for resolving names, you need to add an SRV resource record with the service name _globalnames._msdcs to that forest's forestwide partition. The record must specify the FQDN of the DNS server that hosts the GlobalNames zone.

You can deploy a GlobalNames zone by completing the following steps:

1. In DNS Manager, press and hold or right-click the Forward Lookup Zones node and then select New Zone. In the New Zone Wizard, tap or click Next twice to accept the defaults to create a primary zone integrated with Active Directory Domain Services.

2. On the Active Directory Zone Replication Scope page, choose to replicate the zone throughout the forest and then tap or click Next.

3. On the Zone Name page, enter **GlobalNames** as the zone name. Tap or click Next twice, and then tap or click Finish.

4. On every authoritative DNS server in the forest now and in the future, you need to type the following at an elevated Windows PowerShell prompt:

    ```
    Set-DnsServerGlobalNameZone -ComputerName ServerName -Enable $True
    ```

    Here, *ServerName* is the name of the DNS server that hosts the GlobalNames zone. To specify the local computer, just omit the –ComputerName parameter, such as:

    ```
    Set-DnsServerGlobalNameZone -Enable $True
    ```

5. For each server that you want users to be able to access using a single-label name, add an alias (CNAME) record to the GlobalNames zone. In DNS Manager, press and hold or right-click the GlobalZones node, select New Alias (CNAME), and then use the dialog box provided to create the new resource record.

Maintaining and troubleshooting DNS

In Chapter 6, "Architecting DNS infrastructure," and Chapter 7, "Implementing and managing DNS," I discussed how you can install, configure, and manage Domain Name System (DNS) services throughout your organization. As an administrator, maintaining and troubleshooting DNS might also be an important part of your routine workload.

Anytime you are working with DNS—and especially when you are troubleshooting—it's important to remember that issues with DNS can be due to client configuration, internal server configuration, and external server configuration. Although you can control client and internal server configuration, you don't necessarily have any control over external server configuration. Because of this, it's important to be able to determine quickly whether a DNS problem is one you can resolve or an issue with external servers over which you have no control.

Maintaining and monitoring DNS

When using DNS, you can perform many routine tasks to maintain and monitor domain name-resolution services. Key tasks you might need to perform include the following:

- Configuring default application directory partitions and replication scope

- Setting aging and scavenging

- Configuring logging and checking event logs

For performing these administrative tasks, your tools of choice might include DNS Manager, the Dnscmd utility, and the DnsServer Module for Windows PowerShell. Don't forget that for command-line and Windows PowerShell administration you generally need to work with an elevated, administrative command or Windows PowerShell prompt.

Configuring default partitions and replication scope

When the domain controllers running DNS in all the domains of your forest are using Microsoft Windows Server 2008 or later, you can create default application directory partitions for DNS. This reduces DNS replication traffic because DNS changes are replicated only to domain controllers that are also configured as DNS servers. There are two ways to configure default application directory partitions:

- **Forestwide.** Creates a single application directory partition that stores DNS zone data and replicates that data to all DNS servers in the forest. The default partition name is ForestDnsZones.*DnsForestName*, where *DnsForestName* is the domain name of the forest.

- **Domainwide.** Creates a single application directory partition that stores DNS zone data and replicates that data to all DNS servers in a designated domain. The default partition name is DomainDnsZones.*DnsDomainName*, where *DnsDomainName* is the domain name of the domain.

Check the DNS configuration fast

A fast way to check for the default application partitions and other DNS server configuration settings is to use Windows PowerShell. At a Windows PowerShell prompt, type **Get-DnsServer ServerName**, where *ServerName* is the fully qualified name or IP address of a DNS server, such as corpserver03.cpandl.com or 192.168.10.15.

By default, the DNS Server service will try to create the default application directory partitions when you install it. You can verify this by connecting to the primary DNS server in the forest root domain and looking for subdomains of the forest root domain named DomainDnsZones and ForestDnsZones. Figure 8-1 shows an example in which these partitions have been created.

If the DNS Server service is unable to create these partitions, you need to create the partitions manually. To do so, you must use an account that is a member of the Enterprise Admins group. If the default application partitions are currently available, the option to create them should not be available in DNS Manager.

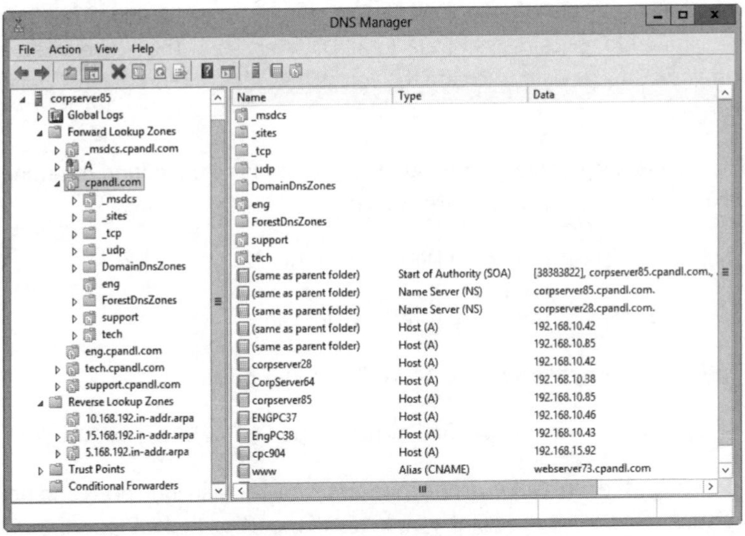

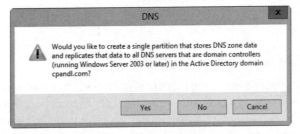

Figure 8-1 The default application partitions.

If the default application partitions have not yet been created, you can create them in DNS Manager by following these steps:

1. In DNS Manager, connect to the DNS server handling the zone for the parent domain of your forest root, such as cpandl.com rather than tech.cpandl.com.

2. Press and hold or right-click the server entry and select Create Default Application Directory Partitions.

3. The first prompt, shown in Figure 8-2, asks Would You Like To Create A Single Partition That Stores DNS Zone Data And Replicates That Data To All DNS Servers That Are Domain Controllers In The Active Directory Domain *DomainName*? If you want to create the DomainDnsZones.Dns-DomainName default partition, tap or click Yes.

Figure 8-2 Creating the default domain partition.

4. The next prompt states Would You Like To Create A Single Partition That Stores DNS Zone Data And Replicates That Data To All DNS Servers In The Active Directory Forest *ForestName*? If you want to create the ForestDnsZones.DnsForestName default partition, tap or click Yes.

When you create Active Directory–integrated zones, you have the option of setting the replication scope. Four replication scopes are available:

- To All DNS Servers In The Active Directory Forest

- To All DNS Servers In The Active Directory Domain

- To All Domain Controllers In The Active Directory Domain

- To All Domain Controllers Specified In The Scope Of This Directory Partition

To check or change the replication scope for a zone in DNS Manager, press and hold or right-click the related domain or subnet entry and select Properties. In the Properties dialog box, the current replication scope is listed to the right of the Replication entry. If you tap or click the related Change button, you can change the replication scope using the dialog box shown in Figure 8-3.

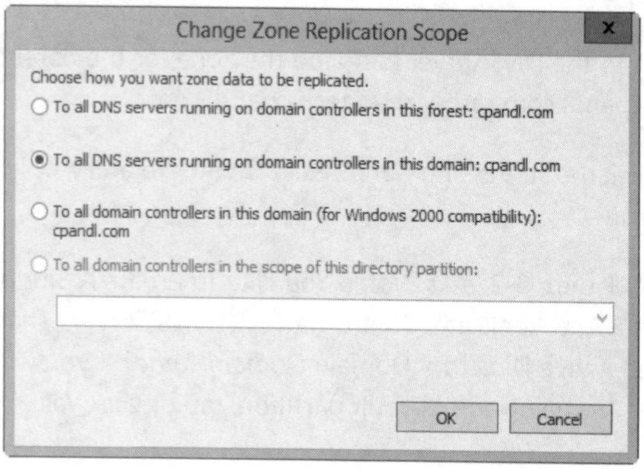

Figure 8-3 Changing the replication scope as necessary.

Setting the aging and scavenging rules

By default, the DNS Server service doesn't clean out old records. In some ways, this is a good thing because you don't want records you created manually to be deleted. However, for records created automatically through dynamic DNS, you might want to clear out old records periodically. Why? Consider the case of systems that register with DNS and then are removed from the network. Records for these systems will not be cleared automatically, which means that the DNS database might contain records for systems that are no longer in use.

DNS can help you clear out old records by using aging and scavenging. These rules determine how long a record created through a dynamic DNS update is valid and, if a record isn't reregistered within the allotted time, whether it can be cleared out. Aging and scavenging rules are set at two levels:

- **Zone.** Zone aging/scavenging properties apply to an individual zone on a DNS server. To set zone-level options, press and hold or right-click a zone entry and select Properties. In the Properties dialog box, select Aging in the General tab. After you select Scavenge Stale Resource Records and then configure the No-Refresh Interval duration and the Refresh Interval duration, tap or click OK.

- **Server.** Server aging/scavenging properties apply to all zones on a DNS server. To set server-level options in DNS Manager, press and hold or right-click a server entry and select Set Aging/Scavenging For All Zones. After you enable and configure aging/scavenging, tap or click OK. You'll see a prompt telling you these settings will be applied to new Active Directory–integrated zones created on the server. To apply these settings to existing zones, select Apply These Settings To The Existing Active Directory–Integrated Zones and then tap or click OK.

In either case, the dialog box you see is similar to the one shown in Figure 8-4. To enable aging/scavenging, select the Scavenge Stale Resource Records check box and then set these intervals:

- **No-Refresh Interval.** Sets a period of time during which a DNS client can't reregister its DNS records. When aging/scavenging is enabled, the default interval is seven days. This means that if a DNS client attempts to reregister its record within seven days of creating it, the DNS server will ignore the request. Generally, this is what you'll want to use because each time a record is reregistered this is seen as a change that must be replicated. The No-Refresh Interval option doesn't affect clients whose IP address has changed and who therefore need to reregister their DNS records. The reason for this is that the previous records are actually deleted and new records are then created.

- **Refresh Interval.** Sets the extent of the refresh window. Records can be scavenged only when they are older than the combined extent of the No-Refresh Interval and the Refresh Interval. When aging/scavenging is enabled, the default No-Refresh Interval is seven days and the default Refresh Interval is seven days. This means their combined extent is 14 days and the DNS server can't scavenge records until they are older than 14 days.

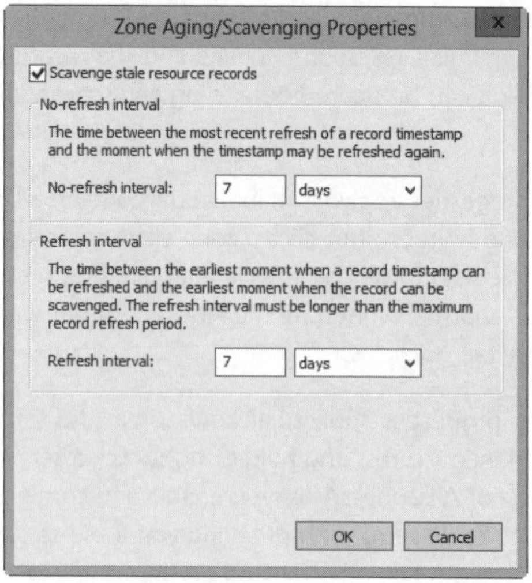

Figure 8-4 Setting aging/scavenging options.

Scavenge stale records manually

In addition to configuring automatic aging/scavenging, you can manually scavenge for stale (old) records. To do this in DNS Manager, press and hold or right-click a server entry and select Scavenge Stale Resource Records. When prompted to confirm the action, select Yes. You can get information about zone aging using Get-DnsServerZoneAging and configure related settings using Set-DnsServerZoneAging. To start scavenging, enter **Start-DnsServerScavenging -ComputerName ServerName**, where *ServerName* is the fully qualified name or IP address of the DNS server to work with, such as NS1.cpandl.com or 10.10.1.52.

Configuring logging and checking DNS Server logs

By default, the DNS Server service is configured to record all types of events (error, warning, and informational events) in the DNS Server log. To change this behavior in DNS Manager, press and hold or right-click a server entry and then select Properties. In the Properties dialog box, tap or click the Event Logging tab. Select the appropriate logging option so that no events, errors only, or errors and warnings are logged, and then tap or click OK.

Using DNS Manager, you can view only DNS-related events that have been logged in the system log by expanding the Global Logs node in the left pane and selecting DNS Events. As Figure 8-5 shows, you then see the current DNS events for the server. The primary events you will want to examine are error and warning events.

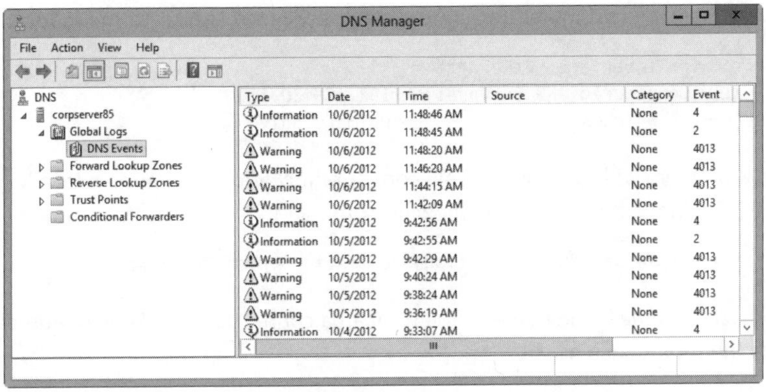

Figure 8-5 Checking the event logs for warnings and errors.

Troubleshooting the DNS client service

Frequently, when you are trying to troubleshoot DNS problems, you will want to start on the client that is experiencing the problem. If you don't find a problem on the client, try troubleshooting the DNS Server service.

Try reregistering the client

If the problem has to do with a client not showing up in DNS, force the client to reregister itself in DNS by typing **ipconfig /registerdns**. For this to work, however, a client's A and PTR records must exist. Although the necessary A and PTR records will be created automatically for clients using dynamically configured DNS records, you must manually create and update the A and PTR records for clients using statically configured records.

Check the client's TCP/IP configuration

If the problem has to do with the client making lookups, start by checking the DNS servers configured for the client to use.

Checking IPv4

You can display IPv4 information by typing **netsh interface ipv4 show dnsserver**. The output will show you the DNS servers for the client. If the DNS servers are configured through DHCPv4, the output will look similar to the following:

```
Configuration for interface "Ethernet"
    DNS servers configured through DHCP:  192.168.20.21
    Register with which suffix:           Primary only
```

If the DNS servers are configured locally, the output will look similar to the following:

```
Configuration for interface "Ethernet"
     Statically Configured DNS Servers:    192.168.20.11
     Register with which suffix:           Primary only
```

If you see a problem with the client's DNS configuration, you can change a locally assigned DNS server IP address by typing the following command:

```
netsh interface ipv4 set dns ConnectionName static ServerIPAddress
```

Here, *ConnectionName* is the name of the local area connection and *ServerIPAddress* is the IP address of the server, such as:

```
netsh interface ipv4 set dns "Ethernet" static 192.168.0.1
```

If you see a problem with a DHCP-assigned DNS server IP address, try renewing the client's IP address lease by typing **ipconfig /renew**.

With Windows PowerShell, you can enter **Get-DnsClientServerAddress –AddressFamily IPv4** to show the DNS servers for the client. The output shows the DNS servers configured for each IPv4 interface but doesn't indicate whether the servers are statically and dynamically assigned. To change locally assigned DNS server IPv4 addresses, you can use Set-DNSClientServerAddress. The basic syntax is:

```
Set-DNSClientServerAddress –InterfaceAlias ConnectionName
–ServerAddresses ("ServerIPAddress1, ServerIPAddress2, … ServerIPAddressN")
```

Such as:

```
Set-DNSClientServerAddress –InterfaceAlias "Ethernet"
–ServerAddresses ("192.168.20.20, 192.168.20.21")
```

Checking IPv6

You can display IPv6 information by typing **netsh interface ipv6 show dnsserver**. The output will show you the DNS servers for the client. If the DNS servers are configured through DHCPv6, the output will look similar to the following:

```
Configuration for interface "Ethernet"
    DNS servers configured through DHCP: fec0:0:0:ffff::1%1
                                         fec0:0:0:ffff::2%1
                                         fec0:0:0:ffff::3%1
        Register with which suffix:      Primary only
```

If the DNS servers are configured locally, the output will look similar to the following:

```
Configuration for interface "Ethernet"
     Statically Configured DNS Servers: fec0:0:0:ffff::1%1
                                        fec0:0:0:ffff::2%1
```

```
                                          fec0:0:0:ffff::3%1
         Register with which suffix:          Primary only
```

If you see a problem with the client's DNS configuration, you can change a locally assigned DNS server IP address by typing the following command:

```
netsh interface ipv6 set dns ConnectionName static ServerIPAddress
```

Here, *ConnectionName* is the name of the local area connection and *ServerIPAddress* is the IP address of the server, such as:

```
netsh interface ipv6 set dns "Ethernet" static fe80::fdc2:3222:ab7e:23b1
```

If you see a problem with a DHCP-assigned DNS server IP address, try renewing the client's IP address lease by typing **ipconfig /renew**.

With Windows PowerShell, you can enter **Get-DnsClientServerAddress –AddressFamily IPv6** to show the DNS servers for the client. The output shows the DNS servers configured for each IPv6 interface but doesn't indicate whether the servers are statically and dynamically assigned. To change locally assigned DNS server IPv6 addresses, you can use Set-DNSClientServerAddress. The basic syntax is:

```
Set-DNSClientServerAddress –InterfaceAlias ConnectionName
–ServerAddresses ("ServerIPAddress1, ServerIPAddress2, … ServerIPAddressN")
```

Check the client's resolver cache

If you don't see a problem with the client's DNS configuration, you will want to check the client's DNS resolver cache. All current Windows operating systems have a built-in DNS resolver cache that caches resource records from query responses that the DNS Client service receives. When performing lookups, the DNS client first looks in the cache. Records remain in the cache until one of the following events occurs:

- Their Time to Live (TTL) expires.

- The system or the DNS Client service is restarted.

- The cache is flushed.

You can display the records in a cache by typing **ipconfig /displaydns** at the command prompt. Records in the cache look like this:

```
Windows IP Configuration

    1.0.0.127.in-addr.arpa
    ----------------------------------------
    Record Name.......... : 1.0.0.127.in-addr.arpa.
    Record Type.......... : 12
```

```
Time To Live.......... : 573686
Data Length.......... : 4
Section.............. : Answer
PTR Record........... : localhost

www.williamstanek.com
---------------------------------------
Record Name.......... : www.williamstanek.com
Record Type.......... : 5
Time To Live.......... : 12599
Data Length.......... : 4
Section.............. : Answer
CNAME Record ........ : williamstanek.com
```

If you suspect a client has stale records in its cache, you can force it to flush the cache. To do so, type **ipconfig /flushdns** at the command prompt.

With Windows PowerShell, you can enter **Get-DnsClientCache | fl** to display the DNS cache. The records in the cache are formatted similarly. To clear the cache, you can use Clear-DnsClientCache.

Perform lookups for troubleshooting

Another useful command to use when troubleshooting DNS is NSLookup. You can use NSLookup to query the default DNS server of a client and check to see the actual records it is using. To perform a basic lookup, just type **NSLookup** followed by the fully qualified domain name (FQDN) of the host to look up. Consider the following example:

```
nslookup www.microsoft.com
```

The response shows the information that the default DNS server has on that host, such as:

```
C:\Documents and Settings\WS>nslookup www.microsoft.com
DNS request timed out.
    timeout was 2 seconds.
Non-authoritative answer:
Name:  www2.microsoft.akadns.net
Addresses:  207.46.244.188, 207.46.156.252, 207.46.144.222, 207.46.245.92
            207.46.134.221, 207.46.245.156, 207.46.249.252, 207.46.156.220
Aliases:  www.microsoft.com, www.microsoft.akadns.net
```

If you want to look up a particular type of record, follow these steps:

1. Type **nslookup** at the command prompt. The prompt changes to >.

2. Type **set query=*RecordType***, where *RecordType* is the type of record, such as **set query=mx**, **set query=soa**, or **set query=ns**.

3. Type the FQDN for the domain in which you want to search, such as **microsoft.com**.

The output shows you matching records in the specified domain, such as:

```
microsoft.com     MX preference = 10, mail exchanger = mailb.microsoft.com

microsoft.com     nameserver = dns1.cp.msft.net
microsoft.com     nameserver = dns1.dc.msft.net
mailb.microsoft.com     internet address = 131.107.3.122
mailb.microsoft.com     internet address = 131.107.3.123
```

Troubleshooting the DNS Server service

If you suspect the DNS problem is on the server itself, you can begin troubleshooting on the server. There are, of course, many troubleshooting techniques. This section covers the key ones you'll want to use.

Check the server's TCP/IP configuration

When you are troubleshooting DNS on a DNS server, start with the server's Transmission Control Protocol/Internet Protocol (TCP/IP) configuration. After you verify or modify the TCP/IP configuration as necessary, you can continue to troubleshoot. DNS servers maintain a cache memory of resource records for the zones they are configured to work with.

Check the server's cache

If you think the problem with DNS is that the server has stale records, you can check the zone information on the DNS server by using the following command:

```
dnscmd ServerName /zoneprint.
```

Here, *ServerName* is the name or IP address of the DNS server and "." indicates that you want to examine the root hints. This list includes the root name servers the server is using. You also can specify the name of a specific zone to examine, such as:

```
dnscmd ServerName /zoneprint eng.cpandl.com
```

If necessary, you can force a server to clear out its cache memory of resource records. To do so, in DNS Manager press and hold or right-click the server entry and select Clear Cache. You can clear the cache at the command prompt by typing the following:

```
dnscmd ServerName /clearcache
```

Here, *ServerName* is the name or IP address of the DNS server whose cache you want to clear.

With Windows PowerShell, you can use Get-DnsServerZone to get a list of available zones and basic information about those zones. To display information about a DNS server's cache, you can use Get-DnsServerCache. To display information about zone aging, you can use Get-DnsServerZoneAging.

You also can use Get-DnsServerStatistics to display detailed statistics. For diagnosing cache issues, you'll want to pay particular attention to the RecordStatistics, RecursionStatistics, and CacheStatistics values.

To clear the DNS server's cache, you can use Clear-DnsServerCache.

Check replication to other name servers

Active Directory replication of changes to DNS zones is automatic. By default, Active Directory checks for changes to zones every 180 seconds. This interval is called the *directory service polling interval*. For advanced configuration needs, you can set the directory service polling interval by using Dnscmd. Type **dnscmd *ServerName* /config /dspollinginterval *Interval***, where *ServerName* is the name or IP address of the DNS server you want to configure and *Interval* is the polling interval in seconds.

If the problem has to do with failure to replicate changes to secondary servers, start by ensuring that zone transfers are enabled, as discussed in the section entitled "Configuring zone transfers" in Chapter 7. If zone transfers are properly configured, try updating the serial number on the zone records on the primary server. In DNS Manager, press and hold or right-click the server entry in DNS Manager and select Update Server Data Files. This increments the serial number for zones as needed, which should trigger zone transfers if they are necessary.

With Windows PowerShell, you use Get-DnsServerDsSetting to work with directory service settings and return a list of all configurable settings. Although Set-DnsServerDsSetting provides parameters for working with each setting, you can modify values using the same technique that is required with Set-DnsServerSetting—and this is what I recommend because it will help ensure that you master this technique for working with multivalued objects.

By storing the returned value from this command in a variable, you can work with the related object (which has the type Microsoft.Management.Infrastructure .CimInstance#DnsServerDsSetting) and access any of the stored values. Consider the following example:

```
$DsSettings = "Get-DnsServerDsSetting –ComputerName CorpServer21"
```

Here, you get directory services settings for CorpServer21 and store the returned value in a variable called $DsSettings. The returned value is an object of type Microsoft.Management .Infrastructure.CimInstance#DnsServerDsSetting. You can access any of the values stored in the object by using the following syntax:

```
$DsSettings.PropertyName
```

Here, *PropertyName* is the name of the property you want to work with. Knowing this, you can display the current value of any property, such as PollingInterval:

```
$DsSettings.PollingInterval
```

If the property is configurable, you also can set the value of the property. Because PollingInterval is a configurable integer value, you can set the property to an integer value, as shown in this example:

```
$DsSettings = "Get-DnsServerDsSetting –ComputerName CorpServer34"
$DsSettings.PollingInterval = 120
```

At this point your changes are stored in the object you are working with and you can make other changes to this object. When you are finished making changes, check your changes by entering the following:

```
$DsSettings
```

To write your changes, you must pass your object to Set-DnsServerSetting using the following syntax:

```
ObjectParam | Set-DnsServerSetting –ComputerName ServerName –Passthru
```

Such as:

```
$DsSettings | Set-DnsServerSetting –ComputerName CorpServer34 –Passthru
```

Examine the configuration of the DNS server

Frequently, DNS problems have to do with a DNS server's configuration. Rather than trying to navigate multiple tabs and dialog boxes to find the configuration details, you can use Dnscmd to help you. You can view a DNS server's configuration by typing **dnscmd *ServerName* /info** at the command prompt, where *ServerName* is the name or IP address of the DNS server you want to check, such as Primary or 10.10.1.52. The output looks like this:

```
Query result:
Server info
    server name             = CorpServer28.cpandl.com
    version                 = 25800306 (6.3 build 9600)
    DS container            = cn=MicrosoftDNS,cn=System,DC=cpandl,DC=com
    forest name             = cpandl.com
    domain name             = cpandl.com
    builtin forest partition = ForestDnsZones.cpandl.com
    builtin domain partition = DomainDnsZones.cpandl.com
    read only DC            = 0
    last scavenge cycle     = not since restart (0)
  Configuration:
    dwLogLevel              = 00000000
    dwDebugLevel            = 00000000
```

```
         dwRpcProtocol             = 00000005
         dwNameCheckFlag           = 00000002
         cAddressAnswerLimit       = 0
         dwRecursionRetry          = 3
         dwRecursionTimeout        = 8
         dwDsPollingInterval       = 180
Configuration Flags:
         fBootMethod                  = 3
         fAdminConfigured             = 1
         fAllowUpdate                 = 1
         fDsAvailable                 = 1
         fAutoReverseZones            = 1
         fAutoCacheUpdate             = 0
         fSlave                       = 1
         fNoRecursion                 = 0
         fRoundRobin                  = 1
         fStrictFileParsing           = 0
         fLooseWildcarding            = 0
         fBindSecondaries             = 0
         fWriteAuthorityNs            = 0
         fLocalNetPriority            = 1
Aging Configuration:
         ScavengingInterval           = 0
         DefaultAgingState            = 0
         DefaultRefreshInterval       = 168
         DefaultNoRefreshInterval     = 168
ServerAddresses:

         Ptr          = 000000DF5514E7C0
         MaxCount     = 2
         AddrCount    = 2
         Addr[0] => af=23, salen=28, [sub=0, flag=00000000] p=13568,
                  addr=fe80::81ff:7053:92ab:bc14
         Addr[1] => af=2, salen=16, [sub=0, flag=00000000] p=13568, addr=192.168.10.42

ListenAddresses:
    NULL IP Array.
Forwarders:

         Ptr          = 000000DF5514E880
         MaxCount     = 3
         AddrCount    = 3
         Addr[0] => af=23, salen=28, [sub=0, flag=00000000] p=13568, addr=fec0:0:0:ffff::1
         Addr[1] => af=23, salen=28, [sub=0, flag=00000000] p=13568, addr=fec0:0:0:ffff::2
         Addr[2] => af=23, salen=28, [sub=0, flag=00000000] p=13568, addr=fec0:0:0:ffff::3

         forward timeout  = 3
         slave            = 1

Command completed successfully.
```

Table 8-1 summarizes, section by section, the output from Dnscmd /Info. Using Dnscmd /Config, you can configure most of these options. The actual subcommand to use is indicated in parentheses in the first column, and examples of acceptable values are indicated in the third column. For example, if you want to set the fBindSecondaries configuration setting to allow maximum compression and efficiency (assuming you are using Microsoft DNS servers or BIND 4.9.4 or later), you type **dnscmd *ServerName* /config /bindsecondaries 0**, where *ServerName* is the name or IP address of the DNS server you want to configure. This overrides the default setting to support other DNS servers.

Table 8-1 DNS server configuration parameters

Section/Entry (Command)	Description	Example/Accepted Values
Server Info		
Server name	The FQDN of the DNS server.	Corpsvr28.cpandl.com
Version	The operating system version and build. Version 6.2 is Windows Server 2012.	23F00206 (6.2 build 9200)
DS container	The directory services container for a DNS server that uses Active Directory–integrated zones.	cn=MicrosoftDNS, cn=System, DC=cpandl,DC=com
Forest name	The name of the Active Directory forest in which the server is located.	cpandl.com
Domain name	The name of the Active Directory domain in which the server is located.	cpandl.com
Builtin domain partition	The default application partition for the domain.	DomainDnsZones.cpandl .com
Builtin forest partition	The default application partition for the forest.	ForestDnsZones.cpandl.com
Read Only DC	The domain controller is read only.	0, false; 1, true
Last scavenge cycle	The last time records were aged/ scavenged.	not since restart (0)
Configuration		
dwLogLevel (/loglevel)	Indicates whether debug logging is enabled. A value other than zeros means it is enabled.	0x0; default, no logging.
dwDebugLevel	The debug logging level, not used. dwLogLevel is used instead.	00000000

Section/Entry (Command)	Description	Example/Accepted Values
dwRpcProtocol (/rpcprotocol)	The RPC protocol used. 5 = 0x1+0x4, meaning TCP/IP and LPC.	0x0; disables remote procedure call (RPC) for DNS. 0x1; default, uses TCP/IP. 0x2; uses named pipes. 0x4; uses LPC.
dwNameCheckFlag (/namecheckflag)	The name-checking flag. By default, DNS names can be in multibyte Unicode format, as indicated by the example entry.	0; Strict RFC (ANSI). 1; Non RFC (ANSI). 2; Multibyte (UTF8). 3; All Names.
cAddressAnswerLimit (/addressanswerlimit)	The maximum number of records the server can send in response to a query.	0; default with no maximum. [5–28]; sets a maximum.
dwRecursionRetry (/recursionretry)	The number of seconds the server waits before trying to contact a remote server again.	3
dwRecursionTimeout (/recursiontimeout)	The number of seconds the server waits before stopping contact attempts.	8
dwDsPollingInterval (/dspollinginterval)	How often, in seconds, Active Directory polls for changes in Active Directory–integrated zones.	180
Configuration Flags		
fBootMethod (/bootmethod)	The source from which the server gets its configuration information.	1; loads from the BIND file. 2; loads from the registry. 3; loads from Active Directory and the registry.
fAdminConfigured	Indicates whether the settings are administrator-configured.	1; default for yes.
fAllowUpdate	Indicates whether dynamic updates are allowed.	1; default, dynamic updates are allowed. 0; dynamic updates are not allowed.
fDsAvailable	Indicates whether Active Directory directory services are available.	1; Active Directory is available. 0; Active Directory isn't available.
fAutoReverseZones (/disableauto reversezone)	Indicates whether automatic creation of reverse lookup zones is enabled.	1; default, enabled. 0; disabled.

Section/Entry (Command)	Description	Example/Accepted Values
fAutoCacheUpdate (/secureresponses)	Indicates how server caching works.	0; default, saves all responses to name queries to cache. 1; saves only records in same DNS subtree to cache.
fSlave (/isslave)	Determines how the DNS server responds when forwarded queries receive no response.	0; default, recursion is enabled. If the forwarder does not respond, the server attempts to resolve the query itself using recursion. 1; recursion is disabled. If the forwarder does not respond, the server terminates the search and sends a failure message to the resolver.
fNoRecursion (/norecursion)	Indicates whether the server performs recursive name resolution.	0; default, DNS server performs recursion if requested. 1; DNS server doesn't perform recursion.
fRoundRobin (/roundrobin)	Indicates whether the server allows round-robin load balancing when there are multiple A records for hosts.	1; default, automatically loads balances using round robin for any hosts with multiple A records. 0; disables round robin.
fStrictFileParsing (/strictfileparsing)	Indicates server behavior when it encounters bad records.	0; default, continues to load and logs error. 1; stops loading DNS file and logs error.
fBindSecondaries (/bindsecondaries)	Indicates the zone transfer format for secondaries. By default, DNS server is configured for compatibility with other DNS server types.	1; for pre-BIND 4.9.4 compatibility. 0; default, enables compression and multiple transfers on Windows secondaries and others with BIND 4.9.4 or later.
fWriteAuthorityNs (/writeauthorityns)	Indicates whether the server writes NS records in the authority section of a response.	0; default, writes for referrals only. 1; writes for all successful authoritative responses.
fLocalNetPriority (/localnetpriority)	Determines the order in which host records are returned when there are multiple host records for the same name.	1; returns records with similar IP addresses first. 0; returns records in the order in which they are in DNS.
Aging Configuration		
ScavengingInterval (/scavenginginterval)	Indicates the number of hours between scavenging intervals.	0x0; scavenging is disabled.

Section/Entry (Command)	Description	Example/Accepted Values
DefaultAgingState (/defaultagingstate)	Indicates whether scavenging is enabled by default in new zones.	0; default, scavenging is disabled. 1; scavenging is enabled.
DefaultRefresh Interval (/defaultrefresh interval)	Indicates the default Refresh Interval in hours.	168 (set in hexadecimal).
DefaultNo RefreshInterval (/defaultno refreshinterval)	Indicates the default No-Refresh Interval in hours.	168 (set in hexadecimal).
ServerAddresses		
Addr Count	The number of IP addresses configured on the server and the IP address used.	2 Addr[0] dr=fe80::81ff:7053:92ab:bc14 Addr[1] addr=192.168.10.42
ListenAddresses		
Addr Count	The number and value of IP addresses configured for listening for requests from clients. Set to NULL IP Array when there are no specific IP addresses designated for listening for requests from clients.	NULL IP Array
Forwarders		
Addr Count	The number and value of IP addresses of servers configured as forwarders. Set to NULL IP Array when there are no forwarders.	3 Addr[0] addr=fec0:0:0:ffff::1 Addr[1] addr=fec0:0:0:ffff::2 Addr[2] addr=fec0:0:0:ffff::3
Forward timeout (/forwardingtimeout)	Timeout for queries to forwarders in seconds.	3
Slave	Indicates whether recursion is enabled.	0; recursion is enabled. 1; recursion is disabled.

Another useful command for troubleshooting DNS Server is Dnscmd /Statistics. This command shows you the following information:

- DNS server time statistics, including server start time, seconds since start, and stats of last cleared date and time

- Details on queries and responses, including total queries received, total responses sent; the number of UDP queries received and sent, UDP responses received and sent; and the number of TCP queries received and sent and TCP responses received and sent

- Details on queries by record, including the exact number of each type of record sent

- Details on failures and where they occurred, including recursion failures, retry limits reached, and partial answers received

- Details on the total number of dynamic updates, the status for each update type; later breakdowns on the number and status of secure updates, the number of updates that were forwarded, and the types of records updated

- Details on the amount of memory used by DNS, including the total amount of memory used, standard allocations, and allocations from standard to the heap

CHAPTER 8

Save the stats to a file

Write the output of Dnscmd /Statistics to a file so that you don't overflow the history buffer in the command prompt. This also enables you to go through the stats at your leisure. Enter **dnscmd ServerName /statistics > FileName**, where *ServerName* is the name or IP address of the DNS server and *FileName* is the name of the file to use, such as **dnscmd corpsvr02 /statistics > dns-stats.txt**. With Windows PowerShell, you can use Get-DnsServer and Get-DnsServerStatistics to display similar information.

Examine zones and zone records

Dnscmd provides several useful commands for helping you pinpoint problems with records. To get started, list the available zones by typing **dnscmd *ServerName* /enumzones**, where *ServerName* is the name or IP address of the DNS server you want to check. The output shows a list of the zones that are configured as follows:

```
Enumerated zone list: Zone count = 11
 Zone name                       Type      Storage       Properties
 .                               Cache     AD-Domain
 _msdcs.cpandl.com               Primary   AD-Forest     Secure
 10.168.192.in-addr.arpa         Primary   AD-Domain     Secure Rev
 15.168.192.in-addr.arpa         Primary   AD-Domain     Secure Rev
 5.168.192.in-addr.arpa          Primary   AD-Domain     Secure Rev
 A                               Primary   AD-Domain     Secure
 cpandl.com                      Primary   AD-Domain     Secure Aging
 eng.cpandl.com                  Primary   AD-Domain     Secure
 support.cpandl.com              Primary   AD-Domain     Secure
```

```
tech.cpandl.com          Primary    AD-Domain      Secure
TrustAnchors             Primary    AD-Forest
```

The zone names you can work with are listed in the first column. The other values tell you the type of zone and the way it's configured, as summarized in Table 8-2. With Windows PowerShell, you can use Get-DnsServerZone to display similar information.

Table 8-2 Zone entries and their meanings

Column/Entry	Description
Type	
Cache	A cache zone (server cache).
Primary	A primary zone.
Secondary	A secondary zone.
Stub	A stub zone.
File	
AD-Forest	Active Directory–integrated with a forestwide replication scope.
AD-Legacy	Active Directory–integrated with a legacy replication scope to all domain controllers in the domain.
AD-Domain	Active Directory–integrated with a domainwide replication scope.
File	Indicates the zone data is stored in a file.
Properties	
Secure	Zone allows secure dynamic updates only and is a forward lookup zone.
Secure Rev	Zone allows secure dynamic updates only and is a reverse lookup zone.
Secure Aging	Zone allows secure dynamic updates only and is configured for aging/scavenging.
Aging	Zone is configured for aging/scavenging but isn't configured for dynamic updates.
Update	Zone is a forward lookup zone configured to allow both secure and nonsecure dynamic updates.
Update Rev	Zone is a reverse lookup zone configured to allow both secure and nonsecure dynamic updates.
Down	Secondary or stub zone hasn't received a zone transfer since startup.

After you examine the settings for zones on the server, you can print out the zone records of a suspect zone by typing **dnscmd *ServerName* /zoneprint *ZoneName*** at the command prompt, where *ServerName* is the name or IP address of the DNS server and *ZoneName* is the name of the zone as reported previously.

Consider the following example:

```
dnscmd corpsvr02 /zoneprint cpandl.com
```

Here, you want to examine the cpandl.com zone records on the CORPSVR02 server. The output from this command shows the records in this zone and their settings. Here is a partial listing:

```
;
;  Zone:     cpandl.com
;  Server:   corpserver28
;  Time:     Sat Nov 15 12:08:51 2014 UTC
;
@ [Aging:3609354] 600 A  192.168.10.85
[Aging:3609352] 600 A  192.168.10.42
3600 NS  corpserver28.cpandl.com.
3600 NS  corpserver85.cpandl.com.
3600 SOA  corpserver28.cpandl.com. hostmaster.cpandl.com. 38383822 900 600 86400 3600
3600 MX  10 mailserver64.cpandl.com.
_msdcs 3600 NS  corpserver28.cpandl.com.

CorpServer28 3600 A  192.168.10.42
CorpServer64 [Aging:3608421] 1200 A  192.168.10.38
CorpServer85 3600 A  192.168.10.85


;
;  Finished zone: 212 nodes and 137 records in 0 seconds

;
```

The Dnscmd /Zoneprint shows all the records, even the ones created by Active Directory. This is particularly useful because it means you don't have to try to navigate the many subfolders in which these SRV records are stored.

Getting DNS server statistics

As part of routine monitoring of DNS, you might want to periodically examine DNS server statistics to ensure that DNS is functioning as expected. DNS server statistics also can be useful when you are trying to diagnose and resolve DNS issues. You can get detailed statistics from a DNS server regarding queries, responses, dynamic updates, and much more using the Get-DnsServerStatistics cmdlet.

NOTE

Because Get-DnsServerStatistics requires administrator privileges, you must run this cmdlet at an elevated, administrator Windows PowerShell prompt. If you use a standard prompt, you'll see an error stating that Get-DnsServerStatistics failed to get zone statistics from the server with a category error showing permission denied.

The basic syntax for Get-DnsServerStatistics is:

```
Get-DnsServerStatistics [-ComputerName ComputerID] [-Zone ZoneName]
```

Use the –ComputerName parameter to specify the DNS server to query. You can specify the computer name using an IPv4 address, an IPV6 address, a host name, or an FQDN. If you don't specify a server to query, Get-DnsServerStatistics assumes you want to query the local server.

Use the –Zone parameter to specify the FQDN of the DNS zone for which you want statistics. If you don't specify a zone, statistics for all primary and secondary zones on the server are returned in the results.

Because the results are returned in a collection of objects, you can store the output returned by Get-DnsServerStatistics in a variable and then examine the properties of this variable to display only the statistics you want to work with. To list the statistics sections you can work with, enter **Get-DnsServerStatistics | Get-Member**. In the following example, you store the output from Get-DnsServerStatistics in the $stats variable and then display only the statistics for dynamic updates:

```
$stats = Get-DnsServerStatistics
$stats.UpdateStatistics
```

You also could do this in one line:

```
(Get-DnsServerStatistics).UpdateStatistics
```

Other types of statistics you can display separately include CacheStatistics, DatabaseStatistics, DnssecStatistics, ErrorStatistics, QueryStatistics, and MemoryStatistics.

CHAPTER 9

Implementing and maintaining WINS

Windows Internet Naming Service (WINS) enables computers to register and resolve Network Basic Input/Output System (NetBIOS) names on Internet Protocol version 4 (IPv4) networks. WINS is not used with IPv6 networks. WINS is maintained primarily for backward support and compatibility with legacy applications and early versions of Microsoft Windows that used WINS for computer name resolution. WINS also is maintained for networks running pre–Windows Server 2008 versions of Windows Server that don't have Active Directory deployed and thus don't require Domain Name System (DNS). On many large networks, WINS is needed to support legacy applications and legacy hooks into Active Directory from upgrades that proceeded from early versions of Windows Server to current versions.

If you are setting up a new network and there are no legacy operating systems, you probably don't need WINS. In that case only DNS is needed because if Active Directory is deployed these computers rely exclusively on DNS for name resolution. Because WINS is not required, you could remove WINS support from the network. Doing so, however, means that legacy applications and services that rely on NetBIOS, such as the computer Browser service, would no longer function.

WINS essentials

Like DNS, WINS is a client/server protocol. All Windows servers have a WINS service that can be installed to provide WINS services on the network. All Windows computers have a WINS client that is installed automatically. The Workstation and Server services on computers are used to specify resources that are available, such as file shares. These resources also have NetBIOS names.

NetBIOS namespace and scope

WINS architecture is very different from DNS. Unlike DNS, WINS has a flat namespace and doesn't use a hierarchy or tree. Each computer or resource on a Windows network has a NetBIOS name, which can be up to 15 characters long. This name must be unique on the network—no other computer or resource can have the same name. Although there are no extensions to this name per se that indicate a domain, a NetBIOS scope can be set in Dynamic Host Configuration Protocol (DHCP).

The NetBIOS scope is a hidden sixteenth character (suffix) for the NetBIOS name. It's used to limit the scope of communications for WINS clients. Only WINS clients with the same NetBIOS scope can communicate with each other. For details on setting the NetBIOS scope for computers that use DHCP, see the section entitled "Configuring TCP/IP options" in Chapter 5, "Configuring DHCP Services."

Inside OUT

Decommissioning WINS

WINS is needed to support legacy applications written to the NetBIOS over TCP/IP interface and to support network browsing for users in pre–Windows Server 2008 environments. If you don't have NetBIOS applications on the network or pre–Windows Server 2008 infrastructure, you don't need to use WINS. That said, before you decommission existing WINS infrastructure, you should ensure that your Active Directory domains and forests don't have legacy hooks that use the NetBIOS over TCP/IP interface. Your network might have legacy hooks that use NetBIOS if trusts were established in your domains and forests under early Windows Server releases and you subsequently upgraded to later releases of Windows Server. If so, you might need WINS to get the trusts verified and reestablished. The only way to be certain that you don't need WINS in a situation where legacy hooks might exist is to perform a fresh install of the network environment with Windows Server 2003 or later and Active Directory operations in Windows Server 2003 Native Mode or higher.

If WINS is no longer needed on your network, you can look to decommission WINS. The best approach to decommissioning WINS is a methodical one that includes clear communication of your plan to decommission WINS throughout the organization as appropriate for IT guidelines. Start by examining the applications and server products in use throughout the organization that use or rely on network connections, such as Exchange Server, Systems Management Server, and Microsoft BackOffice Server. If the product version was developed and released prior to the release of Windows Vista and Windows Server 2008, the product might require NetBIOS naming. After you upgrade or replace applications and server products as appropriate, you can then enter the next phase of the transition in which you stop and then disable the WINS service on your organization's WINS servers. This stops NetBIOS name resolution without uninstalling your WINS servers. During this phase you might find that some applications require WINS for name resolution. If so, you can enable WINS and then make plans to phase out those applications. Once you are certain there is no need for WINS, you can completely decommission WINS by removing the WINS Server feature from your servers.

NetBIOS node types

The way WINS works on a network is determined by the node type set for a client. The node type defines how name services work. WINS clients can be one of four node types:

- **B-Node (Broadcast Node).** Broadcast messages are used to register and resolve names. Computers that need to resolve a name broadcast a message to every host on the local network, requesting the IP address for a computer name. This node type is best for small networks.

- **P-Node (Peer-to-Peer Node).** WINS servers are used to register and resolve computer names to Internet Protocol (IP) addresses. Computers that need to resolve a name send a query message to the server and the server responds. This node type is best if you want to eliminate broadcasts. In some cases, however, resources might not be seen as available if the WINS server isn't updated by the computer providing the resources.

- **M-Node (Mixed Node).** A combination of B-Node and P-Node. WINS clients first try to use broadcasts for name resolution. If this fails, the clients try using a WINS server. Using this node type still results in a lot of broadcast traffic.

- **H-Node (Hybrid Node).** A combination of B-Node and P-Node. WINS clients first try to use a WINS server for name resolution. If this fails, the clients try broadcasts for name resolution. This node type is best for most networks that use WINS servers because it reduces broadcast traffic.

Small networks might not need a WINS server

WINS resolves NetBIOS computer names to IP addresses. Using WINS, the computer name DESKTOP12, for example, could be resolved to an IP address that enables computers on a Microsoft network to find one another and transfer information. On a small network without subnets and with a limited number of computers, WINS clients can rely on broadcasts for name resolution. In this case it isn't necessary to set up a WINS server.

WINS name registration and cache

WINS maintains a database of name-to-IP-address mappings automatically. Whenever a computer or resource becomes available, it registers itself with the WINS server to tell the server the name and IP address that it's using. As long as no other computer or resource on the network is using that name, the WINS server accepts the request and registers the computer or resource in its database.

Name registration isn't permanent. Each name that is registered has a lease period associated with it, which is called its Time to Live (TTL). A WINS client must reregister its name before the lease expires, and it attempts to do so when 50 percent of the lease period has elapsed or when it's restarted. If a WINS client doesn't reregister its name, the lease expires and is marked for deletion from the WINS database. During normal shutdown, a WINS client sends a message to the WINS server requesting the release of the registration. The WINS server then marks the record for deletion. Whenever records are marked for deletion, they are said to be *tombstoned*.

As with DNS clients, WINS clients maintain a cache of NetBIOS names that have been looked up. The WINS cache, however, is designed to hold only names looked up recently. By default, names are cached for up to 10 minutes and the cache is limited to 16 names. You can view entries in the NetBIOS cache by typing **nbtstat –c** at the command prompt.

WINS implementation details

On most networks that use WINS, you'll want to configure at least two WINS servers for name resolution. When there are multiple WINS servers, you can configure replication of database entries between the servers. Replication allows for fault tolerance and load balancing by ensuring that entries in the database of one server are replicated to its replication partners. These replication partners can then handle renewal and release requests from clients as if they held the primary registration in the first place.

WINS supports the following:

- **Persistent connections.** In a standard configuration, replication partners establish and release connections each time they replicate WINS database changes. With persistent connections, replication partners can be configured to maintain a persistent connection. This reduces the overhead associated with opening and closing connections and speeds up the replication process.

- **Automatic replication partners.** Using automatic replication partners, WINS can auto-matically configure itself for replication with other WINS servers. To do this, WINS sends periodic multicast messages to announce its availability. These messages are addressed to the WINS multicast group address (224.0.1.24), and any other WINS servers on the network that are listening for datagrams sent on this group address can receive and process the automatic replication request. After replication is set up with multicast partners, the partners use standard replication with either persistent or nonpersistent connections.

- **Manual tombstoning.** Manual tombstoning allows administrators to mark records for deletion. A record marked for deletion is said to be tombstoned. This state is then replicated to a WINS server's replication partners, which prevents the record from being re-created on a replication partner and then being replicated back to the original server on which it was marked for deletion.

- **Record export.** The record export feature allows administrators to export the entries in the WINS database to a file that can be used for tracking or reporting on which clients are using WINS.

Setting up WINS servers

To turn a computer running Windows Server into a WINS server, you must install the WINS service. This service doesn't require a dedicated server and usually uses limited resources. This means you can install the WINS service on a DNS server, a DHCP server, or a domain controller. The key requirement is that the WINS service can be installed only on a computer with a static IPv4 address. Although you can install WINS on a server with multiple IPv4 addresses or multiple network interfaces, this isn't recommended because the server might not be able to replicate properly with its replication partners. In most cases you won't want to configure a domain controller as a WINS server.

You can install the WINS service by following these steps:

1. In Server Manager, select Add Roles And Features from the Manage menu. This starts the Add Roles And Features Wizard. If the wizard displays the Before You Begin page, read the introductory text and then tap or click Next.

2. On the Installation Type page, Role-Based Or Feature-Based Installation is selected by default. Tap or click Next.

3. On the Server Selection page, you can choose to install roles and features on running servers or virtual hard disks (VHDs). Either select a server from the server pool or select a server from the server pool on which to mount a VHD. If you are adding roles and features to a VHD, tap or click Browse and then use the Browse For Virtual Hard Disks dialog box to locate the VHD. When you are ready to continue, tap or click Next twice.

4. On the Features page, select WINS Server. Tap or click Next. If additional features are required, you'll see an additional dialog box. Tap or click Add Features to close the dialog box, and add the required features to the server installation. When you are ready to continue, tap or click Next.

5. Tap or click Install. When the wizard finishes installing the selected features, tap or click Close.

After you install WINS Server, the WINS console is available on the Tools menu in Server Manager. After you open the WINS console, select the WINS server you are working with to see its entries, as shown in Figure 9-1.

CHAPTER 9

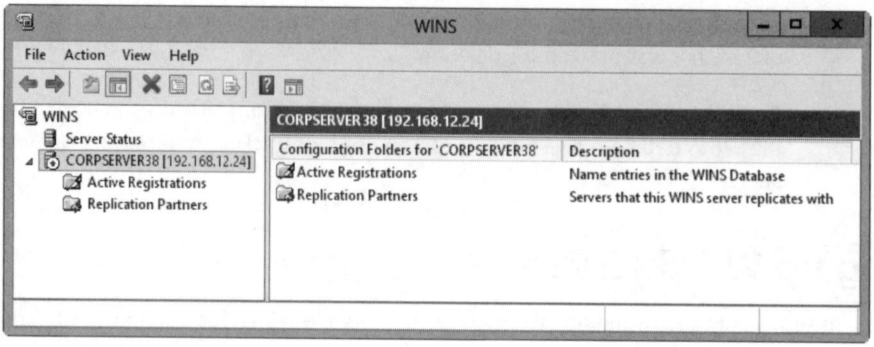

Figure 9-1 The WINS console.

The most important postinstallation task for the WINS service is to configure replication part-ners. However, you should check the Transmission Control Protocol/Internet Protocol (TCP/IP) configuration of the WINS server. It should have only itself listed as the WINS server to use and shouldn't have a secondary WINS server. This prevents the WINS client on the server from reg-istering itself with a different WINS database, which can cause problems.

To set the server's primary WINS server address to its own IP address and clear out any secondaries from the list, open Network And Sharing Center. In Network And Sharing Center, tap or click Change Adapter Settings. In Network Connections, press and hold or right-click the connection you want to work with and then select Properties. In the Properties dia-log box, open the Internet Protocol (TCP/IP) Properties dialog box by double-tapping or double-clicking Internet Protocol Version 4 (TCP/IPv4). Tap or click Advanced to display the Advanced TCP/IP Settings dialog box, and then tap or click the WINS tab. Set the WINS serv-er's IP address as the WINS server to use and remove any additional WINS server addresses. When you're finished, tap or click OK twice and then tap or click Close.

You can remotely manage and configure WINS. Just start the WINS console, press and hold or right-click the WINS node in the left pane, and select Add Server. In the Add Server dialog box, select WINS Server, type the name or IP address of the WINS server, and then tap or click OK.

The command-line counterpart to the WINS console is *Netsh WINS*. From the command prompt on a computer running Windows Server, you can use Netsh WINS to perform all the tasks available in the WINS console and to perform some additional tasks that can't be per-formed in the WINS console. To start Netsh WINS and access a particular WINS server, follow these steps:

1. Start a command prompt and then type **netsh** to start Netsh. The command prompt changes to *netsh>*.

2. Access the WINS context within Netsh by typing **wins**. The command prompt changes to *netsh wins>*.

3. Type **server** followed by the Universal Naming Convention (UNC) name or IP address of the WINS server, such as **\\wins2** or **\\10.10.15.2**. If the WINS server is in a different domain from your logon domain, you should type the fully qualified domain name (FQDN) of the server, such as **\\wins2.cpandl.com**.

4. The command prompt changes to *netsh wins server>*. You can now work with the selected server. If you later want to work with a different server, you can do this without having to start over. Just type **server** followed by the UNC name or IP address of that server.

NOTE

Technically, you don't need to type the double backslashes (\\) when you specify an IP address. You must, however, type \\ when you specify a server's name or FQDN. Because of this discrepancy, you might want to use \\ all the time so that you won't leave it out by accident when you need it.

TROUBLESHOOTING

Resolving WINS replication errors

Most WINS replication errors involve incorrectly configured WINS servers. If you see replication errors in the event logs, check the TCP/IP configuration of your WINS servers. Every WINS server in the organization should be configured as its own primary WINS server, and you should delete any secondary WINS server addresses. This ensures that WINS servers register their NetBIOS names only in their own WINS databases. If you don't configure WINS in this way, WINS servers might register their names with other WINS servers. This can result in different WINS servers owning the NetBIOS names that a particular WINS server registers and, ultimately, lead to problems with WINS itself. For more information on this issue, see Microsoft Knowledge Base article 321208 (*http://support.microsoft.com/default.aspx?scid=kb;en-us;321208*).

Configuring replication partners

When you have two or more WINS servers on a network, you should configure replication between them. When servers replicate database entries with each other, they are said to be *replication partners*.

Replication essentials

WINS servers have two replication roles:

- **Push partner.** A push partner is a replication partner that notifies other WINS servers that updates are available.

- **Pull partner.** A pull partner is a replication partner that requests updates.

By default, all WINS servers have replication enabled and replication partners are configured to use both push and pull replication. After a replication partner notifies a partner that there are changes by using push replication, the partner can request the changes by using pull replication. This pulls the changes down to its WINS database. In addition, all replication is done using persistent connections by default to increase efficiency.

Because replication is automatically enabled and configured, all you have to do to start replication is tell each WINS server about the other WINS servers that are available. On a small network you can do this using the automatic replication partners feature. Because the automatic replication partners feature can cause a lot of broadcast traffic on medium or large networks that contain many clients and servers, you'll probably want to designate specific replication partners to reduce broadcast traffic.

Configuring automatic replication partners

To configure automatic replication partners, follow these steps:

1. Start the WINS console. If the server you want to configure as a partner isn't listed in the console, press and hold or right-click the WINS node in the left pane and select Add Server. In the Add Server dialog box, select WINS Server, type the name or IP address of the WINS server, and then tap or click OK.

2. Expand the server entry, press and hold or right-click the Replication Partners entry in the left pane, and then select Properties. In the Replication Partners Properties dialog box, tap or click the Advanced tab, as shown in Figure 9-2.

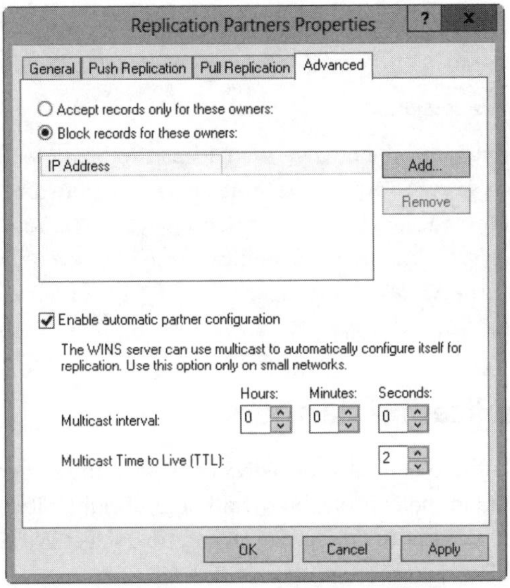

Figure 9-2 Enabling automatic replication.

3. Select the Enable Automatic Partner Configuration check box.

4. Use the Multicast Interval options to set the interval between multicast broadcasts to the WINS server group address. These broadcasts are used to tell other WINS servers about the availability of the server you are configuring. The default interval is 0 minutes, which disables WINS broadcasts.

Inside OUT

Registrations remain until restart

After a server is discovered and added as a partner through multicasting, the server remains as a configured partner until you restart the WINS service or until you restart the server. When WINS is shut down properly, part of the shutdown process is to send messages to current replication partners and remove its registration.

5. Use the Multicast Time To Live (TTL) combo box to specify how many links multicast broadcasts can go through before being discarded. The default is 2, which allows the broadcasts to be relayed through two routers.

6. Tap or click OK.

CHAPTER 9

Inside OUT

Multicast through routers is possible

The Multicast TTL is used to allow the discovery broadcasts to be routed between subnets. This means you can use automatic replication partners on networks with subnets. However, routing isn't automatic just because a datagram has a TTL. You must configure the routers on each subnet to forward multicast traffic received from the WINS multicast group address (224.0.1.24).

Using designated replication partners

To designate specific replication partners, start the WINS console. If the server you want to configure as a partner isn't listed in the console, press and hold or right-click the WINS node in the left pane and select Add Server. In the Add Server dialog box, select WINS Server, type the name or IP address of the WINS server, and then tap or click OK.

Next, expand the server entry, press and hold or right-click the Replication Partners entry in the left pane, and then select New Replication Partners. In the New Replication Partner dialog box, type the name or IP address of the WINS server that should be used as a replication partner and then tap or click OK. The replication partner is added and listed as available in the WINS console. As shown in Figure 9-3, replication partners are listed by server name, IP address, and replication type.

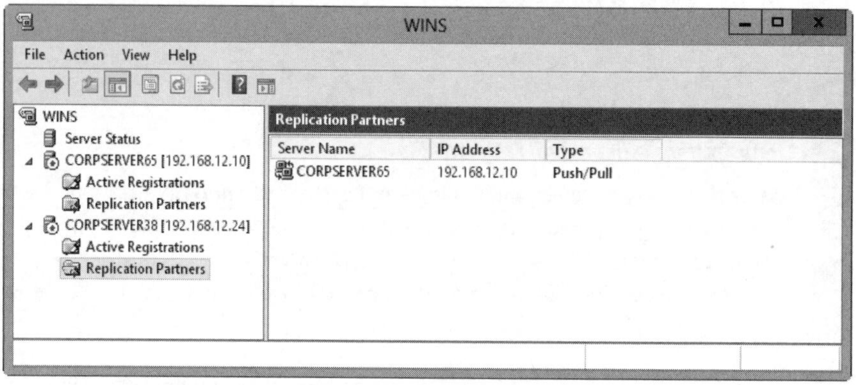

Figure 9-3 Viewing replication partners in the WINS console.

By default, the replication partner is configured to use both push and pull replication in addition to persistent connections. After you configure a replication partner, the configuration is permanent. If you restart a server, you don't need to reconfigure replication partners.

To view or change the replication settings for a replication partner, start the WINS console. Expand the server entry for the server you want to work with and then select the Replication Partners entry in the left pane. Double-tap or double-click the replication partner in the details pane. This displays the replication partner's Properties dialog box. Tap or click the Advanced tab, as shown in Figure 9-4.

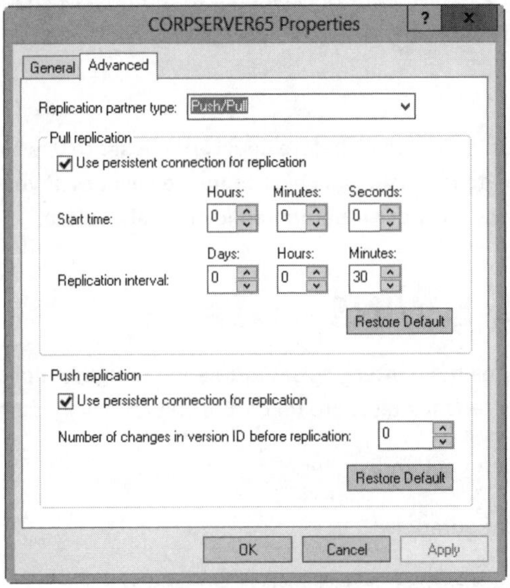

Figure 9-4 Configuring replication partner settings.

The configuration options are used as follows:

- Replication Partner Type   Sets the replication type as push, pull, or push/pull.

- Pull Replication

    - *Use Persistent Connection For Replication*. Configures pull replication so that a persistent connection is used. This reduces the time spent opening and closing connections and improves performance.

    - *Start Time*. Sets the hour of the day when replication should begin, using a 24-hour clock.

    - *Replication Interval*. Sets the frequency of replication. The default is every 30 minutes.

CHAPTER 9

- Push Replication

  - *Use Persistent Connection For Replication.* Configures push replication so that a persistent connection is used. This reduces the time spent opening and closing connections and improves performance.

  - *Number Of Changes In Version ID Before Replication.* Can be used to limit replication by allowing replication to occur only when a set number of changes have occurred in the local WINS database.

NOTE

By default, Number Of Changes In Version ID Before Replication is set to 0, which allows replication at the designated interval whenever there are changes. If you set a specific value, that many changes must occur before replication takes place.

Configuring and maintaining WINS

WINS is fairly easy to configure and maintain after you set it up and configure replication partners. The key configuration and maintenance tasks are related to the following issues:

- Configuring burst handling as the network grows

- Checking server status and configuration

- Checking active registrations and scavenging records if necessary

- Maintaining the WINS database

Configuring burst handling

If you configured the WINS server on a network with more than 100 clients, you should enable burst handling of registrations. As your network grows, you should change the burst-handling sessions as appropriate for the number of clients on the network. To configure burst handling of registration and name refresh requests, start the WINS console. Press and hold or right-click the server entry in the WINS console and then select Properties. In the Properties dialog box, tap or click the Advanced tab, as shown in Figure 9-5.

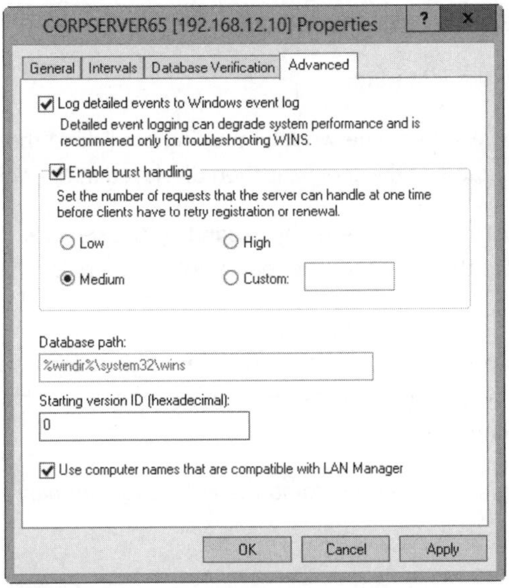

Figure 9-5 Setting burst handling for medium and large networks.

Select the Enable Burst Handling check box, and then select one of the following burst-handling settings:

- Low, for handling up to 300 registration and name refresh requests

- Medium, for handling up to 500 registration and name refresh requests

- High, for handling up to 1,000 registration and name refresh requests

Inside OUT

Set a custom threshold for burst handling

You also can set a custom threshold value for burst handling. To do this, select Custom and then enter a threshold value between 50 and 5,000. For example, if you set the threshold to 5,000, up to 5,000 requests can be queued at once. Keep in mind that you would do this only if your network environment needs this setting. If you set the value to 5,000 but only need a queue that allows up to 100 name registration requests, you would waste a lot of server resources maintaining a very large queue that you don't need.

CHAPTER 9

Checking server status and configuration

Using the WINS console, you can do the following:

- View the status of all WINS servers on the network by tapping or clicking the Server Status entry in the left pane. The status of the servers is then displayed in the right pane.

- View the current replication partners for a server by expanding the server entry and selecting Replication Partners in the left pane. The replication partners for that server are displayed in the right pane.

- View server statistics for startup, replication, queries, releases, registrations, and replication partners by pressing and holding or right-clicking the server entry in the left pane and selecting Display Server Statistics.

Using Netsh WINS, you can view server statistics by typing the following command:

```
netsh wins server ServerName show statistics
```

Here, *ServerName* is the name or IP address of the WINS server you want to work with, such as \\WINS02 or 10.10.12.15. An example of the statistics follows:

```
***You have Read and Write access to the server corpsvr02.cpandl.com***

        WINS Started                            : 8/11/2014 at 12:25:11
        Last initialization                     : 8/13/2014 at 03:12:12
        Last planned scavenging                 : 8/20/2014 at 11:22:24
        Last admin triggered scavenging         : 8/10/2014 at 18:41:31
        Last replicas tombstones scavenging     : 8/22/2014 at 10:31:44
        Last replicas verification scavenging   : 8/24/2014 at 13:42:12
        Last planned replication                : 8/10/2014 at 17:30:59
        Last admin triggered replication        : 8/27/2014 at 09:32:45
        Last reset of counter                   : 9/01/2014 at 19:33:21


Counter Information :
        No of U and G Registration requests = (250 222)
        No of Successful/Failed Queries = (812/67)
        No of U and G Refreshes = (213 144)
        No of Successful/Failed Releases = (68/12)
        No of U. and G. Conflicts = (12 10)


~~~~~~~~~~~~~~~~~~~~~~~~~~~~~~~~~~~~~~~~~~~~~~~~~~~~~~~~~~~~~~~~~~~~~~~~~~~~~~~
WINS Partner IP Address    -No. of Replication    -No. of Comm Failure
~~~~~~~~~~~~~~~~~~~~~~~~~~~~~~~~~~~~~~~~~~~~~~~~~~~~~~~~~~~~~~~~~~~~~~~~~~~~~~~
    192.168.15.18        -      153        -      2
```

These statistics are useful for troubleshooting registration and replication problems. Once they're configured, scavenging and replication are automatic. Problems to look for include the following:

- **Replication.** If there are problems with replication, you should see a high number of communication failures relative to the number of replications. Check the links over which replication is occurring to see if there are intermittent failures or times when links aren't available.

- **Name resolution.** If WINS clients are having problems with name resolution, you'll see a high number of failed queries. You might need to scavenge the database for old records more frequently. Check the server statistics for the renew interval, extinction interval, extinction timeout, and verification interval in the Intervals tab in the server's Properties dialog box.

- **Registration release.** If WINS clients aren't releasing registrations properly, you'll see a high number of failed releases. Clients might not be getting shut down properly.

You can view the configuration details for a WINS server by typing the following command:

```
netsh wins server ServerName show info
```

Here, *ServerName* is the name or IP address of the WINS server. The output looks like this:

```
WINS Database backup parameter
~~~~~~~~~~~~~~~~~~~~~~~~~~~~~~~~~~~~~~~~~~~~~~~~~~~~~~~~~~~~~~~~~~
Backup Dir         :
Backup on Shutdown  : Disabled

Name Record Settings(day:hour:minute)
~~~~~~~~~~~~~~~~~~~~~~~~~~~~~~~~~~~~~~~~~~~~~~~~~~~~~~~~~~~~~~~~~~
Refresh Interval               : 006:00:00
Extinction(Tombstone) Interval : 004:00:00
Extinction(Tombstone) TimeOut  : 006:00:00
Verification Interval          : 024:00:00

Database consistency checking parameters :
~~~~~~~~~~~~~~~~~~~~~~~~~~~~~~~~~~~~~~~~~~~~~~~~~~~~~~~~~~~~~~~~~~
Periodic Checking              : Disabled

WINS Logging Parameters:
~~~~~~~~~~~~~~~~~~~~~~~~~~~~~~~~~~~~~~~~~~~~~~~~~~~~~~~~~~~~~~~~~~

Log Database changes to JET log files     : Enabled
Log details events to System Event Log    : Enabled

Burst Handling Parameters :
~~~~~~~~~~~~~~~~~~~~~~~~~~~~~~~~~~~~~~~~~~~~~~~~~~~~~~~~~~~~~~~~~~
```

```
Burst Handling State                : Enabled
Burst handling queue size           : 500
```

Checking active registrations and scavenging records

Using the WINS console, you can view the active registrations in the WINS database by expanding the server entry, pressing and holding or right-clicking Active Registrations, and choosing Display Records. In the Display Records dialog box, tap or click Find Now without making any selections to see all the available records or use the filter options to specify the types of records you want to view, and then tap or click Find Now. To tombstone a record manually, press and hold or right-click it and then select Delete. This deletes it from the current server, and this deletion is then replicated to other WINS servers—that is, the record will be replicated marked as Tombstoned.

Netsh provides many ways to examine records in the WINS database. Because examining records in the WINS database is something you won't do frequently, the easiest way to do it is to list all available records and write the information to a file you can search. To do this, type the following command:

```
netsh wins server ServerName show database Servers={}
```

Here, *ServerName* is the name or IP address of the WINS server. The output shows you the registration entries in the database as follows:

```
~~~~~~~~~~~~~~~~~~~~~~~~~~~~~~~~~~~~~~~~~~~~~~~~~~~~~~~~~~~~~~~~~~~~~~~~~~~~~~~~~~
     NAME   -T-S-VERSION  -G-   IPADDRESS   -   EXPIRATION DATE
~~~~~~~~~~~~~~~~~~~~~~~~~~~~~~~~~~~~~~~~~~~~~~~~~~~~~~~~~~~~~~~~~~~~~~~~~~~~~~~~~~
Retrieving database from the Wins server 192.168.1.50
CPANDL     [1Bh]-D-A- 2  -U- 192.168.1.50  -7/30/2014 13:18:01 PM
CORPSVR02  [00h]-D-A- 7  -U- 192.168.1.50  -7/30/2014 13:18:01 PM
CORPSVR02  [20h]-D-A- 6  -U- 192.168.1.50  -7/30/2014 13:18:01 PM
CPANDL     [00h]-D-A- 4  -N- 192.168.1.50  -7/30/2014 13:18:01 PM
CPANDL     [1Ch]-D-A- 3  -I- 192.168.1.50  -7/30/2014 13:18:01 PM
CPANDL     [1Eh]-D-A- 1  -N- 192.168.1.50  -7/30/2014 13:18:01 PM
```

WINS automatically scavenges the database to mark old records for deletion. To see when this is done, check the server statistics for the renew interval, extinction interval, extinction timeout, and verification interval in the Intervals tab in the server's Properties dialog box.

You can initiate scavenging (referred to as an *admin-triggered scavenging* in the server statistics) by pressing and holding or right-clicking the server entry in the WINS console and selecting Scavenge Database. To initiate scavenging at the command prompt, type **netsh wins server *ServerName* init scavenge**, where *ServerName* is the name or IP address of the WINS server.

After scavenging, the renew interval, extinction interval, extinction timeout, and verification interval are used to mark each record as follows:

- If the renew interval has not expired, the record remains marked as Active.

- If the renew interval has expired, the record is marked as Released.

- If the extinction interval has expired, the record is marked as Tombstoned.

If the record was tombstoned, it's deleted from the database. If the record is active and was replicated from another server but the verification interval has expired, the record is revalidated.

Maintaining the WINS database

The WINS database, like any database, should be maintained. You should routinely perform the following maintenance operations:

- Verifying the database consistency

- Compacting the database

- Backing up the database

Verifying the WINS database consistency

You can configure WINS to verify the database consistency automatically. This operation checks and verifies the registered names. To configure automatic database consistency checks, follow these steps:

1. Start the WINS console. Press and hold or right-click the WINS node in the left pane and select Add Server. In the Add Server dialog box, select WINS Server, type the name or IP address of the WINS server, and then tap or click OK.

2. Press and hold or right-click the server entry in the WINS console and select Properties. In the Properties dialog box, tap or click the Database Verification tab, as shown in Figure 9-6.

CHAPTER 9

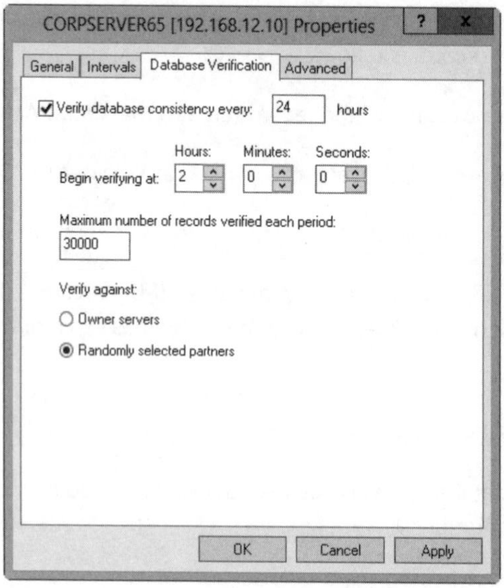

Figure 9-6 Setting automatic verification of the WINS database.

3. Select the Verify Database Consistency Every check box and then set a check interval. Typically, you'll want to perform this operation no more frequently than once every 24 hours.

4. Use the Begin Verifying At section to set the time at which verification checks are started. This time is on a 24-hour clock, and the default time is 2 hours, 0 minutes, and 0 seconds, meaning 2:00 A.M. If you instead want verification checks to begin at 2:00 P.M., you set the time to 14 hours, 0 minutes, and 0 seconds.

5. Set other options as necessary and then tap or click OK.

Compacting the WINS database

The WINS database should be compacted periodically—at least once a month or once every other month, depending on how often computers are added to or removed from your network. In addition to reducing the size of the database by squeezing out unneeded space that has been allocated and is no longer needed, compacting the database can improve performance and make the database more reliable.

At the command prompt, you can compact the WINS database by following these steps:

1. Change to the WINS directory by typing **cd %SystemRoot%\System32\Wins**.

2. Stop the WINS service by typing **net stop wins**.

3. Compact the WINS database by typing **jetpack wins.mdb winstemp.mdb**.

4. Start the WINS service by typing **net start wins**.

NOTE

During the time you're compacting the WINS database, the WINS service will be unavailable. To reduce the impact on network name resolution, schedule WINS maintenance during times when replication and resolution needs are low.

Backing up the WINS database

By default, the WINS database is not backed up—but it should be. You can perform manual or automatic backups. To back up the WINS database manually, follow these steps:

1. Start the WINS console. Press and hold or right-click the server entry and then select Back Up Database.

2. In the Browse For Folder dialog box, select the folder in which the WINS server should store the database backup files and then tap or click OK.

3. The WINS server then writes the backup files to a subfolder of the designated folder called Wins_bak. When it finishes, tap or click OK.

To configure automatic backups of the WINS database, follow these steps:

1. Start the WINS console. Press and hold or right-click the server entry and then select Properties.

2. In the Properties dialog box, tap or click Browse in the General tab.

3. Use the Browse For Folder dialog box to select the folder in which the WINS server should store the database backup files and then tap or click OK. The WINS server will write backup files to a subfolder of the designated folder called Wins_bak.

4. Select Back Up Database During Shutdown.

5. Tap or click OK. Now whenever you shut down the server or the WINS service on the server, the WINS service will back up the database to the designated folder.

CHAPTER 9

Restoring the WINS database

If something happens to the WINS database, you can use the backup files to recover it to the state it was in prior to the problem. To restore the WINS database from backup, follow these steps:

1. Start the WINS console. Press and hold or right-click the server entry, point to All Tasks, and then select Stop. This stops the WINS service.

2. Press and hold or right-click the server entry again and select Restore Database.

3. In the Browse For Folder dialog box, select the parent folder of the Wins_bak folder created during backup (not the Wins_bak folder itself) and tap or click OK.

4. The WINS server then restores the database from backup. When it finishes, tap or click OK.

5. The WINS service will be restarted automatically.

Enabling WINS lookups through DNS

You can enable WINS lookups through DNS. This integration of WINS and DNS provides an additional opportunity to resolve an IP address to a host name when normal DNS lookups fail. Typically, this might be necessary for clients that can't register their IP addresses in DNS using dynamic updates.

You enable WINS name resolution on a zone-by-zone basis from within the DNS console. Follow these steps:

1. In the DNS console, press and hold or right-click the zone you want to work with and then select Properties.

2. In the Properties dialog box, tap or click the WINS or WINS-R tab as appropriate for the type of zone. The WINS tab is used with forward lookup zones, and the WINS-R tab is used with reverse lookup zones.

3. Select Use WINS Forward Lookup or Use WINS Reverse Lookup as appropriate.

4. If you're not using DNS servers running on Windows Server, select Do Not Replicate This Record. This ensures that the WINS record that is created during this configuration won't be replicated to servers that don't support this feature.

5. Type the IP address of a WINS server you want to use for name resolution and then tap or click Add. Repeat this step for other WINS servers that should be used.

6. Tap or click OK.

CHAPTER 9

Active Directory architecture

Active Directory is an extensible directory service that enables you to manage network resources efficiently. A directory service does this by storing detailed information about each network resource, which makes it easier to provide basic lookup and authentication. Being able to store large amounts of information is a key objective of a directory service, but the information must also be organized so that it's easily searched and retrieved.

Active Directory provides for authenticated search and retrieval of information by dividing the physical and logical structures of the directory into separate layers. Understanding the physical structure of Active Directory is important for understanding how a directory service works. Understanding the logical structure of Active Directory is important for implementing and managing a directory service.

Active Directory physical architecture

The physical layer of Active Directory controls the following features:

- How directory information is accessed

- How directory information is stored on the hard disk of a server

Active Directory physical architecture: A top-level view

From a physical or machine perspective, Active Directory is part of the security subsystem. (See Figure 10-1.) The security subsystem runs in user mode. User-mode applications do not have direct access to the operating system or hardware. This means that requests from user-mode applications have to pass through the executive services layer and must be validated before being executed.

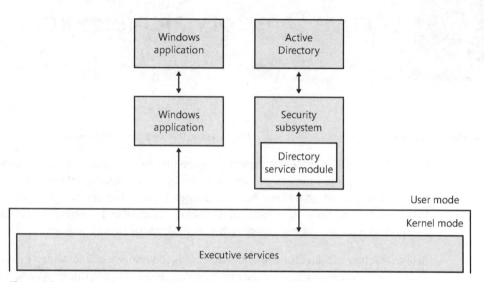

Figure 10-1 Top-level overview of the Active Directory architecture.

NOTE

Being part of the security subsystem makes Active Directory an integrated part of the access-control and authentication mechanism built into Microsoft Windows Server. Access control and authentication protect the resources in the directory.

Each resource in Active Directory is represented as an object. Anyone who tries to gain access to an object must be granted permission. Lists of permissions that describe who or what can access an object are referred to as *access control lists (ACLs)*. Each object in the directory has an associated ACL.

You can restrict permissions across a broader scope by using Group Policy. The security infra-structure of Active Directory uses policy to enforce security models on several objects that are grouped logically. You can also set up trust relationships between groups of objects to allow for an even broader scope for security controls between trusted groups of objects that need to interact. From a top-level perspective, that's how Active Directory works, but to really under-stand Active Directory, you need to delve into the security subsystem.

Active Directory within the Local Security Authority

Within the security subsystem, Active Directory is a subcomponent of the Local Security Authority (LSA). As shown in Figure 10-2, the LSA consists of many components that provide the security features of Windows Server and ensure that access control and authentication function as they should. Not only does the LSA manage local security policy but it also performs the following functions:

- Generates security identifiers (SIDs)

- Provides the interactive process for logon

- Manages auditing

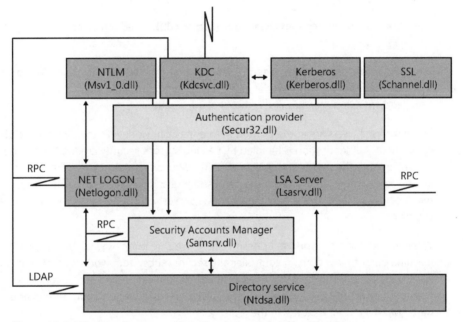

Figure 10-2 Windows Server security subsystem using Active Directory.

When you work through the security subsystem as it is used with Active Directory, you'll find the three following key areas:

- Authentication mechanisms

  - **NTLM (Msv1_0.dll).** Used for Windows NT LAN Manager (NTLM) authentication

  - **Kerberos (Kerberos.dll) and Key Distribution Center (Kdcsvc.dll).** Used for Kerberos V5 authentication

  - **SSL (Schannel.dll).** Used for Secure Sockets Layer (SSL) authentication

  - **Authentication provider (Secur32.dll).** Used to manage authentication

- Logon/access-control mechanisms

    - **NET LOGON (Netlogon.dll).** Used for interactive logon through NTLM. For NTLM authentication, NET LOGON passes logon credentials to the directory service module and returns the SIDs for objects to clients making requests.

    - **LSA Server (Lsasrv.dll).** Used to enforce security policies for Kerberos and SSL. For Kerberos and SSL authentication, LSA Server passes logon credentials to the directory service module and returns the SIDs for objects to clients making requests.

    - **Security Accounts Manager (Samsrv.dll).** Used to enforce security policies for NTLM.

- **Directory service component: Directory service (Ntdsa.dll).** Used to provide directory services for Windows Server. This is the actual module that allows you to perform authenticated searches and retrieval of information.

As you can see, users are authenticated before they can work with the directory service component. Authentication is handled by passing a user's security credentials to a domain controller. After the user is authenticated on the network, the user can work with resources and perform actions according to the permissions and rights the user has been granted in the directory. At least, this is how the Windows Server security subsystem works with Active Directory.

When you are on a network that doesn't use Active Directory, or when you log on locally to a machine other than a domain controller, the security subsystem works as shown in Figure 10-3. Here, the directory service is not used. Instead, authentication and access control are handled through the Security Accounts Manager (SAM). Here, information about resources is stored in the SAM, which itself is stored in the registry.

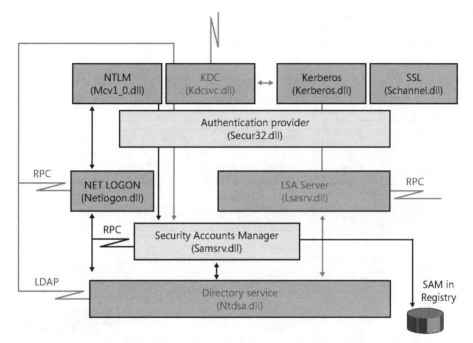

Figure 10-3 Windows Server security subsystem without Active Directory.

Directory service architecture

As you've seen, incoming requests are passed through the security subsystem to the directory service component. The directory service component is designed to accept requests from
many kinds of clients. As shown in Figure 10-4, these clients use specific protocols to interact
with Active Directory.

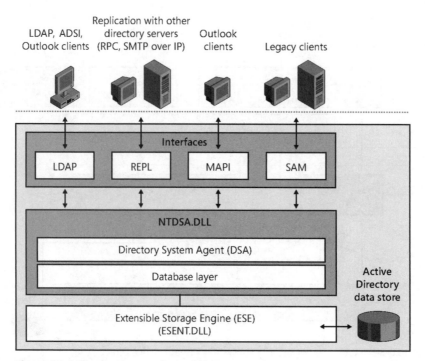

Figure 10-4 The directory service architecture.

Protocols and client interfaces

The primary protocol for Active Directory access is Lightweight Directory Access Protocol (LDAP). LDAP is an industry standard protocol for directory access that runs over Transmission Control Protocol/Internet Protocol (TCP/IP). Active Directory supports LDAP versions 2 and 3. Clients can use LDAP to query and manage directory information—depending on the level of permissions they have been granted—by establishing a TCP connection to a domain controller. The default TCP port used by LDAP clients is 389 for standard communications and 636 for SSL.

Active Directory supports intersite and intrasite replication through the REPL interface, which uses either remote procedure calls (RPCs) or Simple Mail Transfer Protocol over Internet Protocol (SMTP over IP), depending on how replication is configured. Each domain controller is responsible for replicating changes to the directory to other domain controllers, using a multimaster approach. The multimaster approach used in Active Directory allows updates to be made to the directory by any domain controller and then replicated to other domain controllers.

For older messaging clients, Active Directory supports the Messaging Application Programming Interface (MAPI). MAPI allows messaging clients to access Active Directory (which Microsoft Exchange uses for storing information), primarily for address book lookups. Messaging clients use RPCs to establish a connection with the directory service. The RPC Endpoint Mapper uses UDP port 135 and TCP port 135. Current messaging clients use LDAP instead of RPC.

For legacy clients, Active Directory supports the SAM interface, which also uses RPCs. This allows legacy clients to access the Active Directory data store the same way they would access the SAM database. The SAM interface is also used during certain replication activities.

Directory System Agent and database layer

Clients and other servers use the LDAP, REPL, MAPI, and SAM interfaces to communicate with the directory service component (Ntdsa.dll) on a domain controller. From an abstract perspective, the directory service component consists of the following:

- Directory System Agent (DSA), which provides the interfaces through which clients and other servers connect

- Database layer, which provides an application programming interface (API) for working with the Active Directory data store

From a physical perspective, the DSA is really the directory service component and the database layer resides within it. The reason for separating the two is that the database layer performs a vital abstraction. Without this abstraction, the physical database on the disk would not be protected from the applications the DSA interacts with. Furthermore, the object-based hierarchy used by Active Directory would not be possible. Why? Because the data store is in a single data file using a flat (record-based) structure, whereas the database layer is used to represent the flat file records as objects within a hierarchy of containers. Like a folder that can contain files and other folders, a container is simply a type of object that can contain other objects and other containers.

Each object in the data store has a name relative to the container in which it's stored. This name is aptly called the object's *relative distinguished name (RDN)*. An object's full name, also referred to as an object's *distinguished name (DN)*, describes the series of containers, from the highest to the lowest, of which the object is a part.

To make sure every object stored in Active Directory is truly unique, each object also has a globally unique identifier (GUID), which is generated when the object is created. Unlike an object's RDN or DN, which can be changed by renaming an object or moving it to another container, the GUID can never be changed. The DSA assigns it to an object, and it never changes.

The DSA is responsible for ensuring that the type of information associated with an object adheres to a specific set of rules. This set of rules is referred to as the *schema*. The schema is stored in the directory and contains the definitions of all object classes and describes their attributes. In Active Directory the schema is the set of rules that determine the kind of data that can be stored in the database, the type of information that can be associated with a particular object, the naming conventions for objects, and so on.

Inside OUT

The schema saves space and helps validate attributes

The schema serves to separate an object's definition from its actual values. Thanks to the schema, Active Directory doesn't have to write information about all of an object's possible attributes when it creates the object. When you create an object, only the defined attributes are stored in the object's record. This saves a lot of space in the database. Furthermore, because the schema specifies not only the valid attributes but also the valid values for those attributes, Active Directory uses the schema both to validate the attributes that have been set on an object and to keep track of what other possible attributes are available.

The DSA is also responsible for enforcing security limitations. It does this by reading the SIDs on a client's access token and comparing them to the SIDs for an object. If a client has appropriate access permissions, it is granted access to an object. If a client doesn't have appropriate access permissions, it's denied access.

Finally, the DSA is used to initiate replication. Replication is the essential functionality that ensures that the information stored on domain controllers is accurate and consistent with changes that have been made. Without proper replication, the data on servers would become stale and outdated.

Extensible Storage Engine

Active Directory uses the Extensible Storage Engine (ESE) to retrieve information from, and write information to, the data store. The ESE uses indexed and sequential storage with transactional processing, as follows:

- **Indexed storage.** Indexing the data store allows the ESE to access data quickly without having to search the entire database. In this way, the ESE can rapidly retrieve, write, and update data.

- **Sequential storage.** Sequentially storing data means that the ESE writes data as a stream of bits and bytes. This allows data to be read from and written to specific locations.

- **Transactional processing.** Transactional processing ensures that changes to the database are applied as discrete operations that can be rolled back if necessary.

Any data that is modified in a transaction is copied to a temporary database file. This gives two views of the data that's being changed: one view for the process changing the data and one view of the original data that's available to other processes until the transaction is finalized. A transaction remains open as long as changes are being processed. If an error occurs during processing, the transaction can be rolled back to return the object being modified to its original state. If Active Directory finishes processing changes without errors occurring, the transaction can be committed.

As with most databases that use transactional processing, Active Directory maintains a transaction log. A record of the transaction is written first to an in-memory copy of an object, then to the transaction log, and finally to the database. The in-memory copy of an object is stored in the *version store*. The version store is an area of physical memory (RAM) used for processing changes. Typically, the version store is 25 percent of the physical RAM.

The transaction log serves as a record of all changes that have yet to be committed to the database file. The transaction is written first to the transaction log to ensure that even if the database shuts down immediately afterward, the change is not lost and can take effect. To ensure this, Active Directory uses a checkpoint file to track the point up to which transactions in the log file have been committed to the database file. After a transaction is committed to the database file, it can be cleared out of the transaction log.

The actual update of the database is written from the in-memory copy of the object in the version store and not from the transaction log. This reduces the number of disk I/O operations and helps ensure that updates can keep pace with changes. When many updates are made, however, the version store can reach a point at which it's overwhelmed. This happens when the version store reaches 90 percent of its maximum size. When this happens, the ESE temporarily stops processing cleanup operations that are used to return space after an object is modified or deleted from the database.

Although in earlier releases of Windows Server index creation could affect domain controller performance, Windows Server 2012 and Windows Server 2012 R2 allow you to defer index creation to a time when it's more convenient. By deferring index creation to a designated point in time, rather than creating indexes as needed, you can ensure that domain controllers can perform related tasks during off-peak hours, thereby reducing the impact of index creation. Any attribute that is in a deferred index state will be logged in the event log every 24 hours. Look for event IDs 2944 and 2945. When indexes are created, event ID 1137 is logged.

In large Active Directory environments, deferring index creation is useful to prevent domain controllers from becoming unavailable due to building indexes after schema updates. Before you can use deferred index creation, you must enable the feature in the forest root domain. You do this using the *DSHeuristics* attribute of the Directory Services object for the domain. Set the eighteenth bit of this attribute to 1. Because the tenth bit of this attribute typically also is set to 1 (if the attribute is set to a value), the attribute normally is set to the following: 000000000100000001. You can modify the *DSHeuristics* attribute using ADSI Edit or Ldp.exe.

ADSI Edit is a snap-in you can add to any Microsoft Management Console (MMC). Open a new MMC by entering **MMC** at a prompt and then use the Add/Remove Snap-in option on the File menu to add the ADSI Edit snap-in to the MMC. You can then use ADSI Edit to modify the *DSHeuristics* attribute by completing the following steps:

1. Press and hold or right-click the root node and then select Connect To. In the Connection Settings dialog box, choose the Select A Well Known Naming Context option. On the related selection list, select Configuration (because you want to connect to the Configuration naming context for the domain) and then tap or click OK.

2. In ADSI Edit, work your way down to the CN=Directory Service container by expanding the Configuration naming context, the CN=Configuration container, the CN=Services container, and the CN=Windows NT container.

3. Next, press and hold or right-click CN=Directory Service and then select Properties. In the Properties dialog box, select the dsHeuristics properties and then tap or click Edit.

4. In the String Attribute Editor dialog box, type the desired value, such as **000000000100000001**, and then tap or click OK twice.

Ldp is a graphical utility. Open Ldp by typing **ldp** in the Apps Search box or at a prompt. You can then use Ldp to modify the *DSHeuristics* attribute by completing the following steps:

1. Choose Connect on the Connection menu and then connect to a domain controller in the forest root domain. After you connect to a domain controller, choose Bind on the Connection menu to bind to the forest root domain using an account with enterprise administrator privileges.

2. Next, choose Tree on the View menu to open the Tree View dialog box. In the Tree View dialog box, choose CN=Configuration container as the base distinguished name to work with.

3. In the CN=Configuration container, expand the CN=Services container, expand the CN=Windows NT container, and then select the CN=Directory Service container. Next, press and hold or right-click CN=Directory Service and then select Modify.

4. In the Modify dialog box, type the attribute name as **dsHeuristics** and the value as **000000000100000001**.

5. If the attribute already exists, set the Operation as Replace. Otherwise, set the Operation as Add.

6. Tap or click Enter to create an LDAP transaction for this update, and then tap or click Run to apply the change.

NOTE
The value 000000000100000001 is nine zeros with a 1 in the tenth position followed by seven zeros with a 1 in the eighteenth position.

Once the change is replicated to all domain controllers in the forest, they will defer index creation automatically. You must then trigger index creation manually by either restarting domain controllers, which rebuilds the schema cache and deferred indexes, or by triggering a schema update for the RootDSE. In ADSI Edit, you can initiate an update by connecting to the RootDSE. To do this, press and hold or right-click the root node and then select Connect To. In the Connection Settings dialog box, choose the Select A Well Known Naming Context option. On the related selection list, select RootDSE and then tap or click OK. In ADSI Edit, press and hold or right-click the RootDSE node and then select Update Schema Now.

To allow for object recovery and for the replication of object deletions, an object that is deleted from the database is logically removed rather than physically deleted. The way deletion works depends on whether Active Directory Recycle Bin is enabled or disabled.

Deletion without Recycle Bin   When Active Directory Recycle Bin is disabled, as with standard deployments prior to Windows Server 2008 R2, most of the object's attributes are removed and the object's *Deleted* attribute is set to TRUE to indicate that it has been deleted. The object is then moved to a hidden Deleted Objects container where its deletion can be replicated to other domain controllers. (See Figure 10-5.) In this state, the object is said to be *tombstoned*. To allow the tombstoned state to be replicated to all domain controllers, and thus removed from all copies of the database, an attribute called *tombstoneLifetime* is also set on the object. The *tombstoneLifetime* attribute specifies how long the tombstoned object should remain in the Deleted Objects container. The default lifetime is 180 days.

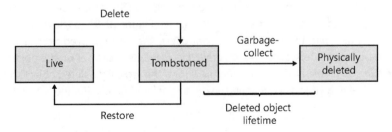

Figure 10-5 Active Directory object life cycle without Recycle Bin.

Inside OUT

The tombstone process

When an object is tombstoned, Active Directory changes the distinguished name so that the object name can't be recognized. Next, Active Directory deletes all of the object's link-valued attributes, and most of the object's non-link-valued attributes are cleared. Finally, the object is moved to the Deleted Objects container.

You can recover tombstoned objects using tombstone reanimation. However, attribute values that were removed are not recovered. This means the link-valued attributes, which include group memberships of user accounts, and the non-link-valued attributes are not recovered.

The ESE uses a garbage-collection process to clear out tombstoned objects after the tombstone lifetime has expired, and it performs automatic online defragmentation of the database after garbage collection. The interval at which garbage collection occurs is a factor of the value set for the *garbageCollPeriod* attribute and the tombstone lifetime. By default, garbage collection occurs every 12 hours. When there are more than 5,000 tombstoned objects to be garbage-collected, the ESE removes the first 5,000 tombstoned objects and then uses the CPU availability to determine if garbage collection can continue. If no other process is waiting for the CPU, garbage collection continues for up to the next 5,000 tombstoned objects whose tombstone lifetime has expired, and the CPU availability is again checked to determine if garbage collection can continue. This process continues until all the tombstoned objects whose tombstone lifetime has expired are deleted or another process needs access to the CPU.

Deletion with Recycle Bin   When Active Directory Recycle Bin is enabled as an option with Windows Server 2008 R2 and later, objects aren't tombstoned when they are initially deleted and their attributes aren't removed. Instead, the deletion process occurs in stages.

In the first stage of the deletion, the object is said to be *logically deleted*. Here, the object's *Deleted* attribute is set to TRUE to indicate that it has been deleted. The object is then moved, with its attributes and name preserved, to a hidden Deleted Objects container where its deletion can be replicated to other domain controllers. (See Figure 10-6.) To allow the logically deleted state to be replicated to all domain controllers, and thus removed from all copies of the database, an attribute called *ms-DeletedObjectLifetime* is also set on the object. The *ms-DeletedObjectLifetime* attribute specifies how long the logically deleted object should remain in the Deleted Objects container. The default deleted object lifetime is 180 days.

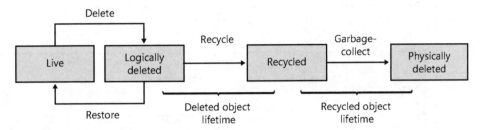

Figure 10-6 Active Directory object life cycle with Recycle Bin.

When the deleted object lifetime expires, Active Directory removes most of the object's attributes, changes the distinguished name so that the object name can't be recognized, and sets the object's *tombstoneLifetime* attribute. This effectively tombstones the object (and the process is the same as the legacy tombstone process).

The recycled object remains in the Deleted Objects container until the recycled object lifetime expires, and it's said to be in the *recycled* state. The default tombstone lifetime is 180 days.

As with deletion without the Recycle Bin, the ESE uses a garbage-collection process to clear out tombstoned objects after the tombstone lifetime has expired. This garbage-collection process is the same as discussed previously.

Data store architecture

After you examine the operating system components that support Active Directory, the next step is to see how directory data is stored on a domain controller's hard disks. As Figure 10-7 shows, the data store has a primary data file and several other types of related files, including working files and transaction logs.

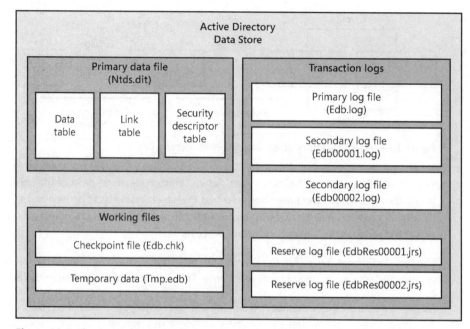

Figure 10-7 The Active Directory data store.

These files are used as follows:

- **Primary data file (Ntds.dit).** Physical database file that holds the contents of the Active Directory data store

- **Checkpoint file (Edb.chk).** Checkpoint file that tracks the point up to which the transactions in the log file have been committed to the database file

- **Temporary data (Tmp.edb).** Temporary workspace for processing transactions

- **Primary log file (Edb.log).** Primary log file that contains a record of all changes that have yet to be committed to the database file

- **Secondary log files (Edb00001.log, Edb00002.log, …).** Additional logs files that are used as needed

- **Reserve log files (EdbRes00001.jrs, EdbRes00002.jrs, …).** Files that are used to reserve space for additional log files if the primary log file becomes full

The primary data file contains three indexed tables:

- **Active Directory data table.** The data table contains a record for each object in the data store, which can include object containers, the objects themselves, and any other type of data that is stored in Active Directory.

- **Active Directory link table.** The link table is used to represent linked attributes. A linked attribute is an attribute that refers to other objects in Active Directory. For example, if an object contains other objects (that is, it is a container), attribute links are used to point to the objects in the container.

- **Active Directory security descriptor table.** The security descriptor table contains the inherited security descriptors for each object in the data store. Windows Server uses this table so that inherited security descriptors no longer have to be duplicated on each object. Instead, inherited security descriptors are stored in this table and linked to the appropriate objects. This makes Active Directory authentication and control mechanisms very efficient.

Think of the data table as having rows and columns; the intersection of a row and a column is a *field*. The table's rows correspond to individual instances of an object. The table's columns correspond to attributes defined in the schema. The table's fields are populated only if an attribute contains a value. Fields can be a fixed or a variable length. If you create an object and define only 10 attributes, only these 10 attributes will contain values. Although some of those values might be fixed length, others might be variable length.

Records in the data table are stored in data pages that have a fixed size of 8 kilobytes (KBs, or 8,192 bytes). Each data page has a page header, data rows, and free space that can contain row offsets. The page header uses the first 96 bytes of each page, leaving 8,096 bytes for data and row offsets.

Row offsets indicate the logical order of rows on a page, which means that offset 0 refers to the first row in the index, offset 1 refers to the second row, and so on. If a row contains long, variable-length data, the data might not be stored with the rest of the data for that row. Instead, Active Directory can store an 8-byte pointer to the actual data, which is stored in a collection of 8 KB pages that aren't necessarily written contiguously. In this way, an object and all its attribute values can be much larger than 8 KBs.

The primary log file has a fixed size of 10 megabytes (MBs). When this log fills up, Active Directory creates additional (secondary) log files as necessary. The secondary log files are also limited to a fixed size of 10 MBs. Active Directory uses the reserve log files to reserve space on disk for log files that might need to be created. Because several reserve files are already created, this speeds up the transactional logging process when additional logs are needed.

By default, the primary data file, the working files, and the transaction logs are all stored in the same location. On a domain controller's system volume, you'll find these files in the %SystemRoot%\NTDS folder. Although these are the only files used for the data store, Active Directory uses other files. For example, policy files and other files, such as startup and shutdown scripts used by the DSA, are stored in the %SystemRoot%\Sysvol folder.

NOTE

A distribution copy of Ntds.dit is also placed in the %SystemRoot%\System32 folder. This is used to create a domain controller when you install Active Directory on a server running Windows Server. If the file doesn't exist, the Active Directory Installation Wizard will need the installation media to promote a member server to be a domain controller.

Inside OUT

The log files have attributes you can examine

When you stop Active Directory Domain Services, you can use the Extensible Storage Engine Utility (esentutl.exe) to examine log file properties. At an elevated command prompt, type **esentutl.exe –ml LogName**, where *LogName* is the name of the log file to examine, such as edb.log, to obtain detailed information on the log file, including the base name, creation time, format version, log sector sizes, and logging parameters. While Active Directory Domain Services is offline, you can also use esentutl.exe to perform defragmentation, integrity checks, and copy, repair, and recovery operations. To learn more about this utility, type **esentutl.exe** at an elevated command prompt. Following the prompts, you can then type the letter corresponding to the operation you want to learn more about. For example, type **esentutl.exe** and then press the D key to learn the defragmentation options.

Active Directory logical architecture

The logical layer of Active Directory determines how you see the information contained in the data store and also controls access to that information. The logical layer does this by defining the namespaces and naming schemes used to access resources stored in the directory. This provides a consistent way to access directory-stored information regardless of type. For example, you can obtain information about a printer resource stored in the directory in much the same way that you can obtain information about a user resource.

To better understand the logical architecture of Active Directory, you need to understand the following topics:

- Active Directory objects

- Active Directory domains, trees, and forests

- Active Directory trusts

- Active Directory namespaces and partitions

- Active Directory data distribution

Active Directory objects

Because so many types of resources can be stored in the directory, a standard storage mechanism was needed and Microsoft developers decided to use the LDAP model for organizing data. In this model, each resource that you want to represent in the directory is created as an object with attributes that define information you want to store about the resource. For example, the user object in Active Directory has attributes for a user's first name, middle initial, last name, and logon name.

An object that holds other objects is referred to as a *container object* or simply a *container*. The data store itself is a container that contains other containers and objects. An object that can't contain other objects is a *leaf object*. Each object created within the directory is of a particular type or class. The object classes are defined in the schema. Some of the object types include:

- User

- Group

- Computer

- Printer

When you create an object in the directory, you must comply with the schema rules for that object class. Not only do the schema rules dictate the available attributes for an object class, they also dictate which attributes are mandatory and which attributes are optional. When you create an object, mandatory attributes must be defined. For example, you can't create a user object without specifying the user's full name and logon name. The reason is that these attributes are mandatory.

Some rules for attributes also are defined in policy. For example, the default security policy for Windows Server specifies that a user account must have a password and that the password must meet certain complexity requirements. If you try to create a user account without a password or with a password that doesn't meet these complexity requirements, the account creation will fail because of the security policy.

The schema also can be extended or changed. This allows administrators to define new object classes, add attributes to existing objects, and change the way attributes are used. However, you need special access permissions and privileges to work directly with the schema. Specifically, you must be a member of the Schema Admins group.

Active Directory domains, trees, and forests

Within the directory, objects are organized using a hierarchical tree structure called a *directory tree*. The structure of the hierarchy is derived from the schema and is used to define the parent–child relationships of objects stored in the directory.

A logical grouping of objects that allows central management of those objects is called a *domain*. In the directory tree, a domain is itself represented as an object. In fact, it's the parent object of all the objects it contains. An Active Directory domain can contain millions of objects. You can create a single domain that contains all the resources you want to manage centrally. In Figure 10-8, a domain object is represented by a large triangle and the objects it contains are as shown.

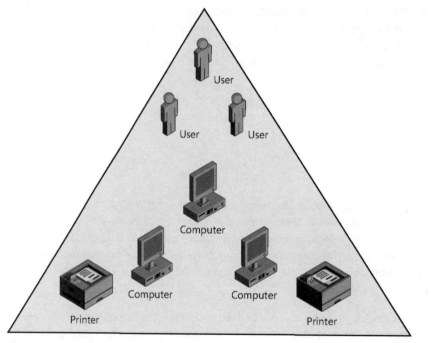

Figure 10-8 An Active Directory domain.

Domains are only one of several building blocks for implementing Active Directory structures. Other building blocks include the following:

- Active Directory trees, which are logical groupings of domains

- Active Directory forests, which are logical groupings of domain trees

As described, a directory tree is used to represent a hierarchy of objects, showing the parent–child relationships between those objects. Thus, when we're talking about a domain tree, we're looking at the relationship between parent and child domains. The domain at the top of the domain tree is referred to as the *root domain* (think of this as an upside-down tree). More specifically, the root domain is the first domain created in a new tree within Active Directory. When talking about forests and domains, there is an important distinction made between the first domain created in a new forest—a forest root domain—and the first domain created in each additional tree within a forest—a root domain.

In the example shown in Figure 10-9, cohovineyard.com is the root domain in an Active Directory forest with a single tree—that is, it's the forest root domain. As such, cohovineyard.com is the parent of the sales.cohovineyard.com domain and the mf.cohovineyard.com domain. The mf.cohovineyard.com domain itself has a related subdomain: bottling.mf.cohovineyard.com. This makes mf.cohovineyard.com the parent of the child domain bottling.mf.cohovineyard.com.

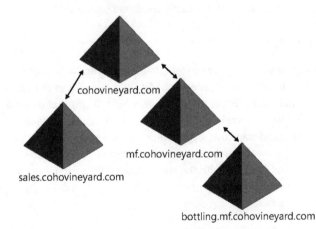

cohovineyard.com

mf.cohovineyard.com

sales.cohovineyard.com

bottling.mf.cohovineyard.com

Figure 10-9 An Active Directory forest with a single tree.

The most important thing to note about this and all domain trees is that the namespace is contiguous. Here, all the domains are part of the cohovineyard.com namespace. If a domain is a part of a different namespace, it can be added as part of a new tree in the forest. In the example shown in Figure 10-10, a second tree is added to the forest. The root domain of the second tree is cohowinery.com, and this domain has cs.cohowinery.com as a child domain.

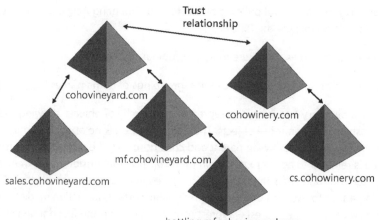

Figure 10-10 An Active Directory forest with multiple trees.

You create a forest root domain by installing Active Directory on a stand-alone server and establishing the server as the first domain controller in a new forest. To add a tree to an existing forest, you install Active Directory on a stand-alone server and configure the server as a member of the forest, but with a domain name that is not part of the current namespace being used. You make the new domain part of the same forest to allow associations called *trusts* to be made between domains that belong to different namespaces.

Active Directory trusts

In Active Directory, two-way transitive trusts are established automatically between domains that are members of the same forest. Trusts join parent and child domains in the same domain tree and join the roots of domain trees. Trusts are transitive, which means that if domain A trusts domain B and domain B trusts domain C, domain A trusts domain C. Because all trusts in Active Directory are two-way and transitive, by default every domain in a forest implicitly trusts every other domain. It also means that resources in any domain are available to users in every domain in the forest. For example, with the trust relationships in place, a user in the sales.cohovineyard.com domain could access a printer or other resources in the cohovineyard.com domain—or even the cs.cohowinery.com domain.

However, the creation of a trust doesn't imply any specific permission. Instead, it implies only the ability to grant permissions. No privileges are automatically implied or inherited by the establishment of a trust relationship. The trust doesn't grant or deny any permission. It exists only to allow administrators to grant permissions.

Several key terms are used to describe trusts, including the following:

- **Trusting domain.** A domain that establishes a trust is referred to as a *trusting domain*. Trusting domains allow access by users from another domain (the trusted domain).

- **Trusted domain.** A domain that trusts another domain is referred to as a *trusted domain*. Users in trusted domains have access to another domain (the trusting domain).

To make it easier for administrators to grant access throughout a forest, Active Directory allows you to designate two types of administrators:

- **Enterprise administrators.** These are the designated administrators of the enterprise. Enterprise administrators can manage and grant access to resources in any domain in the Active Directory forest.

- **Domain administrators.** These are the designated administrators of a particular domain. Domain administrators in a trusting domain can access user accounts in a trusted domain and set permissions that grant access to resources in the trusting domain.

Going back to the example, Tom, an enterprise administrator in this forest, could grant access to resources in any domain in the forest. If Jim, in the sales.cohovineyard.com domain, needed access to a printer in the cs.cohowinery.com domain, Tom could grant this access. Because in this example cs.cohowinery.com is the trusting domain and sales.cohovineyard.com is the trusted domain, Sarah, a domain administrator in the cs.cohowinery.com domain, also could grant permission to use the printer. Bob, a domain administrator for sales.cohovineyard.com, could not grant such permissions, however, because the printer resource exists in a domain other than the one he controls.

To continue working with Figure 10-10, take a look at the arrows that designate the trust relationships. For a user in the sales.cohovineyard.com domain to access a printer in the cs.cohowinery.com domain, the request must pass through the following series of trust relationships:

1. The trust between sales.cohovineyard.com and cohovineyard.com

2. The trust between cohovineyard.com and cohowinery.com

3. The trust between cohowinery.com and cs.cohowinery.com

The *trust path* defines the path that an authentication request must take between the two domains. Here, a domain controller in the user's local domain (sales.cohovineyard.com) would pass the request to a domain controller in the cohovineyard.com domain. This domain controller, in turn, would pass the request to a domain controller in the cohowinery.com domain.

CHAPTER 10

Finally, the request would be passed to a domain controller in the cs.cohowinery.com domain, which would ultimately grant or deny access.

In all, the user's request has to pass through four domain controllers—one for each domain between the user and the resource. Because the domain structure is separate from the network's physical structure, the printer could actually be located right beside the user's desk and the user would still have to go through this process. If you expand this scenario to include all the users in the sales.cohovineyard.com domain, you could potentially have hundreds of users whose requests have to go through a similar process to access resources in the cs.cohowinery .com domain.

Omitting the fact that the domain design in this scenario is very poor—because if many users are working with resources, those resources are ideally in their own domain or in a domain closer in the tree—one solution for this problem would be to establish a *shortcut trust* between the user's domain and the resource's domain. With a shortcut trust, you could specify that cs.cohowinery.com explicitly trusts sales.cohovineyard.com. Now when a user in the sales.cohovineyard.com domain requests a resource in the cs.cohowinery.com domain, the local domain controller knows about cs.cohowinery.com and can directly submit the request for authentication. This means that the sales.cohovineyard.com domain controller sends the request directly to a cs.cohowinery.com domain controller.

Shortcut trusts are designed to help make more efficient use of resources on a busy network. On a network with a lot of activity, the explicit trust can reduce the overhead on servers and on the network as a whole. You shouldn't implement shortcut trusts without careful planning. You should use them only when resources in one domain will be regularly accessed by users in another domain. They don't need to be used between two domains that have a parent–child relationship because a default trust already exists explicitly between a parent domain and a child domain.

With Active Directory, you can also make use of *external trusts*. External trusts are manually configured and are always nontransitive. External trusts can be either one-way or two-way trusts. When you establish a trust between a domain in one forest and a domain in another forest, security principals from the external domain can access resources in the internal domain. In the internal domain, Active Directory creates a foreign security principal to represent each security principal in the external domain. Foreign security principals can be added to domain local groups in the internal domain.

Active Directory namespaces and partitions

Any data stored in the Active Directory database is represented logically as an object. Every object in the directory has a relative distinguished name (RDN). That is, every object has a name relative to the parent container in which it's stored. The relative name is the name of the object itself, and it's also referred to as an object's *common name* (CN). This relative name is stored as an attribute of the object and must be unique for the container in which it's located. Following this, no two objects in a container can have the same common name, but two objects in different containers could have the same name.

In addition to an RDN, objects have a distinguished name (DN). An object's DN describes the object's place in the directory tree and is logically the series of containers from the highest to the lowest of which the object is a part. It's called a distinguished name because it serves to distinguish like-named objects and, as such, must be unique in the directory. No two objects in the directory will have the same distinguished name.

Every object in the directory has a parent, except the root of the directory tree, which is referred to as the rootDSE. The rootDSE represents the top of the logical namespace for a directory. It has no name per se. Although there is only one rootDSE, the information stored in the rootDSE specifically relates to the domain controller on which the directory is stored. In a domain with multiple domain controllers, the rootDSE will have a slightly different representation on each domain controller. The representation relates to the capability and configuration of the domain controller in question. In this way, Active Directory clients can determine the capabilities and configuration of a particular domain controller.

Below the rootDSE, every directory tree has a root domain. The root domain is the first domain created in an Active Directory forest and is also referred to as the forest root domain. After it's established, the forest root domain never changes, even if you add new trees to the forest. The LDAP distinguished name of the forest root domain is DC=*ForestRootDomainName*, where DC is an LDAP identifier for a domain component and *ForestRootDomainName* is the actual name of the forest root domain. Each level within the domain tree is broken out as a separate domain component. For example, if the forest root domain is cohovineyard.com, the domain's distinguished name is DC=cohovineyard,DC=com.

When Active Directory is installed on the first domain controller in a new forest, three containers are created below the rootDSE:

- The Forest Root Domain container, which is the container for the objects in the forest root domain

- The Configuration container, which is the container for the default configuration and all policy information

- The Schema container, which is the container for all objects, classes, attributes, and syntaxes

From a logical perspective, these containers are organized as shown in Figure 10-11. The LDAP identifier for an object's common name is CN. The DN for the Configuration container is CN=configuration,DC=*ForestRootDomainName*, and the DN for the Schema container is CN=schema,CN=configuration,DC=*ForestRootDomainName*. In the cohovineyard.com

CHAPTER 10

domain, the DNs for the Configuration and Schema containers are CN=configuration,DC= cohovineyard,DC=com and CN=schema,CN=configuration,DC=cohovineyard,DC=com, respectively. As you can see, the distinguished name allows you to walk the directory tree from the relative name of the object you are working with to the forest root.

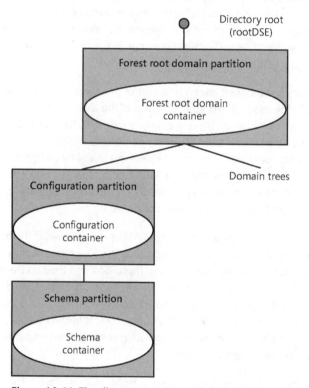

Figure 10-11 The directory tree in a new forest.

As shown in the figure, the Forest Root Domain container and the Configuration and Schema containers exist within their own individual partitions. Active Directory uses partitions to logically apportion the directory so that each domain controller does not have to store a complete copy of the entire directory. To do this, object names are used to group objects into logical categories so that the objects can be managed and replicated as appropriate. The largest logical category is a directory partition. All directory partitions are created as instances of the domainDNS object class.

As far as Active Directory is concerned, a domain is a container of objects that is logically partitioned from other container objects. When you create a new domain in Active Directory, you create a new container object in the directory tree, and that container, in turn, is contained by a domain directory partition for the purposes of management and replication.

Active Directory data distribution

Active Directory uses partitions to help distribute three general types of data:

● Domainwide data, which is data replicated to every domain controller in a domain

● Forestwide data, which is data replicated to every domain controller in a forest

● Application data, which is data replicated to an arbitrary set of domain controllers

Every domain controller stores at least one domain directory partition and two forestwide data partitions: the schema partition and the configuration partition. Data in a domain directory partition is replicated to every domain controller in the domain as a writeable replica.

Forestwide data partitions are replicated to every domain controller in the forest. The configuration partition is replicated as a writeable replica. The schema partition is replicated as a read-only replica, and the only writeable replica is stored on a domain controller that is designated as having the schema operations master role. Other operations master roles also are defined.

Active Directory can replicate application-specific data that is stored in an application partition, such as the default application partitions used with zones in Domain Name System (DNS) that are integrated with Active Directory. Application partition data is replicated on a forest-wide, domainwide, or other basis to domain controllers that have a particular application partition. If a domain controller doesn't have an application partition, it doesn't receive a replica of the application partition.

In addition to full replicas that are distributed for domains, Active Directory distributes partial replicas of every domain in the forest to special domain controllers designated as global catalog servers. The partial replicas stored on global catalog servers contain information on every object in the forest and are used to facilitate searches and queries for objects in the forest. Because only a subset of an object's attributes is stored, the amount of data replicated to and maintained by a global catalog server is significantly smaller than the total size of all object data stored in all the domains in the forest.

Every domain must have at least one global catalog server. By default, the first domain controller installed in a domain is set as that domain's global catalog server. You can change the global catalog server, and you can designate additional servers as global catalog servers as necessary.

CHAPTER 10

Designing and managing the domain environment

As you learned in the previous chapter, the physical structure of Active Directory is tightly integrated with the security architecture of the Microsoft Windows operating system. At a high level, Active Directory provides interfaces to which clients can connect, and the directory physically exists on disk in a database file called Ntds.dit. When you install Active Directory on a computer, the computer becomes a domain controller. When you implement Active Directory, you can have as many domain controllers as you need to support the directory service needs of the organization.

Before you implement or modify the Active Directory domain environment, you need to consider the limitations and architecture requirements for the following processes:

- Replication

- Search and global catalogs

- Compatibility and functional levels

- Authentication and trusts

- Delegated authentication

- Operations masters

Remember that planning for Active Directory is an ongoing process that you should think about whether you are planning to deploy Active Directory for the first time or have already deployed Active Directory in your organization. Why? Because every time you consider making changes to your organizational structure or network infrastructure, you should consider how this affects Active Directory and plan accordingly.

In planning for Active Directory, few things are outside the scope of the design. When you initially deploy Active Directory, you need to develop an Active Directory design and implementation plan that involves every level of your organization and your network infrastructure.

After you deploy Active Directory, any time you plan to change your organizational structure or network infrastructure, you should determine the impact on Active Directory. You then need to plan for and implement any changes to Active Directory that are required.

Design considerations for Active Directory replication

Active Directory uses a multimaster replication model. Every domain controller deployed in the organization is autonomous, with its own copy of the directory. When you need to make changes to standard directory data, you can do so on any domain controller and you can rely on Active Directory's built-in replication engine to replicate the changes to other domain controllers in the organization as appropriate.

As shown in Figure 11-1, the actual mechanics of replication depend on the level and role of a domain controller in the organization. To help manage replication, Active Directory uses partitions in the following ways:

- Forestwide data is replicated to every domain controller in the forest and includes the configuration and schema partitions for the forest. A domain controller designated as the schema master maintains the only writeable copy of the schema data. Every domain controller maintains a writeable copy of the configuration data.

- Domainwide data is replicated to every domain controller in a domain and includes only the data for a particular domain. Every domain controller in a domain has a writeable copy of the data for that domain.

NOTE

Domain controllers designated as Domain Name System (DNS) servers also replicate directory partitions for DNS. Every domain controller that is designated as a DNS server has a copy of the ForestDNSZones and DomainDNSZones partitions. Windows Server 2008 and later support two types of domain controllers: writeable domain controllers and read-only domain controllers. Writeable domain controllers are the standard type of domain controller and are the only type of domain controller with writeable directory partitions. Read-only domain controllers, in contrast, have directory partitions that can be read but not modified. To help make the architecture and design discussions easier to follow, I discuss architecture and design considerations for read-only domain controllers separately, and you'll find a complete discussion in Chapter 15, "Deploying read-only domain controllers."

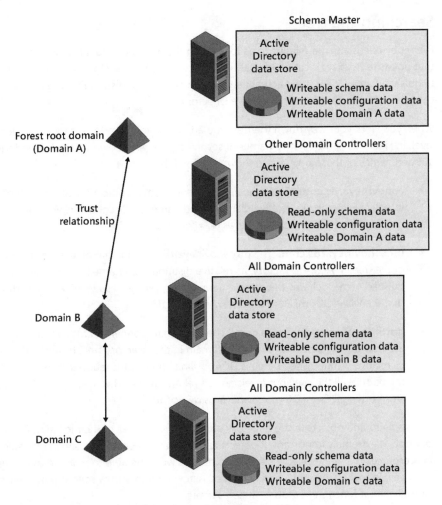

Figure 11-1 Replication of data in the Active Directory data store.

Design considerations for Active Directory search and global catalogs

Active Directory uses the Lightweight Directory Access Protocol (LDAP) model to query and manage directory information. You can locate objects in the directory by using an LDAP query.

Searching the tree

Every object has a name relative to its location in the directory and a distinguished name that points to its exact location in relation to the root of the directory tree. The relative distinguished name (RDN) is the actual name of the object. The distinguished name (DN) is the complete object name as seen by Active Directory.

When you work your way down the tree, you add a naming component for each successive level. In Figure 11-2 the relative names of several objects are shown on the left and the distinguished names of those objects are shown on the right.

- **cohovineyards.com.** The cohovineyards.com domain object is near the top of the tree. In Active Directory, its relative distinguished name is DC=cohovineyards and its distinguished name is DC=cohovineyards,DC=com.

- **mf.cohovineyards.com.** The mf.cohovineyards.com domain object is at the next level of the tree. In Active Directory, its relative distinguished name is DC=mf and its distinguished name includes the path to the previous level and its relative name. This means that the DN is DC=mf,DC=cohovineyards,DC=com.

- **bottling.mf.cohovineyards.com.** The bottling.mf.cohovineyards.com domain object is below the mf.cohovineyards.com domain in the directory tree. In Active Directory, its relative distinguished name is DC=bottling and its distinguished name includes the path to all the previous levels and its relative name. This means that the DN is DC=bottling,DC=mf,DC=cohovineyards,DC=com.

Being able to find objects in the directory efficiently, regardless of their location in the directory tree, is extremely important. If objects can't be easily located, users won't be able to find resources that are available and administrators won't be able to manage the available resources. To make it easier to find resources, Active Directory uses special-purpose domain controllers that function as global catalog servers.

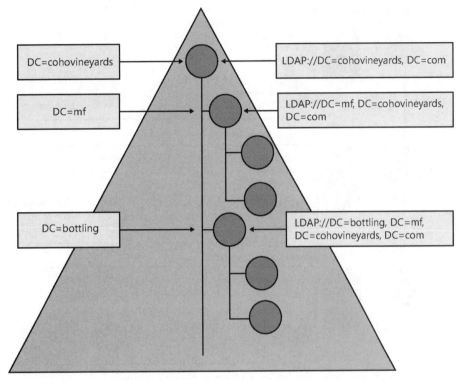

Figure 11-2 Active Directory uses the LDAP model to query and manage the directory.

Accessing the global catalog

A domain controller designated as a global catalog server contains an additional data store called the *global catalog*, as shown in Figure 11-3. The global catalog contains a partial, read-only replica of all the domains in the Active Directory forest. Although the catalog is a partial replica, it does contain a copy of every object in the directory, but only the base attributes of those objects. Queries to global catalog servers are made over TCP port 3268 for standard communications and TCP port 3269 for secure communications.

Global catalog data is replicated to global catalog servers using the normal Active Directory replication process. In an Active Directory forest with domains A, B, and C, this means that any domain controller designated as a global catalog server has a partial replica of all three domains. If a user in domain C searches for a resource located in domain A, the global catalog server in domain C can respond to the query using an attribute that has been replicated to the global catalog without needing to refer to another domain controller. Without a global catalog server, a domain controller in domain C would need to forward the query to a domain controller in domain A.

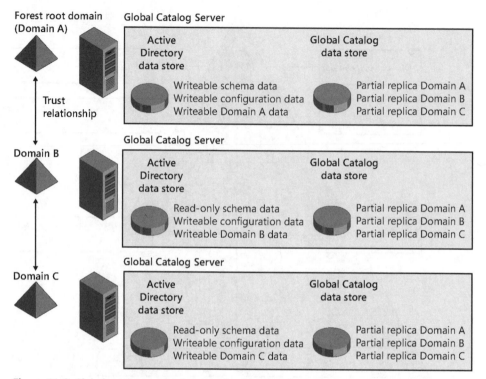

Figure 11-3 Global catalog servers in an Active Directory forest.

Designating global catalog servers

The first domain controller installed in a domain is automatically designated as a global catalog server. You can designate additional domain controllers to be global catalog servers as
well. To do this, you use the Active Directory Sites And Services tool to set the Global Catalog
Server option for the domain controller you want to be a global catalog server.

Start Active Directory Sites And Services by choosing the related option from the Tools menu
in Server Manager. Expand the site you want to work with, such as Default-First-Site-Name,
expand the related Servers node, and then select the server you want to designate as a global
catalog, as shown in Figure 11-4.

> **NOTE**
>
> You also can start Active Directory Sites And Services by typing **Dssite.msc** in the
> Everywhere Search box or at a prompt.

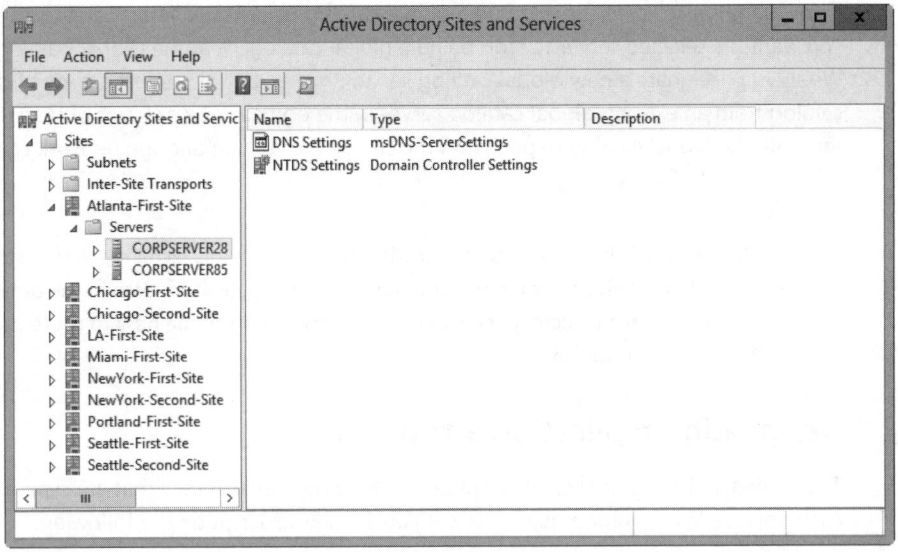

Figure 11-4 Select the server to designate as a global catalog.

In the right pane, press and hold or right-click NTDS Settings and then select Properties. This displays the NTDS Settings Properties dialog box, as shown in Figure 11-5.

Figure 11-5 Configure NTDS settings.

CHAPTER 11

If you want the selected server to be a global catalog, select the Global Catalog check box. If you want the selected server to stop being a global catalog, clear the Global Catalog check box. When you designate a new global catalog server, the server will request a copy of the global catalog from an existing global catalog server in the domain. The amount of time it takes to replicate the global catalog depends on the size of the catalog and the network configuration.

NOTE

Exchange Server is tightly integrated with Active Directory. Exchange Server stores schema data, configuration data, domain data, and application data in the directory. It also uses Active Directory replication topology to determine how to route messages within the organization.

Designating replication attributes

The contents of the global catalog are determined by the attributes that are replicated for each object class. Common object classes you'll work with include the following:

- **Computer.** Represents a computer account in the domain or forest

- **Contact.** Represents a contact in the domain or forest

- **Domain.** Represents a domain

- **Group.** Represents a group account in the domain or forest

- **InetOrgPerson.** Represents a special type of user account, which typically has been migrated from another directory service

- **PrintQueue.** Represents a logical printer (print queue) in the domain or forest

- **Server.** Represents a server account in the domain or forest

- **Site.** Represents an Active Directory site

- **Subnet.** Represents an Active Directory subnet

- **User.** Represents a user account in the domain or forest

Schema administrators can configure additional attributes to be replicated by global catalog servers. The primary reason for replicating additional attributes is to add attributes for which users routinely search. You shouldn't add attributes for which users search infrequently. You should rarely, if ever, remove attributes that are being replicated.

If you are a member of the Schema Admins group, you can manage the attributes that are replicated through the global catalog by using the Active Directory Schema snap-in for the

Microsoft Management Console (MMC). When you start this snap-in, it makes a direct connection to the schema master for the forest.

The Active Directory Schema snap-in is not available by default. You must install this tool by registering its dynamic-link library (DLL). To do this, type the following at an elevated command prompt:

```
regsvr32 schmmgmt.dll
```

After you install this tool, you can add the Active Directory Schema snap-in to a custom console by following these steps:

1. Open a blank MMC in Author mode. Type **mmc** in the Apps Search box. Next, tap or click mmc and then press Enter.

2. In your MMC, choose Add/Remove Snap-in from the File menu in the main window. This displays the Add Or Remove Snap-ins dialog box.

3. The Available Snap-ins list shows all the snap-ins that are available. Select Active Directory Schema and then tap or click Add. The Active Directory Schema snap-in is added to the Selected Snap-ins list.

4. Close the Add Or Remove Snap-ins dialog box by tapping or clicking OK and return to the console you are creating.

After you add the snap-in to a custom console, you can edit the schema for the object whose attribute you want to replicate in the global catalog. In Active Directory Schema, expand the Active Directory Schema node and then select the Attributes node. A list of the attributes for all objects in the directory appears in the right pane, as shown in Figure 11-6.

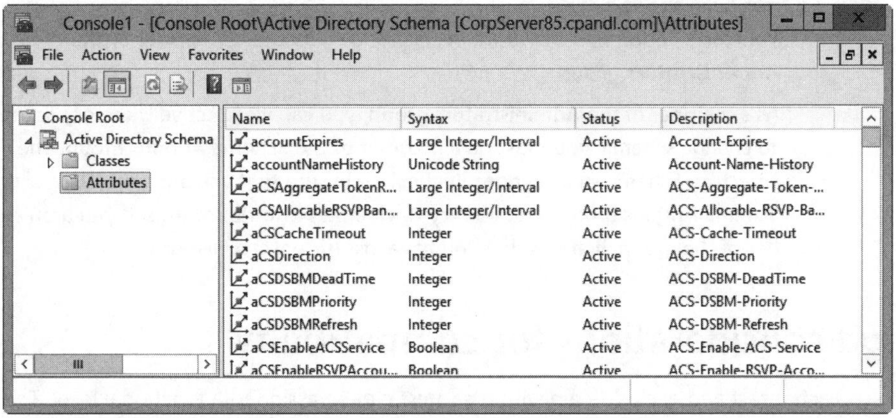

Figure 11-6 View a list of attributes for all objects in the directory.

Double-tap or double-click the attribute you want to replicate to the global catalog. In the attribute's Properties dialog box, mark the attribute to be replicated by selecting the Replicate This Attribute To The Global Catalog check box, as shown in Figure 11-7. If you want the attribute to be indexed in the database for faster search and retrieval, select the Index This Attribute check box. Although indexing an attribute enables it to be found more quickly, each index you create slightly increases the size of the Active Directory database.

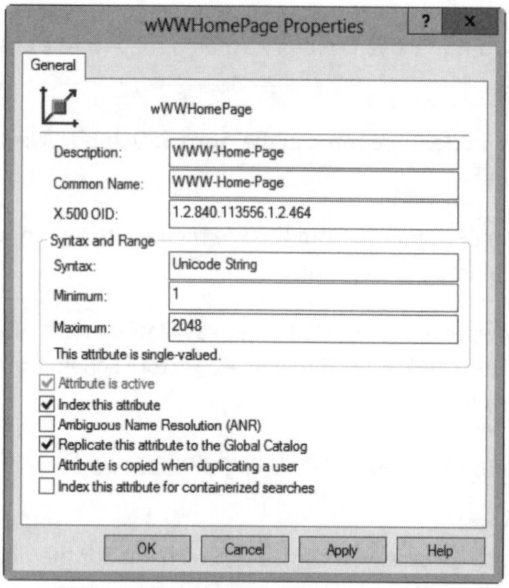

Figure 11-7 Replicate an attribute to the global catalog.

> ## TROUBLESHOOTING
>
> *You can't change an attribute even though you are a member of the Administrators group*
>
> As a member of the Administrators group, you can view Active Directory schema. To change schema, you must be a member of the Schema Admins group. The Active Directory Schema snap-in doesn't check to ensure that you are a member of the Schema Admins group until you try to change attribute settings. If you aren't a member of the group, it states that you have insufficient permissions.

Design considerations for compatibility

Each forest and each domain within a forest can be assigned a functional level. The functional level for a forest is referred to as the *forest functional level*. The functional level for a domain within a forest is referred to as the *domain functional level*. Functional levels affect the inner workings of Active Directory and are used to enable features that are compatible with the installed server versions of the Windows operating system.

Understanding domain functional level

When you set a functional level for a domain, the level of functionality applies only to that domain. This means that other domains in the forest can have different functional levels.

As shown in Table 11-1, there are several domain functional levels. Changing a functional level changes the operating systems that are supported for domain controllers. For example, in Windows 2008 functional level, the domain can have domain controllers running Windows Server 2008 or later.

> **NOTE**
>
> Generally, once you raise the domain functional level you can't lower it. However, there are specific exceptions. When you raise the domain functional level to Windows Server 2012 R2, you can lower it to Windows Server 2012 or Windows Server 2008 R2. If Active Directory Recycle Bin has not been enabled, you can also lower the domain functional level from Windows Server 2012 R2 to Windows Server 2012, Windows Server 2008 R2, or Windows Server 2008. You can't roll back the domain functional level to Windows Server 2003 or lower.

Table 11-1 Domain functional levels

Domain Functional Level	Supported Domain Controllers
Windows Server 2003	Windows Server 2012 R2 Windows Server 2012 Windows Server 2008 R2 Windows Server 2008 Windows Server 2003
Windows Server 2008	Windows Server 2012 R2 Windows Server 2012 Windows Server 2008 R2 Windows Server 2008
Windows Server 2008 R2	Windows Server 2012 R2 Windows Server 2012 Windows Server 2008 R2
Windows Server 2012	Windows Server 2012 R2 Windows Server 2012
Windows Server 2012 R2	Windows Server 2012 R2

Domains operating in Windows Server 2003 mode can use group nesting, group type conversion, universal groups, and migration of security principals. They also can use many improved

Active Directory features, including group nesting, group type conversion, universal groups, easy domain controller renaming, updating logon timestamps, migration of security principals, and Kerberos KDC key version numbers. Applications can use constrained delegation to take advantage of the secure delegation of user credentials through the Kerberos authentication protocol. You can also redirect the Users and Computers containers to define a new well-known location for user and computer accounts.

The Windows Server 2008 domain functional level adds the following features to those available with Windows Server 2003:

- Distributed File System Replication for SYSVOL, which provides more robust and granular replication of SYSVOL

- Advanced Encryption Standard (AES) support for the Kerberos protocol, allowing user accounts to use AES 128-bit or AES 256-bit encryption

- Last interactive logon information, which displays the time of the last successful interactive logon for a user, the number of failed logon attempts since the last logon, and the time of the last failed logon

- Fine-grained password policies, which make it possible for password and account lockout policy to be specified for user and global security groups in a domain

The Windows Server 2008 domain functional level adds support for Active Directory Recycle Bin, managed service accounts, Authentication Mechanism Assurance, and other important Active Directory enhancements. Although Active Directory for Windows Server 2012 has many enhancements, most of these enhancements require using only Windows Server 2012 or later domain controllers. That said, Kerberos Armoring requires the Windows Server 2012 or later domain functional level. Kerberos Armoring also is referred to as Flexible Authentication Secure Tunneling (FAST) and is defined by RFC 6113.

Understanding forest functional level

The forest functional levels are listed in Table 11-2. Generally, once you raise the forest functional level you can't lower it. However, there are specific exceptions. When you raise the forest functional level to Windows Server 2012 R2, you can lower it to Windows Server 2012 or Windows Server 2008 R2. If Active Directory Recycle Bin has not been enabled, you can also lower the forest functional level from Windows Server 2012 R2 to Windows Server 2012, Windows Server 2008 R2, or Windows Server 2008. You can't roll back the forest functional level to Windows Server 2003 or lower.

Table 11-2 Forest functional levels

Forest Functional Level	Supported Domain Controllers
Windows Server 2003	Windows Server 2012 R2 Windows Server 2012 Windows Server 2008 R2 Windows Server 2008 Windows Server 2003
Windows Server 2008	Windows Server 2012 R2 Windows Server 2012 Windows Server 2008 R2 Windows Server 2008
Windows Server 2008 R2	Windows Server 2012 R2 Windows Server 2012 Windows Server 2008 R2
Windows Server 2012	Windows Server 2012 R2 Windows Server 2012
Windows Server 2012 R2	Windows Server 2012 R2

The Windows Server 2003 forest functional level supports linked-value replication to improve the replication of changes to group memberships; domain rename and domain restructure using renaming; and one-way, two-way, and transitive forest trusts. Also supported are dynamic auxiliary classes and the deactivation of schema class objects and attributes.

The Windows Server 2008 forest functional level offers incremental improvements over the Windows Server 2003 forest functional level. When all domains within a forest are operating at this level, you see improvements in both intersite and intrasite replication throughout the organization. Also, domain controllers can use Distributed File System (DFS) replication rather than File Replication Service (FRS) replication. In addition, Windows Server 2008 security principals are not created until the primary domain controller (PDC) emulator operations master in the forest root domain is running Windows Server 2008.

The Windows Server 2008 R2 forest functional level adds the Active Directory Recycle Bin, managed service accounts, and Authentication Mechanism Assurance. The Windows Server 2012 forest functional level adds functionality improvements and support for Kerberos Armoring.

Raising or lowering the domain or forest functional level

You can raise the domain or forest functional level by using either Active Directory Domains And Trusts or Active Directory Administrative Center. Generally, once you raise the domain or forest functional level you can't lower it. However, there are specific exceptions, as discussed previously in this chapter. Keep in mind that if you enabled Active Directory Recycle Bin, you won't be able to lower the forest functional level.

In Active Directory Administrative Center, you can raise the domain functional level by following these steps:

1. The local domain is opened for management by default. If you want to work with a different domain, tap or click Manage and then tap or click Add Navigation Nodes. In the Add Navigation Nodes dialog box, select the domain you want to work with and then tap or click OK.

2. Select the domain you want to work with by tapping or clicking it in the left pane. In the Tasks pane, tap or click Raise Domain Functional Level.

3. The current domain name and functional level are displayed in the Raise Domain Functional Level dialog box.

4. To change the domain functionality, select the new domain functional level by using the list provided and then tap or click Raise.

5. Tap or click OK. The new domain functional level is replicated to each domain controller in the domain. In a large organization this operation can take several minutes or longer.

To raise the forest functional level by using Active Directory Administrative Center, follow these steps:

1. Select the domain you want to work with by tapping or clicking it in the left pane. In the Tasks pane, tap or click Raise Forest Functional Level.

2. The current forest name and functional level are displayed in the Raise Forest Functional Level dialog box.

3. To change the forest functionality, select the new forest functional level by using the list provided and then tap or click Raise.

4. Tap or click OK. The new forest functional level is replicated to each domain controller in each domain in the forest. In a large organization this operation can take several minutes or longer.

In Active Directory Domains And Trusts, you can raise the domain functional level by following these steps:

1. Press and hold or right-click the domain you want to work with and then select Raise Domain Functional Level. The current domain name and functional level appear in the Raise Domain Functional Level dialog box.

2. To change the domain functionality, select the new domain functional level by using the selection list provided and then tap or click Raise.

3. When you tap or click OK, the new domain functional level is replicated to each domain controller in the domain. In a large organization this operation can take several minutes or longer.

To raise the forest functional level by using Active Directory Domains And Trusts, complete the following steps:

1. Press and hold or right-click the Active Directory Domains And Trusts node in the console tree and then select Raise Forest Functional Level. The current forest name and functional level appear in the Raise Forest Functional Level dialog box.

2. To change the forest functionality, select the new forest functional level by using the selection list provided and then tap or click Raise.

3. When you tap or click OK, the new forest functional level is replicated to each domain controller in each domain in the forest. In a large organization this operation can take several minutes or longer.

Although you can raise the domain or forest functional level by using the graphical tools, you need to use Windows PowerShell to lower the domain or forest functional level. Several cmdlets are provided for working with domains and forests, including Get-ADDomain, Get-ADForest, Set-ADDomainMode, and Set-ADForestMode.

You use Get-ADDomain and Get-ADForest to get information about domains and forests, including the fully qualified name of a domain or forest. You use Set-ADDomainMode to raise or lower the domain functional level, and the basic syntax is as follows:

```
Set-ADDomainMode -Identity DomainName -DomainMode NewMode
```

Here, *DomainName* is the fully qualified name of the domain you want to work with and *NewMode* is the desired operating level:

- Use Windows2008Domain to set the Windows Server 2008 domain functional level.

- Use Windows2008R2Domain to set the Windows Server 2008 R2 domain functional level.

- Use Windows2012Domain to set the Windows Server 2012 domain functional level.

- Use Windows2012R2Domain to set the Windows Server 2012 R2 domain functional level.

CHAPTER 11

For example, if the current domain functional level is Windows Server 2012 R2, you could lower the domain functional level in the Cpandl.com domain to Windows Server 2012 by using the following command:

```
Set-ADDomainMode -Identity cpandl.com -DomainMode Windows2012Domain
```

When setting the domain functional level, you also could set the domain context based on the current logon domain. The easiest way to do this is to use the following command:

```
$domain = get-addomain
```

This command gets the domain object for the current logon domain and stores it in the $domain variable. After you get the domain object, you can set the domain functional level for the current logon domain as shown in this example:

```
$domain = get-addomain
Set-ADDomainMode -Identity $domain -DomainMode Windows2012Domain
```

You use Set-ADForestMode to raise or lower the forest functional level, and the basic syntax is as follows:

```
Set-ADForestMode -Identity ForestName -ForestMode NewMode
```

Here, *ForestName* is the fully qualified name of the forest you want to work with and *NewMode* is the desired operating level:

- Use Windows2008Forest to set the Windows Server 2008 forest functional level.

- Use Windows2008R2Forest to set the Windows Server 2008 R2 forest functional level.

- Use Windows2012Forest to set the Windows Server 2012 forest functional level.

- Use Windows2012R2Forest to set the Windows Server 2012 R2 forest functional level.

For example, if the current forest functional level is Windows Server 2012 R2, you could lower the forest functional level in the Cpandl.com forest to Windows Server 2012 by using the following command:

```
Set-ADForestMode -Identity cpandl.com -ForestMode Windows2012Forest
```

When setting the forest functional level, you might want to ensure that you are working directly with the schema master for the forest. The easiest way to do that is to use the following commands:

```
$forest = get-adforest
Set-ADForestMode -Identity $forest -server $forest.SchemaMaster -ForestMode
Windows2012Forest
```

Here, you get the forest object for the current logon forest and store it in the $forest variable. After you get the forest object, you set the forest functional level for the current logon forest and specify that the server you want to work with is the schema master.

Design considerations for Active Directory authentication and trusts

Authentication and trusts are integral parts of Active Directory. Before you implement any Active Directory design or try to modify your existing Active Directory infrastructure, you should have a firm understanding of how both authentication and trusts work in an Active Directory environment.

Universal groups and authentication

When a user logs on to a domain, Active Directory looks up information about the groups of which the user is a member to generate a security token for the user. The security token is needed as part of the normal authentication process and is used whenever a user accesses resources on the network.

Understanding security tokens and universal group membership caching

To generate the security token, Active Directory checks the domain local and global group memberships for the user. All the supported domain functional levels support a special type of group called a *universal group*. Universal groups can contain user and group accounts from any domain in the forest. Because global catalog servers are the only servers in a domain with forestwide domain data, the global catalog is essential for logon.

Because of problems authenticating users when global catalog servers are not available, Windows Server 2003 introduced a technique for caching universal group membership. In a domain with domain controllers running Windows Server 2003 or later, universal group membership caching can be enabled. After you enable caching, the cache is where domain controllers store universal group membership information that they have previously looked up. Domain controllers can then use this cache for authentication the next time the user logs on to the domain. The cache is maintained indefinitely and updated periodically to ensure that it's current. By default, domain controllers check the consistency of the cache every eight hours.

Thanks to universal group membership caching, remote sites running Windows Server 2003 or later domain controllers don't necessarily need to have global catalog servers configured. This gives you additional options when configuring the Active Directory forest. The assignment of security tokens is only part of the logon process. The logon process also includes authentication and the assignment of a User Principal Name (UPN) to the user.

CHAPTER 11

Inside OUT

The User Principal Name (UPN) suffix can be changed

Every user account has a User Principal Name (UPN), which consists of the User Logon Name combined with the at symbol (@) and a UPN suffix. The names of the current domain and the root domain are set as the default UPN suffix. You can specify an alternate UPN suffix to use to simplify logon or provide additional logon security. This name is used only within the forest and does not have to be a valid DNS name. For example, if the UPN suffix for a domain is it.seattle.cpandl.local, you could use an alternate UPN suffix to simplify this to cpandl.local. This would allow the user Williams to log on using williams@cpandl.local rather than williams@it.seattle.cpandl.local.

You can add or remove UPN suffixes for an Active Directory forest and all domains within that forest by completing the following steps:

1. Start Active Directory Domains And Trusts from the Administrative Tools menu.

2. Press and hold or right-click the Active Directory Domains And Trusts node and then tap or click Properties.

3. To add a UPN suffix, in the box provided type the alternate suffix and then tap or click Add.

4. To remove a UPN suffix, in the list provided tap or click the suffix to remove and then tap or click Remove.

5. Tap or click OK.

Enabling universal group membership caching

In a domain with domain controllers, you use the Active Directory Sites And Services tool to configure universal group membership caching. You enable caching on a per-site basis. Start Active Directory Sites And Services by choosing the related option from the Tools menu in Server Manager. Expand and then select the site in which you want to enable universal group membership caching, as shown in Figure 11-8.

In the right pane, press and hold or right-click NTDS Site Settings and then select Properties. This displays the NTDS Site Settings Properties dialog box, as shown in Figure 11-9.

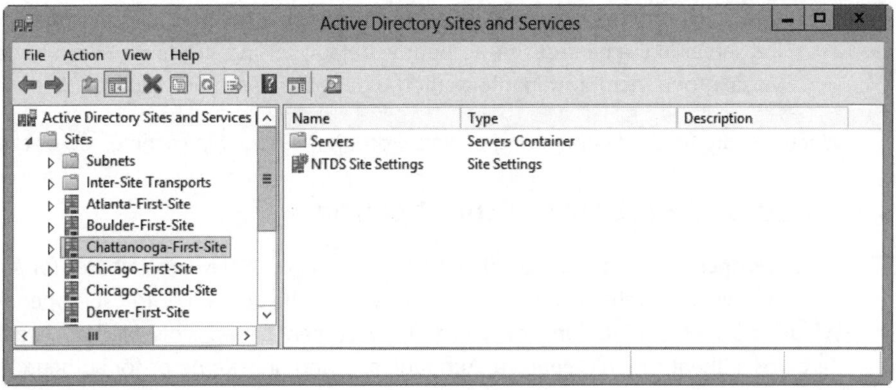

Figure 11-8 Enable caching on a per-site basis.

Figure 11-9 Enable universal group membership caching.

To enable universal group membership caching for the site, select the Enable Universal Group Membership Caching check box and continue as follows:

- If the directory has multiple sites, you can replicate existing universal group membership information from a specific site's cache by selecting the site on the Refresh Cache From list. With this option, universal group membership information doesn't need to be generated and then replicated; it's simply replicated from the other site's cache.

- If the directory has only one site or you'd rather get the information from a global catalog server in the nearest site, accept the default setting <Default>. With this option, universal group membership information is generated and then replicated.

When you are finished configuring universal group membership caching, tap or click OK.

NTLM and Kerberos authentication

Windows operating systems use either NT LAN Manager (NTLM) or Kerberos for authentication. However, in the default configuration, when the domain or forest is operating at
Windows Server 2012 R2 functional level NTLM authentication is disabled by default and only
Kerberos authentication is enabled. Although allowing only Kerberos for authentication is certainly substantially more secure, some older applications require NTLM for authentication and
won't work properly if NTLM authentication is disabled. To resolve this problem, you would
need to enable NTLM for authentication.

With NTLM, an encrypted challenge/response is used to authenticate a user without sending
the user's password over the network. The system requesting authentication must perform a
calculation that proves it has access to the secured NTLM credentials. It does this by sending a
one-way hash of the user's password that can be verified.

NTLM authentication has interactive and noninteractive authentication processes. Interactive
NTLM authentication over a network typically involves a client system from which a user is
requesting authentication and a domain controller on which the user's password is stored. As
the user accesses other resources on the network, noninteractive authentication might take
place as well to permit an already logged-on user to access network resources. Typically, noninteractive authentication involves a client, a server, and a domain controller that manages the
authentication.

To see how NTLM authentication works, consider the situation that arises when a user tries
to access a resource on the network and the user is prompted for a user name and password.
Assuming the resource is on a server that is not also a domain controller, the authentication
process is similar to the following:

1. When prompted, the user provides a domain name, user name, and password. The client
   computer generates a cryptographic hash of the user's password, discards the actual
   password, and then sends the user name to the server as unencrypted text.

2. The server generates a 16-byte random number, called a *challenge*, and sends it to
   the client.

3. The client encrypts the challenge with the hash of the user's password and returns the result, called a *response*, to the server. The server then sends the domain controller the user name, the challenge sent to the client, and the response from the client.

4. The domain controller uses the user name to retrieve the hash of the user's password from the Security Accounts Manager (SAM) database. The domain controller uses this password hash to encrypt the challenge and then compares the encrypted challenge it computed to the response computed by the client. If they are identical, the authentication is successful.

Active Directory uses Kerberos as the default authentication protocol, and NTLM authentication is maintained only for backward compatibility with legacy clients. Whenever a current client tries to authenticate with Active Directory, the client tries to use Kerberos. Kerberos has a number of advantages over NTLM authentication, including the use of mutual authentication. Mutual authentication in Kerberos allows for two-way authentication so that a server can authenticate a client and a client can authenticate a server. Thus, mutual authentication ensures not only that an authorized client is trying to access the network but also that an authorized server is the one responding to the client request.

Kerberos uses the following three main components:

- A client that needs access to resources

- A server that manages access to resources and ensures that only authenticated users can gain access to resources

- A Key Distribution Center (KDC) that acts as a central clearinghouse

Establishing the initial authentication

To act as KDCs, all domain controllers run the Kerberos Key Distribution Center service. With Kerberos authentication, a user password is never sent over the network. Instead, Kerberos authentication uses a shared-secret authentication model. In most cases the client and the server use the user's password as the shared secret. With this technique, authentication works as shown in Figure 11-10.

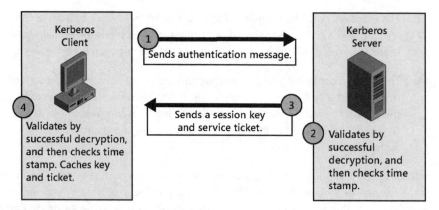

Figure 11-10 The Kerberos authentication process.

The details of the initial authentication of a user in the domain are as follows:

1. When a user logs on to the network, the client sends the KDC server a message containing the user name, the domain name, and a request for access to the network. In the message is a packet of information that has been encrypted using the shared-secret information (the user's password), which includes a time stamp.

2. When the KDC server receives the message, the server reads the user name and then checks the directory database for its copy of the shared-secret information (the user's password). The KDC server then decrypts the secret part of the message and checks the message time stamp. As long as the message time stamp is within five minutes of the current time on the server, the server can authenticate the user. If the decryption fails or the message time stamp is more than five minutes off the current time, the authentication fails. Five minutes is the default value; the allowable time difference can be configured through domain security policy by using the Kerberos policy Maximum Tolerance For Computer Clock Synchronization.

3. After the user is authenticated, the KDC server sends the client a message that is encrypted with the shared-secret information (the user's password). The message includes a session key that the client will use when communicating with the KDC server from now on and a session ticket that grants the user access to the domain controller. The ticket is encrypted with the KDC server's key, which makes it valid only for that domain controller.

4. When the client receives the message, the client decrypts the message and checks the message time stamp. As long as the message time stamp is within five minutes of the current time on the server, the client can then authenticate the server and assume that the server is valid. The client then caches the session key so that it can be used for all

future connections with the KDC server. The session key is valid until it expires or the user logs off. The session ticket is cached as well, but it isn't decrypted.

Accessing resources after authentication

After initial authentication, the user is granted access to the domain. The only resource to which the user has been granted access is the domain controller. When the user wants to access another resource on the network, the client must request access through the KDC. An overview of the process for authenticating access to network resources is shown in Figure 11-11.

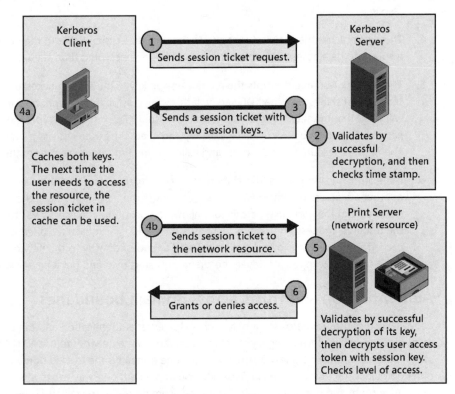

Figure 11-11 The Kerberos authentication process.

The details of an access request for a network resource are as follows:

1. When a user tries to access a resource on the network, the client sends the KDC server a session ticket request. The message contains the user's name, the session ticket the client was previously granted, the name of the network resource the client is trying to access, and a time stamp that is encrypted with the session key.

2.   When the KDC server receives the message, the server decrypts the session ticket using its key. It then extracts the original session key from the session ticket and uses it to decrypt the time stamp, which is then validated. The validation process is designed to ensure that the client is using the correct session key and that the time stamp is valid.

3.   If all is acceptable, the KDC server sends a session ticket to the client. The session ticket includes two copies of a session key that the client will use to access the requested resource. The first copy of the session key is encrypted using the client's session key. The second copy of the session key contains the user's access information and is encrypted with the resource's secret key, which is known only by the KDC server and the network resource.

4.   The client caches the session ticket and then sends the session ticket to the network resource to gain access. This request also contains an encrypted time stamp.

5.   The network resource decrypts the second session key in the session ticket, using the secret key it shares with the KDC server. If this is successful, the network resource has validated that the session ticket came from a trusted KDC. It then decrypts the user's access information by using the session key and checks the user's access permissions. The network resource also decrypts and validates the time stamp sent from the client.

6.   If the authentication and authorization are successful (meaning that the client has the appropriate access permissions), the user is granted the type of access to the network resource that the particular permissions allow. The next time the user needs to access the resource, the session ticket in cache is used—as long as it hasn't expired. Using a cached session ticket allows the client to send a request directly to the network resource. If the ticket has expired, however, the client must start over and get a new ticket.

Authentication and trusts across domain boundaries

Active Directory uses Kerberos security for server-to-server authentication and the establishment of trusts, while allowing legacy clients and servers on the network to use NTLM if necessary. Figure 11-12 shows a one-way trust in which one domain is the trusted domain and the other domain is the trusting domain. Typically, you implement one-way trusts when you have separate account and resource domains. The establishment of the trust allows users in the account domain to access resources in the resource domain.

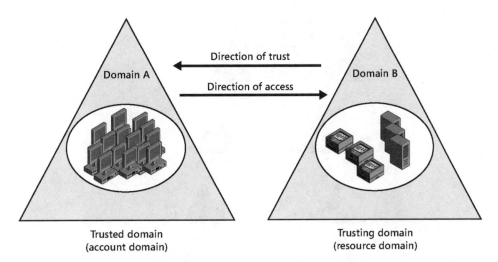

Figure 11-12 One-way trust with a trusted domain and a trusting domain.

Two-way transitive trusts

With Active Directory, trusts are automatically configured between all the domains in a forest and are implemented as two-way transitive trusts. As a result, if the domains shown in Figure 11-12 are domains in the same forest, users in domain A can automatically access resources in domain B and users in domain B can automatically access resources in domain A. Because the trusts are automatically established between all domains in the forest, no setup is involved and there are many more design options for implementing Active Directory domains.

As trusts join parent and child domains in the same domain tree and join the roots of domain trees, the structure of trusts in a forest can be referred to as a *trust tree*. When a user tries to access a resource in another domain, the trust tree is used and the user's request has to pass through one domain controller for each domain between the user and the resource. This type of authentication takes place across domain boundaries. Authentication across domain boundaries also applies when a user with an account in one domain visits another domain in the forest and tries to log on to the network from that domain.

Consider the example shown in Figure 11-13. If a user from domain G visits domain K and tries to log on to the network, the user's computer must be able to connect to a domain controller in domain K. Here, the user's computer sends the initial logon request to the domain K domain controller. When the domain controller receives the logon request, it determines that the user is located in domain G. The domain controller refers the request to a domain controller in the next domain in its trust tree, which in this case is domain J. A domain controller in domain J refers the request to domain I. A domain controller in domain I refers the request to domain H. This process continues through domains A, E, and F until the request finally gets to domain G.

CHAPTER 11

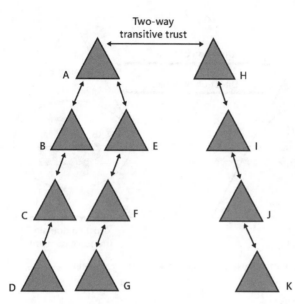

Figure 11-13 A forest with many domains.

Shortcut trusts

You can avoid this rather lengthy referral process if you establish an explicit trust between domain G and domain K, as shown in Figure 11-14. Technically, explicit trusts are one-way transitive trusts, but you can establish a two-way explicit trust by creating two one-way trusts. Thus, unlike standard trusts within the trust tree, which are inherently two-way and transitive, explicit trusts can be made to be two-way if desired. Because they can be used to establish authentication shortcuts between domains, explicit trusts are also referred to as *shortcut trusts*. In this example it was decided to create two one-way trusts: one from domain G to domain K and one from domain K to domain G. With these shortcut trusts in place, users in domain G could visit domain K and be rapidly authenticated and users in domain K could visit domain G and be rapidly authenticated.

If you examine the figure closely, you see that several other shortcut trusts were added to the forest as well. Shortcut trusts were established between B and E and between E and I. Establishing the shortcut trusts in both directions allows for easy access to resources and rapid authentication in several combinations, such as the following:

- Using the B to E shortcut trust, users in domain B can rapidly access resources in domain E.

- Using the B to E and E to I shortcut trusts, users in domain B can also rapidly access resources in domain I.

- Using the B to E shortcut trust, users in domain B can visit domain E and be rapidly authenticated.

- Using the B to E and E to I shortcut trusts, users in domain B can visit domain I and be rapidly authenticated.

The trusts work similarly for users in domain E. Users in domain E have direct access to both domain B and domain I. Imagine that domain B is sales.cohovineyard.com, domain E is mf.cohovineyard.com, and domain I is cs.cohowinery.com, and you might be able to better picture how the shortcut trusts allow users to cut across trees in the Active Directory forest. I hope that you can also imagine how much planning should go into deciding your domain structure, especially when it comes to access to resources and authentication.

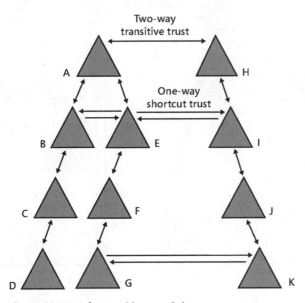

Figure 11-14 A forest with several shortcut trusts.

Authentication and trusts across forest boundaries

You can establish authentication and trusts across forest boundaries as well. One-way external trusts, such as the one depicted in Figure 11-15, are nontransitive. This means that if, as in the example, a trust is established between domain H and domain L only, a user in any domain in forest 1 could access a resource in domain L but not in any other domain in forest 2. The reason for this limitation is that the trust doesn't continue past domain L. It does not matter that a two-way transitive trust does exist between domain L and domain M or that a two-way trust also exists between domain L and domain O.

Windows Server supports cross-forest transitive trusts, also referred to simply as *forest trusts*. With this type of trust, you can establish a one-way or two-way transitive trust between forests to share resources and to authenticate users. With a two-way trust, as shown Figure 11-16, you enable cross-forest authentication and cross-forest authorization. Cross-forest trusts are supported when all domain controllers in all domains of both forests are running Windows Server 2003 or higher and the forest is operating at the Windows Server 2003 or higher functional level.

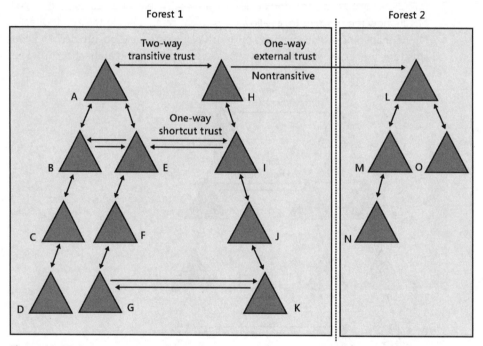

Figure 11-15 A one-way external trust that crosses forest boundaries but is nontransitive.

As discussed earlier in this chapter in the section entitled "NTLM and Kerberos authentication," Kerberos is the default authentication protocol but NTLM can also be used (when permitted and enabled). This allows current clients and servers and older clients and servers to be authenticated. After you establish a two-way cross-forest trust, users get all the benefits of Active Directory regardless of where they sign on to the network. With cross-forest authentication, you ensure secure access to resources when the user account is in one forest and the computer account is in another forest and when the user in one forest needs access to network resources in another trusted forest. As part of cross-forest authorization, administrators can select users and global groups from trusted forests for inclusion in local groups. This ensures the integrity of the forest security boundary while allowing trust between forests.

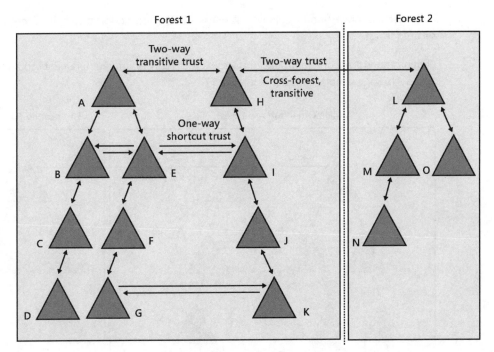

Figure 11-16 A two-way transitive trust between forests.

When you connect two or more forests by using cross-forest trusts, the implementation is referred to as a *federated forest design*. The federated forest design is most useful when you need to join two separate Active Directory structures—for example, when two companies merge, when one company acquires another, or when an organization has a major restructuring. Consider the case in which two companies merge and, rather than migrate their separate Active Directory structures into a single directory tree, the staff decides to link the two forests by using cross-forest trusts. As long as the trusts are two-way, users in forest 1 can access resources in forest 2 and users in forest 2 can access resources in forest 1.

Having separate forests with cross-forest trusts between them is also useful when you want a division or group within the organization to have more autonomy but still have a link to the other divisions or groups. For example, if you are setting up a division that you intend to spin off once it is up and running, you likely will want that division to be in a separate forest with cross-forest trusts between your primary forest and the new forest.

By placing the division or group in a separate forest, you ensure strict security and give that division or group ownership of the Active Directory structure. If users in the forest were to need access to resources in another forest, you could establish a one-way cross-forest trust between the forests. This would allow users in the secured forest to gain access to resources

CHAPTER 11

in the second forest, but it would not allow users in the second forest to gain access to the secured forest.

Organizations that contain groups or divisions with high security requirements could use this approach. For example, consider Figure 11-17.

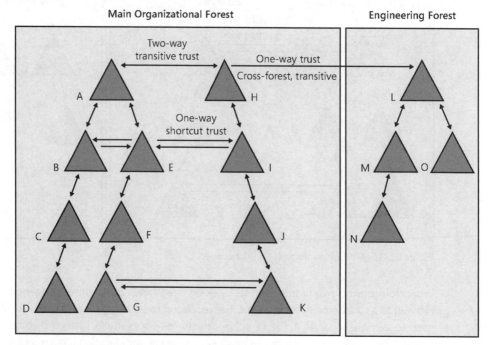

Figure 11-17 A one-way transitive trust between forests.

In this situation the users in the organization's Engineering department need access to resources in other departments, but for security reasons they should be isolated from the rest of the organization. Here, the organization has implemented two forests: a main organizational forest and a separate Engineering forest. Using a one-way cross-forest trust from the main forest to the Engineering forest, the organization allows Engineering users to access other resources, but it ensures that the Engineering department is secure and isolated.

Examining domain and forest trusts

You can examine existing trusts by using Active Directory Domains And Trusts. Start Active Directory Domains And Trusts by choosing the related option from the Tools menu in Server Manager. As shown in Figure 11-18, you see a list of available domains.

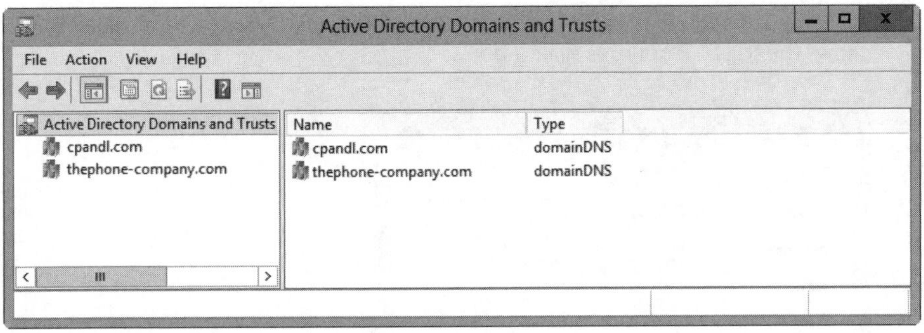

Figure 11-18 Examine trusts in available domains.

To examine the existing trusts for a domain, press and hold or right-click the domain entry and then select Properties. Then, in the domain's Properties dialog box, tap or click the Trusts tab, as shown in Figure 11-19. The Trusts tab is divided into two panels:

- **Domains Trusted By This Domain (Outgoing Trusts).** Lists the domains that this domain trusts (the trusted domains)

- **Domains That Trust This Domain (Incoming Trusts).** Lists the domains that trust this domain (the trusting domains)

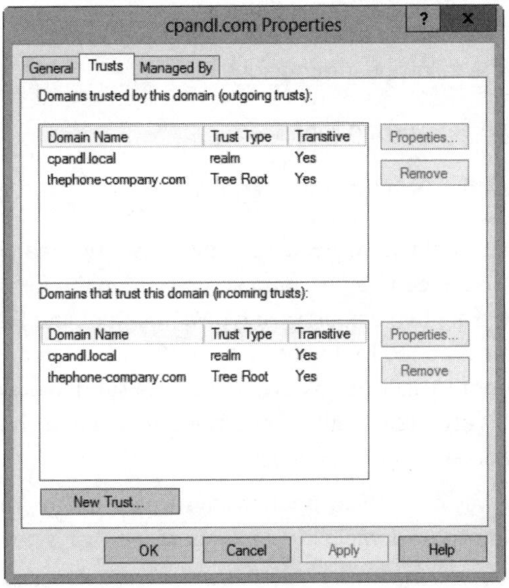

Figure 11-19 Examine the existing trusts of a domain.

CHAPTER 11

To view the details of a particular trust, select it and then tap or click Properties. Figure 11-20 shows the trust's Properties dialog box.

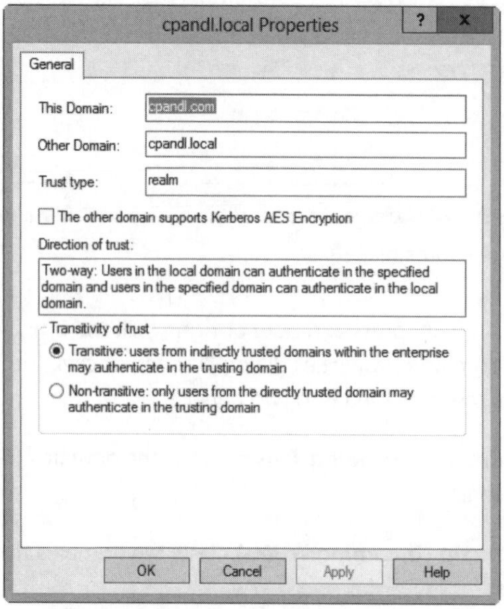

Figure 11-20 Examine the details of an existing trust.

The Properties dialog box contains the following information:

- **This Domain.** The domain you are working with.

- **Other Domain.** The domain with which the trust is established.

- **Trust Type.** The type of trust. By default, two-way transitive trusts are created auto-matically when a new domain is added to a new domain tree within the forest or a sub-domain of a root domain. There are two default trust types: Tree Root and Parent And Child. When a new domain tree is added to the forest, the default trust that is estab-lished automatically is a tree-root trust. When a new domain is a subdomain of a root domain, the default trust that is established automatically is a parent and child trust. Other trust types that might appear include the following:

  - External, which is a one-way or two-way nontransitive trust used to provide access to resources in a domain or to a domain in a separate forest that is not joined by a forest trust

  - Forest, which is a one-way or two-way transitive trust used to share resources between forests

- Realm, which is a transitive or nontransitive trust that can be established as one-way or two-way between a non-Windows Kerberos realm and a Windows Server 2008 or higher domain

- Shortcut, which is a one-way or two-way transitive trust used to speed up authentication and resource access between domain trees

- **Direction Of Trust.** The direction of the trust. All default trusts are established as two-way trusts. This means that users in the domain you are working with can authenticate in the other domain and users from the other domain can authenticate in the domain you are working with.

- **Transitivity Of Trust.** The transitivity of the trust. All default trusts are transitive, which means that users from indirectly trusted domains can authenticate in the other domain.

When setting up trusts, don't forget about the role of DNS in the trusts. The domain controllers in the domains must have access to DNS information about the domain controllers in the other domains. This DNS information can be transferred to the domain's DNS server as a secondary zone, or conditional forwarding can be configured.

Establishing external, shortcut, realm, and cross-forest trusts

All trusts, regardless of type, are established in the same way. For all trusts, there are two sides: an incoming trust and an outgoing trust. To configure both sides of the trust, keep the following in mind:

- For domain trusts, you need to use two accounts: one that is a member of the Domain Admins group in the first domain and one that is a member of the Domain Admins group in the second domain. If you don't have appropriate accounts in both domains, you can establish one side of the trust and allow an administrator in the other domain to establish the other side of the trust.

- For forest trusts, you need to use two accounts: one that is a member of the Enterprise Admins group in the first forest and one that is a member of the Enterprise Admins group in the second forest. If you don't have appropriate accounts in both forests, you can establish one side of the two-way trust and allow an administrator in the other forest to establish the other side of the trust.

- For realm trusts, you need to establish the trust separately for the Windows domain and for the Kerberos realm. If you don't have appropriate administrative access to both the Windows domain and the Kerberos realm, you can establish one side of the trust and allow an administrator to establish the other side of the trust.

CHAPTER 11

To establish a trust, follow these steps:

1. In Active Directory Domains And Trusts, press and hold or right-click the domain for which you want to establish a one-way incoming trust, a one-way outgoing trust, or a two-way trust, and then choose Properties. For a cross-forest trust, this must be the forest root domain in one of the participating forests.

2. In the domain Properties dialog box, tap or click the Trusts tab and then tap or click the New Trust button. This starts the New Trust Wizard. Tap or click Next to skip the welcome page.

3. On the Trust Name page, specify the domain name of the other domain, as shown in Figure 11-21. For a cross-forest trust, this must be the name of the forest root domain in the other forest.

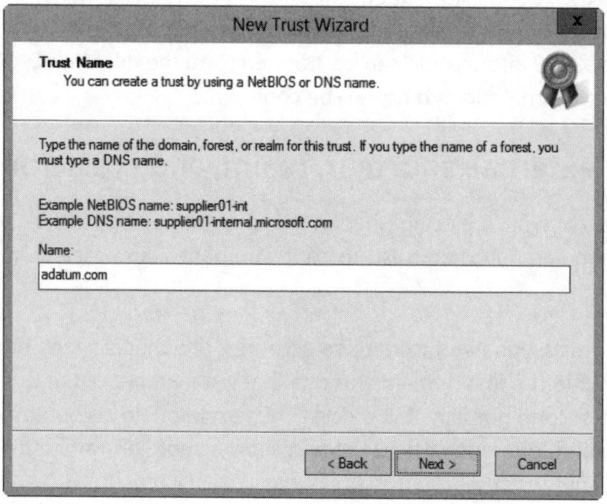

Figure 11-21 Specify the name of the other domain.

4. When you tap or click Next, the wizard tries to establish a connection to the other domain. The options on the next page depend on whether you are connecting to a Windows domain, a Windows forest, or a non-Windows domain:

   - If the domain is determined to be a Windows forest, you have the option of creating an external trust that is nontransitive or a forest trust that is transitive. Choose either External Trust or Forest Trust and then tap or click Next.

   - If the domain is determined to be a Windows domain, it's assumed that you are creating a shortcut trust and the wizard goes directly to the Direction Of Trust page.

- If the domain is determined to be a non-Windows domain, you have the option of creating a realm trust with a Kerberos version 5 realm. Select Realm Trust and then, on the Transitivity Of Trust page, select either Nontransitive or Transitive and then tap or click Next.

5. On the Direction Of Trust page, shown in Figure 11-22, choose the direction of the trust and then tap or click Next. The following options are available:

   - **Two-Way.** Users in the domain initially selected and in the designated domain can access resources in either domain or realm.

   - **One-Way: Incoming.** Users in the domain initially selected will be able to access resources in the designated domain. Users in the designated domain will not be able to access resources in the domain initially selected.

   - **One-Way: Outgoing.** Users in the designated domain will be able to access resources in the domain initially selected. Users in the domain initially selected will not be able to access resources in the designated domain.

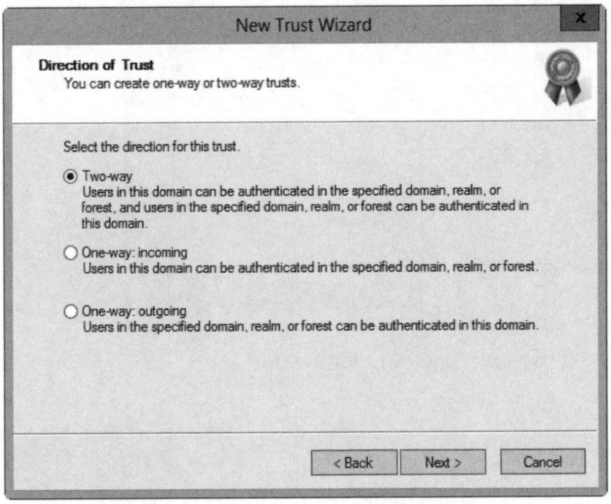

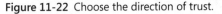

Figure 11-22 Choose the direction of trust.

6. For shortcut or forest trusts, the next page you see is the Sides Of Trust page. To begin using a trust, you must create both sides of the trust. You have the option of setting the sides of the trust for This Domain Only or for Both This Domain And The Specified Domain:

   - If you are creating only one side of the trust, select This Domain Only and then tap or click Next.

- If you are setting both sides of the trust or the administrator from the other domain is at your desk, select Both This Domain And The Specified Domain and then tap or click Next. When prompted, type (or let the other administrator type) the name and password of an appropriate account in the other domain or forest and then tap or click OK.

7. On the Trust Password page, shown in Figure 11-23, type and then confirm the initial password you want to use for the trust. The password is arbitrary but must follow the strong security rules, meaning that it must have at least eight characters, contain a combination of uppercase and lowercase characters, and contain either numerals or special characters.

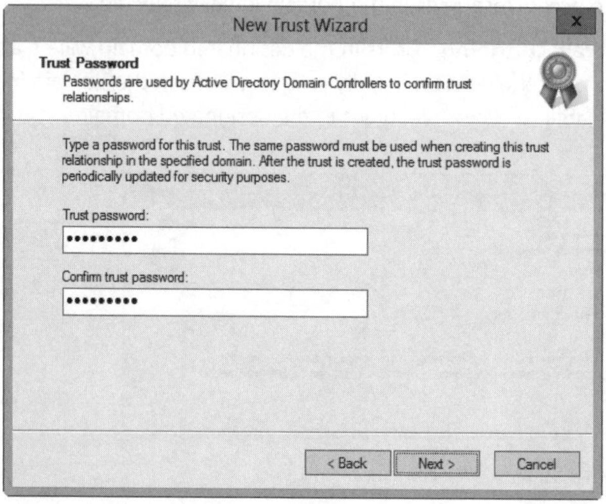

Figure 11-23 Set the initial password for the trust.

Inside OUT

You might need the password

The trust password you use must be the same for both the domain initially selected and the specified domain, so be sure to write down the password so that you can use it when configuring the other side of the trust. After you create the trust, Active Directory periodically updates the password, using an automatic password reset. This helps safeguard the integrity of the trust.

8. For domain or realm trusts, tap or click Next twice to begin the trust creation process.

9. For forest trusts, you can set the outgoing trust authentication level as either Domain-Wide Authentication or Selective Authentication. With Domain-Wide Authentication, users in the trusted domain can be authenticated to use all the resources in the trusting domain (and any trusted domains). This means that authentication is automatic for all users. With Selective Authentication, only the users or groups to which you explicitly grant permission can access resources in the trusting domain. This means that authentication is not automatic and you will need to grant individual access to each server that you want to make available to users in the trusting domain. Tap or click Next twice.

10. After the trust is created, you are given the opportunity to verify the trust.

Verifying and troubleshooting trusts

By default, Windows validates all incoming trusts automatically. If the credentials used to establish the trust are no longer valid, the trust fails verification. If you want to revalidate a trust by providing new credentials or to specify that incoming trusts should not be validated, follow these steps:

1. In Active Directory Domains And Trusts, press and hold or right-click the trusted domain for which you want to verify the incoming trust and then select Properties.

2. In the domain's Properties dialog box, tap or click the Trusts tab, and then tap or click Validate and select one of the following options:

   - If you want to stop validation of the incoming trust, select No, Do Not Validate The Incoming Trust.

   - If you want to revalidate the incoming trust, select Yes, Validate The Incoming Trust and then type the user account and password for an administrator account in the other (trusting) domain.

3. Tap or click OK. For a two-way trust, repeat this procedure for the other (trusting) domain.

You might want to revalidate trusts or specify that incoming trusts should not be validated for the following reasons:

- If clients are unable to access resources in a domain outside the forest, the external trust between the domains might have failed. In this case you should verify the trust for the trusted domain. Note that a PDC emulator must be available to reset and verify the external trust.

- If clients or servers get trust errors within an Active Directory forest, there could be several causes. The time on the clients or servers trying to authenticate might be more than

CHAPTER 11

five minutes off, which is the default maximum time difference allowed for Kerberos authentication. In this case, synchronize the time on the clients and servers. The problem could also be that the domain controller might be down or the trust relationship could be broken. For the latter case, you can run NETDOM to verify or reset the trust.

Delegating authentication

The delegation of authentication is often a requirement when a network service is distributed across several servers, such as when the organization uses web-based application services with front-end and back-end servers. In this environment, a client connects to the front-end servers and the user's credentials might need to be passed to back-end servers to ensure that the user gets access only to information to which the user has been granted access.

Delegated authentication essentials

Delegated authentication is provided through Kerberos using either proxy tickets or forwarded tickets:

- With proxy tickets, the client sends a session ticket request to a domain controller acting as a KDC, asking for access to the back-end server. The KDC grants the session ticket request and sends the client a session ticket with a PROXIABLE flag set. The client can then send this ticket to the front-end server, and the front-end server, in turn, uses this ticket to access information on the back-end server. In this configuration, the client needs to know the name of the back-end server, which in some cases is problematic— particularly if you need to maintain strict security for the back-end databases and don't want their integrity to be compromised.

- With forwarded tickets, the client sends an initial authorization request to the KDC, requesting a session ticket that the front-end server will be able to use to access the back-end servers. The KDC grants the session ticket request and sends it to the client. The client can then send the ticket to the front-end server, which then uses the session ticket to make a network resource request on behalf of the client. The front-end server then gets a session ticket to access the back-end server using the client's credentials.

You also can use *constrained delegation*. Constrained delegation allows you to configure accounts so that they are delegated only for specific purposes. This kind of delegation is based on service principal names, and a front-end server can access only network resources for which delegation has been granted.

Prior to Windows Server 2012, delegation only worked within the same domain and front-end servers needed to be configured with the services that were to be impersonated. Beginning with Windows Server 2012, delegation works across domains and forests and back-end servers can authorize front-end service accounts that can impersonate users against their resources. Administrators can configure back-end server accounts with the accounts that are permitted for impersonation by using New-ADComputer, Set-ADComputer, New-ADServiceAccount, and Set-ADServiceAccount.

Configuring delegated authentication

To use delegated authentication, the user account (and the service or computer account acting on the user's behalf) must be configured to support delegated authentication.

Configuring the delegated user account

For the user account, you must ensure that the account option Account Is Sensitive And Cannot Be Delegated is not selected. By default, it isn't selected. If you want to check this option, use Active Directory Users And Computers, as shown in Figure 11-24. Double-tap or double-click the user's account entry in Active Directory Users And Computers and then tap or click the Account tab. You find the Account Is Sensitive And Cannot Be Delegated check box under Account Options. Scroll through the list until you find it.

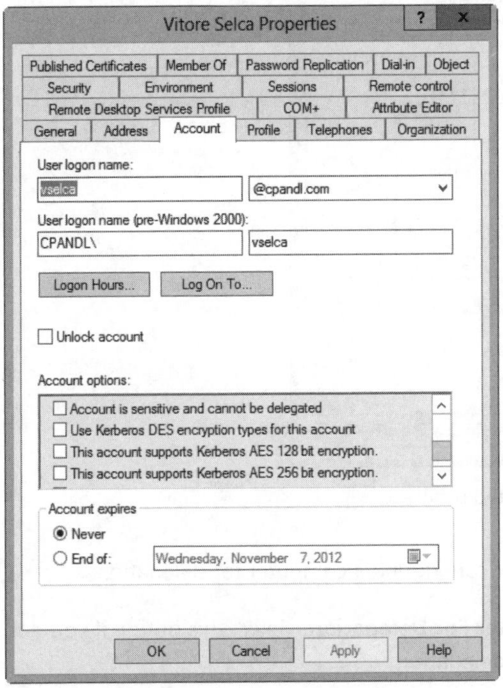

Figure 11-24 Configure delegated authentication.

CHAPTER 11

Configuring the delegated service or computer account

For the service acting on the user's behalf, you must first determine if the service is running under a normal user account or under a special identity, such as LocalSystem. If the service runs under a normal user account, check the account in Active Directory Users And Computers and ensure that the Account Is Sensitive And Cannot Be Delegated check box is not selected. If the service runs under a special identity, you need to configure delegation for the computer account of the front-end server.

In Active Directory Users And Computers, double-tap or double-click the computer account to display its Properties dialog box and then tap or click the Delegation tab, as shown in Figure 11-25.

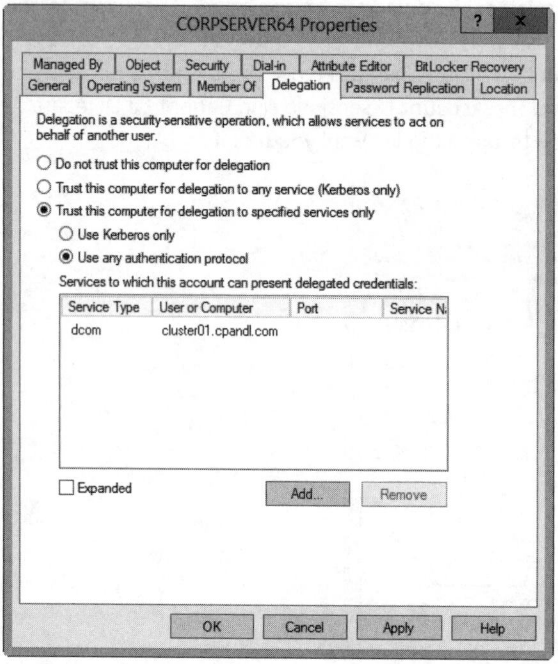

Figure 11-25 Configure the delegated service.

You have the following options for configuring a computer for delegation:

- **Do Not Trust This Computer For Delegation.** Select this option if you don't want the computer to be trusted for delegation.

- **Trust This Computer For Delegation To Any Service (Kerberos Only).** Select this option to use the legacy client level of authentication, which allows the service to make requests for any network resources on the client's behalf.

- **Trust This Computer For Delegation To Specified Services Only.** Select this option to use the Windows Server 2008 and higher levels of authentication, which allows the service to make requests only for specified services. You can then specify whether the client must authenticate using Kerberos only or can use any authentication protocol.

When you are using the Windows Server 2008 and higher levels of authentication, you must next specify the services to which the front-end server can present a client's delegated credentials. To do this, you need to know the name of the computers running the services and the types of services you are authorizing. Tap or click Add to display the Add Services dialog box and then tap or click Users Or Computers to display the Select Users Or Computers dialog box.

In the Select Users Or Computers dialog box, type the name of the computer providing the service, such as **CORPSVR02**, and then tap or click Check Names. If multiple matches are found, select the name or names you want to use and then tap or click OK. If no matches are found, either you entered an incorrect name or you're working with an incorrect location. Modify the name and try again or tap or click Locations to select a new location. To add computers, type a semicolon (;) and then repeat this process. When you tap or click OK, the Add Services dialog box is updated with a list of available services on the selected computer or computers, as shown in Figure 11-26.

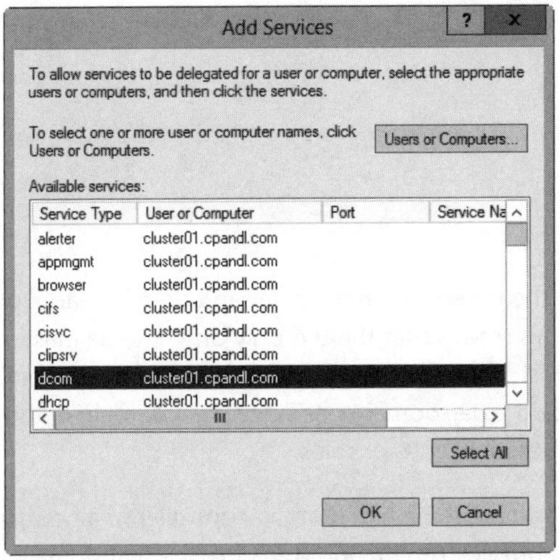

Figure 11-26 The Add Services dialog box is updated with a list of available services for the selected computer or computers.

Use the Add Services dialog box to select the services for which you are authorizing delegated authentication. You can use Shift+click or Ctrl+click to select multiple services. After you select the appropriate services, tap or click OK. The selected services are added to the Services To

Which This Account Can Present Delegated Credentials list. Tap or click OK to close the computer's Properties dialog box and save the delegation changes.

Design considerations for Active Directory operations masters

The multimaster replication model of Active Directory creates a distributed environment that allows any domain controller to be used for authentication and allows you to make changes to standard directory information without regard to which domain controller you use. The approach works well for most Active Directory operations—but not all. Some Active Directory operations can be performed only by a single authoritative domain controller called an *operations master*.

Operations master roles

A designated operations master has a flexible single-master operations (FSMO) role. The five designated roles are as follows:

- Schema master

- Domain naming master

- Relative ID (RID) master

- PDC emulator

- Infrastructure master

As depicted in Figure 11-27, two of the roles—schema master and domain naming master—are assigned on a per-forest basis. This means that there is only one schema master and only one domain naming master in a forest. The other three roles—RID master, PDC emulator, and infrastructure master—are assigned on a per-domain basis. For each domain in the forest, there is only one of each of these operations master roles.

When you install Active Directory and create the first domain controller in a new forest, all five roles are assigned to that domain controller. As you add domains, the first domain controller you install in a domain is automatically designated the RID master, infrastructure master, and PDC emulator for that domain.

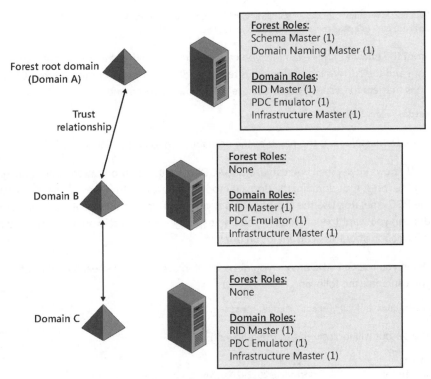

Figure 11-27 Operations masters in forests and domains.

As part of domain design, you should consider how many domain controllers you need per domain and whether you need to transfer operations master roles after you install new domain controllers. In all cases, you'll want to have at least two domain controllers in each domain in the forest. The reasons for transferring the operations master roles depend on several factors. First, you might want to transfer an operations master role to improve perfor-mance, as you might do when a server has too heavy a workload and you need to distribute some of the load. Second, you might need to transfer an operations master role if you plan to take the server with that role offline for maintenance or if the server fails.

You can determine the current operations masters for your logon domain by typing the fol-lowing at a command prompt:

```
netdom query fsmo
```

As shown here, the output lists each role owner by its fully qualified domain name:

```
Schema master            CorpServer26.cpandl.com
Domain naming master     CorpServer26.cpandl.com
PDC                      CorpServer32.tech.cpandl.com
```

CHAPTER 11

```
RID pool manager          CorpServer32.tech.cpandl.com
Infrastructure master     CorpServer41.tech.cpandl.com
```

From the output in this example, you can also determine that the forest root domain is cpandl.com and the current logon domain is tech.cpandl.com. If you want to determine the operations masters for a specific domain, use the following command:

```
netdom query fsmo /d:DomainName
```

Here, *DomainName* is the name of the domain, such as eng.cpandl.com.

In Windows PowerShell you can use Get-ADDomain to get information about domains, including the forest root domain, the domain mode, the infrastructure master, the RID master, and the PDC emulator. Use the *–Identity* parameter to specify the fully qualified name of the domain you want to work with. If you don't specify a domain to work with, the cmdlet displays information about the current logon domain.

When you use Get-ADDomain, you get a lot of information. To streamline this information, you can enter the following:

```
get-addomain | fl forest, *mode, *master, pdc*
```

The output will look similar to the following:

```
forest              : cpandl.com
DomainMode          : Windows2012R2Domain
InfrastructureMaster : CorpServer18.cpandl.com
RIDMaster           : CorpServer18.cpandl.com
PDCEmulator         : CorpServer18.cpandl.com
```

Use Get-ADForest to get information about forests, including the forest mode, the domain naming master, and the schema master. As shown in the following example, the output provides a lot of additional information as well:

```
ApplicationPartitions : {DC=ForestDnsZones,DC=cpandl,DC=com, DC=DomainDnsZones,
DC=cpandl,DC=com}
CrossForestReferences : {}
DomainNamingMaster  : CorpServer18.cpandl.com
Domains             : {cpandl.com}
ForestMode          : Windows2012R2Forest
GlobalCatalogs      : {CorpServer18.cpandl.com}
Name                : cpandl.com
PartitionsContainer : CN=Partitions,CN=Configuration,DC=cpandl,DC=com
RootDomain          : cpandl.com
SchemaMaster        : CorpServer18.cpandl.com
Sites               : {Default-First-Site-Name}
SPNSuffixes         : {}
UPNSuffixes         : {}
```

You can change operations master roles in several ways:

- If you demote a domain controller acting as an operations master, any operations master roles are automatically transferred to other domain controllers.

- If the current operations master is online, you can perform a role transfer, gracefully shifting the role from one domain controller to another.

- If the current operations master has failed *and will not be coming back online*, you can seize the role and forcibly transfer it to another domain controller.

Inside OUT

Recommended placement of operations master roles

Microsoft recommends the following configuration:

- Ideally, you should place the forestwide roles, schema master and domain naming master, on the same domain controller. There is very little overhead associated with these roles, so placement on the same server adds very little load overall. However, you must safeguard this server because these are critical roles in the forest. In addition, the server acting as the domain naming master should also be a global catalog server.

- Ideally, you should place the relative ID master and PDC emulator roles on the same domain controller. The reason for this is that the PDC emulator uses more relative IDs than most other domain controllers. If the relative ID master and PDC emulator roles aren't on the same domain controller, the domain controllers on which they are placed should be in the same Active Directory site and the domain controllers should have a reliable connection between them.

- Ideally, you should not place the infrastructure master on a domain controller that is also a global catalog server. The reason for this is a bit complicated, and there are some important exceptions to note.

The infrastructure master is responsible for updating cross-domain group membership, and it determines whether its information is current or out of date by checking a global catalog and then replicating changes to other domain controllers as necessary. If the infrastructure master and the global catalog are on the same server, the infrastructure master doesn't see that changes have been made and thus doesn't replicate them.

The exceptions are for a single-domain forest or a multidomain forest in which all domain controllers are global catalog servers. In the case of a single-domain forest, there are no cross-group references to update, so it doesn't matter where the infra-structure master is located. In the case of a multidomain forest in which all domain controllers are global catalog servers, all the domain controllers know about all the objects in the forest already, so the infrastructure master doesn't really have to make updates.

Using, locating, and transferring the schema master role

The schema master is the only domain controller in the forest with a writeable copy of the schema container. This means that it is the only domain controller in the forest on which you can make changes to the schema. You make changes to the schema by using the Active Directory Schema snap-in. When you start the Active Directory Schema snap-in, it makes a direct connection to the schema master, allowing you to view the schema for the directory. To make changes to the schema, however, you must use an account that is a member of the Schema Admins group.

By default, the schema master is the first domain controller installed in the forest root domain. You can transfer this role by using the Active Directory Schema snap-in or the NTDSUTIL command-line utility.

To locate the schema master for the current forest, enter the following command at a Windows PowerShell prompt:

```
(Get-ADForest).SchemaMaster
```

Alternatively, open the Active Directory Schema snap-in in a custom console. Press and hold or right-click the Active Directory Schema node and then select Operations Master. The Change Schema Master dialog box, shown in Figure 11-28, shows the current schema master.

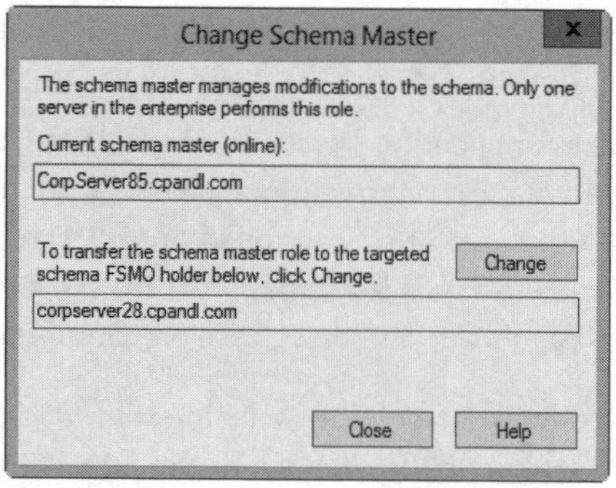

Figure 11-28 View the current schema master.

To transfer the schema master role to another server, follow these steps:

1. Open the Active Directory Schema snap-in in a custom console. Press and hold or right-click the Active Directory Schema node and then select Change Active Directory Domain Controller.

2. In the Change Directory Server dialog box, select This Domain Controller and then select the forest root domain name in the Look In This Domain list. Next, select an available domain controller to which you want to transfer the role and then tap or click OK.

3. In the Change Directory Server dialog box, select This Domain Controller. Next, tap or click the domain controller to which you want to transfer the schema master role and then tap or click OK.

4. Press and hold or right-click the Active Directory Schema node and then select Operations Master. In the Change Schema Master dialog box, tap or click Change. When prompted to confirm, tap or click Yes and then tap or click Close.

Using, locating, and transferring the domain naming master role

The domain naming master is responsible for adding or removing domains from the forest. Any time you create a domain, a remote procedure call (RPC) connection is made to the domain naming master, which assigns the domain a globally unique identifier (GUID). Any time you remove a domain, an RPC connection is made to the domain naming master and the previously assigned GUID reference is removed. If you can't connect to the domain naming master when you are trying to add or remove a domain, you will not be able to create or remove the domain.

To locate the domain naming master for the current forest, enter the following command at a Windows PowerShell prompt:

```
(Get-ADForest).DomainNamingMaster
```

Alternatively, start Active Directory Domains And Trusts. Press and hold or right-click the Active Directory Domains And Trusts node and then select Operations Master.

CHAPTER 11

The Operations Master dialog box, shown in Figure 11-29, shows the current domain naming operations master:

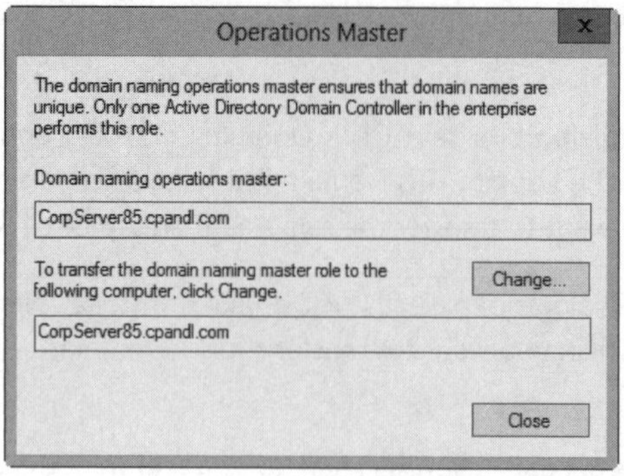

Figure 11-29 View the current domain naming operations master.

To transfer the domain naming master role to another server, follow these steps:

1. In Active Directory Domains And Trusts, press and hold or right-click the Active Directory Domains And Trusts node and then select Change Active Directory Domain Controller.

2. In the Change Directory Server dialog box, select This Domain Controller and then select the forest root domain name in the Look In This Domain list. Next, select an available domain controller to which you want to transfer the role and then tap or click OK.

3. Press and hold or right-click the Active Directory Domains And Trusts node and then select Operations Master. In the Change Operations Master dialog box, tap or click Change. When prompted to confirm, tap or click Yes and then tap or click Close.

Using, locating, and transferring the relative ID master role

The relative ID (RID) master controls the creation of new security principals—such as users, groups, and computers—throughout its related domain. Every domain controller in a domain is issued a block of relative IDs by the RID master. These relative IDs are used to build the security IDs that uniquely identify security principals in the domain. The actual security ID generated by a domain controller consists of a domain identifier, which is the same for every object in a domain, and a unique relative ID that differentiates the object from all other objects in the domain. The block of relative IDs issued to a domain controller is called a *RID pool*. Typically, blocks of relative IDs are issued in lots of 500. When the RID pool on a domain controller is nearly exhausted, the domain controller requests a new block of 500 RIDs. It's the job of the RID master to issue blocks of RIDs, and it does so as long as it's up and running. If a domain controller can't connect to the RID master and for any reason runs out of RIDs, no new objects can be created on the domain controller and object creation will fail. To resolve this problem, the RID master must be made available or the RID master role must be transferred to another server.

Inside OUT

Size the RID pool

Size the RID pool by editing the registry on each domain controller and changing the REG_DWORD value of the RID Block Size value located in HKLM\System \CurrentControlSet\Services\NTDS\RID Values. For Windows Server 2012 and later, the maximum RID pool block size is 15,000. Previously, the maximum was 10,000. If you enter a value greater than 15,000, the RID pool block size will be 15,000. In addition, an error with event ID 16653 and the source as Directory-Services-SAM will be logged each time you start the domain controller.

Because relative IDs are not reused and a finite number of them is available for assignment throughout the lifetime of a domain, older enterprise environments could run out of relative IDs. RID pool exhaustion can seriously affect the domain because no new objects can be created. In an Active Directory domain, $2^{30} - 1$ (1,073,741,823) RIDs are available. Although approximately 1 billion objects sounds like a lot, RIDs could be leaked and lost in earlier releases of Windows Server. If a RID was taken from a RID pool to create an object but the object creation failed, the RID was not available for reuse. If a deleted Domain Controller computer object was restored, the domain controller could repeatedly request a new RID pool block because of a missing *rIDSetReference* attribute and, by itself, could use up the RID pool in about 24 months. Windows Server 2012 and later resolve these and other identified problems that could lead to faster-than-normal depletion of the RID pool.

The newly implemented RID Reuse pool resolves some of these problems. When object creation fails, the RID, instead of being leaked and lost, is placed in the Reuse pool. Because a domain controller checks the Reuse pool for available relative IDs before taking a relative ID from the primary pool, the relative ID can be assigned to the next object created on that domain controller. Keep in mind, however, that rebooting a domain controller clears its RID Reuse pool.

Because the RID master can run out of assigned addresses in its global RID pool space, Windows Server 2012 and later issue periodic RID consumption warnings and also have a soft ceiling for the RID pool. When 10 percent of the global address space is used, the RID master logs an informational event with a RID consumption warning. The RID master logs another RID consumption warning when 10 percent of the remainder is used, and so on, so that the RID consumption warnings become more frequent as more and more of the global space is depleted. The soft ceiling is reached when 90 percent of the available address space is used. As a result, the RID master will not allocate any additional blocks of RIDs until the soft ceiling is removed.

CHAPTER 11

Using Dcdiag, you can check the number of RIDs available by entering the following at a command prompt on the RID master for the domain:

```
dcdiag /test:ridmanager /v | find /i "Available RID Pool"
```

The output will show the available RIDs and be similar to the following:

```
* Available RID Pool for the Domain is 480678 to 1073741823
```

From this output, you know the number of available RIDs and you can infer the number of RIDs that have been used. Here, 480,677 RIDs have been used and 1,073,261,146 RIDs are available. That's 480,678 minus 1 to determine the number of RIDs that have been used and 1,073,741,823 minus 480,677 to determine the number of RIDs available.

If a domain's RID master is running Windows Server 2012 or later, you can double the size of the RID pool by enabling SID compatibility. Enabling SID compatibility unlocks the thirty-first bit of the RID pool, which effectively raises the total number of RIDs available for a domain to $2^{31} - 1$ (2,147,483,647) or approximately 2 billion objects. Set the *sidCompatibilityVersion* property on the RID master to 1 to unlock the thirty-first bit and enable SID compatibility. However, before you implement this change, you must ensure that all other domain controllers in the domain are also running Windows Server 2012 or later or that domain controllers running earlier versions of Windows Server have updates applied to ensure compatibility with this change.

Inside OUT

Removing the soft ceiling on the RID pool

Active Directory blocks further allocations from the global RID pool by setting the *msDS-RIDPoolAllocationEnabled* attribute of the RID *Manager$* object to FALSE. To enable the RID master to allocate blocks of RIDs from the global space, you must set the *msDS-RIDPoolAllocationEnabled* attribute to TRUE.

You can modify the *msDS-RIDPoolAllocationEnabled* attribute by using ADSI Edit or Ldp.exe. This value is set on a per-domain basis. ADSI Edit is a snap-in for MMC.

You can open ADS Edit by typing **AdsiEdit.msc** in the Everywhere Search box or at a prompt. Alternatively, open a new MMC by typing **MMC** at a prompt and then use the Add/Remove Snap-in option on the File menu to add the ADSI Edit snap-in to the MMC.

In ADSI Edit, press and hold or right-click the root node and then select Connect To. In the Connection Settings dialog box, choose the Select A Well Known Naming Context option. On the related selection list, select Default Naming Context and then tap or click OK. In ADSI Edit, work your way down to the CN=System container by expanding the Default naming context and the domain container. With the CN=System container selected in the left pane, press and hold or right-click CN=RID Manager$ and then select Properties. In the Properties dialog box, select the *msDS-RIDPoolAllocationEnabled* property and then tap or click Edit. In the Boolean Attribute Editor dialog box, select True and then tap or click OK twice.

Ldp is a graphical utility. Open Ldp by typing **ldp** in the Apps Search box or at a prompt. In Ldp, choose Connect from the Connection menu to connect to a domain controller in the domain you want to work with. After you connect to a domain controller, choose Bind from the Connection menu to bind to the domain using an account with domain administrator privileges. Next, choose Tree from the View menu to open the Tree View dialog box. In the Tree View dialog box, use the domain container as the base distinguished name (DN) to work with. In the domain container, expand the CN=System container. Next, press and hold or right-click CN=RID Manager$ and then select Modify. In the Modify dialog box, type **msDS-RIDPoolAllocationEnabled** in the Edit Entry Attribute box and then type **True** in the Values box. Because the attribute should already exist, set the Operation value as Replace. Tap or click Enter to create an LDAP transaction for this update and then tap or click Run to apply the change.

In Ldp, choose Connect from the Connection menu to connect to the RID master for the domain you want to work with. After you connect to the RID master, choose Bind from the Connection menu to bind to the domain using an account with domain administrator privileges. Next, choose Modify from the Browse menu to open the Modify dialog box. In the Edit Entry Attribute box, type **sidCompatibilityVersion**. In the Values box, type **1**. Because the attribute shouldn't already exist, set the Operation value as Add. Tap or click Enter to create an LDAP transaction for this update. Ensure that Synchronous is selected as an option and then tap or click Run to apply the change.

To locate the RID master for the current logon domain, enter the following command at a Windows PowerShell prompt:

```
(Get-ADDomain).RIDMaster
```

Alternatively, start Active Directory Users And Computers. Press and hold or right-click the domain you want to work with and then select Operations Masters. The Operations Masters dialog box, shown in Figure 11-30, shows the current RID master in the RID tab.

CHAPTER 11

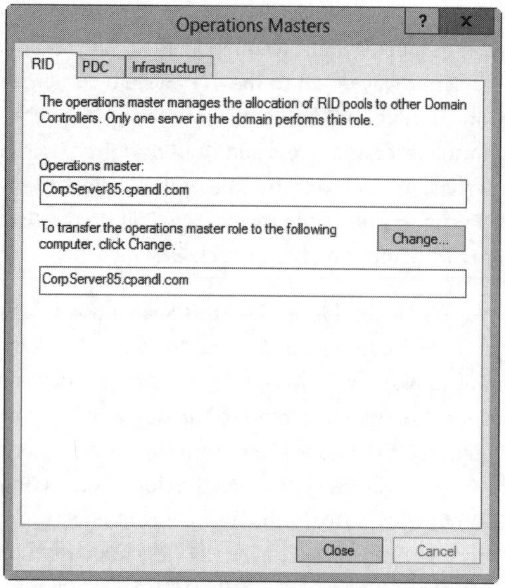

Figure 11-30 View the current RID master.

To transfer the RID master role to another server, follow these steps:

1. In Active Directory Users And Computers, press and hold or right-click the domain node and then select Change Domain Controller. In the Change Directory Server dialog box, select This Domain Controller, select an available domain controller to which you want to transfer the role, and then tap or click OK.

2. Press and hold or right-click the domain node again and then select Operations Masters. In the Operations Masters dialog box, the RID tab is selected by default. Tap or click Change. When prompted to confirm, tap or click Yes and then tap or click Close.

Using, locating, and transferring the PDC emulator role

The PDC emulator role is responsible for processing password changes and also is the default authoritative time server in the forest. All domain controllers in a domain know which server has the PDC emulator role.

When a user changes a password, the change is first sent to the PDC emulator, which in turn replicates the change to all the other domain controllers in the domain. If a user tries to log on to the network but provides an incorrect password, the domain controller checks the PDC emulator to see if it has a recent password change for this account. If so, the domain controller retries the logon authentication on the PDC emulator. This approach is designed to ensure that if a user has recently changed a password, that user is not denied logon with the new password.

Because the PDC emulator is the default time server for the forest, other computers on the network rely on the PDC emulator for time synchronization. To ensure that time synchronization is accurate in the Active Directory forest, you should configure the PDC emulator to synchronize time with a reliable external time source, a reliable internal time source, or a hardware clock. If you want the PDC emulator to use a Network Time Protocol (NTP) time source, type the following at an elevated command prompt:

```
w32tm /config /computer:PDCName /manualpeerlist:time.windows.com
/syncfromflags:manual /update
```

Here, *PDCName* is the fully qualified domain name of the PDC emulator and the */ManualPeerList* option configures the PDC emulator to get its time from *time.windows.com*. Here is an example:

```
w32tm /config /computer:dc05.cpandl.com /manualpeerlist:time.windows.com
/syncfromflags:manual /update
```

You also could get time from pool.ntp.org. The following example sets multiple peer servers so you have alternates should a server not be available:

```
w32tm /config /computer:dc05.cpandl.com /manualpeerlist: 0.pool.ntp.org,1.pool.ntp
.org,2.pool.ntp.org,3.pool.ntp.org
/syncfromflags:manual /update
```

Here, the servers used for time are as follows:

- 0.pool.ntp.org

- 1.pool.ntp.org

- 2.pool.ntp.org

- 3.pool.ntp.org

If you configured a reliable time server in the forest root domain, you can configure the PDC emulator master to synchronize with this server instead by typing the following:

```
w32tm /config /computer:PDCName /syncfromflags:domhier /update
```

Here, the */SyncFromFlags* option configures the PDC emulator to get its time synchronization information from the forest root domain hierarchy.

CHAPTER 11

IMPORTANT

The first domain controller to hold the PDC emulator role is the default authoritative time server for the forest. If the PDC emulator role is moved to a new domain controller, the time server role doesn't move automatically to the new domain controller. In this case you must configure the Windows Time service for the new PDC emulator master role holder and reconfigure the original PDC emulator master role holder to synchronize from the domain and not from an external or internal time source.

Domain computers on the network don't necessarily get their time directly from the PDC emulator. Generally, domain computers follow the directory hierarchy and synchronize time with a domain controller in their local domains. Domain controllers synchronize their time by using a series of queries that help them determine the best time source. A domain controller will make up to six queries:

1. The domain controller queries for parent domain controllers in the same site.

2. The domain controller queries for other domain controllers in the same site.

3. The domain controller queries for a PDC emulator in the same site.

4. The domain controller queries for parent domain controllers in other sites.

5. The domain controller queries for other domain controllers in other sites.

6. The domain controller queries for a PDC emulator in other sites.

NOTE

Parent domain controllers prefer reliable time sources but can also synchronize with nonreliable time sources if that is all that's available. Local domain controllers synchronize only with reliable time sources. Reliable time sources can synchronize only with domain controllers in the parent domain. The PDC emulator can synchronize with a reliable time source in its own domain or any domain controller in the parent domain.

Each query returns a list of domain controllers that can be used as a time source and a relative weighting for each based on reliability and location. A score of 8 is assigned to a domain controller in the same site. A score of 4 is assigned to a domain controller configured as a reliable time source. A score of 2 is assigned to a domain controller in a parent domain. A score of 1 is assigned to a domain controller that is the PDC emulator. Because the weighted scores are cumulative, a same-site PDC emulator would have a score of 9 (8 + 1).

To locate the PDC emulator for the current logon domain, enter the following command at a Windows PowerShell prompt:

```
(Get-ADDomain).PDCEmulator
```

Alternatively, start Active Directory Users And Computers. Press and hold or right-click the domain you want to work with and then select Operations Masters. The Operations Masters dialog box shows the current PDC emulator in the PDC tab.

To transfer the PDC emulator role to another server, follow these steps:

1. In Active Directory Users And Computers, press and hold or right-click the domain node and then select Change Domain Controller. In the Change Directory Server dialog box, select This Domain Controller, select an available domain controller to which you want to transfer the role, and then tap or click OK.

2. Press and hold or right-click the domain node again and then select Operations Master. In the Operations Masters dialog box, click the PDC tab. Tap or click Change. When prompted to confirm, tap or click Yes and then tap or click Close.

Using, locating, and transferring the infrastructure master role

The infrastructure master is responsible for updating cross-domain, group-to-user references. This means that the infrastructure master is responsible for ensuring that changes to the common name of a user account are correctly reflected in the group membership information for groups in other domains in the forest. The infrastructure master does this by comparing its directory data to that of a global catalog. If the data is outdated, it updates the data and replicates the changes to other domain controllers in the domain. If for some reason the infrastructure master is unavailable, group-to-user name references will not be updated and cross-domain group membership might not accurately reflect the actual names of user objects.

To locate the infrastructure master for the current logon domain, enter the following command at a Windows PowerShell prompt:

```
(Get-ADDomain).InfrastructureMaster
```

Alternatively, start Active Directory Users And Computers. Press and hold or right-click the domain you want to work with and then select Operations Masters. The Operations Masters dialog box shows the current infrastructure master in the Infrastructure tab.

To transfer the infrastructure master role to another server, follow these steps:

1. In Active Directory Users And Computers, press and hold or right-click the domain node and then select Change Domain Controller. In the Change Directory Server dialog box, select This Domain Controller, select an available domain controller to which you want to transfer the role, and then tap or click OK.

2. Press and hold or right-click the domain node again and then select Operations Masters. In the Operations Masters dialog box, click the Infrastructure tab. Tap or click Change. When prompted to confirm, tap or click Yes and then tap or click Close.

CHAPTER 11

Seizing operations master roles

When an operations master fails and is not coming back online, you need to seize the role to forcibly transfer it to another domain controller. Seizing a role is a drastic step that you should perform only when the previous role owner *will never be available again*. Don't seize an operations master role when you can transfer it gracefully using the normal transfer procedure. Seize a role only as a last resort.

Before you seize a role and forcibly transfer it, you should determine how up to date the domain controller that will take over the role is with respect to the previous role owner. Active Directory tracks replication changes by using update sequence numbers (USNs). Because of replication latency, domain controllers might not all be up to date. If you compare a domain controller's USN to that of other servers in the domain, you can determine whether the domain controller is the most up to date with respect to changes from the previous role owner. If the domain controller is up to date, you can transfer the role safely. If the domain controller isn't up to date, you can wait for replication to occur and then transfer the role to the domain controller.

For working with Active Directory replication, Windows Server includes Repadmin and Windows PowerShell cmdlets. To display the highest sequence number for a specified naming context on each replication partner of a designated domain controller, type the following at a command prompt:

```
repadmin /showutdvec DomainControllerName NamingContext
```

Here, *DomainControllerName* is the fully qualified domain name of the domain controller and *NamingContext* is the distinguished name (DN) of the domain in which the server is located, such as:

```
repadmin /showutdvec corpserver52 dc=cpand1,dc=com
```

The output shows the highest USN on replication partners for the domain partition:

```
Main-Site\corpserver31    @ USN    678321 @ Time 2014-05-12 04:32:45
Main-Site\corpserver26    @ USN    681525 @ Time 2014-05-12 04:32:45
```

In this example, if CorpServer31 was the previous role owner and the domain controller you are examining has an equal or higher USN for CorpServer31, the domain controller is up to date. However, if CorpServer31 was the previous role owner and the domain controller you are examining has a lower USN for CorpServer31, the domain controller is not up to date and you should wait for replication to occur before seizing the role. You could also use **Repadmin /Syncall** to force the domain controller that is the most up to date with respect to the previous role owner to replicate with all of its replication partners. Note that you can use **Repadmin /Replsingleobject** to replicate a specific object by using its distinguished name.

With Windows PowerShell, you can use the Get-AdReplicationUpToDatenessVectorTable cmdlet to display similar information about USNs. Just follow the cmdlet name with the name of the domain controller to examine, such as:

```
get-adreplicationuptodatenessvectortable corpserver85.cpandl.com
```

The output shows a list of the highest USNs seen by the specified domain controller for every domain controller in the forest. You also can use Sync-ADObject to replicate a specific object.

To seize an operations master role, follow these steps:

1. Open a command prompt on the console of the server you want to assign as the new operations master locally or by means of Remote Desktop.

2. List current operations masters by typing **netdom query fsmo**.

3. Type **ntdsutil**. At the ntdsutil prompt, type **roles**.

4. At the fsmo maintenance prompt, type **connections**.

5. At the server connections prompt, type **connect to server** followed by the fully qualified domain name of the domain controller to which you want to assign the operations master role.

6. After you establish a connection to the domain controller, type **quit** to exit the server connections prompt.

7. At the fsmo maintenance prompt, type one of the following:

    - seize pdc
    - seize rid master
    - seize infrastructure master
    - seize schema master
    - seize domain naming master

8. At the fsmo maintenance prompt, type **quit**.

9. At the ntdsutil prompt, type **quit**.

CHAPTER 11

Organizing Active Directory

Whether you are implementing a new Active Directory environment or updating an existing Active Directory environment, there's a lot to think about when it comes to design. Every Active Directory design is built from the same basic building blocks. These basic building blocks include the following:

- **Domains.** A domain is a logical grouping of objects that allows for central management and control over the replication of those objects. Every organization has at least one domain, which is implemented when Active Directory is installed on the first domain controller.

- **Domain trees.** A domain tree is a single domain in a unique namespace or a group of domains that share the same namespace. The domain at the top of a domain tree is referred to as the *root domain*. Two-way transitive trusts join parent and child domains in the same domain tree.

- **Forests.** A forest is a single domain tree or a group of domain trees that are grouped together to share resources. The first domain created in a new forest is referred to as the *forest root domain*. Domain trees in a forest have two-way transitive trusts between their root domains.

Many organizations have only one domain, and although I'll discuss in this chapter reasons why you might want to have additional domains, domain trees, and forests, you might also want to add structure to a domain. The building block you use to add structure to a domain is the organizational unit (OU), which I'll discuss in depth in this chapter.

Creating an Active Directory implementation or update plan

Creating or modifying an existing domain and forest plan is the most important design decision you make when implementing Active Directory. As such, this isn't a decision you should make alone. When you design Active Directory for an organization of any size, you should get the organization's management involved in the high-level design process.

Involvement doesn't mean letting other groups decide on all aspects of the design. Many complex components have to fit together, and the actual implementation of Active Directory should be the responsibility of the IT group. Involvement means getting feedback from—and working with—the business managers of other groups. This ensures that the high-level design meets their business requirements.

In addition, you almost certainly need to get approval for the high-level design goals with regard to security, access, usability, and manageability. Keep this in mind as you are developing the initial implementation plan. Your plan should start with the highest-level objects and work toward the lowest-level objects. This means that you must take the following steps:

1. Develop a forest plan.

2. Develop a domain plan that supports the forest plan.

3. Develop an organizational unit plan that supports the domain and forest plans.

The sections that follow discuss how to develop the necessary plans. After you have completed the planning and the plans are approved, you can implement the plans.

As part of your Active Directory planning, you should ensure that you meet or exceed your organization's service-level agreements (SLAs) and include the necessary hardware and network plans to make sure your implementation or upgrade is a success. For remote locations, such as branch offices, you should also determine whether read-only domain controllers (RODCs) are appropriate. RODCs are discussed in Chapter 15, "Deploying read-only domain controllers."

Developing a forest plan

Forest planning involves developing a plan for the namespace and administration needs of the organization as a whole. As part of this planning, you should decide who are the owners of the forest or forests you intend to implement. From an administration standpoint, the owners of a forest are the users who are the members of the Schema Admins and Enterprise Admins groups of the forest and the users who are members of the Domain Admins group in the root domain of the forest. Although these users have direct control over the forest structure, they typically don't make the final decisions when it comes to implementing forestwide changes. Typically, the final authority for making forestwide changes is an IT manager or business manager who is requesting changes based on a specific business need or requirement and acting after coordinating with business managers from other groups as necessary.

Forest namespace

The top structure in any Active Directory implementation is the forest root domain. The forest root domain is established when you install Active Directory on the first domain controller in a new forest. Any time you add to an existing forest a new domain that is part of a different namespace, you establish a root domain for a new tree. The name given to a root domain—either the forest root domain itself or the root domain of a new tree in a forest—acts as the base name for all domains later created in that tree. As you add subsequent domains, the domains are added below an established root domain. This makes the domains child domains of a root domain. (See Figure 12-1.)

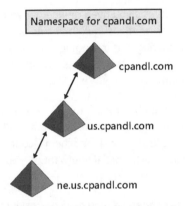

Figure 12-1 A hierarchy of domains.

Regardless of whether your forest uses a single namespace or multiple namespaces, additional domains in the same forest have the following characteristics:

- **Share a common schema.** All domain controllers in the forest have the same schema, and a single schema master is designated for the forest.

- **Share a common configuration directory partition.** All domain controllers in the forest share the same configuration container, and it stores the default configuration and policy information.

- **Share a common trust configuration.** All domains in the forest are configured to trust all the other domains in the forest, and the trust is two-way and transitive.

- **Share a common global catalog.** All domains in the forest have the same global catalog, and it stores a partial replica of all objects in the forest.

- **Share common forestwide administrators.** All domains in the forest have the same top-level administrators, Enterprise Admins and Schema Admins, who have the following roles:

    - Enterprise Admins are the only administrators with forest-level privileges, which allow them to add or remove domains. The Enterprise Admins group is also a member of the local Administrators group of each domain, so, by default, these users can manage any domain in the forest.

- Schema Admins are the only administrators who have the right to modify the schema.

A single forest vs. multiple forests

Part of creating a forest plan is deciding how many forests you need or whether you need additional forests. This isn't an easy decision or a decision that should be made lightly. With a single forest, you have a single top-level unit for sharing and managing resources. You can share information across all domains in the forest. However, this requires a great deal of trust and cooperation among all the groups in the organization.

With multiple forests, you change the dynamic considerably. You no longer have a single top-level unit for sharing and managing resources. You have separate structures that are fully autonomous and isolated from one another. The forests do not share schema, configuration information, trusts, global catalogs, or forestwide administrators. If you want to, you can connect the forests with a cross-forest trust.

If you decide to implement a cross-forest trust between forests, you can control whether a trust is one-way or two-way. You can also control the trust authentication level. Unlike interforest trusts, which are two-way and transitive by default, cross-forest trusts are either two-way or one-way. With a two-way trust, users in either forest have access to resources in the other forest. With a one-way trust, users in one forest have access to resources in the other forest but not vice versa.

The trust authentication level is set on outgoing trusts and is either domainwide or selective. Domainwide authentication is open and implies a certain level of trust because users in the trusted forest can be authenticated to use all of the resources in the trusting forest. Selective authentication is closed and more secure because only the users or groups to which you explicitly grant permission can access resources in the trusting domain.

Inside OUT

Consider the size of the organization

You should consider the size of the organization when deciding on a forest structure. However, the size of an organization alone is not a reason for deploying multiple forests. A forest can contain multiple domains. The domains can be deployed in multiple namespaces. Each domain is a separate unit of administration, and each domain can have millions of objects.

Inside OUT

Geographically separated sites

Geographically separated business units might want completely separate forests or domains. Although there might be business reasons for this, you should not make the decision based on perceived limitations in Active Directory. As long as a connection can be made between locations, there is no need for separate forests or domains. Active Directory sites provide the solution for connecting across limited bandwidth links. With the automatic compression feature for site bridgehead servers, replication traffic is compressed 85 to 90 percent, meaning that it is 10 to 15 percent of its noncompressed size. This means that even low-bandwidth links can often be used effectively for replication. For more information on sites, see Chapter 18, "Active Directory site administration."

Forest administration

Most companies opt to deploy a single forest, and it is only through merger or acquisition that additional forests enter the picture. In part, this is because there is no easy way to merge multiple forests into a single forest if you decide to do so later. To merge forests, you must migrate objects from one forest to the other by using the Active Directory Migration Tool (ADMT). This can be a very long process. For this and other reasons, you should decide from the start how many forests are going to be implemented and you should justify the need for each additional forest. Sometimes, additional forests are deployed because of organizational politics or the inability of business units to decide how to manage the top-level forest functions. At other times, additional forests are deployed to isolate business units or give complete control of the directory to a business unit.

The organization should consider the following factors before creating additional forests:

- Additional forests make it more difficult for users to collaborate and share information. For example, users have direct access to the global catalog and can search for resources easily only for their own forest. You must configure access to resources in other forests, and the users can't directly search for available resources in other forests.

- Additional forests mean additional administrative overhead and duplication of infrastructure. Each forest has its own forest-level configuration and one or more additional domain-level configurations that need to be managed. The ability to share resources and synchronize information across forests must be specifically configured rather than implemented by using built-in trusts and synchronization.

Sometimes, however, you need the additional controls put in place with additional forests to be reasonably sure that administrators from other domains in a forest do not make harmful changes to the directory, which are then replicated throughout the organization. All the domain controllers in a forest are tightly integrated. A change made on one domain controller is replicated to all other domain controllers. Replication is automatic, and there are no security checks other than that the person making the change must have the appropriate permissions in the first place; that is, the person must be a member of the appropriate administrator group for the type of change being made. If such an administrator is acting maliciously in making changes, those changes will be replicated regardless of the effect on the organization.

That said, you can have reasonable assurance about administrative access by putting in place strict administration rules and procedures. With strict rules and procedures, the organization has the following levels of administrators:

- Top-level administrators with enterprisewide privileges who are trusted with forestwide administration. These administrators are members of the Enterprise Admins group.

- High-level administrators with domainwide privileges who are trusted with domain-wide administration. These administrators are members of the Domain Admins, Administrators, Server Operators, or Backup Operators group.

- Administrators who are delegated responsibilities for specific tasks, which might include being a member of the Server Operators, Backup Operators, or a similar group.

To have reasonable assurance that the level of administrative access is appropriate, the organization also needs to physically secure domain controllers, set policies about how administrators use their accounts (such as running tasks as an administrator only when needed for administration), and configure auditing of all actions performed by both users and administrators.

Developing a domain plan

After you determine how many forests are needed based on the current namespace and administration needs of the organization as a whole, you next need to determine the domain structure that needs to be implemented. Whether your organization has an existing Active Directory structure or is implementing Active Directory for the first time, this means assessing the current environment and determining what changes are needed.

You need to thoroughly document the existing infrastructure and determine what—if anything—needs to be restructured, replaced, or upgraded. You also need to determine if it's even possible or practical to update the existing infrastructure as proposed. In some cases you might find that current design is not ideal for updating as proposed and you might need to revise your plans.

That's all acceptable because design is usually an iterative process in which you go from the theoretical to the practical during successive revisions. Just remember that it's difficult to change the domain namespace and the number of forests and domains after you've started implementing the design. Other parts of a design, such as the OU and site structure, are easier to change after implementation.

> NOTE
>
> **For tips and techniques on naming domains and establishing a naming hierarchy, see Chapter 6, "Architecting DNS infrastructure." You'll also find detailed information on using DNS (Domain Name System) with Active Directory in Chapter 7, "Implementing and managing DNS."**

Domain design considerations

Domains enable you to logically group objects for central management and control over the replication of those objects. You use domains to partition a forest into smaller components. As part of domain design, you should consider the following:

- **Replication.** Domains set the replication boundary for the domain directory partition and for domain policy information stored in the Sysvol folder on every domain controller in the domain. Any changes made to the domain directory partition or domain policy information on one of the domain controllers are replicated automatically to the other domain controllers in the domain. Although other directory partitions, such as the schema and configuration, are replicated throughout a forest, the domain information is replicated only within a particular domain. The more objects in the domain container, the more data that potentially needs to be replicated.

- **Resource access.** The trusts between and among domains in a forest do not by themselves grant permission to access resources. A user must be specifically given permission to access a resource in another domain. By default, an administrator of a domain can manage only resources in that domain and can't manage resources in another domain. This means that domain boundaries are also boundaries for resource access and administration.

- **Policy.** The policies that apply to one domain are independent from those applied to other domains. This means that policies for user and computer configuration and security can be applied differently in different domains. Certain policies can be applied only at the domain level. These policies, referred to as *domain security policies*, include password policies, account lockout policies, and Kerberos policies. These policies are applied to all domain accounts.

- **Language.** For organizations in which multiple languages are used, you might want to configure servers within a domain with the same additional languages. This is a consideration for administration purposes but not a requirement.

A single domain vs. multiple domains

With domain design, part of the decision involves the number of domains that are needed. You might need to implement additional domains or continue using a single domain. A single domain is the easiest to manage. It's also the ideal environment for users because it's easier for users to locate resources in a single domain environment than in a multidomain or multitree forest.

Beyond simplicity, there are several other reasons for implementing or keeping a single-domain design, such as the following:

- You do not need to create additional domains to limit administrative access, to delegate control, to create a hierarchical structure, or to enforce most group policies. In Active Directory, you can use OUs for these purposes.

- You might want to make authentication and resource access easier to configure and less prone to problems. A single domain doesn't have to rely on trusts or the assignment of resource access in other domains.

- You might want to make domain structure easier to manage. A single domain has only one set of domain administrators and one set of domain policy. A single domain doesn't need duplicate domainwide infrastructure for domain controllers.

- Your organization might frequently restructure its business units. It's easy to rename OUs, but it's very difficult to rename domains. It's easy to move accounts and resources between OUs, but it's much more difficult to move accounts and resources between domains.

With Active Directory you can have millions of objects in a single domain, so the reason for using multiple domains should not be based solely on the number of objects—although the number of objects is certainly still a factor to consider from a manageability standpoint. That said, using multiple domains sometimes makes sense, particularly if your organization has loosely connected business divisions or business locations with wide geographic separation. For example, if City Power & Light and The Phone Company are two divisions of one company, it might make sense to have a cpandl.com domain and a thephone-company.com domain within the same forest. If City Power & Light has Canadian and United States operations, it might make sense to have can.cpandl.com and us.cpandl.com domains.

Restricting access to resources and needing to enforce different sets of security policies are also reasons for using multiple domains. Using multiple domains creates boundaries for resource access and administration. It also creates boundaries for security policy. So if you need to limit resource access or tighten security controls for both users and administrators, you'll probably want to use multiple domains.

Like additional forests, multiple domains require additional administrative and infrastructure overhead. Each domain has its own domain-level configuration, which requires server hardware and administrators to manage that hardware. Because users might be accessing and authenticating resources across trusts, there is more complexity and there are more points of failure.

Forest root domain design configurations

The forest root domain can be either a dedicated root or a nondedicated root. A dedicated root, also referred to as an *empty root*, is used as a placeholder to start the directory. No user or group accounts are associated with it other than accounts created when the forest root is installed and accounts that are needed to manage the forest. Because no additional user or group accounts are associated with it, a dedicated root domain is not used to assign access to resources. This approach also would enable you to use cpandl.com as your external DNS name and corp.cpandl.com as your internal DNS name. A nondedicated root is used as a normal part of the directory. It has user and group accounts associated with it and is used to assign access to resources.

For an organization that is going to use multiple domains anyway, using a dedicated root domain makes a lot of sense. The forest root domain contains the forestwide administrator accounts (Enterprise Admins and Schema Admins) and the forestwide operations masters (domain naming master and schema master). It must be available when users log on to domains other than their home domain and when users access resources in other domains.

A dedicated root domain is easier to manage than a root domain that contains accounts. It allows you to separate the root domain from the rest of the forest. The separation also helps safeguard the entire directory, which is important because the forest root domain can't be replaced. If the root domain is destroyed and can't be recovered, you must re-create the entire forest.

Changing domain design

Ideally, after you implement a domain structure, the domain names never need to change. In the real world, however, things change. Organizations change their names, merge with other companies, are acquired, or restructure more often than we'd like. With Active Directory, you have several options for changing structure. If you find that you need to move a large number of objects from one domain to another, you can use the ADMT. You can rename domains as long as the forest is running at the Microsoft Windows Server 2003 or higher functional level. Changing the domain design after implementation is difficult, however, and involves using the

Domain Rename utility (Rendom.exe) and other tools, which are built into Windows Server 2008 and later.

NOTE

You can't change domain names if you have deployed Microsoft Exchange Server 2007 or Microsoft Exchange Server 2010. For a complete list of Microsoft applications and servers that do not support Domain Rename, see Microsoft Knowledge Base article 300684 (*http://support.microsoft.com/kb/300684/en-us*).

You can rename domains in the following key ways:

- Rename domains to move them within a domain tree. For example, you could rename a child domain from eng.it.cohowinery.com to eng.cohowinery.com.

- Rename domains so that a new tree is created. For example, you could change the name of a child domain from vineyard.cohowinery.com to cohovineyard.com.

- Rename domains to move them to a new tree. For example, you could change the name of a child domain from it.cohowinery.com to it.cohovineyard.com.

- Rename domains to set new domain names without changing the parent–child structure. For example, if the company name changes from Coho Vineyard to Coho Winery, you could change the existing domain names to use cohowinery.com instead of cohovineyard.com.

You can't use the Domain Rename utility to change which domain is the forest root domain. Although you can change the name of the forest root domain so that it is no longer the forest root *logically*, the domain remains the forest root domain *physically* in Active Directory. It still contains the forestwide administrator accounts (Enterprise Admins and Schema Admins) and the forestwide operations masters (domain naming master and schema master). This occurs because there is no way to change the forest root domain assignment within Active Directory after the forest root has been established.

As you might imagine, renaming a domain in a single-domain forest is the easiest renaming operation. As you increase the number of domains within a forest, you increase the complexity of the Domain Rename operation. Regardless of how many domains you are working with, you should always plan the project completely from start to finish and back up the entire domain infrastructure before trying to implement Domain Rename.

The reason for this planning and backup is that when you rename domains, even if you rename only one domain in a forest of many domains, you must make a change to every domain controller in the forest so that it recognizes the renamed domain. When you are finished, you must reboot each domain controller. If you don't perform the rename change on every domain controller, you must remove from service the domain controllers that did not get the updates. Furthermore, from the time you start the rename operation to the time you reboot domain controllers, the forest is out of service.

To complete the process after renaming a domain and updating domain controllers, you must reboot each workstation or member server in the renamed domain twice. While you are working with domain controllers and other computers that don't use Dynamic Host Configuration Protocol (DHCP) in the renamed domain, you should rename the computer so that the DNS name is correct and make other DNS name changes as appropriate.

Developing an organizational unit plan

So far in this book I've discussed domains, domain trees, and forests. These are the components of Active Directory that can help you scale the directory to meet the needs of any organization regardless of its size. Sometimes, however, what you want to do is not scale the directory but instead create hierarchical structures that represent parts of the organization or limit or delegate administrative access for a part of the organization. This is where OUs come in handy.

Using organizational units

An *organizational unit* (OU) is a logical administrative unit that is used to group objects within a domain. Within a domain, you can use OUs to delegate administrator privileges while limiting administrative access and to create a hierarchy that mirrors the business's structure or functions. So, rather than having multiple domains to represent the structure of the organization or its business functions, you can create OUs within a domain to do this.

At its most basic level, an OU is a container for objects that can contain other OUs and the following objects:

- Computers

- Contacts

- Groups

- inetOrgPerson

- Printers

- Shared Folders

- Users

> **NOTE**
>
> OUs are used to contain objects within a domain. They can't, however, contain objects from other domains.

> **NOTE**
>
> An inetOrgPerson object is used for LDAP compatibility and is defined in Request For Comments (RFC) 2798. Except for having a different object name, you manage inetOrgPerson objects the same way as user objects.

For administrative purposes, you can use OUs in two key ways.

First, you can use OUs to delegate administrative rights. You can use this approach to give someone limited or full administrative control over only a part of a domain. For example, if you have a branch office, you could create an OU for all the accounts and resources at that office and then delegate administration of that OU to the local administrator.

Second, you can use OUs to manage a group of objects as a single unit. Unlike domains, OUs are not a part of the DNS structure. Within Active Directory, OUs are seen as container objects that are part of a domain. In the directory tree they are referenced with the OU= identifier, such as OU=Sales for an OU named Sales. The distinguished name (DN) of an OU includes the path to its parent and its relative name. As you might recall, the DC= identifier is used to reference domain components. This means that the Sales OU in the cpandl.com domain has a DN of OU=Sales,DC=cpandl,DC=com.

Because OUs can contain other OUs, you can have multiple levels of OUs. For example, if you had a United States OU and a Europe OU within the Sales OU, the DNs of these OUs would be OU=USA,OU=Sales,DC=cpandl,DC=com and OU=Europe,OU=Sales,DC=cpandl,DC=com, respectively. When you nest OUs in this way, the nested OUs inherit the Group Policy settings of the top-level OUs by default, but you can override inheritance if you want to use unique Group Policy settings for a particular OU.

From a user perspective, OUs are fairly transparent. Because OUs aren't a part of the DNS structure, users don't have to reference OUs when they log on, when they're authenticating, or when they perform searches of Active Directory. This makes multiple OUs much easier to work with than multiple domains. Also, it's easy to change the names and structures of OUs, which isn't the case with domains.

Using OUs for delegation

Although you'll want to centrally manage Active Directory structure, you can delegate many other administrative tasks related to Active Directory to specific groups or individuals. Delegating administrative rights allows a user to perform a set of assigned administrative tasks for a specific OU. The tasks allowed depend on how you configure delegation, and they include allowing someone to perform the following actions:

- Create, delete, and manage accounts

- Reset user passwords and force password changes at next logon

- Read all user information

- Create, delete, and manage groups

- Modify the membership of a group

- Manage Group Policy links

- Generate Resultant Set of Policy

One of the common reasons for delegating administrative rights is to allow an individual in a department or business unit to reset user passwords. When you delegate this right, you allow a trusted person to change someone's password if the need arises. Because the right is delegated to a user within a particular OU, this right is limited to that specific OU. In many organizations this type of right is granted to Help Desk staff to allow them to reset passwords while preventing them from changing other account properties.

Using OUs for Group Policy

Group Policy allows you to specify a set of rules for computer and user configuration settings. These rules control the working environment for computers and users. Although I'll discuss Group Policy in depth in Chapter 17, "Managing Group Policy," the important thing to know about Group Policy is that you can use it to set default options, to limit options, and to prevent changing options in virtually every aspect of computer and user configuration.

Every domain you create has a default Group Policy rule set, referred to as the Default Domain Policy. Group Policy can also be applied to OUs, which makes OUs important in helping administrators manage groups of accounts and resources in a particular way. By default, OUs inherit the Group Policy settings of their parent object. For top-level OUs within a domain, this means that the Default Domain Policy is inherited by default. For lower-level OUs, this means that the OUs inherit the Group Policy of the OUs above them (and if the higher-level OUs inherit Group Policy from the domain, so do the lower-level OUs).

To manage Group Policy, you can use the Group Policy Management Console (GPMC). Group Policy is a very important part of Active Directory. Not only can you use it to manage the functionality available to users, but you also can use it to enforce security, to standardize desktop configuration, to install software, to specify scripts that should run when a computer starts or shuts down and when a user logs on or logs off, and so on.

CHAPTER 12

Because Group Policy is so important in Active Directory, you should plan your OU structure with Group Policy in mind. You do this by grouping objects that require the same Group Policy settings. For example, if a group of users requires a specific environment configuration to use an application or if a group of users requires a standard set of mapped drives, you can configure this through Group Policy.

Creating an OU design

OUs simplify administration by organizing accounts and resources in ways that best fit the organizational structure. When designing an OU structure, you should plan the structure before you try to implement it. You'll often find that you need multiple levels of OUs. This is fine. The levels of OUs form a hierarchy, much like the hierarchy formed when you use multiple levels of domains. The key thing to understand about any OU design is that it is really for administrators. As such, the design needs to be meaningful for your organization's administrators—and, ideally, it should help make administration easier.

Creating a good OU design isn't always as easy as it seems. Before trying to implement a design, it's a good idea to go through several possible scenarios on paper. Through revisions on paper, you should be able to improve the design substantially. Common design models for OUs are discussed in the sections that follow.

OU design: The division or business unit model

With a division or business unit model, you use OUs to reflect the department structure within the organization. The advantage of this model is that users will know and understand it. The disadvantage of this model is that when the company restructures, you might need to redesign the OU structure.

In the example shown in Figure 12-2, OUs are organized by department within the company and, to allow for separate controls for accounts and resources, the related objects are put in second-level OUs. If you want to have only one level of OUs, you could do this by putting all the objects in the top-level OU.

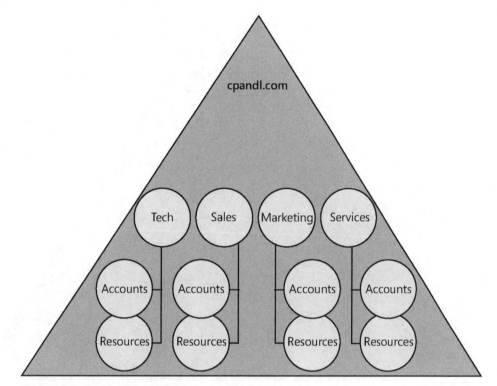

Figure 12-2 The division or business unit model.

OU design: The geographic model

With a geographic model, you use OUs to reflect geographic location. In this model, the top-level OUs represent the largest geographic units, such as continents and the lower-level OUs represent successively smaller geographic units, such as countries/regions. (See Figure 12-3.)

This model has several advantages. A geographic structure is stable. Many companies frequently reorganize internally, but they rarely change geographic structure. Also, when you use a geographic model, it's easy to determine where accounts and resources are physically located.

The disadvantages of this model have to do with its scope. For a global company, this design would put all accounts and resources in a single domain. As a result, changes made to Active Directory at any location would be replicated to every office location. Additionally, the OU structure doesn't relate to the business structure of the organization.

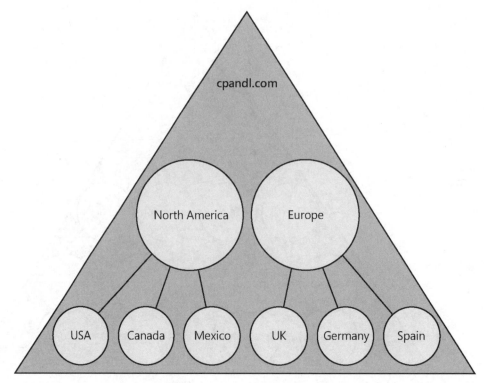

Figure 12-3 The geographic model.

OU design: The cost center model

With a cost center model, you use OUs to reflect cost centers. In this model, the top-level OUs represent the major cost centers within the organization and the lower-level OUs represent geographic locations, projects, or business structures, as shown in Figure 12-4. In a company in which budget is the top priority, the cost center model might be an effective way to reflect this priority. Cost centers could also be independent divisions or business units within the company that have their own management and cost controls.

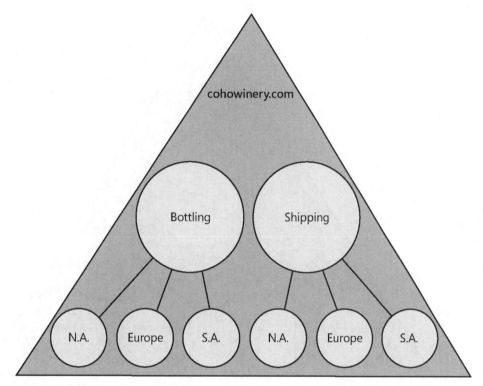

Figure 12-4 The cost center model.

The ability to represent costs and budgets in this way is a definite advantage, but it could also be a disadvantage. Cost center structure is not a structure well known to most administrators, and it might be confusing.

OU design: The administration model

With an administration model, you use OUs to reflect the way resources and accounts are managed. Because this model reflects the business structure of a company, it's very similar to the division or business unit model. The key difference is that the top-level OU is for administrators and second-level OUs are for the business structure. (See Figure 12-5.) If successive levels are needed, they can be organized by resource type, geographic location, project type, or some combination of the three.

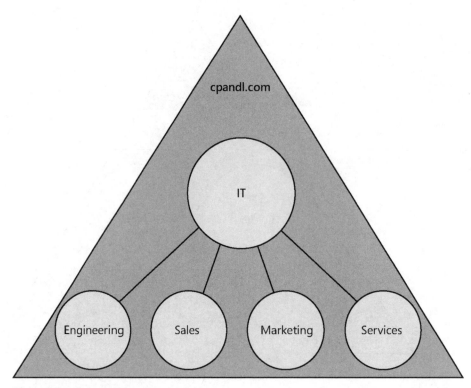

Figure 12-5 The administration model.

In a large company, you might use multiple implementations of this model for each division or business unit. In this case, the top-level administrative group would be for the division or business unit and the second-level OUs would be for groups within the division.

The advantage of this model is that it is designed around the way administrators work and represents the business structure of the company. The disadvantage of this model is that when the company (or divisions within the company) restructures, you might need to redesign the OU structure.

CHAPTER 13

Configuring Active Directory sites and replication

As part of the design of Active Directory Domain Services, you should examine the network topology and determine if you need to manage network traffic between subnets or business locations. To manage network traffic related to Active Directory, you use sites, which can be used to reflect the physical topology of your network. Every Active Directory implementation has at least one site. An important part of understanding sites involves understanding Active Directory replication. Active Directory uses two replication models: one model for replication within sites and one model for replication between sites. To plan your site structure, you need a solid understanding of these replication models.

Working with Active Directory sites

A *site* is a group of Transmission Control Protocol/Internet Protocol (TCP/IP) subnets that are implemented to control directory replication traffic and isolate logon authentication traffic between physical network locations. Each subnet that is part of a site should be connected by reliable, high-speed links. Any business location connected over slow or unreliable links should be part of a separate site. Because of this, individual sites typically represent the individual local area networks (LANs) within an organization and the wide area network (WAN) links between business locations typically mark the boundaries of these sites. However, you can also use sites in other ways.

Sites do not reflect the Active Directory namespace. Domain and site boundaries are separate. From a network topology perspective, a single site can contain multiple TCP/IP subnets as well. However, a single subnet can be in only one site. This means that the following conditions apply:

- A single site can contain resources from multiple domains.

- A single domain can have resources spread out among multiple sites.

- A single site can have multiple subnets.

As you design the site structure, you have many options. Sites can contain a domain or a portion of a domain. A single site can have one subnet or multiple subnets. Note that replication is handled differently *between* sites than it is *within* sites. Replication that occurs within a site is referred to as *intrasite replication*. Replication between sites is referred to as *intersite replication*. Each side of a site connection has one or more designated bridgehead servers.

Figure 13-1 shows an example of an organization that has one domain and two sites at the same physical location. Here, the organization has an East Campus site and a West Campus site. As you can see, the organization has multiple domain controllers at each site. The domain controllers in the East Campus site perform intrasite replication with one another, as do the domain controllers in the West Campus site. Designated servers in each site, referred to as site *bridgehead* servers, perform intersite replication with one another.

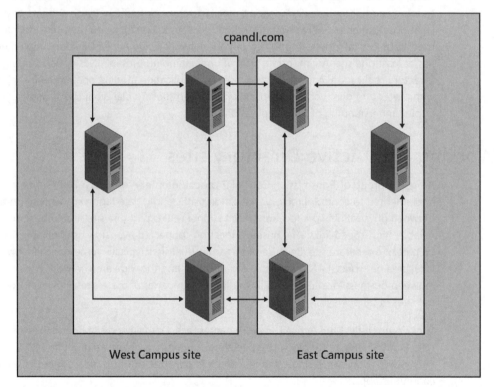

Figure 13-1 Multiple sites at the same location.

Figure 13-2 shows an example of an organization that has two physical locations. Here, the organization has decided to use two domains and two sites. The Main site is for the cohowinery.com domain, and the Seattle site is for the sea.cohowinery.com domain. Again, replication occurs both within and between the sites.

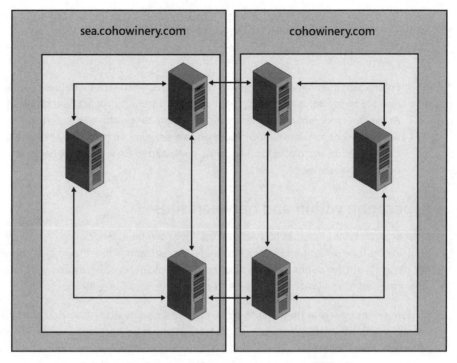

Figure 13-2 Multiple sites at different locations.

Single site vs. multiple sites

One reason to create additional sites at the same physical location is to control replication traffic. Replication traffic between sites is automatically compressed, reducing the amount of traffic passed between sites by 85 to 90 percent of its original size. Because network clients try to log on to network resources within their local site first, you can use sites to isolate logon traffic as well.

It's recommended that each site have at least one domain controller and one global catalog for client authentication. For name resolution and IP address assignment, it's also recommended that each site have at least one Domain Name System (DNS) server and one Dynamic Host Configuration Protocol (DHCP) server. By creating multiple sites in the same physical location and establishing a domain controller, a global catalog, and a DNS and DHCP server within each site, you can closely control the logon process.

You should also design sites with other network resources in mind, including Distributed File System (DFS) file shares, certificate authorities, and Microsoft Exchange servers. You want to configure sites so that clients' network queries can be answered within the site. If every client query for a network resource has to be sent to a remote site, there could be substantial network traffic between sites, which could be a problem over slow WAN links.

NOTE

Enterprises often have branch offices where each branch office is defined as a separate site to control traffic for high-bandwidth–consuming applications rather than Active Directory replication. Here, traffic for high-bandwidth–consuming applications, such as DFS or software control and change management, is carefully managed, but authentication and global catalog traffic is allowed to cross the WAN because it is less bandwidth-intensive.

Replication within and between sites

Most organizations implementing Active Directory have multiple domain controllers. The domain controllers might be located in a single server room where they are all connected to a fast network, or they might be spread out over multiple geographic locations, from which they are connected over a WAN that links the company's various office locations.

All domain controllers in the same forest—regardless of how many domain controllers there are and where the domain controllers are located—replicate information with one another. Although more replication is performed within a domain than between domains, replication between domains still occurs. The same replication model is used in both cases.

When a change is made to a domain partition in Active Directory, the change is replicated to all domain controllers in the domain. If the change is made to an attribute of an object tracked by the global catalog, the change is replicated to all global catalog servers in all the domains of the forest. Similarly, if you make a change to the forestwide configuration or schema partitions, these changes are replicated to all domain controllers in all the domains of the forest.

Authentication within and between domains is also handled by domain controllers. If a user logs in to his or her home domain, the local domain controller authenticates the logon. If a user logs in to a domain other than the home domain, the logon request is forwarded through the trust tree to a domain controller in the user's home domain.

The Active Directory replication model is designed for consistency, but the consistency is loosely defined. By *loosely defined*, I mean that at any given moment the information on one domain controller can be different from the information on a different domain controller. This can happen when Microsoft Windows Server has not yet replicated the changes on the first domain controller to the other domain controller. Over time, Windows Server replicates the changes made to one domain controller to all domain controllers as necessary.

When multiple sites are involved, the replication model is used to store and then forward changes as necessary between sites. In this case, a domain controller in the site where the changes were originally made forwards the changes to a domain controller in another site. This domain controller, in turn, stores the changes and then forwards the changes to all the domain controllers in the second site. In this way, the domain controller on which a change is made doesn't have to replicate directly with all the other domain controllers. Instead, it can rely on the store-and-forward technique to ensure that the changes are replicated as necessary.

Determining site boundaries

When trying to determine site boundaries, you should configure sites so that they reflect the physical structure of your network. Use connectivity between network segments to determine where you should locate site boundaries. Areas of the network that are connected with fast connections should all be part of the same site—unless you have specific requirements for controlling replication or the logon process. Areas of the network that are connected with limited bandwidth or unreliable links should be part of different sites.

As you examine each of the organization's business locations, determine whether placing either writeable domain controllers or read-only domain controllers and other network resources at that location is necessary. If you elect not to place a domain controller at a remote location, you can't make the location a part of a separate site. Not making the location a separate site has the following advantages:

- No Active Directory replication between the business locations

- No remote domain controllers to manage

- No additional site infrastructure to manage

This approach also has the following disadvantages:

- All logon traffic must cross the link between the business locations.

- Users might experience slow logon and authentication when trying to access network resources.

In the end, the decision to establish a separate site might come down to the user experience and the available bandwidth. If you have fast connections between sites—which should be dedicated and redundant—you might not want to establish a separate site for the remote business location. If you have limited bandwidth between business locations and want to maintain the user experience, you might want to establish a separate site and place domain controllers and possibly other network resources at the site. This speeds up the logon and authentication process and enables you to better control the network traffic between sites.

Understanding Active Directory replication

When you are planning the site structure, you need to understand how replication works. As discussed previously, Active Directory uses two replication models, each of which is handled differently. The intrasite replication model is used for replication within sites and is optimized for high-bandwidth connections. The intersite replication model is used for replication between sites and is optimized for limited-bandwidth connections. Before I get into the specifics of replication and the replication models, let's look at the way replication has changed from its early implementations to the present.

Tracking Active Directory replication changes over time

The replication model used for current Windows Server versions has changed in several important ways from the model first implemented. Understanding these changes can inform the way you deploy and work with Active Directory. It can also help ensure that outdated guidance isn't driving configuration decisions.

Originally, the smallest unit of replication was an individual attribute. Upon first examination, this seems to be what is wanted; after all, you don't want to have to replicate an entire object if only an attribute of that object has changed. The problem with this approach is that some attributes are multivalued. That is, they have multiple values. An example is the membership attribute of a universal group. This attribute represents all the members of the universal group.

As a result of this design oversight, when you added or removed a single user from the group, you caused the entire group membership to be replicated. In large organizations a significant amount of replication traffic was often generated because universal groups might have several thousand members. Current Active Directory architecture resolves this problem by replicating only the attribute's updated value. With universal group membership, this means that only the users you've added or removed are updated, rather than the entire group membership.

Intersite replication has also changed. You can turn off compression for intersite replication and enable notification for intersite replication. An improved knowledge consistency checker (KCC) enables Active Directory to support a greater number of sites. These changes affect intersite replication in the following key ways:

- All intersite replication traffic is compressed by default. Although this significantly reduces the amount of traffic between sites, it increases the processing overhead required to replicate traffic between sites on the bridgehead servers. Therefore, if processor utilization on bridgehead servers is a concern and you have adequate bandwidth connections between sites, you might want to disable compression.

- Replication between sites occurs at scheduled intervals according to the site-link configuration. You can enable notification for intersite replication, which allows the bridgehead server in a site to notify the bridgehead server on the other side of a site link that changes have occurred. This enables the other bridgehead server to pull the changes across the site link and thereby get more frequent updates.

- In early implementations the KCC greatly influenced the maximum number of sites you could have in a forest. As a result, there was a practical limit of about 100 sites per forest. With current implementations, the KCC itself is no longer the limiting factor. This means that you can have many hundreds of sites per forest.

NOTE

To turn off compression or enable notification, you need to edit the related site link or connection object. See "Configuring advanced site-link options" in Chapter 18, "Active Directory site administration."

Windows Server 2008 R2 and later support improved load balancing to distribute the workload more evenly among bridgehead servers. Prior to Windows Server 2008 R2, inbound connections from sites primarily targeted one bridgehead server in a site with requests even if multiple bridgeheads were available. Windows Server 2008 R2 and later have load-balancing improvements that help ensure that inbound connections are more evenly balanced when there are multiple bridgehead servers.

Because improved load balancing is a feature of the operating system and doesn't require operating in a Windows Server 2008 R2 or higher forest or domain functional level, you can start taking advantage of the improvements just by upgrading bridgehead servers. It's important to point out that intrasite replication algorithms have not changed—only intersite replication algorithms have changed. This means that these improvements do not apply to intrasite replication. Additionally, this load balancing occurs between two sites and doesn't extend outward in a spanning tree. Thus, the KCC doesn't take into account other sites when load-balancing connections between two sites.

The way load balancing works with multiple domains is slightly different from how it works with a single-domain environment. This is because an existing connection is always used instead of a new one, even if the connection is for a different naming context. Thus, with multiple domains it might appear that load balancing isn't working properly when in fact it is.

The KCC can still have unbalanced connections, such as when domain controllers go offline for extended periods. This unbalance can occur because the KCC does not rebalance connections when offline domain controllers come back online. The KCC prefers to maintain a stable topology rather than try to rebalance the topology.

Inside OUT

Load balancing manually

You can manually force load balancing. To do this, start by deleting the inbound inter-site connections for a domain controller or site. Next, either wait for the KCC to run automatically (which will occur within 15 minutes) or manually run the KCC by entering the following command at an elevated prompt: **repadmin /kcc.**

Don't run the KCC at all your sites simultaneously. If you do, inbound connections all choose the same bridgehead server. The reason this happens is that the system clock seeds the probabilistic choices for inbound connections. To avoid this problem, ensure that there is at least a one-second interval between the times you start the KCC in each site.

Tracking Active Directory system volume changes over time

As with replication, the Active Directory system volume has changed in several important ways since it was first implemented. Understanding these changes can inform the way you deploy and work with Active Directory, and it also can help ensure that outdated guidance isn't driving configuration decisions.

The Active Directory system volume (Sysvol) contains domain policy—as well as scripts used for logon, logoff, shutdown, and startup—and other related files in addition to files stored within Active Directory. The way domain controllers replicate the Sysvol depends on the domain functional level:

- When a domain is running at the Windows Server 2003 functional level, domain controllers replicate the Sysvol by using File Replication Service (FRS).

- When a domain is running at the Windows Server 2008 or higher functional level, domain controllers replicate the Sysvol by using Distributed File System (DFS).

FRS and DFS are replication services that use the Active Directory replication topology to replicate files and folders in the Sysvol shared folders on domain controllers. The way this works is that the replication service checks with the KCC to determine the replication topology that has been generated for Active Directory replication. Then it uses this replication topology to replicate Sysvol files to all the domain controllers in a domain. Because DFS has been significantly enhanced, you'll want to use DFS instead of FRS whenever possible.

Inside OUT

Why DFS instead of FRS?

When used with Active Directory, DFS has several advantages over FRS. DFS was enhanced for Windows Server 2003 R2 and Windows Server 2008. These enhancements not only made DFS easier to manage but also introduced several additional replication and compression technologies. With Windows Server 2003 R2 and later, DFS Replication (DFS-R) and Remote Differential Compression (RDC) are used instead of Rsync to provide up to 300 percent faster replication and 200 to 300 percent faster compression. Operational overhead for managing content and replication also was reduced by 40 percent. Additionally, DFS-R supports automated recovery from database loss or corruption, replication scheduling, and bandwidth throttling. Together, these features make DFS-R significantly more scalable than FRS.

RDC is the secret ingredient associated with enhanced DFS that enables the granular replication of changes—this is what's referred to when you read a vague statement that says DFS allows for the granular replication of the Sysvol. RDC enables granular replication by accurately identifying changes within and across files and transmitting only those changes to achieve significant bandwidth savings. More specifically, RDC detects insertions, removals, or rearrangements of data in files, enabling DFS-R to replicate only the changed file blocks when files are updated. Changes within or across files are called *file deltas*.

In addition to calculating file deltas and transferring only the differences, RDC can copy any similar file from any client or server to another using data that is common to both computers. This further reduces the amount of the data sent and the overall bandwidth requirements for file transfers. Local differencing techniques are used to transform the old version into a new version. The differences between two versions of the file are calculated on the source domain controller and then sent to the DFS client on the target domain controller.

The storage techniques and replication architectures for DFS and FRS are decidedly different. Figure 13-3 shows a conceptual view of how FRS is used with Active Directory on a domain controller. The FRS (Ntfrs.exe) stores FRS topology and schedule information in Active Directory and periodically polls Active Directory to retrieve updated information using Lightweight Directory Access Protocol (LDAP). Most administrator tools that work with FRS use LDAP as well. Internally, FRS makes direct calls to the file system using standard I/O. FRS uses the remote procedure call (RPC) protocol when communicating with remote servers.

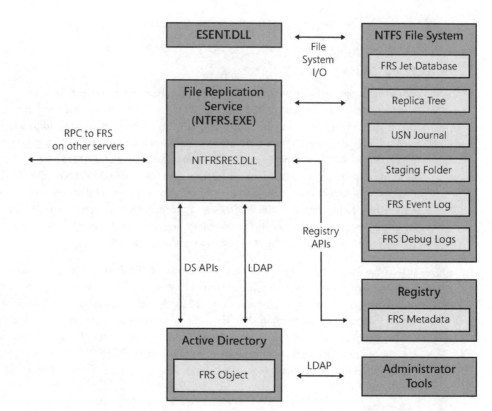

Figure 13-3 A conceptual view of how File Replication Service (FRS) works.

FRS stores various types of data in the NTFS file system, including transactions in the FRS Jet database (Ntfrs.jdb), events and error messages in the FRS Event log (NtFrs.evt), and debug logs stored in the debug log folder (%SystemRoot%\Debug). Esent.dll is a dynamic-link library used by the Jet database to store transactions. Ntfrsres.dll is a dynamic-link library that FRS uses to store events and error messages.

The contents of the replica tree determine what FRS replicates. The replica tree for Active Directory is the Sysvol. The Sysvol contains domain, staging, staging areas, and sysvol folders. The USN journal is a persistent log of changes made to files on an NTFS volume. NTFS uses the USN journal to track information about added, deleted, and modified files. FRS, in turn, uses the USN journal to determine when changes are made to the contents of the replica tree. FRS then replicates changes according to the schedule in Active Directory. FRS stores configuration data in the registry.

Inside OUT

The replica root

The actual replica root begins at the %SystemRoot%\Sysvol\domain folder, but the folder that is actually shared is the %SystemRoot%\Sysvol\sysvol folder. These folders appear to contain the same content because Sysvol uses junction points (also known as reparse points). A junction point is a physical location on a hard disk that points to data that is located elsewhere on the hard disk or on another storage device.

The Sysvol\domain folder contains policies and scripts in separate subfolders. The Sysvol\Staging folder acts as a queue for changed files that need to be replicated. Within the Sysvol\Staging Areas folder, the DomainName folder is a junction point to the Sysvol\staging\domain folder. Within the Sysvol\sysvol folder, the DomainName folder is a junction point to the Sysvol\domain folder.

After a user or the operating system changes a Sysvol file and the file is closed, FRS creates the file in the staging folder by using the backup application programming interfaces (APIs) and replicates the file according to the schedule set in Active Directory. FRS uses the same backup APIs that are used to ensure that Volume Shadow Copy Service–compatible backup programs, such as Windows Backup, can make point-in-time, consistent backups of the replica tree. Before such a program takes a shadow copy of a replica tree, the program instructs FRS to stop requesting new work items. After all currently active items are complete, FRS enters a pause state during which no new items can be processed.

Figure 13-4 shows a conceptual view of how DFS System is used with Active Directory on a domain controller. The DFS (Dfssvc.exe) stores information about stand-alone namespaces in the registry and information about domain-based namespaces in Active Directory.

The stand-alone DFS metadata contains information about the root, root target, links, link targets, and configuration settings defined for each stand-alone namespace. This metadata is maintained in the registry of the root server at HKLM\SOFTWARE\Microsoft\Dfs\Roots \Standalone.

Domain-based root servers have a registry entry for each root under KEY_LOCAL_MACHINE \SOFTWARE\Microsoft\Dfs\Roots\Domain, but these entries do not contain the domain-based DFS metadata. When the DFS service starts on a domain controller using Active Directory with DFS, the service checks this path for registry entries that correspond to domain-based roots. If these entries exist, the root server polls the primary domain controller (PDC) emulator master to obtain the DFS metadata for each domain-based namespace and stores the metadata in memory.

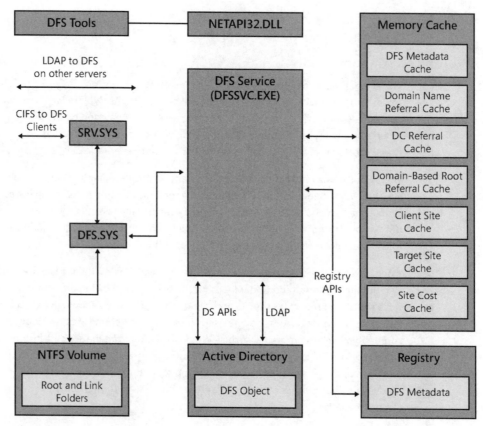

Figure 13-4 A conceptual view of how DFS works.

In the Active Directory data store, the DFS object stores the DFS metadata for a domain-based namespace. The DFS object is created in Active Directory when you install a domain at or raise a domain to at least the Windows Server 2008 domain functional level. Active Directory replicates the entire DFS object to all domain controllers in a domain.

DFS uses a client/server architecture. A domain controller hosting a DFS namespace has both the client and server components, enabling the domain controller to perform local lookups in its own data store and remote lookups in data stores on other domain controllers. DFS uses the Common Internet File System (CIFS) for communication between DFS clients, root servers, and domain controllers. CIFS is an extension of the Server Message Block (SMB) file-sharing protocol.

When a domain controller receives a CIFS request, the SMB Service server driver (Srv.sys) passes the request to the DFS driver (Dfs.sys) and this driver, in turn, directs the request to the

CHAPTER 13

DFS service. Dfs.sys also handles the processing of links when they are encountered during file-system access.

When a client requests a referral for a domain-based namespace, the domain controller first checks its domain-based root referral cache for an existing referral. If the referral cache exists, the domain controller uses the cache to create the referral. If the referral cache does not exist, the domain controller locates the DFS object for that namespace and uses the metadata in the object to create the necessary referral. A referral contains a list of Universal Naming Convention (UNC) paths that the client can use. DFS uses LDAP to retrieve metadata about the domain-based namespace from Active Directory and stores this information in its in-memory cache. Various types of in-memory cache are used:

- Domain Name Referral Cache contains the host names of computers and the fully qualified names of the local domain, all trusted domains in the forest, and domains in trusted forests.

- Domain Controller Referral Cache contains the host names of computers and the fully qualified names of the domain controllers for the list of domains it has cached.

- Domain-Based Root Referral Cache contains a list of root targets that host a given domain-based namespace.

- Client Site Cache stores information about the site in which a client is located (as determined by using a DSAddressToSiteNames lookup).

- Target Site Cache stores information about the site in which a target UNC path is located (as determined using a DSAddressToSiteNames lookup).

- Site Cost Cache contains a mapping of sites to their associated cost information as defined in Active Directory.

After this information is cached, DFS can provide this to clients that are requesting information about DFS namespaces. The physical structures and caches on a domain controller vary according to the type of namespace the server hosts (domain-based or stand-alone). Each root and link in a namespace has a physical representation on an NTFS volume on each domain controller. The DFS root for Active Directory corresponds to the Sysvol shared folder. If a domain controller hosts additional namespaces, the domain controller will have additional roots and links.

Replication architecture: An overview

Active Directory replication is a multipart process that involves a source domain controller and a destination domain controller. From a high level, replication works much as shown in Figure 13-5.

CHAPTER 13

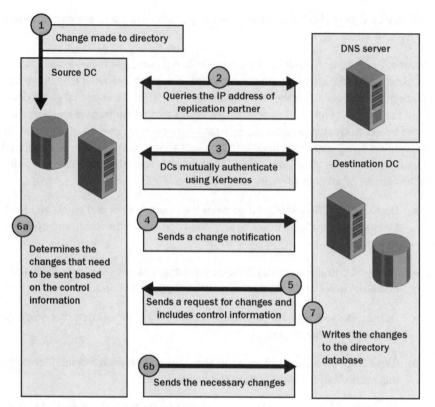

Figure 13-5 An overview of replication.

The step-by-step procedure goes like this:

1. When a user or a system process makes a change to the directory, this change is implemented as an LDAP write to the appropriate directory partition.

2. The source domain controller begins by looking up the IP address of a replication partner. For the initial lookup—or when the destination DNS record has expired—the source domain controller does this by querying the primary DNS server. Subsequent lookups can be done using the local resolver cache.

3. The source and destination domain controllers use Kerberos to mutually authenticate each other.

4. The source domain controller then sends a change notification to the destination domain controller using RPC over IP.

5. The destination domain controller sends a request for the changes using RPC over IP, including information that enables the source domain controller to determine if those changes are needed.

6. Using the information sent by the destination domain controller, the source domain controller determines what changes (if any) need to be sent to the destination domain controller. Then it sends the required changes using RPC over IP.

7. The destination domain controller uses the replication subsystem to write the changes to the directory database.

NOTE

For intersite replication, two transports are available: RPC over IP and Simple Mail Transfer Protocol (SMTP). With this in mind, you can also use SMTP as an alternate transport. SMTP uses TCP port 25.

As you can see from this overview, Active Directory replication depends on the following key services:

- LDAP

- Domain Name System (DNS)

- Kerberos version 5 authentication

- Remote procedure call (RPC)

These Windows services must be functioning properly to allow directory updates to be replicated. Active Directory also uses either FRS or DFS to replicate files in the System Volume (Sysvol) shared folders on domain controllers. The User Datagram Protocol (UDP) and TCP ports used during replication are similar whether FRS or DFS is used. Table 13-1 summarizes the ports that are used.

Table 13-1 Ports used during Active Directory replication

Service/Component	Port	
	UDP	**TCP**
LDAP	389	389
LDAP Secure Sockets Layer (SSL)		686
Global Catalog (LDAP)		3268
Global Catalog (LDAP, SSL)		3269
Kerberos version 5	88	88

Service/Component	Port	
	UDP	TCP
DNS	53	53
RPC		Dynamic
RPC endpoint mapper with DFS		135
Server Message Block (SMB) over IP	445	445
SMTP		25
Kerberos Change/Set Password	464	464

Inside OUT

Intrasite replication essentials

The Active Directory replication model is designed to ensure that there is no single point of failure. In this model every domain controller can access changes to the database and replicate those changes to all other domain controllers. When replication occurs within a domain, the replication follows a specific model that is very different from the replication model used for intersite replication.

With intrasite replication, the focus is on ensuring that changes are rapidly distributed. Intrasite replication traffic is not compressed, and replication is designed so that changes are replicated almost immediately after a change has been made. The main component in Active Directory responsible for the replication structure is the KCC. One of the main responsibilities of the KCC is to generate the replication topology—that is, the way replication is implemented.

As domain controllers are added to a site, the KCC configures a ring topology for intrasite replication with pull replication partners. This model is used for the following reasons:

- In a ring topology model, there are always at least two paths between connected network resources to provide redundancy. Creating a ring topology for Active Directory replication ensures that there are at least two paths that changes can follow from one domain controller to another.

- In a pull replication model, two servers are used. One is designated the push partner; the other is the pull partner. It's the responsibility of the push partner to notify the pull partner that changes are available. The pull partner can then request the changes. Creating push and pull replication partners enables rapid notification of changes and enables updating after a request for changes has been made.

The KCC uses these models to create a replication ring. As domain controllers are added to a site, the size and configuration of this ring change. When there are at least three domain controllers in a site, each domain controller is configured with at least two incoming replication connections. As the number of domain controllers changes, the KCC updates the replication topology.

When a domain controller is updated, it waits approximately 15 seconds before initiating replication. This short wait is implemented in case additional changes are made. The domain controller on which the change is made notifies one of its partners, using an RPC, and specifies that changes are available. The partner can then pull the changes. After replication with this partner completes, the domain controller waits approximately three seconds and then notifies its second partner of changes. The second partner can then pull the changes. Meanwhile, the first partner is notifying its partners of changes as appropriate. This process continues until all the domain controllers have been updated.

Inside OUT

Replicating urgent changes

The 15-second delay for replication applies to all current implementations of Active Directory. However, the delay is overridden to enable the immediate replication of priority changes. Priority (urgent) replication is triggered if you perform one of the following actions:

- Lock out an account or change the account lockout policy (or if an account is locked out automatically due to failed logon attempts)

- Change the domain password policy

- Change the password on a domain controller computer account

- Change the relative ID master role owner

- Change a shared secret password used by the Local Security Authority (LSA) for Kerberos authentication

Urgent replication means that there is no delay to initiate replication. Note that all other changes to user and computer passwords are handled by the designated PDC emulator in a domain. When a user changes a normal user or computer password, the domain controller to which that user is connected immediately sends the change to the PDC emulator. This way the PDC emulator always has the latest password for a user.

This is why the PDC emulator is checked for a new password if a logon fails initially. After the new password is updated on the PDC emulator, the PDC emulator replicates the change using normal replication. The only exception is when a domain controller contacts the PDC emulator requesting a password for a user. In this case the PDC emulator immediately replicates the current password to the requesting domain controller so that no additional requests are made for that password.

Figure 13-6 shows a ring topology that the KCC would construct if there were three domain controllers in a site.

As you can see from the figure, replication is set up as follows:

- DC1 has incoming replication connections from DC2 and DC3.

- DC2 has incoming replication connections from DC1 and DC3.

- DC3 has incoming replication connections from DC1 and DC2.

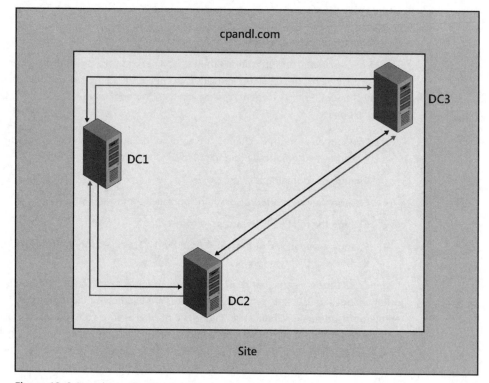

Figure 13-6 Intrasite replication using a ring topology.

If you make changes to DC1, DC1 notifies DC2 of the changes. DC2 then pulls the changes. After replication completes, DC1 notifies DC3 of the changes. DC3 then pulls the changes. Because all domain controllers in the site have now been notified, no additional replication occurs. However, DC2 still notifies DC3 that changes are available. DC3 does not pull the changes, however, because it already has them.

Domain controllers track directory changes using update sequence numbers (USNs). Any time a change is made to the directory, the domain controller assigns the change a USN. Each domain controller maintains its own local USNs and increments their values each time a change occurs. The domain controller also assigns the local USN to the object attribute that changed. Each object has a related attribute called *uSNChanged*. The *uSNChanged* attribute is stored with the object and identifies the highest USN that has been assigned to any of the object's attributes.

To see how this works, consider the following example. The local USN for DC1 is 125. An administrator connected to DC1 changes the password on a user's account. DC1 registers the change as local USN 126. The local USN value is written to the *uSNChanged* attribute of the user object. If the administrator next edits a group account and changes its description, DC1 registers the change as local USN 127. The local USN value is written to the *uSNChanged* attribute of the *Group* object.

NOTE

With replication there is sometimes a concern that replication changes from one domain controller might overwrite similar changes made to another domain controller. However, because object changes are tracked on a per-attribute basis, this rarely happens. It's very unlikely that two administrators would change identical attributes of an object at the same time. By tracking changes on a per-attribute basis, Active Directory effectively minimizes the possibility of any conflict.

Each domain controller tracks not only its local USN but also the local USNs of other domain controllers, in a table referred to as an *up-to-dateness vector*. During the replication process, a domain controller that is requesting changes includes its up-to-dateness vector. The receiving domain controller can then compare the USN values to those it has stored. If the current USN value for a particular domain controller is higher than the stored value, changes associated with that domain controller need to be replicated. If the current value for a particular domain controller is the same as the stored value, changes for that domain controller do not need to be replicated.

Because only necessary changes are replicated, this process of comparing up-to-dateness vectors ensures that replication is very efficient and that changes propagate only when necessary. The up-to-dateness vectors are, in fact, the mechanism that enables domain controllers with redundant connections to know that they've already received the necessary updates.

Inside OUT

Schema changes have priority

Several types of replication changes have priority. If you make changes to object attributes in the schema, these changes take precedence over most other changes. In this case, Active Directory blocks the replication of normal changes and replicates the schema changes. Active Directory continues to replicate schema changes until the schema configuration is synchronized on all domain controllers in the forest. This ensures that schema changes are applied rapidly. Still, it's a good idea to make changes to the schema during off-hours because schema changes need to propagate throughout the forest before other changes, such as resetting passwords, can be made to Active Directory.

Intersite replication essentials

Intrasite replication focuses on speed; intersite replication focuses on efficiency. The primary goal of intersite replication is to transfer replication information between sites while making the most efficient use of the available resources. With efficiency as a goal, intersite replication traffic uses designated bridgehead servers and a default configuration that is scheduled rather than automatic and compressed rather than uncompressed:

- With designated bridgehead servers, the Inter-Site Topology Generator (ISTG) limits the points of replication between sites. Instead of allowing all the domain controllers in one site to replicate with all the domain controllers in another site, the ISTG designates a limited number of domain controllers as bridgehead servers. These domain controllers are then the only ones used to replicate information between sites.

- With scheduled replication, you can set the valid times during which replication can occur and the replication frequency within this scheduled interval. By default, when you configure intersite replication, replication is scheduled to occur every 180 minutes 24 hours a day. When there's limited bandwidth between sites, you might want to change the default schedule to better accommodate the users who also use the link. For example, you might want to allow replication to occur every 180 minutes 24 hours a day on Saturday and Sunday but during the week set the schedule to allow more bandwidth during the day. For example, you might set replication to occur every 60 minutes from 6 A.M. to 8 A.M. and from 7 P.M. to 3 A.M. Monday through Friday.

- With compression, replication traffic is compressed 85 to 90 percent, meaning that it is 10 to 15 percent of its uncompressed size. This means that even low-bandwidth links can often be used effectively for replication. Compression is triggered when the replication traffic is more than 32 kilobytes (KBs) in size.

As discussed previously, there are two key ways to change intersite replication:

- Turn off automatic compression if you have sufficient bandwidth on a link and are more concerned about the processing power used for compression.

- Enable automatic notification of changes to allow domain controllers on either side of the link to indicate that changes are available. Automatic notification allows those changes to be requested rather than making domain controllers wait for the next replication interval.

Regardless of the site-link configuration, replication traffic is sent through dedicated bridgehead servers rather than through multiple replication partners. When changes are made to the directory in one site, those changes replicate to the other site through the designated bridgehead servers. The bridgehead servers then initiate the replication of the changes exactly as was discussed earlier in this chapter in the Inside Out entitled "Intrasite replication essentials," except that the servers can use SMTP instead of RPC over IP if you use SMTP as a transport. Thus, intersite replication is really concerned with getting changes from one site to another across a site link.

Figure 13-7 shows an example of intersite replication using a single dedicated bridgehead server on each side of a site link. In this example, DC3 is the designated bridgehead server for Site 1 and DC4 is the designated bridgehead server for Site 2.

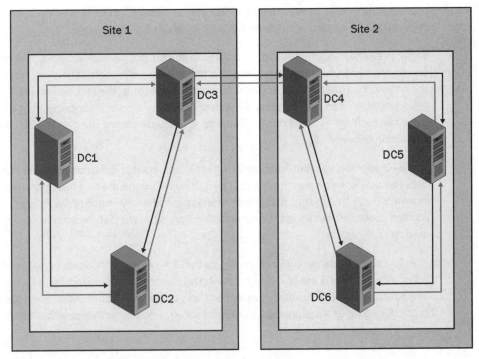

Figure 13-7 Replication between two sites.

As you can see from the figure, replication is set up as follows:

- DC1 has incoming replication connections from DC2 and DC3.

- DC2 has incoming replication connections from DC1 and DC3.

- DC3 has incoming replication connections from DC1 and DC2.

- DC4 has incoming replication connections from DC5 and DC6.

- DC5 has incoming replication connections from DC4 and DC6.

- DC6 has incoming replication connections from DC4 and DC5.

If changes are made to DC1 in Site 1, DC1 notifies DC2 of the changes. DC2 then pulls the changes. After replication completes, DC1 notifies DC3 of the changes. DC3 then pulls the changes. Because all domain controllers in Site 1 have now been notified, no additional replication occurs within the site. However, DC2 still notifies DC3 that changes are available. DC3 does not pull the changes, however, because it already has them.

According to the site-link configuration between Site 1 and Site 2, DC3 notifies DC4 that changes are available. DC4 then pulls the changes. Next, DC4 notifies DC5 of the changes. DC5 then pulls the changes. After replication completes, DC4 notifies DC6 of the changes. DC6 then pulls the changes. Because all domain controllers in Site 2 have now been notified, no additional replication occurs. However, DC5 still notifies DC6 that changes are available. DC6 does not pull the changes, however, because it already has the changes.

So far, I've talked about designated bridgehead servers but haven't said how bridgehead servers are designated. That's because it's a rather involved process. When you set up a site, the knowledge consistency checker (KCC) on a domain controller that Active Directory has designated the Inter-Site Topology Generator (ISTG) is responsible for generating the intersite topology. Each site has only one ISTG, and its job is to determine the best way to configure replication between sites.

The ISTG does this by identifying the bridgehead servers that are to be used. Replication between sites is always sent from a bridgehead server in one site to a bridgehead server in another site. This ensures that information is replicated only once between sites. As domain controllers are added to and removed from sites, the ISTG regenerates the topology automatically.

The ISTG also creates the connection objects that are needed to connect bridgehead servers on either side of a site link. This is how Active Directory logically represents a site link. The ISTG continuously monitors connections and creates new connections when a domain controller acting as a designated bridgehead server is no longer available. In most cases there will be more than one designated bridgehead server, and I discuss why in the next section, "Replication rings and directory partitions."

NOTE

You can manually configure intersite replication in several ways. In addition to using the techniques discussed previously for scheduling, notification, and compression, you can configure site link costs, configure connection objects manually, and designate preferred bridgehead servers.

Replication rings and directory partitions

The KCC is responsible for generating the intrasite replication topology, and the ISTG uses the KCC to generate the intersite replication topology. The KCC always configures the replication topology so that each domain controller in a site has at least two incoming connections if possible, as already discussed. The KCC also always configures intrasite replication so that each domain controller is no more than three hops from any other domain controller. This also means that *maximum replication latency*, the delay in replicating a change across an entire site, is approximately 45 seconds for normal replication.

When there are two domain controllers in a site, each domain controller is the replication partner of the other. When there are between three and seven domain controllers in the domain, each domain controller has two incoming connections and two replication partners. Figure 13-8 shows the replication topology for City Power & Light's Sacramento campus. Here, the network is spread over two buildings that are connected with high-speed interconnects. Because the buildings are connected over redundant high-speed links, the organization uses a single site with three domain controllers in each building. The replication topology for the six domain controllers as shown ensures that no domain controller is more than three hops from any other domain controller.

When the number of domain controllers increases beyond seven, additional connection objects are added to ensure that no domain controller is more than three hops from any other domain controller in the replication topology. To see an example of this, consider Figure 13-9. Here, City Power & Light has built a third building that connects its original buildings to form a U-shaped office complex. The administrators have placed two new domain controllers in Building 3. As a result of adding these domain controllers, some domain controllers now have three replication partners.

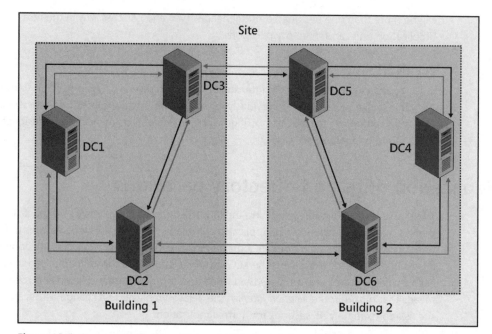

Figure 13-8 Campus replication with two buildings and three domain controllers in each building.

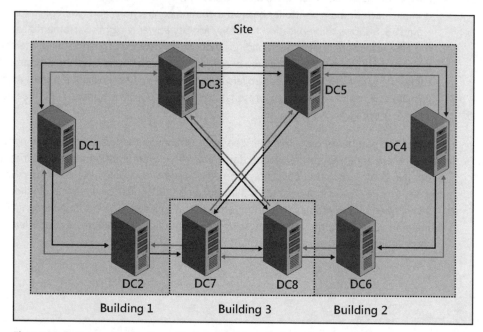

Figure 13-9 Campus replication with three buildings and eight domain controllers.

At this point you might be wondering what role, if any, directory partitions play in the replication topology. After all, from previous discussions you know that Active Directory has multiple directory partitions and that those partitions are replicated in the following ways:

- On a forestwide basis for configuration and schema directory partitions

- On a domainwide basis for the domain directory partition

- On a selective basis for the global catalog partition or other application-specific partitions, which include special application partitions and the ForestDnsZones and DomainDnsZones application partitions used by DNS

In previous discussions I didn't want to complicate things by adding a discussion of partition replication. From a logical perspective, partitions do play an important role in replication. Replication rings, the logical implementation of replication, are based on the types of directory partitions that are available. The KCC generates a replication ring for each kind of directory partition.

Table 13-2 details the replication partners for each kind of directory partition. Replication rings are implemented on a per-directory partition basis. There is one replication ring per directory partition type, and some rings include all the domain controllers in a forest, all the domain controllers in a domain, or only those domain controllers using application partitions.

Table 13-2 Per-directory partition replication rings

Directory Partition	Replication Partners
Configuration directory partition	All the domain controllers in the forest
Schema directory partition	All the domain controllers in the forest
Domain directory partition	All the domain controllers in a domain
Global catalog partition	All domain controllers in the forest that host global catalogs
Application directory partition	All the domain controllers using the application partition on a forestwide, domainwide, or selective basis, depending on the configuration of the application partition
ForestDnsZones directory partition	All the domain controllers in the forest that host DNS
DomainDnsZones directory partition	All the domain controllers that host DNS for that domain

When replication rings are within a site, the KCC on each domain controller is responsible for generating the replication topology and keeping it consistent. When replication rings go across site boundaries, the ISTG is responsible for generating the replication topology and keeping it consistent. Because replication rings are merely a logical representation of replication, the actual implementation of replication rings is expressed in the replication topology by using connection objects. Whether you're talking about intrasite or intersite replication, there is one connection object for each incoming connection. The KCC and the ISTG do not create additional connection objects for each replication ring. Instead, they reuse connection objects for as many replication rings as possible.

When you extend the reuse of connection objects to the way intersite replication is performed, the following is how multiple bridgehead servers might be designated. Typically, each site also has a designated bridgehead server for replicating the domain, schema, and configuration directory partitions. Other types of directory partitions might be replicated between sites by domain controllers that host these partitions. For example, if two sites have multiple domain controllers and only a few have application partitions, a connection object might be created for the intersite replication of the application partition.

Figure 13-10 shows an example of how you might use multiple bridgehead servers. Here, the domain, schema, and configuration partitions replicate from Site 1 to Site 2 and vice versa using the connection objects between DC3 and DC5. A special application partition is replicated from Site 1 to Site 2 and vice versa using the connection objects between DC2 and DC6.

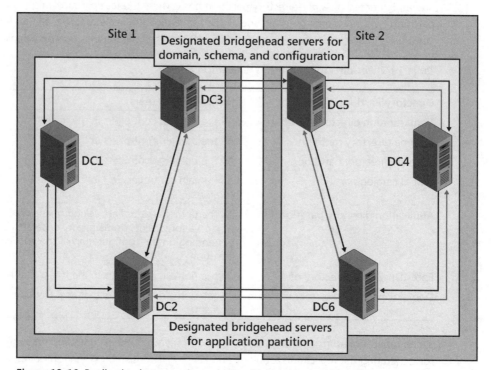

Figure 13-10 Replication between sites using multiple bridgehead servers.

The global catalog partition is a special exception. The global catalog is built from all the domain databases in a forest. Each designated global catalog server in a forest must get global catalog information from the domain controllers in all the domains of the forest. This means that a global catalog server must connect to a domain controller in every domain, and there must be an associated connection object to do this. Because of this, global catalog servers are another reason for having more than one designated bridgehead server per site.

Figure 13-11 provides an example of how replication might work for a more complex environment that includes domain, configuration, and schema partitions in addition to DNS and global catalog partitions. Here, the domain, schema, and configuration partitions replicate from Site 1 to Site 2 and vice versa using the connection objects between DC3 and DC5. The connection objects between DC1 and DC4 replicate the global catalog partition from Site 1 to Site 2 and vice versa. In addition, the connection objects between DC2 and DC6 replicate the DNS partitions from Site 1 to Site 2 and vice versa.

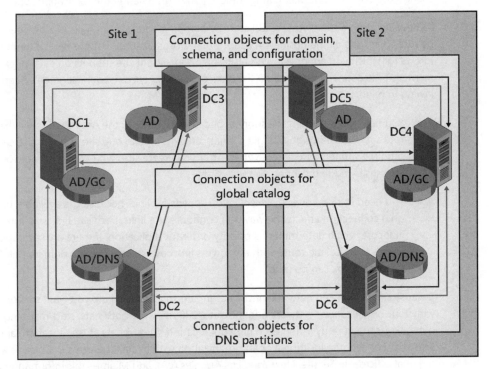

Figure 13-11 Replication in a complex environment.

Developing or revising a site design

Site design depends on your organization's networking infrastructure. As you set out to implement an initial site design, you should start by mapping your organization's existing network topology. Any time you plan to revise your network infrastructure, you must also plan the necessary revisions to your existing site design.

Mapping network infrastructure

Although site design is relatively independent from domain structure, the replication topology depends on how available domain controllers are and how they are configured. The KCC running on each domain controller monitors domain controller availability and configuration, and it updates replication topology as changes occur. The ISTG performs similar monitoring to determine the best way to configure intersite replication. This means that as you implement or change the domain controller configuration, you might change the replication topology.

To develop a site design, you should start by mapping your existing network architecture. Be sure to include all the business locations in the organization that are part of the forest or forests for which you are developing a site plan. Document the subnets on each network segment and the connection speed on the links connecting each network segment. Keep the following in mind:

- You need to document the subnets because each site in the organization will have separate subnets. Although a single subnet can exist only in one site, a single site can have multiple subnets associated with it. After you create sites, you create subnet-to-site associations by adding subnets to these sites.

- You need to document the connection speeds for links because the available bandwidth on a connection affects the way you configure site links. Each site link is assigned a link cost, which determines its priority order for replication. If there are several possible routes to a site, the route with the lowest link cost is used first. If a primary link fails, a secondary link can be used.

Because site design and network infrastructure are so closely linked, you want to work closely with your organization's network administrators. If you wear both hats, start mapping the network architecture by listing each network location, the subnets at that location, and the links that connect the location. For an organization with its headquarters in Chicago and four regional offices—in Seattle, New York, Los Angeles (LA), and Miami—this information might come together as shown in Table 13-3. Notice that I start with the hubs and work my way to the central office. This way, when I finally make this entry, the multiple connections to the central office are all accounted for.

Table 13-3 Mapping network structure

Location	Subnets	Connections
Seattle	10.1.11.0/24, 10.1.12.0/24	256 kilobits per second (Kbps) Seattle–Chicago, 128 Kbps Seattle–LA
LA	10.1.21.0/24, 10.1.22.0/24	512 Kbps LA–Chicago, 128 Kbps LA–Seattle
New York	10.1.31.0/24, 10.1.32.0/24	512 Kbps New York–Chicago, 128 Kbps New York–Miami
Miami	10.1.41.0/24, 10.1.42.0/24	256 Kbps Miami–Chicago, 128 Kbps Miami–New York
Chicago	10.1.1.0/24, 10.1.2.0/24	256 Kbps Seattle–Chicago, 512 Kbps LA–Chicago, 512 Kbps New York–Chicago, 256 Kbps Miami–Chicago

I then use the table to create a diagram similar to the one shown in Figure 13-12, in which I depict each network and the connections among them. I also note the subnets at each location. Although it's also helpful to know the number of users and computers at each location, this information alone isn't enough to help you determine how links connecting sites are used. The only certain way to know that is to monitor the network traffic going over the various links.

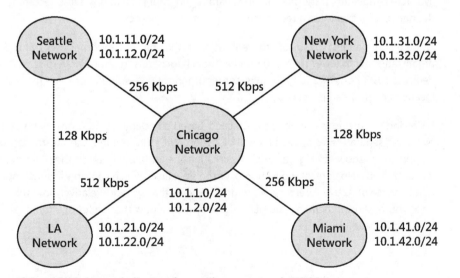

Figure 13-12 Network diagram for a wide area network (WAN).

Creating a site design

After you map the network structure, you are ready to create a site design. Creating a site design involves the following steps:

1. Mapping the network structure to the site structure

2. Designing each individual site

3. Designing the intersite replication topology

4. Considering the impact of site-link bridging

5. Planning the placement of servers in sites

Each of these steps is examined in the sections that follow.

Mapping the network structure to the site structure

To map the network structure to the site structure, start by examining each network location and the speed of the connections between those locations. In general, if you want to make separate network locations part of the same site, the sites should have at least 512 Kbps of available bandwidth. If the sites are in separate geographic locations, I also recommend that the network locations have redundant links for fault tolerance.

These recommended speeds are for replication traffic only, not for other user traffic. Smaller organizations with fewer than 100 users at branch locations might be able to scale down to dedicated 128 Kbps or 256 Kbps links. Larger organizations with 250 or more users at branch locations might need to scale up.

Following the previous example, the Chicago-based company would probably be best served by having separate sites at each network location. With this in mind, the site-to-network mapping is as shown in Figure 13-13. By creating the additional sites at the other network locations, you help control replication over the slow links, which can significantly improve the performance of Active Directory. More good news is that sites are relatively low-maintenance once you configure them, so you get a significant benefit without a lot of additional administration overhead.

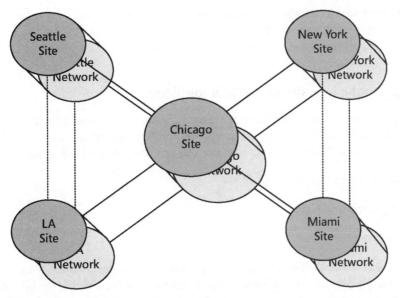

Figure 13-13 Initial site-to-network mapping.

Designing each individual site

After you determine how many sites you will have, you need to consider the design of each site. A key part of the site design is naming the sites and identifying the subnets that are associated with each site. Site names should reflect the physical location of the site. The default site created by Active Directory is Default-First-Site-Name, and most site names should follow a similar naming scheme. Continuing the example, you might use the following site names:

- Seattle-First-Site

- LA-First-Site

- NewYork-First-Site

- Miami-First-Site

- Chicago-First-Site

I used dashes instead of spaces, following the style Active Directory uses for the default first site. I named the sites *City*-First-Site rather than *City*-Site to enable easy revision of the site architecture to include additional sites at each location. Now, if a location receives additional sites, the naming convention is very clear, and it's also very clear that if you have a Seattle-First-Site, a Seattle-Second-Site, and a Seattle-Third-Site, these are all different sites at the Seattle location.

To determine the subnets that you should associate with each site, use the network diagram developed in the previous section. It already has a list of the subnets. In your site documentation, just note the IP subnet associations that are needed and update your site diagram to include the subnets.

Designing the intersite replication topology

After you name the sites and determine subnet associations, you should design the intersite replication topology. You do this by planning the details of replication over each link designated in the initial site diagram. For each site link, plan the following components:

- Replication schedule

- Replication interval

- Link cost

Typically, you want replication to occur at least every 180 minutes, 24 hours a day, 7 days a week. This is the default replication schedule. If you have limited bandwidth, you might need to alter the schedule to allow user traffic to have priority during peak usage times. If bandwidth isn't a concern or if you have strong concerns about keeping branch locations up to date, you might want to increase the replication frequency. In all cases, you should, if possible, monitor any existing links to get a sense of the bandwidth utilization and the peak usage periods.

Calculating the link cost can be a bit complicated. When there are multiple links between locations, you need to think carefully about the appropriate cost of each link. Even if there is only one link between all your sites now, you should set an appropriate link cost now to ensure that if links are added between locations, all the links are used in the most efficient way possible.

Valid link costs range from 1, which assigns the highest possible preference to a link, to 99999, which assigns the lowest possible preference to a link. When you create a new link, the default link cost is set to 100. If you set all the links to this cost, all the links have equal preference for replication. But would you really want replication to go over a 128 Kbps link when you have a 512 Kbps link to the same location? Probably not.

In most cases the best way to set the link cost is to assign a cost based on the available network bandwidth over a link. Table 13-4 provides an example of how this could be done.

Table 13-4 Setting the link cost based on available bandwidth

Available Bandwidth	Link Cost	Preference
10 gigabits per second (Gbps) to 2 Gbps	1	Top
2 Gbps to 1 Gbps	2	Extremely high
1 Gbps to 512 megabits per second (Mbps)	4	Very high
512 Mbps to 256 Mbps	10	Moderately high
256 Mbps to 100 Mbps	20	High
100 Mbps to 10 Mbps	40	Above normal
10 Mbps to 1.544 Mbps	100	Normal
1.544 Mbps to 512 Kbps	200	Below normal
512 Kbps to 256 Kbps	400	Moderately low
256 Kbps to 128 Kbps	800	Low
128 Kbps or less	1600	Very low

You can use the costs in the table to assign costs to each link you identified in your site diagram. After you do this, update your site diagram so that you can determine the route that is used for replication if all the links are working. As Figure 13-14 shows, your site diagram should now show the names of the sites, the associated subnets, and the cost of each link.

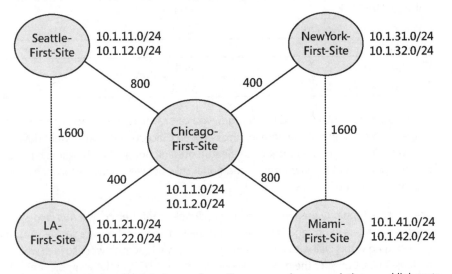

Figure 13-14 Updated site design to show site names, subnet associations, and link costs.

Considering the impact of site-link bridging

By default, Active Directory automatically configures site-link bridges, which make links transitive between sites in much the same way that trusts are transitive between domains. When a site is bridged, any two domain controllers can make a connection across any consecutive series of links. The site-link-bridge cost is the sum of all the costs of the links included in the bridge. Let's calculate the site-link-bridge costs using the links shown in Figure 13-14. Because of site-link bridges, the domain controllers at the Chicago headquarters have two possible routes for replication to each of the branch office locations. The costs of these routes are summarized in Table 13-5.

Table 13-5 Link and bridge costs

Site/Link	Link/Bridge Cost
SEATTLE SITE	
Chicago–Seattle	800
Chicago–LA–Seattle	2000
LA SITE	
Chicago–LA	400
Chicago–Seattle–LA	2400
NEW YORK SITE	
Chicago–New York	400
Chicago–Miami–New York	2400
MIAMI SITE	
Chicago–Miami	800
Chicago–New York–Miami	2000

Knowing the costs of links and link bridges, you can calculate the effects of a network link failure. In this example, if the primary link between Chicago and Seattle went down, replication would occur over the Chicago–LA–Seattle site-link bridge. In this example it's relatively straightforward, but if you introduce additional links between network locations, the scenarios become very complicated very quickly.

The network topology used in the previous example is referred to as a *hub-and-spoke* design. The headquarters in Chicago is the hub, and the rest of the offices are spokes. Automatic site-link bridging works well with a hub-and-spoke design. It doesn't work so well when you have multiple hubs. Consider the example shown in Figure 13-15. In this example, Chicago is the main hub, but because Seattle and LA each have a spoke, they are also considered hubs.

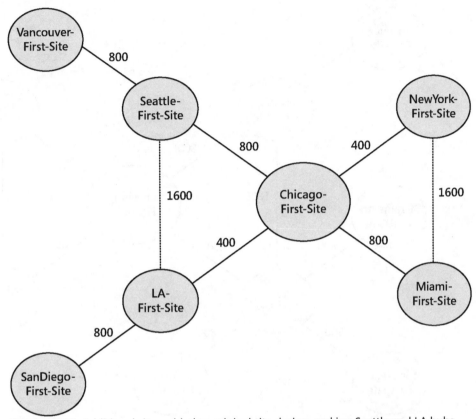

Figure 13-15 Additional sites added to original site design, making Seattle and LA hubs.

Site-link bridging can have unintended consequences when you have multiple hubs and spokes on each hub. Here, when the bridgehead servers in the Chicago site replicate with other sites, they replicate with Seattle, New York, LA, and Miami bridgehead servers as before, but they also replicate with the Vancouver and San Diego bridgehead servers across the site bridge from Chicago–Seattle–Vancouver and from Chicago–LA–San Diego. This means that the same replication traffic could go over the Chicago–Seattle and the Chicago–LA links twice. This can happen because of the rule of three hops for optimizing replication topology.

The repeat replication over the hub links becomes worse as you add spokes. Consider Figure 13-16. Here, the LA hub has connections to sites in Sacramento, San Diego, and San Francisco. As a result of site-link bridging, the same replication traffic could go over the Chicago–LA links four times. This happens because of the rule of three hops for optimizing replication topology.

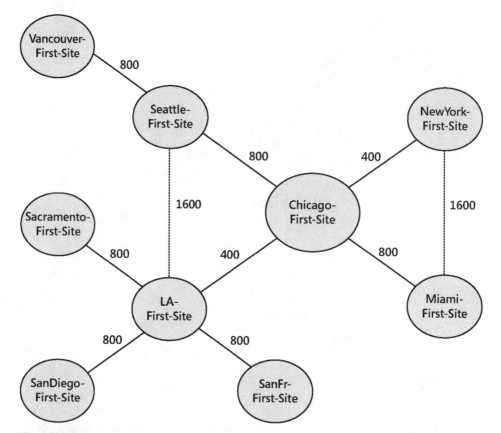

Figure 13-16 A site design with multiple spokes at hubs.

The solution to the problem of repeat replication traffic is to disable automatic site bridging. Unfortunately, the automatic bridging configuration is all or nothing. This means that if you disable automatic site-link bridging and still want to bridge some site links, you must configure those bridges manually. You can enable, disable, and manually configure site-link bridges as discussed in the section entitled "Configuring site-link bridges" in Chapter 18.

Planning the placement of servers in sites

When you finish configuring site links, you should plan the placement of servers in the sites. Think about which types of domain controllers and how many of each will be located in a site. Answer the following questions:

- Will there be domain controllers? If so, how many?

- Will any of the domain controllers host a global catalog? If so, how many?

- Will any of the domain controllers host DNS? If so, how many?

- Will any of the domain controllers have an operations master role? If so, what roles and on which domain controllers?

Think about which Active Directory partitions will be replicated between the sites as a result of the domain controller placement. Also think about any additional partitions that might need to be replicated to a site. Answer the following questions:

- Will domain, configuration, and schema partitions be replicated to the site?

- Will a global catalog be replicated to the site?

- Will ForestDnsZones and DomainDnsZones partitions be replicated to the site?

- Will any special application partitions be replicated to the site? If so, which partitions, how are they used, and which domain controllers will host them?

By answering all these questions, you know what servers will be placed in each site and what information will be replicated between sites. Don't forget about dependent services for Active Directory. At a minimum, each site should have at least one domain controller, a global catalog, and DNS. This configuration enables intrasite replication to occur without having to go across site links for dependent services. To improve the user experience, keep the following in mind:

- Global catalogs are needed for logon (unless universal group membership caching is enabled). If there is a local global catalog, logon can complete without a request having to go across a site link.

- DHCP servers are needed for dynamic IP addressing. If there is a local DHCP server, clients with dynamic IP addressing will be able to start up and get an IP address assignment without having to go across a site link.

- DNS servers are needed for forward and reverse lookups. If there is a local DNS server, clients will be able to perform DNS queries without having to go across a site link.

CHAPTER 14

Implementing Active Directory Domain Services

After you've completed planning, the process of implementing Active Directory Domain Services (AD DS) is similar whether you are installing Active Directory for the first time or extending your existing Active Directory infrastructure. In either case, you need to take the following steps:

1. Install the necessary domain controllers and assign any other needed roles to these servers.

2. Create the necessary organizational units (OUs) and delegate administrative control over these OUs as necessary.

3. Create any necessary user, group, and computer accounts and the resources that are required for use in a domain.

4. Use group policy and local security policy to set default settings for user and computer environments in any domains and OUs you created.

5. Create the necessary sites and configure those sites for use and replication.

In this chapter, I examine the steps for installing domain controllers, creating OUs, and delegating administrative control. Chapter 16, "Managing users, groups, and computers," discusses creating user, group, and computer accounts and related Group Policy. Chapter 17, "Managing Group Policy," discusses managing Group Policy and local security policy. Chapter 18, "Active Directory site administration," discusses creating sites and managing replication.

Preinstallation considerations for Active Directory

Whenever you work with a server role as complex as Active Directory Domain Services, you should take time to carefully consider the physical implementation. As with the installation of Microsoft SQL Server, Microsoft Exchange Server, or Microsoft Internet Information Services (IIS), you should evaluate hardware requirements, plan for the system's backup needs, and consider how the system will be used.

Hardware and configuration considerations for domain controllers

Every domain controller is essentially a database server with a complex replication system, and, as such, when you select hardware for and configure domain controllers, you should use all the care and attention that you'd give to one of your mainstay database servers. The hardware you choose for the domain controllers should be correctly sized.

You should take the following guidelines into consideration:

- **Processor.** The CPU for a domain controller needs to be relatively fast. As soon as you install the second domain controller in a forest, a process called the Knowledge Consistency Checker (KCC) begins running on every domain controller. The KCC is responsible for generating the replication topology and dynamically handling changes and failures within the replication topology. By default, the KCC on every domain controller recalculates the replication topology every 15 minutes. The more complex the replication topology, the more processing power it takes to perform this task. In many cases, even in small domain environments, the calculations the KCC performs considerably increase CPU utilization. This is acceptable for short durations. However, if the domain controller doesn't have a fast enough CPU, generating the replication topology in a complex environment could take several minutes rather than several seconds, which could severely affect the performance of all other processes running on the server.

- **Multiprocessing.** Some installations might benefit from having domain controllers with multiple CPUs. With multiple processors you might see significant performance improvements. However, rather than having a single beefy domain controller, it's better to have multiple domain controllers placed appropriately.

- **Memory.** Domain controllers might use more memory than other servers. In addition to running standard processes, domain controllers must run special processes, such as storage engine processes, knowledge consistency checking, replication, and garbage collection. Therefore, most domain controllers should have at least 4 gigabytes (GBs) of RAM as a recommended starting point for full server installations and 2 GBs of RAM for core server installations. Be sure to monitor memory usage and upgrade as necessary. Ideally, for best performance you want to have enough RAM so that the entire Active Directory tree can reside in physical memory. In large environments, having properly sized RAM can make a substantial difference in performance.

- **Disks.** The data storage capacity you need depends entirely on the number of objects related to users, computers, groups, and resources that are stored in the Active Directory database. The initial installation of Active Directory requires a small amount of available space. By default, the database is stored in the Ntdis.dit database file on the system volume, as are related log files. When the database and log files are stored together, the storage volume should have free disk space of at least 20 percent of the combined size of the database and log files. When the database and log files are stored separately, each storage volume should have free disk space of at least 20 percent of either the database or the log files as appropriate.

- **Data protection.** Domain controllers should use fault-tolerant drives to protect against hardware failure of the system volume and any other volumes used by Active Directory. I recommend using a redundant array of independent disks (RAID), either RAID 1 or RAID 5. Hardware RAID is preferable to software RAID.

When configuring the hardware, you should consider where you will install the files used by Active Directory. Active Directory database and log files are stored by default in the %SystemRoot%\NTDS folder, although the Active Directory system volume (Sysvol)—which is created as a shared folder and contains policy, scripts, and other related files—is stored by default in the %SystemRoot%\SYSVOL folder. These locations are completely configurable during installation; you should consider whether you want to accept the defaults or store the files elsewhere. In large enterprises, you typically get better scalability and performance if you put the database and log files on different volumes, each on a separate drive. The Active Directory Sysvol can usually remain in the default location.

NOTE

If you decide to move the Sysvol, you must move it to an NTFS volume. For security reasons, the database and log folders should be on NTFS volumes as well, but this isn't a requirement.

Active Directory is dependent on network connectivity and the Domain Name System (DNS). You should configure domain controllers to use static Internet Protocol (IP) addresses and have the appropriate primary and secondary DNS servers set in their Transmission Control Protocol/Internet Protocol (TCP/IP) configuration, as discussed in Chapter 3, "Managing TCP/IP networking." If DNS isn't available on the network, you have the opportunity to make DNS available during the installation of Active Directory. Implement DNS as discussed in Chapter 6, "Architecting DNS infrastructure," and Chapter 7, "Implementing and managing DNS," and be sure to configure the DNS server to use itself for DNS resolution. If you previously deployed Microsoft DNS, as discussed in Chapters 6 and 7, the DNS environment should already be set to work with Active Directory.

If you are using a DNS server that does not use Microsoft DNS, you can verify that the DNS server will work properly with Active Directory by using the Domain Controller Diagnostic Utility (Dcdiag.exe). You can run Dcdiag and test the DNS configuration by typing the following command at the command prompt:

```
dcdiag /test:dcpromo /dnsdomain:DomainName /newforest
```

CHAPTER 14

Here, *DomainName* is the name of the DNS domain in which the domain controller is located. Consider the following example:

```
dcdiag /test:dcpromo /dnsdomain:cpandl.com /newforest
```

Here, you run a test of the Active Directory Domain Services Configuration Wizard (Dcpromo .exe) to see if the DNS domain cpandl.com is compatible with creating a new forest. You need to closely examine and resolve any errors in the output of the test.

Configuring Active Directory for fast recovery with storage area networks

Domain controllers are backed up differently than other servers are. To back up Active Directory, you must back up the System State. On Microsoft Windows Server 2012 R2 there are approximately 50,000 system state files, which use approximately 4 GBs of disk space in the default installation. These files must be backed up as a set and can't be divided. To keep the System State intact when you place the volumes related to Active Directory on a storage area network (SAN), you must also place the operating system (system and boot volume) on the SAN. This means that you must then boot from the SAN.

Booting from a SAN and configuring Active Directory so that the related volumes are on a SAN enables several fast recovery scenarios—most of which make use of the Volume Shadow Copy Service (VSS). For instance, suppose that a domain controller is using the C, D, and E volumes: C for the operating system and Sysvol, D for the Active Directory database, and E for the Active Directory logs. By using a third-party backup utility that makes use of VSS, you might be able to use that backup software to create shadow copies of the System State on separate logical unit numbers (LUNs) on the SAN.

On the SAN, let's say that volumes C, D, and E correspond to LUNs 1, 2, and 3 and that the current shadow copy of those volumes is on LUNs 7, 8, and 9. If Active Directory failed at this point, you could recover it by performing the following steps:

1. Use the DiskRAID utility to mask the failed LUNs (1, 2, and 3) so that they are no longer accessible.

2. Use the DiskRAID utility to unmask the shadow-copied LUNs (7, 8, and 9) so that they are usable.

    NOTE The DiskRAID utility is a command-line tool for configuring and managing RAID storage subsystems, such as those associated with network-attached storage (NAS) and SANs. Windows 8.1 and Windows Server 2012 R2 might be the last versions of Windows to support DiskRAID. Storage technologies are in transition from traditional approaches to standards-based approaches. As a result, several popular tools and favored features are being phased out, including DiskRAID.

3. Boot the domain controller to firmware, set the boot device to LUN 6, and then reboot.

4. You've now recovered Active Directory. When the domain controller starts, it will recover the Active Directory database and synchronize with the rest of the domain controllers in the organization through regular replication.

Connecting clients to Active Directory

Network clients connect to Active Directory for logon and authentication and to perform Lightweight Directory Access Protocol (LDAP) lookups. In a standard configuration of Active Directory, communications between clients and servers are secure and use either Server Message Block (SMB) signing or secure channel encryption and signing. Secure communications are used by default because the default security policy for Windows Server 2008 and later has higher security settings than the security policies for previous versions of Windows. All current Windows clients natively support SMB signing, secure channel encryption and signing, or both.

CHAPTER 14

Inside OUT

Secure communications for domain controllers

One reason for configuring secure communications by default is to prevent certain types of security attacks. Secure communications specifically thwart man-in-the-middle attacks, among others. In this attack, a third machine gets between the client and the server and pretends to be the other machine to each. This allows the man-in-the-middle machine to intercept and modify data that is transmitted between the client and the server. With that said, if you must disable secure communications, you can.

To disable the secure communications requirement, follow these steps:

1. Open the related Group Policy Object (GPO) for editing in the Group Policy Management Editor.

2. Expand Computer Configuration, Windows Settings, Security Settings, Local Policies, and then select Security Options.

3. Under Security Options, press and hold or right-click Domain Member: Digitally Encrypt Or Sign Secure Channel Data (Always) and then select Properties.

4. In the Properties dialog box, select Disabled and then tap or click OK.

Installing Active Directory Domain Services

Any server running Windows Server can act as a domain controller. You configure a server as a domain controller by following a two-part process. You add the Active Directory Domain Services (AD DS) role to the server you want to promote to a domain controller and then configure the services by using the Active Directory Domain Services Configuration Wizard.

Active Directory installation options and issues

You have several options for installing Active Directory binaries:

- Use the Add Roles And Features Wizard in Server Manager to add the Active Directory Domain Services role to the server. On the Select Server Roles page, select Active Directory Domain Services and then tap or click Next twice. Tap or click Install.

- Enter the following command at an elevated Windows PowerShell prompt: **install-windowsfeature ad-domain-services –includemanagementtools**.

Both of these installation techniques do the same thing: they prepare the server by installing the AD DS binaries and the related management tools. The AD DS binaries include the Windows components that enable servers to act as domain controllers. The technique you use depends primarily on your personal preference. However, although any administrator can install the AD DS binaries, you might need additional administrator permissions to fully configure a domain controller.

After you install the binaries, you can configure Active Directory Domain Services and promote the server to a domain controller. In Server Manager you have a Notification task labeled Promote This Server To A Domain Controller. Tapping or clicking the related link starts the Active Directory Domain Services Configuration Wizard. At the Windows PowerShell prompt, you use the following cmdlets in the ADDSDeployment module to configure Active Directory Domain Services:

- **Install-ADDSForest.** Installs a new forest root domain. The *–DomainMode* and *–ForestMode* parameters set the domain and forest functional levels, respectively, which have acceptable values of Win2003, Win2008, Win2008R2, Win2012, and Win2012R2. The *–SafeModeAdministratorPassword* parameter sets the recovery password. The *–CreateDNSDelegation* parameter creates a delegation for the domain in DNS, and the *–InstallDNS* parameter installs DNS. The basic syntax and an example follow:

```
install-addsforest –domainname DomainName –DomainMode DomMode
–ForestMode ForMode
–CreateDNSDelegation –installdns –SafeModeAdministratorPassword Password

install-addsforest –domainname cpandl.com –DomainMode Win2012
–ForestMode Win2012
```

```
-SafeModeAdministratorPassword
(convertto-securestring "Str!F#789" -asplaintext)
```

- **Install-ADDSDomain.** Installs a new child or tree domain. The
  –NewDomainName parameter sets the name of the domain, and the
  –ParentDomainName parameter sets the name of the parent domain. The *–DomainType*
  parameter sets the domain type as either *ChildDomain* or *TreeDomain*. The basic syntax
  and an example follow:

```
install-addsdomain -domainname DomainName -parentdomainname ParentDomain
-SafeModeAdministratorPassword Password -DomainMode DomMode
-DomainType DomType -installdns -CreateDNSDelegation

install-addsdomain -domainname eng -parentdomainname cpandl.com
-SafeModeAdministratorPassword (read-host -prompt "Recovery Password:"
-assecurestring) -DomainMode Win2012 -installdns -CreateDNSDelegation
```

- **Install-ADDSDomainController.** Installs an additional domain controller. The
  –InstallationMediaPath parameter sets the path of the folder from which to install media.
  The *–SiteName* parameter specifies the Active Directory site for the domain controller.
  The basic syntax and an example follow:

```
install-addsdomaincontroller -domainname DomainName -CreateDNSDelegation
-installdns -SafeModeAdministratorPassword Password -SiteName Site
-installfrommedia FolderPath

install-addsdomaincontroller -domainname cpandl.com -CreateDNSDelegation
-SafeModeAdministratorPassword (convertto-securestring
    "Str!F#789" -asplaintext)
-installdns -SiteName Seattle-First-Site -installfrommedia d:\Data\ADDS
```

When you configure Active Directory, you are given the option of setting the domain controller type as a domain controller either for a new domain or as an additional domain controller in an existing domain. If you make the domain controller part of a new domain, you can create a new domain in a new forest, a child domain in an existing domain tree, or a new domain tree in an existing forest. In fact, this is how you extend the Active Directory structure from the first domain in a new forest to include additional domains and domain trees.

To configure Active Directory, you must use an account with administrator privileges. The administrator privileges and installation requirements are as follows:

- **Creating a domain controller in a new forest.** If you are creating a domain controller in a new forest, you should log on to the local machine using either the local Administrator account or an account that has administrator privileges on the local machine and then start the installation. Because you are creating the new forest, the server should have a static IP address. After you install DHCP servers in the new forest, you can assign the domain controller a dynamic IP address.

- **Creating a domain controller in a new domain or a new domain tree.** If you are creating a domain controller in a new domain or a new domain tree in an existing forest, you should log on to the local machine using either the local Administrator account or an account that has administrator privileges on the local machine and then start the installation. You will also be required to provide the credentials for an account that is a member of the Enterprise Admins group in the forest of which the domain will be a part.

  Because you are creating a new domain or domain tree, the server should have a static IP address. After you install DHCP servers in the new domain or domain tree, you can assign the domain controller a dynamic IP address.

- **Creating an additional domain controller in an existing domain.** If you are creating an additional domain controller in an existing domain, you should consider whether you want to perform an installation from media rather than creating the domain controller from scratch. With either technique, you need to log on to the local machine using either the local Administrator account or an account that has administrator privileges on the local machine and then start the installation.

  You will also be required to provide the credentials for an account that is a member of the Domain Admins group in the domain of which the domain controller will be a part. Because you are installing an additional domain controller, the server should already be a member of the domain and must have a valid IP address. The IP address can be a static IP address or a dynamic IP address assigned by a DHCP server.

NOTE
Domain controllers that also act as DNS servers should not have dynamic IP addresses. The reason for this is that the IP address of a DNS server should be fixed to ensure reliable DNS operations.

IMPORTANT
The server you want to promote must have appropriately configured TCP/IP settings. This means the server must have an appropriate IP address, as discussed previously. It also might mean that the server needs to have an appropriate subnet mask and default gateway and preferred and alternate DNS server settings.

Before starting an Active Directory installation, you should examine local accounts and check for encrypted files and folders. Because domain controllers do not have local accounts or separate cryptographic keys, making a server a domain controller deletes all local accounts and all certificates and cryptographic keys from the server. Any encrypted data on the server, including data stored using the Encrypting File System (EFS), must be decrypted before installing Active Directory or it will be permanently inaccessible. However, this isn't an issue for BitLocker Driver Encryption. With BitLocker Driver Encryption you don't need to decrypt entire drives, but you do need to disable BitLocker before you run Dcpromo.

Inside OUT

Finding encrypted files

To search an entire volume for encrypted files, change directories to the root directory by using the CD command and then examine the entire contents of the directory by using the EFSInfo utility as follows:

```
efsinfo /s:DriveDesignator /i | find ": Encrypted"
```

Here, *DriveDesignator* is the drive designator of the volume to search, such as C, as shown in the following example:

```
efsinfo /s:c: /i | find ": Encrypted"
```

Here, *EFSInfo* is used to search the root directory of C and all its subdirectories and display the encryption status of all files and folders. Because you care about only the encrypted files and folders, you pipe the output to the Find utility and search it for the string ": Encrypted", which is a text string that appears only in the output for encrypted files and folders.

To add the first domain controller that runs Windows Server 2012 R2 to an existing Active Directory infrastructure, the Active Directory Domain Services Configuration Wizard automatically runs Adprep.exe as needed for the forest and domain. This is a new feature for Windows Server 2012 R2. Preparing the forest and domain includes updating the Active Directory schema as needed, creating new objects and containers as needed, and modifying security descriptors and access control lists as needed. For forest prep, the account you use must be a member of the Schema Admins group, the Enterprise Admins group, and the Domain Admins group of the domain that hosts the schema master, which is, by default, the forest root domain. For domain prep, you must use an account that can log on to the infrastructure master and is a member of the Domain Admins group. For read-only domain controller (RODC) prep, you must use an account that is a member of the Enterprise Admins group.

Using the Active Directory Domain Services Configuration Wizard

With Windows Server 2012 R2, Active Directory Domain Services installation and configuration tasks are performed through Server Manager. You no longer have to run an installation wizard and a separate command-line promotion task. Instead, you use the Add Roles And Features Wizard to add the Active Directory Domain Services role to the server and then promote the server to a domain controller by using the Active Directory Domain Services Configuration Wizard. The basic steps are as follows:

1. In Server Manager, tap or click Manage and then tap or click Add Roles And Features. This starts the Add Roles And Features Wizard. If the wizard displays the Before You Begin page, read the Welcome message and then tap or click Next.

2. On the Select Installation Type page, select Role-Based Or Feature-Based Installation and then tap or click Next.

3. On the Select Destination Server page, the server pool shows servers you added for management. Tap or click the server you are configuring and then tap or click Next.

4. On the Select Server Roles page, select Active Directory Domain Services and then tap or click Next twice. Tap or click Install. This runs the Active Directory Domain Services Configuration Wizard.

5. When the initial installation task completes, you need to tap or click Promote This Server To A Domain Controller to start the Active Directory Domain Services Configuration Wizard. If you closed the Add Roles And Features Wizard window, you need to tap or click the Notifications icon and then tap or click Promote This Server To A Domain Controller.

6. If the computer is currently a member server, the wizard takes you through the steps needed to install Active Directory Domain Services, which might include running Adprep.exe automatically to prepare the directory schema in the forest and domain for Windows Server 2012 R2. Upgrading the forest requires credentials that include group memberships in Enterprise Admins, Schema Admins, and Domain Admins for the forest root domain. Upgrading a domain other than the forest root domain requires credentials that include group memberships in Domain Admins.

NOTE

If you haven't previously run adprep /domainprep /gpprep in each domain, you need to manually perform this task. Server Manager for Windows Server 2012 R2 will not prepare Group Policy for you. Note that Group Policy needs to be prepared only the first time you deploy domain controllers running Windows Server 2003 SP1 or later. Adprep /gpprep modifies the access control entries (ACEs) for all GPO folders in the SYSVOL directory to grant read access to all enterprise domain controllers. This level of access is required to support Resultant Set of Policy (RSoP) for site-based policy and causes the NT File Replication Service (NTFRS) to resend all GPOs to all domain controllers.

It's also important to point out that the Active Directory Domain Services Configuration Wizard doesn't prepare a domain for RODCs when you install the first writeable Windows Server 2012 R2 domain controller. Instead, domains are prepared for RODCs automatically when you promote the first unstaged RODC in a domain. You also can manually prepare a domain for RODCs by running Adprep.exe /rodcprep.

To automatically create or update a DNS delegation, the account you use must be a member of the DNS Admins group in the domain.

The way you continue depends on whether you are creating an additional domain controller for an existing domain, creating a new domain in a new forest, or creating a new domain tree or domain in an existing forest.

Creating additional domain controllers for an existing domain

To create an additional domain controller for an existing domain, follow these steps:

1. Start the Active Directory Domain Services Configuration Wizard as discussed previously. On the Deployment Configuration page, shown in Figure 14-1, choose Add A Domain Controller To An Existing Domain.

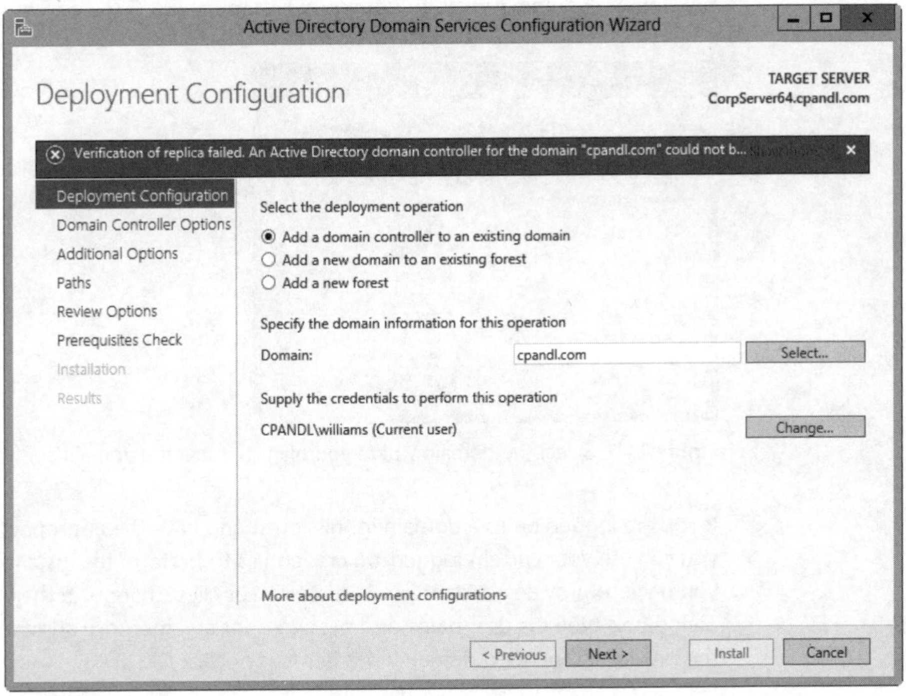

Figure 14-1 Add the domain controller to an existing domain.

IMPORTANT

Note the verification error shown in Figure 14-1. If the server doesn't have appropriate TCP/IP settings, the wizard won't be able to connect to a domain controller in the target domain and you'll see the error shown in the figure. You can see this same verification error for other reasons as well: if you type an invalid domain name or if all the domain controllers in the specified domain are offline. You need to correct the problem before you can continue.

A verification error also occurs if you enter the wrong password when setting credentials. Here, the error states: "Verification of replica failed. The wizard cannot access the list of domains in the forest. The user name or password is incorrect." Although the wizard checks the credentials when you enter them to ensure that the user name and password are valid, the wizard doesn't verify user credential permissions until just before installation.

2. In the Domain box, type the full DNS name of the domain in the forest where you plan to install the domain controller, such as **cpandl.com**. To select a domain in the forest from a list of available domains, tap or click Select. Next, in the Select A Domain dialog box, tap or click the domain to use and then tap or click OK. (See Figure 14-2.)

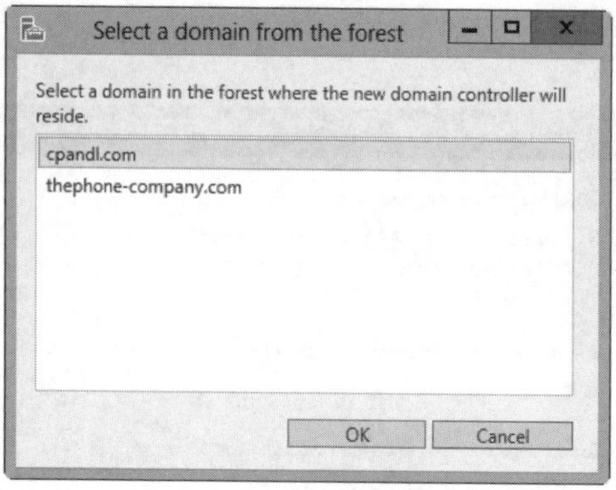

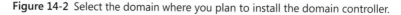

Figure 14-2 Select the domain where you plan to install the domain controller.

3. If you are logged on to a domain in this forest and have the appropriate permissions, you can use your current logged-on credentials to perform the installation. Otherwise, you need to provide alternate credentials. Tap or click Change. In the Windows Security dialog box, type the user name and password for an enterprise administrator account in the previously specified domain and then tap or click OK.

4. When you tap or click Next, the wizard performs several preliminary checks and then displays the Domain Controller Options page, shown in Figure 14-3. The wizard does the following:

- Checks any user credentials you entered to ensure that the user name and password are valid. The wizard doesn't verify user credential permissions until the prerequisite checks, which occur just before installation.

- Determines the available Active Directory sites. The most appropriate site for the server's current subnet is selected by default on the Domain Controller Options page.

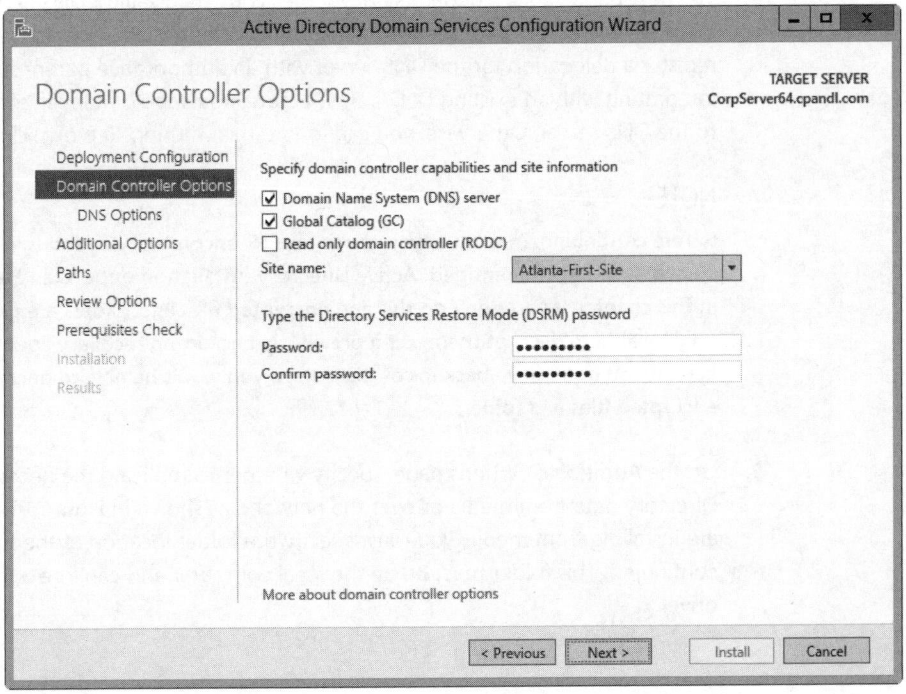

Figure 14-3 Set primary options for the domain controller.

5. Select additional installation options as permitted. The domain controller can be a DNS server, a global catalog server, or both. To ensure high availability of directory services, all domain controllers should provide DNS and global catalog services. Domain Name System (DNS) Server is selected by default if the current domain already hosts DNS on its domain controllers (based on the Start of Authority query in DNS). Global Catalog (GC) is always selected by default.

6. Select the Active Directory site in which you want to locate the domain controller. By default, the wizard selects the site with the most correct subnet. If there is only one site, the wizard selects that site automatically. No automatic selection is made if the server does not belong to an Active Directory subnet and multiple sites are available.

7. Type and confirm the password that should be used when you want to start the computer in Directory Services Restore mode. Be sure to track this password carefully. This special password is used only in Restore mode and is different from the Administrator account password. (It is the local Administrator password, which is in the local database of domain controllers; this database is normally hidden.) To continue, tap or click Next.

8. The next page you see depends on whether you are installing DNS Server. If you are installing the DNS Server service as an additional option, the wizard next attempts to register a delegation for the DNS server with an authoritative parent zone. If you are integrating with an existing DNS infrastructure, you should manually create a delegation to the DNS server. Otherwise, you can ignore this warning. Tap or click Next to continue.

NOTE

Before continuing, make sure you check for EFS-encrypted files and folders as discussed in the section entitled "Active Directory installation options and issues" earlier in this chapter. If you don't do this and encrypted files and folders are present, you will only be able to decrypt them using previously backed-up recovery agent EFS private keys. If you don't have backups of these keys, you won't be able to decrypt previously encrypted files and folders.

9. On the Additional Options page, specify whether to replicate the necessary Active Directory data from media or over the network, as shown in Figure 14-4. When you are installing from media, you must specify the folder location of the media before continuing. This folder must be on the local computer and can't be a mapped network drive.

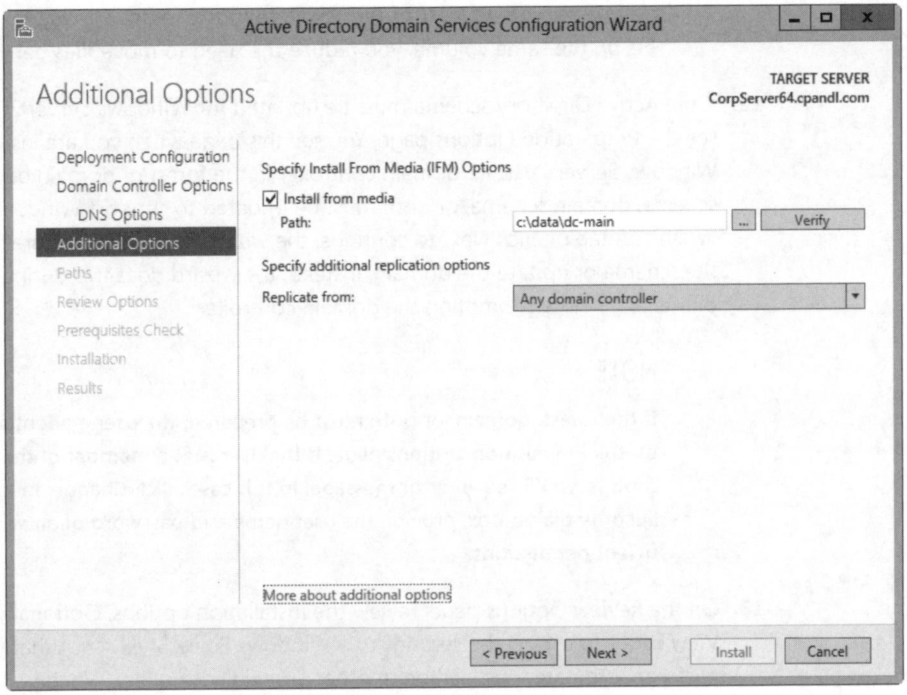

Figure 14-4 Specify whether to replicate over the network or from media.

10. If you choose to replicate data over the network, you can choose a replication partner for the installation or all replication from any available domain controller. When you install a domain controller and do not use backup media, all directory data is replicated from the replication partner to the domain controller you are installing. Because this can be a considerable amount of data, you typically want to ensure that both domain controllers are located in the same site or connected over reliable, high-speed networks.

11. On the Paths page, select a location in which to store the Active Directory database folder, log folder, and SYSVOL. Keep the following in mind when configuring these locations:

    ■ The default location for the database and log folders is a subfolder of %SystemRoot%\NTDS. As discussed in the section entitled "Hardware and configuration considerations for domain controllers" earlier in this chapter, you get better performance if these folders are on two separate volumes, each on a separate drive.

    ■ The default location for the SYSVOL folder is %SystemRoot%\Sysvol. In most cases you'll want to accept the default because the replication services store their database in a subfolder of the %SystemRoot% folder anyway. By keeping the folders on the same volume, you reduce the need to move files between drives.

12. If the Active Directory schema must be updated for Windows Server 2012 R2, you'll see the Preparation Options page. You see this page when you are installing the first Windows Server 2012 R2 domain controller in the forest or domain because the forest schema, domain schema, or both must be updated to support Windows Server 2012 R2. When you tap or click Next to continue, the wizard doesn't use Adprep.exe to extend the schema or update the domain. Instead, the wizard does this during the installation phase, just before promoting the domain controller.

NOTE

If the forest, domain, or both must be prepared, the user credentials are checked on the Preparation Options page. If the user isn't a member of the appropriate groups, you'll see an error message. In this case, click Change. In the Windows Security dialog box, provide the user name and password of an account with sufficient permissions.

13. On the Review Options page, review the installation options. Optionally, tap or click View Script to export the settings to a Windows PowerShell script that you can use to perform automated installation of other domain controllers. When you tap or click Next, the wizard performs preliminary checks to verify that the domain and forest are capable of supporting a new Windows Server 2012 R2 domain controller. The wizard also displays information about security changes that could affect older operating systems.

14. When you tap or click Install, the wizard uses the options you selected to install and configure Active Directory. This process can take several minutes. Keep the following in mind:

- If you specified that the DNS Server service should be installed, the server will also be configured as a DNS Server at this time.

- Because you are installing an additional domain controller in an existing domain, the domain controller needs to obtain updates of all the directory partitions from other domain controllers and will do this by initiating a full synchronization. The only way to avoid this is to make a media backup of Active Directory on an existing domain controller, start the Active Directory Domain Services Configuration Wizard in Advanced mode, and then specify the backup media to use during installation of Active Directory.

15. When the wizard finishes configuring Active Directory, you receive a prompt informing you that the computer will be restarted. After the server restarts, Active Directory will be completely configured and the server can then act as a domain controller.

After installing Active Directory, you should verify the installation by doing the following (in no particular order):

- Examine the log of the installation, which is stored in the Dcpromo.log file in the %SystemRoot%\Debug folder. As shown in Figure 14-5, the log is very detailed and takes you through every step of the installation process, including the creation of direc-tory partitions and the securing of the registry for Active Directory.

```
                                   DCPROMO - Notepad                          _  □  x

File  Edit  Format  View  Help
10/02/2014 11:53:00 [INFO] Promotion request for replica domain controller
10/02/2014 11:53:00 [INFO] DnsDomainName  cpandl.com
10/02/2014 11:53:00 [INFO]      ReplicaPartner  CorpServer28.cpandl.com
10/02/2014 11:53:00 [INFO]      SiteName  Default-First-Site-Name
10/02/2014 11:53:00 [INFO]      DsDatabasePath  C:\Windows\NTDS, DsLogPath  C:\Windows\NTDS
10/02/2014 11:53:00 [INFO]      SystemVolumeRootPath  C:\Windows\SYSVOL
10/02/2014 11:53:00 [INFO]      Account (NULL)
10/02/2014 11:53:00 [INFO]      Options  1179840
10/02/2014 11:53:00 [INFO] Validate supplied paths
10/02/2014 11:53:00 [INFO] Validating path C:\Windows\NTDS.
10/02/2014 11:53:00 [INFO]      Path is a directory
10/02/2014 11:53:00 [INFO]      Path is on a fixed disk drive.
10/02/2014 11:53:00 [INFO] Validating path C:\Windows\NTDS.
10/02/2014 11:53:00 [INFO]      Path is a directory
10/02/2014 11:53:00 [INFO]      Path is on a fixed disk drive.
10/02/2014 11:53:00 [INFO] Validating path C:\Windows\SYSVOL.
10/02/2014 11:53:00 [INFO]      Path is on a fixed disk drive.
10/02/2014 11:53:00 [INFO]      Path is on an NTFS volume
10/02/2014 11:53:00 [INFO] Start the worker task
10/02/2014 11:53:00 [INFO] Request for promotion returning 0
10/02/2014 11:53:00 [INFO] Forcing time sync
10/02/2014 11:53:00 [INFO] Forcing a time sync with CorpServer28.cpandl.com
10/02/2014 11:53:00 [INFO] Searching for a domain controller for the domain cpandl.com that
contains the account CORPSERVER85$
```

Figure 14-5 Examine the log of the installation.

- Verify that replication is working as expected. One way to show the replication status is to enter **repadmin /showrepl** at a command prompt. You can also verify whether the domain controller has any incoming replication requests to process. To do this, enter **repadmin /queue** at an elevated command prompt.

- Check for DNS updates in the DNS console, shown in Figure 14-6. If you added a domain controller to an existing domain, DNS is updated to add SRV records for the server, and these are in the appropriate subfolders of the zone, such as _tcp and _udp. If you created a new domain, DNS is updated to include a forward lookup zone for the domain.

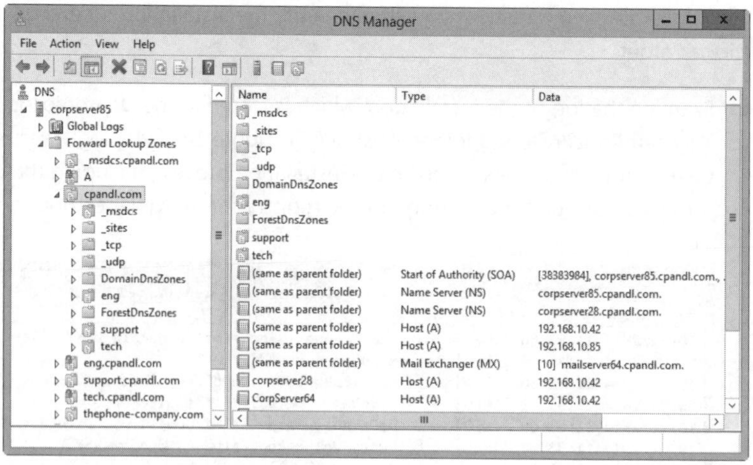

Figure 14-6 Check for DNS updates.

- Check for updates in Active Directory Users And Computers. For example, check to make sure the new domain controller is listed in the Domain Controllers OU, as shown in Figure 14-7.

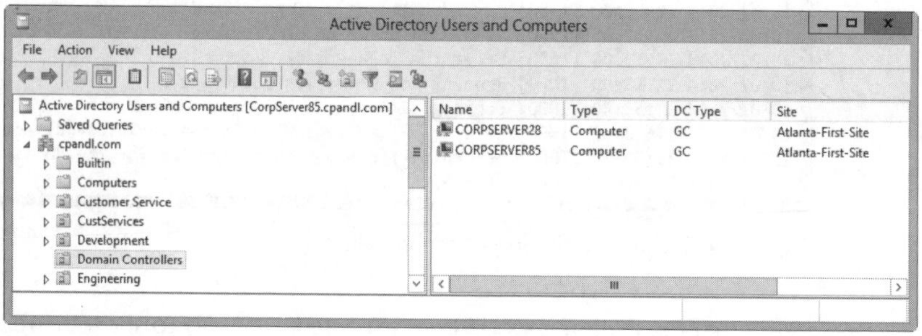

Figure 14-7 Check for updates in Active Directory Users And Computers.

If you created a new domain, the following containers are created and populated as appropriate:

- Builtin contains the built-in accounts for administration, including Administrators and Account Operators.

- Computers contains computer accounts for the domain.

- Domain Controllers contains the domain controller accounts and should have an account for the domain controller you installed.

- ForeignSecurityPrincipals is a container for security principals from other domain trees.

- Users is the default container for user accounts in the domain.

Creating new domains in new forests

To create a new domain in a new forest, follow these steps:

1. Start the Active Directory Domain Services Configuration Wizard as discussed previously. The wizard uses the credentials of the built-in Administrator account to create the forest root.

   ### NOTE

   If the server doesn't have an appropriate IP address, you see a warning about the invalid IP address or improper network configuration and you need to correct the problem before you can continue.

2. On the Deployment Configuration page, select Add A New Forest. Type the full DNS name for the new root domain in the new forest. Domain names are not case-sensitive and use the letters A to Z, the numerals 0 to 9, and the hyphen (-) character. The name must have at least two naming components. Each component of the domain name must be separated by a dot (.) and can't be longer than 63 characters. Following this, thephone-company.com is a valid domain name, but thephone-company is not.

3. When you tap or click Next, the wizard determines whether the name you entered is already in use on your network. If the name is already in use, you need to enter a different name or go back and make a different configuration selection. Keep in mind that the domain should not have the same name as an external DNS. If the external DNS name is thephone-company.com, you should use a different name for your internal forest to avoid compatibility issues.

4. On the Domain Controller Options page, shown in Figure 14-8, choose the desired functional level for the new Active Directory forest. The forest functional level can be set to Windows Server 2003, Windows Server 2008, Windows Server 2008 R2, Windows Server 2012, or Windows Server 2012 R2. For a complete discussion of forest functional levels, see the section entitled "Domain design considerations" in Chapter 12, "Organizing Active Directory," and the section entitled "Understanding forest functional level" in Chapter 11, "Designing and managing the domain environment."

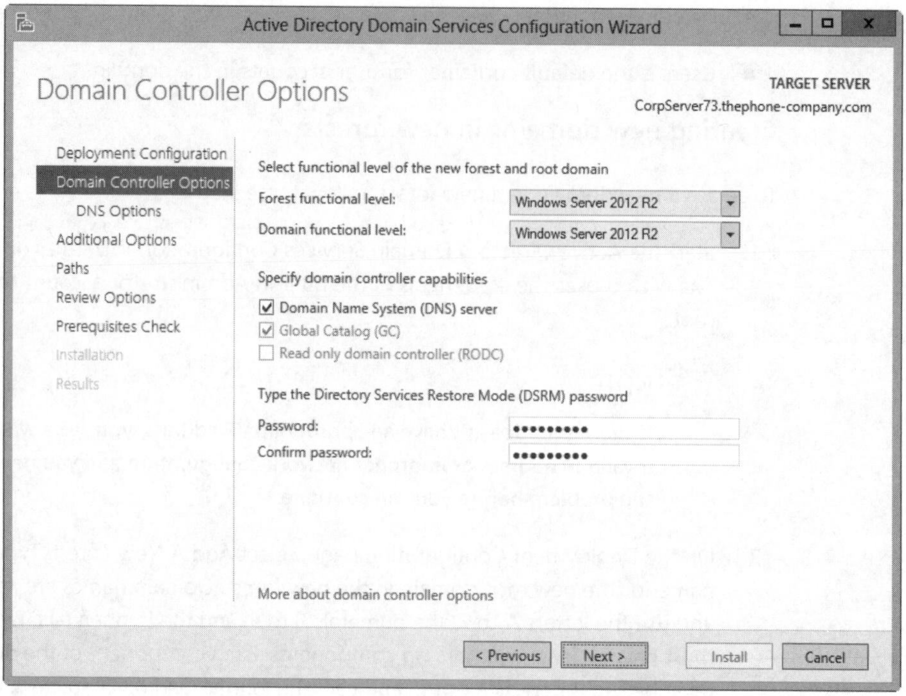

Figure 14-8 Choose the functional level and options for the new domain in a new forest.

5.   Choose the desired functional level for the new domain. The domain functional level can't be set lower than the forest functional level. For example, if you set the forest functional level to Windows Server 2008 R2, you can set the domain functional level to Windows Server 2008 R2, Windows Server 2012, or Windows Server 2012 R2. See the section entitled "Domain design considerations" in Chapter 12 and the section entitled "Understanding domain functional level" in Chapter 11 for a complete discussion of domain functional levels.

6.   As permitted, select additional installation options. When you are creating a new forest root domain, the first domain controller must be a global catalog and can't be an RODC. The domain controller also can be a DNS server, and the related option is selected by default.

7.   Type and confirm the password that should be used when you want to start the computer in Directory Services Restore mode. Be sure to track this password carefully. This special password is used only in Restore mode and is different from the Administrator account password. To continue, tap or click Next.

8. The next page you see depends on whether you are installing DNS Server. If you are installing the DNS Server service as an additional option, the wizard next attempts to register a delegation for the DNS server with an authoritative parent zone. If you are integrating with an existing DNS infrastructure, you should manually create a delegation to the DNS server. Otherwise, you can ignore this warning. Tap or click Next to continue.

> ## NOTE
> If you choose to let the wizard install DNS Server, the DNS Server service will be installed and the domain controller will also act as a DNS server. A primary DNS zone will be created as an Active Directory–integrated zone with the same name as the new domain you are setting up. The wizard will also update the server's TCP/IP configuration so that its primary DNS server is set to itself.

9. When you tap or click Next, the wizard examines the network environment and attempts to register the domain and the domain controller in DNS. When you are installing a new forest root domain and DNS Server, you can't configure DNS options or DNS delegation. When you elect not to install DNS Server and have existing DNS infrastructure, however, you can create a DNS delegation using the related option and you can also provide alternate credentials. In this case the credentials you provide must have the right to update the DNS zone.

10. The wizard uses the domain name to generate a default NetBIOS name. You can accept the wizard-generated name or type a new NetBIOS name of up to 15 characters and then tap or click Next to continue.

11. The rest of the installation proceeds as previously discussed. Continue with steps 11–15 and the post-installation checks discussed in the previous section, "Creating additional domain controllers for an existing domain."

Creating a new domain or domain tree within an existing forest

To create a new domain or domain tree within an existing forest, follow these steps:

1. Start the Active Directory Domain Services Configuration Wizard as discussed previously. If the server doesn't have an appropriate IP address, you see a warning about the invalid IP address or improper network configuration and you need to correct the problem before you can continue.

2. On the Deployment Configuration page, you need to choose one of the following:

   - **Choose Add A New Domain To An Existing Forest and then choose Child Domain as the domain type.** Choose these options to establish the first domain controller in a domain that is a child domain of an existing domain. By choosing these options, you are specifying that the necessary parent domain already exists.

CHAPTER 14

For example, you would choose these options if the parent domain cpandl.com had already been created and you wanted to create the tech.cpandl.com domain as a child of this domain.

For Parent Domain Name, type or select the fully-qualified name of the parent domain, such as **cpandl.com**. Next, type the name of the new child domain in the New Domain Name box. Be sure to provide a valid, single-label name for the child domain, such as **tech** rather than **tech.cpandl.com**. The name must follow DNS domain name requirements. This means the name can use the letters A to Z, the numerals 0 to 9, and the hyphen (-) character. Following this, thephone-company .com is a valid domain name but thephone-company is not.

- **Choose Add A New Domain To An Existing Forest and then choose Tree Domain as the domain type.** Choose these options to establish a new domain tree that is separate from any existing trees in the existing Active Directory forest. By choosing these options, you specify that there isn't an existing parent domain with which you want to associate the new domain. For example, you should choose this option if the cohowinery.com domain already exists and you want to establish the cohovineyard.com domain in a new tree in the existing forest.

  For Forest Name, type the fully-qualified name of the forest root domain, such as **cpandl.com**. Next, type the fully-qualified name of the new tree domain in the New Domain Name box. The name must have at least two naming components. Each component of the domain name must be separated by a dot (.) and can't be longer than 63 characters. Use only the letters A to Z, the numerals 0 to 9, and the hyphen (-) character.

3. The rest of the installation proceeds as previously discussed. Continue with steps 3–15 and the post-installation checks discussed in the previous section, "Creating additional domain controllers for an existing domain." Note that you do not have the option to install from media or replicate from an existing domain controller, so the Additional Options page does not appear.

Additionally, if you created a new domain, you also need to configure DNS so that name resolution works appropriately with any existing domains. Normally, when you create a new domain, a DNS delegation is created automatically during the installation process. This delegation, created in the parent DNS zone, transfers name-resolution authority and provides an authoritative referral to other DNS servers and clients of the new zone.

Several resource records, which point to the DNS server as authoritative for the zone, are created as well:

- A name server (NS) resource record to establish the delegation and specify that the server is an authoritative server for the delegated subdomain

- A host (A or AAAA) resource record to resolve the name of the server

Creating the delegation ensures that computers in other domains can resolve DNS queries for computers in the subdomain. The wizard can create the delegation records only on Microsoft DNS servers. If the parent DNS domain zone resides on third-party DNS servers, such as Berkeley Internet Name Domain (BIND), you see a warning prompt stating that the records can't be created and you need to create the records manually.

The wizard creates the required resource records in the parent DNS zone, and then it verifies the records after you click Next on the Domain Controller Options page. If the wizard can't verify that the records exist in the parent domain, the wizard provides you with the option to either create a new DNS delegation for a new domain or update the existing delegation and then continue with the new domain controller installation.

Creating a DNS delegation during installation requires credentials that have permissions to update the parent DNS zones. If you don't want to or can't create the delegation during the installation, that's okay, because you can manually create and validate the delegation before or after the installation.

CHAPTER 14

Inside OUT

Creating a zone delegation for a subdomain

To create a zone delegation in DNS Manager, press and hold or right-click the parent domain and then click New Delegation. Use the New Delegation Wizard to create the delegation as discussed in the section entitled "Configuring subdomains and delegating authority" in Chapter 7.

If zone delegation is not possible at all, you can use other methods for providing name resolution from other domains to the hosts in the subdomain. As an example, the DNS administrator of another domain could configure conditional forwarding, stub zones, or secondary zones to resolve names in the subdomain. To enable name resolution for computers within the new domain, you typically want to create secondary zones for all existing domains in the new domain and set up zone transfers. To enable name resolution into the new domain from existing domains, you typically want to create a secondary zone in existing domains for the new domain and set up zone transfers.

Performing an Active Directory installation from media

Whenever you install an additional domain controller in an existing domain, you should consider whether you want to perform an installation from media rather than create the domain controller from scratch. Doing so allows the Active Directory Domain Services Configuration Wizard to get the initial data for the Configuration, Schema, and Domain directory partitions and, optionally, get the SYSVOL from backup media rather than performing a full synchronization over the network.

This not only reduces the amount of network traffic—which is especially important when installing domain controllers in remote sites that are connected by low-bandwidth WAN links—but also can greatly speed up the process of installing an additional domain controller and getting the directory partition data synchronized. This means that rather than having to replicate the full data across the network, the domain controller needs to get only the changes made since the backup media was made. This can mean that only several megabytes of replication traffic are generated rather than several gigabytes. On a busy or low-bandwidth network this can be very important.

> ### NOTE
>
> **Installing Active Directory from media is not designed to be used to restore failed domain controllers. To restore failed domain controllers, you should use System State restore because this ensures that all the data that needs to be restored is recovered as necessary, including registry settings, Sysvol data, and Active Directory data.**

In Windows Server 2008 or later, you can create installation media by restoring a System State backup of a domain controller. Windows Server 2008 or later versions also give you the option of performing an installation from media backup. A media backup is preferred to a System State backup because it includes only directory data. In contrast, a System State backup includes over 50,000 files that require several gigabytes of space, not including the directory data.

Regardless of which technique you want to use, there are a few guidelines you should follow when installing Active Directory from backup media:

- Always try to use the most recent media backup of Active Directory. This reduces the number of updates that must replicate to the domain controller, which in turn minimizes the post-installation replication traffic.

- Always use a backup of a domain controller in the same domain in which the new domain controller is being created, and always use a backup from another domain controller running the *same version of Windows Server*.

- Always copy the backup to a local drive on the server for which you are installing Active Directory. You can't use backup media from Universal Naming Convention (UNC) paths or mapped drives.

- Never use backup media that is older than the deleted object lifetime of the domain. The default value is 60 days. If you try to use backup media older than 60 days, the Active Directory installation fails. For more information about the deleted object lifetime and why it's important, see the section "Extensible Storage Engine," in Chapter 10, "Active Directory architecture."

With these guidelines in mind, you can create an additional domain controller from backup media by completing the following steps:

1. Open an elevated command prompt window. At the command prompt, type **ntdsutil**. This starts the Directory Services Management Tool.

2. At the ntdsutil prompt, type **activate instance ntds**. This sets Active Directory as the directory service instance to work with.

3. Type **ifm** to access the install from a media prompt and then type one of the following commands, where *FolderPath* is the full path to the folder in which to store the Active Directory backup media files:

   - **Create Full *FolderPath*.** Creates a full writeable installation media backup of Active Directory. You can use the media to install a writeable domain controller or a read-only domain controller.

   - **Create RODC *FolderPath*.** Creates a read-only installation media backup of Active Directory. You can use the media to install a read-only domain controller. The backup media does not contain security credentials, such as passwords.

   - **Create Sysvol Full *FolderPath*.** Creates a full writeable installation media backup of Active Directory and the Sysvol. You can use the media to install a writeable domain controller or a read-only domain controller. The Sysvol files include computer and user scripts and Group Policy settings.

   - **Create Sysvol RODC *FolderPath*.** Creates a read-only installation media backup of Active Directory and the Sysvol. You can use the media to install a read-only domain controller.

4. Ntdsutil then creates snapshots of Active Directory partitions. When it's finished creating the snapshots, Ntdsutil mounts the snapshots as necessary and then defragments the media backup of the Active Directory database. The progress of the defragmentation is shown as a percentage complete.

5. Ntdsutil copies registry data related to Active Directory. If you are creating backup media for the Sysvol, Ntdsutil also creates backups of all policy settings, scripts, and other data stored on the Sysvol. When it finishes this process, Ntsdsutil unmounts any snapshots it was working with. The backup process should complete successfully. If it doesn't, note and resolve any problems that prevented successful creation of the backup media, such as the target disk running out of space or insufficient permissions to copy to the folder path.

6. Type **quit** at the ifm prompt and type **quit** at the ntdsutil prompt.

CHAPTER 14

7. Copy the backup media to a local drive on the server for which you are installing Active Directory.

8. On the server you want to make a domain controller, start the Active Directory Domain Services Configuration Wizard. Follow all the same steps as you would if you were adding a domain controller to the domain without media. After you select additional domain controller options and get past any DNS prompts, you see the Additional Options page, shown previously in Figure 14-4. On this page, select Install From Media and then type the folder location of the backup media files or tap or click the options button to find this location.

9. You can now complete the installation as discussed in the section entitled "Creating additional domain controllers for an existing domain" earlier in this chapter. Continue with the rest of the steps and perform the post-installation checks as well.

You can create an additional domain controller using a System State backup by completing the following steps:

1. Create a System State backup on a domain controller in the domain by using Windows Backup or by typing the following at an elevated command prompt:

   ```
   wbadmin start systemstatebackup -backupTarget:VolumeName
   ```

   Here, *VolumeName* is the storage location for the backup, such as F:.

2. Restore the System State backup to an alternate location by using Windows Backup or by typing the following at an elevated command prompt:

   ```
   wbadmin start systemstaterecovery -backupTarget:VolumeName
   -recoveryTarget:OtherLocation
   ```

   Here, *VolumeName* is the storage location that contains the System State backup you want to recover, such as F:, and *OtherLocation* is the alternate folder location in which the backup should be restored, such as F:\NTDSRestore.

3. Copy the backup media to a local drive on the server for which you are installing Active Directory.

4. On the server you want to make a domain controller, start the Active Directory Domain Services Configuration Wizard in Advanced Installation mode. Follow the same steps that you would if you were adding a domain controller to the domain without media. After you select additional domain controller options and get past any DNS prompts, you see the Additional Options page, shown previously in Figure 14-4. On this page, select Install From Media and then type the folder location of the backup media files or tap or click the options button to find this folder.

5. You can now complete the installation as discussed in the section entitled "Creating additional domain controllers for an existing domain" earlier in this chapter. Continue with the rest of the steps and perform the post-installation checks as well.

Cloning virtualized domain controllers

Windows Server 2012 R2 includes enhancements that ensure that virtualized domain controllers work properly. After you virtualize the first domain controller in a domain, you can clone the machine to easily add domain controllers to the domain.

Using clones of virtualized domain controllers

When you clone a domain controller, you make a copy of an existing virtual domain controller's virtual hard disk or virtual machine. The clone domain controller determines that it's a copy because the value of the VM-Generation ID supplied by the virtual machine will be different from the value of the VM-Generation ID stored in the directory.

The clone also looks for a DCCloneConfig.xml file in the directory where the directory resides, %windir%\NTDS, or the root of a removable media drive. This triggers an update whereby the new VM-Generation ID is stored in the directory, the clone's invocationID is reset, and any update sequence numbers (USNs) previously allocated from the RID pool are discarded.

The clone then continues provisioning itself. Using the security context of the domain controller whose copy it represents, the clone contacts the PDC emulator, which also must be running Windows Server 2012 R2 but doesn't have to be running in a virtualized environment. The PDC emulator verifies that the requesting domain controller is authorized for cloning.

Once the PDC emulator verifies the clone, the PDC emulator creates a new machine identity—including a new security identifier, account, and password that identifies the clone as a replica domain controller—and then sends this information back to the clone. The clone uses this information to finalize the configuration of Active Directory Domain Services.

> NOTE
> You can create multiple clones at the same time in batches. Generally, you should not try to create more than 16 clones at the same time. This number is controlled by the maximum number of outbound replication connections, which is 16 by default for Distributed File System Replication.

CHAPTER 14

Creating a clone virtualized domain controller

Deploying a clone virtualized domain controller is a multistep process that involves the following steps:

1. Grant the source virtualized domain controller the permission to be cloned. Any virtualized domain controller in the same domain as the domain controller can be prepared for cloning. In Active Directory Administrative Center, press and hold or right-click the source virtualized domain controller and then choose Add To Group. In the Select Groups dialog box, type **Cloneable Domain Controllers** and then tap or click OK. Once the group membership change is replicated to the PDC emulator, you can continue. If the Cloneable Domain Controllers group is not found, the PDC emulator might not be hosted on a domain controller that runs Windows Server 2012 R2, which is a prerequisite.

   IMPORTANT

   As a security best practice, don't add servers to the Cloneable Domain Controllers group until you are ready to perform cloning operations. After cloning operations are complete and you verify the operation, remove the servers from the Cloneable Domain Controllers group.

2. On the source virtualized domain controller, run the Get-ADDCCloningExcludedApplicationList cmdlet at an elevated Windows PowerShell prompt to identify installed applications or services on the source domain controller that have not been evaluated for cloning. Either correct any problems with these applications and services or remove them prior to cloning. For any remaining applications and services that can be safely cloned, run the command again with the –GenerateXML parameter. This provisions the applications and programs in the CustomDCCloneAllowList.xml file.

3. On the source virtualized domain controller, run the New-ADDCCloneConfigFile cmdlet at an elevated Windows PowerShell prompt to generate the configuration file for the clone. Set the host name, TCP/IP configuration, and optionally, the Active Directory site, as shown in this example:

```
New-ADDCCloneConfigFile -CloneComputerName "VCorpServer18" -Static
-IPv4Address "192.168.10.34" -IPv4SubnetMask "255.255.255.0"
-IPv4DefaultGateway "192.168.10.1" -IPv4DNSResolver "192.168.10.38"
-SiteName "Seattle-First-Site"
```

4. Export a copy of the virtualized domain controller. Before you can copy the virtualized domain controller, you must shut down the source domain controller and then delete any associated snapshots. Deleting snapshots merges any AVHD files into the base VHD, which ensures that you create a clone from the newest directory version and get the

correct configuration. To shut down the source domain controller, enter the following at an elevated Windows PowerShell prompt:

```
Stop-VM –Name SourceDC –ComputerName HyperVHost
```

Here, *SourceDC* is the source virtualized domain controller and *HyperVHost* is the server hosting the virtualized domain controller, such as

```
Stop-VM –Name VCorpServer01 –ComputerName VHostServer12
```

To delete snapshots of the source domain controller, enter the following at an elevated Windows PowerShell prompt:

```
Get-VMSnapshot SourceDC | Remove-VMSnapshot –IncludeAllChildSnapshots
```

Here, *SourceDC* is the source virtualized domain controller, such as

```
Get-VMSnapshot VCorpServer01 | Remove-VMSnapshot –IncludeAllChildSnapshots
```

Finally, copy the virtualized domain controller. To do this, enter the following at an elevated Windows PowerShell prompt:

```
Export-VM –Name SourceDC –ComputerName HyperVHost -Path FolderPath
```

Here, *SourceDC* is the source virtualized domain controller, *HyperVHost* is the server hosting the virtualized domain controller, and *FolderPath* sets the save location, such as

```
Export-VM –Name VCorpServer01 –ComputerName VHostServer12 -Path d:\VMs\VServer01
```

5. Import the copy of the virtualized source domain controller and rename it. If you plan to run the virtualized domain controller on a different Hyper-V host, copy the contents of the save folder to a folder on that host. Import the virtualized source domain controller by entering the following at an elevated Windows PowerShell prompt:

```
Import-VM –Path FolderPath –Copy –GenerateNewId
```

Here, *FolderPath* sets the folder path to the save location, such as

```
Import-VM –Name -Path d:\VMs\VServer01
```

Rename the virtualized source domain controller by entering the following at an elevated Windows PowerShell prompt:

```
Rename-VM -Name OrigDCName -NewName NewDCName
```

Here, *OrigDCName* is the name of the original source domain controller and *NewDCName* is the new name for the new virtualized domain controller, such as

```
Rename-VM -Name VCorpServer01 -NewName VCorpServer02
```

While the source domain controller is offline, you can create multiple clones as well. Just repeat the import-and-rename process, making sure each clone has a different save location for its required files. You can use the *–VhdDestinationPath* parameter to set the location for virtual hard disks for a virtual machine, the *–SnapshotFilePath* parameter to set the path for the Snapshot store, the *–SmartPagingFilePath* parameter to set the path for the smart paging folder, and the *–VirtualMachinePath* parameter to set the path for the virtual machine configuration folder. These paths all can be set to the same destination.

Finalizing the clone deployment

After you copy, import, and export the clone or clones, you can finalize the deployment. To do this, follow these steps:

1. Restart the source domain controller to bring it back online. To start the source domain controller, enter the following at an elevated Windows PowerShell prompt:

   ```
   Start-VM –Name SourceDC –ComputerName HyperVHost
   ```

   Here, *SourceDC* is the source virtualized domain controller and *HyperVHost* is the server hosting the virtualized domain controller, such as

   ```
   Start-VM –Name VCorpServer01 –ComputerName VHostServer12
   ```

2. Start each clone in turn to bring it online for the first time. To start a clone, enter the following at an elevated Windows PowerShell prompt:

   ```
   Start-VM –Name NewDC –ComputerName HyperVHost
   ```

   Here, *NewDC* is the name of the clone and *HyperVHost* is the server hosting the virtualized domain controller, such as

   ```
   Start-VM –Name VCorpServer02 –ComputerName VHostServer45
   ```

3. Make sure the cloning completed successfully by logging on to the clone and checking its configuration. If you can't log on normally, the clone might be operating in Directory Services Recovery Mode. At this point, just restarting the clone might resolve the problem.

Troubleshooting the clone deployment

If the clone does not return to a normal mode on the next reboot, try logging on using Directory Services Recovery Mode. Type **.\Administrator** as the user and the DSRM password. You find errors related to cloning by reviewing the following:

- The System event log

- The Directory Service event log

- The Dcpromo log

In the Dcpromo log, which is stored in the %SystemRoot%/Debug folder, look for entries regarding the state of the directory-cloning process. If the entries state that cloning can't be retried, the virtual machine could not be set up as a clone virtualized domain controller. Delete the virtual machine on the Hyper-V host and re-create the clone.

If the errors you see relate to cloning and cloning can be retried, you need to remove the DS Restore Mode boot flag so that Active Directory Domain Services can configure itself again. To do this, follow these steps:

1. After you fix the cause of any errors, type **msconfig** in the Apps Search box and then press Enter to start the System Configuration utility. Alternatively, you could press Windows key+R, type **msconfig**, and then press Enter.

2. In the Boot tab, under Boot Options, clear Safe Boot and then tap or click OK. When prompted to restart the server, tap or click Yes.

3. When the virtual machine restarts, Active Directory attempts to finalize the cloning and provision itself again. Log on to the clone and determine whether the problems are resolved.

If entries in the Dcpromo log indicate that cloning succeeded, other types of problems might relate to the following items:

- Promotion, the directory configuration, incompatible applications, and services in the allow list (CustomDCCloneAllowList.xml). Incompatible applications and services must be removed.

- Invalid or duplicated IP address or other improper TCP/IP settings or an invalid Active Directory site listed in the config file (Dccloneconfig.xml). TCP/IP and site settings must be corrected as appropriate.

- Invalid or duplicate MAC address. The machine address must be valid and unique.

- An invalid or duplicate host name. The clone can't have the same host name as the source domain controller.

- The PDC emulator being unavailable. The PDC emulator must be reachable by a remote procedure call (RPC).

- The domain controller not having appropriate permissions. The domain controller must be a member of Cloneable Domain Controllers. The Allow A DC To Create A Clone Of Itself permission must be set on the domain root for the Cloneable Domain Controllers group.

If the domain controller is not advertising itself as available, check the Directory Service, System, Application, and DFS Replication event logs for errors and take corrective action as appropriate. Otherwise, if the domain controller is advertising itself as available, troubleshoot as you would any other newly promoted domain controller.

Uninstalling Active Directory

When you uninstall Active Directory, you demote the domain controller and make it a work-group server. You uninstall Active Directory Domain Services by following these steps:

1. In Server Manager, tap or click Manage and then tap or click Remove Roles And Features. This starts the Remove Roles And Features Wizard. If the wizard displays the Before You Begin page, read the Welcome message and then tap or click Next.

2. On the Select Installation Type page, select Role-Based Or Feature-Based Installation and then tap or click Next.

3. On the Select Destination Server page, the server pool shows servers you added for management. Tap or click the server you are configuring and then tap or click Next.

4. On the Remove Server Roles page, clear Active Directory Domain Services. An additional prompt is displayed warning you about dependent features, such as Group Policy Management and the AD DS management tools. If you tap or click the Remove Features button, the wizard removes the dependent features and Active Directory Domain Services. If you want to keep related management tools, clear the Remove Management Tools check box and then tap or click Continue.

5. You see the Validation Results dialog box, shown in Figure 14-9. Tap or click Demote This Domain Controller. This starts the Active Directory Domain Services Wizard.

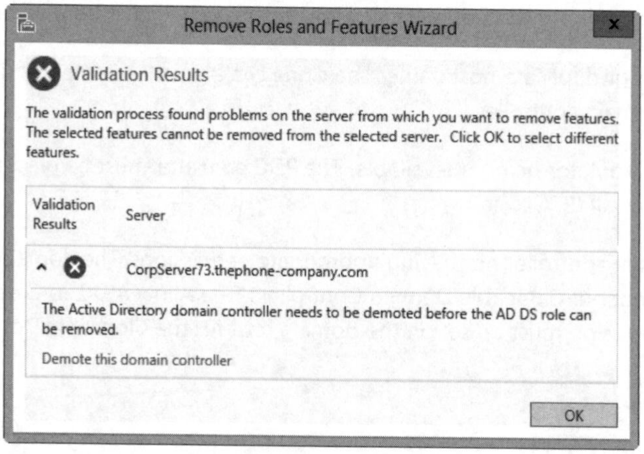

Figure 14-9 Demote the domain controller.

When the Active Directory Domain Services Configuration Wizard starts, you see the Credentials page shown in Figure 14-10. You must be a member of the Domain Admins group to remove an additional domain controller from a domain and a member of the Enterprise Admins group to remove the last domain controller from a domain. If you are logged on with an account that has appropriate permissions for uninstalling Active Directory, you can use your current logged-on credentials. Otherwise, tap or click Change and then use the options in the Windows Security dialog box to enter the user name and password for an account that does have the appropriate permissions.

If this is the last domain controller in the domain and you want to permanently remove the domain from the forest, select the Last Domain Controller In The Domain check box before you continue. After you remove the last domain controller in the domain, you can no longer access any application partition data, domain accounts, or encrypted data. Therefore, before you uninstall the last domain controller in a domain, you should examine domain accounts and look for encrypted files and folders.

> **NOTE**
> Because the deleted domain no longer exists, its accounts and cryptographic keys are no longer applicable, which results in the deletion of all domain accounts and all certificates and cryptographic keys from the server. You must decrypt any encrypted data on the server, including data stored using the EFS, before removing Active Directory or the data will be permanently inaccessible.

CHAPTER 14

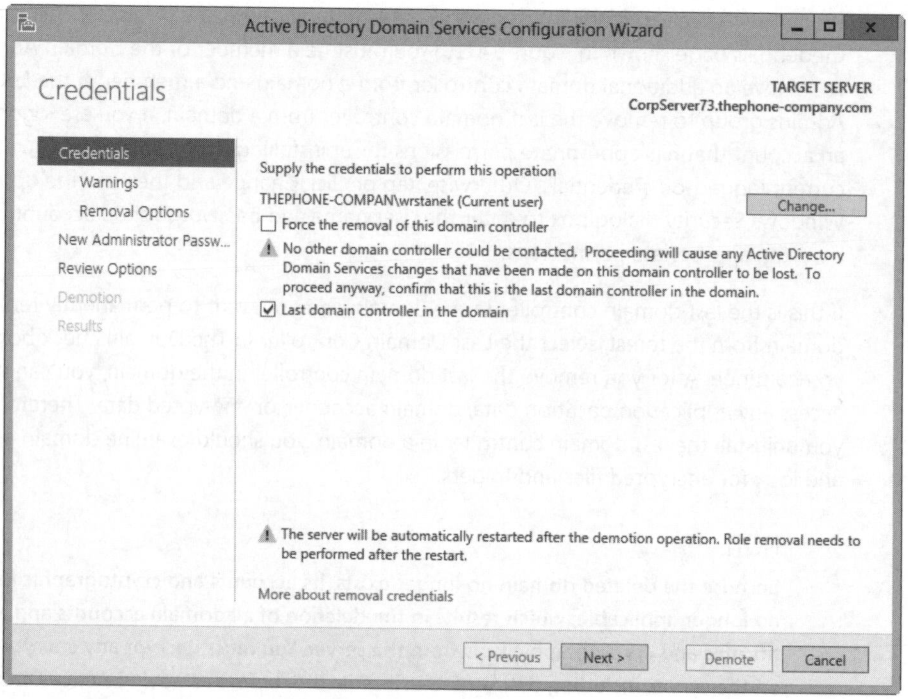

Figure 14-10 Removing Active Directory from a server.

Inside OUT

Forcing the removal of a domain controller

As Figure 14-10 shows, you also have the option of forcing the removal of the domain controller. Force a removal only when the domain controller can't contact other domain controllers and you can't resolve the network problems that are preventing communications. If you force a removal, you need to clean up orphaned metadata from the directory.

Forcing a removal demotes the domain controller without removing the domain controller object's metadata from Active Directory. As a result, the metadata remains in Active Directory on other domain controllers in the forest. Any unreplicated changes on the domain controller—such as new user accounts, modified settings, or changed passwords—are lost as well.

Finally, after you force a removal of Active Directory, you should ensure that the decommissioned domain controller is never reconnected to the network without first being formatted and re-created.

When you are ready to continue, tap or click Next. The Active Directory Domain Services Configuration Wizard then examines the Active Directory forest, checking the credentials you provided and attempting to determine related functions that the domain controller performs, such as DNS Server and Global Catalog. If additional functions are found, you must select Proceed With Removal to continue.

Inside OUT

Considerations for removing global catalogs

If you run the Active Directory Domain Services Configuration Wizard on a domain controller that is also a global catalog server, you see a warning prompt about this because you don't want to remove the last global catalog from the domain accidentally. If you remove the last global catalog from the domain, users won't be able to log on to the domain. A quick way to determine the global catalog servers in a domain is to type the following command at a command prompt:

```
dsquery server -domain DomainName | dsget server -isgc -dnsname
```

Here, *DomainName* is the name of the domain you want to examine. Consider the following example:

```
dsquery server -domain cpandl.com | dsget server -isgc -dnsname
```

Here, you are examining the cpandl.com domain to obtain a list of the global catalog servers according to their DNS names. The output is shown in two columns, for example:

```
dnsname                 isgc
corpsvr15.cpandl.com    no
corpsvr17.cpandl.com    yes
```

The first column is the DNS name of each domain controller in the domain. The second column is a flag that indicates whether the domain controller is also a global catalog. Thus, if the *isgc* value is set to yes for a domain controller, it is also a global catalog server.

On the Removal Options page, you have several additional removal options. If this domain controller is also hosting the last DNS Server for the zone, you can select Remove This DNS Zone to force the removal of DNS Server. You also can elect to remove application partitions. Tap or click View Partitions to confirm which application partitions should be deleted.

Next, you are prompted to type and confirm the password for the local Administrator account on the server. This is necessary because domain controllers don't have local accounts but member or stand-alone servers do. Therefore, this account will be re-created as part of the Active Directory removal process. Tap or click Next.

On the Review Options page, review your selections. Optionally, tap or click Export Settings to export the settings to a Windows PowerShell script that you can use to perform an automated demotion of other domain controllers. When you tap or click Demote, the wizard uses the options you selected to demote the domain controller. This process can take several minutes. Keep the following in mind:

- If there are updates to other domains in the forest that have not been replicated, the domain controller replicates these updates. Then the wizard begins the demotion process.

- If the domain controller is also a DNS server, the DNS data in the ForestDnsZones and DomainDnsZones partitions is removed. If the domain controller is the last DNS server in the domain, this results in the last replica of the DNS information being removed from the domain. All associated DNS records are lost and might need to be re-created.

At this point the actions that the Active Directory Domain Services Configuration Wizard performs depend on whether you are removing an additional domain controller or removing the last domain controller from a domain. If you are removing an additional domain controller from a domain, the wizard does the following:

- Removes Active Directory and all related services from the server and makes it a member server in the domain

- Changes the computer account type and moves the computer account from the Domain Controllers container in Active Directory to the Computers container

- Transfers any operations master roles from the server to another domain controller in the domain

- Updates DNS to remove the domain controller SRV records

- Creates a local Security Accounts Manager (SAM) account database and a local Administrator account

If you are removing the last domain controller from a domain, the wizard verifies that there are no child domains of the current domain before continuing. If child domains are found, the removal of Active Directory fails with an error telling you that you can't remove Active Directory. When the domain being removed is a child domain, the wizard notifies a domain controller in the parent domain that the child domain is being removed. For a parent domain in its own tree, the wizard notifies a domain controller in the forest root domain. Either way, the domain object is either tombstoned or logically deleted and this change is then replicated to other domain controllers. The domain object and any related trust objects are also removed from the forest.

As part of removing Active Directory from the last domain controller in a domain, all domain accounts, all certificates, and all cryptographic keys are removed from the server. The wizard creates a local SAM account database and a local Administrator account. It then changes the computer account type to a stand-alone server and puts the server in a new workgroup.

Creating and managing organizational units

Organizational units (OUs) are logical administrative units that can help you limit the scope of a domain. They can contain many types of objects, including those for computers, contacts, groups, printers, or users. Because they can also contain other OUs, you can build a hierarchy of OUs within a domain. You can also use OUs to delegate administrator privileges on a limited basis.

Creating an OU

Several tools are available for creating OUs. Typically, the tool you use depends on what other administrative tasks you might need to perform. For example, if you are creating an OU to add resources to it, you might want to use either Active Directory Users And Computers or Active Directory Administrative Center. If you are creating an OU to apply Group Policy to it, you might want to use Group Policy Management.

As long as you use an account that is a member of the Administrators group, you'll be able to create OUs anywhere in the domain. The only exception is that you can't create OUs within the default containers created by Active Directory.

> NOTE
> You can create OUs within the Domain Controllers container. This is possible because this container is created as an OU. Creating OUs within Domain Controllers is useful if you want to organize domain controllers.

When you work with Active Directory Users And Computers, you are connected to your login domain by default. If you want to create OUs in a different domain, press and hold or right-click the Active Directory Users And Computers node in the console tree and then select Change Domain. In the Change Domain dialog box, type the name of the domain to which you want to connect and then tap or click OK. Alternatively, in the Change Domain dialog box, you can tap or click Browse to open the Browse For Domain dialog box to find the domain to which you want to connect.

You can now create the OU. If you want to create a top-level OU (that is, an OU that has the domain container as its parent), press and hold or right-click the domain node in the console tree, point to New, and then select Organizational Unit. If you want to create a lower-level OU, press and hold or right-click the OU in which you want to create the new OU, point to New, and then select Organizational Unit.

In the New Object–Organizational Unit dialog box, type a new name for the OU, as shown in Figure 14-11, and then tap or click OK. Although the OU name can be any string of up to 256 characters, the best OU names are short and descriptive.

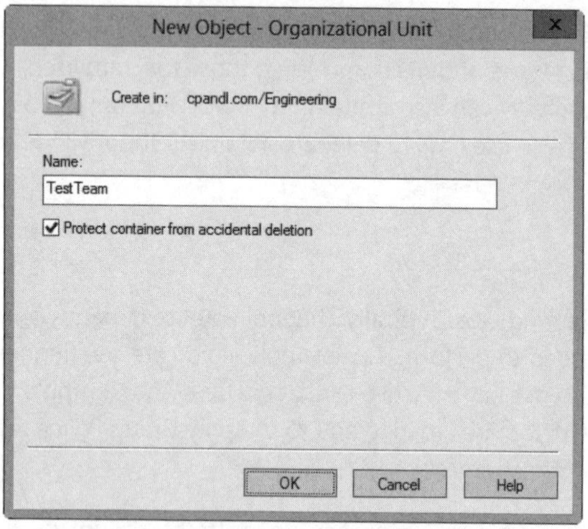

Figure 14-11 Specify the name of the OU to create.

Inside OUT

Understanding deletion protection for OUs

When you create a new OU, the Protect Container From Accidental Deletion check box is selected automatically. This prevents any user or administrator in the domain from deleting the OU accidentally. Before you can delete a protected OU, you must clear this protection flag. In Active Directory Administrative Center, this is a standard property in the Properties dialog box. In Active Directory Users And Computers, this is an advanced property in the Object tab, and you must enable the Advanced Features view by choosing Advanced Features from the View menu before you can clear or select it. Therefore, to delete an OU, you must complete the following steps:

1. In Active Directory Users And Computers, enable the Advanced Features view by choosing Advanced Features from the View menu.

2. Press and hold or right-click the OU and then select Properties.

3. In the Object tab of the Properties dialog box, clear the Protect Object From Accidental Deletion check box and then tap or click OK.

4. In Active Directory Users And Computers, press and hold or right-click the OU and then select Delete.

5. When prompted to confirm, tap or click Yes.

Creating OUs in Active Directory Administrative Center is similar. When you work with Active Directory Administrative Center, you are connected to your login domain by default. If you want to create OUs in a different domain, tap or click Manage and then select Add Navigation Nodes.

In the Additional Navigation Nodes dialog box, shown in Figure 14-12, you see available domains for the forest in the Columns list. To add a node for a listed domain, select it in the Columns list, tap or click the Add (>>) button, and then tap or click OK. To add a node for a domain that isn't listed, click Connect To Another Domain, enter the fully-qualified domain name, and then tap or click OK. Either way, a management node for the domain should be added to the console.

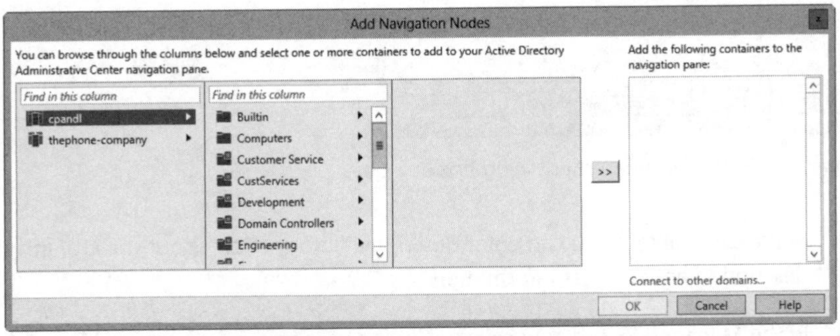

Figure 14-12 Select the domain that you want to manage.

If you want to create a top-level OU in Active Directory Administrative Center, press and hold or right-click the domain node in the console tree, point to New, and then select Organizational Unit. If you want to create a lower-level OU, press and hold or right-click the OU in which you want to create the new OU, point to New, and then select Organizational Unit. In the Create Organizational Unit dialog box, type a new name for the OU and then tap or click OK.

Setting OU properties

OUs have properties that you can set to add descriptive information. This helps other adminis-trators know how the OU is used.

To set the properties of an OU in Active Directory Users And Computers, press and hold or right-click the OU and then select Properties. This displays the OU's Properties dialog box, as shown in Figure 14-13.

Figure 14-13 The OU Properties dialog box.

- In the General tab, you can enter descriptive information about the OU, including a text description and address information.

- In the Managed By tab, you can specify the user or contact responsible for managing the OU. This gives a helpful point of contact for questions regarding the OU.

- In the Object tab, you can determine the canonical name of the OU object and specify whether the OU should be protected from accidental deletion.

- In the COM+ tab, you can specify the COM+ partition of which the OU should be a member (if any).

- In the Attribute Editor tab, you can view and set attributes of the OU object.

Similar options for setting the properties of an OU are available in Active Directory Administrative Center. Press and hold or right-click the OU and then select Properties to open the OU's Properties dialog box. COM+ and Attribute Editor options are available on the Extensions panel.

Creating or moving accounts and resources for use with an OU

After you create an OU, you might want to place accounts and resources in it. In either Active Directory Users And Computers or Active Directory Administrative Center, you follow one of these procedures:

- You create accounts in the OU. To do so, press and hold or right-click the OU, point to New, and then select the type of object to create, such as Computer, Group, or User.

- You move existing accounts or resources to an OU. To do so, select the accounts or resources in their existing container. Using Ctrl+Tap or click or Shift+Tap or click, you can select and move multiple accounts or resources as well. Next, press and hold or right-click the accounts or resources and then select Move. In the Move dialog box, select the container to which you want to move the accounts or resources and then tap or click OK.

Delegating the administration of domains and OUs

When you create domains and OUs, you'll often want to be able to delegate control over them to specific individuals. This is useful if you want to give someone limited administrative privileges for a domain or OU. Before you delegate administration, you should carefully plan the permissions to grant. Ideally, you want to delegate the permissions that allow a user to perform necessary tasks but prevent your delegate from performing tasks he or she should not. Often, figuring out the tasks that a user with limited administrative permissions should be able to perform requires talking to the department or office manager or to the user.

Understanding delegation of administration

You delegate control of Active Directory objects to grant users permission to manage users, groups, computers, OUs, or other objects stored in Active Directory. You can grant permissions in the following ways:

- **Grant full control over an OU.** Useful when you have local administrators within departments or at branch offices and want them to be able to manage all objects in the OU. Among other things, this allows local administrators to create and manage accounts in the OU.

- **Grant full control over specific types of objects in an OU.** Useful when you have local administrators who should be able to manage only specific types of objects in an OU. For example, you might want local administrators to be able to manage users and groups but not to be able to manage computer accounts.

- **Grant full control over specific types of objects in a domain.** Useful when you want to allow a user to manage only specific types of objects in a domain. Rather than adding the user as a member of the Administrators group, you grant the user full control over specific objects. For example, you might allow the user to manage user and group accounts in the domain but not to perform other administrative tasks.

- **Grant rights to perform specific tasks.** Useful when you want to allow a user to perform a specific task. For example, you might want to allow a department manager to read information related to user accounts in Active Directory Users And Computers, or you might want to allow help desk staff to reset user passwords.

When you delegate permissions, be sure to keep in mind how inheritance works in Active Directory. As you might recall from previous discussions of permissions, lower-level objects inherit permissions from top-level objects. In a domain, the top-level object is the domain object itself. This has the following results:

- Any user designated as an administrator for a domain automatically has full control over the domain.

- If you grant permissions at the domain level, the user has those permissions for all OUs in the domain as well.

- If you grant permissions in a top-level OU, the user has those permissions for all OUs that are created within the top-level OU.

Delegating administration

To delegate administration of a domain or OU, follow these steps:

1. In Active Directory Users And Computers, press and hold or right-click the domain or OU for which you want to delegate administration and then select Delegate Control. When the Delegation Of Control Wizard starts, tap or click Next.

2. On the Users Or Groups page shown in Figure 14-14, tap or click Add to display the Select Users, Computers, Or Groups dialog box.

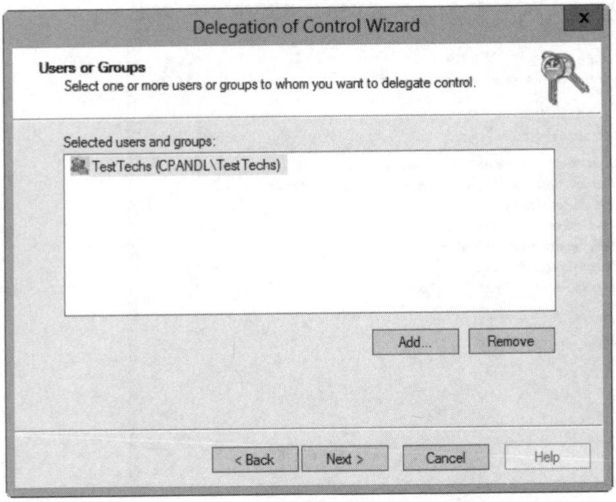

Figure 14-14 Select the users and groups to whom you want to delegate control.

3. The default location is the current domain. Tap or click Locations to see a list of the available domains and other resources that you can access. Because of the built-in transitive trusts, you can usually access all the domains in the domain tree or forest.

4. Type the name of a user or group account in the selected or default domain and then tap or click Check Names. The options available depend on the number of matches found as follows:

   - If a single match is found, the dialog box is automatically updated as appropriate and the entry is underlined.

   - If no matches are found, you either entered an incorrect name part or you're working with an incorrect location. Modify the name and try again or tap or click Locations to select a new location.

   - If multiple matches are found, select the name or names you want to use and then tap or click OK.

5. To add users or groups, type a semicolon (;) and then repeat this process.

6. When you tap or click OK, the users and groups are added to the Selected Users And Groups list in the Delegation Of Control Wizard. Tap or click Next to continue.

7. On the Tasks To Delegate page, shown in Figure 14-15, a list of common tasks is provided. If you want to delegate any of these common tasks, select the tasks. Afterward, tap or click Next and then tap or click Finish. Skip the remaining steps that follow.

CHAPTER 14

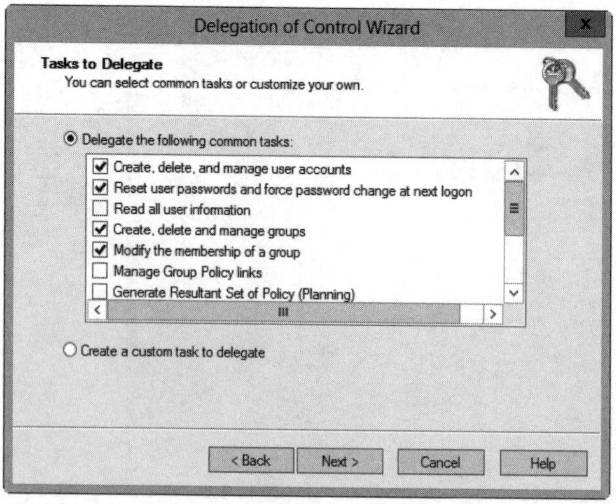

Figure 14-15 Select the tasks to delegate or choose to create a custom task.

8. If you want to create a custom task to delegate, choose Create A Custom Task To Delegate and then tap or click Next. On the Active Directory Object Type page, shown in Figure 14-16, you can now choose to delegate management of all objects in the container or limit the delegation to specific types of objects.

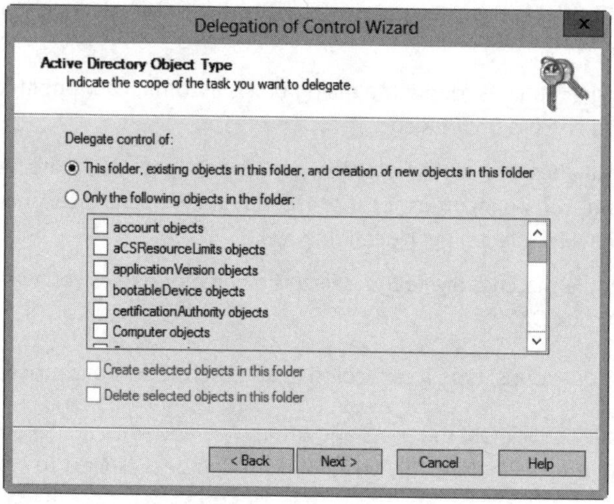

Figure 14-16 Delegate the control of tasks.

9. On the Permissions page, shown in Figure 14-17, you can select the levels of permissions to delegate for the previously selected objects. You can choose to allow Full Control over the object or objects or you can delegate specific permissions.

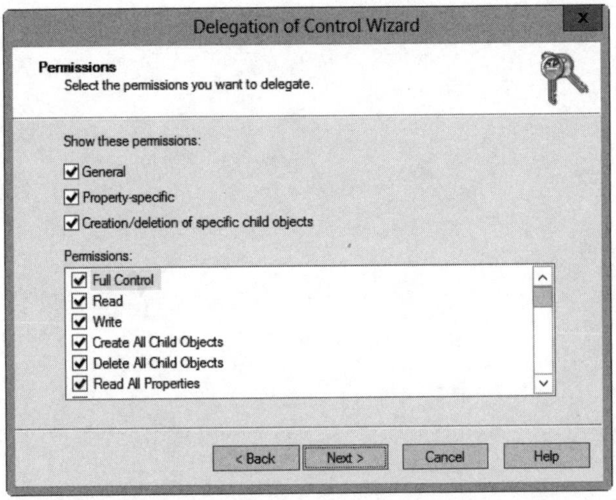

Figure 14-17 Specify the permissions to delegate for the previously selected objects.

10. Tap or click Next and then tap or click Finish.

Deploying read-only domain controllers

In the previous chapter you learned about installing domain controllers using a standard read/writeable installation. That chapter, however, did not discuss read-only domain controllers (RODCs) or describe the differences between read-only domain controllers and read/writeable domain controllers (RWDCs), which is exactly what this chapter is about. After you work with RODCs and RWDCs for a time, you'll understand why it's important to consider them as separate and distinct from each other.

When working with RODCs, keep in mind that they represent a paradigm shift. Although many enterprises continue to use writeable domain controllers at all office locations, enterprises increasingly use RWDCs only in their data centers and on trusted networks–they deploy RODCs everywhere else. The primary reason for this paradigm shift is that RODCs offer improved security and reduced risk compared to their RWDC counterparts. RODCs also can have lower hardware requirements because they use fewer processor and memory resources than RWDCs.

That said, you should also understand that the infrastructure and techniques related to RODCs might change. For this reason, I discuss RODCs with a look to the future and also deviate from common terminology in my references to RODCs and RWDCs. My hope is that my many years' experience with RODCs and RWDCs will help you successfully deploy both of them in your organization and that when you do so, you'll do so by prefacing the installation plans with enough caveats to see you safely through the changes.

Introducing read-only domain controllers

When the domain and forest are operating at the Microsoft Windows Server 2003 functional level or higher, you have the option of deploying RODCs. An RODC is an additional domain controller that hosts a read-only replica of a domain's Active Directory data store. RODCs are designed to be placed in locations that require fast and reliable authentication services but that aren't necessarily secure. This makes RODCs ideally suited to the needs of branch offices where a domain controller's physical security can't be guaranteed.

Only Windows Server 2008 and later releases of Windows Server can act as RODCs. Typically, you do not need to make any changes to client computers to allow them to use an RODC.

RODCs support the same features as RWDCs and can be used in both Core Server and Full Server installations. Except for passwords and designated, nonreplicated attributes, RODCs store the same objects and attributes as writeable domain controllers. These objects and attributes are replicated to RODCs using unidirectional replication from a writeable domain controller acting as a replication partner. Because no changes are written directly to RODCs, writeable domain controllers acting as replication partners do not have to pull changes from RODCs. This reduces the workload of bridgehead servers in the hub site and the scope of your replication monitoring efforts. See Figure 15-1 for a top-level overview of how the replication of data works.

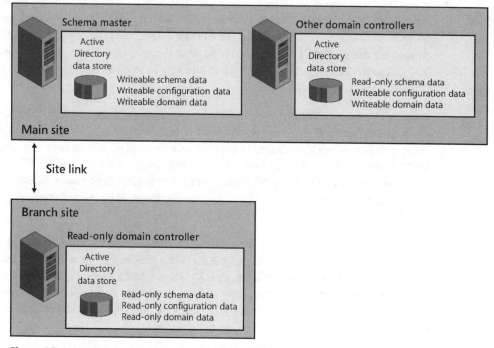

Figure 15-1 An overview of replication of read-only Active Directory data.

Although Active Directory clients and applications can access the directory to read data, the clients are not able to write changes directly to an RODC. Instead, they are referred to a writeable domain controller in a hub site. This prevents changes made by malicious users at branch locations from corrupting the Active Directory forest.

Inside OUT

Test your applications before deploying RODCs

Test all your applications that work with Active Directory before deploying RODCs. Most applications that work with Active Directory are read-intensive and do not require write access. Some applications, however, update information that's stored in Active Directory and expect this capability always to be available. If an application tries to write to an RODC, it's referred to a writeable domain controller (DC) running Windows Server 2008 or later. If the write operation succeeds, subsequent read operations might fail because the application will attempt to read from the RODC, which might not have received the updates through replication yet. To ensure proper operations, you should update applications that require write access to the directory to use binding calls to writeable domain controllers.

You can install the Domain Name System (DNS) Server service on an RODC. When you do this, the RODC receives a read-only replica of all application directory partitions that are used by DNS, including ForestDNSZones and DomainDNSZones. (See Figure 15-2.) Clients can query DNS on the RODC for name resolution as they would query any other DNS server. As with Active Directory data, the DNS server on an RODC does not support client updates directly.

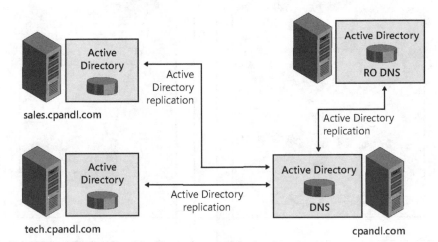

Figure 15-2 Replication of read-only DNS data.

The RODC does not register name server (NS) resource records for any Active Directory–integrated zone that it hosts. When a client attempts to update its DNS records on an RODC, the RODC returns a referral to another DNS server and the client can then attempt the update with this DNS server. In the background, the DNS server on the RODC then attempts to pull the updated record from the DNS server that made the update. This replication request is only for the updated DNS record. The entire list of changed zone or domain data does not get replicated during this special replication request.

Because RODCs by default do not store passwords or credentials other than for their own computer accounts and the Kerberos Ticket Granting (krbtgt) accounts, RODCs pull user and computer credentials from a writeable domain controller running Windows Server 2008 or later and clients can, in turn, authenticate against an RODC, as shown in Figure 15-3. You must explicitly allow any other credentials to be cached on that RODC using Password Replication Policy. If it's allowed by a Password Replication Policy that is enforced on the writeable domain controller, an RODC retrieves and then caches credentials as necessary until the credentials change. Because only a subset of credentials is stored on an RODC, the number of credentials that can possibly be compromised is limited.

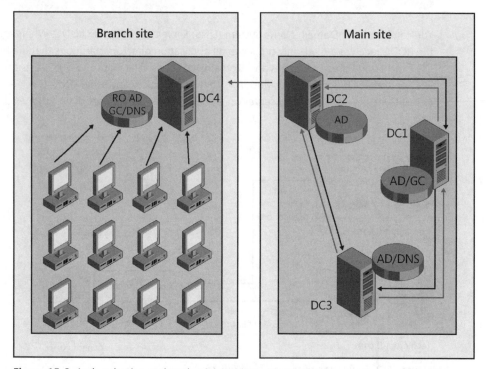

Figure 15-3 Authentication and credential caching with an RODC.

The RODC is advertised as the Key Distribution Center (KDC) for the branch office. After an account is authenticated, the RODC attempts to contact and pull the user credentials or computer credentials from a writeable domain controller that is running Windows Server 2008 or later in the hub site. The hub site can be any Active Directory site with writeable domain controllers running Windows Server 2008 or later.

The writeable domain controller recognizes that the request is coming from an RODC because of the use of the special Kerberos Ticket Granting account of the RODC. The Password Replication Policy that is enforced at the writeable domain controller determines whether a user's credentials or a computer's credentials can be replicated to the RODC. If the Password Replication Policy allows it, the RODC pulls and then caches the credentials from the writeable domain controller. After the credentials are cached on the RODC, the RODC can directly service that user's or computer's logon requests until the credentials change. This limits the exposure of credentials if an RODC is compromised.

NOTE

The RODC uses a different Kerberos Ticket Granting account and password than the KDC on a writeable domain controller uses when it signs or encrypts Ticket-Granting Ticket (TGT) requests. This provides cryptographic isolation between KDCs in different branches and prevents a compromised RODC from issuing service tickets to resources in other branches or in a hub site.

RODCs reduce the administration burden on the enterprise by allowing any domain user to be delegated as a local administrator without granting any other rights in the domain. This creates a clear separation between domain administrators and delegated administrator users at branch offices. An RODC can't act as an operations master role holder. Although RODCs can pull information from domain controllers running Windows Server 2003, RODCs can only pull updates of the schema, configuration, and domain partitions from a writeable domain controller running Windows Server 2008 or later in the same domain and a partial attribute set of the other domain partitions in the forest (the global catalog). Although RODCs can host a global catalog, they can't act as bridgehead servers or hold operations master roles.

Design considerations for read-only replication

Before you can deploy any RODCs in a domain, the primary domain controller (PDC) emulator operations master role holder for the domain must be running Windows Server 2008 or later. Also, you must ensure that a bidirectional communications path is open between the RODC and the PDC emulator. To accommodate this requirement, you might need to modify router and firewall configurations.

RODCs are designed to be placed in sites that have no other domain controllers. Consider the example shown in Figure 15-4. Here, the organization has one domain and two sites at the same physical location. Because the East Campus site is used for the organization's primary operations and is more secure from a physical perspective, the administrative staff decided to configure this site with the writeable domain controllers and the operations masters for the domain. Because the West Campus site is less secure from a physical perspective, the administrative staff decided to remove all other domain controllers and place only a read-only domain controller in this site.

NOTE

You can't place RODCs from the same domain in the same site. However, you can place an RODC in a site with RWDCs from the same domain or different domains or RODCs from different domains. Doing so has a number of constraints and requires additional planning.

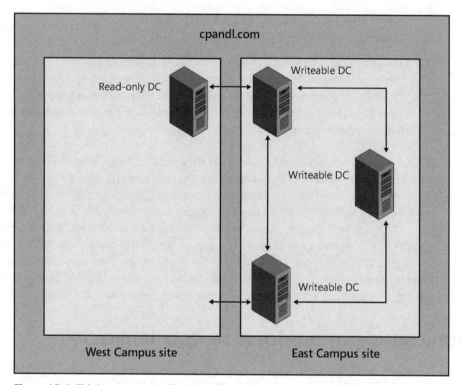

Figure 15-4 This is an example of placing domain controllers within domains.

RODCs perform inbound replication only by pulling data from a designated replication partner. RODCs can't perform outbound replication and therefore can't be a source domain controller for any other domain controller. An RODC can replicate data from a domain controller running Windows Server 2003 or later. However, it can replicate updates of the domain partition only from a domain controller located in the same domain that's running Windows Server 2008 or later.

Table 15-1 lists the specific partitions that can be replicated and the permitted replication partners. Only an RODC also configured as a DNS server can obtain the application partitions containing DNS data. In contrast, writeable domain controllers running Windows Server 2003 or later can perform inbound and outbound replication of all available partitions.

Table 15-1 Replicating directory partitions with RODCs

Directory Partition	Replication Partner
Schema	DC running Windows Server 2003 or later
Configuration	DC running Windows Server 2003 or later
Domain	DC running Windows Server 2008 or later
Application	DC running Windows Server 2003 or later
DNS	DC running Windows Server 2003 or later with Active Directory–integrated DNS zones
Global catalog	DC running Windows Server 2003 or later

Generally speaking, you should place writeable domain controllers in hub sites and read-only domain controllers in spoke sites. This configuration can relieve the inbound replication load on bridgehead servers because RODCs never replicate any changes. Consider the example shown in Figure 15-5. In this example, Main Site is the hub site and there are four branch office sites: Site A, Site B, Site C, and Site D. In this example, sites are connected in several ways with redundant pathways. However, the site link with the lowest cost is always the link between Main Site and a particular branch site.

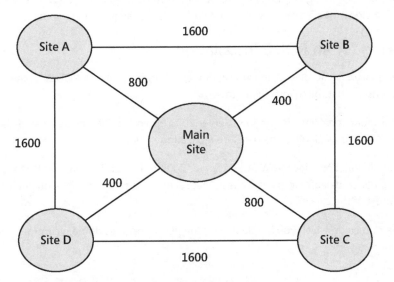

Figure 15-5 Placing domain controllers within sites.

To put an RODC in any branch site, you should place a domain controller running Windows Server 2008 or later for the same domain in Main Site to replicate the domain partition to the RODC. Placing only a domain controller running Windows Server 2003 in Main Site permits the RODC in the branch site to replicate the schema, configuration, and application directory partitions, but not the domain partition.

The replication schedule for site links can cause delays in receiving directory updates when replicating to other sites across a wide area network (WAN). To improve replication performance, RODCs immediately refer many types of write operations to a writeable domain controller, and this can cause unscheduled network traffic over WAN links. Additionally, for these select operations, RODCs immediately attempt inbound replication of individual changes:

- Password changes made using the Security Accounts Manager (SAM) interface rather than the Lightweight Directory Access Protocol (LDAP)

- DNS updates in which a client attempts to make a DNS update and is then referred to the DNS server where the updates are registered

Installing RODCs

RODCs can cache passwords for accounts. After an RODC has cached the password for a user, it remains in the Active Directory database until the user changes the password or the Password Replication Policy for the RODC changes in such a way that the user's password should no longer be cached. Accounts that will not have credentials cached on the RODC can still use the RODC for domain logon. The RODC retrieves the credentials from its RWDC replication partner. The credentials, however, will not be cached for subsequent logons using the RODC.

Preparing for an RODC installation

You can install an RODC only in an existing domain. Before you install RODCs in any domain, you must ensure that the following are true:

- Forest functional level is Windows Server 2003 or higher. This ensures that linked-value replication is available to help ensure replication consistency.

- Domain functional level is Windows Server 2003 or higher. This ensures that Kerberos constrained delegation is available so that security calls can be impersonated under the context of the caller.

- The domain in which you are deploying the RODC includes domain controllers running Windows Server 2003 or later.

- The domain controller that holds the PDC emulator operations master role is running Windows Server 2008 or later, and the RODC can communicate over a secure channel with the PDC emulator.

- At least one domain controller running Windows Server 2008 or later for the same domain must be located in the site closest to the site that includes the RODC. To ensure that the RODC can replicate all directory partitions, this domain controller must be a global catalog server.

- To run the DNS server on the RODC, another domain controller running Windows Server 2008 or later must be running in the domain and hosting the primary or Active Directory–integrated DNS domain zone. A standard or Active Directory–integrated DNS zone on an RODC is always a read-only copy of the zone file.

- You must run the **adprep /rodcprep** command before installing any RODCs in a domain. You need to do this only once for a domain. This ensures that the RODC can replicate DNS partitions. This is *not* required for new forests with only domain controllers that run Windows Server 2008 or later or when you are not using Active Directory–integrated DNS in the existing forest.

When you install an RODC, you can do the following:

- **Configure the Password Replication Policy.** The Password Replication Policy controls whether user and group passwords are replicated to the RODC. You can configure Denied Accounts for passwords that are never replicated and Allowed Accounts for passwords that are always replicated. See the section entitled "Managing Password Replication Policy" later in this chapter for more information.

- **Delegate administrative permissions.** By delegating administrative permissions, you allow a specified user or group to act as the local administrator of the RODC. Delegating permissions in this way grants the user or group no other administrative permissions in the domain. For ease of administration, you should create a new group for this purpose prior to deploying an RODC. See the section entitled "Delegating administrative permissions" later in this chapter for more information.

- **Install from media.** When you install from media, the RODC can get the required directory data from a local or shared folder rather than from over the network. Performing an RODC installation from media reduces directory-replication traffic over the network. You must create the media before installing the RODC, as discussed in the section entitled "Installing an RODC from media" later in this chapter.

- **Stage the deployment.** Typically, you use a staged deployment to allow a user who might not otherwise have appropriate permissions to deploy an RODC. You do this by creating the RODC in two phases. First, an administrator prestages the RODC by creating an RODC account in the domain. Then, a server is attached to the account during the installation of Active Directory Domain Services.

Installing an RODC

You can install an RODC as an additional domain controller in a domain using a standard deployment or a staged deployment. If you haven't run **adprep /rodcprep** in the domain previously, which might be required (as noted earlier), you must run this command now. The Active Directory Domain Services Configuration Wizard will not prepare a domain for RODCs.

To install an RODC in an existing domain, follow these steps:

1. In Server Manager, tap or click Manage and then tap or click Add Roles And Features. This starts the Add Roles And Features Wizard. If the wizard displays the Before You Begin page, read the Welcome message and then tap or click Next.

2. On the Select Installation Type page, select Role-Based Or Feature-Based Installation and then tap or click Next.

3. On the Select Destination Server page, the server pool shows servers you added for management. Tap or click the server you are configuring and then tap or click Next.

4. On the Select Server Roles page, select Active Directory Domain Services and then tap or click Next twice. Tap or click Install. This runs the Active Directory Domain Services Configuration Wizard.

5. When the initial installation task completes, you need to tap or click Promote This Server To A Domain Controller to start the Active Directory Domain Services Configuration Wizard. If you closed the Add Roles And Features Wizard window, you need to tap or click the Notifications icon and then tap or click Promote This Server To A Domain Controller.

6. On the Deployment Configuration page, shown in Figure 15-6, select Add A Domain Controller To An Existing Domain.

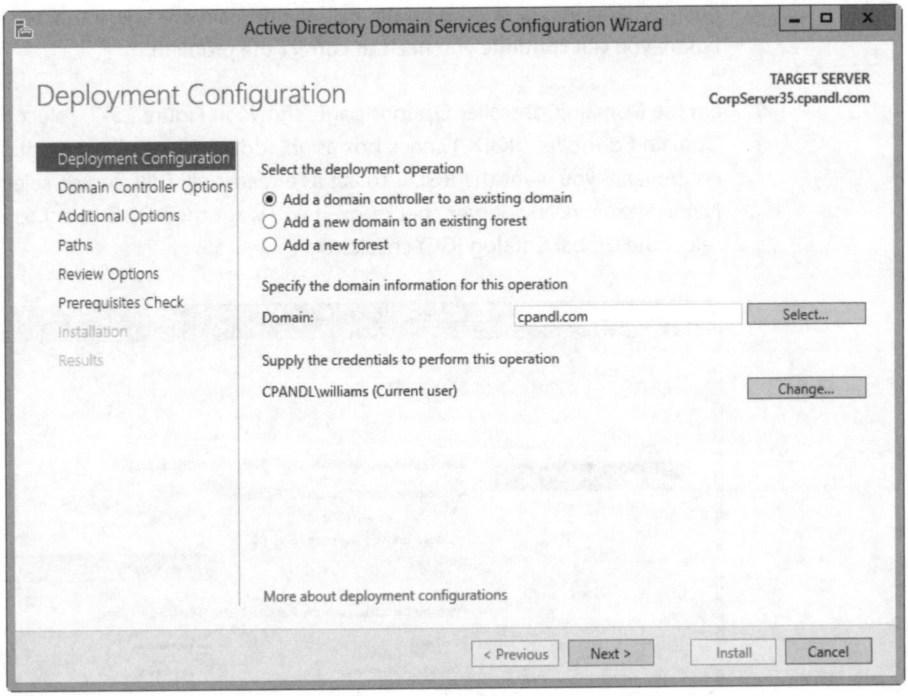

Figure 15-6 Add the domain controller to an existing domain.

7. In the Domain box, type the full DNS name of the domain in the forest where you plan to install the domain controller, such as **cpandl.com**. To select a domain in the forest from a list of available domains, tap or click Select. Next, in the Select A Domain dialog box, tap or click the domain to use and then tap or click OK.

8. If you are logged on to a domain in this forest and have the appropriate permissions, you can use your current logged-on credentials to perform the installation. Otherwise, you need to provide alternate credentials. Tap or click Change. In the Windows Security dialog box, type the user name and password for an enterprise administrator account in the previously specified domain and then tap or click OK.

IMPORTANT

When you tap or click Next, the wizard performs several preliminary checks on the Deployment Configuration page. If the server doesn't have appropriate TCP/IP settings, the wizard won't be able to connect to a domain controller in the target domain. If the user name and password you entered are invalid, you'll see an error. However, the wizard doesn't verify that the account has appropriate permissions until the prerequisite checks, which occur just before installation. Finally, you'll also see an error if the domain name you entered is invalid or if the domain can't be contacted. In each case, before you can continue you need to correct the problem.

9. On the Domain Controller Options page, shown in Figure 15-7, select the Read-Only Domain Controller (RODC) check box as an additional installation option for the domain controller. If you want the RODC to act as a read-only DNS server, select the Domain Name System (DNS) Server check box. If you want the RODC to act as a global catalog, select the Global Catalog (GC) check box.

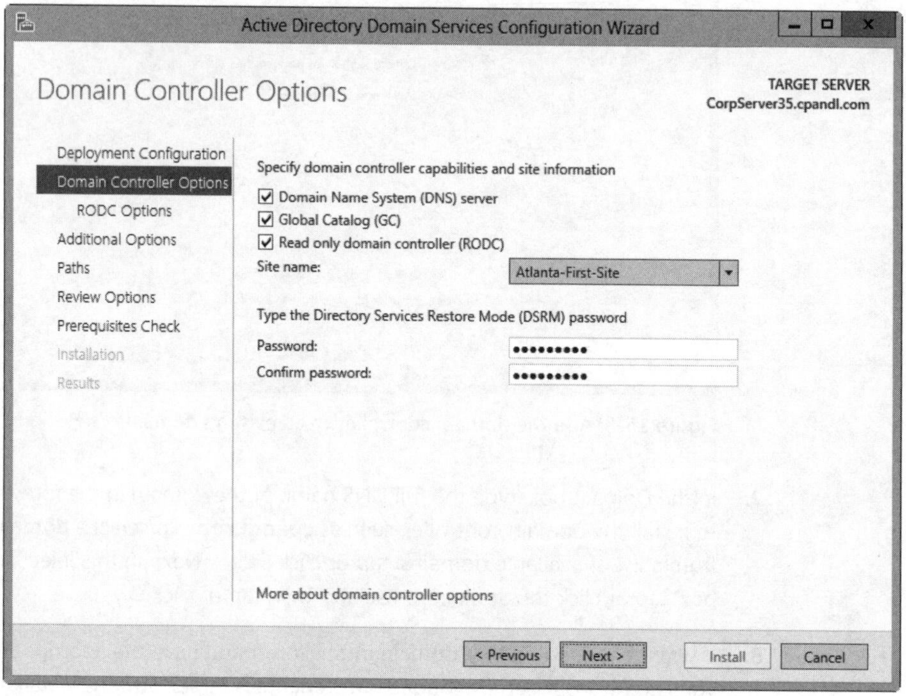

Figure 15-7 Set options for the RODC.

10. Select the Active Directory site in which you want to locate the domain controller. By default, the wizard selects the site with the most correct subnet. If there is only one site, the wizard selects that site automatically. No automatic selection is made if the server does not belong to an Active Directory subnet and multiple sites are available.

11. Type and confirm the password that should be used when you want to start the computer in Directory Services Restore Mode. Be sure to track this password carefully. This special password is used only in Restore mode and is different from the

Administrator account password. (It's the local Administrator password, which is in the local database of domain controllers; this database normally is hidden.) Tap or click Next.

12. You'll next be able to configure the Password Replication Policy for the RODC. (See Figure 15-8.) Add or remove any users or groups for which you want to allow or deny password replication. For more information, see the section entitled "Allowing or denying accounts in Password Replication Policy" later in this chapter. Tap or click Next to continue.

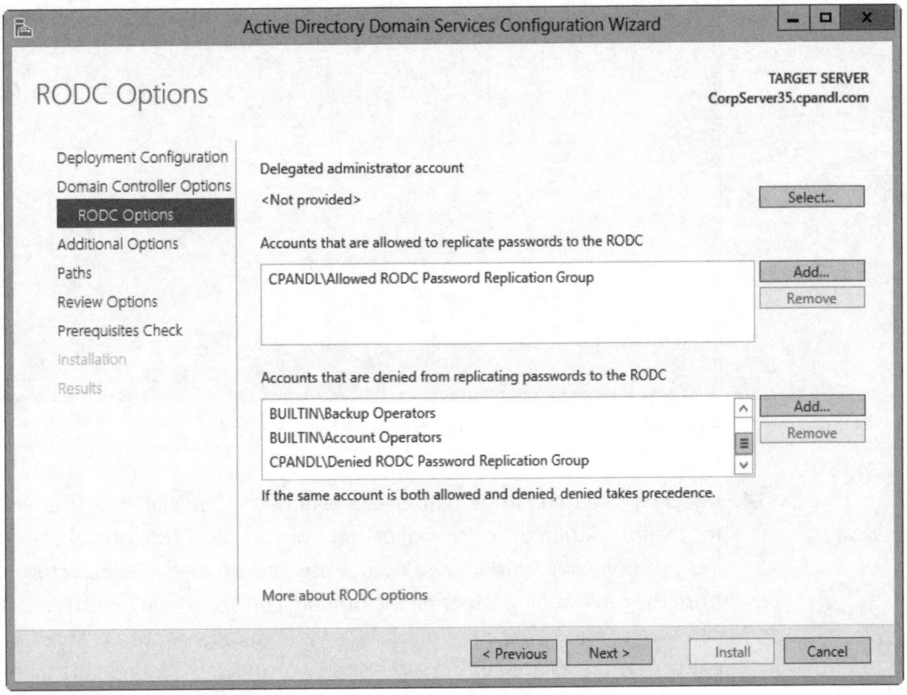

Figure 15-8 Configure the Password Replication Policy.

13. On the Additional Options page, specify whether to replicate the necessary Active Directory data from media or over the network, as shown in Figure 15-9. When you are installing from media, you must specify the folder location of the media before continuing. This folder must be on the local computer and can't be a mapped network drive.

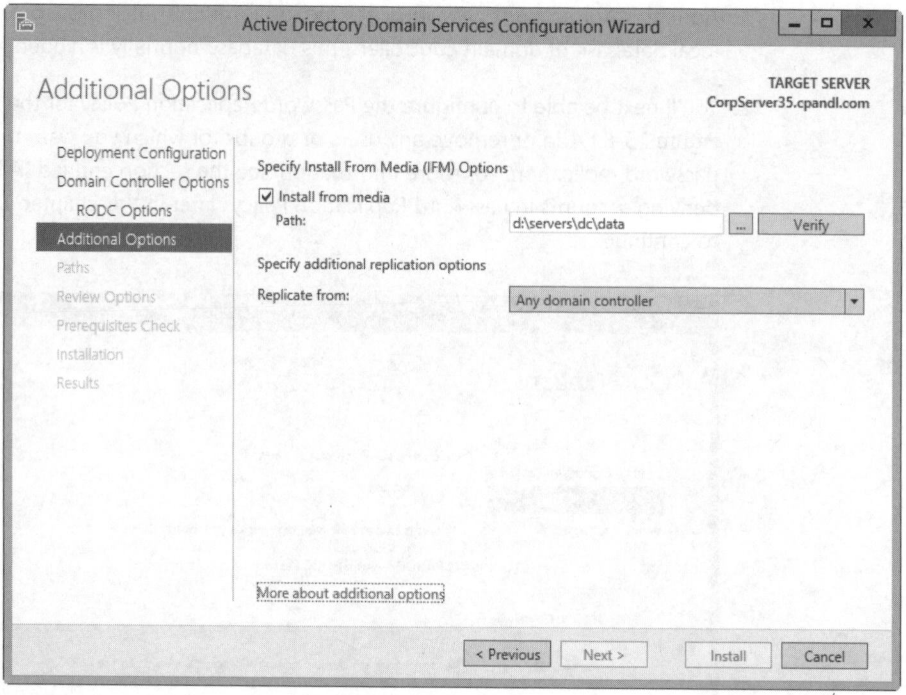

Figure 15-9 Set the Install From Media options.

14. If you choose to replicate data over the network, you can choose a replication partner for the installation or for all replication from any available domain controller. When you install a domain controller and do not use backup media, all directory data is replicated from the replication partner to the domain controller you're installing. Because this can be a considerable amount of data, you typically want to ensure that both domain controllers are located in the same site or connected over reliable high-speed networks.

15. On the Paths page, select a location in which to store the Active Directory database folder, log folder, and SYSVOL. When configuring these locations, keep the following in mind:

   - The default location for the database and log folders is a subfolder of %SystemRoot%\NTDS. As discussed in the section entitled "Hardware and configuration considerations for domain controllers" in Chapter 28, "Implementing Active Directory Domain Services," you'll get better performance if these folders are on two separate volumes, each on a separate disk.

- The default location for the SYSVOL folder is %SystemRoot%\Sysvol. In most cases you'll want to accept the default because the replication services store their database in a subfolder of the %SystemRoot% folder anyway. By keeping the folders on the same volume, you reduce the need to move files between drives.

16. On the Review Options page, review the installation options. Optionally, tap or click View Script to export the settings to a Windows PowerShell script that you can use to perform automated installation of other domain controllers. When you tap or click Next, the wizard performs preliminary checks to verify that the domain and forest are capable of supporting a new Windows Server 2012 R2 domain controller. The wizard also displays information about security changes that could affect older operating systems.

17. When you tap or click Install, the wizard uses the options you selected to install and configure Active Directory. This process can take several minutes. Keep the following in mind:

   - If you specified that the DNS Server service should be installed, the server will also be configured as a DNS server at this time.

   - Because you are installing an additional domain controller in an existing domain, the domain controller needs to obtain updates of all the directory partitions from other domain controllers and will do this by initiating a full synchronization. The only way to avoid this is to make a media backup of Active Directory on an existing domain controller, start the Active Directory Domain Services Configuration Wizard in Advanced mode, and then specify the backup media to use during the installation of Active Directory.

18. When the wizard finishes configuring Active Directory, you are shown a prompt stating that the computer will be restarted. After the server restarts, Active Directory will be completely configured and the server can then act as a domain controller.

Verify the installation by checking the Dcpromo.log file in the %SystemRoot%\Debug folder. Next, check for DNS updates in the DNS console. Because you added a domain controller, DNS should be updated with SRV records for the server, and these are in the appropriate subfolders of the zone, such as _tcp and _udp. In Active Directory Users And Computers, you should see the domain controller listed in the Domain Controllers OU, as shown in Figure 15-10.

CHAPTER 15

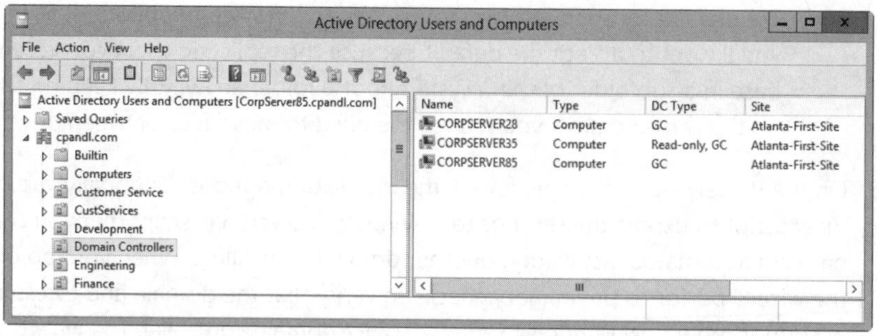

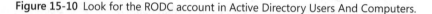

Figure 15-10 Look for the RODC account in Active Directory Users And Computers.

Installing an RODC from media

You can create the necessary installation media by completing these steps:

1. Log on to a domain controller for the domain in which you are creating the RODC.

2. At an elevated command prompt, type **ntdsutil**.

3. At the ntdsutil prompt, type **activate instance ntds**.

4. At the ntdsutil prompt, type **ifm**.

5. You can now create a copy of the directory data with or without the Sysvol.

   a. To create a copy of directory data without the Sysvol data, type **create RODC** **SaveFolder**, where *SaveFolder* is an empty folder into which you want to write the RODC data, such as C:\RODC. Ntdsutil then performs a number of housekeeping tasks while creating the snapshot for the RODC media. While it performs these tasks, the output will look similar to the following:

```
Creating snapshot for RODC media...
Snapshot set {09a1fe9b-4224-4094-a6a9-9f4f49cee068} generated successfully.
Snapshot {de9f9bb6-ebc0-4913-ac8b-3d49f5c32975} mounted as
C:\$SNAP_201410131424_VOLUMEC$\
Initiating DEFRAGMENTATION mode...
    Source Database: C:\$SNAP_201410131424_VOLUMEC$\Windows\NTDS\ntds.dit
    Target Database: c:\rodc\Active Directory\ntds.dit

                Defragmentation  Status (% complete)

    0    10   20   30   40   50   60   70   80   90  100
    |----|----|----|----|----|----|----|----|----|----|
    ..................................................

Converting Full DC IFM media to Read-only DC IFM media...
```

```
Records scanned:       4443
Records scanned:        202
Read-only DC IFM media conversion completed successfully.

              Securing  Status (% complete)

       0    10   20   30   40   50   60   70   80   90  100
       |----|----|----|----|----|----|----|----|----|----|
       .................................................

3328 pages seen
1564 blank pages seen
0 unchanged pages seen
2 unused pages zeroed
1683 used pages seen
0 pages with unknown objid
82270 nodes seen
16 flag-deleted nodes zeroed
0 flag-deleted nodes not zeroed
0 version bits reset seen
0 orphaned LVs
Snapshot {de9f9bb6-ebc0-4913-ac8b-3d49f5c32975} unmounted.
IFM media created successfully in c:\rodc
```

   b. To create a copy of directory data with the Sysvol data, type **create sysvol rodc**
   SaveFolder, where *SaveFolder* is a different, empty folder into which you want to
   write Sysvol data for the RODC, such as C:\SysvolSave. Ntdsutil then performs a
   number of housekeeping tasks while creating the snapshot of the Sysvol. While it
   performs these tasks, the output will look similar to the following:

```
Creating snapshot for RODC media...
Snapshot set {510f93b4-d2ef-4800-b4e4-82926bad7c85} generated successfully.
Snapshot {35c61a1b-5072-462f-b2bb-c340799d7094} mounted as
C:\$SNAP_201410131428_VOLUMEC$\
Snapshot {35c61a1b-5072-462f-b2bb-c340799d7094} is already mounted.
Initiating DEFRAGMENTATION mode...
     Source Database: C:\$SNAP_201410131428_VOLUMEC$\Windows\NTDS\ntds.dit
     Target Database: c:\rodc-sysvol\Active Directory\ntds.dit

              Defragmentation  Status (% complete)

       0    10   20   30   40   50   60   70   80   90  100
       |----|----|----|----|----|----|----|----|----|----|
       .................................................

Converting Full DC IFM media to Read-only DC IFM media...
Records scanned:       4443
Records scanned:        202
Read-only DC IFM media conversion completed successfully.

              Securing  Status (% complete)
```

```
    0    10   20   30   40   50   60   70   80   90  100
    |----|----|----|----|----|----|----|----|----|----|
    .................................................
```

```
3328 pages seen
1564 blank pages seen
0 unchanged pages seen
2 unused pages zeroed
1683 used pages seen
0 pages with unknown objid
82270 nodes seen
16 flag-deleted nodes zeroed
0 flag-deleted nodes not zeroed
0 version bits reset seen
0 orphaned LVs
Copying SYSVOL...
Copying c:\rodc-sysvol\SYSVOL
Copying c:\rodc-sysvol\SYSVOL\cpandl.com
Copying c:\rodc-sysvol\SYSVOL\cpandl.com\Policies
...
Copying c:\rodc-sysvol\SYSVOL\cpandl.com\scripts
Snapshot {35c61a1b-5072-462f-b2bb-c340799d7094} unmounted.
IFM media created successfully in c:\rodc-sysvol
```

6. Copy the save folder and its entire contents to a local folder on the RODC. The amount of data written to the save folder will vary depending on the number of objects and the properties those objects contain in the directory.

Because you created installation media for an RODC, passwords are not included in the data. You can use this same technique to create installation media for writeable domain controllers. In step 5, instead of typing **create rodc**, type **create full**. Instead of typing **create sysvol rodc**, type **create sysvol full**. That's it; it's that easy. However, a full copy of the directory data contains passwords and other critically important security data that require additional safeguards.

Staging an RODC

You stage deployment to allow a user who might not otherwise have appropriate permissions to deploy an RODC. You do this by creating the RODC in two phases. First, an administrator prestages the RODC by creating an RODC account in the domain. Then the server you are promoting is attached to the account during the installation of Active Directory Domain Services. To perform either task, you need to use an account that is a member of the Domain Admins group. You also can delegate permission to a user or group that allows attaching the RODC.

You can pre-create the RODC account by following these steps:

1. Start the Active Directory Domain Services Installation Wizard. Do one of the following:

    - In Active Directory Users And Computers, connect to the domain where the RODC will be added, press and hold or right-click the related Domain Controllers node, and then select Pre-Create Read-Only Domain Controller Account.

    - In Active Directory Administrative Center, connect to the domain where the RODC will be added, select the related Domain Controllers node in the console tree, and then, under Tasks, select Pre-Create Read-Only Domain Controller Account.

2. By default, the wizard uses Basic Installation mode. Select Use Advanced Mode Installation before tapping or clicking Next to continue.

3. If the server doesn't have an appropriate IP address, you'll see the Configure TCP/IP page. This page displays a warning about the invalid IP address or improper network configuration, and you need to correct the issue before you can continue.

4. When you tap or click Next, you'll see the Network Credentials page. If you are logged on to a domain in this forest and have the appropriate permissions, you can use your current logged-on credentials to perform the installation. Otherwise, select Alternate Credentials, tap or click Set, type the user name and password for an enterprise administrator account in the previously specified domain, and then tap or click OK.

5. When you tap or click Next, the wizard examines the Active Directory forest and domain configuration. On the Specify The Computer Name page, shown in Figure 15-11, enter the name of the computer that will be the RODC and confirm that the fully qualified domain name is the one you expected. If the fully qualified domain name isn't the one you expected, you might have selected the wrong domain before starting the wizard.

CHAPTER 15

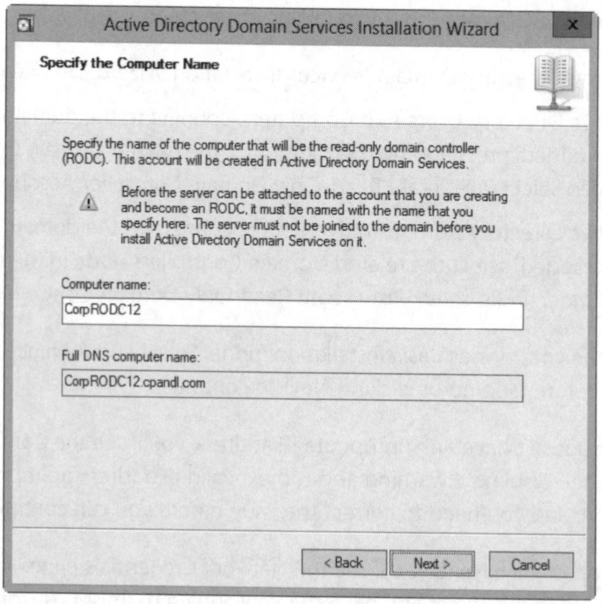

Figure 15-11 Specify the name of the server that will be promoted.

6. When you tap or click Next, the wizard verifies the source domain and the computer name and then loads a list of sites in the Active Directory forest. On the Select A Site page, select the site in which the domain controller should be located and then tap or click Next.

7. When you tap or click Next, the wizard validates the site name, examines the DNS configuration, and attempts to determine whether any authoritative DNS servers are available. If you want the RODC to act as a read-only DNS server, select the DNS Server check box. If you want the RODC to act as a global catalog, select the Global Catalog check box. When you are ready to continue, tap or click Next.

8. If you are installing the DNS Server service as an additional option and the server doesn't have static IP addresses for both Internet Protocol version 4 (IPv4) and Internet Protocol version 6 (IPv6), you'll see a warning prompt regarding the server's dynamic IP address or addresses. Tap or click Yes only if you plan to use the dynamic IP address or addresses, despite the possibility that this could result in an unreliable DNS configuration. Tap or click No if you plan to change the IP configuration before continuing.

9. Configure the Password Replication Policy for the RODC, as shown in Figure 15-12. Add or remove any users or groups for which you want to allow or deny password replication. For more information, see the section entitled "Allowing or denying accounts in Password Replication Policy" later in this chapter. Tap or click Next to continue.

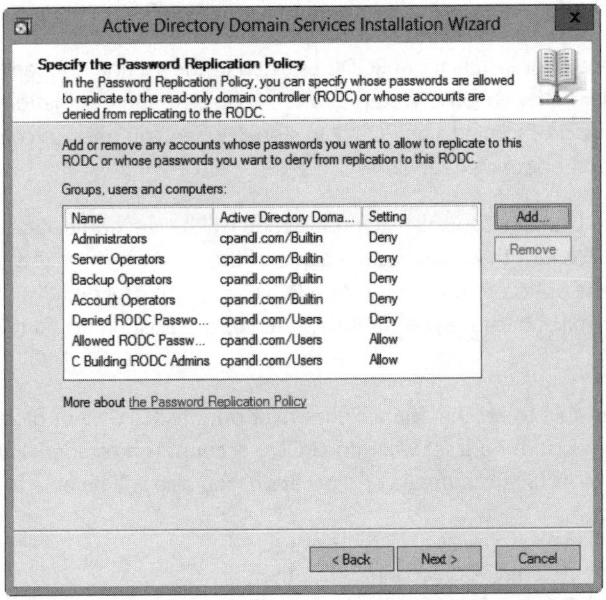

Figure 15-12 Configure the Password Replication Policy.

10. Configure delegation. The delegated user or group will be able to attach the RODC and also will have local administrative permissions on the RODC. Tap or click Set, use the Select User Or Group dialog box to specify a delegated user or group, and then tap or click OK.

11. Tap or click Next. Review the installation options. Optionally, tap or click Export Settings to save these settings to an answer file that you can use to perform unattended installations of other RODCs. When you tap or click Next again, the wizard uses the options you selected to configure the account in Active Directory.

12. When the wizard finishes configuring Active Directory, tap or click Finish. In the Domain Controllers container, an account is created for the RODC with the type set as Unoccupied DC Account. This indicates that the account is staged and ready for a server to be attached to it.

Any user who is a member of Domain Admins can attach a server to the RODC account, and so can any user or group that was delegated permission when setting up the RODC account. To attach a server to the account, do the following:

1. If a server with the server name specified as the RODC account name isn't already set up, configure this server and add it for management in Server Manager.

2. Follow the steps for installing an RODC as listed in the section entitled "Installing an RODC" earlier in the chapter. In step 3, when you select the destination server, select the server you are promoting to an RODC. In step 8, when you need to confirm permissions, enter the appropriate credentials.

3. In step 9, the Domain Controllers Options page will have a notification that states, "A pre-created account that matches the name of the target server exists in the directory." You'll have the option to use the existing RODC account (the default) or to reinstall the domain controller. Because you want to attach to the existing account, use the existing account.

4. You won't be able to set the domain controller options for DNS or global catalogs because these options are set when the RODC account is prestaged. However, you will be able to install from media or replication. You also will be able to set the directory paths.

You also can pre-create an RODC account using the Add-ADDSReadOnlyDomainControllerAccount cmdlet. Use the *–DomainControllerAccountName* parameter to specify the name of the account, the *–DomainName* parameter to specify the domain in which to create the account, and the *–SiteName* parameter to specify the Active Directory site for the account. Here is an example:

```
add-addsdomaincontrolleraccount -domaincontrolleraccountname corpserver15
-domainname tech.cpandl.com -sitename chicago-first-site
```

Once you stage the account, you can use the Install-ADDSDomainController cmdlet to promote the server that you want to be the RODC. Use the *–ExistingAccount* parameter to attach the server to the existing account, as shown in this example:

```
install-addsdomaincontroller -domainname tech.cpandl.com –useexistingaccount
-credential (get-credential)
```

Managing Password Replication Policy

When you deploy an RODC, you must configure the Password Replication Policy on the writeable domain controller that will be its replication partner. The Password Replication Policy acts as an access control list (ACL) and determines whether an RODC should be permitted to cache a password for a particular user or group. After the RODC receives an authenticated user or computer logon request, it refers to the Password Replication Policy to determine whether it should cache the password for the account.

Working with Password Replication Policy

You can configure Password Replication Policy in several ways:

- Allow no accounts to be cached for the strictest control, such as when the physical security of the RODC can't be guaranteed.

- Allow few accounts to be cached for strong control, such as when the physical security of the RODC is good but can't be reasonably assured at all times.

- Allow many accounts to be cached for less strict control, such as when the physical security of the RODC can be reasonably assured at all times (and you also might want to configure TPM and BitLocker).

NOTE
The fewer account passwords replicated to RODCs, the less risk that security could be breached if an RODC is compromised. The more account passwords replicated to RODCs, the greater the risk involved if an RODC is compromised.

Password Replication Policy is managed on a per-computer basis. The computer object for an RODC is updated to include the following multivalued directory attributes that contain security principals (users, computers, and groups):

- *msDS-Reveal-OnDemandGroup*, which defines the Allowed Accounts list

- *msDS-NeverRevealGroup*, which defines the Denied Accounts list

- *msDS-RevealedUsers*, which defines the Revealed Accounts list

- *msDS-AuthenticatedToAccountList*, which defines the Authenticated To list

The RODC uses these attributes together to determine whether an account password can be replicated and cached. The passwords for Denied Accounts are never replicated and cached. The passwords for Allowed Accounts can always be replicated and cached. Whether a password is cached or not doesn't depend on whether a user or computer has logged on to the domain through the RODC. At any time, an RODC can replicate the passwords for Allowed Accounts and administrators can also prepopulate passwords for Allowed Accounts using Active Directory Users And Computers.

During an advanced installation of an RODC, you can configure the initial Password Replication Policy settings. To support RODCs, Windows Server 2008 and later use several built-in groups:

- **Enterprise Read-Only Domain Controllers.** Every RODC in the Active Directory forest is a member of this group automatically. Membership in this group is required for proper operations.

- **Read-Only Domain Controllers.** Every RODC in the Active Directory domain is a member of this group automatically. Membership in this group is required for proper operations.

- **Allowed RODC Password Replication Group.** You can manage Allowed Accounts using the Allowed RODC Password Replication Group. Passwords for members of this group are always replicated to RODCs.

- **Denied RODC Password Replication Group.** You can manage Denied Accounts using the Denied RODC Password Replication Group. Passwords for members of this group are never replicated to RODCs.

By default, the Allowed RODC Password Replication Group has no members. Also by default, the Allowed RODC Password Replication Group is the only Allowed Account defined in Password Replication Policy.

By default, the Denied RODC Password Replication Group contains the following members:

- Cert Publishers

- Domain Admins

- Domain Controllers

- Enterprise Admins

- Group Policy Creator Owners

- Read-Only Domain Controllers

- Schema Admins

- The domainwide krbtgt account

Also by default, the Denied Accounts list contains the following security principals, all of which are built-in groups:

- Account Operators

- Administrators

- Backup Operators

- Denied RODC Password Replication Group

- Server Operators

Allowing or denying accounts in Password Replication Policy

Each RODC has a separate Password Replication Policy. To manage the Password Replication Policy, you must be a member of the Domain Admins group. The easiest way to manage Password Replication Policy is to do the following:

- Add accounts for which passwords should not be replicated to the Denied RODC Password Replication Group.

- Add accounts for which passwords should be replicated to the Allowed RODC Password Replication Group.

You can also edit Password Replication Policy settings directly. To edit the Password Replication Policy for an RODC, follow these steps:

1. In Active Directory Users And Computers, ensure that Active Directory Users And Computers points to a writeable domain controller that is running Windows Server 2008 or later. Press and hold or right-click the Active Directory Users And Computers node and then select Change Domain Controller. As shown in Figure 15-13, the domain controller to which you are connected should be a writeable domain controller—that is, it should not list RODC under DC Type. If you are connected to an RODC, change to a writeable domain controller. Tap or click Cancel or OK as appropriate.

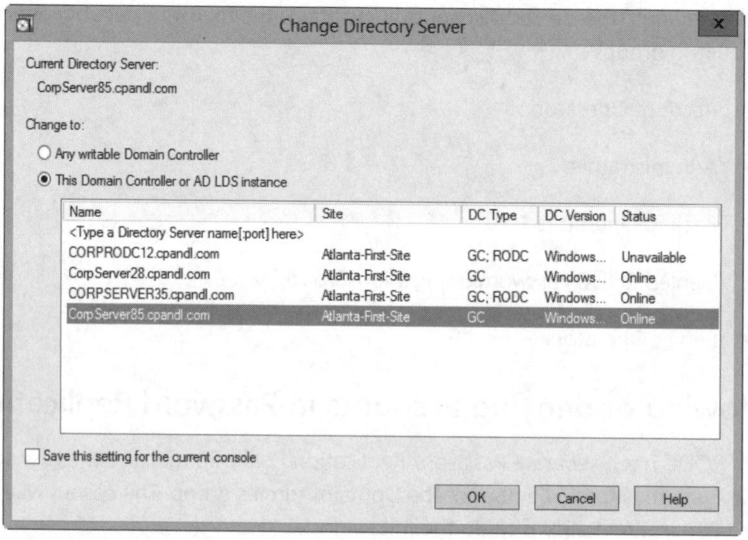

Figure 15-13 Make sure you are connected to a writeable domain controller.

2. In Active Directory Users And Computers, expand the domain node and then select Domain Controllers.

3. In the details pane, press and hold or right-click the RODC computer account and then choose Properties.

4. In the Password Replication Policy tab, shown in Figure 15-14, you'll see the current settings for Password Replication Policy on the RODC.

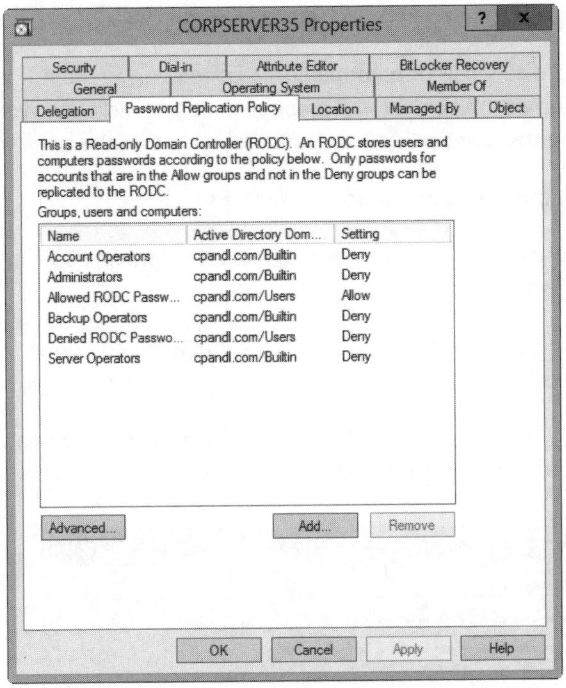

Figure 15-14 Review the current Password Replication Policy settings for the RODC.

5. You can now do the following:

- **Define an Allowed Account.** Tap or click Add, select Allow Passwords For The Account To Replicate To This RODC, and then tap or click OK. In the Select Users, Contacts, Computers, Or Groups dialog box, type an account name and then tap or click Check Names. If the account name is listed correctly, tap or click OK to add it to the Password Replication Policy as an Allowed Account.

- **Define a Denied Account.** Tap or click Add, select Deny Passwords For The Account To Replicate To This RODC, and then tap or click OK. In the Select Users, Contacts, Computers, Or Groups dialog box, type an account name and then tap or click Check Names. If the account name is listed correctly, tap or click OK to add it to the Password Replication Policy as a Denied Account.

- **Remove an account from Password Replication Policy.** Select the account name in the Groups, Users And Computers list, and then tap or click Remove. When prompted to confirm, tap or click Yes.

Viewing and managing credentials on an RODC

You can review cached credentials or prepopulate credentials using the Advanced Password Replication Policy dialog box. When you are prepopulating user accounts, you should also consider prepopulating the passwords of computer accounts that the users will be using.

To view and work with this dialog box, follow these steps:

1. In Active Directory Users And Computers, expand the domain node and then select Domain Controllers.

2. In the details pane, press and hold or right-click the RODC computer account and then choose Properties.

3. In the Password Replication Policy tab, tap or click Advanced to display the Advanced Password Replication Policy dialog box shown in Figure 15-15.

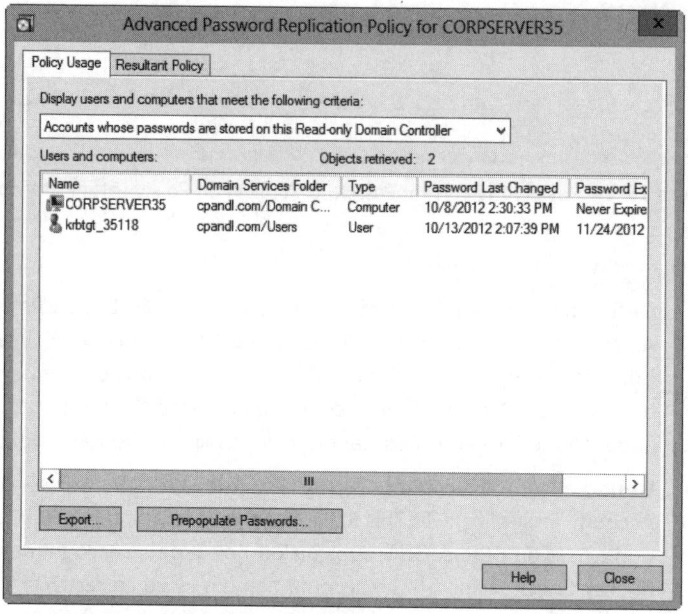

Figure 15-15 Review stored credentials.

4. You now have the following options:

- Accounts for which passwords are stored on the RODC are displayed by default. To view accounts that have been authenticated to this RODC, on the Display Users And Computers That Meet The Following Criteria list, select Accounts That Have Been Authenticated To This Read-Only Domain Controller.

- To prepopulate passwords for an account, tap or click Prepopulate Passwords. In the Select Users Or Computers dialog box, type an account name and then tap or click Check Names. If the account name is listed correctly, tap or click OK to add a request that its password be replicated to the RODC. When prompted to confirm, tap or click Yes. The password is then prepopulated. Tap or click OK.

Determining whether an account is allowed or denied access

To determine whether an account is allowed or restricted, you can use Resultant Set of Policy (RSoP) to examine all related group memberships and determine exactly what rules apply. Follow these steps:

1. In Active Directory Users And Computers, expand the domain node and then select Domain Controllers.

2. In the details pane, press and hold or right-click the RODC computer account and then choose Properties.

3. In the Password Replication Policy tab, tap or click Advanced to display the Advanced Password Replication Policy dialog box.

4. In the Resultant Policy tab, tap or click Add.

5. In the Select Users Or Computers dialog box, type an account name and then tap or click Check Names. If the account name is listed correctly, tap or click OK to display the RSoP, as shown in Figure 15-16.

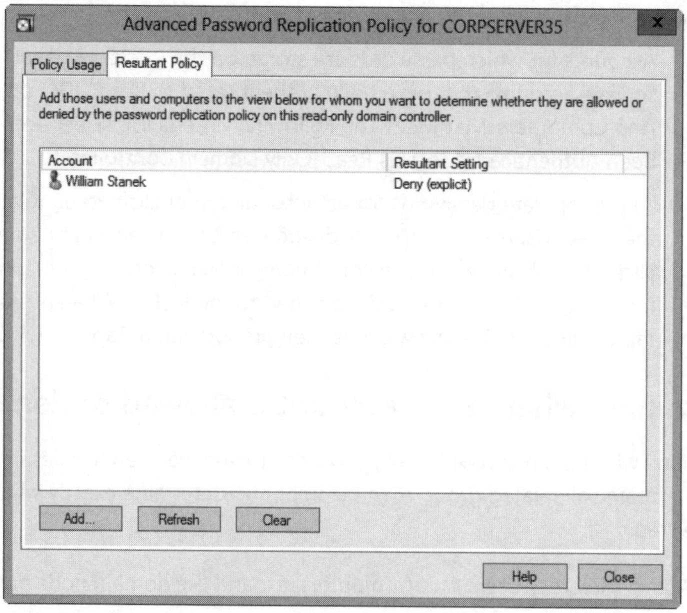

Figure 15-16 Determine whether an account is allowed or denied access using Resultant Set of Policy.

Resetting credentials

If an RODC is compromised or stolen, you can reset the passwords for all accounts for which credentials were cached on the RODC by following these steps:

1.   In Active Directory Users And Computers, ensure that Active Directory Users And Computers points to the writeable domain controller that is running Windows Server 2008 or later. Press and hold or right-click the Active Directory Users And Computers node and then select Change Domain Controller. The domain controller to which you are connected should be a writeable domain controller—that is, it should not list RODC under DC Type. If you are connected to an RODC, change to a writeable domain controller. Tap or click Cancel or OK as appropriate.

2.   In Active Directory Users And Computers, expand the domain node and then select Domain Controllers.

3.   In the details pane, press and hold or right-click the RODC computer account and then choose Delete.

4.   When prompted to confirm, tap or click Yes.

5. When prompted again, specify whether you want to reset all passwords for user accounts, computer accounts, or both, that were cached on this RODC. If you reset user account passwords, the affected users won't be able to log on until they contact you or the help desk to obtain a new password. If you reset computer account passwords, the affected computers will be disjoined from the network and won't be able to connect to the domain until they are rejoined.

6. You want to export the list of cached accounts to a file, and this is the default selection. Tap or click Browse to select a save location and set a file name for the account list. The password for every user whose account is listed in this file has been reset.

7. Tap or click Delete. When prompted, confirm that you really want to delete all metadata for the RODC by tapping or clicking OK.

Delegating administrative permissions

During the configuration of an RODC, you have an opportunity to specify user or group accounts that should be delegated administrative permissions. After the initial configuration, you can add or remove administrative permissions using Dsmgmt.

To grant administrative permissions to an additional user, follow these steps:

1. At an elevated command prompt, type **dsmgmt**.

2. At the dsmgmt prompt, type **local roles**.

3. At the local roles prompt, type **show role administrators** to list current administrators. In the default configuration, no users or groups are listed.

4. At the local roles prompt, type **add** *Domain\User* **administrators** to grant administrative permissions, where *Domain* is the domain in which the user account is located and *User* is the account name, such as **CPANDL\williams**.

5. Confirm the addition by typing **show role administrators**.

6. Type **quit** twice to exit Dsmgmt.

To remove administrative permissions, follow these steps:

1. At an elevated command prompt, type **dsmgmt**.

2. At the dsmgmt prompt, type **local roles**.

3. At the local roles prompt, type **show role administrators** to list current administrators. In the default configuration, no users or groups are listed.

4. At the local roles prompt, type **remove *Domain\User* administrators** to remove administrative permissions for a specified user, where *Domain* is the domain in which the user account is located and *User* is the account name, such as **CPANDL\williams**.

5. Confirm the removal by typing **show role administrators**.

6. Type **quit** twice to exit Dsmgmt.

Managing users, groups, and computers

Managing users, groups, and computers will probably be a significant part of your duties and responsibilities as an administrator. Managing users, groups, and computers encapsulates the important duties of a system administrator because of the way you must balance convenience, performance, fault tolerance, and security.

In this chapter you'll learn how to manage domain accounts. Although local system accounts are discussed, they are not the primary focus. Also, Microsoft Windows 8 and Windows Server 2012 and later add a special type of local account called a Microsoft account. You can think of Microsoft accounts as synchronized accounts. When you connect a local or domain account to a Microsoft account, the account becomes a connected local or connected domain account.

Managing domain user accounts

The next part of this chapter is dedicated to helping you plan, manage, and administer user accounts securely and efficiently. Windows operating systems have come a long way since the early days of Windows Server, and you now have many options for managing users.

Configuring user account policies

Because domain controllers share the domain accounts database, user account policies must be consistent across all domain controllers. The way consistency is ensured is by having domain controllers obtain user account policies only from the domain container and allowing only one top-level account policy for domain accounts. The one top-level account policy allowed for domain accounts is determined by the highest-precedence Group Policy Object (GPO) linked to the domain container. This top-level account policy is then enforced by the domain controllers in the domain. Domain controllers always obtain the top-level account policy from the highest-precedence GPO linked to the domain container. By default, this is the Default Domain Policy GPO.

When a domain is operating at the Windows Server 2008 or higher functional level, you can use two object classes in the Active Directory schema to fine-tune the way account policy is applied:

- Password Settings Container

- Password Settings Object

The default Password Settings Container (PSC) is created under the System container in the domain, and it stores the Password Settings Objects (PSOs) for the domain. Although you can't rename, move, or delete the default PSC, you can add to this container PSOs that define the various sets of secondary account policy settings you want to use in your domain. You can then apply the desired secondary account policy settings to users, inetOrgPersons, and global security groups, as discussed later in this chapter in the section "Creating Password Settings Objects and applying secondary settings."

Local account policy is used for local logon

Local account policies can be different from the domain account policy, such as when you specifically define an account policy for local accounts in local GPOs (LGPOs). For example, if you configure an account policy for LGPOs, when users log on to Active Directory they'll obtain their account policy from the Default Domain Policy instead of from the LGPOs. The only exception is when users log on locally to their machines instead of logging on to Active Directory; in that case, any account policy applied to an applicable local GPO is applied and enforced.

Some security options are also obtained from the Default Domain Policy GPO

Two policies in Computer Configuration\Windows Settings\Security Settings\Local Policies\Security Options also behave like account policies. These policies are Network Access: Allow Anonymous SID/NAME Translation and Network Security: Force Logoff When Logon Hours Expire. For domain accounts, the settings for these policies are obtained only from the Default Domain Policy GPO. For local accounts, the settings for these policies can come from a local organizational unit (OU) GPO, if one is defined and applicable.

As discussed in Chapter 17, "Managing Group Policy," account policies in a domain are configured through the policy editors accessible from the Group Policy Management Console (GPMC). When you are editing policy settings, you'll find account policies under Computer

Configuration\Windows Settings\Security Settings\Account Policies. To change Group Policies, you must be a member of the Administrators, Domain Admins, or Enterprise Admins group in Active Directory. Members of the Group Policy Creator Owners group can also modify Group Policy for the domain.

The account policies for a domain contain three subsets: Password Policy, Account Lockout Policy, and Kerberos Policy. Although secondary account policies include Password Policy and Account Lockout Policy, they do not include Kerberos Policy. Kerberos Policy can be set only at the domain level for the top-level account policy.

Enforcing Password Policy

Password policies for domain user accounts and local user accounts are very important in preventing unauthorized access. There are six settings for password policies that enable you to control how passwords are managed. When you are setting the top-level account policy for the Default Domain Policy, these policies are located in Computer Configuration\Windows Settings\Security Settings\Account Policies\Password Policy. (See Figure 16-1.) When you are setting the secondary account policy for a PSO, you configure these settings using similarly named object attributes.

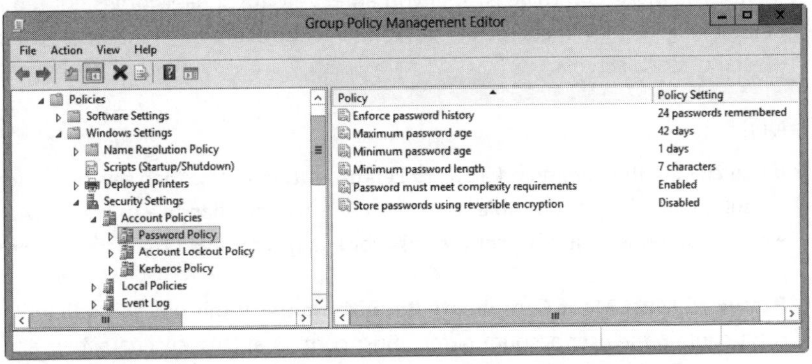

Figure 16-1 Manage Password Policy in the Default Domain Policy.

The settings are as follows:

- **Enforce Password History.** When users change their passwords, this setting determines how many old passwords will be maintained and associated with each user. The maximum value is 24. If you enter zero (0), a password history is not kept. On a domain controller, the default is 24 passwords; on a stand-alone server, it's zero passwords.

- **Maximum Password Age.** This determines when users are required to change their passwords. For example, if this is set to 90 days, on the ninety-first day the user will be required to change his or her password. The default on domain controllers is 42 days.

The minimum number of days is zero, which effectively means that the password never changes. The maximum number of days is 999. In an environment where security is critical, you probably want to set the value low. In contrast, in environments where security is less stringent, you could set the password age high (rarely requiring users to change passwords). Additionally, when security is critical and two-factor authentication is used, you might want to consider using a higher setting than you typically would.

- **Minimum Password Age.** This setting determines how long users must use passwords before they are allowed to change the password. It must be more than zero days for the Enforce Password History policy to be effective. In an environment where security is critical, you should set this to a shorter time; where security is not as tight, you should set it to a longer time. This setting must be configured to be less than the Maximum Password Age policy. The maximum value is 998. If you enter zero (0), a password can be changed immediately. The default is one day on a domain controller and zero days on stand-alone servers.

- **Minimum Password Length.** This is the number of characters that sets the minimum requirement for the length of the password. Again, an environment where security is more critical might require longer passwords than one with reduced security requirements. The maximum value is 14. If you enter zero (0), a password is not required. The default length is seven characters on domain controllers. The default is zero characters on stand-alone servers.

NOTE

If you change the Minimum Password Length setting to less than seven characters (the default), you might not be able to create a new user or change a user's password. To work around this limitation, set the password length to seven characters or more.

- **Password Must Meet Complexity Requirements.** If this policy is defined, passwords can't contain the user account name, must contain at least six characters, and must contain three of the four complexity groups: uppercase letters, lowercase letters, numerals, and special nonalphabetical characters, such as the percentage sign (%) and the asterisk (*). (Complexity requirements are enabled by default on domain controllers and disabled by default on stand-alone servers.)

- **Store Passwords Using Reversible Encryption.** This is an additional policy that allows for plain text encryption of passwords for applications that might need it. By default, this feature is disabled. Enabling this policy is basically the same as storing passwords as plain text, and this policy is used when applications use protocols that need information about the user's password. Because this policy degrades the overall security of the domain, you should use it only when absolutely necessary (and preferably not on a domain-joined server).

Configuring Account Lockout Policy

Account Lockout Policy is invoked after a local user or a domain user has been locked out of his or her account. There are three settings for account lockout policies:

- **Account Lockout Duration.** If a user becomes locked out, this setting determines how long the user will be locked out before the user account is unlocked. There is no default setting because this setting is dependent on the account lockout threshold setting. The range is from 0 to 99,999 minutes. When this is set to zero, the account will be locked out indefinitely and, in that case, will require an administrator to unlock it.

- **Account Lockout Threshold.** This setting determines how many failed attempts at logon Windows Server permits before a user will be locked out of the account. The range is from 0 to 999. If this setting is zero, the account will never be locked out and the Account Lockout Duration security setting is disabled. The default setting is zero.

- **Reset Account Lockout Counter After.** This setting is the number of minutes after a failure to log on before the logon counter is reset to zero. This value must be less than or equal to the Account Lockout Duration setting if the Account Lockout Threshold policy is enabled. The valid range is from 1 to 99,999 minutes.

When you are setting the top-level account policy for the Default Domain Policy, these policies are located in Computer Configuration\Windows Settings\Security Settings\Account Policies\Account Lockout Policy. When you are setting the secondary account policy for a PSO, you configure these settings using similarly named object attributes.

Setting Kerberos Policy

Kerberos is an authentication system designed to ensure the secure exchange of information, as discussed in the section entitled "NTLM and Kerberos authentication" in Chapter 11, "Designing and managing the domain environment." Windows Server has five settings for Kerberos Policy, which are applied only to domain user accounts. The policies, which are described in the following list, can be set only for the top-level account policy, and they are located in Computer Configuration\Windows Settings\Security Settings\Account Policies \Kerberos Policy:

- **Enforce User Logon Restrictions.** If you want to validate every session ticket request against the user rights, keep the default setting enabled.

- **Maximum Lifetime For Service Ticket.** The default is 600 minutes, but this setting must be greater than 10 minutes and it also must be less than or equal to what is configured for the Maximum Lifetime For User Ticket setting. The setting does not apply to sessions that have already been validated.

- **Maximum Lifetime For User Ticket.** This is different from the Maximum Lifetime For Service Ticket setting. Maximum Lifetime For User Ticket sets the maximum amount of time that a ticket can be used before either a new one must be requested or the existing one is renewed, whereas the Maximum Lifetime For Service Ticket setting is used to access a particular service. The default is 10 hours.

- **Maximum Lifetime For User Ticket Renewal.** This user account security policy object configures the maximum amount of time the ticket can be used. The default is seven days.

- **Maximum Tolerance For Computer Clock Synchronization.** Sometimes workstations and servers have different local clock times. You can use this setting to configure a tolerance level (defaults to five minutes) for this possible difference so that Kerberos authentication does not fail.

Using Authentication Policies

Authentication policies are an advanced configuration option for large enterprises. You can use authentication policies for several reasons, including to restrict the authentication methods available to user, service, and computer accounts and to specify access control conditions that restrict the devices that can request Kerberos tickets for user, service, and computer accounts.

If you want to use authentication policies and related options, the Active Directory domain must be operating at the Windows Server 2012 R2 or higher functional level. Authentication policies are enforced during initial Kerberos authentication and whenever a user, computer, or service requests access to a server's services. You use authentication policy silos to identify the users, computers, managed services accounts, and group managed service accounts to which you want to apply authentication settings, to fine-tune which accounts are to be protected, and to define explicitly permitted accounts.

Several object classes in the Active Directory schema were implemented to support authentication policies and silos, including

- **Authentication Policies container.** Used to store Authentication Policy objects in Active Directory Domain Services.

- **Authentication Policy object.** Used to configure Kerberos Ticket-Granting Ticket properties and specify authentication conditions based on account type.

- **Authentication Policy Silos container.** Used to store Authentication Policy Silo objects in Active Directory Domain Services.

- **Authentication Policy Silo object.** Defines the authentication policy or policies to be applied to accounts that inherit this object.

When you use Windows Server 2012 R2, a default Authentication Policies container is created under the System container in a domain and it stores the Authentication Policy objects
(APOs). You can add APOs to the Authentication Policies Container to define the various sets
of authentication settings you want to use.

You use authentication policies in conjunction with the Protected Users security group. Any
accounts that should have additional protections should be added to the Protected Users
group, restricted using an Authentication Policy object, and then optionally identified in
an authentication policy silo to fine-tune the way controls are applied. Membership in the
Protected Users group ensures that only Kerberos can be used for authentication. Otherwise, if
NTLM is used for authentication, access control conditions that you define in policies will not
be properly applied.

Authentication policies can be configured in auditing only or enforce mode. With auditing
only mode, policy restrictions are audited rather than enforced. With enforced mode, policy
restrictions are strictly enforced.

In Active Directory Administrative Center, you create and manage authentication policies using
the options on the Authentication\Authentication Policies node. To create an authentication
policy, select the Authentication\Authentication Policies node in the left pane. Next, under
Tasks, select New and then select Authentication Policy. In the Create Authentication Policy
dialog box, use the options provided to define the new policy and specify access control conditions for each type of account to which the policy will apply.

Authentication Policy silos allow you to apply authentication policies in several ways. When
you create the object, you can specify a single authentication policy to apply to all member
accounts or use a separate authentication policy for each type of security principal. As part of
creating the authentication policy silo, you also can specify explicitly permitted accounts.

In Active Directory Administrative Center, you create and manage authentication silos using
the options on the Authentication\Authentication Policy Silos node. To create an authentication policy silo, select the Authentication\Authentication Policies node in the left pane. Next,
under Tasks, select New and then select Authentication Policy Silo. Use the options in the
Create Authentication Policy Silo dialog box to create the authentication policy silo.

Creating Password Settings Objects and applying secondary settings

When you want to fine-tune the way account policy is applied, you need to create a password
settings policy and add users, inetOrgPersons, and global security groups as members of the
password settings policy. A password settings policy is simply a global security group that
applies the desired secondary PSO rather than the default PSO. Afterward, you have to create

a Password Settings Object with attributes that define the desired policy settings and then link this object to the password settings policy.

Password settings policies can have attributes for all the settings that can be defined in the Default Domain Policy except Kerberos settings, including the following settings: Account Lockout Duration, Account Lockout Threshold, Enforce Password History, Maximum Password Age, Minimum Password Age, Minimum Password Length, Passwords Must Meet Complexity Requirements, Reset Account Lockout After, and Store Passwords Using Reversible Encryption.

IMPORTANT
User objects have three settings that override the settings in a PSO: Reversible Password Encryption Required, Password Not Required, and Password Does Not Expire. You can configure these settings in the *userAccountControl* attribute of a *User* object.

Before you start, you should consider how you will organize your password settings policies. In most cases you'll want to create password settings policies that closely resemble the OUs in your domain. To do this, you create password settings policies with the same names as your OUs and then add users, inetOrgPersons, and global security groups as members of these groups as appropriate to reflect the organizational structure of your OUs.

You can create the password settings policy and define its members using either Active Directory Users And Computers or Active Directory Administrative Center, as discussed later in this chapter in the section entitled "Managing groups." By default, only members of the Administrators, Domain Admins, or Enterprise Admins group can create PSOs. You can create a PSO and set its attributes using Active Directory Administrative Center. At the Windows PowerShell prompt, you can create PSOs using the New-ADFineGrainedPasswordPolicy cmdlet.

When you work with Active Directory Administrative Center, you are connected to your logon domain by default. If you want to work with objects in a different domain, tap or click Manage and then select Add Navigation Nodes. In the Additional Navigation Nodes dialog box, you'll see available domains for the forest in the Columns list. To add a node for a listed domain, select it in the Columns list, tap or click the Add (>>) button, and then tap or click OK. To add a node for a domain that isn't listed, select Connect To Another Domain, enter the fully qualified domain name (FQDN), and then tap or click OK.

Inside OUT

Understanding PSO precedence

A user, inetOrgPerson, or global security group can have multiple PSOs linked to it. This can occur either because of membership in multiple groups that each have different PSOs applied to them or because multiple PSOs are applied directly to the object. However, only one PSO is applied as the effective policy and only the settings from that PSO affect the user, inetOrgPerson, or group. The settings from other PSOs do not apply and can't be merged in any way.

Active Directory determines the applicable PSO according to the precedence value assigned to its *msDS-PasswordSettingsPrecedence* attribute. This attribute has an integer value of 1 or greater. A lower value for the precedence attribute indicates that the PSO has a higher priority than other PSOs. For example, suppose an object has three PSOs linked to it. One PSO has a precedence value of 5, one PSO has a precedence value of 8, and the other PSO has a precedence value of 12. In this case, the PSO that has the precedence value of 5 has the highest priority and is the one applied to the object.

If multiple PSOs are linked to a user or group, the PSO that is applied is determined as follows:

1. A PSO that is linked directly to the user object is applied. If more than one PSO is linked directly to the user object, the PSO with the lowest precedence value is applied.

2. If no PSO is linked directly to the user object, all PSOs that are applicable to the user, based on the user's global group memberships, are compared and the PSO with the lowest precedence value is applied.

3. If no PSO is linked directly or indirectly to the user object, the Default Domain Policy is applied.

Microsoft recommends that you assign each PSO in the domain a unique precedence value. However, you can create multiple PSOs with the same precedence value. If multiple PSOs have the same precedence value, the PSO with the lowest globally unique identifier (GUID) is applied. Typically, this means that Active Directory will apply the PSO with the earliest creation date.

The user object has three attributes that override the settings that are present in the applicable PSO: Reversible Password Encryption Required, Password Not Required, and Password Does Not Expire. You can set these attributes in the *userAccountControl* attribute of the user object in Active Directory Users And Computers or Active Directory Administrative Center.

CHAPTER 16

To create a password settings policy and define its attributes, follow these steps:

1. In the left pane of Active Directory Administrative Center, you can use the List view or Tree view. Select the Tree view.

2. In the Tree view, expand the System container for the domain you want to work with and then select the Password Settings Container to view any previously created password settings policies in the main pane.

3. Under Tasks, select New and then select Password Settings. This opens the Create Password Settings dialog box, shown in Figure 16-2.

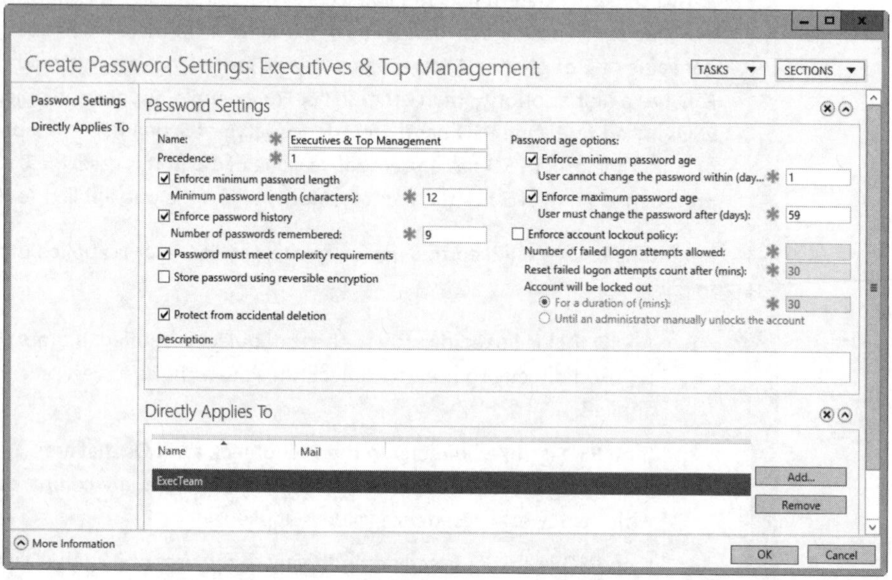

Figure 16-2 Specify a name for the password settings policy and then configure its settings.

4. In the Name box, type a descriptive name for the password settings policy.

5. In the Precedence box, type the precedence order for the policy. When multiple password settings policies apply to a user, the precedence of the policy determines which settings are applied. A policy with a precedence of 1 always has precedence over a policy with a lower precedence.

6. As appropriate, use the following options to define the policy settings:

    -   **Enforce Minimum Password Length.** Sets the minimum password length for user accounts. The maximum value is 14. If you enter zero (0), a password is not required.

- **Enforce Password History.** Sets the password history length. The maximum value is 24. If you enter zero (0), a password history is not kept.

- **Password Must Meet Complexity Requirements.** Sets the password complexity status for passwords as either false or true. In most cases you'll want to turn on this feature to ensure that users enter complex passwords.

- **Store Password Using Reversible Encryption.** Sets the reversible encryption status for passwords as either true or false. In most cases you'll want to turn off this feature to ensure that passwords are stored with strong encryption.

- **Enforce Minimum Password Age.** Sets the minimum password age in days. The maximum value is 998 days. If you enter zero (0), a password can be changed immediately.

- **Enforce Maximum Password Age.** Sets the maximum password age in days. The maximum value is 999 days. If you enter zero (0), passwords never expire.

7. If you also want to enforce lockout policy, select Enforce Account Lockout Policy and then use the following options to configure lockout settings:

   - **Number Of Failed Logon Attempts Allowed.** Specifies how many failed attempts at logon are allowed before a user is locked out. The maximum value is 999. If you enter zero (0), accounts will never be locked.

   - **Reset Failed Logon Attempts Count After.** Specifies the number of minutes after a logon failure before the logon counter is reset. The valid range is from 1 to 99,999 minutes.

   - **Account Will Be Locked Out.** Specifies how long a user will be locked out before the account is unlocked automatically. You can set a specific duration with a valid range from 1 to 99,999 minutes, or you can specify that the account will be locked out until an administrator unlocks it.

8. Under Directly Applies To, click Add. This displays the Select Users Or Groups dialog box, which you can use to specify an account to which this password settings policy will apply. Repeat this step to apply the policy to multiple accounts.

9. Tap or click OK.

NOTE

You can link a PSO to other types of groups in addition to global security groups. However, when the Resultant Set of Policy (RSoP) is determined for a user or group, only PSOs that are linked to global security groups, user objects, and inetOrgPerson objects are considered. PSOs that are linked to distribution groups or other types of security groups are ignored.

Understanding user account capabilities, privileges, and rights

All user accounts have specific capabilities, privileges, and rights. When you create a user account, you can grant the user specific capabilities by making the user a member of one or more groups. This gives the user the capabilities of these groups. You then assign additional capabilities by making a user a member of the appropriate groups or withdraw capabilities by removing a user from a group.

Some capabilities of accounts are built in. The built-in capabilities of accounts are assigned to groups and include the group's automatic capabilities. Although built-in capabilities are predefined and unchangeable, they can be granted to users by making the users members of the appropriate group or delegated by specifically granting the capability—for example, the ability to create, delete, and manage user accounts. This capability is assigned to administrators and account operators. Thus, if a user is a member of the Administrators group, the user can create, delete, and manage user accounts.

Other capabilities of accounts—such as permissions, privileges, and logon rights—can be assigned. The access permissions for accounts define the operations that can be performed on network resources. For example, permissions control whether a user can access a particular shared folder. The privileges of an account grant permissions to perform specific tasks, such as the ability to change the system time. The logon rights of an account grant logon permissions, such as the ability to log on locally to a server.

An important part of an administrator's job is being able to determine and set permissions, privileges, and logon rights as necessary. Although you can't change a group's built-in capabilities, you can change a group's default privileges and logon rights. For example, you could revoke network access to a computer by removing a group's right to access the computer from the network.

Assigning user rights

The most efficient way to assign a user right is to make the user a member of a group that already has that right. Sometimes, however, you might want a user to have a particular right but not have all the other rights of the group. One way to resolve this problem is to give the user the right directly. Another way to resolve this is to create a special group for users that need the right. This is the approach used with the Remote Desktop Users group, which Microsoft created to grant the Allow Logon Through Remote Desktop Services right to groups of users.

You assign user rights through the Local Policies node of Group Policy. You can set local policies on a per-computer basis using a computer's local security policy or on a domain or OU
basis through an existing Group Policy for the related domain or OU. When you do this, the
local policies apply to all accounts in the domain or OU.

Assigning user rights for a domain or OU

You can assign user rights for a domain or OU by completing the following steps:

1. In Group Policy Management Console, select the policy you want to work with and then
   press and hold or right-click Edit. Access the User Rights Assignment node by working
   your way down the console tree. Expand Computer Configuration, Windows Settings,
   Security Settings, Local Policies, and User Rights Assignment, as shown in Figure 16-3.

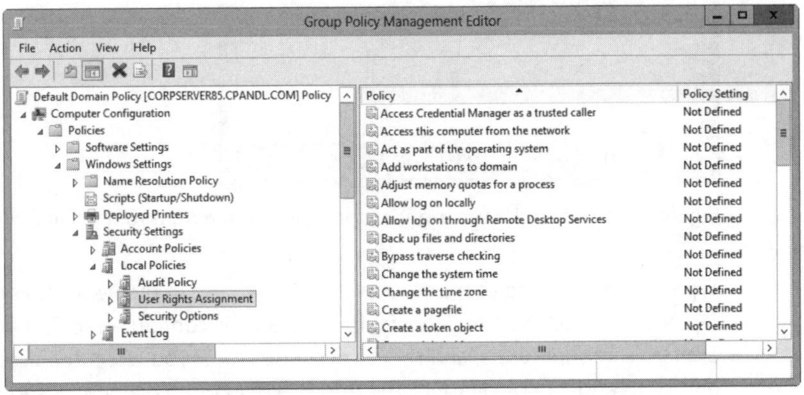

Figure 16-3 Configure user rights in Group Policy.

2. To configure a user right, double-tap or double-click a user right or press and hold
   or right-click it and select Properties. This opens a Properties dialog box, as shown in
   Figure 16-4. If the policy isn't defined, select Define These Policy Settings. To apply the
   right to a user or group, tap or click Add User Or Group. Then, in the Add User Or Group
   dialog box, tap or click Browse. This opens the Select Users, Computers, Or Groups
   dialog box.

CHAPTER 16

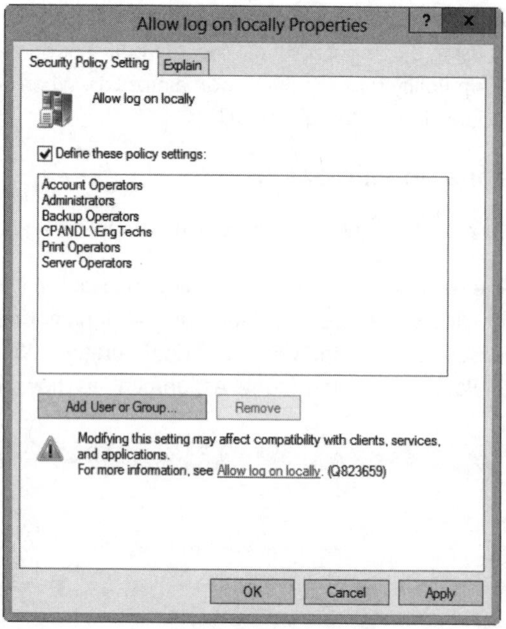

Figure 16-4 Define the user right and then assign the right to users and groups.

3. Type the name of the user or group you want to use in the field provided and then tap or click Check Names. By default, the search is configured to find built-in security principals, groups, users, and service accounts. After you select the account names or groups to add, tap or click OK. The Add User Or Group dialog box should now show the selected accounts. Tap or click OK again.

4. The Properties dialog box is updated to reflect your selections. If you made a mistake, select a name and remove it by tapping or clicking Remove. When you're finished granting the right to users and groups, tap or click OK.

Assigning user rights on a specific computer

User rights can also be applied to a specific computer. However, remember that domain and OU policy take precedence over local policy. This means that any settings in these policies will override settings you make on a local computer.

You can apply user rights locally by completing the following steps:

1. Start local security policy by choosing the related option from the Tools menu in Server Manager. All computers, even domain controllers, have local security policy. Settings available in the Local Security Policy console are a subset of the computer's local policy.

2. Under Security Settings, expand Local Policies and then select User Rights Assignment.

3. Double-tap or double-click the user right you want to modify. The Properties dialog box shows current users and groups that have been given the user right.

4. You can apply the user right to additional users and groups by tapping or clicking Add User Or Group. This opens the Select Users, Computers, Or Groups dialog box, which you can use to add users and groups.

5. Tap or click OK twice to close the open dialog boxes.

NOTE

If the options in the Properties dialog box are dimmed, it means the policy has been set at a higher level and can't be overridden locally.

Creating and configuring domain user accounts

As a member of the Administrators, Account Operators, Enterprise Admins, or Domain Admins group, you can use Active Directory Users And Computers or Active Directory Administrative Center to create user accounts. The process is similar regardless of which tool you use.

Follow these steps to create a user account in Active Directory Users And Computers:

1. By default, you are connected to your logon domain. If you want to create accounts in a different domain, press and hold or right-click the Active Directory Users And Computers node in the console tree and then select Change Domain. In the Change Domain dialog box, type the name of the domain to which you want to connect and then tap or click OK. Alternatively, you can tap or click Browse to find the domain to which you want to connect in the Browse For Domain dialog box.

2. You can now create the user account. Press and hold or right-click the container in which you want to create the user, point to New, and then select User. This will start the New Object–User Wizard.

    When you create a new user, you're prompted for the first name, initials, last name, full name, and logon name, as shown in Figure 16-5. The pre–Windows 2000 logon name then appears automatically. This logon name is used with early releases of Windows.

CHAPTER 16

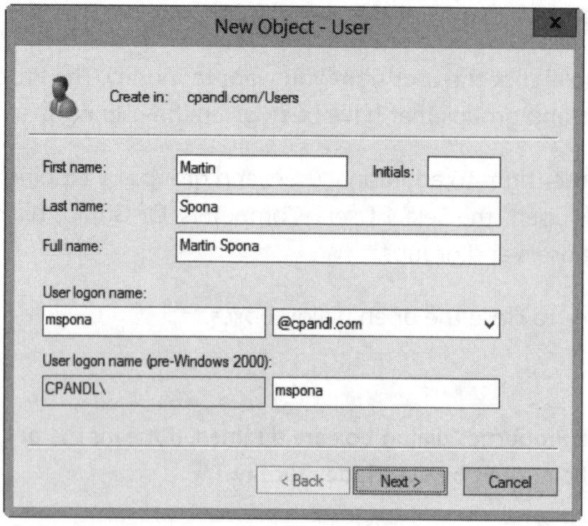

Figure 16-5 Create a user account.

3. When you tap or click Next, you can set the user's password and account options. The password must meet the complexity requirements set in Group Policy. As shown in Figure 16-6, these options are as follows: User Must Change Password At Next Logon, User Cannot Change Password, Password Never Expires, and Account Is Disabled.

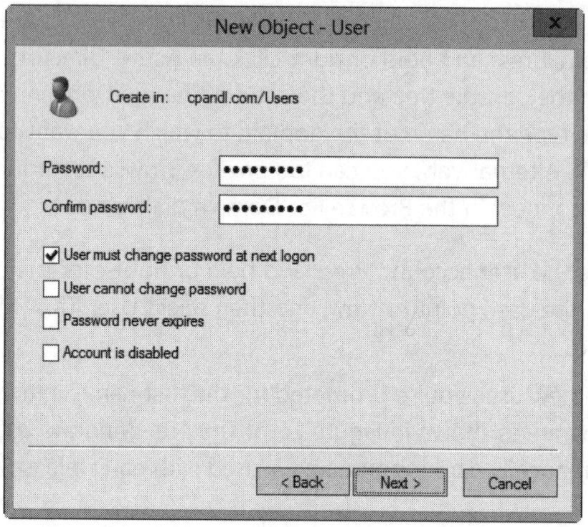

Figure 16-6 Set the user's password and account options.

4. Tap or click Next and then tap or click Finish. If you use a password that doesn't meet the complexity requirements of Group Policy, you'll see an error and you'll have to tap or click Back to change the user's password before you can continue.

Inside OUT

Creating user accounts using Windows PowerShell

With Windows PowerShell, you can create user accounts using the New-ADUser cmdlet and set account properties using the Set-ADUser, Set-ADAccountPassword, Set-ADAccountControl, and Enable-ADAccount cmdlets. With New-ADUser, use *–DisplayName* to set the display name, *–GivenName* to set the first name, *–Initials* to set the middle initial, *–Surname* to set the last name, and *–Name* to set the full name. You also need to specify the user principal name (UPN), whether the account should be enabled, and the account password. You do this using the *–UserPrincipalName*, *–Enabled*, and *–AccountPassword* parameters, respectively. Here is an example:

```
New-ADUser –DisplayName "William R. Stanek" –GivenName "William" –Initials "R"
–Name "William R. Stanek" –SamAccountName "WilliamS" -Enabled $true
-AccountPassword (ConvertTo-SecureString "ChangePasswordNow!" –AsPlainText
-force) -PassThru
```

To bulk create user accounts, you can import the account details from a text file containing a list of column headings on the first line followed by the details of each account you want to create on separate lines, as shown in this example:

```
DisplayName,GivenName,FullName,SamName
Peter Brehm,Peter,Peter Brehm,peterb
Oliver Kiel,Oliver,Oliver Kiel,oliverk
```

If you saved this file with the name *newusers.csv* in the c:\scripts\data folder, you could then use the following script to bulk create accounts:

```
$NewUsers = import-csv c:\scripts\data\newusers.csv
ForEach ($User in $NewUsers) { New-ADUser –DisplayName $User.FullName
-GivenName $User.GivenName –Name $User.FullName –SamAccountName
$User.SamName-Enabled $true -ChangePasswordAtLogon $true -AccountPassword
(ConvertTo-SecureString "ChangePasswordNow!" -AsPlainText -force) -PassThru }
```

Or you could use the file to create the accounts directly from the prompt by entering the following command all on one line:

```
import-csv c:\scripts\data\newusers.csv | ForEach { New-ADUser
-DisplayName $_.FullName –GivenName $_.GivenName –Name $_.FullName
-SamAccountName $_.SamName -Enabled $true -ChangePasswordAtLogon $true
-AccountPassword
(ConvertTo-SecureString "ChangePasswordNow!" -AsPlainText -force) -PassThru }
```

Obtaining effective access

In Active Directory, user accounts are defined as objects—as are group and computer accounts. This means that user accounts have security descriptors that list the users and groups that are granted access. Security descriptors also define ownership of the object and specify the permissions that those users and groups have been assigned with respect to the object.

Individual entries in the security descriptor are referred to as *access control entries (ACEs)*. Active Directory objects can inherit ACEs from their parent objects. This means that permissions for a parent object can be applied to a child object. For example, all members of the Account Operators group inherit permissions granted to this group.

Because of inheritance, sometimes it isn't clear whether a particular user, group, or computer has permission to work with another object in Active Directory. This is where the Effective Access tool comes in handy. You use this tool to examine the permissions that a user, group, or computer has with respect to another object. For example, if you want to determine what permissions, if any, a user who has received delegated control has over another user or group, you can use Effective Access to do that.

IMPORTANT

The Effective Access tool is available in Active Directory Users And Computers—but only if you are in the Advanced Features view. Choose Advanced Features from the View menu if necessary.

In Active Directory Users And Computers or Active Directory Administrative Center, double-tap or double-click the user, group, or computer for which you are trying to determine the effective permissions of another user or group. If you are working with Active Directory Administrative Center, open the Extensions panel.

Next, tap or click the Advanced button in the Security tab to open the Advanced Security Settings dialog box. Tap or click the Effective Access tab. Next, tap or click Select A User, type the name of the user or group for which you want to see the effective permissions with regard to the previously selected object, and then tap or click OK.

When you tap or click View Effective Access, the effective permissions for the selected user or group in relation to the previously selected object appear, as shown in Figure 16-7. The Effective Access column has check marks showing which permissions are in effect. If there are no effective permissions, none of the permissions' check boxes are selected.

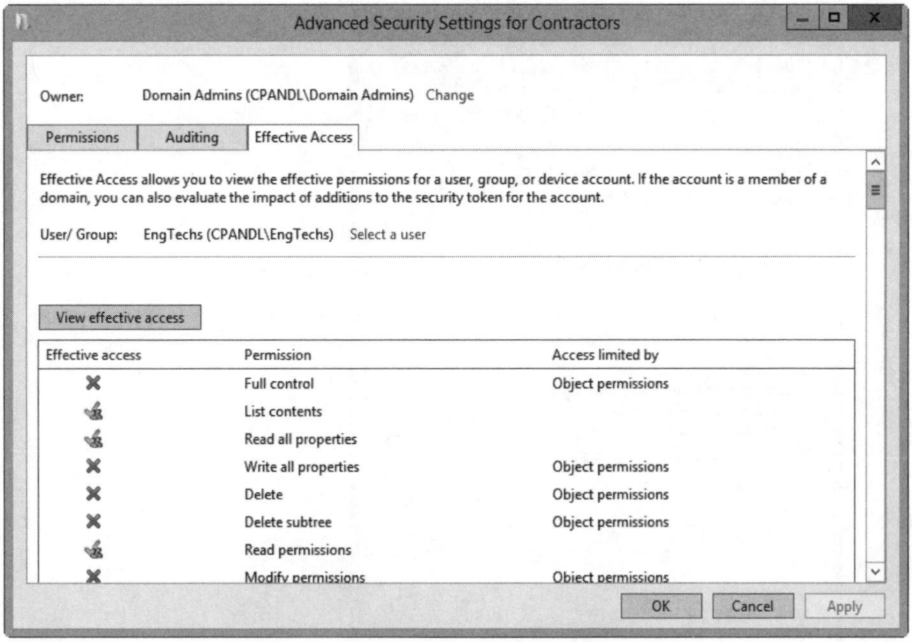

Figure 16-7 Obtain effective access for a user, group, or computer.

Configuring account options

Every user account created in Active Directory has account options that control logon hours, the computers to which a user can log on, account expiration, and so on. To manage these settings for a user, double-tap or double-click the user account in Active Directory Users And Computers or Active Directory Administrative Center. Next, click the Account tab or Account panel as appropriate.

Figure 16-8 shows an account Properties dialog box for Active Directory Users And Computers. You'll find similar options for the Properties dialog box that opens when you are working with Active Directory Administrative Center.

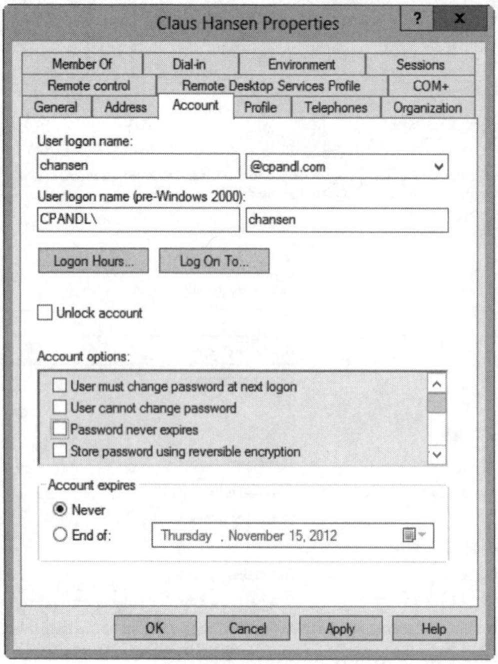

Figure 16-8 The user account Properties dialog box displays logon settings.

Below the general account name fields, the available options are divided into three main areas. The first area that you can configure controls two computer options: Logon Hours and Log On To.

- **Setting Logon Hours.** To configure when a user can log on to the domain, tap or click Logon Hours. By default, users can log on 24 hours a day, seven days a week. To deny a user a specific day or time, select the area you want to restrict the user from logging on to and then select the Logon Denied option, as shown in Figure 16-9. For example, this option can be used to restrict shift workers to certain hours or to restrict working days to weekdays.

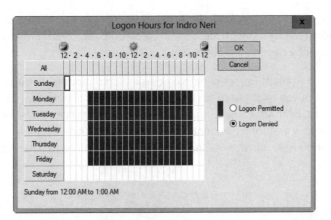

Figure 16-9 Configure logon hours for a specific user.

- **Configuring Logon Computer.** When you tap or click Log On To, you can restrict which computers a user can log on from. The default setting allows users to log on from all computers. To restrict which computers a user can log on from, choose The Following Computers, as shown in Figure 16-10. Type a host name or a fully qualified domain name in the Computer Name field, such as **Workstation18** or **Workstation .cpandl.com**. Tap or click Add. Repeat this procedure to set other logon computers.

NOTE

Earlier releases of Windows required the NetBIOS protocol to restrict which computers a user can log on from. This requirement has been phased out.

Figure 16-10 Specify which computers the user can log on to.

CHAPTER 16

Below the Logon Hours and Log On To buttons is the Unlock Account check box. If the user has become locked out by trying to log on with the wrong password too many times, you can unlock the account by clearing this check box.

Finally, you use the Account Expires panel to set expiration options for the account. The default is Never, but you might need to configure this setting for some users. For example, temporary workers, contract workers, summer help, or consultants might be working on your network for only a specified amount of time. If you know how long they need access to resources in your domain, you can use the Account Expires settings to automate the disabling of their accounts.

Disabling accounts

In most network environments, administrators to whom the task of managing users has been delegated will not be able to remove users immediately upon their leaving the organization, which creates a window of vulnerability. Yet when accounts have scheduled end points, you can schedule them to be disabled on a specific date. So it's a good idea to schedule accounts to be disabled if you are sure that the user will no longer be working. If the account is automatically disabled but the user needs access, the user will let you know. But if the account is not disabled automatically, it can present a big security problem. To handle this on an enterprise level, many businesses are reviewing (or implementing) provisioning applications to automate the process of taking away access to company resources when employees leave the company.

Configuring profile options

User accounts also can have profiles, logon scripts, and home directories associated with them. To configure these options, double-tap or double-click a user account in Active Directory Users And Computers or Active Directory Administrative Center. Next, click the Profile tab or the Profile panel as appropriate.

Figure 16-11 shows the Profile tab in the Properties dialog box that opens when you are working with Active Directory Users And Computers. Similar options are available on the Profile panel of the Properties dialog box that opens when you are working with Active Directory Administrative Center.

As the figure shows, you can set the following options in the Profile tab:

- **Profile Path.** Sets the location of the roaming user profile for the user, such as \\FileServer32\profiles\%UserName%. Profiles provide the environment settings for users. Each time a user logs on to a computer, that user's profile is used to determine desktop and Control Panel settings, the availability of menu options and applications, and so on.

- **Logon Script.** As the name implies, logon scripts are accessed when users log on to their accounts. Logon scripts set commands that should be executed each time a user logs on. One user or many users can use a single logon script, and, as the administrator, you control which users run which scripts. You can specify a logon script to use by typing the path to the logon script in the Logon Script field. Be sure to set the full path to the logon script, such as **\\FileServer81\LogonScripts\enteam.vbs**.

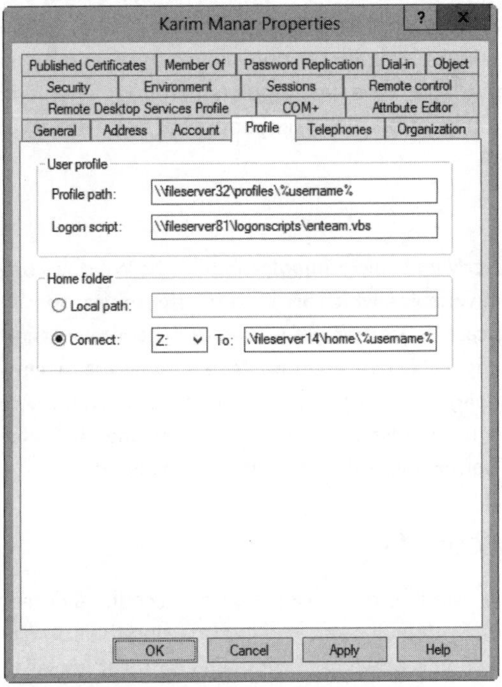

Figure 16-11 Configure paths for User Profile settings.

NOTE

You shouldn't use scripts to set environment variables. Environment settings used by scripts aren't maintained for subsequent user processes.

- **Home Folder.** A home folder can be assigned to each user account. Users can store their personal files in and retrieve them from this directory. Many applications use the home folder as the default for File Open and Save As operations, helping users find their resources easily. Home directories can be located on a user's local hard disk drive or on a shared network drive. If you don't assign a home folder, Windows Server uses a default local home folder.

To specify a home folder, do either of the following:

- Specify a local home folder by tapping or clicking the Local Path option button and then typing the path to the home folder on the user's computer. Here's an example: **C:\Home\%UserName%**.

- Specify a network home folder by selecting the Connect option button in the Home Folder section and then selecting a drive letter for the home folder. For consistency, you should use the same drive letter for all users. Also, be sure to select a drive letter that won't conflict with any currently configured physical or mapped drives. To avoid problems, you might want to use Z as the drive letter. After you select the drive letter, type the complete path to the home folder, using the Universal Naming Convention (UNC) notation, such as **\\FileServer14 \Home\%UserName%**.

NOTE

%UserName% refers to the *UserName* environment variable. The Windows operating system has many environment variables, which are used to refer to user-specific and system-specific values. In this case, %UserName% is used to dynamically assign the user name as appropriate for the applicable user account. Keep in mind that when a user's account and user name are changed, it can create a problem that prevents access to the user's home folder. To resolve this problem, you just need to rename the folder, and the good news is that the folder permissions will not need to be changed.

Troubleshooting user accounts

When a user logs on to the network using his or her domain user account, a domain control-ler validates the account credentials. By default, users can log on using their domain user accounts even if the network connection is down or no domain controller is available to authenticate the user's logon. However, the user must have previously logged on to the com-puter and have valid, cached credentials. If the user has no cached credentials on the com-puter and the network connection is down or no domain controller is available, the user will not be able to log on to the domain.

Each member computer in a domain can cache up to 10 credentials by default. Authentication also can fail if the system time on the member computer deviates from the logon domain controller's system time more than is allowed in the Kerberos Policy: Maximum Tolerance For Computer Clock Synchronization setting. The default tolerance is five minutes for member computers.

Users' accounts can be disabled by administrators or locked out due to Account Lockout Policy. When a user tries to log on using an account that is disabled or locked out, the user sees a prompt that says that the user can't log on because that user's account is disabled or locked out. The prompt also tells the user to contact an administrator.

Active Directory Users And Computers shows disabled accounts with a red warning icon next to the account name. To enable a disabled account, press and hold or right-click the account in Active Directory Users And Computers and then select Enable Account. You can search the entire domain for users with disabled accounts by typing **dsquery user –disabled** at a command prompt. To enable a disabled account from the command line, type **dsmod user UserDN –disabled no**.

When a user account has been locked out by the Account Lockout Policy, the account can't be used for logging on until the lockout duration has elapsed or an administrator resets the account. If the account lockout duration is indefinite, the only way to unlock the account is to have an administrator reset it. In Active Directory Users And Computers, you can unlock an account by pressing and holding or right-clicking the locked account and then selecting Properties. In the Account tab of the Properties dialog box, select the Unlock Account check box and then tap or click OK.

Additionally, when account logon failure auditing is enabled, logon failure is recorded in the security log on the logon domain controller. Auditing policies for a site, domain, or OU GPO are stored under Computer Configuration\Windows Settings\Security Settings\Local Policies \Audit Policy.

Maintaining user accounts

User accounts are easy to maintain after they've been configured. Most of the maintenance tasks you need to perform involve user profiles and group membership, which are covered in separate sections of this chapter. Other than these areas, you might need to perform the following tasks:

- Delete user accounts

- Disable, enable, or unlock user accounts

- Move user accounts

- Rename user accounts

- Reset a user's domain password

CHAPTER 16

- Set logon scripts and home folders

- Create a local user account password backup

Each of these tasks is examined in the sections that follow.

Deleting user accounts

Each user account created in the domain has a unique security identifier (SID), and that SID is never reused. If you delete an account, you can't create an account with the same name and regain all the permissions and settings of the previously deleted account. The SID for the new account will be different from the old one, and you will have to redefine all the necessary permissions and settings. Because of this, you should delete accounts only when you know they are not going to be used again. If you are unsure, disable the account rather than delete it.

To delete an account, select the account in either Active Directory Users And Computers or Active Directory Administrative Center and then press Delete. When prompted to confirm the deletion, tap or click Yes. The account is permanently deleted. Deleting a user account doesn't delete a user's on-disk data. It only deletes the user account from Active Directory. This means that the user's profile and other personal data will still be available on disk until you manually delete it.

CAUTION

The permissions on users are internally characterized within Active Directory by unique SIDs that are allocated when the user is created. If you delete a user account and then re-create it, it will have a new SID and thus new permissions.

Disabling and enabling user accounts

If you need to deactivate a user account temporarily so that it can't be used for logon or authentication, you can do this by disabling the account. Although disabling an account makes it unusable, you can later enable the account so that it can be used again. To disable an account in Active Directory Users And Computers, press and hold or right-click the account and then select Disable Account. To disable an account in Active Directory Administrative Center, press and hold or right-click the account and then select Disable.

Next, when you are notified by a prompt that the account has been disabled, tap or click OK. A circle with a down arrow is added to the account's icon to show that it is disabled. If you later need to enable the account, you can do so by pressing and holding or right-clicking the account and then selecting either Enable Account or Enable, depending on which management tool you are using.

Moving user accounts

When a user changes departments, you might need to move the user account to a new container in Active Directory Users And Computers or Active Directory Administrative Center. To move a user account, press and hold or right-click the account and then select Move. The Move dialog box appears, which you can use to select the container to which you want to move the user account. Alternatively, you can drag the user account into a new container. You can also select multiple users to move by using Windows keyboard shortcuts, such as Ctrl, and then selecting multiple users or by using Shift and selecting the first and last users.

Renaming user accounts

Active Directory tracks objects by their SID. This allows you to safely rename user, computer, and group accounts without worrying about having to change access permissions as well. That said, the process of renaming a user account is not as easy as the process of renaming other types of accounts. The reason is that users have several name components that are all related to a user's last name, including a full name, display name, and user logon name. So when a person's last name changes as the result of a marriage, adoption, or divorce, you need to update not only the user's account name in Active Directory but also the rest of the related name components.

To simplify the process of renaming user accounts, Active Directory Users And Computers provides the Rename User dialog box (shown in Figure 16-12), which you can use to rename a user's account and all the related name components. Active Directory Administrative Center doesn't have this simple renaming tool.

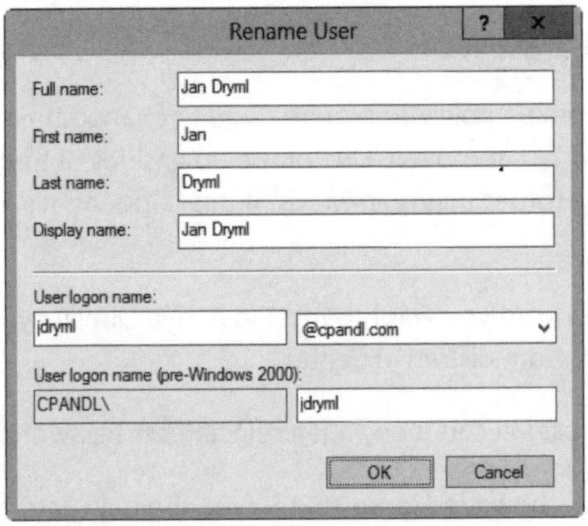

Figure 16-12 Rename a user account.

CHAPTER 16

With the addition of the Rename User dialog box, the process for renaming user accounts is as follows:

1. Find the user account that you want to rename in Active Directory Users And Computers.

2. Press and hold or right-click the user account and then select Rename. Active Directory Users And Computers highlights the account name for editing. Press the Backspace or Delete key to erase the existing name and then press Enter to open the Rename User dialog box.

3. Make the necessary changes to the user's name information and then tap or click OK. If the user is logged on, you'll see a warning prompt telling you that the user should log off and then log back on using the new account logon name.

4. The account is renamed, and the SID for access permissions remains the same. You might still need to modify other data for the user in the account's Properties dialog box, including the following:

    - **User Profile Path.** As necessary, change the Profile Path information in the Profile tab and then rename the corresponding directory on disk.

    - **Logon Script Name.** If you use individual logon scripts for each user, change the Logon Script Name value in the Profile tab and then rename the logon script on disk.

    - **Home Folder.** As necessary, change the home folder path in the Profile tab and then rename the corresponding directory on disk.

Resetting a user's domain password

One of the good things about using domain policy to require users to change their passwords is that the overall security of the network is improved. One of the downsides of frequent password changes is that users occasionally forget their passwords. If this happens, it's easy to fix it by doing the following:

1. Find the user account whose password you want to reset in Active Directory Users And Computers or in Active Directory Administrative Center.

2. Press and hold or right-click the user account and then select Reset Password.

3. In the Reset Password dialog box, shown in Figure 16-13, type the new password and then confirm it for the user by typing it again.

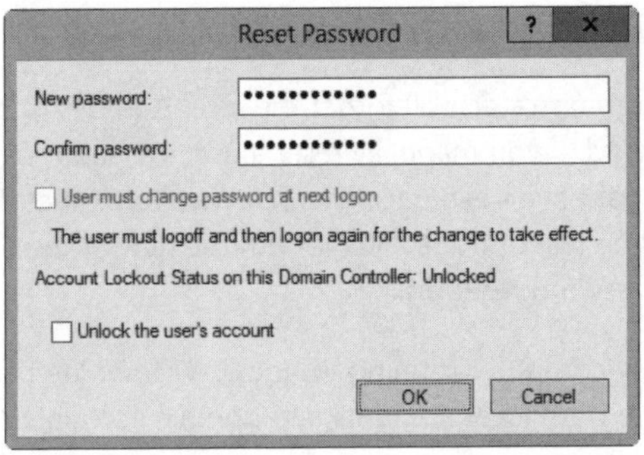

Figure 16-13 Configure the new password for the selected user.

4. If the account status is listed as locked, select the Unlock The User's Account check box.

5. Tap or click OK.

NOTE

The password change is immediately replicated to the primary domain controller (PDC) emulator, as discussed in the section entitled "Using, locating, and transferring the PDC emulator role" in Chapter 11. This makes the password available for the user to log on anywhere in the domain.

Unlocking user accounts

Whenever users violate Group Policy—such as when they fail to change their passwords before they expire or exceed the limit for bad logon attempts—Active Directory locks their accounts. After an account is locked, the user can no longer log on. Because accounts also can be locked because someone is trying to break into an account, you shouldn't automatically unlock accounts. Instead, either wait until the user asks you to unlock the account or go speak to the user when you notice that the user's account has been locked.

You can unlock accounts by completing the following steps:

1. In Active Directory Users And Computers, press and hold or right-click the locked account and then select Properties.

2. In the Properties dialog box, click the Account tab.

3. Clear the Unlock Account check box and then tap or click OK.

This option is not available in Active Directory Administrative Center.

Creating a user account password backup

Sometimes a user (or even an administrator) will forget the local Administrator's password or another user's account password. If you manually reset a user's account password and the user has encrypted email, files that have been encrypted, or passwords that the user uses for Internet accounts, that data will be lost or not available with the new or reset password. To prevent this, you can create a password reset disk.

You can make a reset disk for any computer running Windows Vista or later, except for domain controllers. Reset disks can be for both local accounts and domain accounts. When creating a reset disk, be careful of the following:

- You are not allowed to simultaneously create a reset disk and change your password from the Logon screen.

- You do not have to create a new reset disk each time you change a user's password; you need to create the reset disk only once for an account.

- Users should create their own reset disks for each account they use.

Follow these steps to make a password reset disk:

1. Press Ctrl+Alt+Del and then tap or click the Change A Password option.

2. Tap or click Create A Password Reset Disk to start the Forgotten Password Wizard.

3. In the Forgotten Password Wizard, read the introductory message. Insert the USB flash drive you want to use and then tap or click Next.

4. Select the USB flash drive you want to use in the drive list. Tap or click Next.

5. Type the current password for the account in the text box provided and then tap or click Next.

6. After the wizard creates the password reset disk, remove the disk and then tap or click Finish.

Store the USB flash drive in a secure place because now anyone can use it to gain access to the account. If a user is unable to log in because the user forgot the password, you can use the password reset disk to create a new password and log in to the account using this password by following these steps:

1. On the Log On screen, tap or click the arrow button without entering a password. The Reset Password option should be displayed. If the user has already entered the wrong password, the Reset Password option might already be displayed.

2. Insert the USB flash device containing the password recovery file and then tap or click Reset Password to start the Reset Password Wizard.

3. In the Reset Password Wizard, read the introductory message and then tap or click Next.

4. Insert the disk into drive A or insert the USB flash key containing the password recovery file and then tap or click Next.

5. Select the device you want to use in the drive list and then tap or click Next.

6. On the Reset The User Account Password page, type and confirm a new password for the user.

7. Type a password hint and then tap or click Next. Tap or click Finish.

Inside OUT

How the password reset disk works

The reset disk process generates a public/private key pair. No passwords are stored on the reset disk. The reset disk contains the private key, and the public key encrypts the account password. When a user forgets the account password, the restore process uses the private key on the reset disk to decrypt the current password and create a new one that is encrypted with the same key. Data is not lost because the same encryption is used for any other encrypted data.

Managing groups

Active Directory groups are objects that can hold users, contacts, computers, or other groups. When you want to manage users, computers, and other resources—such as files, directories, printers, network shares, and email distribution lists—using groups can decrease administration time and improve network performance.

Understanding groups

Types of groups and the group scope are essential topics in planning and managing an efficient network. Planning an environment that uses Active Directory and groups is critical—failing to plan or taking shortcuts can negatively affect network traffic and create more administrative work in the long run.

CHAPTER 16

Two types of groups are used in Windows Server: security groups and distribution groups.

- Security groups are used to control access to resources. This is the kind of group you will probably use most often, and it might already be familiar to you. Security groups are listed in discretionary access control lists (DACLs). DACLs are part of an object's descriptor and are used to define permissions on objects and resources.

- Distribution groups are used for unsecured email lists and can include contacts who are not domain users. Distribution lists do not use the functionality of the DACL permissions that security groups do. Distribution groups are not security-enabled, but they can be used by email servers such as Microsoft Exchange Server.

Windows Server uses three group scopes: domain local, global, and universal. The group scope determines the types of objects that can be included as members of a group and the permissions and rights those objects can be granted. In practice, you will almost always use security groups rather than distribution groups because they include distribution group functionality and are the only types of groups that have DACLs.

Domain Local Groups Consider using domain local groups first when you are giving groups or users access to local domain resources. For instance, if you have a domain named north-wind.com and you want users or groups in that local domain to access a shared folder in the northwind.com local domain, you could create a domain local group called SalesPersons, insert into the SalesPersons group the users and global groups to whom you want to give access to the shared folder, and then assign the SalesPersons group permissions on the resource.

Access policies for domain local groups are not stored in Active Directory. This means that they do not get replicated to the global catalog and thus queries performed on the global catalog will not return results from domain local groups. This is because domain local groups can't be determined across domains.

Global Groups Use global groups to give users or groups access to resources according to how they have been organized. For instance, users from the Marketing and Development departments could be put in separate global groups to simplify the administration of their need to access resources such as printers and network shares. Global groups can be nested to grant access to any domain in the forest.

Universal Groups Universal groups have very few fundamental restrictions. Universal groups can be a tempting shortcut for administrators to use because they can be used across domains in the forest. Memberships in universal groups can be drawn from any domain, and permissions can be set within any domain. However, using universal groups as your main method of grouping users, groups, and computers has a significant caveat.

Universal groups are stored in the global catalog, and whenever changes are made to a universal group the changed properties must be replicated to other domain controllers configured as global catalog servers. The replication of individual property changes rather than entire objects is an improvement for Windows Server that should allow wider use of universal groups without causing network bottlenecks or slowed performance during authentication and global catalog changes.

Creating a group

You can create groups in the Users container or in a new OU that you created in the domain. Use either Active Directory Users And Computers or Active Directory Administrative Center to create groups. Whichever tool you use, the process is similar.

To create a group, start Active Directory Users And Computers. Press and hold or right-click the Users container or the OU into which you want to place the group, point to New, and then select Group. This displays the New Object–Group dialog box shown in Figure 16-14. Type a group name and then choose an option in both the Group Scope and Group Type areas. Tap or click OK to create the group.

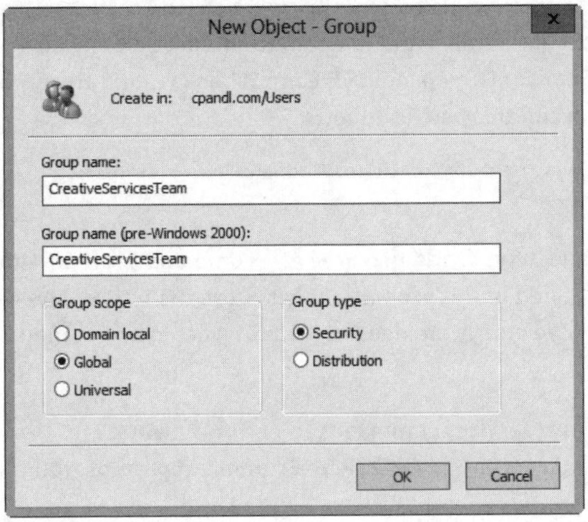

Figure 16-14 Create a group.

Windows Server has three group scopes and two group types from which you can select. This allows you to create six combinations of groups. To create new groups, you must be a member of the Account Operators group, the Domain Admins group, or the Enterprise Admins group.

NOTE

The built-in accounts for Active Directory in Windows Server are located in two places. Built-in domain local groups—such as Administrators, Account Operators, and Backup Operators—are located in the Builtin container. Built-in global groups—such as Domain Admins—are located in the Users container, as are built-in universal groups such as Enterprise Admins and Schema Admins.

Inside OUT

Creating group accounts at the command line

At the command line, you can create groups using DSADD. For groups, AD path strings describe the group's location in the directory, from the group name to the actual containers in which it is stored. You specify that the group is a security group by using **–secgrp yes**. You specify that the group is a distribution group by using **–secgrp no**. You specify the scope of the group by using **–scope u** for universal, **–scope g** for global, and **–scope l** for domain local.

For example, if you want to create a global security group called SeattleServices in the Services OU for the cpandl.com domain, the full path to this group object is CN=SeattleServices,OU=Services,DC=cpandl,DC=com. When creating the group object using DSADD, you must specify this path as follows:

```
dsadd group "CN=SeattleServices,OU=Services,DC=cpandl,DC=com" –secgrp yes
–scope g
```

For the full syntax and usage, type **dsadd group /?** at a command prompt. Although quotation marks aren't required in this example, I always use them to ensure that I don't forget them when they actually are needed, such as when name components contain spaces.

You can also use the directory services commands to perform many group-management tasks. Using DSGET GROUP at a command prompt, you can

- Determine whether a group is a security group by typing **dsget group GroupDN –secgrp**.

- Determine group scope by typing **dsget group GroupDN –scope**.

- Determine the members of a group by typing **dsget group GroupDN –members**, where *GroupDN* is the distinguished name of the group.

- Determine the groups of which a group is a member by typing **dsget group GroupDN –memberof**. You can add the **–expand** option to display the recursively expanded list of groups of which a group is a member.

Using DSMOD GROUP at a command prompt, you can

- Change group scope using **dsmod group GroupDN –scope u** for universal, **–scope g** for global, and **–scope l** for domain local.

- Add members by typing **dsmod group GroupDN –addmbr MemberDN**, where *GroupDN* is the distinguished name of the group and *MemberDN* is the distinguished name of the account or group you want to add to the designated group.

- Remove members by typing **dsmod group GroupDN –rmmbr MemberDN**.

- Convert the group to a security group using **dsmod group GroupDN –secgrp yes** or to a distribution group using **dsmod group GroupDN –secgrp no**.

Adding members to groups

The easiest way to add users to a group is to press and hold or right-click the user in the details pane of Active Directory Users And Computers and then select Add To A Group. The Select Groups dialog box appears, and you can select the group of which the user is to become a member. You can also get to the same dialog box by pressing and holding or right-clicking on the user name, selecting Properties, tapping or clicking the Member Of tab, and then tapping or clicking Add. The process is similar for Active Directory Administrative Center.

NOTE
To add multiple users to a group, select more than one user using Shift+click or Ctrl+click and follow the same steps.

If you want to add both users and groups as members of a group, you can do this by performing the following steps:

1. Double-tap or double-click the group entry in Active Directory Users And Computers. This opens the group's Properties dialog box.

2. In the Members tab, tap or click Add to add accounts to the group.

3. Use the Select Users, Contacts, Computers, Or Groups dialog box to choose users, computers, and groups that should be members of the currently selected group. Tap or click OK.

4. Repeat steps 2 and 3 as necessary to add more users, computers, and groups as members.

5. Tap or click OK.

CHAPTER 16

Deleting a group

Deleting a group is as simple as pressing and holding or right-clicking the group name within Active Directory Users And Computers or Active Directory Administrative Center and then selecting Delete. You should be very careful when deleting groups because, although the deletion does not remove the user accounts contained by the group, the permissions you assigned to the group are lost and can't be recovered by merely re-creating the group with the same name.

> ### CAUTION
> The permissions on groups are internally characterized within Active Directory by unique SIDs that are allocated when the group is created. If you delete a group and then re-create it, it will have a new SID and thus new permissions.

Modifying groups

There are a number of modifications, property changes, and management procedures you might want to apply to groups. You can change the scope, change the members and other groups contained in the group, move a group, delegate the management of a group, and send mail to a group.

Finding a group

When you have a substantial number of groups, you can use the search function to locate the one you need to manage. In Active Directory Users And Computers, just press and hold or right-click the domain or OU and then select Find. In the Find Users, Contacts, And Groups dialog box, you can specify what type of object to find, change the starting point, or structure a search query from the available tabs. After the query has run, you can perform many administrative or management functions on the objects returned in the results window.

In Active Directory Administrative Center, just press and hold or right-click the domain or OU and then select Search Under This Node. In the main pane under Global Search, type the name of the object to find and then tap or click Search.

Inside OUT

Saved queries in Active Directory

In Active Directory Users And Computers, you can reuse and save queries. This allows you to find groups quickly and repeatedly when you want to manage and modify them. You can locate the Saved Queries folder in the default position at the top of the Active Directory Users And Computers console tree (left pane). You can't save queries from the Find menu when you press and hold or right-click a group. You can save them only by using the Saved Query procedure that is found in the uppermost part of the tree in Active Directory Users And Computers and creating a new query.

Managing computer accounts

You manage and configure computer accounts by using Active Directory Users And Computers or Active Directory Administrative Center. Whichever tool you use, the process is similar.

By default, computer accounts are stored in the Computers container and domain controller accounts are stored in the Domain Controllers container. Computer accounts also can be stored in other containers, such as the OUs you created. You can join computers to or remove computers from a domain by using Computer Management or the System tool in Control Panel.

Creating a computer account in Active Directory

You can create two types of computer accounts: standard computer accounts and managed computer accounts. Managed computer accounts are available when you install Windows Deployment Services in your domain.

To create a new computer account, start Active Directory Users And Computers. Press and hold or right-click the container in which you want to create the new computer account, point to New, and then select Computer. This starts the New Object–Computer Wizard shown in Figure 16-15.

CHAPTER 16

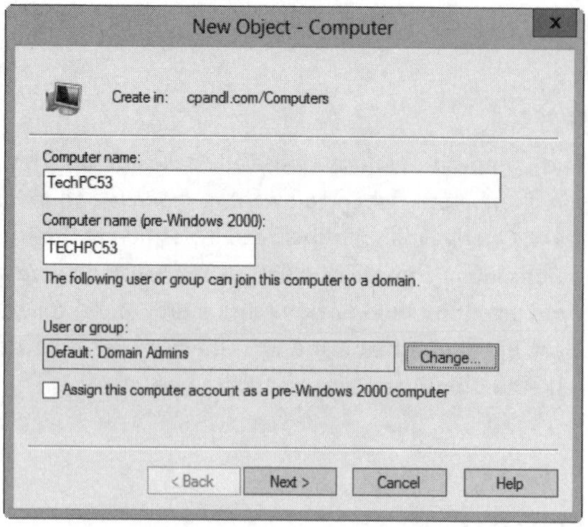

Figure 16-15 Create a computer account.

Type a computer name. By default, only members of the Administrators, Account Operators, Enterprise Admins, or Domain Admins group can join computers to the domain. To allow a different user or group to join the computer to the domain, tap or click Change and then use the Select User Or Group dialog box to select a user or group account that is authorized to join the computer to the domain.

If this account will be used with applications written for legacy operating systems, select Assign This Computer Account As A Pre–Windows 2000 Computer. If Windows Deployment Services are not installed, tap or click OK to create the computer account. Otherwise, you can create the account by tapping or clicking Next twice and then tapping or clicking Finish.

As an alterarnive, you can configure the computer as a managed PC. To do this, tap or click Next to display the Managed page. Select the This Is A Managed Computer check box and then type the computer's globally unique identifier/universally unique identifier (GUID/UUID). On the Host Server page, you have the option to specify which host server to use for remote installation or to allow any available host server to be used for remote installation. To select a host server, select The Following Remote Installation Server. In the Find dialog box, tap or click Find Now to display a list of all remote installation servers in the organization. Tap or click the host server you want to use and then tap or click OK to close the Find dialog box. Tap or click Next and then tap or click Finish.

NOTE

Creating a computer account doesn't join the computer to the domain. It merely creates the account to simplify the process of joining a domain. You can, however, create a computer account when you join a computer to a domain.

Inside OUT

Creating computer accounts at the command line

You can create computer accounts using DSADD as well. To do this, you need to know the Active Directory service path string you want to use. For example, suppose that you want to create a computer account called CustServicePC27 in the Computers container for the cpandl.com domain. The full path to this computer object is CN=CustServicePC27,CN=Computers,DC=cpandl,DC=com. When creating the computer object using DSADD, you must specify this path as follows:

```
dsadd computer "CN=CustServicePC27,CN=Computers,DC=cpandl,DC=com"
```

Here, CN= is used to specify the common name of an object and DC= is used to specify a domain component. With Active Directory path strings, you will also see OU=, which is used to specify the name of an organizational unit object. For the full syntax and usage, type **dsadd computer /?** at a command prompt. Although quotation marks aren't required in this example, I always use them to ensure that I don't forget them when they actually are needed, such as when name components contain spaces.

You can also use the directory services commands to perform many computer management tasks. Use DSMOD COMPUTER to set properties, disable accounts, and reset accounts. Use DSMOVE COMPUTER to move computer accounts to a new container or OU. Use DSRM COMPUTER to remove the computer account.

Joining computers to a domain

When you join a computer to a domain, you must supply the credentials for creating a new computer account in Active Directory. The new computer will be placed in the default Computers container in Active Directory. You must be a member of the Administrators group on the local computer to join it to the domain. Windows Server allows any authenticated user to join workstations to the domain—up to a total of 10 (by default)—provided that you already created the necessary computer accounts. To join a server to a domain, you must be a member of the Administrators, Account Operators, Domain Admins, or Enterprise Admins group.

To join a server or workstation to a domain, follow these steps:

1. Ensure that the client's DNS server settings point to a domain controller or DNS server. These settings are often obtained through DHCP.

2. In the Computer Name tab of the System Properties dialog box, tap or click Change. This displays the Computer Name/Domain Changes dialog box.

CHAPTER 16

3. Select the Domain option, type the name of the domain to join, and then tap or click OK.

4. In the Windows Security prompt, type the name and password of an account with permission to add the computer to the specified domain or to remove the computer from a previously specified domain and then tap or click OK.

5. When prompted that your computer has joined the domain you specified, tap or click OK.

6. You'll see a prompt stating that you need to restart the computer. Tap or click OK.

7. Tap or click Close and then tap or click Restart Now to restart the computer.

TROUBLESHOOTING

The computer won't join the domain

If you have problems joining the computer to the domain, there might be an existing computer in the domain with the same name. In this case you change the computer name and then repeat this procedure. The computer must also have Transmission Control Protocol/Internet Protocol (TCP/IP) properly configured. If you suspect a problem with the TCP/IP configuration, ping the loopback address 127.0.0.1 to ensure that TCP/IP is installed correctly and then check the configuration settings by typing **ipconfig /all** at the command prompt.

Moving a computer account

A corporation might make organizational changes that require you to move a computer account. You can move the computer account from one container to another. Plan and test moving the computer account to ensure that possible conflicts in permissions or rights don't occur. You can use the Effective Permissions tool in planning mode to simulate moving computer accounts and to determine if conflicts could occur.

To move a computer account, you can drag the computer object from one container to another within the details pane of Active Directory Users And Computers. Alternatively, you can press and hold or right-click the computer account name, select Move, and then select the container to which you want to move the account using the Move dialog box. You can't move computer accounts for domain controllers across domains. You must first demote the domain controller and then move the computer account.

Disabling a computer account

Security issues, such as viral attacks or rogue user actions, might require you to temporarily disable a computer account. Perhaps a critical software bug has caused an individual computer to repeatedly try to receive authentication from a domain controller. You disable a computer account to prevent it from authenticating until you fix the problem.

You disable a computer account by pressing and holding or right-clicking it in Active Directory Users And Computers and selecting Disable Account. This prevents the computer from logging on to the domain but doesn't remove the related account from Active Directory. Active Directory Administrative Center doesn't have an option for disabling computer accounts.

Deleting a computer account

When you delete a computer account, you can't just re-create a new computer account with the same name and access. The SID of the original computer account will be different from that of the new account.

To remove a computer account, press and hold or right-click the computer account in either Active Directory Users And Computers or Active Directory Administrative Center and then select Delete.

Managing a computer account

Managing a remote computer is a common task when troubleshooting server or workstation problems. You can configure management settings such as shares, system settings, services and applications, and the event log of the remote computer. Be careful when changing settings or restarting services on remote machines.

Press and hold or right-click the computer account name in Active Directory Users And Computers and then select Manage to bring up Computer Management for that computer. This option is not available in Active Directory Administrative Center.

Resetting a computer account

Computer accounts have passwords, just like user accounts. Unlike user accounts, however, computer account passwords are managed and maintained automatically. To perform this automated management, computers in the domain store a computer account password, which is changed every 30 days by default, and a secure channel password for establishing secure communications with domain controllers.

The secure channel password is also updated by default every 30 days, and both passwords must be synchronized. If the secure channel password and the computer account password get out of sync, the computer won't be allowed to log on to the domain and a domain authentication error message will be logged for the Netlogon service with an event ID of 3210 or 5722.

If this happens, you need to reset the computer account password. One way to do this is to press and hold or right-click the computer account in Active Directory Users And Computers and select Reset Account. You then need to remove the computer from the domain (by making the computer a member of a workgroup or another domain) and then rejoin the computer to the domain.

> ### TROUBLESHOOTING
>
> #### *Rejoining the domain without restarting*
>
> You can save yourself a restart by joining the computer to the NetBIOS name of the domain if it's currently joined to the fully qualified name of the domain, or vice versa. This saves a restart to get into Workgroup mode and then back to Domain mode. As examples, if a computer is joined to Cpandl.com, join the computer to the CPANDL domain, but if a computer is joined to the CPANDL domain, join the computer to the Cpandl.com domain.

Troubleshooting computer accounts

As an administrator, you might see a variety of problems related to computer accounts. When you are joining a computer to a domain, you might experience problems due to incorrect network settings. The computer joining the domain must be able to communicate with the domain controller in the domain. You can resolve connectivity problems by configuring the computer's Local Area Network connection settings appropriately for the domain to which you are connecting. Be sure to check the IP address, default gateway, and DNS server settings. Keep in mind that if the DNS server isn't set in DHCP and DNS is pointing to a different server that isn't a domain controller for the domain you want to join, the computer will not be able to join the domain.

Another common problem is related to insufficient permissions. The user joining the computer to the domain must have appropriate permissions in the domain. Be sure to use an account with appropriate permissions to join the domain.

After a computer is joined to a domain, you sometimes might see problems with the computer password or the trust between the computer and the domain. Diagnosing a password/trust problem is straightforward. If you try to access or browse resources in the domain and are prompted for a user name and password when you normally are not, you might have a password/trust problem with the computer account. For example, if you are trying to connect to a remote computer in Computer Management and you are repeatedly prompted for a user name and password where you weren't previously, the computer account password should probably be reset.

You can verify a password/trust problem by checking the System event log. Look for an error with event ID 3210 generated by the NETLOGON service. The related error message should read as follows:

```
This computer could not authenticate with RESOURCENAME, a Windows domain controller for
domain DOMAINNAME, and therefore this computer might deny logon requests. This inabil-
ity to authenticate might be caused by another computer on the same network using the
same name or the password for this computer account is not recognized. If this message
appears again, contact your system administrator.
```

As part of the troubleshooting process, you should always check the status of the account in Active Directory Users And Computers. A disabled account has a circle with a down arrow. A deleted account will no longer be listed, and you won't be able to search for and find it in the directory. If a user was trying to connect to a resource on a remote computer, the computer to which the user was connecting should have a related error or warning event in the event logs.

If the related computer account is disabled or deleted, you will be denied access to remote resources when connecting to those resources from this computer. As an example, if you are trying to access FileServer75 from CustServicePC83, you will be denied access if the computer account is disabled or deleted. The system event log on the remote computer (FileServer75) should log related NETLOGON errors specifically related to the computer account, such as the following with event ID 5722:

```
The session setup from the computer CORPPC18 failed to authenticate. The name(s) of
the account(s) referenced in the security database is CORPPC18$. The following error
occurred: Access is denied.
```

With Kerberos authentication, a computer's system time can affect authentication. If a computer's system time deviates from the permitted norms set in Group Policy, the computer will fail authentication.

If you are still experiencing problems, check the computer's group membership and the container in which it's located in Active Directory. Computer accounts, like user accounts, can be made members of specific groups and are placed in a specific container in Active Directory. The group membership of a computer determines many permissions with regard to security and resource access. Changing a computer's group membership can significantly affect security and resource access. The container in which a computer is placed determines how Group Policy is applied to the computer. Moving a computer to a different container or OU can significantly affect the way policy settings are applied.

Recovering deleted accounts

Active Directory Recycle Bin allows you to undo the accidental deletion of Active Directory objects in much the same way as you can recover deleted files from the Windows Recycle Bin. Before you can use the Recycle Bin, you must raise the domain and forest functional levels to the Windows Server 2008 R2 level or higher and then you must enable the feature. Keep in mind that once you enable Active Directory Recycle Bin you will not be able to lower the domain or forest functional level below the Windows Server 2008 R2 level.

Enabling Active Directory Recycle Bin

When an Active Directory object is deleted and the Recycle Bin is enabled, the object is put in a state referred to as *logically deleted*. The object's distinguished name is altered and it's moved to the Deleted Objects container, where it remains for the period of time set in the deleted object lifetime value, which is 180 days by default.

You enable the Recycle Bin for use by following these steps:

1. In Active Directory Administrative Center, the local domain is opened for management by default. If you want to work with a different domain, tap or click Manage and then tap or click Add Navigation Nodes. In the Add Navigation Nodes dialog box, select the domain you want to work with and then tap or click OK.

2. Select the domain you want to work with by tapping or clicking it in the left pane. In the Tasks pane, tap or click Enable Recycle Bin and then tap or click OK in the confirmation dialog box.

IMPORTANT

Enabling the Recycle Bin is a forestwide change. When you enable the Recycle Bin in one domain of a forest, Active Directory replicates the change to all domain controllers in all domains of the forest. Thus, every domain in the forest will have its own Recycle Bin.

After you enable the Recycle Bin, Active Directory will begin replicating the change to all domain controllers in the forest. Once the change is replicated, the Recycle Bin will be available for use. If you then tap or click Refresh in Active Directory Administrative Center, you'll see that a Deleted Objects container is available for each domain you select.

Recovering objects from the Recycle Bin

When Active Directory Recycle Bin is enabled, you can easily recover deleted objects. To do this, you use Active Directory Administrative Center. Domains using the Recycle Bin will have a Deleted Object container. In this container you'll see a list of deleted objects, as shown in Figure 16-16.

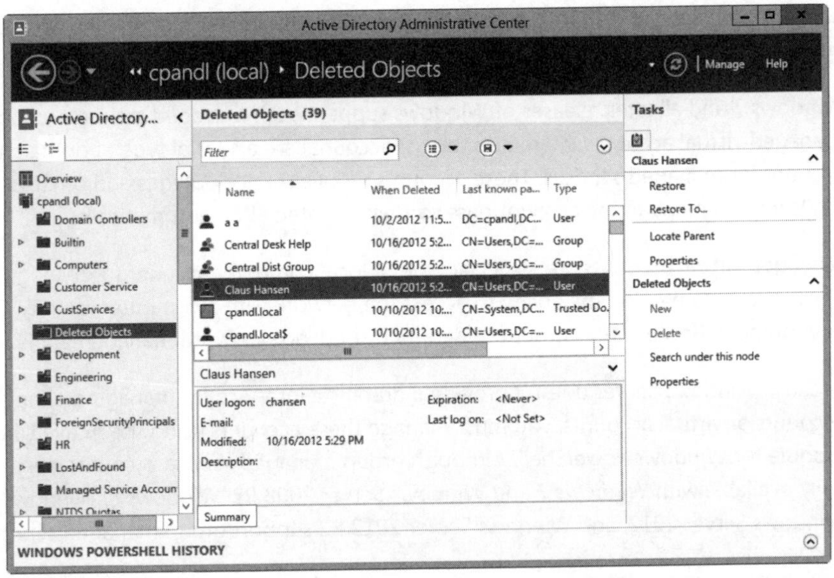

Figure 16-16 The Deleted Objects container contains a list of deleted objects.

As discussed in the section entitled "Extensible Storage Engine" in Chapter 10, "Active Directory architecture," deleted objects remain in the Deleted Objects container for the deleted object lifetime value, which is 180 days by default. Each deleted object is listed by name, and you can see when it was deleted, the last known parent, and the type. When you select a deleted object by tapping or clicking it, you can use the options in the Tasks pane to work with it. The Restore option restores the object to its original container. For example, if the object was deleted from the Users container, it's restored to this container.

The Restore To option restores the object to an alternate container within its original domain or to a different domain within the current forest. Specify the alternate container in the Restore To dialog box. For example, if the object was deleted from the Users container in the eng.cpandl.com domain, you could restore it to the Technology OU in the tech.cpandl.com domain.

Working with managed service accounts

Application servers and database servers often use service accounts. On a local computer you can configure the application to run as a built-in user account, such as Local Service, Network Service, or Local System. Although these service accounts are easy to configure and use, they usually are shared among multiple applications and services and can't be managed on a domain level. If you configure the application to use a domain account, you can isolate the privileges for the application. However, you must then manually manage the account password and any Service Principal Names (SPNs) required for Kerberos authentication.

Windows 7 and all later releases of Windows support both managed service accounts and managed virtual accounts. Managed service accounts are a special type of domain user account for managed services. These accounts reduce service outages and other issues by having Windows manage the account password and related SPNs automatically.

Managed virtual accounts are a special type of local computer account for managed services. These accounts provide the ability to access the network with a computer identity in a domain environment. Because the computer identity is used, no password management is required.

Because Windows Server doesn't provide a graphical interface for managing either service accounts or virtual accounts, you must manage these accounts using the Active Directory module for Windows PowerShell. Although group managed service accounts were not originally available with Windows 7 and Windows Server 2008 R2, Windows 8, Windows 8.1, Windows Server 2012, and Windows Server 2012 R2 support group managed service accounts.

Group managed service accounts provide the same functionality as standard managed service accounts but extend that functionality over multiple servers. For example, when a client computer connects to a service hosted by a server farm, mutual authentication can't succeed unless all the instances of the services use the same principal. By using a group managed service account, you allow each server in the farm to use the same service principal, which is managed by Windows itself rather than individually by the administrator.

Currently, group managed service accounts are the default type of service account for Windows 8, Windows 8.1, Windows Server 2012, and Windows Server 2012 R2. Thus, by default, managed service accounts can span multiple computers.

You can add the account to more than one computer at a time as necessary to support clustered nodes, network load-balancing server farms, and so on. If you want to restrict a managed service account to a single computer, you must set the *–RestrictToSingleComputer* option when creating the account. Don't forget that a single computer can have multiple managed service accounts as well.

In the Active Directory schema, managed service accounts are represented by *msDS-ManagedServiceAccounts*. This object class inherits its attributes from the *Computer* object class, but the objects also are users. Managed service accounts use the same password-update mechanism as regular computer accounts. Thus, the password for the account is updated whenever the computer updates its password, which by default occurs every 30 days. Managed service accounts can automatically maintain their Kerberos SPN and support delegation.

NOTE

By default, all managed service accounts are created in the Managed Service Accounts container in Active Directory. This container is visible in Active Directory Users And Computers when you display advanced features. Additionally, it's important to note that some applications, such as SQL Server and IIS, make extensive use of Kerberos and know how to register themselves with SPNs. If an application supports writing its own SPNs, managed service accounts will work for automatic SPN management.

Like standard computer accounts, managed service accounts do not use either domain or fine-grained password policies. Instead, they use a randomly generated 240-byte (120-character) password. Managed service accounts can't perform interactive logons or be locked out like user accounts can be. You can add managed service accounts to groups by using Active Directory Users And Computers or Add-ADGroupMember.

Creating managed service accounts

With managed service accounts, you create an actual account, which is stored by default in the Managed Service Accounts container in Active Directory. Next, you associate the account with a computer in Active Directory and then install the managed service account on a local server to add it to the account as a local user. Finally, you configure the local service to use the account. Put another way, you must do the following:

1. Create the managed service account.

2. Associate the account with a computer in Active Directory.

3. Install the managed service account on the computer that was associated.

4. Configure the local service to use the account.

You use Windows PowerShell cmdlets to install, uninstall, and reset passwords for managed service accounts. After a managed service account has been installed, you can configure a service or application to use the account and no longer have to specify or change passwords because the computer maintains the account password. You can also configure the SPN on the service account without requiring domain administrator privileges.

To create a managed service account, you use New-ADServiceAccount. The basic syntax is as follows:

```
New-ADServiceAccount -DisplayName DisplayName -SamAccountName SAMName
-Name Name [-RestrictToSingleComputer]
```

DisplayName is the display name for the account, *SAMName* is the pre–Windows 2000 name of the account, and *Name* is the pre–Windows 2000 name of the account, such as:

```
New-ADServiceAccount -DisplayName "SQL Agent Account"
-SamAccountName sqlagent -Name "SQL Agent"
```

By default, the account is created as a group service account. The account will have a randomly generated 240-byte (120-character) password and is created in the Managed Service Accounts container. The account is enabled by default as well, but you can create the account in a disabled state by adding *–Enabled $false*. If you need to pass in credentials to create the account, use the *–Credential* parameter as shown in this example:

```
$cred = Get-Credential
New-ADServiceAccount -DisplayName "IIS Updates Pool"
-SamAccountName pool1 -Name "IIS Updates Pool" -Credential $cred
```

Group managed service accounts are listed in Active Directory Users And Computers. However, you shouldn't use this management tool to work with the account. Instead, you should work with group managed service accounts using Get-ADServiceAccount, Set-ADServiceAccount, and Remove-ADServiceAccount. Get-ADServiceAccount retrieves information about one or more managed service accounts. Set-ADServiceAccount configures properties on an existing managed service account. Remove-ADServiceAccount deletes a managed service account from Active Directory.

After you create a managed service account in Active Directory, you associate it with a target computer in Active Directory using Add-ADComputerServiceAccount. You use Remove-ADComputerServiceAccount to remove a computer association from Active Directory. The basic syntax for Add-ADComputerServiceAccount is as follows:

```
Add-ADComputerServiceAccount [-Identity] ComputerName
[-ServiceAccount] MSAName
```

ComputerName is the name of the target computer, and *MSAName* is the name of the managed service account, such as

```
Add-ADComputerServiceAccount IISServer38 WebServicesAccount
```

Sometimes, you'll need to pass in credentials to create the account. To do this, use the *–Credential* parameter as shown in this example:

```
$cred = Get-Credential
Add-ADComputerServiceAccount IISServer24 FarmFourServicesAccount
```

You can install the account on a local computer by using Install-ADServiceAccount. The basic syntax is this:

```
Install-ADServiceAccount [-Identity] ServiceAccountId
```

ServiceAccountId is the display name or SAM account name of the service account, such as

```
Install-ADServiceAccount sqlagent
```

If you need to pass in credentials to create the account, use the *–Credential* parameter. Use Uninstall-ADServiceAccount to uninstall an account.

Configuring managed service accounts for use

You can configure a service to run with the managed service account by following these steps:

1. In Server Manager, tap or click Tools and then tap or click Computer Management. As necessary, connect to the computer you want to manage. In the left pane, press and hold or right-click the Computer Management node and then tap or click Connect To Another Computer. Enter the host name, fully qualified domain name, or IP address of the remote server and then tap or click OK.

2. In the left pane, expand the Services And Applications node and then select the Services node. Press and hold or right-click the name of the service you want to work with and then tap or click Properties.

3. In the Log On tab, select This Account and then type the name of the managed service account in the format DomainName\AccountName, or tap or click Browse to search for the account.

4. Confirm that the password box is blank and then tap or click OK.

5. Select the name of the service and then tap or click Start to start the service, or tap or click Restart to restart the service as appropriate. Confirm that the newly configured account name appears in the Log On As column for the service.

   ### NOTE
   In the Services snap-in console, you'll see a dollar sign ($) at the end of the account name. When you use the Services snap-in console to configure the logon as an account, the Service Logon Right logon right is automatically assigned to the account. If you use a different tool, the account has to be explicitly granted this right.

Deleting managed service accounts

If a managed service account is no longer being used on a computer, you might want to uninstall the account. Before you do this, however, you should check the Services snap-in to ensure that the account isn't being used. To uninstall a managed service account from a local computer, use Uninstall-ADServiceAccount. The basic syntax is shown here:

```
Uninstall-ADServiceAccount -Identity ServiceAccountId
```

ServiceAccountId is the display name or SAM account name of the service account, such as

```
Uninstall-ADServiceAccount -Identity sqlagent
```

If you need to pass in credentials to uninstall the account, use the –*Credential* parameter.

Managed service account passwords are reset on a regular basis based on the password reset requirements of the domain, but you can reset the password manually if needed. To reset the password for a managed service account, use Reset-ADServiceAccountPassword. The basic syntax is as follows:

```
Reset-ADServiceAccountPassword -Identity ServiceAccountId
```

ServiceAccountId is the display name or SAM account name of the service account, such as

```
Reset-ADServiceAccountPassword -Identity sqlagent
```

If you need to pass in credentials to reset the password, use the –*Credential* parameter. You can modify the default password change interval for managed service accounts by using the domain policy Domain Member: Maximum Machine Account Password Age under Local Policy\Security Options. Group Policy settings under Account Policies\Password Policy are not used to modify managed service account password-reset intervals, and the NLTEST /SC_CHANGE_PWD command can't be used to reset managed service account passwords.

Moving managed service accounts

To move a managed service account from a source computer to a new destination computer, complete the following steps:

1.   On the source computer, configure any services that are using the managed account to use a different account and then run Uninstall-ADServiceAccount.

2.   On the new destination computer, run Install-ADServiceAccount and then use the Services snap-in console to configure the service to run with the managed service account.

To migrate a service from a user account to a managed service account, complete the following steps:

1.   Create a new managed service account in Active Directory by using New-ADServiceAccount.

2.   Install the managed service account on the appropriate computer by using Install-ADServiceAccount and then use the Services snap-in console to configure the service to run with the managed service account.

3. You also might need to configure the access control lists on the service resources for the service management account.

Using virtual accounts

Virtual accounts require very little management. They can't be created or deleted, and they don't require any password management. Instead, they exist automatically and are represented by the machine identity of the local computer.

With virtual accounts, you configure a local service to access the network with a computer identity in a domain environment. Because the computer identity is used, no account needs to be created and no password management is required.

You can configure a service to run with a virtual account by following these steps:

1. In Server Manager, tap or click Tools and then tap or click Computer Management. As necessary, connect to the computer you want to manage. In the left pane, press and hold or right-click the Computer Management node and then tap or click Connect To Another Computer. Enter the host name, fully qualified domain name, or IP address of the remote server and then tap or click OK.

2. In the left pane, expand the Services And Applications node and then select the Services node. Press and hold or right-click the name of the service you want to work with and then tap or click Properties.

3. In the Log On tab, select This Account and then type the name of the service account in the format SERVICE\ComputerName.

4. Confirm that the password box is blank and then tap or click OK.

5. Select the name of the service and then tap or click Start to start the service, or tap or click Restart to restart the service. Confirm that the newly configured account name appears in the Log On As column for the service.

NOTE

In the Services snap-in console, you'll see a dollar sign ($) at the end of the account name. When you use the Services snap-in console to configure the logon as an account, the Service Logon Right logon right is automatically assigned to the account. If you use a different tool, the account has to be explicitly granted this right.

CHAPTER 16

Managing Group Policy

Group Policy is designed to simplify administration by allowing administrators to configure user and computer settings in Active Directory Domain Services and then have those policies automatically applied to computers throughout an organization. This not only provides for the central management of computers but also helps automate key administrative tasks. Using Group Policy, you can accomplish the following tasks:

- Configure security policies for account lockout, passwords, Kerberos, and auditing

- Redirect special folders, such as a user's Documents folder, to centrally managed network shares

- Lock down computer desktop configurations

- Define logon, logoff, shutdown, and startup scripts

- Automate the installation of application software

- Maintain Microsoft Internet Explorer and configure standard settings

Some of these features—such as security policies and folder redirection—have been discussed in previous chapters. Other features are discussed in this chapter. The focus of this chapter, however, is on the management of Group Policy, which is the most challenging aspect of implementing Group Policy in an organization.

NOTE

Under the Computer Configuration and User Configuration nodes, you find two nodes: Policies and Preferences. Settings for general policies are listed under the Policies node. Settings for general preferences are listed under the Preferences node. When referring to settings under the Policies node, I'll typically use shortcut references, such as User Configuration\Administrative Templates\Windows Components, rather than User Configuration\Policies\Administrative Templates: Policy Definitions\Windows Components. This shortcut reference tells you the policy setting being discussed is under User Configuration rather than Computer Configuration and can be found under Administrative Templates\Windows Components.

Understanding Group Policy

You can think of Group Policy as a set of rules that help you manage users and computers. Like any set of rules, Group Policy is effective only under certain conditions.

NOTE

Like Active Directory, Group Policy has gone through several revisions. As a result of these revisions, some policies work only with a version of the Microsoft Windows operating system that is compatible with a particular revision. For example, some group policies are compatible with Windows 7 or later and Windows Server 2008 or later, and others are compatible only with Windows XP Professional and Windows Server 2003 or only with Windows Vista and Windows Server 2008.

Local and Active Directory Group Policy

Two types of group policies are available. The first type is Local Group Policy, which is stored locally on individual computers in the %SystemRoot%\System32\GroupPolicy folder and applies only to a particular computer. Every computer running Windows has one or more local group policies. For a computer in a workgroup, Local Group Policy is the only Group Policy available. A computer in a domain also has a Local Group Policy, but it is not the only Group Policy available. This is where the second type of Group Policy, called Active Directory Group Policy (or more commonly just "Group Policy"), comes into the picture.

Active Directory Group Policy is stored in the Sysvol folder used by Active Directory for replicating policies, and it is represented logically as an object called a Group Policy Object (GPO). A GPO is simply a container for the policies you configure and their settings that can be linked to sites, domains, and organizational units (OUs) in your Active Directory structure. You can create multiple GPOs, and by linking those objects to different locations in your Active Directory structure, you can apply the related policy settings to the users and computers in those Active Directory containers.

When you create a domain, two Active Directory group policies are created:

- **Default Domain Controllers Policy GPO.** A default GPO created for the Domain Controllers OU and applicable to all domain controllers in a domain as long as they are members of this OU

- **Default Domain Policy GPO.** A default GPO created for and linked to the domain within Active Directory

You can create additional GPOs as necessary and link them to the sites, domains, and OUs you've created. Linking a GPO to Active Directory structure is how you apply Group Policy. For example, you could create a GPO called Technology Policy and then link it to the Technology OU. The policy then applies to that OU.

Group Policy settings

Group Policy applies only to users and computers. Although you can use groups to specify the users to whom a particular policy applies, the actual policies are applied only to member users. Group Policy settings are divided into two categories: Computer Configuration and User Configuration. Computer Configuration contains settings that apply to computers. User Configuration contains settings that apply to user accounts.

Figure 17-1 shows the Default Domain Policy for a computer. As you can see in the figure, both Computer Configuration–related and User Configuration–related settings are divided into three major classes, each of which contains several subclasses of settings:

- **Software Settings.** You use these to install software on computers and then maintain it by installing patches or upgrades. You can also uninstall software.

- **Windows Settings.** You use these to manage key Windows settings for both computers and users, including scripts and security. For users, you can also manage Remote Installation Services, folder redirection, and Internet Explorer maintenance.

- **Administrative Templates.** You use these to control registry settings that configure the operating system, Windows components, and applications. Administrative templates are implemented for specific operating-system versions.

CHAPTER 17

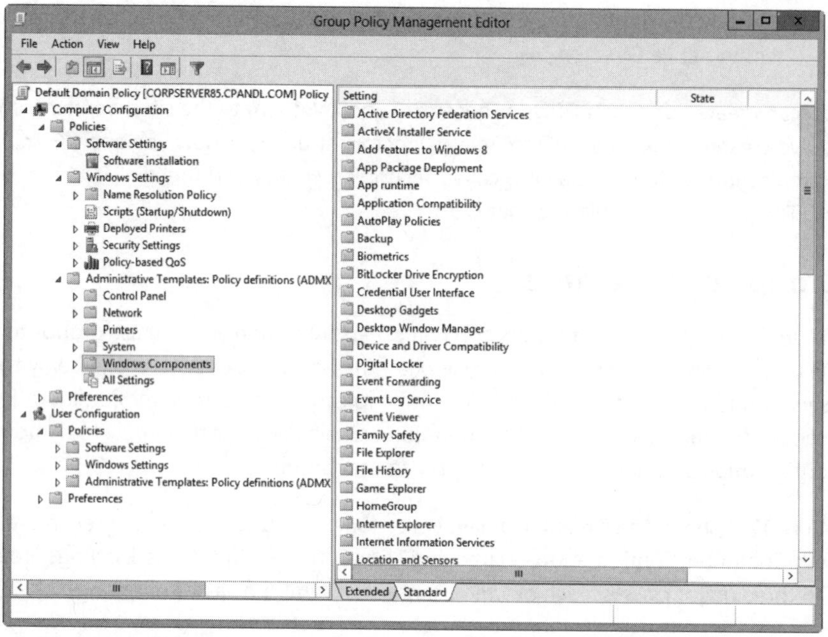

Figure 17-1 The Default Domain Policy includes Computer Configuration–related and User Configuration–related settings.

Group Policy architecture

Within the Windows operating system, the components of Group Policy have separate server and client implementations. (See Figure 17-2.) Each Group Policy client has client-side extensions that are used to interpret and apply Group Policy settings. The client-side extensions are implemented as dynamic-link libraries (DLLs) that are installed with the operating system. The main DLL for processing Administrative Templates is Userenv.dll.

The Group Policy engine running on a client triggers the processing of policy when one of two events occurs: either the system is started or a user logs on to the computer. When a system is started and the network connection is initialized, computer policy settings are applied.

Administrators and others who are delegated permissions in Group Policy can use Group Policy Management Editor to manage Group Policy. This snap-in for the Microsoft Management Console (MMC) provides the three top-level classes (Software Settings, Windows Settings, and Administrative Templates) that can be managed and makes use of a number of extensions. These extensions provide the functionality you can use to configure various Group Policy settings. Some client-side extensions don't have specific implementations on the server because they are registry-based and can be configured through Administrative Templates.

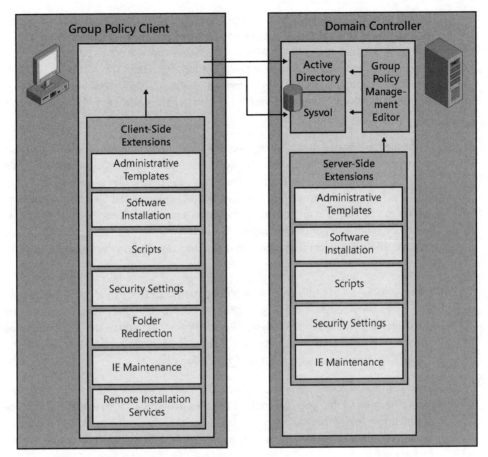

Figure 17-2 Review Group Policy architecture.

Although GPOs are represented logically in Active Directory and replicated through normal replication, most server-side Group Policy components are represented on the Sysvol as physical files. The default location for the Sysvol folder is %SystemRoot%\Sysvol with the subfolder %SystemRoot%\Sysvol\sysvol shared as Sysvol. Within the shared Sysvol folder, you'll find subfolders organized by domain and the globally unique identifier (GUID) of each GPO created in a particular domain.

Administrative templates

Windows Server displays the registry-based policy settings in the Administrative templates. Registry-based policy settings are defined using a standards-based, XML file format called ADMX. This format replaces the ADM format previously used with Windows XP Professional and Windows Server 2003.

CHAPTER 17

You can edit GPOs using ADMX files only on computers running current Windows operating systems. The reason for this is that current Windows operating systems have policy editors that have been updated to work with ADMX. That being said, the policy editors automatically read and display Administrative Template policy settings from both the ADMX and ADM files. This means any custom ADM files you created will still be available. However, the policy editors will exclude ADM files that were included by default in earlier releases of Windows because the ADMX files supersede these files.

ADMX files are divided into language-neutral files ending with the .admx file extension and language-specific files ending with the .adml extension. The language-neutral files ensure that a GPO has identical core policies. The language-specific files allow policies to be viewed and edited in multiple languages. Because the language-neutral files store the core settings, policies can be edited in any language for which a computer is configured, thus allowing one user to view and edit policies in English and another to view and edit policies in Spanish, for example. The mechanism that determines the language used is the language pack installed on the computer.

Unlike ADM files, ADMX files are not stored in individual GPOs by default. Language-neutral ADMX files are installed in the %SystemRoot%\PolicyDefinitions folder. Language-specific ADMX files are installed in the %SystemRoot%\PolicyDefinitions\LanguageCulture folder. Each subfolder is named after the appropriate International Organization for Standardization (ISO) language/culture name, such as en-US for U.S. English.

When you start a policy editor, it automatically reads in ADMX files from the policy definitions folders. Because of this, you can copy ADMX files that you want to use to the appropriate policy definitions folder to make them available when you are editing GPOs. If the policy editor is running when you copy the file or files, you must restart the policy editor to force it to read in the file or files.

Because of these changes, only the current state of a setting is stored in the GPO and the details related to the settings are stored in the ADMX files. This reduces the amount of storage space used as the number of GPOs increases and also reduces the amount of data being replicated throughout the enterprise. As long as you edit GPOs using current Windows operating systems, new GPOs will contain neither ADM nor ADMX files inside the GPO.

Implementing Group Policy

As discussed previously, there are two types of Group Policy: Local Group Policy and Active Directory Group Policy. Local Group Policy applies to a local machine only, and there is only one local GPO per local machine. Active Directory Group Policy, in contrast, can be implemented separately for sites, domains, and OUs.

In an effort to streamline management of Group Policy, Microsoft removed management features from Active Directory–related tools and moved to a primary console called Group Policy Management Console (GPMC). The GPMC is a feature that you can add to any installation of Windows Server by using the Add Features Wizard. The GPMC is also included with Windows desktop operating systems and is available as a download from the Microsoft website. After you add the GPMC to a server, it's available on the Administrative Tools menu.

When you want to edit a GPO in the GPMC, the GPMC opens Group Policy Management Editor, which you use to manage the policy settings. Also available are Group Policy Starter GPO Editor and Local Group Policy Object Editor. You use Group Policy Starter GPO Editor to create and manage Starter Group Policy objects, which are meant to provide a starting point for new policy objects that you use throughout your organization. When you create a new policy object, you can specify a starter GPO as the source or basis of the new object. You use Local Group Policy Object Editor to create and manage policy objects for the local computer rather than using those settings for an entire site, domain, or organizational unit.

When you use any of these tools to create a new GPO or modify an existing GPO in Active Directory (but not with local policy), the related changes are made on the domain controller acting as the PDC emulator if it is available. The PDC emulator is used so that there is a central point of contact for GPO creation and editing, and this in turn helps ensure that only one administrator is granted access to edit a particular GPO at a time. This also simplifies replication of the changes because changes are always replicated from the same point of origin—the PDC emulator. However, if the PDC emulator can't be reached or is otherwise unavailable when you try to work with GPOs, you are given the opportunity to choose to make changes on the domain controller to which you are currently connected or on any available domain controller.

Working with Local Group Policy

Current Windows operating systems support multiple Local Group Policy Objects (LGPOs) on a single computer (as long as the computer is not a domain controller). Previously, computers had only one LGPO. Having multiple LGPOs allows you to do the following:

- Have a top-level LGPO, referred to simply as *Local Group Policy*. Local Group Policy is the only LGPO that allows both computer configuration and user configuration settings to be applied to all users of the computer.

- Assign a different LGPO to each general user type. There are two general user types: Administrators, which includes only the user accounts that are members of the local Administrators group, and Non-Administrators, which includes only the user accounts that are not members of the local Administrators group. Administrators Local Group Policy and Non-Administrators Local Group Policy contain only user configuration settings.

- Assign a different LGPO to each local user. User-specific Group Policy is applied to a specific user or group and contains only user configuration settings.

These multiple LGPOs act as policy layers, and Windows processes them in the following order:

1. Local Group Policy

2. Administrators and Non-Administrators Group Policy

3. User-specific Local Group Policy

When computers are being used in a stand-alone configuration rather than in a domain configuration, you might find that multiple LGPOs are useful because you no longer have to explicitly disable or remove settings that interfere with your ability to manage a computer before performing administrator tasks. Instead, you can implement one LGPO for administrators and another LGPO for nonadministrators. In a domain configuration, however, you might not want to use multiple LGPOs. In domains, most computers and users already have multiple Group Policy Objects applied to them—adding multiple Local Group Policy Objects to this already varied mix can make managing Group Policy confusing. This is especially true when you consider that a setting in one LGPO could possibly conflict with a setting in another LGPO, which, in turn, could conflict with domain GPO settings.

Windows resolves conflicts in settings by overwriting any previous setting with the last-read and most current setting (unless blocking or enforcing is enabled). Regardless, the final setting applied is the one that Windows uses. When Windows resolves conflicts, only the enabled or disabled state of settings matters. If a setting is set as Not Configured, this has no effect on the state of the setting from a previous policy application. You can simplify domain administration by disabling processing of all Local Group Policy Objects. You do this by enabling the Turn Off Local Group Policy Objects Processing policy setting in a domain Group Policy Object. In Group Policy, this setting is located under Computer Configuration\Administrative Templates\System\Group Policy. When this setting is enabled, as shown in Figure 17-3, computers in the domain process only domain-based policy.

You can access the top-level Local Group Policy Object in several ways. One way is to type the following command at a command prompt:

```
gpedit.msc /gpcomputer:"%computername%"
```

This command starts Group Policy Object Editor in an MMC and tells Group Policy Object Editor to target the local computer. Here, *%ComputerName%* is an environment variable that sets the name of the local computer and must be enclosed in double quotation marks as shown. To access Local Group Policy on a remote computer, type the following command at a command prompt:

```
gpedit.msc /gpcomputer: "RemoteComputer"
```

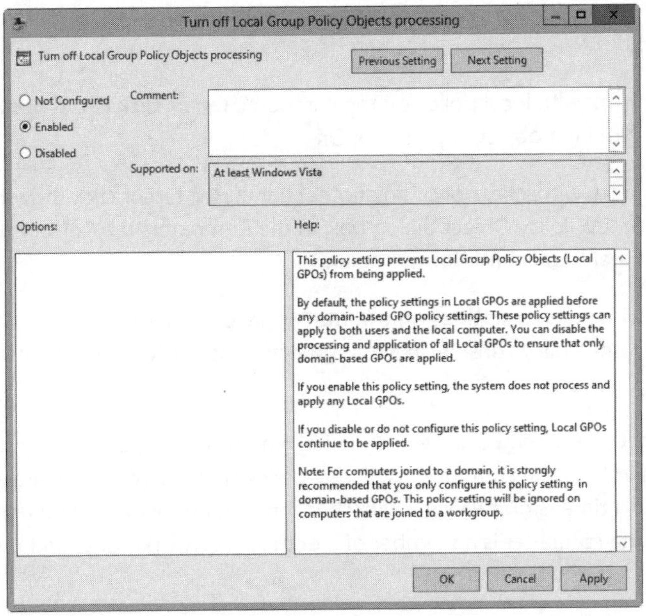

Figure 17-3 Simplify administration by configuring the processing of only domain-based policy.

Here, *RemoteComputer* is the host name or fully qualified domain name (FQDN) of the remote computer, such as

```
gpedit.msc /gpcomputer: "CorpServer08"
```

If you're working with Windows PowerShell already and don't want to open a command prompt (or enter **cmd** to change to the command prompt from within Windows PowerShell), you can open Group Policy Editor while targeting a specify computer. To do this, you must enclose the entire argument string in single quotation marks, such as

```
gpedit.msc '/gpcomputer: "CorpServer08"'
```

You are required to enclose the complete argument string in single quotation marks to ensure that Windows PowerShell passes the command arguments to the command prompt for interpretation rather than trying to parse and interpret the command arguments.

You can also manage the top-level local policy on a computer by following these steps:

1. Type **mmc** into the Apps Search box and then press Enter.

2. In the Microsoft Management Console, tap or click File and then select Add/Remove Snap-in.

3. In the Add Or Remove Snap-ins dialog box, select Group Policy Object Editor and then tap or click Add.

4. If you want to work with local policy on the computer, tap or click Finish because local computer is the default object. Tap or click OK.

5. If you want to work with local policy on another computer, tap or click Browse. In the Browse For A Group Policy Object dialog box, in the Computers tab, select Another Computer and then tap or click Browse again.

If you want to work with security settings only in the top-level Local Group Policy Object, you can use the Local Security Policy console. In Server Manager, select Tools and then select Local Security Policy.

In Group Policy Object Editor and Local Security Policy, you can configure security settings that apply to users and the local computer itself. Any policy changes you make are applied to that computer the next time Group Policy is refreshed. The settings you can manage locally depend on whether the computer is a member of a domain or a workgroup, and they include the following:

- Account policies for passwords, account lockout, and Kerberos

- Event logging options for configuring log size, access, and retention options for the application, system, and security logs

- Local policies for auditing, user rights assignment, and security options

- Security restriction settings for groups, system services, registry keys, and the file system

- Security settings for wireless networking, public keys, and Internet Protocol security (IPsec)

- Software restrictions that specify applications that aren't allowed to run on the computer

Figure 17-4 shows the Local Group Policy Editor. You configure Local Group Policy in the same way that you configure Active Directory–based Group Policy. To apply a policy, you enable it and then configure any additional or optional values as necessary. An enabled policy setting is turned on and active. If you don't want a policy to apply, you must disable it. A disabled policy setting is turned off and inactive.

CHAPTER 17

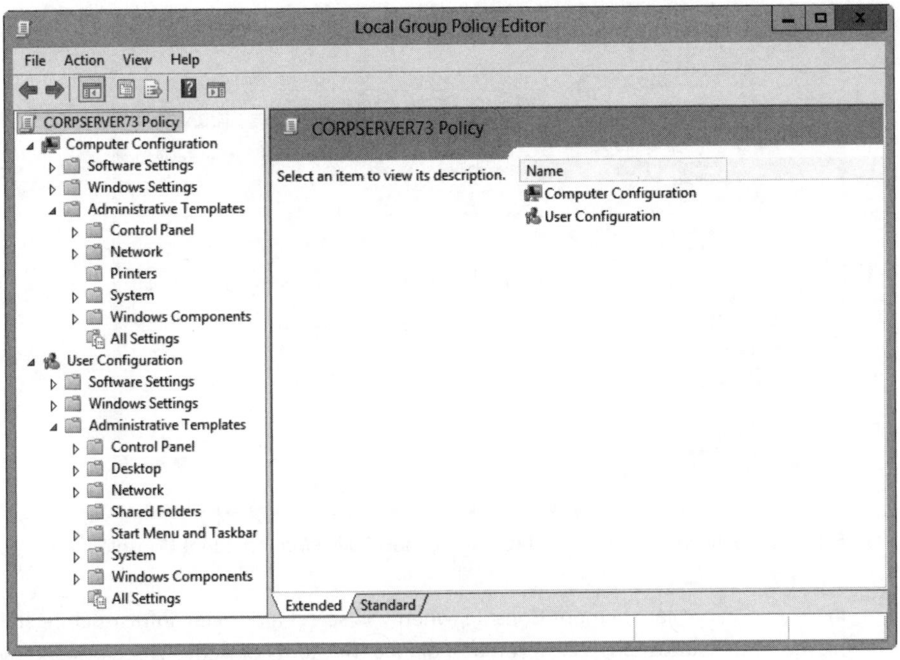

Figure 17-4 Configure local policy using the Local Group Policy Editor.

Working with Group Policy Management Console

Group Policy Management Console (GPMC) provides an integrated interface for working with GPOs. You can install GPMC using the Add Roles And Features Wizard. Alternatively, you can install GPMC by entering the following command at an elevated Windows PowerShell prompt: **install-windowsfeature gpmc**. When you install GPMC, several related snap-ins and tools are installed as well. The sections that follow provide an overview of using GPMC.

Using Group Policy Management Console

You can run Group Policy Management Console from the Tools menu in Server Manager. When you start Group Policy Management Console, the tool connects to Active Directory running on the domain controller acting as the PDC emulator for your logon domain and it obtains a list of all GPOs and OUs in that domain. It does this using Lightweight Directory Access Protocol (LDAP) to access the directory store and the Server Message Block (SMB) protocol to access the Sysvol. The result, as shown in Figure 17-5, is that for each domain to which you are connected, you have all the related GPOs and OUs available to work with in one location.

CHAPTER 17

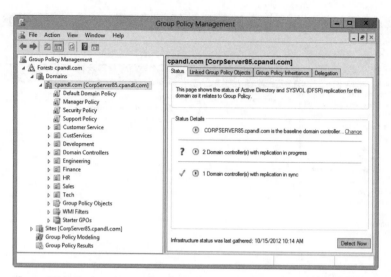

Figure 17-5 Review the results of running Group Policy Management Console.

In Group Policy Management Console, when you select a domain, infrastructure status is displayed in the Status tab, telling you at a glance the status of Active Directory and Sysvol replication for the domain. The status is gathered from a configurable baseline domain controller. If no status is available, just tap or click Detect Now. To change the baseline domain controller, tap or click Change, select a new baseline domain controller, and then tap or click OK.

The status details tell you the number of domain controllers that have their GPO information synchronized with the baseline domain controller and the number of domain controllers with replication in progress. Domain controllers with replication in progress do not have the same GPO information as the baseline domain controller.

The reason codes for in-progress replication can be related to Active Directory or the SYSVOL folder. With Active Directory, the reason codes and meanings are as follows:

- **Accessibility.** The Active Directory service can't be contacted on the specified domain controller.

- **ACLs.** The Active Directory permissions for a specific GPO or GPOs are different from the baseline domain controller.

- **Created Date.** The created date stored in Active Directory for a specific GPO or GPOs is different from the baseline domain controller.

- **GPO Version.** The GPO version information in Active Directory is different from the baseline domain controller.

- **Modified Date.** The modified date stored in Active Directory for a specific GPO or GPOs is different from the baseline domain controller.

- **Number of GPOs.** The total number of GPOs in Active Directory is different from the baseline domain controller.

With the SYSVOL folder, the reason codes and their meanings are as follows:

- **Accessibility.** The SYSVOL folder can't be contacted on the specified domain controller.

- **ACLs.** The SYSVOL permissions on a specified GPO or GPOs are different from the baseline domain controller.

- **GPO Contents.** The contents of the SYSVOL folder for a specified GPO or GPOs are different from the baseline domain controller.

- **GPO Version.** The GPO version information in the GPT.ini file is different from the baseline domain controller.

- **Number of GPOs.** The total number of GPOs in the SYSVOL folder is different from the baseline domain controller.

To give further information for troubleshooting, helpful links are provided with each message.

Accessing forests, domains, and sites in Group Policy Management Console

Working with forests, domains, and sites in Group Policy Management Console is fairly straightforward, as the following list describes:

- **Accessing forests.** The forest root is listed for each forest to which you are connected. You can connect to additional forests by pressing and holding or right-clicking the Group Policy Management node in the console tree and selecting Add Forest. In the Add Forest dialog box, shown in Figure 17-6, type the name of a domain in the forest to which you want to connect and then tap or click OK. As long as there is an external trust to the domain, you can establish the connection and obtain forest information—even if you don't have a forest trust with the entire forest.

CHAPTER 17

Figure 17-6 Type the name of the domain to which you want to connect.

- **Accessing domains.** You can view the domain to which you are connected in a forest by expanding the forest node and then expanding the related Domains node. By default, you are connected to your logon domain in the current forest. If you want to work with other domains in a particular forest, press and hold or right-click the Domains node in the designated forest and then select Show Domains. In the Show Domains dialog box, which has the same options as the Show Sites dialog box, select the options for the domains you want to work with and clear the options for the domains you don't want to work with. Then tap or click OK.

- **Accessing sites.** Because Group Policy is primarily configured for domains and OUs, sites are not shown by default in GPMC. If you want to work with the sites in a particular forest, press and hold or right-click the Sites node in the designated forest and then select Show Sites. In the Show Sites dialog box, shown in Figure 17-7, select the check boxes for the sites you want to work with and clear the check boxes for the domains you don't want to work with. Then tap or click OK.

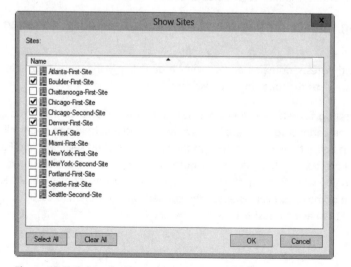

Figure 17-7 Select the sites you want to work with.

Creating and linking a new GPO in Group Policy Management Console

In Group Policy Management Console, you can create and link a new GPO by completing the following steps:

1. Access the domain or OU you want to work with in Group Policy Management Console. Do this by expanding the forest node and the related Domains node as necessary, with the following guidelines:

    -   If you select a domain node, you see a list of the current GPOs and OUs in the domain.

    -   If you select an OU node, you see a list of the current GPOs for the OU (if any).

2. Press and hold or right-click the domain or OU node and select Create A GPO In This Domain, And Link It Here.

3. In the New GPO dialog box, type a descriptive name for the GPO, such as **Support Policy**. If you want to use a starter GPO as the source for the initial settings, select the starter GPO to use from the Source Starter GPO drop-down list. Tap or click OK.

    #### NOTE

    Group Policy Management Console doesn't let you create and link a new GPO for sites. You can, however, use Group Policy Management Console to link a site to an existing GPO. For more information, see the section entitled "Linking to an existing GPO in Group Policy Management Console" later in this chapter.

The new GPO is added to the current list of linked GPOs. If you select the domain or OU node, you can change the preference order of the GPO by selecting it in the Linked Group Policy Objects tab and then tapping or clicking the Move Link Up or Move Link Down button to change the preference order. (See Figure 17-8.) For more information on how preference order works, see the section entitled "Group Policy inheritance" later in this chapter.

CHAPTER 17

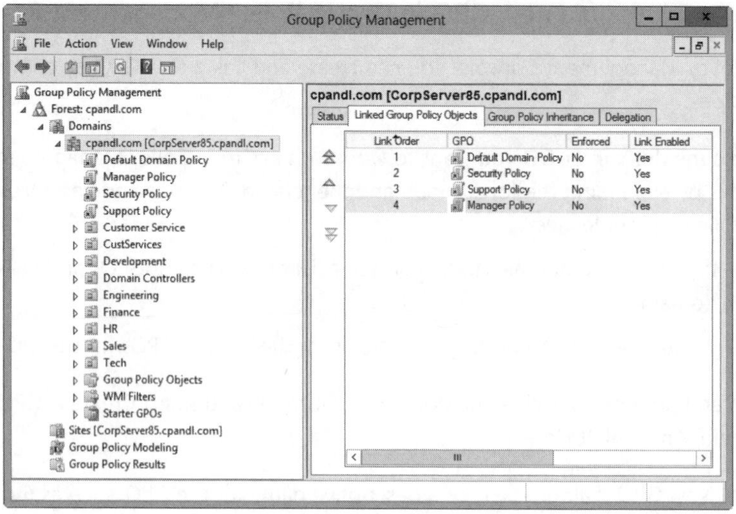

Figure 17-8 Change the preference order of a GPO.

Editing an existing GPO in Group Policy Management Console

In Group Policy Management Console, you can edit an existing GPO linked to the selected container by pressing and holding or right-clicking it and then selecting Edit. This displays the Group Policy Object Editor console. You can then make changes to Group Policy as necessary. The changes will be applied the next time Active Directory is refreshed, according to the inheritance and preference options used by Active Directory.

Linking to an existing GPO in Group Policy Management Console

Linking a GPO to a container applies the object to the container. In Group Policy Management Console, you can link an existing GPO to a domain, OU, or site by completing the following steps:

1. Access the domain or OU you want to work with in Group Policy Management Console. Do this by expanding the forest node and the related Domains node as necessary.

2. Press and hold or right-click the domain, OU, or site node and select Link An Existing GPO.

3. In the Select GPO dialog box, shown in Figure 17-9, select the GPO to use and then tap or click OK.

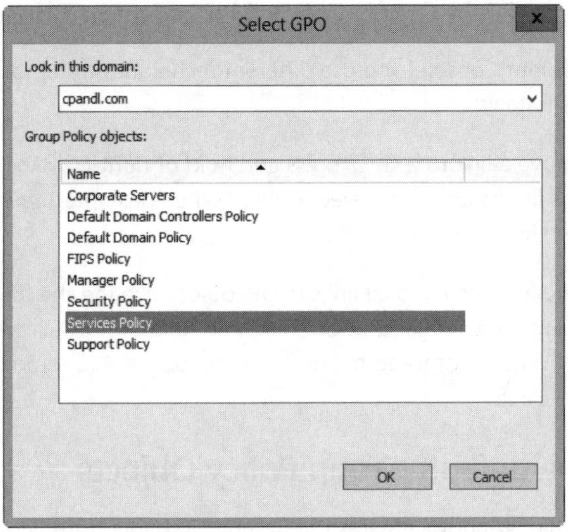

Figure 17-9 Select the GPO that you want to link to the currently selected container.

4. The linked policy will be applied the next time Active Directory is refreshed, according to the inheritance and preference options used by Active Directory.

Working with starter GPOs

Any time you create a new GPO in Group Policy Management Console, you can base the new GPO on a starter GPO. Because the settings of the starter GPO are imported into the new GPO, you can use a starter GPO to define the base configuration settings for a new GPO. In the enterprise, you'll want to create different categories of starter GPOs either based on the users and computers with which they will be used or based on the required security configurations.

To create a starter GPO, follow these steps:

1. In Group Policy Management Console, expand the entry for the forest you want to work with and then double-tap or double-click the related Domains node to expand it.

2. Press and hold or right-click the Starter GPOs node and then select New. In the New Starter GPO dialog box, type a descriptive name for the new starter GPO, such as **Standard User GPO**. If you want, you can enter comments describing the GPO's purpose. Tap or click OK.

3. Press and hold or right-click the new GPO and then select Edit. In Group Policy Object Editor, configure policy settings as necessary and then close Group Policy Object Editor.

CHAPTER 17

Deleting an existing GPO in Group Policy Management Console

In Group Policy Management Console, you use different techniques to remove GPO links and the GPOs themselves, as follows:

- If you want to remove a link to a GPO, press and hold or right-click the GPO in the container to which it is linked and then select Delete. When prompted to confirm that you want to remove the link, tap or click OK.

- If you want to remove a GPO and all links to the object, expand the forest, the Domains node, and the Group Policy Objects node. Press and hold or right-click the GPO and then select Delete. When prompted to confirm that you want to remove the GPO and all links to it, tap or click OK.

Working with the default Group Policy Objects

When you create a domain, Windows creates the Default Domain Controllers Policy GPO and the Default Domain Policy GPO. These default GPOs are essential to the operation and processing of Group Policy. By default, in the precedence order of GPOs, Default Domain Controllers Policy GPO is the highest-precedence GPO linked to the Domain Controllers OU and Default Domain Policy GPO is the highest-precedence GPO linked to the domain.

Although the Default Domain Policy GPO is a complete policy set that includes settings for managing the many policy areas discussed previously, this GPO isn't meant for the general management of Group Policy. You should edit the Default Domain Policy GPO only to manage the default settings for Account Policies (and three specific policies that I'll mention in a moment).

The areas of Account Policy you manage through the Default Domain Policy GPO are as follows:

- **Password Policy.** Determines the default password policies for domain controllers, such as the password history and minimum password length settings

- **Account Lockout Policy.** Determines the default account lockout policies for domain controllers, such as the account lockout duration and account lockout threshold

- **Kerberos Policy.** Determines default Kerberos policies for domain controllers, such as the maximum tolerance for computer clock synchronization

The Default Domain Policy GPO is the only GPO through which Account Policies should be set. To manage other areas of policy, you should create a new GPO and link it to the domain or to an appropriate OU within the domain. This is because only the Account Policy settings for the GPO linked to the domain level with the highest precedence in Active Directory are applied, and, by default, this is the Default Domain Policy GPO.

A few additional policy settings should be managed through the GPO linked to the domain level, and they have the highest precedence as well. These policies—located under Computer Configuration, Windows Settings, Security Settings, Local Policies, Security Options in Group Policy—are as follows:

- **Accounts: Rename Administrator Account.** Configure this policy setting if you want to rename the Administrator account throughout the domain. This sets a new name for the built-in Administrator account so that it's better protected from malicious users. It's important to point out that this specifically affects the logon name of the account and not the display name. The display name will continue to be set to Administrator (or whatever you've set it to). Further, if you or another administrator changes the logon name for this account through Active Directory Users And Computers, the logon name will automatically change back to what is set in policy the next time Group Policy is refreshed.

- **Accounts: Rename Guest Account.** Configure this policy setting if you want to rename the Guest account throughout the domain. This sets a new name for the built-in Guest account so that it's better protected from malicious users. It's important to point out that this specifically affects the logon name of the account and not the display name. The display name will continue to be set to Guest (or whatever you've set it to). Further, if you or another administrator changes the logon name for this account through Active Directory Users And Computers, the logon name will automatically change back to what is set in policy the next time Group Policy is refreshed.

- **Network Access: Allow Anonymous SID/Name Translation.** This policy determines whether an anonymous user can request security identifier (SID) attributes for another user. In most configurations this setting is disabled by default. If this setting is enabled, a malicious user could use the well-known Administrator's SID to obtain the real name of the built-in Administrator account, even if the account has been renamed.

- **Network Security: Force Logoff When Logon Hours Expire.** Configure this policy setting if you want to force users to log off from the domain when logon hours expire. For example, if you set the logon hours from 7 A.M. to 7 P.M. for the user, the user will be forced to log off at 8 P.M.

The Default Domain Controllers Policy GPO is designed to ensure that all domain controllers in a specified domain have the same security settings. This is important because all domain controllers in an Active Directory domain are equal. If there were different security settings on each domain controller, different domain controllers might behave differently, and this would be bad, bad, bad. If one domain controller has a specific policy setting, this policy setting should be applied to all domain controllers to ensure consistent behavior across a domain.

CHAPTER 17

Because all domain controllers are placed in the Domain Controllers OU by default, any security setting changes you make apply to all domain controllers by default. You should use the Default Domain Controllers Policy GPO only to set user rights and to audit policies. Audit Policy determines default auditing policies for domain controllers, such as logging event success, failure, or both. User Rights Assignment determines the default user rights assignment for domain controllers, such as the Log On As A Service right and the Allow Log On Locally right.

CAUTION

If you move a domain controller out of the Domain Controllers OU, you could impair domain management, which could lead to inconsistent behavior during logon and authentication. To prevent problems, any time you move a domain controller out of the Domain Controllers OU you should thereafter carefully manage its security settings. As an example, whenever you make security changes to the Default Domain Controllers Policy GPO, you should ensure that those security changes are applied to domain controllers stored in OUs other than the Domain Controllers OU.

Managing Group Policy through delegation

In Active Directory, administrators are automatically granted permissions for performing different Group Policy management tasks. Other individuals can be granted such permissions through delegation. You delegate to allow a user who is not a member of Enterprise Admins or Domain Admins to perform any management tasks.

Managing GPO creation rights

In Active Directory, administrators are able to create GPOs in a domain and anyone who has created a GPO in a domain has the right to manage that GPO. You can determine who can create GPOs in a domain by following these steps:

1. In Group Policy Management Console, expand the entry for the forest you want to work with, expand the related Domains node, and then select the Group Policy Objects node.

2. As shown in Figure 17-10, the users and groups who can create GPOs in the selected domain are listed in the Delegation tab.

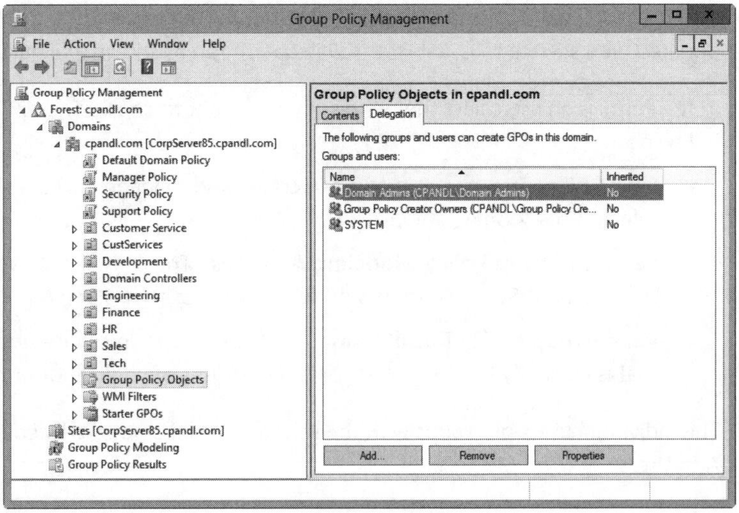

Figure 17-10 Determine creation rights for GPOs.

You can delegate the permission to create GPOs (and thus implicitly grant users or groups the ability to manage the GPOs they create). To grant GPO creation permission to a user or group, follow these steps:

1. In Group Policy Management Console, expand the entry for the forest you want to work with, expand the related Domains node, and then select the Group Policy Objects node.

2. In the right pane, select the Delegation tab. The current GPO creation permissions for individual users and groups are listed. To grant the GPO creation permission to another user or group, tap or click Add.

3. In the Select User, Computer, Or Group dialog box, select the user or group and then tap or click OK.

4. The options in the Delegation tab are updated appropriately. If you later want to remove the GPO creation permission, access the Delegation tab, select the user or group, and then tap or click Remove.

Reviewing Group Policy management privileges

Group Policy Management Console gives you several ways to determine who can manage Group Policy. You can determine Group Policy permissions for a specific site, domain, or OU by following these steps:

1. In Group Policy Management Console, expand the entry for the forest you want to work with and then expand the related Domains or Sites node as appropriate.

CHAPTER 17

2. When you select the domain, site, or OU you want to work with, the right pane is updated with several tabs. Select the Delegation tab as shown in Figure 17-11.

3. In the Permission list, select the permission you want to check. The options are the following:

    ■ **Link GPOs.** The user or group can create and manage links to GPOs in the selected site, domain, or OU.

    ■ **Perform Group Policy Modeling Analyses.** The user or group can determine the Resultant Set of Policy (RSoP) for the purposes of planning.

    ■ **Read Group Policy Results Data.** The user or group can determine the RSoP that is currently being applied for the purposes of verification or logging.

4. The individual users or groups with the selected permissions are listed under Groups And Users.

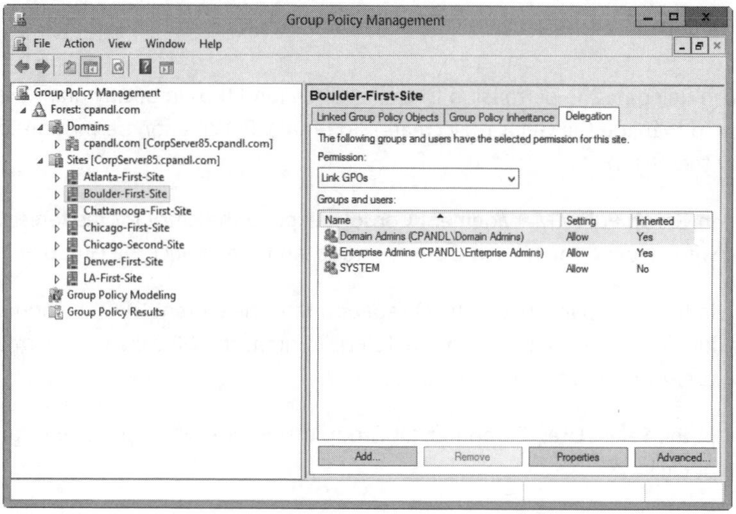

Figure 17-11 Determine permissions for a site, domain, or OU.

You can determine which users or groups have access to a particular GPO and what permissions have been granted to them by following these steps:

1. In Group Policy Management Console, expand the entry for the forest you want to work with, expand the related Domains node, and then select the Group Policy Objects node.

2. When you select the GPO whose permissions you want to check, the right pane is updated with several tabs. Select the Delegation tab as shown in Figure 17-12.

3.   The permissions for individual users and groups are listed. You'll see three general types of allowed permissions:

- **Read.** Enables the user or group to view the GPO and its settings.

- **Edit Settings.** Enables the user or group to view the GPO and its settings. The user or group can also change settings but can't delete the GPO or modify its security.

- **Edit Settings, Delete, Modify Security.** Enables the user or group to view the GPO and its settings. The user or group can also change settings, delete the GPO, and modify the security of the GPO.

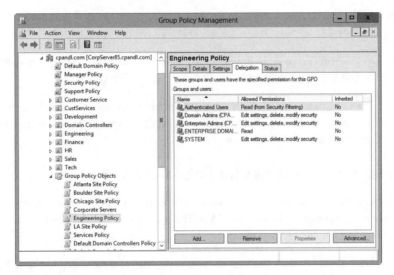

Figure 17-12 Determine permissions on a GPO.

Delegating Group Policy management privileges

You can allow a nonadministrative user or a group (including users and groups from other domains) to work with a domain, site, or OU GPO by granting one of three specific permissions:

- **Read.** Permits the user or group to view the GPO and its settings.

- **Edit Settings.** Permits the user or group to view the GPO and its settings. The user or group can also change settings but can't delete the GPO or modify its security.

- **Edit Settings, Delete, Modify Security.** Permits the user or group to view the GPO and its settings. The user or group can also change settings, delete the GPO, and modify the security of the GPO.

CHAPTER 17

You can grant these permissions to a user or group by following these steps:

1. In Group Policy Management Console, expand the entry for the forest you want to work with, expand the related Domains node, and then expand the Group Policy Objects node.

2. Select the GPO you want to work with in the left pane. In the right pane, select the Delegation tab.

3. The current permissions for individual users and groups are listed. To grant permissions to another user or group, tap or click Add.

4. In the Select User, Computer, Or Group dialog box, select the user or group and then tap or click OK.

5. In the Add Group Or User dialog box, select the permission to grant: Read, Edit Settings, or Edit Settings, Delete, Modify Security. Tap or click OK.

6. The options in the Delegation tab are updated to reflect the permissions granted. If you later want to remove this permission, access the Delegation tab, select the user or group, and then tap or click Remove.

Delegating privileges for links and RSoP

You can allow a nonadministrative user or a group (including users and groups from other domains) to manage GPO links and RSoP. The related permissions can be granted in any combination and are defined as follows:

*   **Link GPOs.** Permits the user or group to create and manage links to GPOs in the selected site, domain, or OU

*   **Perform Group Policy Modeling Analyses.** Permits the user or group to determine RSoP for the purposes of planning

*   **Read Group Policy Results Data.** Permits the user or group to determine RSoP that is currently being applied for the purposes of verification or logging

You can grant these permissions to a user or group by following these steps:

1. In Group Policy Management Console, expand the entry for the forest you want to work with and then expand the related Domains or Sites node as appropriate.

2. In the left pane, select the domain, site, or OU you want to work with. In the right pane, select the Delegation tab.

3. In the Permission list, select the permission you want to grant. The options are Link GPOs, Perform Group Policy Modeling Analyses, and Read Group Policy Results Data.

4. The current permissions for individual users and groups are listed. To grant the selected permission to another user or group, tap or click Add.

5. In the Select User, Computer, Or Group dialog box, select the user or group and then tap or click OK.

6. In the Add Group Or User dialog box, specify how the permission should be applied. To apply the permission to the current container and all child containers, select This Container And All Child Containers. To apply the permission only to the current container, select This Container Only. Tap or click OK.

7. The options in the Delegation tab are updated to reflect the permissions granted. If you later want to remove this permission, access the Delegation tab, select the user or group, and then tap or click Remove.

Managing Group Policy inheritance and processing

GPOs can be linked to sites, domains, and OUs in Active Directory. When you create and link a GPO to one of these containers in Active Directory, the GPO is applied to the user and computer objects in that container according to the inheritance and preference options used by Active Directory. Computer-related policies are processed during startup of the operating system. User-related policies are processed when a user logs on to a computer. After they are applied, Group Policy settings are automatically refreshed at a specific interval to ensure that they are current. Group Policy settings can also be refreshed manually.

Group Policy inheritance

Active Directory uses inheritance to determine how Group Policy is applied. By default, Group Policy settings are inherited from top-level containers by lower-level containers. The order of inheritance goes from the site level to the domain level to the OU level. This means that the Group Policy settings for a site are passed down to the domains within the site and the settings for a domain are passed down to the OUs within that domain.

When multiple group policies are in place, the policies are applied in the following order:

- **Local group policies.** All computers running Windows have Local Group Policy. The local policy is applied first.

- **Site group policies.** Policies linked to sites are processed second. If there are multiple site policies, they are processed synchronously in the listed preference order.

- **Domain group policies.** Policies linked to domains are processed third. If there are multiple domain policies, they are processed synchronously in the listed preference order.

- **OU group policies.** Policies linked to top-level OUs are processed fourth. If there are multiple top-level OU policies, they are processed synchronously in the listed preference order.

- **Child OU group policies.** Policies linked to child OUs are processed fifth. If there are multiple child OU policies, they are processed synchronously in the listed preference order. When there are multiple levels of child OUs, policies for higher-level OUs are applied first and policies for lower-level OUs are applied next.

If multiple policies modify the same settings, the order in which policies are applied determines which policy settings take effect. Most policies have three configuration options: Not Configured, Enabled, and Disabled. The default state of most policies is Not Configured, meaning the policy setting is not configured and does not apply. If a policy is set to Enabled, the policy is enforced and applies to users and computers that are subject to the GPO. If a policy is set to Disabled, the policy is not enforced and does not apply to users and computers that are subject to the GPO.

To override a policy that is enabled in a higher-level container, you can specifically disable it in a lower-level policy. For example, if the user policy Prohibit Access To The Control Panel is enabled for a site, users in the site should not be able to access Control Panel. However, if domain policy specifically disables the user policy Prohibit Access To The Control Panel, users in the domain would be able to access Control Panel. In contrast, if the domain policy was set to Not Configured, the policy setting would not be modified and would be inherited as normal from the higher-level container.

To override a policy that is disabled in a higher-level container, you can specifically enable it in a lower-level policy. For example, if the user policy Force Automatic Setup For All Users is disabled for a domain, users in the domain would be able to choose whether they wanted to use automatic setup for Work Folders. However, if the Engineering OU policy specifically enables the user policy Force Automatic Setup For All Users, Work Folders would be set up automatically for users in the Engineering OU. Again, if the OU policy was instead set to Not Configured, the policy setting would not be modified and would be inherited as normal from the higher-level container.

Changing link order and precedence

The order of inheritance for Group Policy goes from the site level to the domain level and then to each nested OU level. When multiple policy objects are linked to a particular level, the link order determines the order in which policy settings are applied. Linked policy objects are always applied in link ranking order. Lower-ranking policy objects are processed before higher-ranking policy objects.

As shown in Figure 17-13, these policies will be processed from the lowest link order to the highest. Here the Mobile Devices Policy (with link order 2) will be processed before the Technology Policy (with link order 1). Because Technology Policy settings are processed after Mobile Devices Policy settings, Technology Policy settings have precedence and take priority.

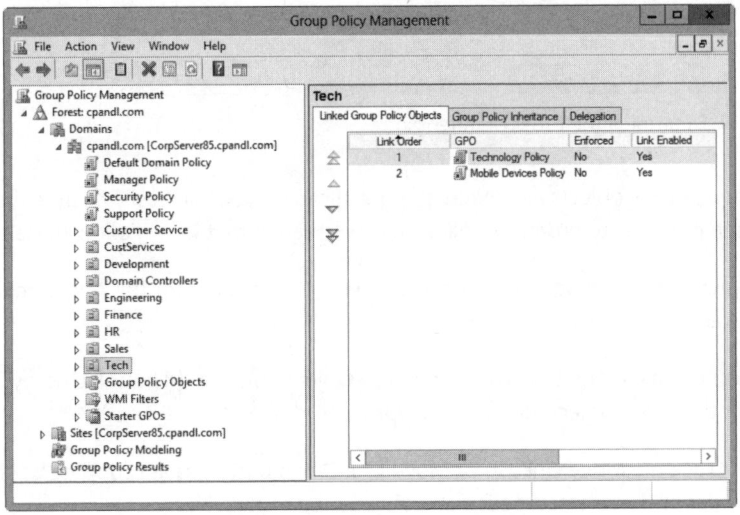

Figure 17-13 Determine the policy-processing order.

To view all inherited GPOs, tap or click the Group Policy Inheritance tab, as shown in Figure 17-14. The precedence order shows exactly how policy objects are being processed for a site, domain, or OU. As with link order, lower-ranking policy objects are processed before higher-ranking policy objects. Here, the Manager Policy (with precedence 4) will be processed first, then Support Policy (with precedence 3), and so on. Because Default Domain Policy is processed last, any policy settings configured in this policy object are final and will override those of other policy objects (unless inheritance blocking or enforcing is used).

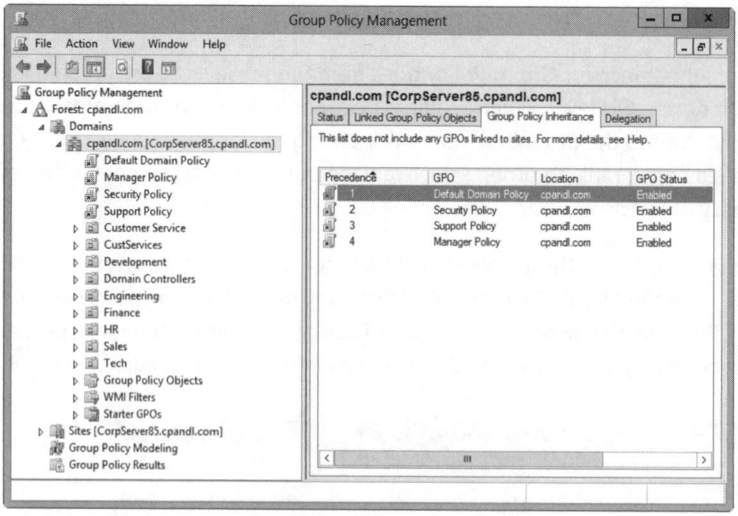

Figure 17-14 Determine the order of inheritance.

When multiple policy objects are linked at a specific level, you can easily change the link order (and thus the precedence order) of policy objects linked at that level. Follow these steps:

1. In Group Policy Management Console, select the container for the site, domain, or OU you want to work with.

2. In the right pane, the Linked Group Policy Objects tab should be selected by default. Select the policy object you want to work with.

3. Tap or click the Move Link Up or Move Link Down button as appropriate to change the link order of the selected policy object.

4. When you are done changing the link order, confirm that policy objects are being processed in the expected order by checking the precedence order in the Group Policy Inheritance tab.

Overriding inheritance

As you know, Group Policy settings are inherited from top-level containers by lower-level containers. If multiple policy objects modify the same settings, the order in which the policy objects are applied determines which policy settings take effect. Essentially, the order of inheritance goes from the site level to the domain level to the OU level. This means that Group Policy settings for a site are passed down to the domains within the site and the settings for a domain are passed down to the OUs within that domain.

You can override policy in two key ways:

- **Disable an enabled (and inherited) policy.** When a policy is enabled in a higher-level policy object, you can override inheritance by disabling the policy in a lower-level policy object. By disabling the policy in a lower-level policy object, you override the policy that is enabled in the higher-level container. For example, if the user policy Prohibit Use Of Internet Connection Sharing On Your DNS Domain Network is enabled for a site, users in the site should not be able to use Internet Connection Sharing. However, if domain policy specifically disables this user policy, users in the domain would be able to use Internet Connection Sharing. In contrast, if the domain policy was set to Not Configured, the policy setting would not be modified and would be inherited as normal from the higher-level container.

- **Enable a disabled (and inherited) policy.** When a policy is disabled in a higher-level policy object, you can override inheritance by enabling the policy in a lower-level policy object. By enabling the policy in a lower-level policy object, you override the policy that is disabled in the higher-level container. For example, if the user policy Allow Shared Folders To Be Published is disabled for a domain, users in the domain would not be able to publish shared folders in Active Directory. However, if the Support Team OU policy specifically enables this user policy, users in the Support Team OU would be able to publish shared folders in Active Directory. Again, if the OU policy was set to Not Configured, the policy setting would not be modified and would be inherited as normal from the higher-level container.

Overriding inheritance is a basic technique for changing the way inheritance works. As long as a policy is not blocked or enforced, this technique will achieve the desired effect.

Blocking inheritance

Sometimes you will want to block inheritance so that no policy settings from higher-level containers are applied to users and computers in a particular container. When inheritance is blocked, only configured policy settings from policy objects linked at that level are applied. This means that all GPOs from all higher-level containers are blocked (as long as there is no policy enforcement).

Domain administrators can use inheritance blocking to block inherited policy settings from the site level. OU administrators can use inheritance blocking to block inherited policy settings from both the domain level and the site level. Here are some examples of inheritance blocking in action:

- You don't want a domain to inherit any site policies, so you configure the domain to block inheritance from higher-level containers. Because inheritance is blocked, only the configured policy settings from policy objects linked to the domain are applied.

Although blocking inheritance of a site policy doesn't affect the inheritance of the domain policy objects by OUs, it does mean that OUs in that domain will not inherit site policies either.

- You don't want an OU to inherit any site or domain policies, so you configure the OU to block inheritance from higher-level containers. Because inheritance is blocked, only the configured policy settings from policy objects linked to the OU are applied. If the OU contains other OUs, inheritance blocking won't affect inheritance of policy objects linked to this OU, but the child OUs will not inherit site or domain policies.

Using Group Policy Management Console, you can block inheritance by pressing and holding or right-clicking the domain or OU that should not inherit settings from higher-level containers and selecting Block Inheritance. If Block Inheritance is already selected, selecting it again removes the setting. When you block inheritance in Group Policy Management Console, a blue circle with an exclamation point is added to the container's node in the console tree. The notification icon provides a quick way to tell whether any domain or OU has the Block Inheritance setting enabled.

Enforcing inheritance

To prevent administrators who have authority over a container from overriding or blocking the inherited Group Policy settings, you can enforce inheritance. When inheritance is enforced, all policy settings from higher-level policy objects are inherited and applied regardless of the policy settings in lower-level policy objects. Thus, the enforcement of inheritance is used to supersede the overriding and blocking of policy settings.

Forest administrators can use inheritance enforcement to ensure that policy settings from the site level are applied and to prevent the overriding or blocking of policy settings by both domain administrators and OU administrators. Domain administrators can use inheritance enforcement to ensure that policy settings from the domain level are applied and to prevent the overriding or blocking of policy settings by OU administrators. Here are some examples of inheritance enforcement in action:

- As a forest administrator, you want to ensure that domains inherit a particular site policy, so you configure the site policy so that inheritance is enforced. Because inheritance is enforced, all policy settings from the site policy are applied regardless of whether domain administrators have tried to override or block policy settings from the site level. The enforcement of the site policy also affects the inheritance for OUs in the affected domains. OUs in the affected domains will inherit the site policy regardless of whether overriding or blocking has been used.

- As a domain administrator, you want to ensure that OUs within the domain inherit a particular domain policy, so you configure the domain policy so that inheritance is enforced. Because inheritance is enforced, all policy settings from the domain policy are applied regardless of whether OU administrators have tried to override or block policy settings from the domain level. The enforcement of the domain policy also affects the inheritance for child OUs within the affected OUs. Child OUs within the affected OUs will inherit the domain policy regardless of whether overriding or blocking has been used.

Using Group Policy Management Console, you enforce policy inheritance by expanding the container to which the policy is linked, pressing and holding or right-clicking the policy, and then selecting Enforced. If Enforced is already selected, selecting it again removes the enforcement. In Group Policy Management Console, you can determine which policies are inherited and which policies are enforced in two ways:

- Select a policy object anywhere in Group Policy Management Console and then view the related Scope tab in the right pane. If the policy is enforced, the Enforced column under Links will have a Yes entry. After you select a policy object, you can press and hold or right-click a location entry in the Scope tab to display a shortcut menu. You can use this shortcut menu to manage linking and policy enforcement.

- Select a domain or OU container in Group Policy Management Console and then view the related Group Policy Inheritance tab in the right pane. If the policy is enforced, you'll see an (Enforced) entry in the Precedence column.

Filtering Group Policy application

By default, GPOs apply to all users and computers in the container to which the GPO is linked. The GPO applies to all users and computers in this way because of the security settings on the GPO, which specify that Authenticated Users have Read permission and Apply Group Policy permission. Thus, the policy affects all users and computers with accounts in the domain. Permissions are also assigned to administrators and the operating system. All members of the Enterprise Admins and Domain Admins groups and the LocalSystem account have permission to edit GPOs and to manage their security.

You can modify which users and computers are affected by a particular GPO by changing the accounts for which the Apply Group Policy permission is set. In this way, you can selectively apply a GPO, which is known as *filtering* Group Policy. For example, say that you create a Technology OU with separate Group Policy objects for users and managers. You want the user GPO to apply to all users who are members of the TechUsers group and the manager GPO to apply to all users who are members of the TechMgrs group. To do this, you must configure the user policy so that the Read and Apply Group Policy permissions apply to the TechUsers group only, and you must configure the manager policy so that the Read and Apply Group Policy permissions apply to the TechMgrs group only.

Before you selectively apply a GPO, you must carefully consider the types of policies it sets. If the GPO sets computer policies, you must ensure that the computer accounts are included so that the computer reads the GPO and applies it at the startup of networking. If the GPO sets user policies, you must ensure that the groups of which the users are members or the individual user accounts are included so that the Group Policy engine reads the GPO and applies it when users log on.

Use the following guidelines to help you determine how permissions should be configured:

- **Group Policy should be applied to all members of a group.** Add the group to the access control list (ACL) for the GPO. Set Read to Allow and set Apply Group Policy to Allow. The Group Policy Object will then be applied to all members of the group except those who are members of another group for which Read or Apply Group Policy is set to Deny.

- **Group Policy should not be applied to members of a group.** Add the group to the ACL for the GPO. Set Read to Deny and set Apply Group Policy to Deny. The Group Policy Object will not be applied to any members of the group, regardless of which other groups members belong to.

- **Membership in this group should not determine whether Group Policy is applied.** Remove the group from the ACL for the GPO or clear both the Allow and Deny check boxes for the Read permission and the Apply Group Policy permission. After you do this, membership in the group will not determine whether the GPO is applied.

You can selectively apply a GPO by completing the following steps:

1. In Group Policy Management Console, select the policy in a container to which the GPO is linked or in the Group Policy Objects node.

2. In the details pane, select the Delegation tab and then tap or click the Advanced button in the lower-right corner of the dialog box. This displays the policy's Security Settings dialog box, as shown in Figure 17-15.

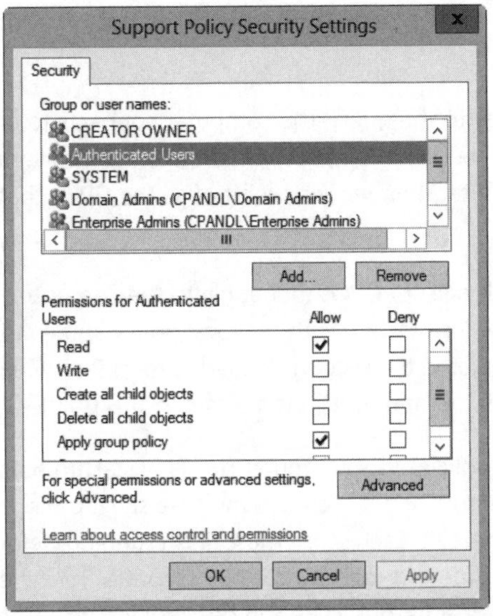

Figure 17-15 Access the security settings for a GPO.

3. You can then add or remove groups as necessary. After a group is added, you can select the Allow or Deny check box for the Read and Apply Group Policy permissions as necessary.

4. When you are finished configuring the ACL for the GPO, tap or click OK until all open dialog boxes are closed.

Group Policy processing

Group Policy settings are divided into two categories:

- **Computer Configuration settings.** Policies that apply to computer accounts only

- **User Configuration settings.** Policies that apply to user accounts only

Normally, Computer Configuration settings are applied during the startup of the operating system and User Configuration settings are applied when a user logs on to a computer. The sequence of events is often important in troubleshooting system behavior. The events that take place during startup and logon are as follows:

1. When the client computer starts, networking is started as part of the normal system startup. The computer reads the registry to determine the Active Directory site in which the computer is located. The computer then sends a query to its primary Domain

Name System (DNS) server to determine the Internet Protocol (IP) addresses of domain controllers in the site.

2.   When the DNS server replies to the query, the computer connects to a domain controller in the local site. The client computer and domain controller authenticate each other. The client computer then requests a list of all the GPOs that apply to the computer.

3.   The domain controller sends a list of GPOs that apply to the computer. The computer processes and applies the GPOs, starting with the local policy and continuing as discussed earlier in the chapter in the section entitled "Group Policy inheritance." Note that only the Computer Configuration settings are sent at this point.

4.   After processing computer policies, the computer runs any startup scripts. Startup scripts are hidden from view by default, and if there are multiple startup scripts the scripts run in sequential order by default. Each script must finish running before the next one can be started. The default time-out for scripts is 600 seconds. Both the synchronous processing of scripts and their time-out value can be modified using Group Policy.

5.   When a user logs on to the computer and is validated, the computer loads the user profile and then requests a list of all the GPOs that apply to the user.

6.   The domain controller sends a list of GPOs that apply to the user. The computer processes and applies the GPOs, starting with the local policy and continuing as discussed earlier in the chapter in the section entitled "Group Policy inheritance." Although only the User Configuration settings are sent and applied at this point, note that any computer policy settings that overlap user policy settings are overwritten by default. User policy settings have precedence by default.

7.   After processing user policies, the computer runs any logon scripts. Logon scripts are hidden from view by default, and if there are multiple logon scripts the scripts run asynchronously by default. Thus, unlike startup scripts for which each script must finish running before the next one can be started, logon scripts are all started and run simultaneously. The default time-out for scripts is 600 seconds.

8.   The user interface, as defined in the user's profile and governed by the policy settings that are in effect, is displayed. If the user logs off the computer, any logoff scripts defined for the user are run. If the user shuts down the computer, logging off is part of the shutdown process, so the user is first logged off and any logoff scripts defined for the user are run. Then the computer runs any shutdown scripts defined for the computer.

CHAPTER 17

Inside OUT

All Group Policy processing is handled as a refresh

Technically, all Group Policy processing is handled as a Group Policy refresh. Thus, processing during startup and logon is technically a refresh, which is handled as discussed later in this chapter in the section entitled "Group Policy refresh." The most important note about refresh is that if the client computer detects that it's using a slow network connection, only Security Settings and Administrative Templates are processed. Although there is no way to turn off the processing of these extensions, you can configure other extensions so that they are processed even across a slow network connection. For more information, see the section entitled "Modifying Group Policy refresh" later in the chapter.

Modifying Group Policy processing

You can modify Group Policy processing by disabling a policy in whole or in part. Disabling a policy is useful if you no longer need a policy but might need to use that policy again in the future. Disabling part of a policy is useful so that the policy applies to either users or computers, not both. You can also modify Group Policy processing as part of troubleshooting.

In Group Policy Management Console, you can enable and disable policies partially or entirely by completing the following steps:

1. In Group Policy Management Console, select the container for the site, domain, or OU you want to work with.

2. In the right pane, select the Details tab and then use the GPO Status selection menu to choose a status as one of the following:

   - **Enabled.** Allows the processing of the policy object and all its settings

   - **All Settings Disabled.** Disallows the processing of the policy object and all its settings

   - **Computer Configuration Settings Disabled.** Disables the processing of Computer Configuration settings, which means only User Configuration settings are processed

   - **User Configuration Settings Disabled.** Disables the processing of User Configuration settings, which means only Computer Configuration settings are processed

CHAPTER 17

3. When prompted to confirm that you want to change the status of this GPO, tap or click OK.

Modifying user policy preference using loopback processing

When a user logs on, the client computer applies User Configuration settings. Because user policy settings have precedence by default, any computer policy settings that overlap user policy settings are overwritten. However, for some computers (particularly special-use computers in classrooms, labs, or public places), you might want to restrict the computer to a specific configuration. In this case, you might not want less-restrictive user policy settings to be applied.

To change the default behavior that gives preference to user policy, you can enable the loopback processing policy. By enabling the loopback processing policy, you ensure that the Computer Configuration settings always apply. Loopback processing can be set in one of two ways: either with Replace or Merge. When you use the Replace option, user settings from the computer's GPOs are processed and the user settings in the user's GPOs are not processed. This means the user settings from the computer's GPOs replace the user settings normally applied to the user.

When you use the Merge option, user settings in the computer's GPOs are processed first, then user settings in the user's GPOs are processed, and then user settings in the computer's GPOs are processed again. This processing technique combines the user settings in the computer and user GPOs. If there are any conflicts, the user settings in the computer's GPOs have preference and overwrite the user settings in the user's GPOs.

To configure loopback processing, follow these steps:

1. Start Group Policy Object Editor. In Group Policy Management Console, press and hold or right-click the Group Policy Object you want to modify and then select Edit.

2. Double-tap or double-click the Configure User Group Policy Loopback Processing Mode in the Computer Configuration\Administrative Templates\System\Group Policy folder.

3. Define the policy by selecting Enabled, as shown in Figure 17-16, and then use the Mode selection menu to set the processing mode as either Replace or Merge.

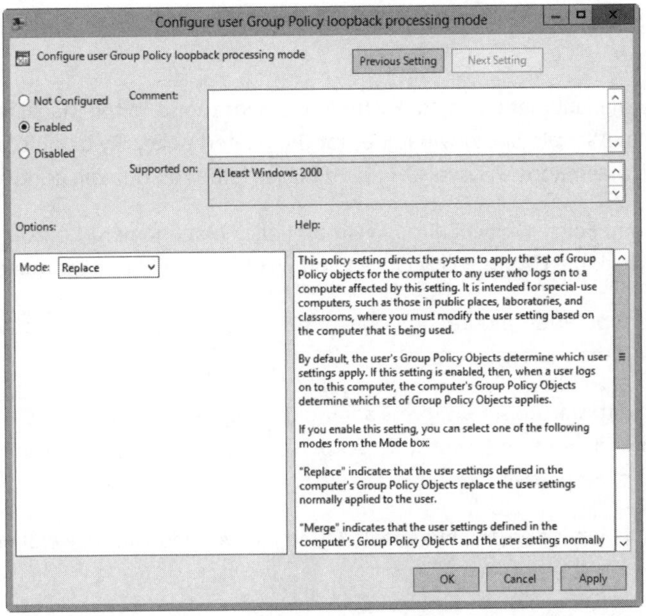

Figure 17-16 Configure loopback processing to give the Computer Configuration settings preference.

4.   Tap or click OK. All current Windows operating systems support this policy.

Using scripts in Group Policy

You can configure computer startup and shutdown scripts and user logon and logoff scripts. You can write these scripts as command-shell batch scripts ending with the .bat or .cmd extension, as scripts that use the Windows Script Host (WSH), or as scripts that use Windows PowerShell. WSH is a feature of Windows Server that lets you use scripts written in a scripting language, such as Microsoft JScript and Microsoft VBScript.

Configuring computer startup and shutdown scripts

You can assign computer startup and shutdown scripts as part of a Group Policy Object. In this way, all computers in a site, domain, or OU run scripts automatically when they're started or shut down.

CHAPTER 17

To configure a script that should be used during computer startup or shutdown, follow these steps:

1. For easy management, copy the scripts you want to use to the Machine\Scripts\Startup or Machine\Scripts\Shutdown folder for the related policy. By default, policies are stored in the %SystemRoot%\Sysvol\Domain\Policies folder on domain controllers.

2. Start Group Policy Object Editor. In Group Policy Management Console, press and hold or right-click the Group Policy Object you want to modify and then select Edit.

3. In the Computer Configuration node, double-tap or double-click the Windows Settings folder and then select Scripts.

4. To work with startup scripts, press and hold or right-click Startup and then select Properties. To work with shutdown scripts, press and hold or right-click Shutdown and then select Properties.

5. The Scripts tab is selected by default. If you are working with PowerShell scripts, select the PowerShell Scripts tab.

6. Tap or click Show Files. If you copied the computer script to the correct location in the Policies folder, you should see the script.

7. Tap or click Add to assign a script. This opens the Add A Script dialog box. In the Script Name field, type the name of the script you copied to the Machine\Scripts\Startup folder or the Machine\Scripts\Shutdown folder for the related policy. Repeat this step to add other scripts.

8. During startup or shutdown, scripts are run in the order in which they're listed in the Properties dialog box. Use the Up or Down button to reposition scripts as necessary.

9. To delete a script, select the script in the Script For list and then tap or click Remove.

10. If you are working with PowerShell scripts, you can elect to run PowerShell scripts before or after other types of scripts. To specify your preference, use the Run Scripts In The Following Order list.

Configuring user logon and logoff scripts

You can assign logon and logoff scripts as part of a Group Policy Object. In this way, all users in a site, domain, or OU run scripts automatically when they log on or log off.

To configure a script that should be executed when a user logs on or logs off, complete the following steps:

1. For easy management, copy the scripts you want to use to the User\Scripts\Logon folder or to the User\Scripts\Logoff folder for the related policy. By default, policies are stored in the %SystemRoot%\Sysvol\Domain\Policies folder on domain controllers.

2. Start Group Policy Object Editor. In Group Policy Management Console, press and hold or right-click the Group Policy Object you want to modify and then select Edit.

3. Double-tap or double-click the Windows Settings folder in the User Configuration node and then tap or click Scripts.

4. To work with logon scripts, press and hold or right-click Logon and then select Properties. To work with logoff scripts, press and hold or right-click Logoff and then select Properties.

5. The Scripts tab is selected by default. If you are working with PowerShell scripts, select the PowerShell Scripts tab.

6. Tap or click Show Files. If you copied the user script to the correct location in the Policies folder, you should see the script.

7. Tap or click Add to assign a script. This opens the Add A Script dialog box. In the Script Name field, type the name of the script you copied to the User\Scripts\Logon folder or the User\Scripts\Logoff folder for the related policy. Repeat this step to add other scripts.

8. During logon or logoff, scripts are executed in the order in which they're listed in the Properties dialog box. Use the Up or Down button to reposition scripts as necessary.

9. To delete a script, select the script in the Script For list and then tap or click Remove.

10. If you are working with PowerShell scripts, you can elect to run PowerShell scripts before or after other types of scripts. To specify your preference, use the Run Scripts In The Following Order list.

Applying Group Policy through security templates

Security templates take the guesswork out of configuring a computer's initial security. You use security templates to apply customized sets of Group Policy definitions that are security related. These policy definitions generally affect the following components:

- Account policy settings that control security for passwords, account lockout, and Kerberos

- Local policy settings that control security for auditing, user rights assignment, and other security options

- Event log policy settings that control security for event logging

- Restricted groups policies that control security for local group membership and administration

- System services policy settings that control the startup mode for local services

- File system policy settings that control security for the local file system

- Registry policy settings that control the values of security-related registry keys

Working with security templates

Security templates can be imported into any GPO. The templates are stored in the %SystemRoot%\Security\Templates folder by default, and you can access them using the Security Templates snap-in. You can also use the snap-in to create new templates. The standard template for domain controllers is DC Security, which contains the default security settings for a domain controller.

After you select the template that you want to use, you should go through each setting that the template will apply and evaluate how the setting will affect your environment. If a setting doesn't make sense, you should modify or delete it as appropriate.

You use the Security Templates snap-in only for viewing templates. You apply templates using the Security Configuration And Analysis snap-in. You can also use Security Configuration And Analysis to compare the settings in a template to the existing settings on a computer. The results of the analysis will highlight areas in which the current settings don't match those in the template. This is useful to determine whether security settings have changed over time.

You can access the security snap-ins by completing the following steps:

1. Tap or click Start, type **mmc** into the Search box, and then press Enter.

2. In the Microsoft Management Console, click File and then select Add/Remove Snap-in.

3. In the Add Or Remove Snap-ins dialog box, select Security Templates and then tap or click Add.

4. Select Security Configuration And Analysis and then tap or click Add. Tap or click OK.

5. By default, the Security Templates snap-in looks for security templates in the %SystemDrive%\Users\%UserName%\Documents\Security\Templates folder. To add other search paths, choose New Template Search Path from the Action menu.

6. Select the template location to add from the Browse For Folder dialog box, such as %SystemRoot%\Security\Templates. Tap or click OK.

You can create a new template by following these steps:

1. In the Security Templates snap-in, press and hold or right-click the search path where the template should be created and then select New Template.

2. Type a name and description for the template in the text boxes provided.

3. Tap or click OK to create the template. The template will have no settings configured, so you need to modify the settings carefully before the template is ready for use.

Applying security templates

You use the Security Templates snap-in to view existing templates or to create new templates. After you create a template or determine that you want to use an existing template, you can configure and analyze the template by completing the following steps:

1. Access the Security Configuration And Analysis snap-in. Press and hold or right-click the Security Configuration And Analysis node and then select Open Database. This displays the Open Database dialog box.

2. Type a new database name in the File Name field and then tap or click Open. The Import Template dialog box is displayed. Select the security template that you want to use and then tap or click Open.

3. Press and hold or right-click the Security Configuration And Analysis node and then select Analyze Computer Now. When prompted to set the error log path, type a new path or tap or click OK to use the default path.

4. Wait for the snap-in to complete the analysis of the template. Afterward, review the findings and update the template as necessary. You can view the error log by pressing and holding or right-clicking the Security Configuration And Analysis node and choosing View Log File.

5. When you're ready to apply the template, press and hold or right-click the Security Configuration And Analysis node and select Configure Computer Now. When prompted to set the error log path, tap or click OK. The default path should be fine.

6. View the configuration error log by pressing and holding or right-clicking the Security Configuration And Analysis node and choosing View Log File. Note any problems and take action as necessary.

CHAPTER 17

Maintaining and troubleshooting Group Policy

Most Group Policy maintenance and troubleshooting tasks are related to determining when a policy is refreshed and applied and then changing the refresh options to ensure that the policy is applied as expected. Thus, maintaining and troubleshooting Group Policy require a keen understanding of how Group Policy refresh works and how it can be changed to meet your needs. You also need tools for modeling and viewing the GPOs that would be applied, or have been applied, to users and computers. Group Policy Management Console provides these tools through the Group Policy Modeling Wizard and the Group Policy Results Wizard, both of which you can use instead of running the Resultant Set Of Policy (RSoP) Wizard in logging mode or planning mode.

Group Policy refresh

Computer policies are applied when a computer starts, and user policies are applied when a user logs on. After the policies are applied, Group Policy settings are automatically refreshed to ensure that they are current. The default refresh interval for domain controllers is every five minutes. For all other computers, the default refresh interval is every 90 minutes, with up to a 30-minute variation to avoid overloading the domain controller with numerous client requests at the same time.

Change the refresh interval through Group Policy

If you like, you can change the Group Policy refresh interval. The related policies are stored in the Computer Configuration\Administrative Templates\System\Group Policy folder. To set the refresh interval for domain controllers, configure the Set Group Policy Refresh Interval For Domain Controllers policy. Select Enabled, set the refresh interval, and then tap or click OK. To set the refresh interval for all other computers, configure the Group Policy Refresh Interval For Computers policy. Select Enabled, set the refresh interval and random offset, and then tap or click OK.

During Group Policy refresh, the client contacts an available domain controller in its local site. If one or more of the GPOs defined in the domain have changed, the domain controller provides a list of all the GPOs that apply to the computer and to the user who is currently logged on, as appropriate. The domain controller does so regardless of whether the version numbers on all the listed GPOs have changed.

By default, the computer processes the GPOs only if the version number of at least one of the GPOs has changed. If any one of the related policies has changed, all of the policies have to be processed again. This is required because of inheritance and the interdependencies within policies. Security Settings are a noted exception to the processing rule. By default, Security

Settings are refreshed every 16 hours (960 minutes) regardless of whether GPOs contain changes. Also, if the client computer detects that it's connecting over a slow network connection, it tells the domain controller and only the Security Settings and Administrative Templates are transferred over the network, which means only the Security Settings and Administrative Templates are applied.

Modifying Group Policy refresh

Group Policy refresh can be changed in several ways. First, client computers determine that they are using a slow network connection by pinging the domain controller to which they are connected with a 0-byte packet. If the response time from the domain controller is more than 10 milliseconds, the computer pings the domain controller three times with a 2-kilobyte (KB) message packet to determine if it is on a slow network. The computer uses the average response time to determine the network speed. By default, if the connection speed is determined to be less than 500 kilobits per second (Kbps), the computer interprets that as a slow network connection—in which case it notifies the domain controller. As a result, only the Security Settings and Administrative Templates in the applicable GPOs are sent by the domain controller.

IMPORTANT

Windows 8.1 and Windows Server 2012 R2 support policies related to connections on cellular and broadband networks as well. Because these types of networks can incur usage charges, they are referred to as *costed networks***, and you'll find related policies under Computer Configuration\Administrative Templates\Network. In Group Policy under the Network folder, you also can specify that wireless WAN (WWAN) connections should always be treated as slow links.**

You can configure slow-link detection using the Configure Group Policy Slow Link Detection policy, which is stored in the Computer Configuration\Administrative Templates\System\Group Policy folder. To configure this policy, follow these steps:

1. Start Group Policy Object Editor. In Group Policy Management Console, press and hold or right-click the Group Policy Object you want to modify and then select Edit.

2. Double-tap or double-click the Configure Group Policy Slow Link Detection policy in the Computer Configuration\Administrative Templates\System\Group Policy folder.

3. Define the policy by selecting Enabled, as shown in Figure 17-17, and then use the Connection Speed combo box to specify the speed that should be used to determine whether a computer is on a slow link. For example, if you want connections less than 384 Kbps to be deemed slow connections, you type **384**. If you want to disable slow-link detection, type **0** (zero) in the Connection Speed box.

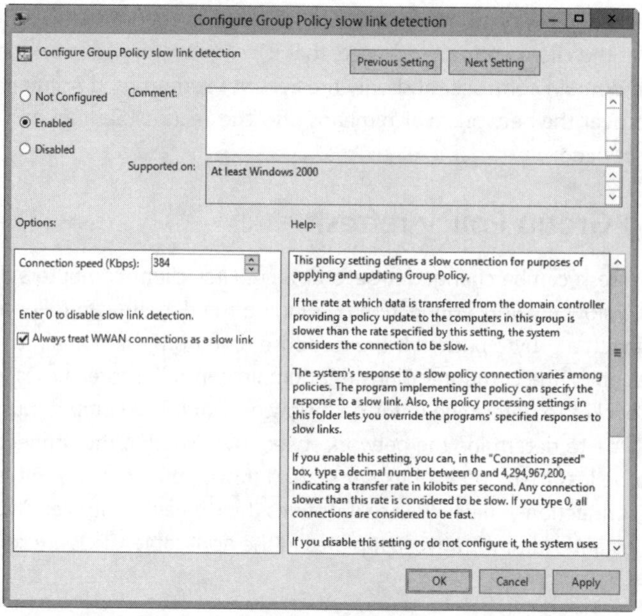

Figure 17-17 Configure slow-link detection as necessary.

4. You also can specify that WWAN connections should always be treated as slow links. Tap or click OK.

If there is any area of Group Policy for which you want to configure refresh, you can do this in Group Policy Object Editor. The related policies are stored in the Computer Configuration\Administrative Templates\System\Group Policy folder and include Applications Policy Processing, Data Sources Policy Processing, Devices Policy Processing, Disk Quota Policy Processing, Drive Maps Policy Processing, EFS Recovery Policy Processing, Environment Policy Processing, and several dozen other specific areas of policy processing.

NOTE
You use Registry Policy Processing to control the processing of all other registry-based extensions.

To configure the refresh of an extension, follow these steps:

1. Start Group Policy Object Editor. In Group Policy Management Console, press and hold or right-click the Group Policy Object you want to modify and then select Edit.

2. Double-tap or double-click the policy in the Computer Configuration\Administrative Templates\System\Group Policy folder.

3. Define the policy by selecting Enabled, as shown in Figure 17-18. The options you have differ slightly depending on the policy selected. They include the following:

- **Allow Processing Across A Slow Network Connection.** Select this option to ensure that the extension settings are processed even on a slow network.

- **Do Not Apply During Periodic Background Processing.** Select this option to override refresh when extension settings change after startup or logon.

- **Process Even If The Group Policy Objects Have Not Changed.** Select this option to force the client computer to process the extension settings during refresh even if the settings haven't changed.

- **Background Priority.** Determines when background processing occurs. If you select Idle, the background processing of the related policy occurs only when the computer is idle. Other processing options are for the lowest activity levels, below-normal activity levels, or normal activity levels.

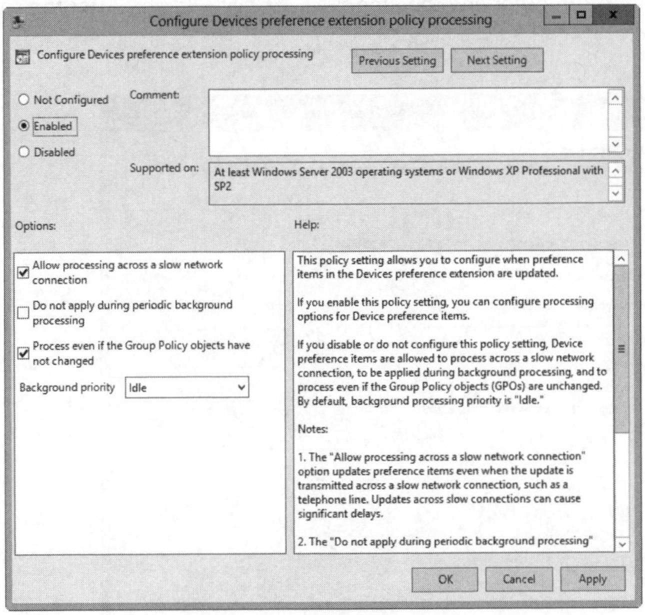

Figure 17-18 Change the way refresh works as necessary.

4. Tap or click OK.

CHAPTER 17

Viewing applicable GPOs and the last refresh

In Group Policy Management Console you can view all of the GPOs that apply to a computer and to the user logged on to that computer. You can also view the last time the applicable GPOs were processed (refreshed). To do this, you run the Group Policy Results Wizard.

To start the Group Policy Results Wizard and view applicable GPOs and the last refresh, follow these steps:

1. Start Group Policy Management Console. Press and hold or right-click Group Policy Results and then select Group Policy Results Wizard.

2. When the Group Policy Results Wizard starts, tap or click Next. On the Computer Selection page shown in Figure 17-19, select This Computer to view information for the local computer. If you want to view information for a remote computer, select Another Computer and then tap or click Browse. In the Select Computer dialog box, type the name of the computer and then tap or click Check Names. After the correct computer account is selected, tap or click OK.

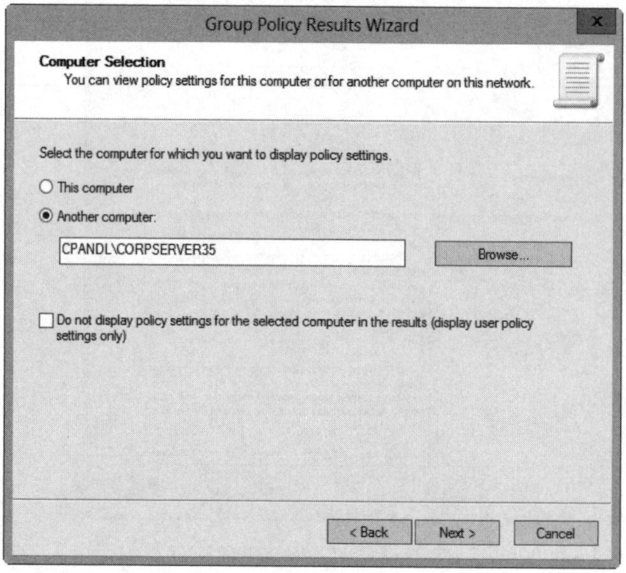

Figure 17-19 Select the computer to work with.

3. In the Group Policy Results Wizard, tap or click Next. On the User Selection page, shown in Figure 17-20, select the user whose policy information you want to view. You can view policy information for any user who has logged on to the computer.

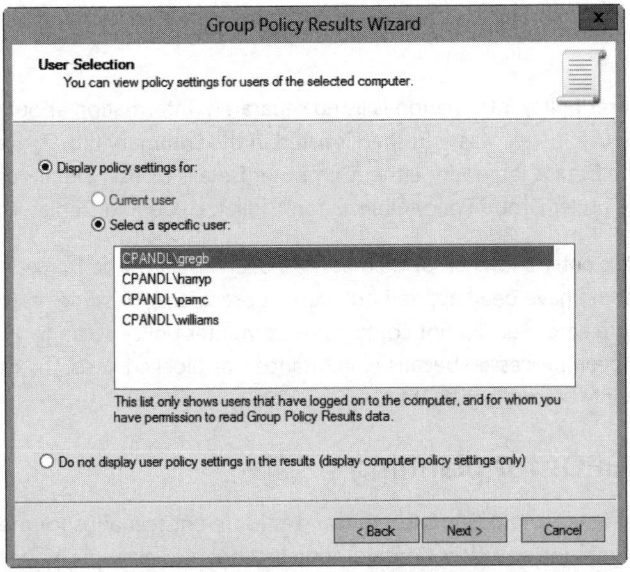

Figure 17-20 Select the user whose policy information you want to view.

4. Tap or click Next twice. After the wizard gathers the policy information, tap or click Finish. The wizard then generates a report, the results of which are displayed in the details pane, as shown in Figure 17-21.

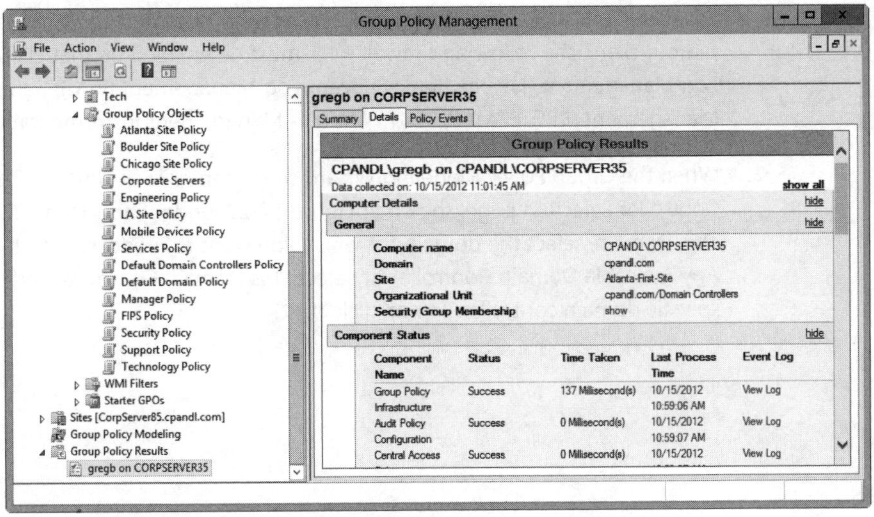

Figure 17-21 Use the report to view policy information.

5. On the report, tap or click Show All to display all of the policy information that was gathered.

Computer and user policy information is listed separately. Information about the last time the computer or user policy was refreshed is listed in the Summary tab. To view all applicable GPOs, look in the Details tab under either Computer Details or User Details as appropriate. You'll see entries under Group Policy Objects for Applied GPOs and Denied GPOs.

The Applied GPOs entry shows all GPOs that have been applied. The Denied GPOs entry shows all GPOs that should have been applied but weren't processed for some reason—for example, because they were empty or did not contain any computer policy settings. The GPO also might not have been processed because inheritance was blocked. If so, the reason denied is Blocked Scope Of Management (SOM).

Modeling GPOs for planning

In Group Policy Management Console, you can test different scenarios for modifying Computer Configuration and User Configuration settings. For example, you can model the effect of a slow link or the use of loopback processing. You can also model the effect of moving a user or computer to another container in Active Directory or adding the user or computer to an additional security group. To do this, you run the Group Policy Modeling Wizard.

To start the Group Policy Modeling Wizard and test various scenarios, follow these steps:

1. Start Group Policy Management Console. Press and hold or right-click Group Policy Modeling and then select Group Policy Modeling Wizard. If you run the results against a remote client, the following firewall rules must be enabled on that client: Remote Event Log Management (NP-In), Remote Event Log Management (RPC), Remote Event Log Management (RPC_EPMAP), and Windows Management Instrumentation (WMI-In).

2. When the Group Policy Modeling Wizard starts, tap or click Next. On the Domain Controller Selection page, shown in Figure 17-22, under Show Domain Controllers In This Domain, select the domain for which you want to model results. Next, either select Any Available Domain Controller or select This Domain Controller and then select a specific domain controller. Tap or click Next.

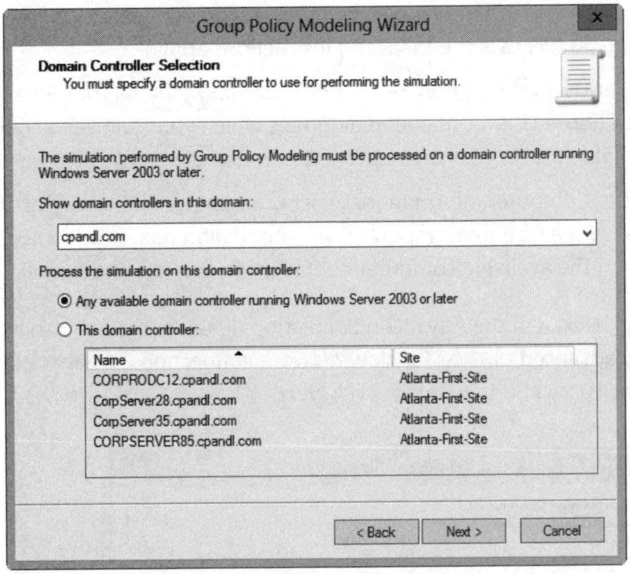

Group Policy Modeling Wizard

Domain Controller Selection
You must specify a domain controller to use for performing the simulation.

The simulation performed by Group Policy Modeling must be processed on a domain controller running Windows Server 2003 or later.

Show domain controllers in this domain:

cpandl.com

Process the simulation on this domain controller:

⦿ Any available domain controller running Windows Server 2003 or later

○ This domain controller:

Name	Site
CORPRODC12.cpandl.com	Atlanta-First-Site
CorpServer28.cpandl.com	Atlanta-First-Site
CorpServer35.cpandl.com	Atlanta-First-Site
CORPSERVER85.cpandl.com	Atlanta-First-Site

< Back   Next >   Cancel

Figure 17-22 Select the domain controller for which you want to model results.

3. On the User And Computer Selection page, shown in Figure 17-23, select the modeling options for users and computers.

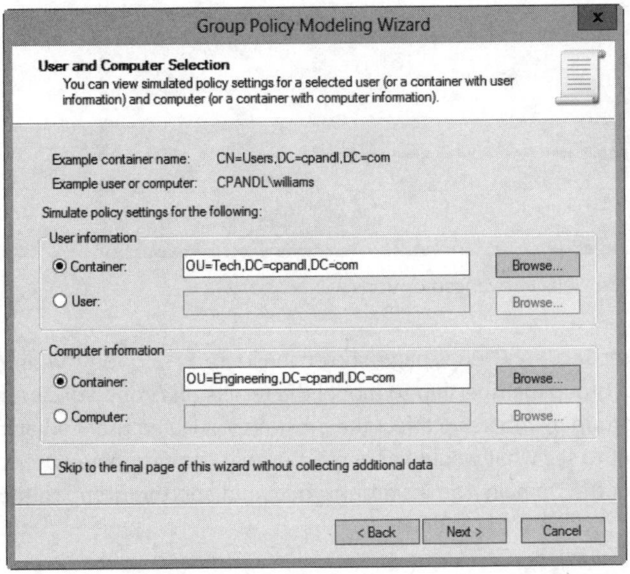

Group Policy Modeling Wizard

User and Computer Selection
You can view simulated policy settings for a selected user (or a container with user information) and computer (or a container with computer information).

Example container name: CN=Users,DC=cpandl,DC=com
Example user or computer: CPANDL\williams

Simulate policy settings for the following:

User information

⦿ Container: OU=Tech,DC=cpandl,DC=com   Browse...

○ User: Browse...

Computer information

⦿ Container: OU=Engineering,DC=cpandl,DC=com   Browse...

○ Computer: Browse...

☐ Skip to the final page of this wizard without collecting additional data

< Back   Next >   Cancel

Figure 17-23 Select the modeling options for users and computers.

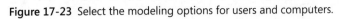

CHAPTER 17

Typically, you'll want to model policy for a specific container using user and computer information. In this case the following instructions apply:

- Under User Information, select Container and then tap or click Browse to display the Choose User Container dialog box, which you can use to choose any of the available user containers in the selected domain.

- Under Computer Information, select Container and then tap or click Browse to display the Choose Computer Container dialog box, which you can use to choose any of the available computer containers in the selected domain.

4. Tap or click Next. On the Advanced Simulation Options page, shown in Figure 17-24, select any advanced options for slow network connections, loopback processing, and sites as necessary and then tap or click Next.

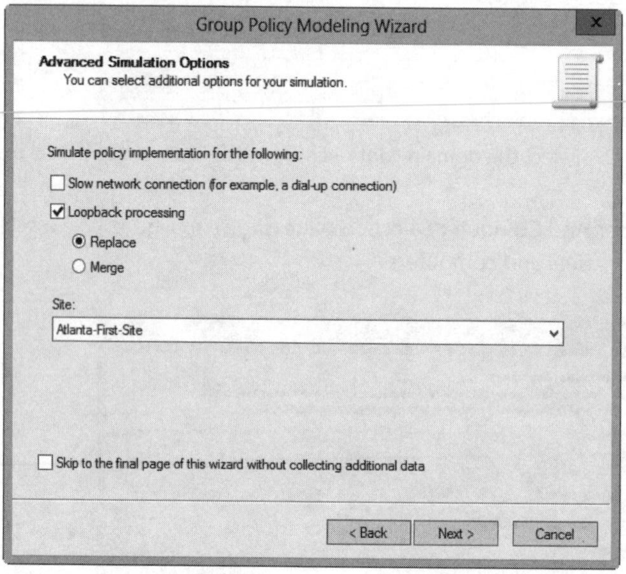

Figure 17-24 Select advanced options as necessary.

5. On the User Security Groups page, shown in Figure 17-25, you can simulate changes to security group membership to model the results on Group Policy. Any changes you make to group membership affect the previously selected user container. For example, if you want to see what would happen if a user in the designated user container were a member of the Domain Admins group, you could add this group to the Security Groups list. Tap or click Next to continue.

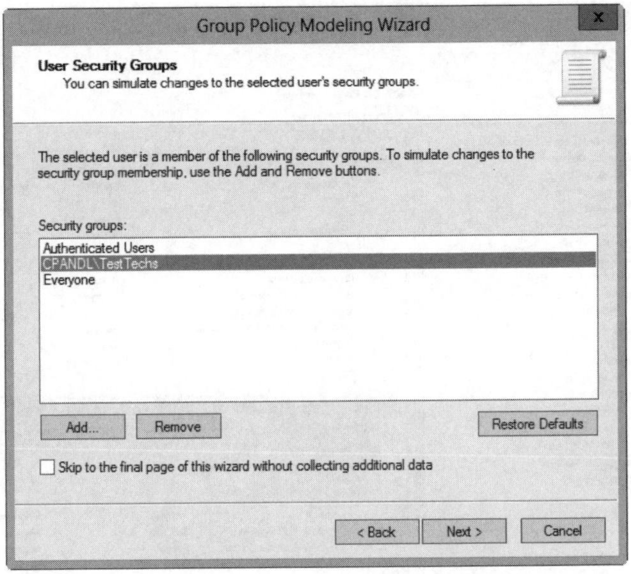

Figure 17-25 Simulate changes to security groups for users.

6. On the Computer Security Groups page, you can simulate changes to security group membership to model the results on Group Policy. Any changes you make to group membership affect the previously selected computer container. For example, if you want to see what would happen if a computer in the designated computer container were a member of the Domain Controllers group, you could add this group to the Security Groups list. Tap or click Next to continue.

7. Windows Management Instrumentation (WMI) filters can be linked to GPOs. By default, it's assumed that the selected users and computers meet all the WMI filter requirements, which is what you usually want for modeling, so tap or click Next twice to skip the WMI Filters For Users and WMI Filters For Computers pages.

8. To complete the modeling, tap or click Next and then tap or click Finish. The wizard then generates a report, the results of which are displayed in the details pane.

9. The name of the modeling report is generated based on the containers you chose and is highlighted for editing. Type a new name as required and then press the Tab key. On the report, select the Details tab and then tap or click Show All to display all of the policy information that was modeled. Figure 17-26 shows an example. Note that the details show how long client-side extensions took to process, the last time an extension was processed, and where GPOs are linked. Detailed event log information from the latest policy application is available as well.

CHAPTER 17

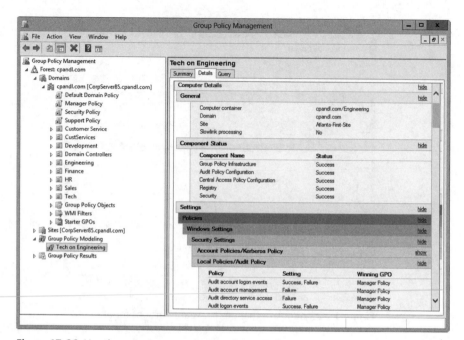

Figure 17-26 Use the report to examine the Group Policy model.

Refreshing Group Policy manually

You can refresh Group Policy manually using Invoke-GPUpdate. If you enter
Invoke-GPUpdate at a Windows PowerShell prompt, both the Computer Configuration
settings and the User Configuration settings in Group Policy are refreshed on the local computer. Add the *–Computer* parameter to refresh Group Policy on a remote computer, such as

```
Invoke-GPUpdate - Computer EngPC18
```

You can also selectively refresh Group Policy. If you want to refresh only Computer
Configuration settings, enter **Invoke-GPUpdate /Target:computer** at the Windows
PowerShell prompt. If you want to refresh only User Configuration settings, enter
Invoke-GPUpdate /Target:user at the Windows PowerShell prompt. By default, only policy
settings that have changed are processed and applied. You can change this behavior by using
the */Force* parameter. This parameter forces a refresh of all policy settings.

You can also use Invoke-GPUpdate to log off a user or restart a computer after Group Policy is
refreshed. This is useful because some Group Policy Objects are applied only when a user logs
on or when a computer starts. To log off a user after a refresh, add the */Logoff* parameter. To
restart a computer after a refresh, add the */Boot* parameter.

You also can perform a remote update using Group Policy Management Console. Remote update uses a remote connection to create a task in the task scheduler of the remote computers on which you want to refresh Group Policy. The task executes within 10 minutes and runs a *Gpupdate /Force* command on the local machine (this command works the same as *Invoke-GPUpdate /Force*). Because this feature uses a remote connection, the following firewall rules must be enabled on clients: Remote Scheduled Tasks Management (RPC), Remote Scheduled Tasks Management (RPC-EPMAP), and Windows Management Instrumentation (WMI-In).

In Group Policy Management Console, you can perform remote updates at the OU level by pressing and holding or right-clicking the OU that contains the computer objects you want to update and then selecting Group Policy Update. Next, when prompted to confirm, tap or click Yes. The *Gpupdate /Force* command is then scheduled to run on all computers in the selected OU and any child OUs of that OU. A results dialog box identifies computers that were contacted and had the task scheduled.

Backing up GPOs

With Windows PowerShell, you can backup GPOs using Backup-GPO. In Group Policy Management Console you also can back up GPOs so that you can restore them later to recover Group Policy to the state it was in when the backup was performed. The ability to back up and restore GPOs is one of the reasons that Group Policy Management Console is more useful than the older Group Policy tools that come with Windows Server. Be sure to keep in mind that you can back up and restore GPOs only when you have installed Group Policy Management Console.

You can back up either an individual GPO in a domain or all GPOs in a domain by completing the following steps:

1. Start Group Policy Management Console. Expand the forest, the Domains node, and the Group Policy Objects node.

2. If you want to back up all GPOs in the domain, press and hold or right-click the Group Policy Objects node and then select Back Up All.

3. If you want to back up a specific GPO in the domain, press and hold or right-click the GPO and then select Back Up.

4. In the Back Up Group Policy Object dialog box, shown in Figure 17-27, tap or click Browse and then use the Browse For Folder dialog box to set the location in which the GPO backup should be stored. This location can be a local folder or a network share.

CHAPTER 17

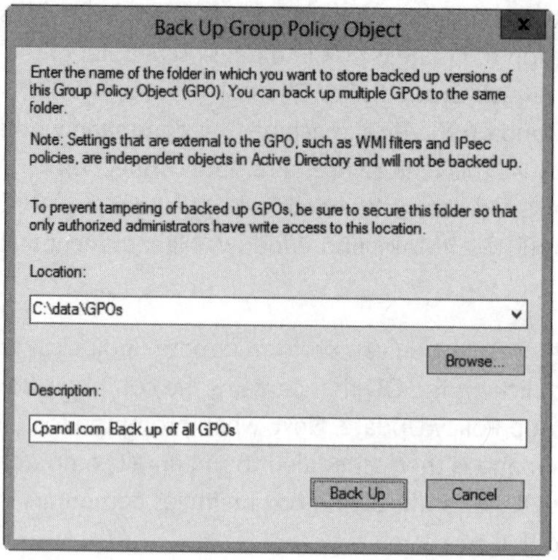

Figure 17-27 Set the backup location and description.

5. In the Description field, type a clear description of the contents of the backup.

6. Tap or click Back Up to start the backup process. The Backup dialog box, shown in Figure 17-28, shows the progress and status of the backup. If a backup fails, check the permissions on the GPO and the folder to which you are writing the backup. To create a backup, you need Read permission on a GPO and Write permission on the backup folder. By default, members of the Domain Admins and Enterprise Admins groups should have these permissions.

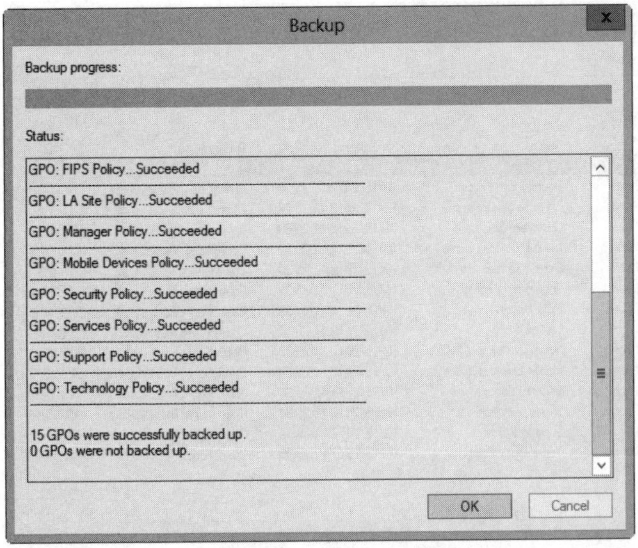

Figure 17-28 The Backup dialog box shows the backup progress and status.

Restoring GPOs

With Windows PowerShell, you can restore GPOs to their original location using Restore-GPO or restore to any location using Import-GPO. Using Group Policy Management Console, you also can restore a GPO to the state it was in when it was backed up. Group Policy Management Console tracks the backup of each GPO separately, even if you back up all GPOs at once. Because version information is also tracked according to the backup time stamp and description, you can restore the last version of each GPO or a particular version of any GPO.

You can restore a GPO by completing the following steps:

1. Start Group Policy Management Console. Expand the forest, the Domains node, and then the Group Policy Objects node.

2. If you want to restore all GPOs in the domain, press and hold or right-click the Group Policy Objects node and then select Manage Backups. This displays the Manage Backups dialog box. (See Figure 17-29.)

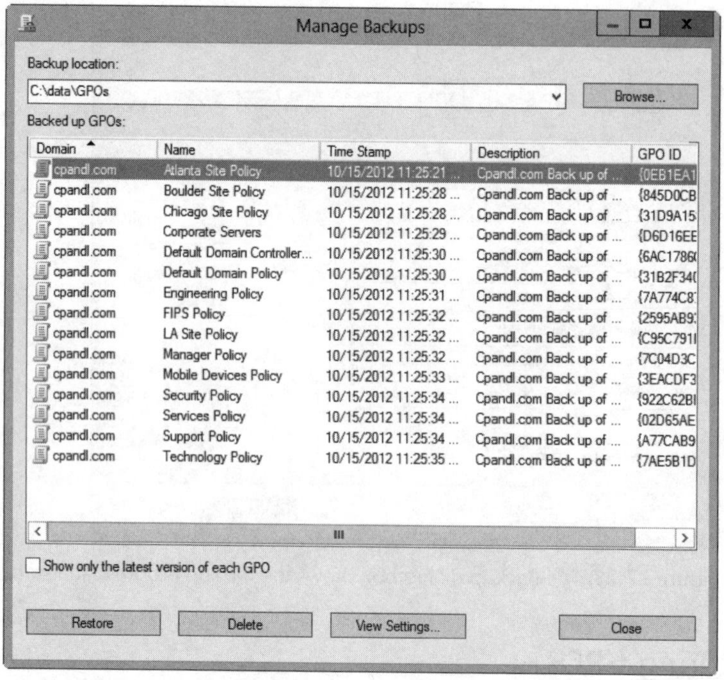

Figure 17-29 Use the Manage Backups dialog box to restore a GPO.

3. In the Backup Location field, type the folder path to the backup or tap or click Browse to use the Browse For Folder dialog box to find the folder.

4. All GPO backups in the designated folder are listed under Backed Up GPOs. To show only the latest version of the GPOs according to the time stamp, select the Show Only The Latest Version Of Each GPO check box.

5. Select the GPO you want to restore. If you want to confirm its settings, tap or click View Settings and then verify that the settings are as expected using Internet Explorer. When you are ready to continue, tap or click Restore. Confirm that you want to restore the selected GPO by tapping or clicking OK.

6. The Restore dialog box, shown in Figure 17-30, shows the progress and status of the restore. If a restore fails, check the permissions on the GPO and the folder from which you are reading the backup. To restore a GPO, you need Edit, Delete, and Modify permissions on the GPO and Read permission on the folder containing the GPO backup. By default, members of the Domain Admins and Enterprise Admins groups should have these permissions.

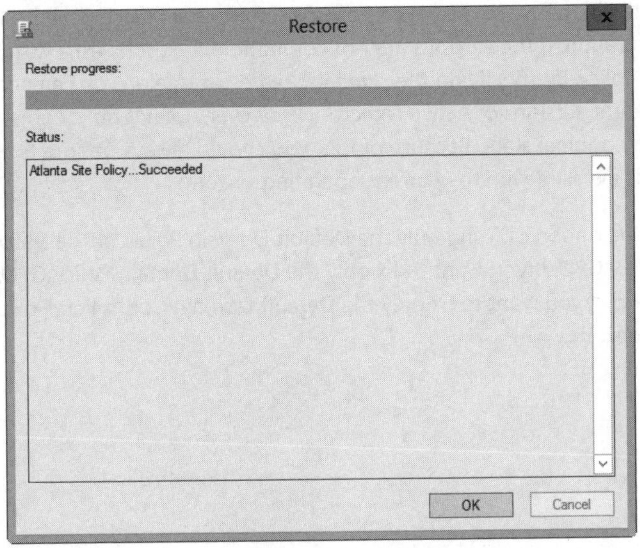

Figure 17-30 The Restore dialog box shows the restore progress and status.

7. Tap or click OK and then either restore additional GPOs as necessary or tap or click Close.

Fixing default Group Policy

The Default Domain Policy GPO and the Default Domain Controllers Policy GPO are vital to the health of Active Directory in a domain. If for some reason these policies become corrupted, Group Policy will not function properly. To resolve this, you must run the Dcgpofix utility. This utility restores the default GPOs to their original, default state, meaning the state they are in when you first install Active Directory in a new domain. You must be a member of Domain Admins or Enterprise Admins to run Dcgpofix.

By default, when you run Dcgpofix, both the Default Domain Policy and Default Domain Controllers Policy GPOs are restored and you will lose any base changes made to these GPOs. The only exceptions are for the following extension settings: Remote Installation Services (RIS), Security Settings, and Encrypting File System (EFS). These extension settings are maintained separately and will not be lost. Nondefault Security Settings are not maintained, however. All other extensions settings are restored to their default post-installation state, and any changes you made are lost.

Before you run Dcgpofix, you should make a backup of the current Default Domain Policy and Default Domain Controllers Policy GPOs. To run Dcgpofix, log on to a domain controller in the domain in which you want to fix default Group Policy and then type **dcgpofix** at the command prompt. Dcgpofix checks the Active Directory schema version number to

CHAPTER 17

ensure compatibility between the version of Dcgpofix you are using and the Active Directory schema configuration. If the versions are not compatible, Dcgpofix exits without fixing the default Group Policy. By specifying the *Ignoreschema* parameter, you can enable Dcgpofix to work with different versions of Active Directory. However, default policy objects might not be restored to their original state. Because of this, you should always be sure to use the version of Dcgpofix that is installed with the current operating system.

You also have the option of fixing only the Default Domain Policy or the Default Domain Controllers Policy GPO. If you want to fix only the Default Domain Policy GPO, type **dcgpofix /target: domain**. If you want to fix only the Default Domain Controllers Policy GPO, type **dcgpofix /target: dc**.

Active Directory site administration

In this chapter I discuss the administration of sites, subnets, site links, and related components. Active Directory sites are used to control directory replication traffic and to isolate logon authentication traffic between physical network locations. Every site has one or more subnets associated with it. Ideally, each subnet that is part of a site should be connected by reliable high-speed links. Any physical location connected over slow or unreliable links should be part of a separate site, and these individual sites are linked to other sites using site links.

Managing sites and subnets

When you install Active Directory Domain Services in a new forest, a new site called the Default-First-Site-Name is created. As you add domains and domain controllers to the forest, these domains and domain controllers are added to this site as they are installed—unless you configured other sites and associated subnets with those sites as necessary.

The administration of sites and subnets involves determining the sites and subnets you need and creating those sites and subnets. All sites have one or more subnets associated with them. It is, in fact, the subnet assignment that tells Active Directory where the site boundaries are established. As you create additional sites, you might also need to specify which domain controllers are part of the sites. You do this by moving domain controllers to the site containers with which they should be associated. Thus, the most common administrative tasks for sites involve the following:

- Creating sites

- Creating subnets and associating them with sites

- Moving domain controllers between sites

Creating an Active Directory site

As part of Active Directory design, which is discussed in Chapter 13, "Configuring Active Directory sites and replication," you must consider whether separate sites are needed. If your organization has multiple locations with limited bandwidth or unreliable connections between locations, you will typically want to create additional sites. In some cases you might also want to create additional sites to separate network segments even if they are connected with high-speed links; the reason for doing this is to isolate logon authentication traffic between the network segments.

To create an additional site, follow these steps:

1. Start Active Directory Sites And Services. In Server Manager, select Tools and then select Active Directory Sites And Services.

Connect to the forest you want to work with

Active Directory Sites And Services is used to view a single forest. If your organization has multiple forests, you might need to connect to another forest. To do this, press and hold or right-click the Active Directory Sites And Services node in the console tree and then select Change Forest. In the Change Forest dialog box, type the name of the root domain in the forest to which you want to connect and then tap or click OK.

2. Press and hold or right-click the Sites container in the console tree and then select New Site. This displays the New Object–Site dialog box, as shown in Figure 18-1.

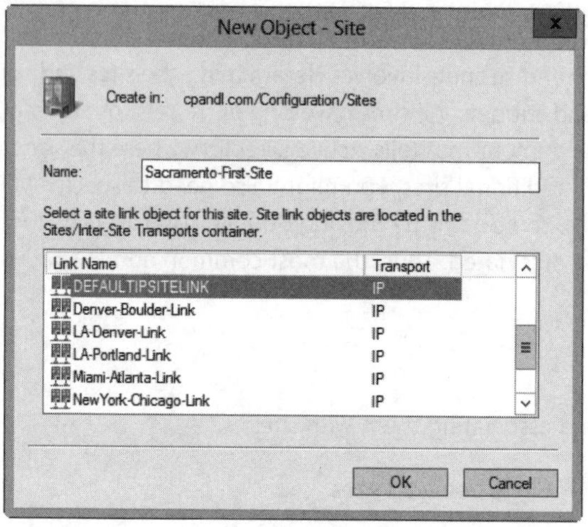

Figure 18-1 Use the New Object–Site dialog box to create a new site.

3. In the New Object–Site dialog box, type a descriptive name for the site. The site name serves as a point of reference for administrators and should clearly depict the purpose or physical location of the site.

4. Choose which site link will be used to connect this site to other sites. If the site link you want to use doesn't exist, that's okay—the site must exist before you can create links to it. Select the default site link DEFAULTIPSITELINK for now and change the site-link settings after you create the necessary site link or links.

5. When you are ready to continue, tap or click OK. A prompt is displayed detailing the steps you must complete to finish the site configuration. Tap or click OK again. As the prompt explains, you should do the following:

   - Ensure that the links to this site are appropriate by creating the necessary site links. The catch here is that both endpoints in a site link—the sites you want to link—must exist before you can create a site link.

   - Create subnets and associate them with the site. This tells Active Directory the network addresses that belong to a site.

Each site should have one or more domain controllers. Ideally, this domain controller should also be a global catalog server. Because of this, you should install one or more domain controllers in the site or move existing domain controllers into the site.

With Windows PowerShell, you can create sites using New-ADReplicationSite. The basic syntax is

```
New-ADReplicationSite SiteName
```

where *SiteName* is the name of the site to create, such as

```
New-ADReplicationSite Denver-First-Site
```

If you want to create multiple sites, you can bulk create the sites using Windows PowerShell. To do this, you'll want to create a file in Notepad and then import this file when creating the sites in Windows PowerShell. If you use Import-CSV for the import operation, the file should be created as a plain-text file and named with the .csv extension. Additionally, the file should begin with a column header entry and have each value on a separate line. To see how this works, consider the following example file named MySites.csv:

```
name
Denver
LA
Seattle
NY
Miami
```

Here, the column header is name and the sites to create are Denver, LA, Seattle, NY, and Miami. You can import the MySites.csv file and create these sites by entering the following:

```
Import-CSV -path C:\MySites.csv | New-ADReplicationSite
```

CHAPTER 18

Creating a subnet and associating it with a site

You create subnets and associate them with sites to allow Active Directory to determine the network segments that belong to the site. Any computer with an Internet Protocol (IP) address on a network segment associated with a site is considered to be located in the site. A site can have one or more subnets associated with it. Each subnet, however, can be associated with only one site.

You can create a subnet and associate it with a site by completing the following steps:

1. In Active Directory Sites And Services, press and hold or right-click the Subnets container in the console tree and select New Subnet. This displays the New Object–Subnet dialog box, as shown in Figure 18-2.

2. In the Prefix field, type the address prefix for the subnet. As discussed in the section entitled "Network prefix notation" in Chapter 2, "Networking with TCP/IP," the address prefix for a network address consists of the network ID address followed by a forward slash followed by the number of bits in the network ID. Typically, the subnet address ends with a 0, such as 192.168.1.0, except when subnetting is used. For example, if the network address is 192.168.1.0 and the subnet mask is 255.255.255.0, you should enter the address prefix as 192.168.1.0/24.

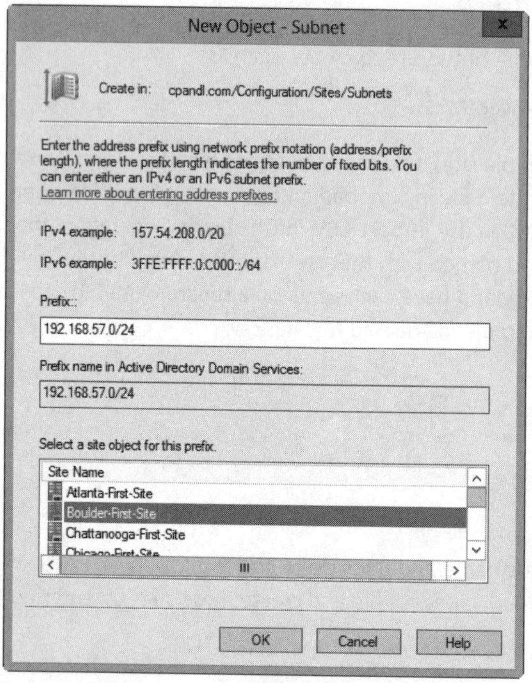

Figure 18-2 Use the New Object–Subnet dialog box to create a new subnet.

3. Select the site with which the subnet should be associated and then tap or click OK. If you ever need to change the site association for the subnet, double-tap or double-click the subnet in the Subnets folder and then, in the General tab, use the Site selection menu to change the site association.

With Windows PowerShell, you can create a subnet and associate it with a site using New-ADReplicationSubnet. The basic syntax is

```
New-ADReplicationSubnet -name AddressPrefix -site SiteName
```

where *AddressPrefix* is the address prefix of the subnet and *SiteName* is the name of the site with which to associate the subnet, such as

```
New-ADReplicationSubnet -name 192.168.1.0/24 -site Boulder-First-Site
```

Associating domain controllers with a site

After you associate subnets with a site, any domain controllers you install will automatically be located in the site where the IP address subnet matches the IP address of the domain controller. If the IP address of the domain controller does not map to a specific site, the domain controller usually is added to the site of the domain controller that provides the replication source for Active Directory Domain Services.

Any domain controllers installed before you established the site and subnets associated with it will not be moved to the site automatically. You must manually move existing domain controllers if necessary. In addition, if you associate a subnet with a different site, you might need to move domain controllers in that subnet to the new site.

Before you can move a domain controller from one site to another, you must determine in which site the domain controller is located. One way to do this is to use the Servers nodes for each site in Active Directory Sites And Services. You can also do this by typing the following command at a command prompt:

```
dsquery server -s DomainControllerName | dsget server -site
```

Here, *DomainControllerName* is the fully qualified domain name of the domain controller, such as

```
dsquery server -s corpserver92.cpandl.com | dsget server -site
```

The output of this command is the name of the site in which the designated domain controller is located.

With Windows PowerShell, you can use Get-ADDomainController to identify the site in which a domain controller is located. The basic syntax is

```
(Get-ADDomainController DomainControllerName).Site
```

where *DomainControllerName* is the IP address, host name, or fully qualified domain name of the domain controller, such as

```
(Get-ADDomainController CorpServer18).Site
```

You can create a list of all domain controllers in the current logon domain and the sites that are associated with it by entering the following command:

```
Get-ADDomainController -Filter * | ft hostname,site
```

You can move a domain controller to a site by completing the following steps:

1. Start Active Directory Sites And Services. Domain controllers associated with a site are listed in the site's Servers node. To locate the domain controller that you want to move, expand the site node and then expand the related Servers node.

2. Press and hold or right-click the domain controller and then select Move. This displays the Move Server dialog box.

3. In the Move Server dialog box, select the site that should contain the server and then tap or click OK.

Another way to move a domain controller from one site to another is to drag the domain controller from its current site to the new site. But don't move a domain controller to a site arbitrarily. Move a domain controller to a site only if it's on a subnet associated with the site.

With Windows PowerShell, you can move a domain controller into a site using Move-ADDirectoryServer. To do this, first get the domain controllers you want to work with using Get-ADDomainController and then move the domain controllers into a specific site using Move-ADDirectoryServer, as shown in the following example:

```
Get-ADDomainController CorpServer18 | Move-ADDirectoryServer -Site LA-First-Site
```

Here, you move CorpServer18, a domain controller, into LA-First-Site.

Managing site links and inter-site replication

Site links are used to connect two or more sites for the purpose of replication. When you install Active Directory in a new forest, a new site link called DEFAULTIPSITELINK is created. As you add sites to the forest, these sites are included in the default site link unless you config-ured other site links. If all of the network connections between sites are the same speed and priority, the default configuration can work. In this case, the inter-site replication configuration for all sites will have the same properties. If you were to change these properties, the changes would affect the replication topology for all sites. By creating additional site links, you can configure different replication properties when the network connections between sites have different speeds and priorities.

Creating additional site links helps the designated Inter-Site Topology Generator (ISTG) for a site prioritize the site links and determine when a site link should be used. It doesn't, however, change the way inter-site replication works. Replication traffic between sites is always sent from a bridgehead server in one site to a bridgehead server in another site. Although it's the job of the ISTG to generate the inter-site replication topology and designate bridgehead servers, you can manually designate bridgehead servers as well. After you establish site links and designate bridgehead servers as necessary, you might want to change the way replication between sites is handled. For example, you might want to disable compression or enable notification so that changes can be replicated more quickly between sites.

Following this, the most common administrative tasks related to site links involve the following:

- Creating site links

- Configuring site-link bridges

- Determining the ISTG

- Configuring site bridgehead servers

- Setting site-link replication options

Before looking at these administrative tasks, however, let's look at the available replication transports.

Understanding IP and SMTP replication transports

When you create a site link, you have to select a replication transport protocol. Two replication transports are available: IP and Simple Mail Transfer Protocol (SMTP). All replication connections within sites are synchronous and use RPC over IP. In this configuration, domain controllers establish an RPC-over-IP connection with a single replication partner at a time and replicate Active Directory changes. By default, the remote procedure call (RPC) connection uses dynamic port mapping. During replication, a replication client establishes a connection to a server on the RPC endpoint mapper port 135 and determines which port is to be used for replication on the server. Any additional replication traffic is sent over the ports defined in Table 13-1, "Ports used during Active Directory replication," in Chapter 13. When RPC over IP is used for inter-site replication, these same ports are used. If there are firewalls between the sites, the appropriate ports on the firewalls must be opened to allow replication to occur.

Because RPC over IP is synchronous, both replication partners must be available at the time the connection is established. This is important because of the transitive nature of site links.

For example, if Site 1 has a link to Site 2 and Site 2 has a link to Site 3, there is an automatic bridge between Site 1 and Site 3 that allows Site 1 to replicate traffic directly to Site 3. Because of this, you must carefully configure site-link schedules so that all potential RPC-over-IP replication partners are available as necessary—more on this in a moment.

You can also configure replication between sites to use SMTP. By using SMTP as the transport, all replication traffic is converted to email messages that are sent between the sites. Because SMTP replication is asynchronous, it can be a good choice when you do not have a permanent connection between sites or when you have unreliable connections between sites. It's also a good choice when you have to replicate between locations over the public Internet.

Before you use SMTP as the replication protocol, there are several important considerations. First, you can use SMTP only to replicate information between domain controllers in different domains because the domain directory partition can't be replicated using SMTP—only the configuration, schema, and global catalog directory partitions can be replicated. Second, SMTP messages are digitally signed and encrypted to ensure that replication traffic is secure even if replication traffic is routed over the public Internet. All domain controllers that will use SMTP for replication require additional components to create, digitally sign, and then encrypt email messages. Specifically, you must install the SMTP Server feature on each domain controller and you must install a Microsoft certificate authority (CA) in your organization. The certificates from the CA are used to digitally sign and encrypt the SMTP messages sent between the sites.

Configure replication through firewalls

If you plan to use SMTP for replication, you must open port 25 on the firewall between sites. Port 25 is the default port used for SMTP. Although SMTP has definite security advantages over standard IP, you can encrypt RPC communications between domain controllers using IP security (IPsec) and then open the appropriate ports on your firewalls for RPC over IP. Encrypting the RPC traffic between domain controllers would then be a viable alternative for replication over the public Internet when you have a dedicated connection between sites.

Creating a site link

After you create the sites that your organization needs, you can create site links between those sites to better manage inter-site replication. Each site link must have at least two sites associated with it. These sites establish the endpoints or transit points for the link. For example, if you create a site link and add Portland-First-Site and LA-First-Site to the link, the Portland and LA sites are the endpoints for the link and the ISTG will use the link to create the connection objects that are required to replicate traffic between these sites.

Before you create a site link, you should determine the transport that you want to use, as discussed previously in the section of this chapter entitled "Understanding IP and SMTP replication transports." You should also consider the following:

- **Link cost.** The cost for a site link determines the relative priority of the link in relation to other site links that might be available. If there are multiple possible routes to a site, the route with the lowest link cost is used first. If a primary link fails, a secondary link can be used. Typically, the link cost reflects the bandwidth available for a specific connection. It also can reflect the actual cost of sending traffic over a particular link if the organization has to pay a fee based on bandwidth usage.

- **Replication schedule.** The replication schedule determines the times during the day when the site link is available for replication. By default, replication is allowed 24 hours a day. If you have a limited-bandwidth connection or you want user traffic to have priority at certain times of the day, you might want to configure a different availability schedule.

- **Replication interval.** The replication interval determines the intervals at which the bridgehead servers in each site check to see if directory updates are available. By default, the interval is set to 180 minutes. Following this, if the replication schedule is configured to allow replication from 7 P.M. to 7 A.M. each day, the bridgehead servers will check for updates daily at 7 P.M., 10 P.M., 1 A.M., 4 A.M., and 7 A.M.

You can create a site link between two or more sites by completing the following steps:

1. Start Active Directory Sites And Services. If your organization has multiple forests, you might need to connect to another forest. To do this, press and hold or right-click the Active Directory Sites And Services node in the console tree and then select Change Forest. In the Change Forest dialog box, type the name of the root domain in the forest to which you want to connect and then tap or click OK.

2. Expand the Sites container and then expand the Inter-Site Transports container. Press and hold or right-click the container for the transport protocol you want to use (either IP or SMTP) and select New Site Link. This displays the New Object–Site Link dialog box, as shown in Figure 18-3.

3. In the New Object–Site Link dialog box, type a descriptive name for the site link. The site name serves as a point of reference for administrators and should clearly depict the sites the link connects.

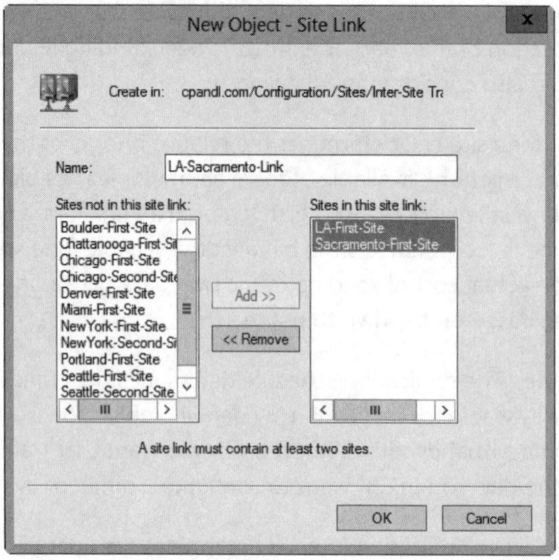

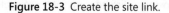

Figure 18-3 Create the site link.

4.   In the Sites Not In This Site Link list, select a site that should be included in the link and then tap or click Add to add the site to the Sites In This Site Link list. Repeat this process for each site you want to add to the link. The link must include at least two sites.

5.   Tap or click OK to close the New Object–Site Link dialog box.

6.   In Active Directory Sites And Services, the site link is added to the appropriate transport folder (IP or SMTP). Select the transport folder in the console tree and then double-tap or double-click the site link in the right pane. This displays the Link Properties dialog box, as shown in Figure 18-4.

7.   Use the Cost combo box to set the relative cost of the link. The default cost is 100. For pointers on determining what cost to use, see the sections entitled "Mapping network infrastructure" and "Designing the inter-site replication topology" in Chapter 13.

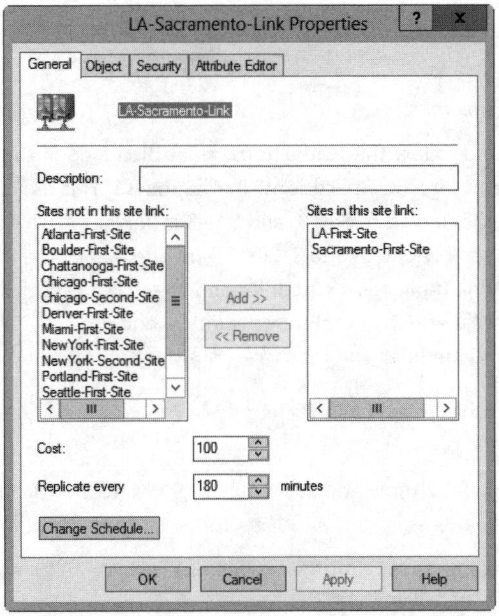

Figure 18-4 Set the site-link properties.

8. Use the Replicate Every combo box to set the replication interval. The default interval is 180 minutes.

9. By default, the site link is available for replication 24 hours a day. To set a different schedule, tap or click Change Schedule and then use the Schedule For dialog box to set the desired replication schedule. When you are finished, tap or click OK.

10. Tap or click OK to close the site link's Properties dialog box.

Inside OUT

The transitive nature of site links

Site links are transitive and follow the "three hops" rules discussed in the section entitled "Replication rings and directory partitions" in Chapter 13. This means that if Site 1 is linked to Site 2, Site 2 is linked to Site 3, and Site 3 is linked to Site 4, the domain controllers in Site 1 can replicate with Site 2, Site 3, and Site 4. Because of the transitive nature of site links, site-link replication schedules and intervals for each site link are combined to determine the effective replication window and interval. To see the impact of combining replication schedules and intervals, consider the following examples:

- Site 1 to Site 2 link has a replication schedule of 7 P.M. to 7 A.M. and an interval of 60 minutes.

- Site 2 to Site 3 link has a replication schedule of 9 P.M. to 5 A.M. and an interval of 60 minutes.

- Site 3 to Site 4 link has a replication schedule of 1 P.M. to 3 A.M. and an interval of 180 minutes.

Because of the overlapping windows and intervals, replication between Site 1 and Site 2 could occur every 60 minutes from 7 P.M. to 7 A.M. Replication between Site 1 and Site 3 could occur every 60 minutes from 9 P.M. to 5 A.M. Replication between Site 1 and Site 4 could occur every 180 minutes from 9 P.M. to 3 A.M. This occurs because the replication availability window must overlap for replication to occur using transitive links.

If the site-replication schedules do not overlap, replication is still possible between multiple sites. To see how replication would work if schedules do not overlap, consider the following example:

- Site 1 to Site 2 link has a replication schedule of 11 P.M. to 3 A.M. and an interval of 60 minutes.

- Site 2 to Site 3 link has a replication schedule of 6 P.M. to 9 P.M. and an interval of 60 minutes.

- Site 3 to Site 4 link has a replication schedule of 1 A.M. to 5 A.M. and an interval of 180 minutes.

Assuming there are no alternate links between the sites, replication between Site 1 and Site 2 could occur every 60 minutes from 11 P.M. to 3 A.M. Site 1 would not be able to replicate with Site 3 and Site 4, however. Instead, Site 2 would replicate changes to Site 3 every 60 minutes from 6 P.M. to 9 P.M. daily. Site 3, in turn, would replicate changes to Site 4 every 180 minutes from 1 A.M. to 5 A.M. daily. In this configuration, there is significant replication latency (delay). Changes made at 5 P.M. in Site 1 would not be replicated to Site 2 until 11 P.M. On the following day the changes would be replicated to Site 3 at 6 P.M., and then at 1 A.M. on the third day the changes would be replicated to Site 4.

With Windows PowerShell, you can create a site link using New-ADReplicationSiteLink. The basic syntax is

```
New-ADReplicationSiteLink SiteLinkName -SitesIncluded Sites
-Cost Cost -ReplicationFrequencyInMinutes Minutes
```

Here, *SiteLinkName* is the name of the site link to create, *Sites* is a comma-separated list of sites to include, *Cost* sets the relative cost of the link, and *Minutes* sets the replication interval, such as

```
New-ADReplicationSiteLink LA-Sacramento-Link -SitesIncluded LA-First-Site,
Sacramento-First-Site -Cost 100 -ReplicationFrequencyInMinutes 180
```

Configuring replication schedules for site links

You can manage the replication schedule for site links in one of two ways: globally or individually. By default, IP site links use individual replication schedules and replicate within these schedules according to the replication interval. In contrast, by default, SMTP site links ignore individual replication schedules and replicate only according to the replication interval. You can control whether global or individual schedules are used by following these steps:

1. Start Active Directory Sites And Services. Expand the Sites container and then expand the Inter-Site Transports container. Press and hold or right-click the container for the transport protocol you want to work with (either IP or SMTP) and then select Properties. This displays a Properties dialog box. (See Figure 18-5.)

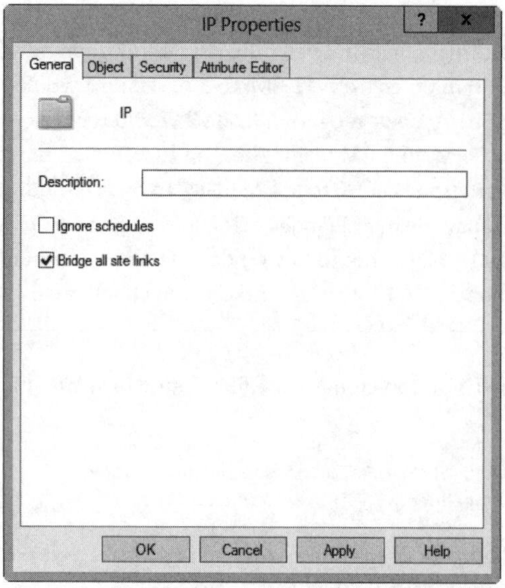

Figure 18-5 Configure global replication.

2. You can now configure global replication for the selected transport. To ignore individual replication schedules on site links, select the Ignore Schedules check box. To use individual schedules, clear the Ignore Schedules check box. Tap or click OK.

When you use individual schedules, you can manage the times when replication is permitted by setting a replication schedule for each site link. By default, replication is available 24 hours a day, 7 days a week. To better manage the traffic flow over inter-site links, you might need to change the permitted replication times. For example, if you find that a particular link is too saturated at specific times of the day, you might want to limit replication to ensure that users have more bandwidth for collaboration and communication.

When individual schedules are allowed, you can configure a site link's replication schedule by following these steps:

1. Start Active Directory Sites And Services. Expand the Sites container, expand the Inter-Site Transports container, and then select the container for the transport protocol you want to work with (either IP or SMTP).

2. In the details pane, press and hold or right-click the site link you want to configure and then select Properties.

3. Tap or click Change Schedule. You can now set the valid and invalid replication hours using the Schedule For SiteLink dialog box. In this dialog box each hour of the day and night is a field that you can turn on and off.

- Hours that are allowed are filled in with a dark bar—you can think of these hours as being turned on.

- Hours that are disallowed are blank—you can think of these hours as being turned off.

4. To change the setting for an hour, tap or click it. Then select either Replication Not Available or Replication Available.

Scheduling features are listed in Table 18-1.

Table 18-1 Scheduling features

Feature	Function
All	Allows you to select all the time periods
Day of week buttons	Allows you to select all the hours in a particular day
Hourly buttons	Allows you to select a particular hour for all the days of the week
Replication Available	Sets the allowed replication hours
Replication Not Available	Sets the disallowed replication hours

NOTE

When you set replication hours, you'll save yourself a lot of work in the long run if you consider peak usage times and use a moderately restricted time window. For example, you might be tempted to restrict replication from 8 A.M. to 6 P.M. every weekday on a limited-bandwidth link. However, such a wide restriction would not allow replication during the day. Instead, you might want to allow replication from 10 A.M. to 1 P.M. and from 6 P.M. to 6 A.M.

Configuring site-link bridges

By default, all site links are transitive, which allows Active Directory to automatically configure site-link bridges between sites. When a site is bridged, any two domain controllers can make a connection across any consecutive series of links as long as the site links are all using the same transport. The site-link bridge cost is the sum of all the links included in the bridge.

A significant advantage of automatically created site-link bridges is that fault tolerance is built in whenever there are multiple possible routes between sites. Another significant advantage is that Active Directory automatically manages the site-link bridges and the ISTG monitors for changes and reconfigures the replication topology accordingly—all without any administrator involvement required. Site-link bridges are discussed in more detail in Chapter 13 in the section entitled "Considering the impact of site-link bridging."

You can enable or disable site-link bridges on a per-transport basis. By default, both the IP and SMTP transports have site-link bridging enabled. If you disable site-link bridging, Active Directory will no longer manage site-link bridges for the transport. You must then create and manage all site-link bridges for that transport. Any sites you add to a site-link bridge are considered to be transitive with each other. Site links that are not included in the site-link bridge are not transitive.

To see how this works, consider the previous example, in which Site 1 is linked to Site 2, Site 2 is linked to Site 3, and Site 3 is linked to Site 4. If you disable site-link bridging and then create a site-link bridge that includes Site 1, Site 2, and Site 3, only those sites would have a transitive site link. Site 4 would be excluded. This means that Site 1 could replicate changes to Site 2 and Site 1 could replicate changes to Site 3. Site 1 could not, however, replicate changes to Site 4. Only Site 3 could replicate changes to Site 4. This would occur because adjacent sites can always replicate changes with each other.

NOTE

One reason to create site-link bridges manually is to reduce the processing overhead on the designated ISTGs in each site. When you disable transitive links, the ISTGs no longer have to create and manage the site-link bridges, and this reduces the number of computations required to create the inter-site replication topology.

To turn off transitive site links and manually configure site-link bridges, follow these steps:

1. Start Active Directory Sites And Services. Expand the Sites container and then expand the Inter-Site Transports container. Press and hold or right-click the container for the transport protocol you want to work with (either IP or SMTP) and then select Properties. This displays a Properties dialog box, as shown previously in Figure 18-5.

2. Clear the Bridge All Site Links check box and then tap or click OK. If you later want to enable transitive links and have Active Directory ignore the site-link bridges you created, you can select the Bridge All Site Links check box.

After you disable transitive links, you can manually create a site-link bridge between two or more sites by completing the following steps:

1. In Active Directory Sites And Services, expand the Sites container and then expand the Inter-Site Transports container. Press and hold or right-click the container for the transport protocol you want to use (either IP or SMTP) and then select New Site Link Bridge. This displays the New Object–Site Link Bridge dialog box, as shown in Figure 18-6.

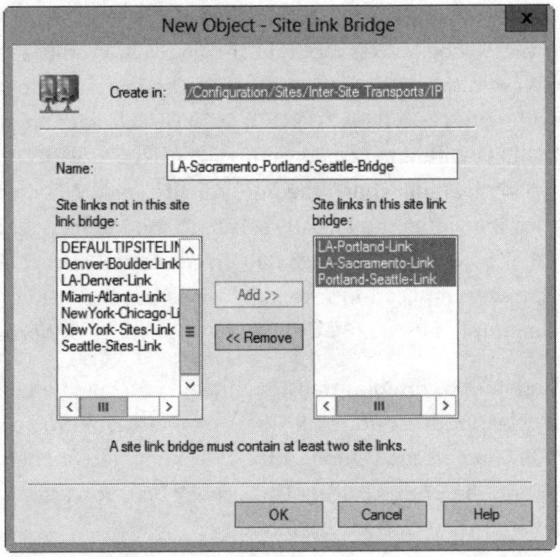

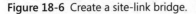

Figure 18-6 Create a site-link bridge.

2. In the New Object–Site Link Bridge dialog box, type a descriptive name for the site-link bridge. This name serves as a point of reference for administrators and should clearly depict all the site links that are part of the bridge.

3. In the Site Links Not In This Site Link Bridge list, select a site link that should be included in the bridge and then tap or click Add to add the site link to the Site Links In This Site Link Bridge list. Repeat this process for each site link you want to add to the bridge. The bridge must include at least two site links.

4. Tap or click OK to close the New Object–Site Link Bridge dialog box.

Inside OUT

Inter-site transport options

In Active Directory Sites And Services, you can control the way site links work by using the Bridge All Site Links and Ignore Schedules check boxes in the IP Properties and SMTP Properties dialog boxes and as discussed earlier in this chapter in the sections entitled "Configuring replication schedules for site links" and "Configuring site-link bridges."

Selecting or clearing these check boxes modifies the flag values on the *Options* attribute, which you can view in the Attribute Editor tab in the related Properties dialog box. The *Options* attribute has two flags: IGNORE_SCHEDULES, with an enabled value of 1, and BRIDGES_REQUIRED, with an enabled value of 2. IGNORE_SCHEDULES enables or disables the use of individual replication schedules for site links. When you override the replication schedule for individual site links by selecting the Ignore Schedules check box, you are setting the IGNORE_SCHEDULES flag on the *Options* attribute. When you allow each site link to have a replication schedule by clearing the Ignore Schedules check box, you are clearing the IGNORE_SCHEDULES flag on the *Options* attribute.

BRIDGES_REQUIRED enables or disables transitive site links. When you disable transitive site links by clearing the Bridge All Site Links check box, you are setting the BRIDGES_REQUIRED flag on the *Options* attribute. When you enable transitive site links by selecting the Bridge All Site Links check box, you are clearing the BRIDGES_REQUIRED flag on the *Options* attribute.

With Windows PowerShell, you can create a site-link bridge using New-ADReplicationSiteLinkBridge. The basic syntax is

```
New-ADReplicationSiteLink SiteLinkBridgeName –SiteLinksIncluded SiteLinks
```

Here, *SiteLinkBridgeName* is the name of the site-link bridge to create and *SiteLinks* is a comma-separated lists of site links to include, such as

```
New-ADReplicationSiteLinkBridge LA-Sacramento-Portland-Seattle-Bridge
–SiteLinksIncluded LA-Portland-Link,LA-Sacramento-Link,Portland-Seattle-Link
```

Determining the ISTG

Each site has an ISTG that is responsible for generating the inter-site replication topology. As your organization grows and you add domain controllers and sites, the load on the ISTG can grow substantially because each addition means that the ISTG must perform additional calculations to determine and maintain the optimal topology. When the ISTG is calculating the replication topology, its processor typically will reach 100 percent utilization. As the topology becomes more and more complex, the process will stay at maximum utilization longer and longer.

Because the ISTG could get overloaded, you should monitor the designated ISTG in a site more closely than other domain controllers. At the command line, you can determine the ISTG for a particular site by typing **repadmin /istg "site:***SiteName***"**, where *SiteName* is the name of the site that you want to work with, such as **repadmin /istg "site:Denver-First-Site"**. If you want to examine the site in which your computer is located, just type **repadmin /istg**.

With Windows PowerShell, use Get-ADReplicationSite to determine the ISTG for a site. You can do the following:

- Enter **Get-ADReplicationSite** to identify the ISTG for the site in which your computer is located.

- Enter **Get-ADReplicationSite** *Identity*, where *Identity* is the distinguished name of the site, to determine the ISTG for a particular site, such as **Get-ADReplicationSite CN=Atlanta-First-Site,CN=Sites,CN=Configuration,DC=cpandl,DC=com**.

- Enter **Get-ADReplicationSite –Server** *DomainServiceOrServerName*, where *DomainOrServerName* is the host name or fully qualified name of the domain service or domain controller to work with, such as **Get-ADReplicationSite –Server Tech .Cpandl.com** or **Get-ADReplicationSite –Server DC17.Cpandl.com**.

You also can determine the ISTG by completing the following steps:

1. In Active Directory Sites And Services, expand the Sites container and then select the site whose ISTG you want to locate in the console tree.

2. In the details pane, double-tap or double-click NTDS Site Settings.

3. In the NTDS Site Settings Properties dialog box, the current ISTG is listed in the Inter-Site Topology Generator panel, as shown in Figure 18-7.

Figure 18-7 Locate the ISTG.

Configuring site bridgehead servers

Replication between sites is performed by bridgehead servers in each site. A bridgehead server is a domain controller designated by the ISTG to perform inter-site replication. Bridgehead servers are discussed in detail in the sections of Chapter 13 entitled "Inter-site replication essentials" and "Replication rings and directory partitions."

As with the ISTG role, operating as a bridgehead server can add a significant load to a domain controller. This load increases with the number and frequency of replication changes. Because of this, you should also closely monitor the designated bridgehead servers to make sure they don't become overloaded.

When you have domain controllers that are already overloaded or not equipped to handle the additional load of being a bridgehead server, you might want to control which domain controllers operate as bridgehead servers. You do this by designating preferred bridgehead servers in a site.

Determine bridgehead servers

You can list the bridgehead servers in a site by typing the following command at a command prompt: **repadmin /bridgeheads site:SiteName**, where *SiteName* is the name of the site, such as **repadmin /bridgeheads site:Seattle-First-Site**. If you omit the *site:SiteName* values, the details for the current site are returned. With Windows PowerShell, use GetADReplicationSiteLinkBridge to get information about site-link bridges. Enter **Get-ADReplicationSiteLinkBridge Identity**, where *Identity* is the distinguished name of a specific site link to examine, such as **Get-ADReplicationSiteLinkBridge "CN=Denver-LA,CN=IP,CN=Inter-Site Transports,CN=Sites,CN=Configuration ,DC=cpandl,DC=com"**.

When you are designating bridgehead servers, you have several important things to consider. First, after you designate a preferred bridgehead server, the ISTG will use only the preferred bridgehead server for inter-site replication. This means that if the domain controller acting as the bridgehead server goes offline or is unable to replicate for any reason, inter-site replication will stop until the server is again available for replication or until you change the preferred bridgehead server configuration options. In the latter case, you need to do one of the following:

- Remove the server as a preferred bridgehead server and then specify a different preferred bridgehead server.

- Remove the server as a preferred bridgehead server and then allow the ISTG to select the bridgehead servers that should be used.

Because you can designate multiple preferred bridgehead servers, you can prevent this situation just by specifying more than one preferred bridgehead server. When there are multiple preferred bridgehead servers, the ISTG attempts to load-balance connections between the servers you designated as the preferred bridgehead servers. If a server fails, the other preferred bridgehead servers handle the load of the failed server.

An additional consideration when designating preferred bridgehead servers is that you must configure a bridgehead server for each partition that needs to be replicated. This means that you must configure at least one domain controller with a replica of each directory partition as a bridgehead server. If you don't do this, the replication of the partition will fail and the ISTG will log an event in the Directory Services event log detailing the failure. Consider the example shown in Figure 18-8.

CHAPTER 18

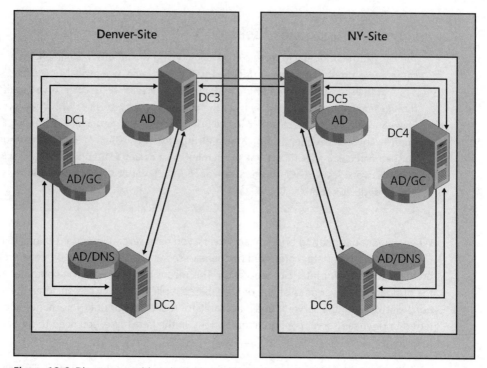

Figure 18-8 Directory partitions in separate sites must have a designated bridgehead server.

Here, the Denver-Site and the NY-Site are part of the same domain, ThePhone-Company. com. Each site has a global catalog and a DNS server that is integrated with Active Directory. In this configuration the bridgehead servers must replicate the following directory partitions: domain, configuration, schema, global catalog, and DNS (for the Domain Name System). If you designate DC3 and DC5 as the preferred bridgehead servers, only the domain, configuration, and schema directory partitions are replicated. This means that replication for the global catalog and the DNS partition would fail and the ISTG would log an event in the Directory Services event log specifying the reason for the failure. In contrast, if you designate DC1 and DC2 as the preferred bridgehead servers for the Denver site and DC4 and DC6 as the preferred bridgehead servers for the NY site, all the directory partitions are replicated.

To configure a domain controller as a preferred bridgehead server, complete the following steps:

1. Start Active Directory Sites And Services. Domain controllers associated with a site are listed in the site's Servers node. To locate the domain controller that you want to work with, expand the site node and then expand the related Servers node.

2. Press and hold or right-click the server you want to designate as a preferred bridgehead and then select Properties.

3. In the Properties dialog box, shown in Figure 18-9, you have the option of configuring the server as a preferred bridgehead server for either IP or SMTP. Select the appropriate transport in the Transports Available For Inter-Site Data Transfer list and then tap or click Add. If you later want the server to stop being a preferred bridgehead, select the transport in the This Server Is A Preferred Bridgehead Server For The Following Transports list and then tap or click Remove.

Figure 18-9 Designating a preferred bridgehead server.

4. Tap or click OK.

Configuring advanced site-link options

After you configure sites and site links, you might want to—or need to—optimize the configuration options to better suit the needs of your organization. Using site-link options, you can manage compression and notification during replication. You do this by editing the *Options* attribute on either the site-link object or the connection object related to the site link you want to modify. Only members of the Enterprise Admins group can change these options.

CHAPTER 18

You can configure a site-link object's *Options* attribute by following these steps:

1. Start Active Directory Sites And Services. Expand the Sites container and then expand the Inter-Site Transports container. Select the transport protocol you want to work with (either IP or SMTP). Next, press and hold or right-click the site link you want to modify and then select Properties.

2. In the Properties dialog box, tap or click the Attribute Editor tab. Scroll through the list of attributes until you find the *Options* attribute. When you find this attribute, select it and then tap or click Edit.

3. In the Integer Attribute Editor dialog box, you can now do the following:

    -   Type **1** to enable notification for inter-site replication. This means that the bridgehead servers on either side of the link will no longer use compression. Use this option only when you have sufficient bandwidth for a site connection and are concerned about high processor utilization on the affected bridgehead servers.

    -   Type **2** to enable two-way synchronization for inter-site replication. This means that bridgehead servers on either side of the link can synchronize changes at the same time. This allows simultaneous synchronization in two directions for faster updates. Use this setting only on links with sufficient bandwidth to handle two-way sync traffic.

    -   Type **4** to turn off compression for inter-site replication. This means that the bridgehead servers on either side of the link can notify each other that changes have occurred. This allows the bridgehead server receiving the notification to pull the changes across the site link and thereby get more frequent updates.

    -   Use combinations of the flag values to set multiple flags. For example, a value of 5 means that compression will be turned off and notification for inter-site replication will be enabled.

    -   Tap or click Clear to reset the *Options* attribute to its default value of *<not set>*. When the *Options* attribute is not set, notification for inter-site replication is disabled and compression is turned on.

4. Tap or click OK twice.

Monitoring and troubleshooting replication

When you have problems with replication, you'll find that monitoring is an important part of your diagnostics and troubleshooting process. Several tools are available to help you, including the Replication Administrator (RepAdmin), which is a command-line utility.

Using the Replication Administrator

You run the Replication Administrator from the command line. Most command-line parameters accept a list of the domain controllers you want to work with (called DCList) and can be specified as follows:

- * is a wildcard that includes all domain controllers in the enterprise.

- *PartialName** is a partial server name that includes a wildcard to match the remainder of the server name.

- *Site:SiteName* includes only domain controllers in the named site.

- *Gc:* includes all global catalog servers in the enterprise.

Knowing this, you can perform many tasks using the Replication Administrator. These tasks are summarized in Table 18-2.

Table 18-2 Key Replication Administrator commands

Command to Type	Description
repadmin /bridgeheads DCList [/verbose]	Lists bridgehead servers.
repadmin /failcache DCList	Lists failed replication events that were detected by the knowledge consistency checker (KCC).
repadmin /istg DCList [/verbose]	Lists the name of the ISTG for a specified site.
repadmin /kcc DCList [/async]	Forces the KCC to recalculate the intrasite replication topology for a specified domain controller. By default, this recalculation occurs every 15 minutes. Use the /Async options to start the KCC and not wait for it to finish the calculation.
repadmin /latency DCList [/verbose]	Lists the amount of time between inter-site replications using the ISTG Keep Alive time stamp.
repadmin /queue DCList	Lists tasks waiting in the replication queue.
repadmin /replsummary DCList	Displays a summary of the replication state.
repadmin /showcert DCList	Displays the server certificates loaded on the specified domain controllers.
repadmin /showconn DCList	Displays the connection objects for the specified domain controllers. It defaults to the local site.
repadmin /showctx DCList	Lists computers that have opened sessions with a specified domain controller.
repadmin/showoutcalls DCList	Lists calls that were made by the specified server to other servers but that have not yet been answered.

CHAPTER 18

Command to Type	Description
repadmin /showrepl DCList	Lists the replication partners for each directory partition on the specified domain controller.
repadmin /showtrust DCList	Lists all domains trusted by a specified domain.

Using PowerShell to monitor and troubleshoot replication

The ActiveDirectory module includes cmdlets for monitoring and troubleshooting replication. Type **Get-Help *–Ad*** to see a complete list of cmdlets for working with Active Directory or **Get-Help *-AdReplication*** to see a list of commands specific to replication. Of all these commands, the ones you'll use the most for troubleshooting are the following:

- Get-ADReplicationPartnerMetadata
- Get-ADReplicationFailure
- Sync-ADObject

Get-ADReplicationPartnerMetadata returns information about the configuration and state of replication for a domain controller, including the date and time of the last replication attempt and the date and time of the last successful replication. The basic syntax is

```
Get-ADReplicationPartnerMetadata -target ServerName
```

Here, *ServerName* is the name of the domain controller to check, or you can use * to look at all domain controllers in the forest, such as

```
Get-ADReplicationPartnerMetadata -target CorpServer25
```

or

```
Get-ADReplicationPartnerMetadata -target *
```

Get-ADReplicationFailure returns information about recent replication errors, including the most recent failures and the partners a domain controller failed to contact. The basic syntax is

```
Get-ADReplicationFailure -target ObjectName -scope [server|site|domain|forest]
```

Here, *ObjectName* is the name of the object to check and *scope* sets the scope of the search. This example checks all domain controllers in the named site:

```
Get-ADReplicationFailure -target Seattle-First-Site -scope site
```

You use Sync-ADObject to perform immediate replication of changes related to a specific object. Typically, you'll use it with another cmdlet, such as Get-ADDomainController. Consider the following scenario:

- The TestTeam group was deleted accidentally, and you recovered the group from the Active Directory Recycle Bin. Now you want to restore the group throughout the domain. The command you use to do this is as follows:

```
Get-ADDomainController -filter * | foreach {Sync-ADObject -object
"cn=testteam,cn=users,dc=cpand1,dc=com" -source corpserver85
-destination $_.hostname}
```

Monitoring replication

Using the Performance Monitor, you can perform in-depth monitoring and analysis of Active Directory. You open the Performance Monitor by choosing the related option from the Tools menu in Server Manager. You can track the performance of multiple domain controllers from a single, monitoring server using Performance Monitor's remote monitoring capabilities.

Directory Services is the performance object you'll use for monitoring Active Directory. Several hundred performance counters are available for selection. Most counters have a prefix that reflects the aspect of Active Directory to which the counter relates. These prefixes include the following:

- **AB.** AB counters relate to the Address Book in Active Directory.

- **ATQ.** ATQ counters relate to the Asynchronous Thread Queue in Active Directory.

- **DRA.** DRA counters relate to the Directory Replication Agent in Active Directory.

- **DS.** DS counters relate to the Directory Service in Active Directory.

- **LDAP.** LDAP counters relate to the Lightweight Directory Access Protocol in Active Directory.

- **SAM.** SAM counters relate to the Security Accounts Manager in Active Directory.

The way domain controllers replicate the SYSVOL depends on the domain functional level. When a domain is running at Microsoft Windows 2000 native or Windows Server 2003 functional level, domain controllers replicate the SYSVOL using File Replication Service (FRS). When a domain is running at Windows Server 2008 functional level, domain controllers replicate the SYSVOL using Distributed File System (DFS).

When Distributed File System (DFS) is used to replicate the Sysvol files between domain controllers, you can monitor the Distributed File System using the DFS Replicated Folders, DFS Replication Connections, and DFS Replication Service Volumes objects. When File Replication

Service (FRS) is used to replicate the Sysvol files between domain controllers, you can monitor File Replication Service using the *FileReplicaConn* and *FileReplicatSet* monitoring objects. Each object has a number of counters that can be used to track the status and health of replication.

You can specify counters to monitor by following these steps:

1. In the Performance Monitor console, expand the Monitoring Tools node and then select the Performance Monitor node.

2. Tap or click the Add (+) button on the toolbar or press Ctrl+I. In the Add Counters dialog box, use the Select Counters From Computer list to select the counter to monitor.

3. Double-tap or double-click the object you want to work with on the Available Counters list. Specify counters to track by selecting them in the Select Counters From Computer list and then tapping or clicking Add. You can learn more about counters by selecting the Show Description check box.

4. When you are finished adding counters, tap or click OK.

If you like, you also can configure performance logging and performance alerting:

-   Events related to Active Directory are also logged in the event logs. Active Directory–related events, including NTDS replication events, are logged in the Directory Service log on the domain controller.

-   Events related to DFS are recorded in the DFS Replication log on the domain controller. The primary source for events is DFSR, which is the DFS Service itself.

-   Events related to FRS are recorded in the File Replication Service log on the domain controller. The primary source for events is NtFrs, which is the File Replication Service itself.

Modifying inter-site replication for testing

Occasionally, when you are testing or troubleshooting inter-site replication, you might need to temporarily modify the way inter-site replication works. You can modify the way inter-site replication works by editing the *Options* attribute on a bridgehead server's server object. Only members of the Enterprise Admins group can change these options.

You can configure a server object's *Options* attribute by following these steps:

1. Start Active Directory Sites And Services. Domain controllers associated with a site are listed in the site's Servers node. To locate the domain controller that you want to work with, expand the site node and then expand the related Servers node.

2. In the left pane, select the bridgehead server you want to work with. Next, press and hold or right-click the related NTDS Settings node and then select Properties.

3. In the Properties dialog box, tap or click the Attribute Editor tab. Scroll through the list of attributes until you find the *Options* attribute. When you find this attribute, select it and then tap or click Edit.

4. In the Integer Attribute Editor dialog box, you can now do the following:

   - Type **2** to disable inbound replication. This means that the bridgehead server will no longer perform inbound replication. The server will still accept replication connections and also perform outbound replication.

   - Type **4** to disable outbound replication. This means that the bridgehead server will no longer perform outbound replication. The server will still accept replication connections and also perform inbound replication.

   - Type **8** to prevent connections from forming replication partnerships. This means that the bridgehead servers will not allow connections to be established for inbound or outbound replication. Existing connections will continue, but no new connections will be established.

   - Use combinations of the flag values to set multiple flags. For example, a value of *14* means that inbound and outbound replication are disabled and that servers are prevented from forming replication partnerships.

   - Tap or click Clear to reset the *Options* attribute and undo your changes. When the *Options* attribute is not set, notification for inter-site replication is disabled and compression is turned on.

5. Tap or click OK twice.

NOTE

When the original value for the *Options* attribute is *1*, the server hosts a global catalog and you must add 1 to all values you enter to ensure that the server can continue to act as a global catalog. When you are finished testing, you can restore the original settings by entering a value of *1*.

CAUTION

Setting these options changes the way the KCC works and also might disable the KCC's ability to automatically generate replication topology. Before you make any changes, note the current value of the *Options* attribute. Typically, the attribute has a value of *<not set>* or *1*. When the original value is *<not set>*, you can tap or click Clear to reset the *Options* attribute and undo your changes. Failure to restore your changes after testing or troubleshooting can cause replication failure throughout the enterprise.

Deploying print services

Print services have changed substantially over the years, and the changes offer many additional features and improvements. The techniques you need to master to successfully deploy print services are what this chapter is about. You'll find detailed discussions on print services architecture, print server selection and optimization, printer hardware selection and optimization, printer connection deployment, and more.

Understanding print services

In a perfect world the printers used by an organization would be selected after careful planning. You'd select the best printer for the job based on the expected use of the printer and the features required. The reality is that in many organizations, departments and individuals separately purchase printers without giving much thought to how the printer will be used. Someone sees that a printer is needed, and a printer is purchased. The result is that many organizations have a hodgepodge of printers. Some printers are high-volume and others are low-volume, low-cost. The high-volume printers are designed to handle heavy daily loads from multiple users, and the low-volume, low-cost printers are designed to handle printing for small groups or individuals. If you are responsible for printers in your department or the organization as a whole, you might want to look at ways to consolidate or standardize so that the hodgepodge of printers spread around the department or throughout the organization is easier to manage and maintain.

All printers, regardless of type, have one thing in common: a device is needed to manage the communication between the printer and the client computers that want to print to the printer. This device is called a print server. In most cases a print server is a computer running the Microsoft Windows operating system. When a Windows computer acts as a print server, it provides many services. It provides clients with the drivers they need for printing. It stores documents that are spooled for printing and maintains the associated print queue. It provides for security and auditing of printer access.

From a process perspective, it helps to understand how printing works so that you can better manage and troubleshoot printing problems. The way printing works depends on the data type of the printer driver being used. There are two main data types for printer drivers:

- **Enhanced Meta File (EMF).** EMF uses the Printer Control Language (PCL) page description language. EMF documents are sent to the print server with minimal processing and are then further processed on the print server.

- **RAW.** RAW is most commonly used with the PostScript page description language. RAW documents are fully processed on clients before being sent to a print server and aren't modified by the print server.

When you print a document, many processes are involved. Figure 19-1 shows the standard EMF printing process.

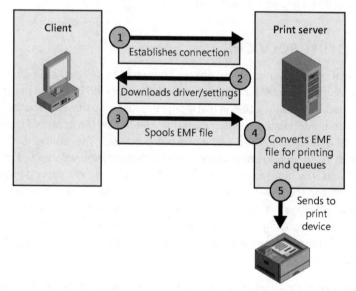

Figure 19-1 This is the standard EMF printing process.

Here, the client establishes a connection to the print server. If it needs a print driver or if a new driver is available, it downloads the driver and the associated settings. The client first uses the print driver to partially render the document into EMF and then spools the EMF file to the print server. The print server converts the EMF file to final form and then queues the file to the printer queue (printer). When the document reaches the top of the print queue, it is sent to the physical print device.

Figure 19-2 shows the standard RAW printing process. Here, the client establishes a connection to the print server. If it needs a print driver or if a new driver is available, it downloads the driver and the associated settings. The client then fully processes the file for printing and spools the RAW file to the print server. The print server queues the file to the logical print device (printer). When the document reaches the top of the print queue, it is sent to the physical print device.

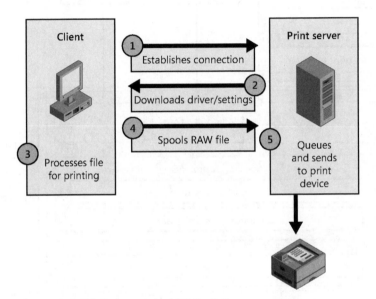

Figure 19-2 This is the standard RAW printing process.

Okay, so that's the version from 10,000 feet—the fine details are much more complicated, as Figure 19-3 shows. The model can be applied to the mechanics of the initial printing of a document on a client to the handling on the print server to the actual printing on the print device.

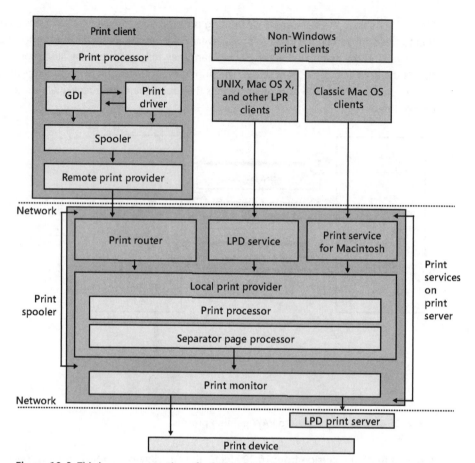

Figure 19-3 This is a representation of printing from the client to the server to the print device.

Print drivers are stored in the %SystemRoot%\System32\Spool\Drivers folder on the print server. Assuming that a client already has the current print drivers, the printing process works like this:

1. On a client running Windows, the application from which you're printing calls the Graphics Device Interface (GDI), which uses the printer driver to determine how to format the document for the selected print device. The GDI is responsible for any necessary preprocessing (converting into EMF or RAW format) of the document, which, depending on the printer driver type and configuration settings, might or might not be necessary. When it's finished with the document, the GDI passes the document to the local print spooler (Winspool.drv).

2. The local print spooler makes a remote procedure call (RPC) connection to the Print Spooler service (Spoolsv.exe) on the print server. The Print Spooler service calls the print router (Spoolss.dll). The print router makes an RPC connection to the remote print provider (Win32spl.dll) on the client. The remote print provider then connects directly to the Print Spooler service on the print server and sends the document.

3. The local print provider on the print server saves the document in the print queue as a print job. By default, all print jobs for all printers on a print server are stored in the %SystemRoot%\System32\Spool\Printers folder. The primary spool file has a .spl extension, and the control information needed to print the spool file is stored in a .shd file.

4. The local print provider is responsible for any necessary postprocessing of the document, which, depending on the printer driver type and configuration settings, might or might not be necessary. The local print provider uses the print processor to do any necessary processing or conversion and the separator page processor to insert any separator pages if necessary. The local print provider processes the document when it reaches the top of the print queue and before it sends the print job to the print monitor.

5. The print monitor sends the print job to the physical print device, where it's actually printed. The way spooling works depends on the print queue configuration and the printer buffer. If possible, the entire document is transferred to the print device. Otherwise, the print monitor sends the print job gradually as the printer buffer allows.

Like the Registry, printing is one of those areas of the Windows operating system that is obfuscated by varying use of terminology. From a user perspective, a printer is the device that prints documents. From a technical perspective, a logical print device or printer is a software component used for printing. Because it is where documents are queued before printing, it is also referred to as a print queue. When you add or install a printer on a Windows system, you're installing the software—the logical print device—as opposed to the physical print device itself.

Windows Server has built-in support for both 32-bit and 64-bit printer drivers. Support for 64-bit printer drivers is important because systems running 64-bit editions of Windows need 64-bit drivers. As with previous versions of Windows, printer drivers are installed automatically on clients when they first try to print to a new printer device on a print server.

Windows uses two types of printer drivers. Printer drivers that operate in kernel mode are Type 2 drivers. With a kernel-mode driver, an error with a printer driver can cause the server to crash. This happens because the driver is running in the operating system kernel process. Printer drivers that operate in user mode are Type 3 drivers. User-mode drivers operate in a process separate from the operating system kernel process, which means that an error in a user-mode driver affects only its related process. In Windows Server, printer drivers operate in user mode and kernel-mode drivers are supported only for backward compatibility.

Inside OUT

Automatic restart of services is for errors only

An error in a user-mode driver typically means that the Print Spooler process hangs up and has to be restarted. Because Windows Server is configured by default to restart the Print Spooler process automatically within one minute if it stops with an error or hangs up, no administrator action is required.

When a service is configured to restart automatically, the restart is performed only when an error occurs. Two general types of errors can occur: either the service will hang up and stop responding or the service will stop running and exit with an error code. In these cases automatic restart can usually recover the service and get the service to resume normal operations. If you stop a service manually, automatic restart does not take place.

In Windows Server, the Microsoft Universal Printer Driver (Unidrv) provides core printing functions that printer driver manufacturers can use. These functions are implemented in the two primary print engines:

- **Unidrv.dll.** Provides the core printing functions for PCL print devices. Uses EMF-formatted files.

- **PScript5.dll.** Provides core printing functions for PostScript print devices. Uses RAW-formatted files.

The availability of these print engines gives printer manufacturers several options for developing printer drivers. They can create a minidriver that implements only the unique functionality of a particular print device and rely on the appropriate print engine for print services, or they can make their own custom driver that uses its own print engine.

Inside OUT

Automatic print driver distribution on clusters

On clusters, any print driver that you install on a virtual cluster is automatically distributed from the cluster spooler resource to all nodes of the cluster. This is an important feature that simplifies installation and management of print clusters. Administrators must install drivers only once rather than once in each node in the cluster. Because Remote Desktop Services and print services can coexist, the two services can be installed on the same nodes in a cluster.

Planning for printer deployments and consolidation

Print servers and printers are the key components needed for printing. You can size and optimize both print servers and printers in many ways.

Optimize and monitor after installation

After sizing and optimization, you should consider optimizing the way printing is handled using print queues. To better support deployed print services, you can periodically monitor performance, check for and install print driver upgrades, and prepare for print server failure.

Sizing print server hardware and optimizing configuration

The maximum load and performance level of a print server depends on its configuration. You can configure print servers in many ways, and, as a print server's workload changes over time, so should its configuration. As the workload of the print server scales, so does the amount of processing and memory required to handle print services. Any computer, including a desktop-class system, can act as a print server. Although most Windows desktop systems are limited to 10 active connections, Windows Server systems are not limited in this way.

You should consider the print server's central processing unit (CPU) speed, total random access memory (RAM), and network card speed. When PCL printers and EMF print drivers are used, most of the document processing is performed on the server and the server will need a fairly fast processor and sufficient RAM to process documents. When PostScript printers and RAW print drivers are used, most of the document processing is performed on clients before documents are transferred to the server and the server's processor speed and memory are less important. In many cases a printer server will provide services for multiple printers, so there's a good chance that some of the printers will be PCL and some of the printers will be PostScript. In this case the processing power and total RAM of the print server are again important.

Complex print jobs, such as those containing high-resolution graphics, can use additional resources on the print server. They require more memory to process and more processing power. The number of clients connecting to a print server can also affect resource requirements:

- Most print clients running Windows establish RPC connections to print servers. With RPC, a connection between a client and server remains open as long as there are one or more open handles. Typically, applications open handles to a print server when a user prints but don't close those open handles until the user shuts down or exits the application. If a user accesses the printer folder or views the printer queue on the print server, this opens handles to the print server because the folders or queues are open as well. As a result, there can be many open handles to a print server using resources even when a printer server isn't busy.

- Most non-Windows clients establish Server Message Block (SMB) connections to print servers. If Line Printer Daemon (LPD) Service is configured, SMB clients running non-Windows operating systems can use the Line Printer Remote (LPR) service to communicate with the LDP service on the print server. Because these clients maintain their own printer spools, the print server acts as the gateway between the client and the printer. These clients use very few resources on the server, but they have very few options.

Print servers must have sufficient disk space to handle print jobs. The amount of disk space required depends on the size of print jobs and the number of print jobs that are queued for printing at any one time. It also depends on the print server configuration because in some cases a print server can be configured to save documents after they have been spooled for faster reprinting. By default, print jobs are spooled to files on the print server's system drive (%SystemRoot%\System32\Spool\PRINTERS), but this is completely configurable, as discussed in the section entitled "Configuring print spool, logging, and notification settings" in Chapter 20, "Managing and maintaining print services."

Print servers perform a substantial number of disk input/output (I/O) operations. To ensure optimal performance, you should consider moving the spool folder to a separate drive or array of drives that isn't used for other purposes. A separate drive should help ensure that disk space isn't a constraint on the number of jobs the print server can handle and that the disk I/O operations related to the spooler are separate from those of other disk I/O operations.

NOTE

Paging and spooling are both disk I/O-intensive operations. In a large enterprise deployment, you might want to consider using separate disks for paging and spooling.

The network interfaces on a print server are also important but often overlooked. The print server needs sufficient connectivity to communicate with both clients and printers. When possible, network cards should operate at 100 megabits per second (Mbps) or higher.

Sizing printer hardware and optimizing configuration

Many types of printers are available, including inkjet and laser. Both types have advantages and disadvantages.

Inkjet printers typically have lower upfront costs but higher costs later because they often require more maintenance and use consumables (ink cartridges) more quickly. A typical inkjet printer will print several hundred pages before you have to replace its ink cartridges. Higher-capacity cartridges are available for some business-class models. As part of periodic maintenance, you must perform nozzle checks to check for clogged nozzles and then clean the print heads if they are clogged. You might also need to align the print heads periodically.

Laser printers typically have higher upfront costs and moderate incremental costs because these printers typically require less maintenance and use consumables (ink cartridges and drum/fuser kits) less frequently. A typical laser printer will print thousands of pages before you have to replace ink cartridges and tens of thousands of pages or more before you have to replace the drum, fuser, or transfer components. Higher-capacity ink cartridges are also available for most business-class models. Replacing the ink cartridges, drum, fuser, and transfer components are the key maintenance tasks.

Use laser printers for high-volume printing

In most cases laser printers have a lower per-sheet print cost than inkjet printers. This is true for black-and-white and color printing. Because of the lower cost, longer life cycle of consumables, and less frequent preventative maintenance schedule, laser printers typically are better suited to high-volume printing.

Most business-class printers can be expanded. The options available depend on the printer model, and they can include the following:

- **RAM expansion modules.** The amount of RAM on a printer determines how much information it can buffer. At a minimum, a printer should be sized so that the average document being printed can be buffered in RAM in its entirety. As the workload of the printer increases, the RAM should allow for buffering of multiple documents simultaneously, which enables faster and more efficient printing.

Consider the type of document being printed

Most word-processing documents are relatively small—several hundred pages of text use only a few hundred kilobytes. When you add graphics, such as with presentations or PDF files, even files with few pages can use several megabytes of disk space. Digital art, computer-aided design (CAD), and other types of files with high-resolution graphics can use hundreds of megabytes.

- **Paper or envelope trays.** Add-on paper or envelope trays can improve performance substantially—more than you'd think. If a group within the organization routinely prints with different paper sizes or prints transparencies or envelopes, you should consider getting an add-on tray to accommodate the additional paper size or type. Otherwise, every time someone prints to the alternate paper size or type, the printer will stop and wait for the user to insert the right kind of paper. On a busy printer this can lead to big delays in printing, frustrated users, and major problems. Additionally, if the needs are specialized and frequent enough, you might want to consider providing a dedicated printer. Although this has a higher initial cost, it can be a productivity boost for both the users with special requirements and everyone who has to work around them.

- **Duplexers.** Duplexers allow for printing on both sides of a sheet of paper. If a printer has a duplexer, Windows Server will use that feature automatically to reduce the amount of paper the printer uses. This doesn't necessarily save time, but it does mean that the printer's tray will have to be refilled less frequently. Users can, of course, change the default settings and elect not to duplex.

- **Internal hard disks.** An internal hard disk shifts much of the printing burden from the print server to the printer itself. A printer with an internal hard disk is able to store many documents internally and queue them for printing directly. Because the documents are stored on the printer, printing is more efficient and can be quicker than if the printer had to wait for documents to be transferred over the network. Finally, don't forget that there are significant security implications where sensitive documents are concerned, so internal hard disks on printers should be treated with the same care as hard disks on servers.

Many groups of users have specific needs, so if you're purchasing a printer for a particular group, be sure to ask the group about its needs, which might include the following:

- **Photo printing.** Usually an option for inkjet printers rather than laser printers

- **Large-format printing.** The capability to print documents larger than 11 by 17 inches

Both inkjet and laser printers are available in direct-attached and network-attached models. Direct-attached printers (more commonly known as local printers) connect directly to a print server by a universal serial bus (USB) or FireWire (IEEE 1394) interface. For faster transmission speeds and easier configuration, consider printers with USB 2, USB 3, or FireWire interfaces and stay away from those with slower USB 1 interfaces. USB and FireWire interfaces are also fully Plug and Play–compliant.

Network-attached printers have a network card and connect to the network like other devices with network cards or built-in wireless networking. A printer with a built-in network interface gives you flexibility in where you place the printer relative to the print server. Unlike a local printer, which must be placed in close proximity to the print server, you can place a network-attached printer just about anywhere with a network connection. If you have a choice, choose a network-attached printer over a local printer.

Inside OUT

The ins and outs of color printing

If your organization is considering color printers, you should look closely at the type of ink or toner cartridges the printer uses. Most business-class color printers have separate cartridges for each basic color—cyan, magenta, and yellow—and black. Some high-end printers have additional cartridges for producing true-to-life colors, and these printers are often referred to by the number of ink/toner cartridges, such as a six-color printer. Look closely at the capacity options for cartridges. Some printers can use both standard-capacity and high-capacity cartridges, but not always for both color and black ink. For example, you might be able to use high-capacity blank ink cartridges that can print up to 4500 pages but only standard-capacity color cartridges that can print up to 1500 pages.

If a group or individual needs a printer for photo printing, it's important to consider whether special photo ink/toner cartridges are available. For example, many inkjet printers have the option to use a photo ink cartridge. This special cartridge prints digital photos with richer colors that are more true to life. Also, don't assume that a color laser printer will be able to print on specialty photo paper because this might not be the case. See the section entitled "Configuring color profiles" in Chapter 20 for details on how Integrated Color Management (ICM) is used.

Whether you are working with an inkjet or laser printer, you should determine the number of pages printed per minute and the recommended monthly print volume or duty cycle. Most color printers print in monochrome slightly faster than they print in color. In a small office you might be able to use a printer that prints 20 to 25 pages a minute, but in a workgroup setting you might find that you need a printer that prints 45 to 50 pages a minute.

When you find a printer that prints at a suitable rate, look at the printer's monthly duty cycle. The monthly duty cycle is a gauge of how robust the printer is and how many pages it can print each month. For example, a printer with a monthly duty cycle of 35,000 pages could handle printing a maximum of 35,000 pages each month (though this probably is not recommended on a sustained basis and if users really print that many pages each month, you'll probably find that the printer is unable to keep up with its workload or that it has frequent problems requiring maintenance).

Inside OUT

Printer duty cycles and consumables

A printer's monthly duty cycle might be completely different from its recommended monthly print volume. Typically, a printer's monthly duty cycle is the maximum number of pages per month that a printer can handle in ideal conditions, and the recommended monthly print volume (which might be substantially less) is what the printer really can handle for optimal performance. Thus, just because a printer is listed as having a huge monthly duty cycle, it doesn't mean that users can print that number of pages each month. As an example, an enterprise-class printer might have a monthly duty cycle of 250,000 pages but a recommended monthly print volume of 5000 to 20,000 pages—a substantial difference. Also consider the consumables for a printer. For example, an enterprise-class printer might have a standard black print cartridge that can print up to 10,000 pages and a high-capacity black print cartridge that can print up to 20,000 pages. Based on this capacity, if users really printed 250,000 pages a month, you would need to change the standard black print cartridge almost every day.

Most laser printers require periodic replacement of drum, fuser, and transfer components. These components are the laser printer's dirty little secret. Most printer manufacturers do not list drum, fuser, or transfer component life cycles with product information. In fact, in a search of printer manufacturer websites at the time I was writing this book, I found that most manufacturers list toner cartridges as replacements parts on the printer pages but list drum, fuser, and transfer components separately. I had to search separately for "drum," "fuser," and "transfer kit" to find the necessary replacement kits. With some high-end printers, the necessary replacement kits might not even be available for direct purchase, requiring your organization to have a service contract or obtain the kit from a third-party source.

One of the reasons it's so hard to find information about these components is that they can be expensive. Consider, for example, an enterprise-class color laser printer. These high-speed, high-capacity laser printers designed for large offices typically have a transfer kit, a fuser kit, and four separate drum kits—one each of black, cyan, yellow, and magenta. Based on 5 percent average coverage per printed page, the fuser kit might yield 100,000 pages and cost around $280, the black drum might yield 40,000 pages and cost around $300, each of the color drums might yield 20,000 pages and cost around $475, and the transfer kit might yield 200,000 pages and cost about $380. Thus, if users print 120,000 monochrome pages and 120,000 color pages each year, your total costs in drum, fuser, and transfer components alone would be around $9,000. Because your toner cartridge cost would be about another $2,500 per year, the total annual cost of all printer consumables would be around $11,500.

Setting up print servers

Windows Server allows you to set up local printers and network-attached printers. You can share either type of printer on the network so that it's available to other computers and users. The computer sharing the printer is called a print server, regardless of whether it's actually running a server version of the Windows operating system.

As discussed previously, you can configure more than one logical print device (printer) for a physical print device. The key reason to do this is if you want to use different options, such as when you want to create a priority or scheduled print queue. If you configure multiple printers, you must use a different local name and share name each time. Other than that, you can choose the identical initial settings each time and modify them as desired.

Installing a print server

You configure a server as a printer server by adding the Print And Document Services role. Follow these steps to install and configure this role:

1. In Server Manager, tap or click Manage and then tap or click Add Roles And Features or select Add Roles And Features in the Quick Start pane. This starts the Add Roles And Features Wizard. If the wizard displays the Before You Begin page, read the Welcome text and then select Next.

2. On the Installation Type page, Role-Based Or Feature-Based Installation is selected by default. Select Next.

3. On the Server Selection page, you can choose to install roles and features on running servers or virtual hard disks. Either select a server from the server pool or select a server from the server pool on which to mount a virtual hard disk (VHD). If you're adding roles and features to a VHD, tap or click Browse and then use the Browse For Virtual Hard Disks dialog box to locate the VHD. When you're ready to continue, select Next.

4. On the Select Roles page, select Print And Document Services. When you're ready to continue, select Next three times.

5. On the Select Role Services page, select one or more of the following role services (see Figure 19-4) and then tap or click Next:

   - **Print Server.** Configures the server as a print server and installs the Print Management console. You can use the Print Management console to manage multiple printers and print servers, to migrate printers to and from other print servers, and to manage print jobs.

- **Line Printer Daemon (LPD) Service.** Installs and starts the TCP/IP Print Server (LPDSVC) service, which allows UNIX-based or other computers that are using the Line Printer Remote (LPR) service to print to shared printers on this server.

- **Distributed Scan Server.** Establishes the server as a scan server, which is used to run scan processes. Scan processes are rules that define scan settings and control delivery of scanned documents on your network. The Scan Management snap-in is installed when you install this role service. Scan Management enables you to manage Web Services on Devices (WSD)–enabled scanners, scan servers, and scan processes.

- **Internet Printing.** Creates a website where authorized users can manage print jobs on the server. It also lets users who have Internet Printing Client installed connect and print to the shared printers on the server using the Internet Printing Protocol (IPP). The default Internet address for Internet Printing is http://*ServerName*/Printers, where *ServerName* is a placeholder for the actual internal or external server name, such as http://PrintServer24/Printers or http://www.adatum.com/Printers.

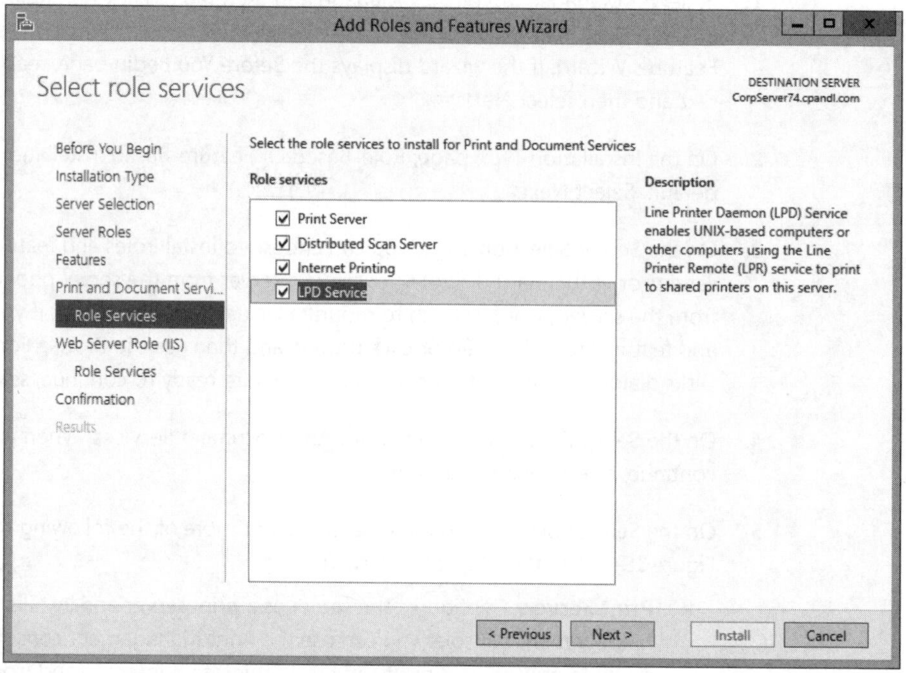

Figure 19-4 Select the role services to install for the printer.

6. When you install Internet Printing, you must also install Web Server (IIS) and Windows Process Activation Service. You'll be prompted to automatically add the required role

CHAPTER 19

services. If you tap or click Yes to continue and install these role services, you'll have the opportunity to add other role services for Web Server (IIS). Select Add Features to continue.

7. After you review the installation options and save them as necessary, select Install to begin the installation process. The Installation Progress page tracks the progress of the installation. If you close the wizard, select the Notifications icon in Server Manager and then select the link provided to reopen the wizard.

8. When Setup finishes installing the Print And Document Services role, the Installation Progress page will be updated to reflect this. Review the installation details to ensure that all phases of the installation were successfully completed.

9. When you install Distributed Scan Server, you'll get a notification that additional configuration is required. Select the link provided to open Scan Management, which you can use to specify scanners to manage. In Scan Management, expand the Scan Management node in the left pane, press and hold or right-click the Managed Scanners node, and then select Manage to open the Add Or Remove Scanners dialog box. Use the Add Or Remove Scanners dialog box to identify the distributed scanners in your organization.

Inside OUT

Getting required binary source files

If the server on which you want to install the Print And Document Services role doesn't have all the required binary source files, the server gets the files through Windows Update by default or from a location specified in Group Policy. You also can specify an alternate path for the required source files by tapping or clicking the Specify An Alternate Source Path link, entering that alternate path in the box provided, and then tapping or clicking OK. For network shares, enter the UNC path to the share, such as \\FileServer18\WinServer12R2\. For mounted Windows images, enter the WIM path prefixed with WIM: and including the index of the image to use, such as WIM:\\FileServer18\WinServer12R2\install.wim:4.

You have several additional options for adding required binaries. At an elevated command prompt, you can enter DISM /Online /Enable-Feature /FeatureName:PrintServer /All /LimitAccess /Source:E:\Sources\SxS, where E: is a mounted ISO or DVD. At an elevated shell prompt, you can enter Enable-WindowsOptionalFeature -Online –FeatureName "PrintServer" -All -LimitAccess Source "E:\Sources\SxS", where E: is a mounted ISO or DVD.

> **NOTE**
> When you install Distributed Scan Server, a security group called Scan Operators is added to the Users container in Active Directory Domain Services (AD DS) for the current logon domain. Any users who need to manage the Distributed Scan service should be added to this group.

Printer sharing controls access to printers that are attached to the computer. However, printer sharing is disabled by default. In File Explorer, select Network in the left pane. On the toolbar in Network Explorer, select Network and then select Network And Sharing Center. In Network And Sharing Center, select Change Advanced Sharing Settings in the left pane. Select the network profile for the network for which file and printer sharing should be enabled. Typically, this is the Domain profile. Standard file and printer sharing controls network access to shared resources. To enable file and printer sharing, select Turn On File And Printer Sharing to enable file and printer sharing.

When you configure a computer running Windows Server as a print server, you'll find several management tools, including the Print Management console and the Printbrm.exe command-line tool. You'll find the Print Management console on the Tools menu in Server Manager. Printbrm.exe is in the %SystemRoot%\System32\Spool\Tools folder.

You'll also find a set of scripts for managing print services from the command line. These scripts are stored in the %SystemRoot%\System32\Printing_Admin_Scripts folder and include the following:

- **PrnCnfg.** A script for managing printer configuration settings, including printer name, printer properties, and printer sharing

- **PrnDrvr.** A script for listing and managing print drivers

- **PrnJobs.** A script for viewing and managing print jobs in a print queue

- **PrnMngr.** A script for installing printers and managing printers configured on a computer

- **PrnPort.** A script for creating and managing Transmission Control Protocol/Internet Protocol (TCP/IP) ports for printers

- **PrntQctl.** A script for managing print queues

- **Pubprn.** A script for printer publishing in Active Directory

Installing network printers automatically

Print Management can automatically detect all network printers located on the same subnet as the computer on which the console is running. After detection, Print Management can automatically install the appropriate printer drivers, set up print queues, and share the printers. To automatically install network printers and configure a print server, follow these steps:

1. Start Print Management by tapping or clicking Tools in Server Manager and then selecting Print Management.

2. In Print Management, expand the Print Servers node by double-tapping or double-clicking it and then press and hold or right-click the entry for the local or remote server you want to work with.

3. Select Add Printer. This starts the Network Printer Installation Wizard.

4. On the Print Installation page, select Search The Network For Printers and then tap or click Next.

5. The wizard will then search the local subnet for network printers. As shown in Figure 19-5, if printers are found, you'll see a list of printers by name, IP address, and status. Tap or click a printer to install, tap or click Next, and then continue this procedure to install the automatically detected printer.

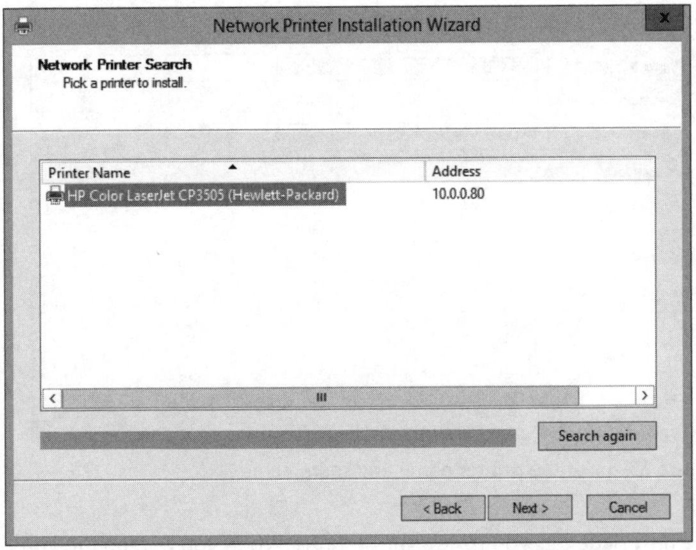

Figure 19-5 Printers located by the wizard are listed by name and IP address.

If a printer you want to use is not listed, you should ensure that the printer is turned on and online and then repeat this procedure. If a printer you want to use is turned on and online but is not listed, see "Adding network-attached printers" to complete the installation.

6. The wizard automatically detects the TCP/IP port configuration of the selected printer and then communicates with the printer to obtain the information required to configure the printer. Afterward, the wizard sets the default name and share name of the printer, as shown in Figure 19-6. The printer is configured as a shared resource as well.

The printer name is the name you encounter when you work with the printer in Print Management. The share name is the name that users use when they work with the printer. The printer name and share name can be up to 256 characters and can include spaces. In a large organization you'll want the share name to be logical and helpful in locating the printer. For example, you might want to give the name Twelfth Floor NE to the printer that points to a print device in the northeast corner of the twelfth floor.

Optionally, enter information in the Location and Comment text boxes that will help users locate and identify the printer. For example, you might want to specify the printer location as: Floor 3 in Building 204.

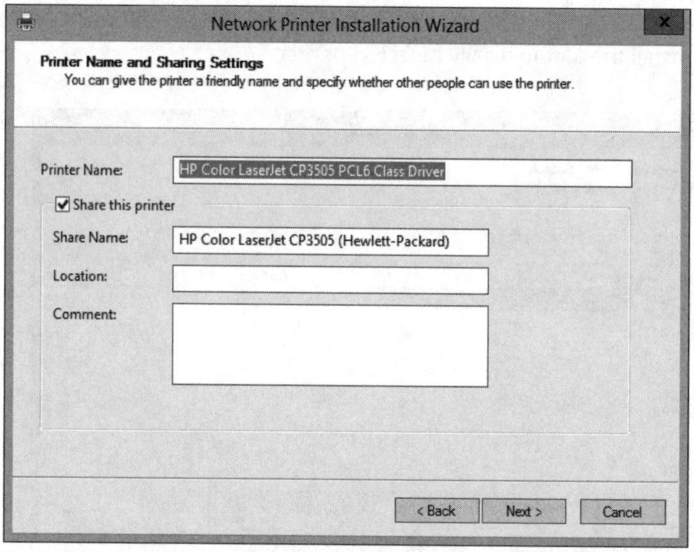

Figure 19-6 Set the printer name and share name.

7. The next page lets you review the settings. When you're ready to complete the installation, tap or click Next.

8. When you share a printer, Windows Server automatically makes drivers available so that users can download them when they first connect to the printer. The status page should confirm that printer driver and printer installation were successful. If there was a problem with the installation, note the errors listed. For example, someone might have turned off the printer while you were trying to configure it. If so, you'll need to turn on the printer and repeat this procedure.

9. If you'd like to print a test page on the printer, select the Print Test Page check box and then tap or click Finish. Otherwise, just tap or click Finish.

10. By default, the printer share is not listed in Active Directory. Listing the printer share in Active Directory enables users to search for and find the printer more easily. If you want the printer share to be listed in Active Directory, select the Printers node in the left pane, press and hold or right-click the printer in the main window, and then select List In Directory.

11. By default, print jobs are sent to the print server, where they are rendered, and then they are sent to the printer. You can change this behavior by using Branch Office Direct Printing. With Branch Office Direct Printing, print jobs are rendered on client computers and then sent directly to the printer. If you want to enable direct printing, select the Printers node in the left pane, press and hold or right-click the printer in the main window, and then select Enable Branch Office Direct Printing.

Adding physically attached print devices

Most physically attached print devices are connected to a computer directly through a USB cable. You can configure physically attached printers as local print devices or as network print devices. The key difference is that a local device is accessible only to users logged on to the computer and a network device is accessible to network users as a shared print device. Remember that the workstation or server you're logged on to becomes the print server for the device you're configuring. If the computer is sleeping or turned off, the printer will not be available.

You can install physically attached print devices locally by logging on to the print server you want to configure; you can install the print devices remotely through Remote Desktop. If you're configuring a local Plug and Play printer and are logged on to the print server, installing a print device is a snap. After the printer is installed, you need to configure it for use.

To set up a local printer, you'll need to use an account that's a member of the Administrators group or the Print Operators group. You can install and configure a print device by following these steps:

1. Turn on the printer and then connect the print device to the server by using the appropriate cable.

2.   If Windows Server automatically detects the print device, Windows begins installing the device and the necessary drivers. If the necessary drivers aren't found, you might need to insert the printer's driver disk into the CD/DVD drive.

3.   If Windows Server doesn't detect the print device automatically, you need to install the print device manually, as described in the next set of instructions.

4.   After you install the printer, you can configure it. In Print Management, expand the Print Servers node and the node for the server you want to work with. When you select the Printers node for the server you are configuring, you'll find a list of available printers in the main pane. Press and hold or right-click the printer you want to configure and then tap or click Manage Sharing. This displays the printer's Properties dialog box with the Sharing tab selected, as shown in Figure 19-7.

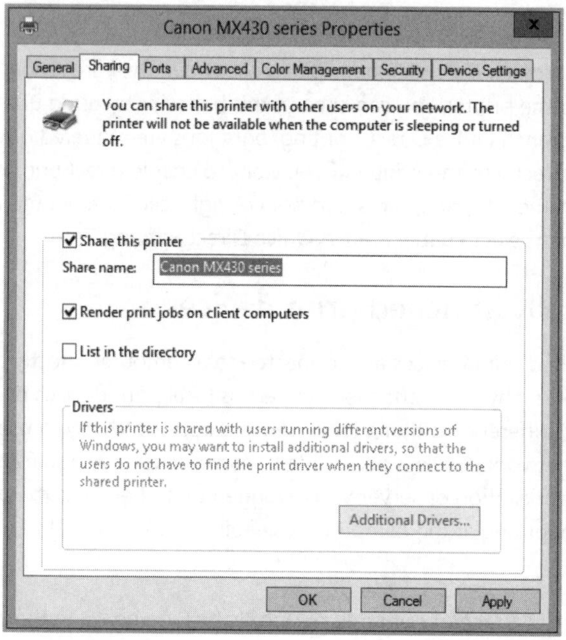

Figure 19-7 Configure the printer by using the Properties dialog box.

5.   When you select the Share This Printer check box, Windows Server sets the default share name to the name of the printer. You can enter a different name for the printer share in the Share Name text box.

6.   By default, the Render Print Jobs On Client Computers check box is selected, which configures the printer for Branch Office Direct Printing. With Branch Office Direct Printing, print jobs are rendered on client computers and then sent directly to the

printer. If you want print jobs to be sent to the print server for rendering and then sent to the printer, clear the Render Print Jobs On Client Computers check box.

7. Listing the printer share in Active Directory enables users to search for and find the printer more easily. If you want the printer share to be listed in Active Directory, select the List In The Directory check box.

8. Tap or click OK.

Sometimes Windows Server won't detect your printer. In this case, follow these steps to install the print device:

1. In Print Management, expand the Print Servers node and the node for the server you want to work with.

2. Press and hold or right-click the server's Printers node and then tap or click Add Printer to start the Network Printer Installation Wizard.

3. On the Printer Installation page, shown in Figure 19-8, select Add A New Printer Using An Existing Port and then choose the appropriate LPT, COM, or USB port. You can also print to a file. If you do, Windows Server 2012 R2 prompts users for a file name each time they print. Tap or click Next.

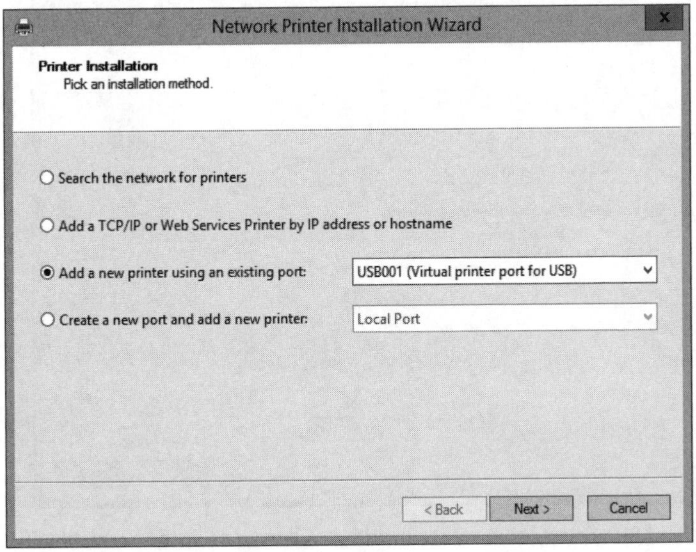

Figure 19-8 Choose the existing port to use.

4.   On the Printer Driver page, shown in Figure 19-9, choose one of the following options:

- If Windows detected the printer type on the selected port and a compatible driver was found automatically, a printer driver is listed that reflects the printer manufacturer and model and the Use The Printer Driver That The Wizard Selected option is selected by default. To accept this setting, tap or click Next.

- If a compatible driver is not available and you want to choose an existing driver installed on the computer, select the Use An Existing Printer Driver On The Computer option. After you choose the appropriate driver from the selection list, tap or click Next.

- If multiple drivers are available for a printer, such as both PCL and PostScript drivers, and you want to use a driver other than the selected default, select the Use An Existing Printer Driver On The Computer option. After you choose the appropriate driver from the selection list, tap or click Next.

- If a compatible driver is not available and you want to install a new driver, select Install A New Driver and then tap or click Next. You must now specify the print device manufacturer and model. This enables Windows Server 2012 R2 to assign a printer driver to the print device. After you choose a print device manufacturer, choose a printer model.

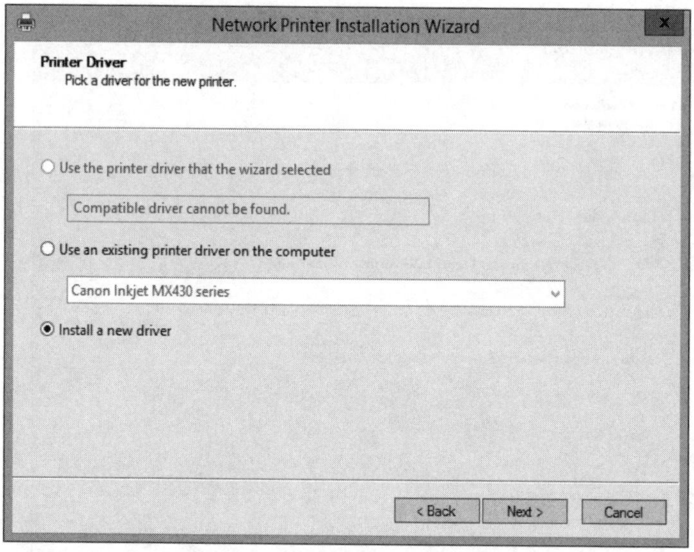

Figure 19-9 Select the driver to use for the printer or install a new driver.

NOTE
If a driver for the specific printer model you're using isn't available, you often can select a generic driver or a driver for a similar print device. Consult the print device documentation for pointers. Note also that if the device manufacturer and model you're using aren't displayed in the list, tap or click Windows Update. Windows will then connect to the Windows Update website to update the list of printers to show additional models. This automatic driver provisioning process can take several minutes. When the update process is complete, you should be able to select your printer manufacturer and model. If you can't, download the driver from the manufacturer's website and then extract the driver files. Tap or click Have Disk. In the Install From Disk dialog box, tap or click Browse. In the Locate File dialog box, locate the .inf driver file for the device and then tap or click Open.

5. Assign a name to the printer. This is the name that will be listed in Print Management. Next, specify whether the printer is available to remote users. To create a printer accessible to remote users, select the Share This Printer option and then enter a name for the shared resource. In a large organization you'll want the share name to be logical and helpful in locating the printer. For example, you could give the name Twelfth Floor NE to the printer that points to the print device in the northeast corner of the twelfth floor.

6. If you like, you can enter a location description and comment. This information can help users find a printer and determine its capabilities. Tap or click Next.

7. The final page lets you review the settings. When you're ready to complete the installation, tap or click Next.

8. After Windows installs the printer driver and configures the printer, you'll get a status page. Ensure that the driver and printer installation succeeded before continuing. If there were errors, you need to correct any problems and repeat this process. To test the printer, select Print Test Page and then tap or click Finish.

When the Network Printer Installation Wizard finishes installing the new printer, the Printers folder will have an additional icon with the name set the way you specified. You can change the printer properties and check printer status at any time. For more information, see the section entitled "Managing printer properties" in Chapter 20.

If you repeat this process, you can create additional printers for the same print device. All you need to do is change the printer name and share name. Having additional printers for a single print device makes it possible for you to set different properties to serve different needs. For example, you could have a high-priority printer for print jobs that need to be printed immediately and a low-priority printer for print jobs that aren't as urgent.

Adding network-attached printers

Network-attached printers are printers that have their own network cards or a wireless network card. Most network-attached printers use the RAW protocol or the LPR protocol to communicate over a standard TCP/IP port.

Network-attached printers are configured as network print devices so that they're accessible to network users as shared print devices. Remember that the server on which you configure the print device becomes the print server for the device you're configuring.

Inside OUT

Printing to UNIX print servers

Sometimes users might want to print to a UNIX print server. To do this, you must install the LPR Port Monitor feature on the users' computers.

On Windows 8.1, you can install the LPR Port Monitor feature using the Windows Features dialog box. In Control Panel, select Programs. On the Programs page, under Programs And Features, tap or click Turn Windows Features On Or Off. In the Windows Features dialog box, expand the Print And Document Services node by double-tapping or double-clicking it, select the LPR Port Monitor check box, and then tap or click OK.

On Windows Server, you can install the LPR Port Monitor feature using the Add Features Wizard. In Server Manager, select Manage and then select Add Roles And Features. This starts the Add Roles And Features Wizard. On the Select Features page, select LPR Port Monitor and then tap or click Next. Tap or click Install. When the wizard finishes installing the feature, tap or click Close.

You can set up a network-attached printer using an account that is a member of the Administrators group or Print Operators group. Follow these steps:

1. Make sure the printer is connected to the network and turned on. One way to do this is to ping the printer's IP address. As a final check of the printer, you might want to print its configuration or check its network settings to ensure that it has the appropriate IP address and subnet mask.

2. In Print Management, expand the Print Servers node and the node for the server you want to work with. Start the Network Printer Installation Wizard by pressing and holding or right-clicking the server's Printers node and then selecting Add Printer.

3. On the Printer Installation page, shown in Figure 19-10, select Add A TCP/IP Or Web Services Printer By IP Address Or Hostname and then tap or click Next.

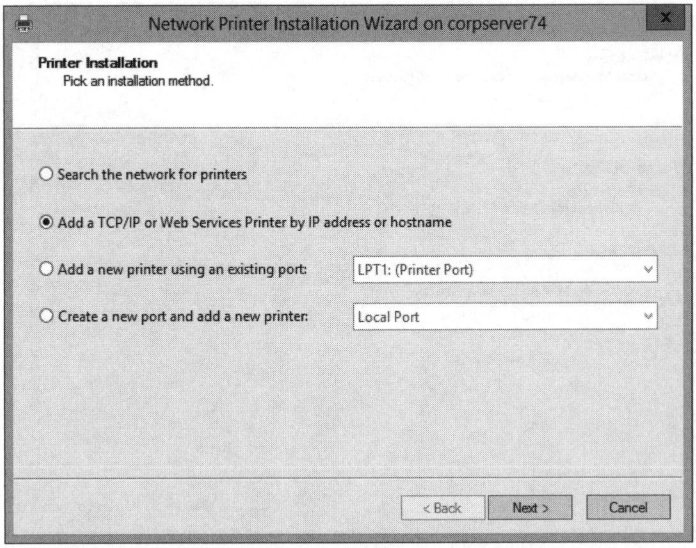

Figure 19-10 Configure the printer by IP address or hostname.

4.   On the Printer Address page, shown in Figure 19-11, choose one of the following options in the Type Of Device list:

   ■   **Autodetect.** Choose this option if you're unsure of the printer device type. Windows Server will then try to detect the type of device automatically.

   ■   **TCP/IP Device.** Choose this option if you're sure that the printer is a TCP/IP device.

   ■   **Web Services Printer.** Choose this option if you're sure that the printer is a Web Services for Devices (WSD)–capable printer.

   ■   **Web Services Secure Printer.** Choose this option if you're sure that the printer supports WSD Secure Printing.

NOTE

With WSD Secure Printing, print servers can create a private secure channel to the print device on the network without the need for additional security technologies such as IPsec. However, users and computers that work with the secure printer must be members of an Active Directory domain. You use the domain settings to manage printer permissions, and Active Directory Domain Services acts as the trust arbitrator between the print server and the printer.

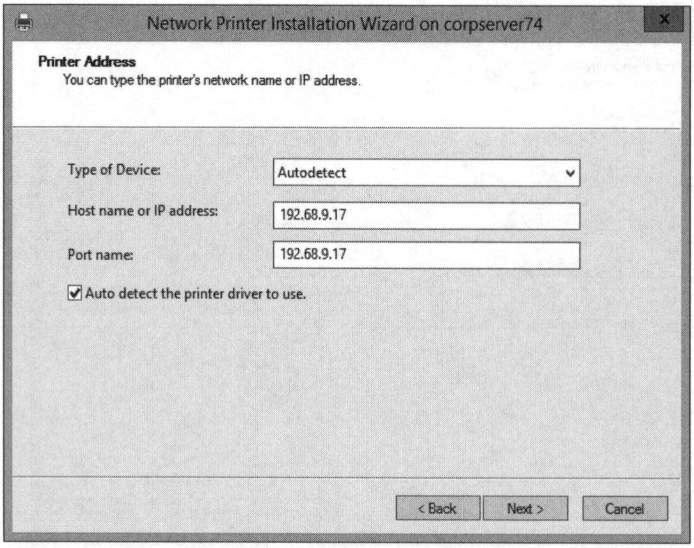

Figure 19-11 Enter the printer's address information.

5. Enter the host name or IP address for the printer in the Host Name Or IP Address text box, such as 192.168.5.87. With the Autodetect and TCP/IP Device options, the wizard will set the port name to the same value. Because this port name must be unique on the print server, you can't have two printers with the same port name on a print server. If you're configuring multiple printers on the print server, be sure to write down the port-to-printer mapping.

6. The Auto Detect The Printer Driver To Use check box is selected by default. When you tap or click Next, the wizard will look for the printer on the network and automatically configure the print device. If the wizard is unable to find the print device or needs additional information, select the printer device type using the Standard list, as shown in Figure 19-12.

NOTE

If the wizard is unable to find the print device on the network, make sure that you entered the printer name or IP address correctly. If you have, make sure the device is on, that it's properly configured, and that the network is set up correctly. If the wizard still can't detect the printer, select the device type and continue with the installation. Keep in mind that you might need to change the standard TCP/IP port monitor settings before you can use the printer. You can do this by selecting Custom and tapping or clicking Settings, or you can perform the necessary changes later. Both techniques are discussed later in this chapter in the section entitled "Changing standard TCP/IP port monitor settings."

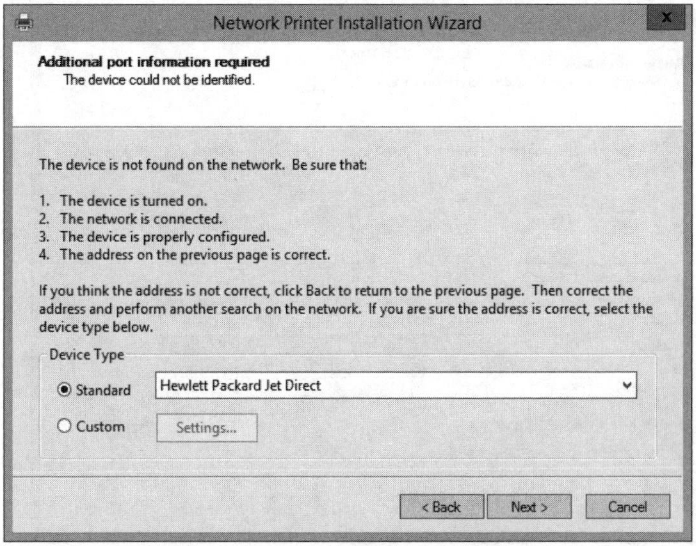

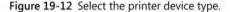

Figure 19-12 Select the printer device type.

7. On the Printer Driver page, choose one of the following options:

    ■ If Windows detected the printer type on the selected port and a compatible driver was found automatically, a printer driver is listed according to the printer manufacturer and model and the Use The Printer Driver That The Wizard Selected option is selected by default. To accept this setting, just tap or click Next.

    ■ If a compatible driver is not available and you want to choose an existing driver installed on the computer, select the Use An Existing Driver option. After you use the selection list to choose the appropriate driver, tap or click Next.

    ■ If a compatible driver is not available and you want to install a new driver, select Install A New Driver and then tap or click Next. As shown in Figure 19-13, you can now specify the print device manufacturer and model. Tap or click Next. This allows Windows Server to assign a printer driver to the print device. After you choose a print device manufacturer, choose a printer model. If the print device manufacturer and model you're using aren't displayed in the list, tap or click Have Disk to install a new driver. For example, if you have an HP LaserJet printer, you'd choose HP as the manufacturer and then you would choose the printer's model name and number.

CHAPTER 19

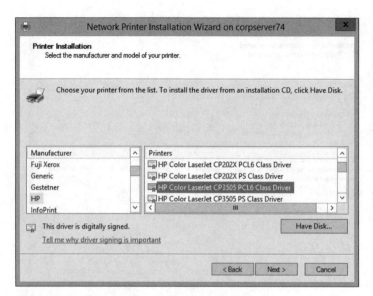

Figure 19-13 If the device wasn't automatically detected, you need to specify the device type and then specify the printer manufacturer and model.

NOTE

If the device manufacturer and model you're using aren't displayed in the list, download the driver from the manufacturer's website and extract the driver files. Tap or click Have Disk. In the Install From Disk dialog box, tap or click Browse. In the Locate File dialog box, locate the .inf driver file for the device and then tap or click Open. Keep in mind that even if there isn't an exact match, you can often choose a similar printer that has a compatible driver. Additionally, if you have a postscript printer and can't find the exact driver or a similar driver, you can often use just about any available postscript driver. Whenever you choose to use a similar or nonexact driver, be sure to print test documents to determine whether the printer is printing correctly.

8. On the Printer Name And Sharing Settings page, shown in Figure 19-14, assign a name to the printer. This is the name you'll see in Print Management.

9. Specify whether the printer is available to remote users. To create a printer accessible to remote users, select the Share This Printer check box and enter a name for the shared resource. In a large organization you'll want the share name to be logical and helpful in locating the printer.

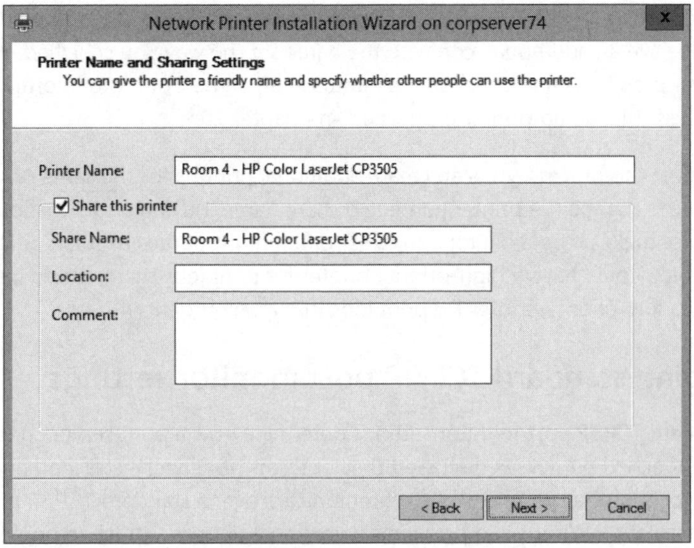

Figure 19-14 Set the printer name and share name.

10. If you like, you can enter a location description and comment. This information can help users find a printer and determine its capabilities.

11. Tap or click Next to continue. The final page lets you review the settings. When you're ready to complete the installation, tap or click Next.

12. After Windows installs the printer driver and configures the printer, you'll see a status page. Before continuing, make sure that the driver and printer installation succeeded. If there were errors, you'll need to correct any problems and repeat this process. To test the printer, select Print Test Page and then tap or click Finish. To install another printer, select Add Another Printer and then tap or click Finish.

By default, the printer share is not listed in Active Directory. Listing the printer share in Active Directory makes it possible for users to search for and find the printer more easily. If you want the printer share to be listed in Active Directory, select the Printers node in the left pane, press and hold or right-click the printer in the main window, and then select List In Directory.

By default, print jobs are sent to the print server, where they are rendered, and then they are sent to the printer. You can change this behavior by using Branch Office Direct Printing. With Branch Office Direct Printing, print jobs are rendered on client computers and then sent directly to the printer. If you want to enable direct printing, select the Printers node in the left pane, press and hold or right-click the printer in the main window, and then select Enable Branch Office Direct Printing.

When the Network Printer Installation Wizard finishes installing the new printer, the Printers folder will have an additional icon with the name set the way you specified. You can change the printer properties and check printer status at any time. For more information, see the section entitled "Managing printer properties" in Chapter 20.

If you repeat this process, you can create additional printers for the same print device. All you need to do is change the printer name and share name. Having additional printers for a single print device makes it possible for you to set different properties to serve different needs. For example, you could have a high-priority printer for print jobs that need to be printed immediately and a low-priority printer for print jobs that aren't urgent.

Changing standard TCP/IP port monitor settings

The standard TCP/IP port monitor settings determine how a print server connects to a network-attached printer. As discussed previously, most network-attached printers use the RAW protocol or the LPR protocol to communicate over a standard TCP/IP port. If the Network Printer Installation Wizard had problems detecting a network-attached printer, there is a good chance that the printer was set up to use the RAW protocol and port 9100. Typically, this is what you want because many current printers use the RAW protocol over TCP port 9100.

To view or change a printer's standard TCP/IP port monitor settings, follow these steps:

1. In Print Management, press and hold or right-click the printer and select Properties. In the printer's Properties dialog box, tap or click the Ports tab. The port used by the printer is selected and highlighted by default. Tap or click Configure Port.

2. In the Configure Standard TCP/IP Port Monitor dialog box, shown in Figure 19-15, select the protocol that the printer uses, either RAW or LPR, as follows:

   - When you select Raw, the Raw Settings panel is available and you can set a port number. Because the default port number used by most Raw printers is 9100, this value is filled in for you. Change the default setting only if the printer documentation instructs you to do so.

   - When you select LPR, the LPR Settings panel is available. Set the queue name to be used by the port. If you're unsure, use the queue name the printer documentation instructs you use.

   ### NOTE

   With LPR, you also have the option to enable LPR Byte Counting. When you select this check box, the print server counts the bytes in a document before sending it to the printer and the printer can use the byte count to verify that a complete document has been received. However, this option slows down printing and uses processor resources on the print server.

3. When you're finished configuring the TCP/IP port monitor settings, tap or click OK.

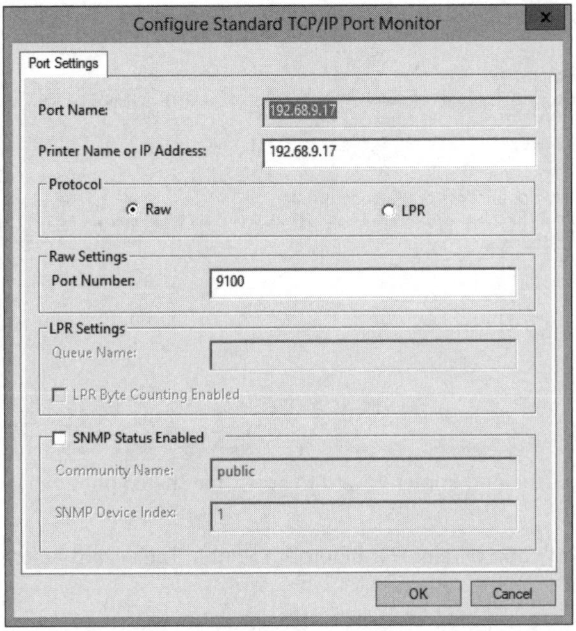

Figure 19-15 Configure the protocol and settings for the TCP/IP port.

Connecting users to shared printers

After you configure and share a printer, users on client computers can connect to it. The technique is similar for all versions of Windows.

Accessing shared printers

Computers running Windows can install print drivers automatically. All you need to do is connect the client computer to the shared printer.

You can create a connection to the printer on a Windows 7 system by following these steps:

1. With the user logged on, tap or click Start and then tap or click Devices And Printers. In Devices And Printers, tap or click Add A Printer to start the Add Printer Wizard, shown in Figure 19-16.

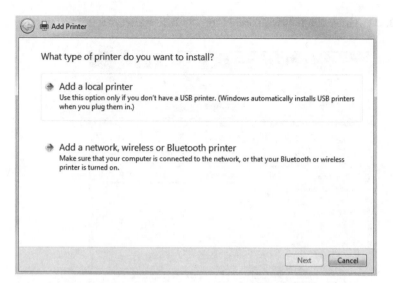

Figure 19-16 Use the Add Printer Wizard to access the shared printer.

2. Select Add A Network, Wireless Or Bluetooth Printer. The wizard searches for available devices.

3. If the printer you want is listed in the Select A Printer list, tap or click it and then tap or click Next.

4. If the printer you want isn't listed in the Select A Printer list, tap or click The Printer That I Want Isn't Listed. On the Find A Printer By Name Or TCP/IP Address page, do one of the following:

   - To browse the network for shared printers, choose Find A Printer In The Directory, Based On Location Or Feature and then tap or click Next. Tap or click the printer to use and then tap or click Select.

   - To specify the printer to use by its share path, choose Select A Shared Printer By Name. Enter the UNC path to the shared printer, such as **\\PrintServer32\Room5**, or the web path to an Internet Printer, such as **http://PrintServer23/Printers/IPrinter18/.printer**.

   - To specify a printer to use by TCP/IP address or host name, select Add A Printer Using A TCP/IP Address Or Hostname and then tap or click Next. Choose a device type and then enter the host name or IP address for the printer, such as **192.168.1.42**. If you select the Autodetect or TCP/IP Device options, the wizard will set the port name to the same value, but you can also choose a different value. Tap or click Next.

5. On the Type A Printer Name page, the printer name is set for you. You can accept the default name or enter a new name. Tap or click Next to install the printer and then tap or click Finish. The user can now print to the network printer by selecting the printer in an application. The Device And Printers folder on the user's computer shows the new network printer as well.

You can create a connection to the printer on a Windows 8.1 system by following these steps:

1. Open Devices And Printers by tapping or clicking View Devices And Printers in Control Panel under the Hardware And Sound heading.

2. In Devices And Printers, tap or click Add A Printer. The Add Printer Wizard attempts to detect the printer automatically.

    If the wizard finds the printer you want to work with, tap or click it in the list provided, follow the prompts, and skip the rest of the steps in this procedure.

    If the wizard doesn't find the printer, tap or click The Printer That I Want Isn't Listed and then complete the rest of this procedure.

3. As shown in Figure 19-17, the Find A Printer By Other Options page provides several options for finding the printer you want. You can find the printer in Active Directory, select a shared printer by its name, add a printer using a TCP/IP address or hostname, and more. If the printer you want is discoverable on the network, the easiest option to use is Add A Bluetooth, Wireless Or Network Discoverable Printer.

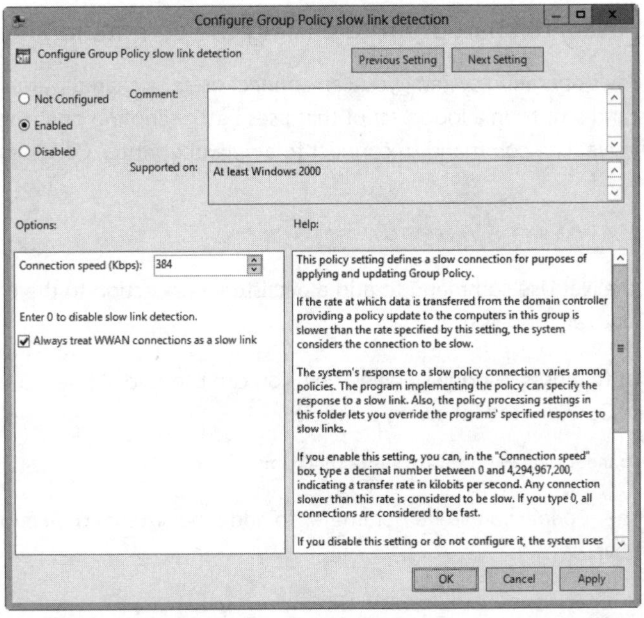

Figure 19-17 Use the Add Printer Wizard to access the shared printer.

4. After you select Add A Bluetooth, Wireless Or Network Discoverable Printer, the wizard tries to detect available printers. In the list of available printers, select the printer you want to use and then tap or click Next.

5. If prompted, install the printer driver on your computer. Complete the additional steps in the wizard and then tap or click Finish. You can confirm that the printer is working by printing a test page.

6. If the wizard doesn't find the printer, repeat the previous procedure and choose another option. Note also that if you have trouble connecting to the printer, you might want to try the following as part of troubleshooting:

    - Ensure that a firewall isn't blocking connectivity to the printer. You might need to open a firewall port to enable access between the computer and the printer.

    - Ensure that the printer is turned on and connected to the same network as the computer. If your network consists of multiple connected subnets, try to connect the printer to the same network subnet. You can determine the subnet by looking at the computer's IP address.

    - Ensure that the printer is configured to broadcast its presence on the network. Most network printers automatically do this.

    - Ensure that the printer has an IP address and proper network settings. If DHCP is configured on the network, DHCP assigns IP addresses automatically as printers connect to the network.

Connecting users to shared printers using the command line and scripts

With any Windows operating system, you can connect users to shared printers using the command line and scripts. In a logon script that uses batch scripting or at the command line, you can use the Net Use command to connect to a network printer. Consider the following example:

```
net use \\corpsvr02\engmain /persistent:yes
```

Here, you use the Net Use command to add a persistent connection to the EngMain printer on CORPSVR02. That's all there is to it.

In a logon script that uses Windows PowerShell, you can use Add-Printer to connect to a network printer. Consider the following example:

```
Add-Printer -ConnectionName \\printsvr14\HpColor
```

Here, you use the -ConnectionName parameter to add a persistent connection to the HpColor printer on PrintSvr14.

You could also use Microsoft VBScript in a logon script to set a printer connection. With VBScript you must initialize the variables and objects you plan to use and then call the AddWindowsPrinterConnection method of the Network object to add the printer connection. If you like, you can also use the SetDefaultPrinter method of the Network object to set the printer as the default for the user. After you're done using variables and objects, it's good form to free the memory they use by setting them to vbEmpty. Consider the following example:

```
Option Explicit
Dim wNetwork, printerPath
Set wNetwork = WScript.CreateObject("WScript.Network")
printerPath = "\\corpsvr02\engmain"

wNetwork.AddWindowsPrinterConnection printerPath
wNetwork.SetDefaultPrinter printerPath

Set wNetwork = vbEmpty
Set printerPath = vbEmpty
```

Here, you use the AddWindowsPrinterConnection method to add a connection to the EngMain printer on CORPSVR02. You then use the SetDefaultPrinter method to set the printer as the default for the user.

Deploying printer connections

As you've seen, it's fairly easy to connect to shared printers. That said, you can make the process even easier by deploying printer connections to computers or users by means of the Group Policy objects (GPOs) that Windows applies. When choosing whether to deploy printer connections to computers or users, keep the following in mind:

- Deploy to groups of computers when you want all users of the computers to access the printers. For per-computer connections, Windows adds or removes printer connections when the computer starts.

- Deploy to groups of users when you want users to be able to access the printers from any computer they log on to. For per-user connections, Windows adds or removes printer connections when the user logs on.

To deploy printer connections to computers running Windows Vista or later, you must follow these steps:

1. In Print Management, expand the Print Servers node and the node for the server you want to work with.

2. Select the server's Printers node. In the main pane, press and hold or right-click the printer you want to deploy and then select Deploy With Group Policy. This displays the Deploy With Group Policy dialog box, shown in Figure 19-18.

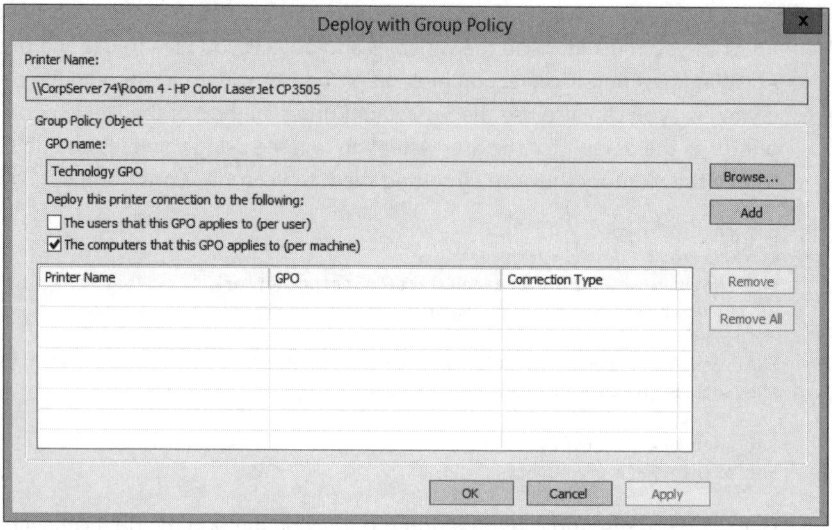

Figure 19-18 Choose the GPO you want to work with.

3. Tap or click Browse. In the Browse For Group Policy Object dialog box, select the GPO to use and then tap or click OK.

4. Do one or both of the following and then tap or click Add to create a print connection entry:

   - To deploy the printer connection on a per-user basis, select the The Users That This GPO Applies To (Per User) check box under Deploy This Printer Connection To The Following.

   - To deploy the printer connection on a per-computer basis, select the The Computers That This GPO Applies To (Per Machine) check box under Deploy This Printer Connection To The Following.

5. Repeat steps 3 and 4 to deploy the printer connection to other GPOs.

6. Tap or click OK to save the GPO changes.

To deploy printer connections to computers running versions of Windows earlier than Windows Vista, follow these steps:

1. In the Group Policy Management Console (GPMC), press and hold or right-click the GPO for the site, domain, or organizational unit you want to work with and then select Edit. This opens the policy editor for the GPO.

2. In the Group Policy Management Editor, do one of the following:

   - To deploy the printer connections on a per-computer basis, double-tap or double-click the Windows Settings folder in the Computer Configuration node. Then tap or click Scripts.

   - To deploy the printer connections on a per-user basis, double-tap or double-click the Windows Settings folder in the User Configuration node. Then tap or click Scripts.

3. Using File Explorer, copy PushPrinterConnections.exe from the %SystemRoot%\System32 folder to the Computer\Scripts\Startup, User\Scripts\Logon or the User\Scripts\Logoff folders for the related policy. Policies are stored in the %SystemRoot%\Sysvol\Domain \Policies folder on domain controllers.

4. In the Group Policy Management Editor, press and hold or right-click Startup Or Logon and then select Properties.

5. In the Startup Or Logon Properties dialog box, tap or click Show Files. If you copied the executable to the correct location in the Policies folder, you should see the executable.

6. In the Startup Or Logon Properties dialog box, tap or click Add. This displays the Add A Script dialog box.

7. In the Script Name text box, type PushPrinterConnections.exe and then tap or click OK.

Configuring point and print restrictions

In Group Policy the Point And Print Restrictions setting controls security warnings and elevation prompts when users point and print and when drivers for printer connections need to be configured. This setting is found in the Administrative Templates for Computer Configuration under the Printers node.

Table 19-1 summarizes how the Point And Print Restrictions setting is used. Note that prior to Windows 7 and Windows Vista Service Pack 2, Point And Print Restrictions were implemented by using User Configuration policy. If you configure Point And Print Restrictions in User Configuration policy, computers running Windows Vista Service Pack 2, Windows 7, and later versions of Windows will ignore the settings.

Table 19-1 Point and Print Restrictions

When The Policy Setting Is...	The Policy Works As Follows
Enabled	Clients can point and print to any server. You can configure clients to show or hide warning and elevation prompts when users point and print and when a driver for an existing printer connection needs to be updated.
Not Configured	Clients can point and print to any server in the forest. Clients also will not show a warning and elevation prompt when users point and print or when a driver for an existing printer connection needs to be updated.
Disabled	Clients can point and print to any server. Clients also will not show a warning and elevation prompt when users point and print or when a driver for an existing printer connection needs to be updated.

By default, Windows allows a user who is not a member of the local Administrators group to install only trustworthy printer drivers, such as those provided by Windows or in digitally signed printer driver packages. When you enable the Point And Print Restrictions setting, you also allow users who are not members of the local Administrators group to install printer connections deployed using Group Policy that include additional or updated printer drivers that are not in the form of digitally signed printer driver packages. If you do not enable this setting, users might need to provide the credentials of a user account that belongs to the local Administrators group.

You can enable and configure the Point And Print Restrictions setting in Group Policy by following these steps:

1. In the Group Policy Management Console (GPMC), press and hold or right-click the GPO for the site, domain, or organizational unit you want to work with and then select Edit. This opens the policy editor for the GPO.

2. In the Group Policy Management Editor, expand Administrative Templates for Computer Configuration and then select the Printers node.

3. In the main pane, double-tap or double-click Point And Print Restrictions. In the Point And Print Restrictions Properties dialog box, shown in Figure 19-19, select Enabled.

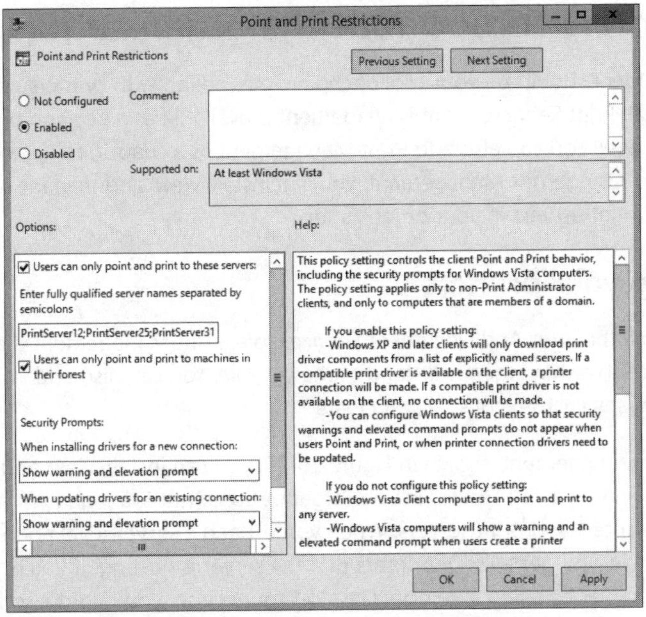

Figure 19-19 Configure point and print restrictions.

4. When you enable pointing and printing restrictions, you can configure policy so that users can only point and print to a named list of servers. To enforce this restriction, select the related check box and enter a list of fully qualified server names separated by semicolons. To remove this restriction, clear the Users Can Only Point And Print To These Servers check box.

5. When you enable pointing and printing restrictions, you can configure policy so that users can only point and print to servers in their forest. To enforce this restriction, select the related check box. To remove this restriction, clear the Users Can Only Point And Print To Machines In Their Forest check box.

6. When you install drivers for a new connection, Windows Vista and later clients can either show or not show a warning or elevation prompt. Use the related selection list to choose the desired option.

7. When you update drivers for an existing connection, Windows Vista and later clients can either show or not show a warning or elevation prompt. Use the related selection list to choose the desired option. Tap or click OK to save your policy settings.

Managing printers throughout the organization

Print Management should be your tool of choice for working with printers and print servers. After you install Print Services, Print Management is available as an option on the Tools menu in Server Manager. You can also add Print Management as a snap-in to any custom console you've created. Using Print Management, you can install, view, and manage all of the printers and Windows print servers in your organization.

Managing your printers

After you install the Print And Document Services role, Print Management is available on the Tools menu in Server Manager as a stand-alone console. You can also add Print Management as a snap-in to any custom console you create.

By using Print Management, shown in Figure 19-20, you can install, view, and manage the printers and Windows print servers in your organization. Print Management also displays the status of printers and print servers. When you expand a server-level node and select the Printers node, you get a list of printers that the server is hosting. If you're accessing the selected print server by using a Remote Desktop connection, you might also find entries for printers being redirected from your logon computer. Redirected printers are listed identified with a (redirected) suffix.

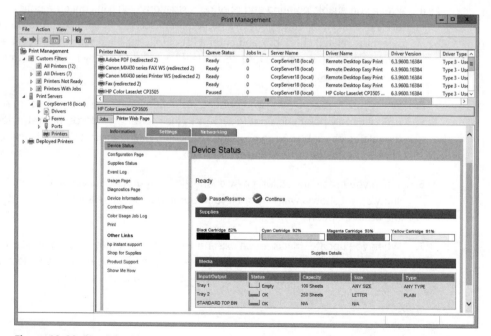

Figure 19-20   Use Print Management to work with print servers and printers throughout your organization.

By default, Print Management enables you to manage local print servers. You can manage and monitor other print servers in the organization by adding them to the console. Additionally, to manage a remote print server, you must be a member of the local Administrators group on the print server or a member of the Domain Admins group in the domain of which the print server is a member.

When you select a print server's Printers node, the main pane lists the associated printer queues by printer name, queue status, number of jobs in a queue, and server name. If you press and hold or right-click Printers and then tap or click Show Extended View, you can turn on Extended view. Extended view makes it easy to track the status of both printers and print jobs by displaying information about the status of a print job, its owner, the number of pages, the size of the job, when it was submitted, its port, and its priority.

In addition, when a printer has a webpage, Extended view displays a Printer Web Page tab that lets you directly access the printer's webpage. This webpage provides details about the printer's status, its physical properties, and its configuration, and it sometimes allows remote administration.

You can add print servers to Print Management by following these steps:

1. In Print Management, press and hold or right-click the Print Servers node in the left pane and then tap or click Add/Remove Servers.

2. In the Add/Remove Servers dialog box, shown in Figure 19-21, you'll find a list of the print servers you previously added. Do one of the following and then tap or click Add To List:

    ■ In the Add Servers list, enter or paste the names of the print servers you want to add. Use commas to separate computer names.

    ■ Tap or click Browse to display the Select Print Server dialog box. Tap or click the print server you want to use and then tap or click Select Server.

3. Repeat the previous step as necessary and then tap or click OK.

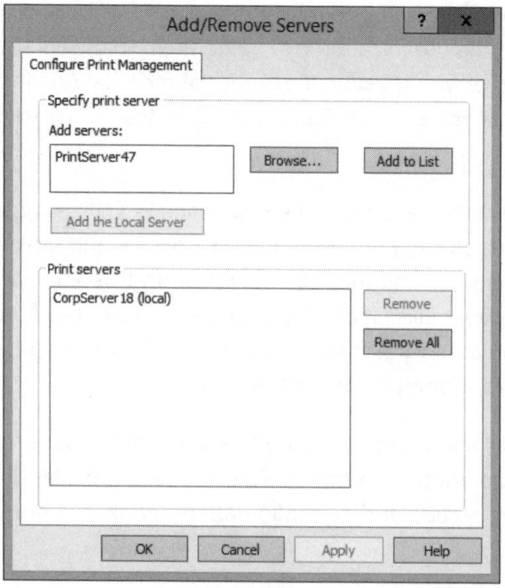

Figure 19-21 Add print servers to Print Management so that you can manage and monitor them.

You can remove print servers from Print Management by following these steps:

1. In Print Management, press and hold or right-click the Print Servers node in the left pane and then tap or click Add/Remove Servers.

2. In the Add/Remove Servers dialog box, you'll find a list of the print servers that are being monitored. Under Print Servers, select one or more servers and then tap or click Remove.

Migrating printers and print queues

You can use the Printer Migration Wizard to move printers and their print queues from one print server to another. This is an efficient way to consolidate multiple print servers or replace an older print server.

When you move printers, the server on which the printers are currently located is the source server and the server to which you want to move the printers is the destination server. With this in mind, you can move printers to a new print server by following these steps:

1. In Print Management, press and hold or right-click the source server and then tap or click Export Printers To A File. This starts the Printer Migration Wizard.

2. On the initial page, shown in Figure 19-22, note the printer-related objects that will be exported and then tap or click Next.

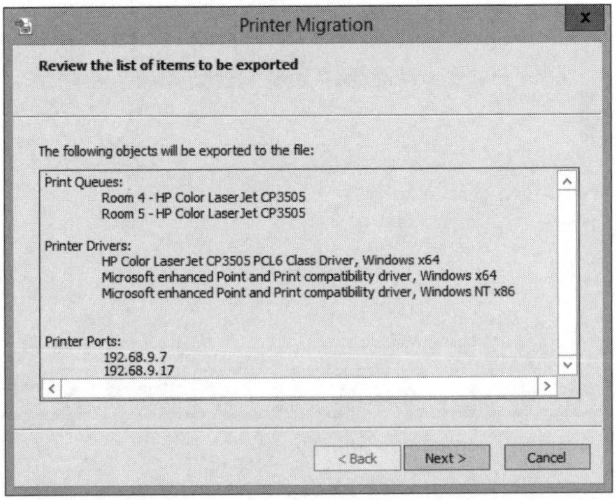

Figure 19-22 Review the printer objects to be exported.

3. On the Select The File Location page, tap or click Browse. In the dialog box provided, select a save location for the printer migration file. After you enter a name for the file, tap or click Save.

4. Printer migration files are saved with the .printerExport extension. Tap or click Next to save the printer settings to this file.

5. After the wizard completes the export process, tap or click Open Event Viewer to review the events generated during the export process. If an error occurred during processing, you can use the event entries to determine what happened and what possible actions to take to resolve the problem. When you're finished, exit the Event Viewer.

6. On the Exporting page, tap or click Finish to exit the Printer Migration Wizard.

7. In Print Management, press and hold or right-click the destination server and then tap or click Import Printers From A File. This launches the Printer Migration Wizard.

8. On the Select The File Location page, tap or click Browse. In the dialog box provided, select the printer migration file you created previously, as shown in Figure 19-23, and then tap or click Open.

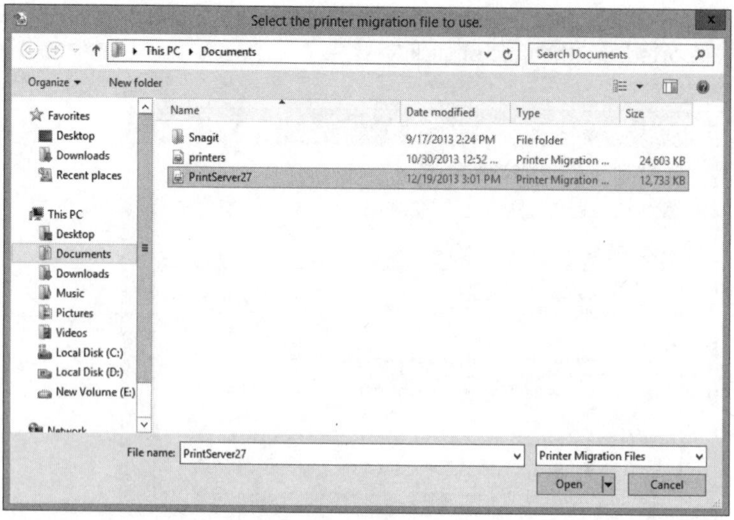

Figure 19-23 Select the printer migration file.

9. Tap or click Next. Note the objects that will be imported and then tap or click Next. On the Select Import Options page, shown in Figure 19-24, choose one of the following options in the Import Mode selection list:

    - **Keep Existing Printers.** When you choose this option and existing printer queues have the same names as those you're importing, the wizard will create copies to ensure that the original printer queues and the imported printer queues are both available.

    - **Overwrite Existing Printers.** When you choose this option and existing printer queues have the same names as those you're importing, the wizard will overwrite the existing printer queues with the information from the printer queues you're importing.

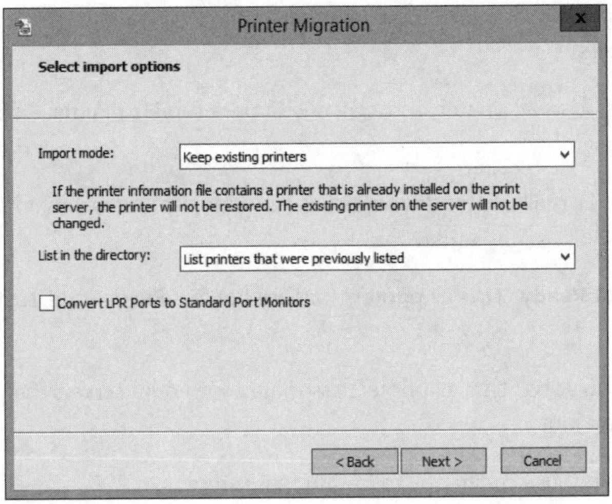

Figure 19-24 Choose the import options for the migration.

10. On the Select Import Options page, choose one of the following options for the List In The Directory list:

   ■ **List Printers That Were Previously Listed.** Choose this option to ensure that only printers that were previously listed are listed in Active Directory.

   ■ **List All Printers.** Choose this option to ensure that all printers are listed in Active Directory.

   ■ **Don't List Any Printers.** Choose this option to ensure that no printers are listed in Active Directory.

11. Tap or click Next to begin the import process. After the wizard completes the import process, tap or click Open Event Viewer to review the events generated during the import process. If an error occurred during processing, you can use the event entries to determine what happened and what possible actions to take to resolve the problem. When you're finished, exit the Event Viewer.

12. On the Importing page, tap or click Finish to exit the Printer Migration Wizard.

Monitoring printers and printer queues automatically

You can use printer filters to display only the printers, printer queues, and printer drivers that meet specific criteria. Through automated notification, you can also use printer filters to automate monitoring of printers.

In Print Management you can view existing filters by expanding the Custom Filters node. If you expand the Custom Filters node and then select a filter, the main pane will show all printers or print drivers that match the filter criteria. Print Management includes the following default printer filters:

- **All Printers.** Lists all printers associated with print servers that have been added to the console

- **All Drivers.** Lists all printer drivers associated with print servers that have been added to the console

- **Printers Not Ready.** Lists all printers that are not in a Ready state, such as those with errors

- **Printers With Jobs.** Lists all printers associated with print servers that have active or pending print jobs

You can create a new custom filter by following these steps:

1. In Print Management, press and hold or right-click the Custom Filters node and then select Add New Printer Filter. This starts the New Printer Filter Wizard.

2. On the Printer Filter Name And Description page, enter a filter name and description. If you'd like the number of matching items to be displayed after the filter name, select the Display The Total Number Of Items Next To The Name Of The Filter check box. Tap or click Next.

3. On the Define A Printer Filter page, define the filter by specifying Field, Condition, and Value to match in the first row. If you want to further narrow the possible matches, define additional criteria as necessary in the second, third, and subsequent rows. When you're ready to continue, tap or click Next.

NOTE

When you use filters for monitoring and notification, you'll use the Queue Status text box most. This text box enables you to receive notification when a printer has a specific status. You can match the following status values: Attention Required, Busy, Deleting, Door Open, Error, Initializing, IO Active, Manual Feed Required, No Toner/Ink, Not Available, Offline, Out Of Memory, Out Of Paper, Output Bin Full, Page Punt, Paper Jam, Paper Problem, Paused, Printing, Processing, Ready, Toner/Ink Low, Waiting, and Warming Up.

NOTE

When you are matching conditions, you can match when an exact condition exists or does not exist. For example, if you want to be notified only of conditions that need attention, you can look for Queue Status conditions that are not exactly the following: **Deleting, Initializing, Printing, Processing, Warming Up, and Ready.**

4. On the Set Notifications page, you can specify whether to send an email, run a script, or both when the specified criteria are met. Tap or click Finish to complete the configuration.

You can modify an existing custom filter by follow these steps:

1. In Print Management, expand the Custom Filters node. Select and then press and hold or right-click the filter you want to work with. From the shortcut menu, choose Properties.

2. In the filter's Properties dialog box, use the options provided to manage the filter settings. This dialog box has the following three tabs:

   ■ **General.** Shows the name and description of the printer filter. Enter a new name and description as necessary.

   ■ **Filter Criteria.** Shows the filter criteria. Enter new filter criteria as necessary.

   ■ **Notification.** Shows the email and script options. Enter new email and script options as necessary.

Managing and maintaining print services

When you point to Print in an application and click, the document is supposed to print on a printer somewhere. Most users don't care to know how or why printing works; they only care that it works. In that respect, printing is like networking services—something most people take for granted until it doesn't work the way they expect it to or it stops working altogether. The problem with this way of thinking is that, next to file and networking services, print services are one of the most used features of the Microsoft Windows operating system. It takes a lot of behind-the-scenes work to ensure that printing is as easy as point and click.

Managing printer permissions

By default, everyone with access to the network can print to a shared printer. This means that any user with a domain account or any user logged on as a guest can print to any available printer. Because this isn't always what is wanted, you might want to consider whether you need to restrict access to a printer. Restricting access to printers ensures that only those users with appropriate permissions can use a printer.

With specialty printers, such as those used for color or large-format printing, you'll find that restricting access to specific groups or individuals makes the most sense. But you might also want to restrict access to other types of printers. For example, you might not want everyone with network access to be able to print. Instead, you might want only users with valid domain accounts to be able to print. While you are configuring printer security, you might also want to configure printer auditing to track who is using printers and what they are doing.

Understanding printer permissions

Printer permissions set the maximum allowed access level for a printer. These permissions are applied whenever someone tries to print, whether the person is connected locally or remotely, and they include both special and standard permissions.

Special permissions are assigned individually and include the following:

- **Read Permissions.** Allows users to view permissions

- **Change Permissions.** Allows users to change permissions

- **Take Ownership.** Allows users to take ownership of a printer, its print jobs, or both

The standard printer permissions available are the following:

- **Print.** With this permission, users can connect to a printer and submit documents for printing. They can also manage their own print jobs. If a user or group has Print permission, it also has the special permission called Read Permissions for any documents it prints.

- **Manage This Printer.** With this permission, users have complete control over a printer and can set printer permissions. This means that they can share printers, change permissions, assign ownership, pause and restart printing, and change printer properties. If a user or group has Manage Printers permission, it also has the special permissions called Read Permissions, Change Permissions, and Take Ownership for any documents on the printer.

- **Manage Documents.** With this permission, users can manage individual print jobs. This allows them to pause, restart, resume, or cancel documents. It also allows them to change the order of documents in the queue. It doesn't, however, allow them to print because this permission is assigned separately. If a user or group has Manage Documents permission, it also has the special permissions called Read Permissions, Change Permissions, and Take Ownership for the printer.

By default, the permissions on printers are assigned as shown in Table 20-1.

Table 20-1 Default Printer Permissions

Group	Print	Manage Documents	Manage This Printer
Creator Owner		Yes	
Everyone	Yes		
All Application Packages	Yes	Yes	
Administrators	Yes	Yes	Yes

As you examine printer permissions, keep in mind that if a user is a member of a group that is granted printer permissions, the user also has those permissions and the permissions are cumulative. This means that if one group of which the user is a member has Print permission and another has Manage Printers permission, the user has both permissions. To override this behavior, you must specifically deny a permission.

CHAPTER 20

TROUBLESHOOTING

Check permissions on the spool folder

By default, the spool folder is located on the system drive. The default permissions give Full Control to Administrators and the System user. System is the account under which the Print Spooler service runs, and this account needs Full Control to be able to create and manage spool files. Administrators are given full control so that they can spool documents and clear out the spool folder if necessary. Creator Owner has special permissions that grant Full Control so that anyone who prints a document can manage it. Users are given Read & Execute, Read, and List Folder Contents permissions so that an authenticated user can access the spool folder and create files and folders. If these permissions get changed, print spooling might fail.

Configuring printer permissions

To view or manage the permissions of a printer, press and hold or right-click the printer in Print Management and then select Properties. In the Properties dialog box, tap or click the Security tab, shown in Figure 20-1. You can now view the users and groups that have printer permissions and the type of permissions they have.

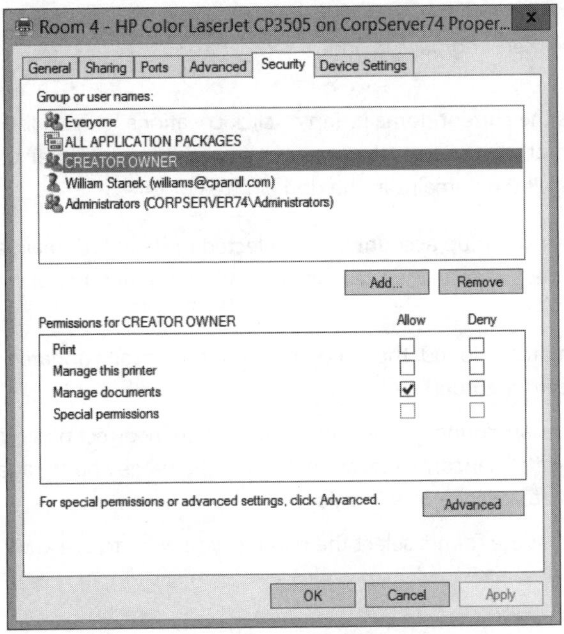

Figure 20-1 View or set printer permissions.

To grant or deny printer permissions, follow these steps:

1. In Print Management, expand the Print Servers node and the node for the server you want to work with.

2. Select the server's Printers node. In the main pane, press and hold or right-click the printer you want to work with and then select Properties.

3. In the printer Properties dialog box, tap or click the Security tab. In the Security tab, tap or click Add. This opens the Select Users, Computers, Service Accounts, Or Groups dialog box, as shown in Figure 20-2.

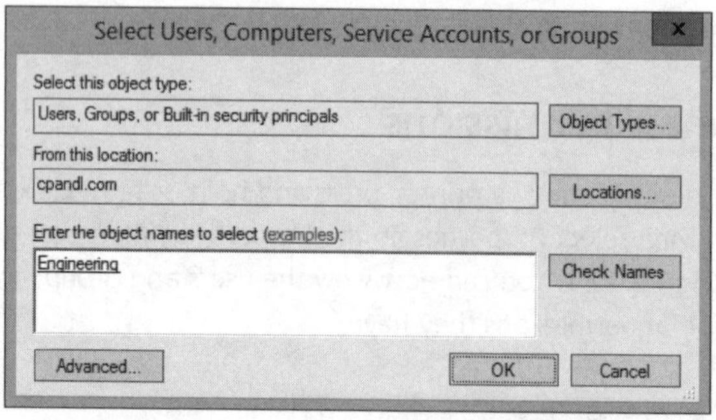

Figure 20-2 Specify the users or groups to add.

4. The default location is the current domain. Tap or click Locations to see a list of the available domains and other resources that you can access. Because of transitive trusts, you can usually access all the domains in the domain tree or forest.

5. Type the name of a user or group account in the selected or default domain and then tap or click Check Names. The options available depend on the number of matches found, as follows:

   - When a single match is found, the dialog box is automatically updated as appropriate and the entry is underlined.

   - When no matches are found, you've either entered an incorrect name part or you're working with an incorrect location. Modify the name and try again or tap or click Locations to select a new location.

   - If multiple matches are found, select the name(s) you want to use and then tap or click OK.

6. To add users or groups, type a semicolon (;) and then repeat this process.

7. When you tap or click OK, the users and groups are added to the Group Or User Names list for the printer.

8. Configure access permissions for each user and group added by selecting an account name and then allowing or denying access permissions. If a user or group should be granted access permissions, select the check box for the permission in the Allow column. If a user or group should be denied access permissions, select the check box for the permission in the Deny column.

    ## NOTE

    If you give a group a permission, such as Print, the related special permission, Read Permissions, is also granted. For this reason you usually don't need to configure special permissions for printers.

9. When you're finished, tap or click OK.

Assigning printer ownership

The owner of a printer has permission to manage its documents. By default, the System user is listed as the current owner of a printer. Ownership can be transferred to an administrator, a user, a group, or a service account. You can take ownership using the printer's Properties dialog box. Press and hold or right-click the printer and then select Properties. In the Security tab of the Properties dialog box, display the Advanced Security Settings dialog box by tapping or clicking Advanced.

The current owner is listed, as shown in Figure 20-3. To change the printer owner, select Change. Use the options provided in the Select User, Computer, Service Account, Or Group dialog box to select a new owner.

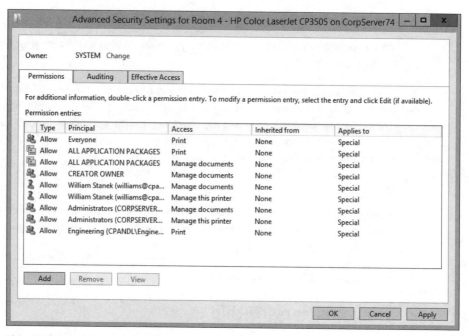

Figure 20-3 Assign printer ownership.

Auditing printer access

Auditing printer access can help you track who is accessing printers and what they are doing. You configure auditing policies on a per-printer basis. In Print Management, press and hold or right-click the printer to be audited and then select Properties. In the Properties dialog box, tap or click the Security tab and then tap or click Advanced. In the Advanced Security Settings dialog box, tap or click the Auditing tab, shown in Figure 20-4.

Now use the Auditing Entries list box to select the users, groups, or computers whose actions you want to audit. To add specific accounts, tap or click Add to open the Auditing Entry For... dialog box. Next, tap or click Select A Principal and then use the Select User, Computer, Service Account, Or Group dialog box to choose an account name to add. If you want to audit actions for all users, use the special group Everyone. Otherwise, select the specific user groups, users, or both that you want to audit. When you tap or click OK, you'll be able to use the Auditing Entry For... dialog box, as shown in Figure 20-5, to specify the permissions for the user, computer, service account, or group.

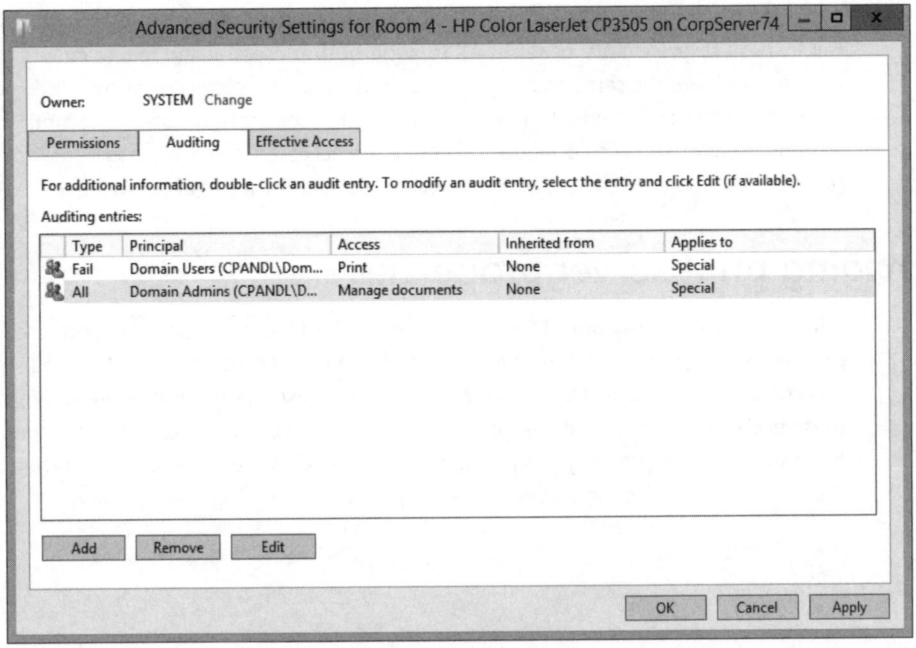

Figure 20-4 Specify the users and groups to which auditing should apply.

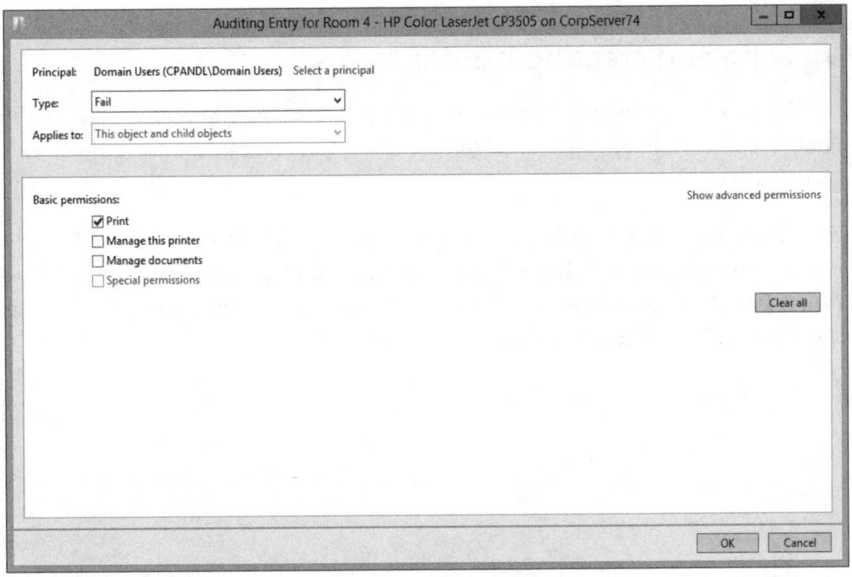

Figure 20-5 Specify the actions to audit for the designated user, group, or computer.

After you make a selection, under Applies To select Success to audit successful events, select Fail to audit failure events, or select All to audit both successful and failure events. The events you can audit are the same as the printer permissions discussed previously. When you're finished, tap or click OK. Repeat this process to audit other users, groups, or computers. Any time printers for which you've configured auditing are accessed, the action is written to the system's security log, where it's stored for your review. The security log is accessible from Event Viewer.

Managing print server properties

Print server properties control the global settings for all printers on a server. You can access print server properties from Print Management. In Print Management, when you select a server node you'll see additional nodes for Drivers, Forms, Ports, and Printers. By selecting these nodes, you can determine the drivers, forms, ports, and printers that are configured on the print server. By pressing and holding or right-clicking the print server and then selecting Properties, you can configure settings for all printers, including the following:

- Forms

- Ports

- Drivers

- Advanced settings

Viewing and creating printer forms

Print servers use forms to define the standard sizes for paper, envelopes, and transparencies. Print servers have many predefined forms from which you can choose, but you can also define your own forms.

To view the current settings for a printer form, press and hold or right-click the print server in Print Management and then select Properties. Then tap or click the Forms tab, as shown in Figure 20-6. Use the Forms On list to select the form you want to view. The form settings are shown in the Form Description (Measurements) area.

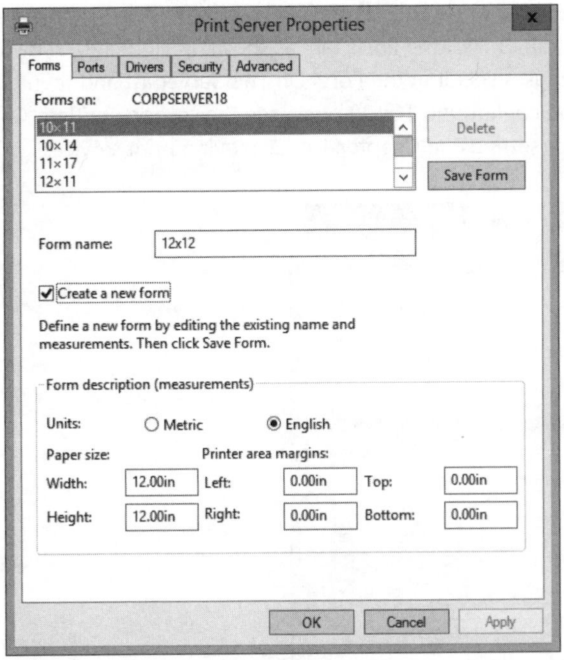

Figure 20-6 View and configure forms for paper, envelopes, and transparencies.

To create a new form, follow these steps:

1. Access the Forms tab of the Print Server Properties dialog box. Use the Forms On list box to select the existing form on which you want to base the new form.

2. Select the Create A New Form check box and then enter a name for the form in the Form Name field.

3. Use the fields in the Form Description (Measurements) area to set the paper size and margins. When you are finished, tap or click the Save Form button to save the form.

Although you can't change or delete the default forms, you can delete forms that users have created. In Print Management, select the Forms node for the server, press and hold or right-click the form, and then select Delete.

Viewing and configuring printer ports

Ports are used to define the interfaces and TCP/IP addresses to which the print server can connect. Using the Print Server Properties dialog box, you can view and manage all the ports configured for use on the printer server. This gives you one location for viewing, adding, deleting, and configuring ports.

To work with ports, press and hold or right-click the print server in Print Management and then select Properties. Then tap or click the Ports tab, as shown in Figure 20-7. If you want to view or change a port's settings, select it in the Ports On This Server list and then tap or click Configure Port. For details on configuring TCP/IP ports, see the section entitled "Changing standard TCP/IP port monitor settings" in Chapter 19, "Deploying print services."

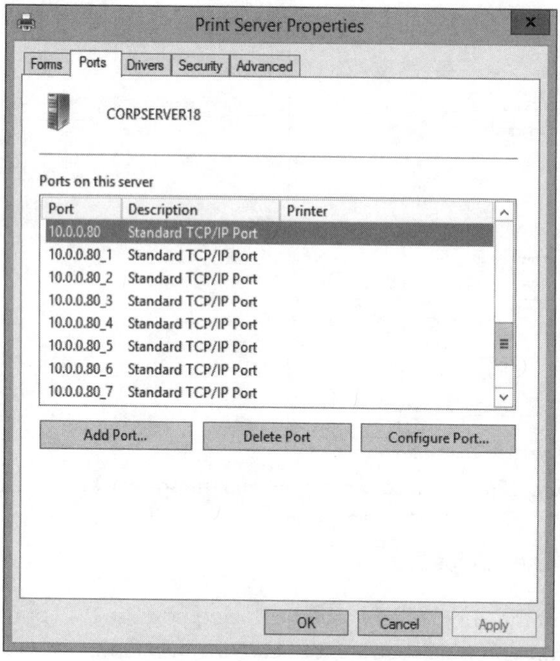

Figure 20-7 View and configure printer ports.

Viewing and configuring print drivers

As discussed later in this chapter in the section entitled "Installing and updating print drivers on clients," printer clients download print drivers the first time they access a printer and any time the print drivers have been updated. After you've configured each printer so that clients can download drivers, you can manage the installed printer drivers through the Print Server Properties dialog box. As with ports, the key here is convenience. You can not only view all the print drivers that are available but also add and remove drivers.

To work with drivers, press and hold or right-click the print server in Print Management and then select Properties. Then tap or click the Drivers tab. As shown in Figure 20-8, drivers are listed by

- **Name.** Typically, this is the manufacturer and model number of the printer.

- **Processor.** The chip architecture for the listed driver.

- **Type.** The driver type, such as Type 4 - User Mode.

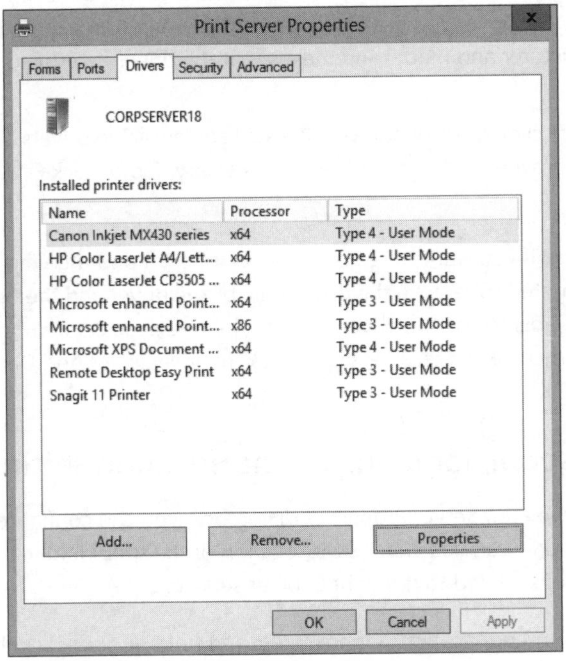

Figure 20-8 View and configure print drivers.

You can now do the following:

- **View driver properties and file associations.** If you select a driver and tap or click Properties, you'll see detailed information on the driver, which includes all the files associated with the driver. These include all related help, configuration, data, driver settings, and dependent files.

- **Add or update an existing print driver.** If you want to add or update an existing print driver, tap or click Add to start the Add Printer Driver Wizard and then follow these steps:

   1. In the Add Printer Driver Wizard, tap or click Next. On the Processor Selection page, choose the processors of all computers that will be connecting to this printer from the network, such as x64 and x86. To install additional print drivers for clients, you need access to the installation files for the appropriate driver version either on the network or on disc.

2. On the Printer Driver Selection page, choose the manufacturer and model of the printer for which you are adding support. If the print device manufacturer and model you're using aren't displayed in the list or you have a newer driver from the manufacturer, tap or click Have Disk to install a new driver. In either case, make sure the driver you use is digitally signed. This is indicated after you select a manufacturer and model and means that the driver is certified for use by Microsoft.

3. When you tap or click Next, Windows will install any available drivers and then prompt you to provide additional drivers as necessary. Tap or click Finish when you are done.

- **Remove print drivers.** If you want to remove a driver, select it and then tap or click Remove. You are prompted to remove the driver only or the driver and the driver package. If you want to be able to use the driver again in the future, select Remove Driver Only and then tap or click OK. Otherwise, tap or click Remove Driver And Driver Package and then tap or click OK.

Configuring print spool, logging, and notification settings

Using the Advanced tab of the Print Server Properties dialog box, you can configure properties related to spooling. Not only can you change the location of the spool folder, but you can also control notification actions related to the Print Spooler service.

To configure the print spool and notification settings, press and hold or right-click the print server and then select Properties. Then tap or click the Advanced tab. As shown in Figure 20-9, you can configure the following options:

- **Spool Folder.** Shows the current location of the print spool folder. To change the spool folder location, type a new folder path, tap or click Apply, and then, when prompted, tap or click Yes.

Spooling changes immediately

The changes to the spool folder will occur immediately. This means that the Print Spooler folder will look to this folder for documents to print and any previously spooled documents in the old spool folder will not print. Because of this, you should allow all current documents to print before changing the spool folder location.

Inside OUT
Setting permissions on the new print spool folder

The security on the selected folder will not be changed, and this could affect spooling of files to the selected folder. For best results, you should set security permissions on the new folder so they are the same as the original spool folder, as discussed in the section entitled "Understanding printer permissions" earlier in this chapter. You can use Windows PowerShell to copy the permissions on the original spool folder to the new spool folder. At an elevated Windows PowerShell prompt, enter the following command:

```
Get-Acl OrigFolderPath | Set-Acl -Path NewFolderPath
```

where *OrigFolderPath* is the path to the original spool folder and *NewFolderPath* is the path to the new spool folder, such as

```
Get-Acl C:\Spool | Set-Acl -Path D:\Spool
```

- **Beep On Errors Of Remote Documents.** Windows clients can display a warning balloon in the notification area when a document has failed to print. This warning is displayed for 10 seconds or until clicked.

- **Show Informational Notifications For Local Printers.** Displays the status of all jobs sent to this print server on the computer of the user who submitted the print job.

- **Show Informational Notifications For Network Printers.** Displays the status of print jobs sent by users on this computer to print services on other print servers.

CHAPTER 20

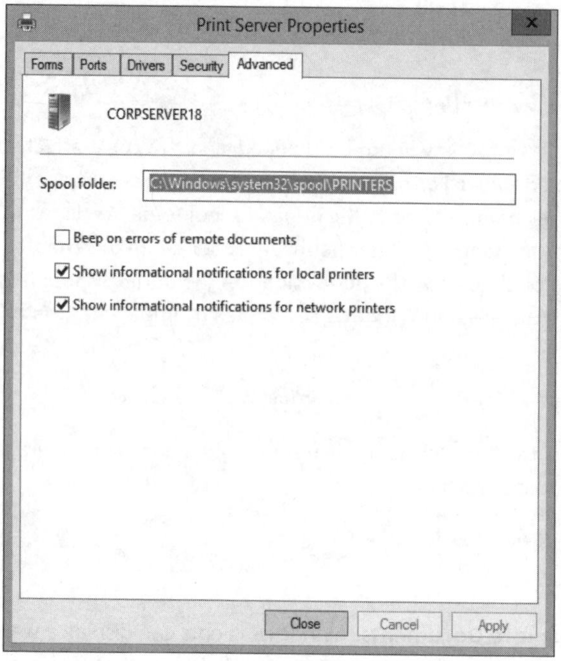

Figure 20-9 Configure the print spool, logging, and notification.

Managing printer properties

Printer properties control the settings for an individual printer. You can access a printer's properties in Print Management. In Print Management, press and hold or right-click the printer and select Properties.

> ### NOTE
> The specific properties displayed depend to some extent on the make and model of the printer you are working with. Because of this, some of the settings described below won't necessarily apply to all printers.

Setting general properties, printing preferences, and document defaults

To help users find printers and ensure that they don't have to waste time trying to configure default settings, such as paper size and paper tray to use, you should take a close look at the general properties, printing preferences, and document defaults assigned to a printer after you install it. Although this will take you a few minutes to go through, it will save users much more time, especially when you consider that this is something that every user in the organization would otherwise have to do.

As Figure 20-10 shows, the general settings are accessed from the General tab of the printer's Properties dialog box.

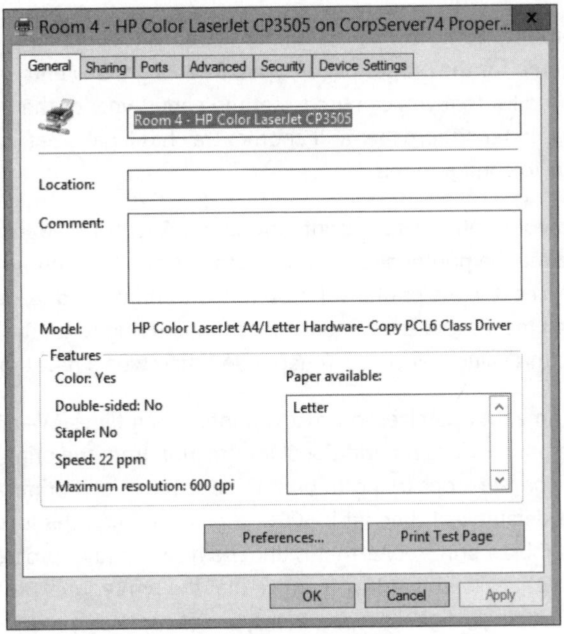

Figure 20-10 Configure general settings.

In Print Management, press and hold or right-click the printer and then select Properties. In the General tab, you can view or change the following options:

- **Local printer name.** The name of the printer on the print server

- **Location.** The location description of the printer

- **Comment.** An additional comment about the printer

To make sure the printer is ready for use, you should next go through the printing preferences and device settings to configure the settings that will be used by default on the printer. Tap or click Preferences in the lower portion of the General tab. Check the settings in the following tabs:

- **Layout.** Controls the paper orientation and page order for printing

- **Paper/Quality.** Controls the paper source (tray), the media (paper type), and the printing preference for black and white or color

In the Printing Preferences dialog box, tap or click OK. Then, in the printer's Properties dialog box, tap or click the Device Settings tab, as shown in Figure 20-11. Check the following device settings and change them as necessary and as they apply to your printer:

- **Form To Tray Assignment.** Form To Tray Assignment options ensure that the printer paper trays are configured for the proper paper types. Selecting a tray entry highlights it and displays a selection list that you can use to set the paper type for the tray. For example, if one tray has letter-sized paper and another tray has legal-sized paper, you'd use the related settings to configure this.

- **Job Timeout.** Job Timeout optimizes the print job wait times. Job Timeout specifies the maximum amount of time the printer allows for a job to get from the computer to the printer. If this time is exceeded, the printer will stop trying to print the document. The default value is 0, which means that the printer will continue trying to print a document indefinitely. To change this value, select Job Timeout and then type a new timeout.

- **Wait Timeout.** Wait Timeout optimizes in-process printing wait times. Wait Timeout specifies how long the printer waits for additional information from the print server. If this time elapses, the printer stops trying to print the document and prints an error message. Typically, the default wait timeout is 300 seconds. Although this is sufficient for most types of print jobs, a print server that is under a heavy load or processing very complex documents might exceed this. If you notice that the printer unexpectedly stops printing photos, CAD drawings, digital art, or other types of complex documents, try increasing the wait timeout to resolve this problem. To change this value, select Wait Timeout and then type a new timeout.

- **Installed Memory/Installable Options.** Installed Memory (sometimes known as Installable Options) tells the computer about the amount of memory installed on the printer. Although you should never use a value less than the default setting for the printer, you can use this option to tell the print server about additional RAM that you installed on the printer. This ensures that the computer knows that the extra RAM is available. To change this value, select Installed Memory and then choose the appropriate value on the selection list.

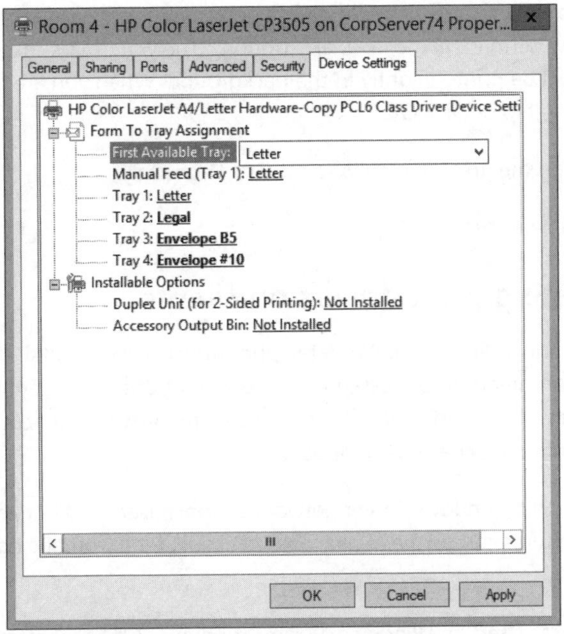

Figure 20-11 Configure Form To Tray Assignment and other device settings.

Setting overlays and watermarks for documents

In secure environments it might be necessary to set a watermark in the background of every page that is printed. A watermark is a word or phrase, such as DRAFT, CONFIDENTIAL, or TOP SECRET, that is printed lightly in the background of every page using a very large font size—typically 72-point Courier. If your printer supports this feature, you can print the watermark in the background of every page or only on the first page of a document.

To clear or set a default watermark for all printed documents, follow these steps:

1. In Print Management, press and hold or right-click the printer and select Properties. In the General tab, tap or click Preferences. Then, in the Printing Preferences dialog box, browse the available tabs until you see Watermarks options. Typically this tab is labeled Overlays or Effects, but it depends on the printer.

2. To clear a default watermark, select None as the watermark type. Then tap or click OK and skip the remaining steps.

3. To set a default watermark, select a watermark type. Sometimes you can select an existing type, such as CONFIDENTIAL, COPY, DRAFT, FINAL, ORIGINAL, or PROOF.

4. To create a new watermark, tap or click Add or Edit and then use the Watermark Details dialog box to set the watermark name, text, and options. The watermark text sets the word or phrase that will be printed lightly in the background. When you are finished creating the watermark, tap or click OK.

5. To set the watermark on the first page only, select First Page Only.

6. Tap or click OK to save your settings.

Installing and updating print drivers on clients

When a print server runs Windows Server 2008 or later, print drivers can be installed and updated automatically on clients, as discussed in the section of Chapter 19 entitled "Understanding print services." A client downloads print drivers the first time it accesses a printer and any time the print drivers have been updated.

By default, printers installed on a Windows Server network support user-mode drivers. Drivers for several processor architectures can be made available to clients for automatic download, including the following:

- **x86 user-mode drivers.** Used on Windows systems running 32-bit processors for Intel x86-based architectures

- **x64 user-mode drivers.** Used on Windows systems running 64-bit processors

You confirm and configure print driver availability on a per-printer basis by following these steps:

1. In Print Management, press and hold or right-click the printer you want to work with and then select Properties.

2. In the Properties dialog box, tap or click the Sharing tab and then tap or click Additional Drivers. This displays the Additional Drivers dialog box, as shown in Figure 20-12.

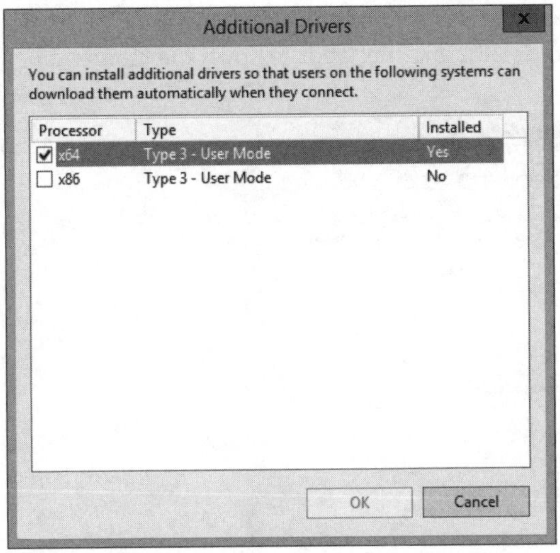

Figure 20-12 Select the additional operating systems that should be supported.

3. Select the check box for any client drivers you want to install and then tap or click OK.

4. To install additional print drivers for clients, you need access to the installation files for the appropriate driver version, either on the network or on disk.

After you've installed the print drivers for clients, clients will download them when they first connect to the printer that you've configured on the print server.

Configuring printer sharing and publishing

When you set up a printer, you are given the chance to share it. If you share a printer, it's published in Active Directory automatically. Users can search for published printers in a variety of ways, including when a user is attempting to connect to a network printer using the Add Printer Wizard. You can check or change the printer sharing and publishing options using the Sharing tab of the printer's Properties dialog box. In Print Management, press and hold or right-click the printer and then select Properties.

In the Sharing tab, you have the following options, as shown in Figure 20-13:

- **Share This Printer.** Selecting this check box shares the printer so that it's accessible to users, as discussed in the section of Chapter 19 entitled "Connecting users to shared printers."

- **Render Print Jobs On Client Computers.** Shifts the print job processing to the client computer rather than to the print server. Use this option to reduce the workload on the print server.

- **List In The Directory.** For a shared printer, selecting this check box lists the printer in Active Directory and clearing the check box removes the listing from Active Directory.

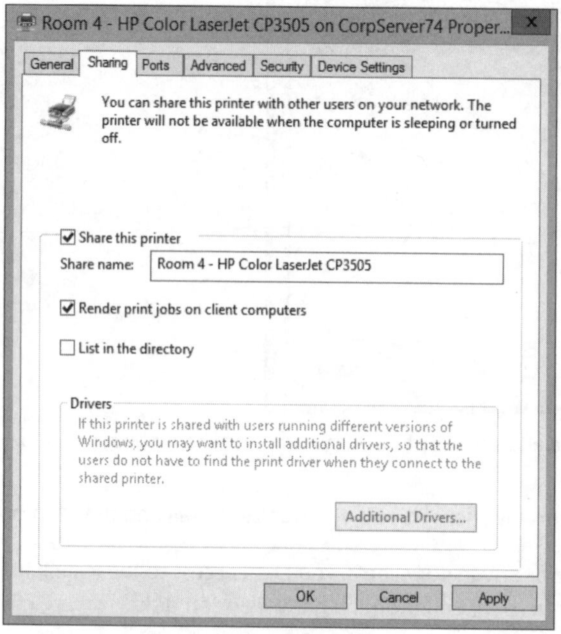

Figure 20-13 Configure sharing settings.

A screen shot of the Sharing tab in a printer's Properties dialog box, showing configuration for sharing settings.

NOTE

When you select the Render Print Jobs On Client Computers option in the Sharing tab, this is the same as pressing and holding or right-clicking the printer and selecting Enable Branch Office Direct Printing. These options render print jobs on client computers and then send the print jobs directly to the printer. Otherwise, print jobs are sent to the print server, where they are rendered, and then sent to the printer.

Optimizing printing through queues and pooling

A printer queue is a logical print device. You can have one logical print device associated with a printer, or you can have multiple logical print devices associated with a printer. The latter option gives you more flexibility and can help improve printing in general, especially if you create different logical print devices for different purposes and educate users on how they should be used. With multiple logical print devices, you can use print queue priority and scheduling settings to control how and when a logical print device is used.

Configuring queue priority and scheduling

Queue priority lets you prioritize printing based on the type of document being printed. Queue scheduling lets you schedule when documents in a queue can be printed—it doesn't restrict spooling to the queue, only printing from the queue. Print queue priority and scheduling settings can be used separately or together. Consider the following scenarios:

- **A printer has a normal queue and a priority queue.** You configure the normal queue so that it can be used for all routine print jobs. You configure the priority queue so that it is used for all urgent print jobs. Because the priority queue has a higher priority than the normal queue, any documents printed to the priority queue are printed before and preempt documents in the normal queue. To ensure that the priority queue isn't abused, you might want to restrict access to those individuals or groups that actually have priority printing needs on a printer.

- **A printer has a normal queue and a scheduled bulk queue.** You configure the normal queue so that it can be used any time for all routine print jobs. You configure the bulk print queue so that it is used for large documents and only after hours or during nonpeak hours. Any document spooled to the normal queue can be printed immediately. Any document spooled to the bulk queue is printed only within the scheduled availability hours, which keeps large documents from tying up the printer and causing a lengthy backup of other documents during peak usage times. If you set the priority of the bulk queue to be lower than that of the normal queue, the normal queue will always have priority.

To set printer availability schedule and priority, follow these steps:

1. In Print Management, press and hold or right-click the printer and then select Properties. Then tap or click the Advanced tab, as shown in Figure 20-14.

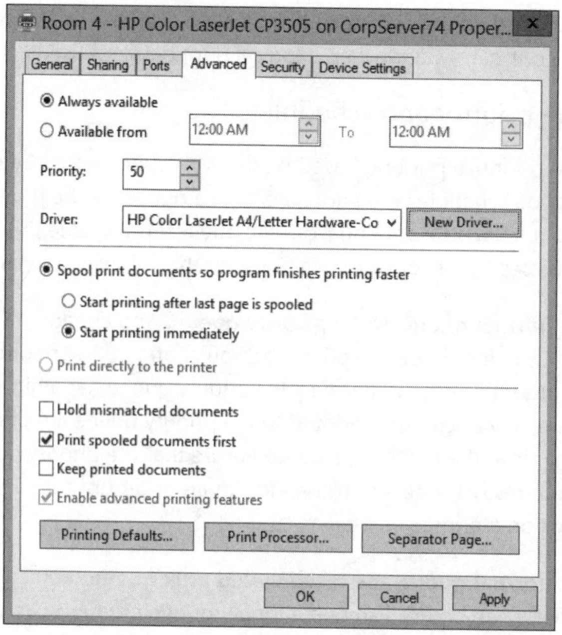

Figure 20-14 Use the Advanced tab to set the printer availability schedule and priority.

2. Printers are either always available or available only during the hours specified. Select Always Available to make the printer available at all times or select Available From to set specific hours of operation.

3. Use the Priority box to set the default priority for the print queue. The priority range goes from 1, which is the lowest priority, to 99, which is the highest priority. Print jobs always print in order of priority, and jobs with higher priority print before jobs with lower priority. The priority you use is assigned to all print jobs spooled to this printer.

4. If you are configuring a priority queue, click the Security tab and configure permissions to allow only those users and groups that you want to print at this priority. Remove or deny print permissions for users and groups that should have a different priority level. These users will use the normal priority queue that you've configured for the printer. If you haven't configured a normal priority queue yet, do so now.

5. When you are finished, tap or click OK. Repeat this process for all other logical print devices you configured for this printer.

Configuring printer pooling

Using a technique called printer pooling, you can associate a single logical print device with multiple physical print devices. In this configuration you have one print queue but multiple printers and the print server sends jobs to the first available physical printer. To take advantage of printer spooling, the printers must use the same printer driver. Typically, this means that they must be from the same manufacturer and be the same model. They must also have the same amount of memory installed.

Figure 20-15 shows an example of printer pooling. As the figure shows, the advantage of printer pooling is that users see a single print queue but multiple printers are available to handle their print jobs. Behind the scenes, administrators are free to add or remove physical printers without affecting the users' configuration.

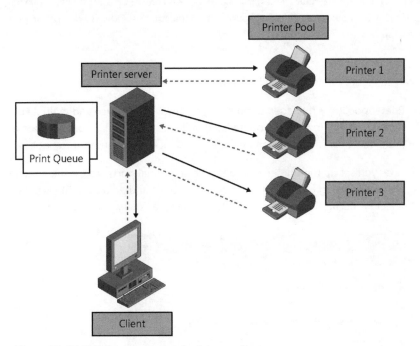

Figure 20-15 This is an example of printer pooling.

Printer pooling is useful in several scenarios:

- **Print-capacity scaling.** To scale print capacity, you can place two, three, four, or more identical printers side by side and then use printer pooling to effectively double, triple, quadruple, or more, your printing capacity. In this arrangement, users have one queue for printing to these printers and the only changes you must make are on the print server. On the print server, you enable printer pooling so that the first available printer prints a document.

- **Printer maintenance and replacement.** Printer pooling can facilitate printer maintenance and replacement as well. If you must maintain or repair a printer that is part of a printer pool, you can take it offline whenever necessary without affecting print operations. Users will still be able to print to the print queue, and the additional printers in the pool will handle printing for their documents.

Cluster the print server

Printer pooling provides high availability and fault tolerance for the printers themselves. It doesn't provide high availability or fault tolerance for the print server. If a group of users requires high performance and high reliability, you can set up a print cluster. Setting up a print cluster provides additional capacity and fault tolerance should one of the print servers stop responding.

You can configure printer pooling by following these steps:

1. Printer pooling is managed using a single logical print device and multiple ports. This means that you must add a printer so that it uses a particular port and then add one additional port for each additional physical print device you want to pool.

2. After you set up the printer and configure additional ports, access the printer's Properties dialog box. In Print Management, press and hold or right-click the printer and select Properties. Then tap or click the Ports tab, as shown in Figure 20-16.

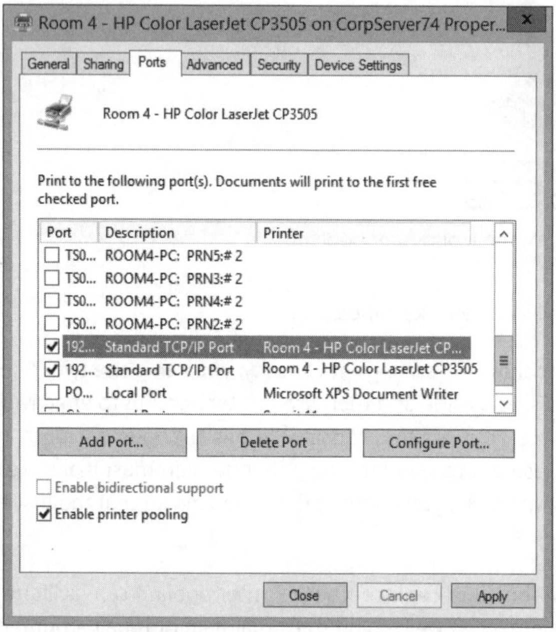

Figure 20-16 Select the ports to use for pooling.

3. Select the Enable Printer Pooling check box and then select the check boxes for all the ports to which printers in the pool are attached. These ports can be local ports or network ports. As long as the physical print devices to which they connect are identical, meaning they are from the same manufacturer, are the same model, and have the same amount of memory installed, you should be able to pool the printers.

4. When you are finished configuring printer pooling, tap or click OK.

Put pooled printers next to each other and consider using separator pages

Printer pooling works best when the pooled printers are all in the same location. You might want to put the printers back to back or side by side. It also helps if you use separator pages. Separator pages help keep print jobs organized and make it easier for users to identify which printouts are theirs.

Configuring print spooling

The way print spooling is configured on a printer affects how clients perceive printing performance and the actual printing options. You can configure printers to start printing immediately after a print job is received or to wait until the last page is spooled. If a print server's drives are full or can't be written to, you can change printer spooling settings so clients can print directly. Although this can slow down printing on a busy printer, it allows clients to continue printing. Other spooling options allow you to keep printed documents for faster reprinting and to hold mismatched documents so that jobs using alternate types of paper or envelopes don't cause the printer to stop and wait.

To configure print spooling options, access the printer's Properties dialog box. In Print Management, press and hold or right-click the printer and select Properties. Then tap or click the Advanced tab. You can now use the following options to configure print spooling:

-   **Spool Print Documents So Program Finishes Printing Faster.** Spools print jobs to the print server, allowing clients to finish faster so they can perform other tasks.

-   **Start Printing After Last Page Is Spooled.** Ensures that the entire document is spooled to the print server and available to the printer when printing begins. This option gives more control over the print job. If printing is canceled or not completed, the job won't be printed. If a higher-priority job becomes available, that job will print first.

-   **Start Printing Immediately.** Reduces the time it takes to print by allowing the printing to begin immediately when the print device isn't already in use. This option is preferred

if you want print jobs to complete faster and if you want to ensure that the client finishes printing faster.

- **Print Directly To The Printer.** Turns off spooling completely, and documents are sent directly to the printer. This option can seriously degrade print performance. Use this option only if there is a problem writing to the spool folder and you want to ensure that printing can continue.

- **Hold Mismatched Documents.** Holds documents that don't match the setup for the print device without affecting other documents in the print queue. This speeds up the overall printing throughput by keeping the printer from waiting for alternate paper and envelope types. For example, if a user prints a transparency, rather than stopping print-ing and waiting for the user to insert transparency paper, the printer holds the docu-ment and continues printing.

- **Print Spooled Documents First.** Allows jobs that have completed spooling to print before jobs in the process of spooling without regard to priority. The document with the highest priority that is already spooled will print even if a higher-priority document is in the process of spooling. This speeds up the overall printing throughput by keeping the printer from waiting for documents that are in the process of spooling.

- **Keep Printed Documents.** Keeps a copy of documents in the print queue in case users need to print the document again. When this option is selected, if a user reprints a document that's already in the queue, the document can be taken directly from the queue rather than having to be transferred and spooled again. In most cases you'll want to consider selecting this check box only when users print specialty types of documents that can take a long time to transfer and spool. Selecting this check box substantially increases the amount of disk space required for spooling. Because keeping printed doc-uments has significant security implications for sensitive documents, internal hard disk drives on printers should be treated with the same care as hard disk drives on servers.

- **Enable Advanced Printing Features.** Enables advanced printing features for metafile (EMF) spooling, including Page Order, Booklet Printing, and Pages Per Sheet. Typically, this check box is selected because metafile spooling is desired.

Viewing the print processor and default data type

Almost every printer has a print processor. The default print processor for Windows systems is Winprint. Other print processors can be installed when you set up a printer. The print proces-sor and the default data type for the processor determine how much processing the printer performs. As discussed previously, the RAW data type is processed on the client and minimally processed on the print server. The EMF data type is sent to the print server for processing.

Generally speaking, you do not need to change either the print processor or the default data type. However, if you want to determine the print processor and default data type used by a printer, you can access the printer's Properties dialog box, tap or click the Advanced tab, and then tap or click Print Processor. This displays the Print Processor dialog box. As shown in Figure 20-17, the current Print Processor and Default Data Type are selected and highlighted by default.

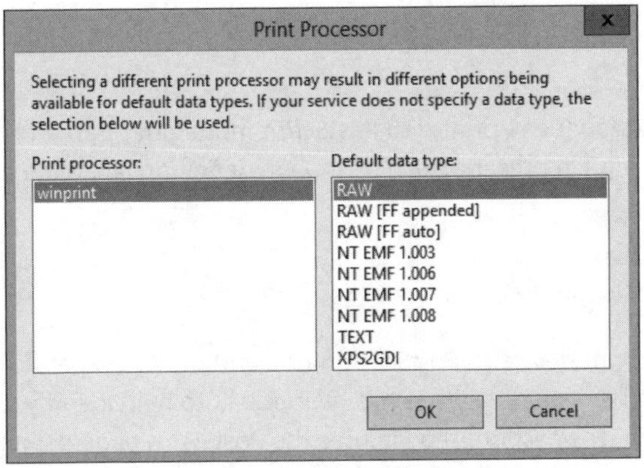

Figure 20-17 The current Print Processor and Default Data Type are selected.

Configuring separator pages

On a busy printer or when you use printer pooling, you might need some help keeping print jobs organized so that users can easily find their print jobs among other print jobs. This is where separator pages come in handy. Separator pages are used at the beginning of each print job to help identify the related document and who printed it.

Using separator pages

By default, printers don't use separator pages. If you want to use separator pages, you must configure them on a per-printer (logical print device) basis. Windows Server includes four default separator pages. These default separator pages are stored in the %SystemRoot% \System32 folder and are defined using standard American Standard Code for Information Interchange (ASCII) text. This means that you can view and edit them using any standard text editor, including Notepad.

The default separator pages include the following types:

- **Pcl.sep.** Sets the print device to PCL mode and prints a separator page before each document. The separator page shows the print job ID, date, and time. The Pcl.sep file uses the PCL page definition language and has the following contents:

```
\
\H1B\L%-12345X@PJL ENTER LANGUAGE=PCL
\H1B\L&l1T\0
\M\B\S\N\U
\U\LJob : \I
\U\LDate: \D
\U\LTime: \T
\E
```

- **Pscript.sep.** Sets a dual-language printer to PostScript mode but doesn't print a separator page. The Pscript.sep file uses the PostScript page definition language and has the following contents:

```
\
\H1B\L%-12345X@PJL ENTER LANGUAGE=POSTSCRIPT\0
```

- **Sysprint.sep.** Sets the print device to PostScript mode and prints a separator page before each document. The separator page has banner text to help identify who printed the document and when. The Sysprint.sep file uses the PostScript page definition language. The key definition assignments are the following:

```
@L/name (@N@L) def
@L/jobid(@I@L) def
@L/date (@D@L) def
@L/time (@T@L) def
```

- **Sysprtj.sep.** Sets the print device to PostScript mode and prints a separator page before each document. The Sysprtj.sep file uses the PostScript page definition language and is essentially an alternate version of the Sysprint.sep that uses a different version of the banner text.

You can install other separator pages in the %SystemRoot%\System32 folder. Some printers install their own separator pages. Typically, they do this because they can't use any of the standard separator pages. For example, Minolta QMS MagiColor Laser printers install their own separator page. The default name of this separator page is Msep01_b.sep. The contents of this file are as follows:

```
\
\M\B\S\N\U
\U\LJob : \I
\U\LDate: \D
\U\LTime: \T
\E
```

Here, the user name is printed in banner text and then job ID, date, and time are printed in standard text. It's important to know what the definitions look like in a separator page because you can customize all separator pages. The way you do this is to modify existing definitions or add definitions.

Setting a separator page

To use one of the default separator pages, access the printer's Properties dialog box, tap or click the Advanced tab, and then tap or click Separator Page to display the Separator Page dialog box shown in Figure 20-18. Do one of the following:

- If you are logged on locally to the print server, tap or click Browse. This opens a Find dialog box in the %SystemRoot%\System32 folder so you can easily choose available separator pages. Be sure to select a separator page that uses the same page description language as the printer and then tap or click Open. Then, in the Separator Page dialog box, tap or click OK.

- If you are accessing the print server remotely, enter the full path to the separator page, such as **C:\Windows\System32\sysprint.sep**. Be sure to specify a separator page that uses the same page description language as the printer and then tap or click OK.

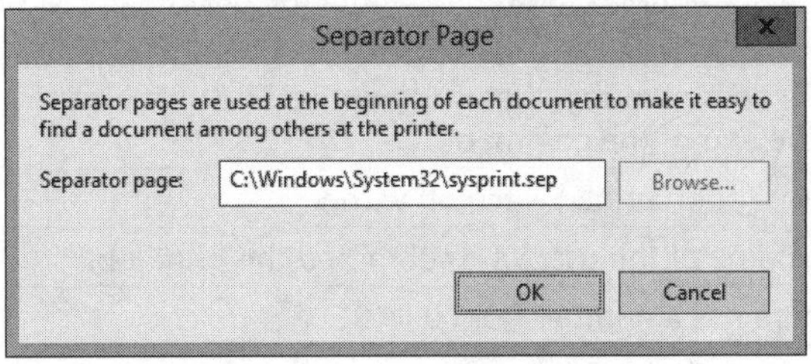

Figure 20-18 Select a separator page.

Test the separator page

After you select a separator page, you should print a test document to ensure that printing works as expected. To do this, tap or click Print Test Page in the General tab of the printer's Properties dialog box. If there's a printing error, you've chosen an incompatible separator page and will need to try a different one.

Customizing separator pages

You can customize separator pages for your organization. Although PCL, PostScript, and other types of separator pages use a different syntax, they all use the same variables. These variables are summarized in Table 20-2.

Table 20-2 Separator Page Variables

Variable	Usage
B	Turns on banner printing of text for which each character is block printed using pound signs (#) until you exit banner printing with the U variable.
D	Prints the date the document was printed using the default date format.
E	Inserts a page break. Typically used at the end of the separator page so that the document starts printing on a new sheet of paper.
F*filepath*	Prints the contents of the specified text file to the separator page. The specified file must contain only text, and the formatting of the text is not retained.
H*nn*	Sets a printer-specific code, which is used to control printer functions. Refer to the printer manual for control codes that might be available.
I	Prints the job ID. The job ID is set when a document is spooled to the printer.
L*text*	Prints the literal text following the variable until the next escape code or variable is reached.
L%	Marks the start of comment text that isn't printed. The next escape code or variable marks the end of the comment.
M	Turns on emphasis (bold) print. Switch off with S.
N	Prints the logon name of the user who submitted the print job.
N	Skips n lines, where n is a number from 0 to 9.
S	Switches off emphasis (bold) print.
T	Prints the time the document was printed using the default time format.
U	Turns off banner text printing.
W*nn*	Sets the line character width. Any lines with more characters than the specified width are truncated. The default width is 80 characters.

Knowing the available variables and their meaning, you can now examine the separator page listings shown previously to see exactly what they are doing.

Now that you know what the variables mean, take another look at Pcl.sep:

1. The first line sets the escape code for the separator page:

\

2. On the second and third lines, the separator page uses control codes to set the page description language to PCL:

    ```
    \H1B\L%-12345X@PJL ENTER LANGUAGE=PCL
    \H1B\L&l1T\0
    ```

3. On the fourth line, the separator page switches to bold banner text mode and then prints the name of the logon user:

    ```
    \M\B\S\N\U
    ```

    ### NOTE

    The order of these elements must be as follows: Enable Emphasis (M), Enable Banner Text (B), Stop Emphasis (S), Print Name (N), Stop Banner Text (U). If you don't follow this order, the emphasis, banner text format, or both might be enabled for the entire separator page.

4. On lines 5 through 8, the separator page prints literal text followed by a value—either the job ID, date, or time:

    ```
    \U\LJob : \I
    \U\LDate: \D
    \U\LTime: \T
    ```

5. On the last line, the separator page inserts a page break:

    ```
    \E
    ```

The PostScript separator pages are a bit more difficult to follow but have similar definitions. With PostScript, @ typically is used as an escape character to mark the start of variables instead of \. However, the first line of the separator page specifies the escape code that will be used.

With both PCL and PostScript, you have two options for customizing separator pages: you can either try to edit the existing separator pages or create your own. Before you edit an existing separator page, you should make a backup copy and work with the copy instead of the original file. If you elect to make your own separator page, you can do so using Notepad.

When you start from scratch, you can use either \ and @ as escape codes or use $. Set the escape code on the first line of the document and stick with the escape code you start with. With that in mind, if you want to print out the user name, date, and time in bold banner text, you would create a separator page with the following contents:

```
$
$M$B$S$N$U
$M$B$S$D$U
```

```
$M$B$S$T$U
$E
```

You would then save the file to the %SystemRoot%\System32 folder and name it with the .sep extension, such as Working.sep. To use the custom separator page, set it as the one to use, as discussed previously.

Configuring color profiles

With more and more color printers being used, it has become increasingly important to ensure that color printers accurately reproduce colors. Windows Server supports Integrated Color Management (ICM). ICM uses color profiles to ensure that colors are printed consistently. A color profile is a file that describes the color characteristics of a particular device.

Display devices and print devices have separate profiles. Typical displays can't show the same set of colors that a color printer can reproduce. The reason for this is that displays and printers use completely different processes to produce color. To help reduce the disparity between what is displayed and what is printed, you can use color management techniques, and this is where color profiles become important.

By default, Windows includes only a few color profiles. When you install a color printer or graphics software on a computer, additional color profiles typically are installed. All color profiles are stored in the %SystemRoot%\System32\Spool\Drivers\Color folder. In most cases color profiles installed with a printer are set as the defaults to use.

To view or configure color profiles, follow these steps:

1. In Print Management, press and hold or right-click the printer and select Properties. In the Color Management tab, tap or click Color Management.

> ### Create a separate printer for experimenting
>
> **Before you change the default color profiles, you might want to create a separate printer (logical print device). This way you can experiment with the printer's color settings without affecting other users.**

2. Tap or click the All Profiles tab to view a summary of all color profiles that are currently available. To add a profile, tap or click Add and then use the Install Profile dialog box to browse for and select the profile you want to use. To remove a profile, select the profile, tap or click Remove, and then tap or click Yes when prompted to confirm.

3. To associate a color profile with a device, tap or click the Devices tab. In the Device list, select the device you want to configure and then select Use My Settings For This

Device. Under Profiles Associated With This Device, you'll see a list of profiles associated with the device (if any) and the current default (if any). Tap or click Add to add a profile association for the selected device. To make a selected profile the default profile, tap or click Set As Default Profile.

4. Tap or click Close.

> ## Copy needed color profiles to the print server
>
> Color profiles available to users, such as graphic designers using Adobe Photoshop or Adobe Illustrator, are installed with the software. These profiles will exist on the user's desktop but not on the print server. To make the profiles available for use, you can copy available profiles from a user's desktop to the print server.

Managing print jobs

To manage a printer and its print jobs, you can use Print Management's extended view. To display the extended view, press and hold or right-click the Printers node and then select Show Extended View. Now when you select a printer, the lower portion of the main window will display the related print queue. Alternately, you can access a separate management window for the printer. In Print Management, just press and hold or right-click the printer you want to work with and select Open Printer Queue.

Pausing, starting, and canceling all printing

Occasionally, you might find that you must temporarily pause printing so that you can replace a toner cartridge, clear a paper jam, or perform some other maintenance procedure. To do this, press and hold or right-click the printer in Print Management and then select Pause Printing. You can resume printing later by pressing and holding or right-clicking the printer and then selecting Resume Printing.

If you need to clear all documents out of the print queue, you can do this as well. Press and hold or right-click the printer in Print Management and then select Cancel All Jobs. When prompted to confirm the action, tap or click Yes.

Viewing print jobs

Every document in the process of printing is shown in the extended view or in the printer queue window. Documents are listed by the following information:

- **Document Name.** The full name of the document

- **Job Status.** The print status of the document

- **Owner.** The user who printed the document

- **Pages.** The number of pages in the document

- **Size.** The file size of the document

- **Submitted.** The date and time the document was spooled to the printer

- **Port.** The ports used for printing

Managing a print job and its properties

When you select a document in the extended view or the printer queue window, you can manage it. To stop the document from printing or, if it's being printed, to pause printing, press and hold or right-click the document and then select Pause. You can enable or resume printing later by pressing and holding or right-clicking the document and selecting Resume. If you need to clear out a document from the print queue, press and hold or right-click the document and then select Cancel. When prompted to confirm the action, tap or click Yes.

You can change a document's properties by pressing and holding or right-clicking the document and selecting Properties. This opens the document's Properties dialog box, as shown in Figure 20-19. To change a document's properties when it's in the process of printing, you should pause the print job first.

Typically, you might want to edit a document's properties to set its priority. For example, if someone printed a very long document and you want to ensure that other documents print before it, you could lower the long document's priority. Similarly, if there's an important document that you want to be printed ahead of other documents, you can raise that document's priority.

> ### TROUBLESHOOTING
>
> *Clear out stuck documents*
>
> The Print Spooler service is configured to restart automatically if there's a problem. Sometimes it won't completely freeze or it will hang up in such a way that it can't be restarted automatically. You can tell this because the print queue will have error documents that you can't clear manually. In this case, restart the Print Spooler service manually. From the Administrative Tools menu, choose Services. In the Services console, select and then press and hold or right-click Print Spooler. From the shortcut menu, choose Start or Restart as appropriate. When you are logged on to the printer server or issuing remote commands, you can enter Restart-Service Spooler at an elevated Windows PowerShell prompt to restart the Spooler service.

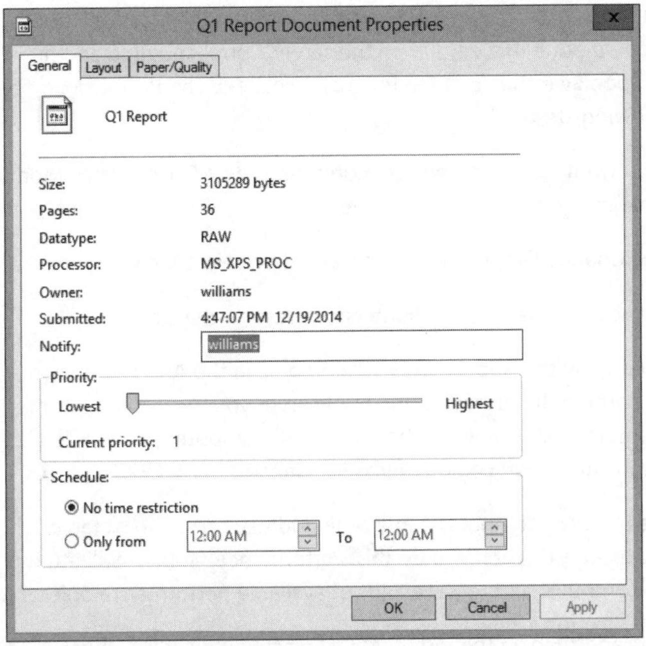

Figure 20-19 You can change the properties of documents in the print queue.

Printer maintenance and troubleshooting

Regular printer maintenance is an important part of printer administration. In addition to checking the print queue periodically for stuck documents and clearing them out as discussed earlier in this chapter in the section entitled "Managing print jobs," you should check to see how the print server is performing. As part of routine maintenance, you should also prepare for print server failure by periodically backing up the print server configuration. Finally, when things go wrong, you must perform troubleshooting.

Monitoring print server performance

Monitoring print server performance can help you track usage statistics and determine whether a print server is performing as expected. It can also help you determine whether changes or upgrades are needed and plan for future needs. You monitor print server performance using the performance objects available in System Monitor. You access System Monitor from within the Performance Monitor console. Tap or click Start, Programs or All Programs, Administrative Tools, Performance or type **perfmon** at the command line.

Get started by following the techniques discussed in Chapter 11, "Comprehensive performance analysis and logging," of *Windows Server 2012 R2 Inside Out: Configuration, Storage, &*

Essentials (Microsoft Press 2014), to establish performance baselines and detect performance bottlenecks. After you've done this, zero in on the server's print spooling and queuing performance using the SpoolSv instance of the Process object and the Print Queue object, as explained in the following steps:

1. On a server you want to use for remote monitoring, start Performance Monitor and then select Performance Monitor in the left pane.

2. Tap or click the Change Graph Type button and then select View Report.

3. Select and then delete the default counters by pressing the Delete key.

4. Press Ctrl+I to display the Add Counters dialog box. In the Add Counters dialog box, type the UNC name or IP address of the print server you want to monitor remotely in the Select Counters From Computer box. The UNC computer name or IP address begins with \\. So, for instance, you could enter \\PrintServer02 or \\192.168.12.15.

5. After you type the UNC computer name or IP address, press Tab or tap or click the Performance Object list. When you do this, Performance Monitor will attempt to connect to the remote computer and retrieve a list of available performance objects to monitor.

6. Choose Process and then, in the Instances Of Selected Object list, choose Spoolsv, as shown in Figure 20-20.

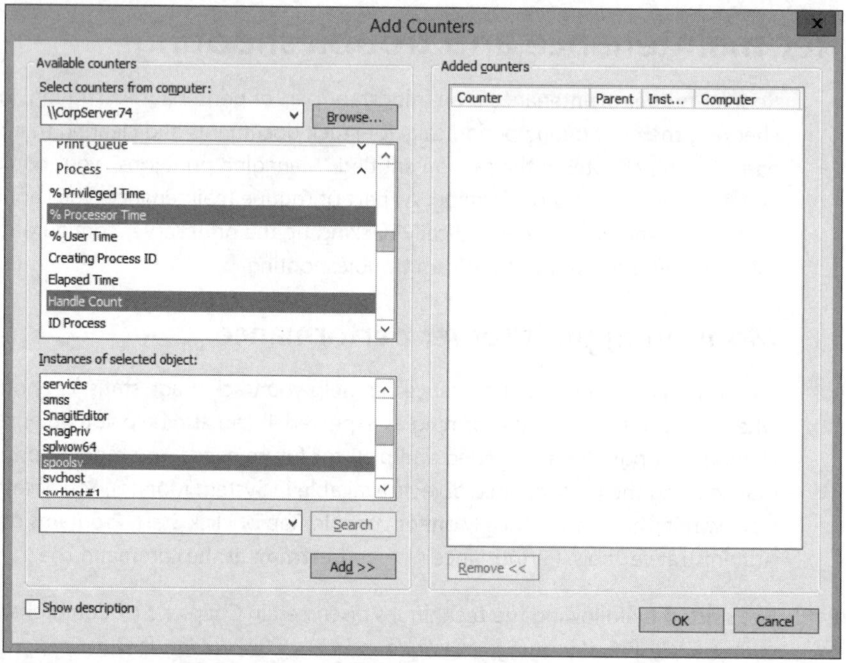

Figure 20-20 Monitor the Process object's Spoolsv instance.

7. Choose the following counters in the Select Counters From List box:

-   **% Processor Time.** Shows the percentage of elapsed time of all process threads used by the Print Spooler service. A dedicated print server that is very busy will have a relatively high percentage of processor time.

-   **Handle Count.** Shows the total number of handles open by the Print Spooler process. This is important to track because each open handle uses resources and open handles can be from clients that aren't actively printing.

-   **Virtual Bytes/Virtual Bytes Peak.** Shows the current/peak size in bytes of the virtual address space used by the Print Spooler process.

-   **Page File Bytes.** Shows the current amount in bytes of the virtual memory that the Print Spooler process has reserved in the paging file.

-   **Pool Paged Bytes.** Shows the current size in bytes of the paged pool used by the Print Spooler process. Memory in the paged pool can be written to disk when it's not in use.

-   **Pool Nonpaged Bytes.** Shows the current size in bytes of the nonpaged pool used by the Print Spooler process. Memory in the nonpaged pool can't be written to disk and must remain in physical memory.

-   **Working Set/Working Set Peak.** Shows the current/peak size in bytes of the set of memory pages (working set) used by the Print Spooler process.

8. Tap or click Add to add the selected counters to the chart.

9. Under Performance Object, expand the Print Queue object and then choose All Instances to track all print queues on the server (see Figure 20-21).

CHAPTER 20

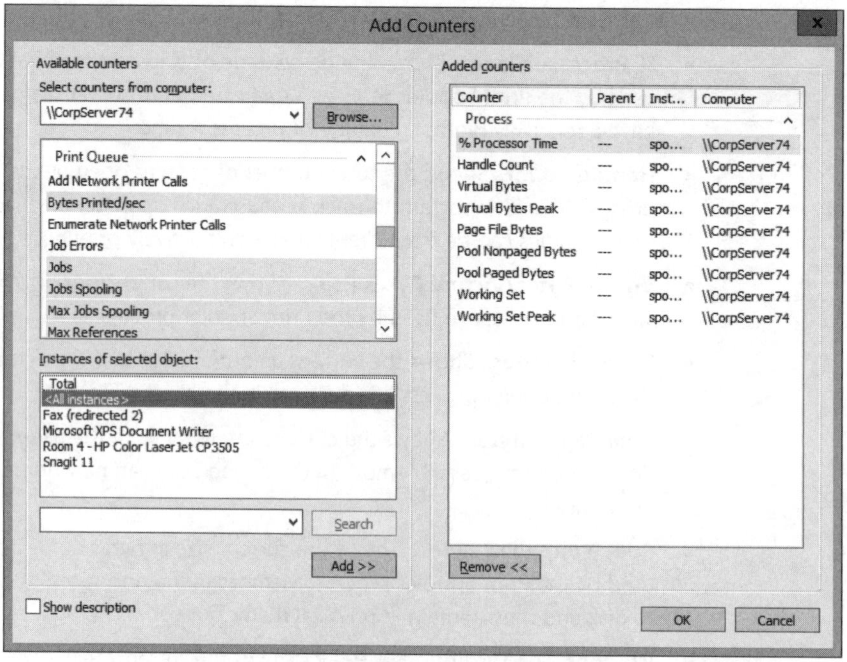

Figure 20-21 Monitor All Instances of select counters for the Print Queue object.

10. Choose the following counters in the Select Counters From Computer list:

- **Bytes Printed/Sec.** Shows the number of bytes printed per second and is a relative indicator of how busy a printer is.

- **Jobs.** Shows the current number of print jobs in a print queue.

- **Jobs Spooling/Max Jobs Spooling.** Shows the current/peak number of print jobs being spooled to the print queue. These are incoming print jobs.

- **Job Errors.** Shows the total number of job errors in a print queue since the last restart. Job errors can occur if there are problems transferring print jobs to the printer. A relatively high number of job errors can indicate networking problems or problems with network cards.

- **References/Max References.** Shows the current/peak number of handles open to a print queue. This is important to track because each open handle uses resources and open handles can be from clients that aren't actively printing.

- **Not Ready Errors.** Shows the total number of printer not ready errors in a print queue since the last restart. These errors occur if the printer is waiting or not ready for printing.

- **Out Of Paper Errors.** Shows the total number of out of paper errors in a print queue since the last restart. If a printer is frequently running out of paper, paper might not be getting refilled often enough or you might need an additional paper tray.

- **Total Jobs Printed.** Shows the total number of jobs printed on a print queue since the last restart. This is a relative indicator of how busy a printer is.

- **Total Pages Printed.** Shows the total number of pages printed on a print queue since the last restart. This is a relative indicator of how busy a printer is.

NOTE

Total Pages Printed doesn't show pages printed by non-Windows clients.

11. Tap or click Add to add the selected counters to the chart and then tap or click OK.

You can now monitor the print server to determine activity levels and how many system resources are being used for printing.

Preparing for print server failure

As part of your print services optimization and maintenance process, you should consider how you are going to handle printer and print server failure. Several techniques have been discussed previously for increasing availability and fault tolerance. These techniques include print queue pooling and print clusters, as discussed earlier in this chapter in the section entitled "Optimizing printing through queues and pooling." Because these options aren't practical for all environments, you should have other backup plans ready.

Start by considering how you would handle printer failure. If you have an identical printer available as a spare, you can configure this printer to take the place of the failed printer. As long as the printer uses the same print drivers, users can access it from the same print queue. If you have other printers available, you could show users how to access one of these printers or, ideally, already have a second printer added for use on their computers as a backup in case the primary printer fails. Trust me; you'll have happier users if you do this.

Next, consider how you would handle print server failure, which could mean that several printers are inaccessible. It's often a good idea to have a secondary print server available if a primary print server fails. You could then switch users from the primary print server to the secondary print server. Assuming the print server is already configured to provide print services for the printers originally serviced by the primary print server, you could just tell users how to access the print queues on the secondary print server.

A more complete disaster recovery plan for a print server would be similar to the following:

1. As part of periodic backups, back up the printer configuration on the print server using the Export Printers To A File option in Print Management. This creates a .printerExport file that you can store on a network share that is itself regularly backed up to tape.

2. If the primary print server failed, you would disconnect the primary server from the network. Then use the Import Printers To A File option to restore the .printerExport file containing the printer configuration on the secondary server.

3. You would then change the secondary print server's IP address and computer name to match that of the original print server. Users would then be able to access printers and resume printing. Alternatively, you could temporarily add a secondary IP address to the secondary print server if you use primarily IP addresses to describe printers or you could modify DNS to point the old host name to the secondary print server.

Solving printing problems

Windows Server automatically restarts spooling if the Print Spooler service hangs up due to errors, which takes a lot of guesswork out of troubleshooting. However, if the Print Spooler has a critical problem, such as when the disk drive on which the spool folder is located runs out of space, the Print Spooler can stop running.

Printer troubleshooting essentials

When you are troubleshooting printing problems, as when troubleshooting any problems, first try to figure out where the problem is and then try to fix it. As with most problems, you'll usually want to start with the client experiencing the printing problem before you start troubleshooting on the print server. Of course, the printer might also have a problem and the network might be a culprit as well. So this gives you four key areas to examine:

*   **Client/Application software.** The client or the application software on the client might be improperly configured. This could include problems with print drivers, permissions, and print settings.

*   **Printer hardware.** The printer might have a problem. This could include being out of paper, being out of toner, or having a paper jam.

*   **Printer server.** The print server might have a problem. This could include the spool folder running out of space, permissions set for a printer or the spool folder, print drivers used by the server, and device status.

*   **Network connectivity.** The network might have a problem, or the network card on the client, server, or printer might be misconfigured or bad.

TROUBLESHOOTING

Running out of space might indicate a deeper problem

Occasionally, the .spl and .shd files won't get cleared out of the spool folder. This can happen if print spooling is not functioning as it should. To correct this problem, manually clear out the print spooler folder and then restart the Print Spooler service. And if Windows won't allow you to delete the files, stop the Print Spooler service first, delete the files, and restart the service.

Start by trying to figure out which area has a problem. If the user is asking you directly for help, make sure the user is connected to the right printer and knows which print device is associated with the printer he or she is using. Try printing to the printer from your machine. You can print a test page from the printer's Properties dialog box by tapping or clicking Print Test Page in the General tab. If you can print a test page, printing is working and the problem might have to do with permissions or the user's system or configuration. Try printing from someone else's computer. If this succeeds, the problem might be with this particular user's system or configuration. If this fails, try printing from the print server. If this fails, the problem might be with the printer configuration or with the network.

While you are printing test pages, be sure to keep track of the printer status. Most current printers have a mini Hypertext Transfer Protocol (HTTP) server and an online status page that you can check just by typing the printer's IP address in your web browser. If you can't check current status that way, press and hold or right-click the Printers node in Print Management and then select Show Extended View. In the main pane, select the printer. You can then view the printer's current jobs by tapping or clicking the Jobs tab in the lower portion of the main pane. Tap or click the Printer Web Page tab to download the printer's webpage and view the current status of the printer (as shown in Figure 20-22).

You can then press and hold or right-click the printer entry and select Open Printer Queue to access its management window. If there's a document with an error status at the top of the print queue, remove it, which should restore printing, and then see the section entitled "Configuring print spooling" earlier in this chapter to see how you can try to prevent that type of error from happening again. If all documents have a printing error or if each time you clear out a bad document from the queue the status changes to Error-Printing, there might be a problem with the network or the printer itself. If the title bar shows that the printer is paused, tap or click Printer and then select Pause Printing to resume printing.

Hopefully, after performing these procedures you'll have isolated the problem to a particular area or have a better understanding of where the problem might exist. With that said, let's delve into specific scenarios and troubleshooting options.

CHAPTER 20

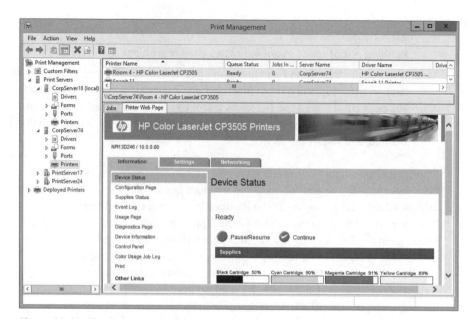

Figure 20-22 Check the status of the remote printer.

Inside OUT

Solve the printing problem with a clear plan

Few things frustrate users more than printing going awry. One of the most important things you can do is to communicate with the user or users having the problem, but don't do this too many times. Don't forget that your account might have permissions and privileges that other user accounts don't, so you might want to have a default user account for troubleshooting. In this case you would log on to your computer or a spare computer at your desk and try printing. Try to solve the problem without taking over a user's machine for troubleshooting. If you must access a user's machine, do this when you are fairly sure the problem is specific to a user or a group of users. If you can't resolve the problem within a reasonable amount of time or you know it's going to be a long time, such as when the print server has stopped working, you should consider implementing your recovery plan, as discussed earlier in this chapter in the section entitled "Preparing for print server failure."

NOTE

If you can't check the status of the printer online, don't spend more than five minutes on a printer problem without walking over to the printer and checking its status. Most printers with an error status will have a blinking yellow light, and the display will state the problem. Also, you might want to check the event logs on the print server for error or warning events.

Comprehensive printer troubleshooting

When someone says there is a printing problem, you should try to determine who is affected by the problem. Try printing from your machine and other machines. Try printing from the print server. Hopefully, after taking these steps you'll know whether the problem affects

- Everyone, meaning no one can print. In these circumstances the problem likely has to do with the printer itself or the network. Perform the following actions:

  - Check the printer status either by walking over to the printer or by using a browser to check the printer's status page. (Try typing the printer's IP address in your web browser.) Then check the event logs on the print server. Look for error or warning events that might indicate a problem.

  - Check the print queue (logical print device). Look to see if the printer is paused or if there are documents with a status of Error-Printing. Clear out these documents by pressing and holding or right-clicking them and selecting Cancel.

  - Print or check the configuration of the printer. Someone might have set it to use Dynamic Host Configuration Protocol (DHCP) and might not have made a reservation for it. In this case, if the printer was shut down and then restarted, it might have a different IP address. The printer port would then point to the wrong IP address. Check the printer's subnet mask as well.

  - Check the network. See if you can ping the printer's IP address from your system and from other systems. At the command line, type **ping *PrinterIP***, where *PrinterIP* is the IP address of the printer. If you can't ping the printer's IP address from any system, the printer might be turned off or its network cable might be disconnected. The printer might also have a bad network card. The problem could also be in the switch into which the printer is plugged or with routing to the printer.

  - Determine the last time the printer worked and if the printer configuration has been changed since then. If the printer never worked, it might not have been configured correctly in the first place. If the printer configuration was changed, change the configuration back to the previous settings if possible. If you suspect a problem with the print driver, try reinstalling it or installing a new driver as discussed earlier in this chapter in the section entitled "Viewing and configuring print drivers."

  - Check the free space on the volume on which the spool folder is located. If the volume is low on space or out of space, the print server won't be able to create spool files and, therefore, documents won't print. Also check the permissions on the spool folder. If the permissions are set incorrectly, the spooling won't work. See the sections entitled "Configuring print spool, logging, and notification settings" and "Understanding printer permissions" earlier in this chapter.

- Check the print monitor and separator page settings to ensure that they are correct. If an incorrect print monitor is set, the printer might print garbled pages or might not print at all. Try using the RAW data type or the EMF data type to see if this clears up the problem. If the separator page is set incorrectly, the printer might print the contents of the separator page or it might not print at all. See the sections entitled "Viewing the print processor and default data type" and "Configuring separator pages" earlier in this chapter.

- Check the Print Spooler service. It's configured for automatic restart, but if restart fails twice within a minute the Print Spooler service won't try to start again. Also, if the print queue has error documents and you can't clear them out, it's usually the fault of the Print Spooler. In this case, restart the service manually. In the Administrative Tools folder, select Services and then select Print Spooler in the right pane. Press and hold or right-click Print Spooler and select Start or Restart as appropriate.

- Some people—meaning some users—can't print, and some can. If some people can't print, the problem likely has to do with the permissions, the application software, or the network. Perform the following actions:

  - Check the network using a computer in the same subnet as the people having the problem. See if you can ping the printer's IP address. At the command line, type **ping *PrinterIP***, where *PrinterIP* is the IP address of the printer. If you can't ping the printer's IP address from any system on the subnet, a switch or routing between the user's computer and the printer might be bad or disconnected. This happens a lot if local switches/hubs are under people's desks.

  - Check the printer permissions and the permissions on the spool folder to see if the groups of which the users are members have appropriate access. If the permissions are set incorrectly, the spooling won't work. See the sections entitled "Configuring print spool, logging, and notification settings" and "Understanding printer permissions" earlier in this chapter.

  - Check the print monitor. The print monitor must use the correct data type. See "Viewing the print processor and default data type" earlier in this chapter.

  - Check the application being used for printing. The application might be incorrectly configured, or the default printer might not be what users think it is.

  - Check the error message generated when printing. If the client gets an error stating it must install a printer driver when connecting to a printer, this means that the correct drivers are installed on the server but aren't available to the client. See the section entitled "Installing and updating print drivers on clients" earlier in this chapter.

● One person, meaning only one user, can't print. If only one person can't print, the problem likely has to do with application software, the user's computer, or permissions. Start with the user's computer and perform the following actions:

- Check the application being used for printing. The application might be incorrectly configured, or the default printer might not be what the user thinks it is.

- Check the user's computer. The Print Spooler service must be running for the user to print. The computer must have sufficient temporary space to generate the initial spool file. The computer must have other essential services configured. The list goes on. Essentially, if you suspect the problem has to do with that specific computer, it's best if you restart the computer.

- Check to make sure the user's computer can connect over the network to other resources. Try pinging the router or the printer in question.

- Check the error message generated when printing. If the client gets an error stating it must install a printer driver when connecting to a printer, this means that the correct drivers are installed on the server but aren't available to the client. See the section entitled "Installing and updating print drivers on clients" earlier in this chapter. If the client gets an Access Denied error, this is a permissions issue.

- Check the printer permissions and the permissions on the spool folder to see if the user or groups of which the user is a member have appropriate access. If the permissions are set incorrectly, the spooling won't work. See the sections entitled "Configuring print spool, logging, and notification settings" and "Understanding printer permissions" earlier in this chapter.

Resolving garbled or incorrect printing

If the printer prints garbled or incorrect pages, this can be a sign that the printer is incorrectly configured. You should check the print driver and the port monitor settings. You might want to reinstall the print driver as discussed in earlier in this chapter in the section entitled "Viewing and configuring print drivers." You might want to change the port monitor data type to RAW or EMF to see if this clears up the problem. See the section entitled "Viewing the print processor and default data type" earlier in this chapter.

To resolve this problem, check the following:

● Ensure that the complete document is transferred to the printer before printing starts by selecting the Start Printing After Last Page Is Spooled option. See the section entitled "Configuring print spooling" earlier in this chapter.

- Try using the RAW data type or the EMF data type to see if this clears up the problem. See the section entitled "Viewing the print processor and default data type" earlier in this chapter.

- Try removing any separator page that is used because this might be setting the printer page description language incorrectly. See the section entitled "Configuring separator pages" earlier in this chapter.

- Try clearing the Enable Advanced Printing Features check box in the Advanced tab. This disables metafile spooling. Typically, non-Windows clients use SMB connections and spool RAW-formatted files to the print server. See the section entitled "Configuring print spooling" earlier in this chapter.

Backup and recovery

Every Microsoft Windows Server system on your network represents a major investment of time, resources, and money. It requires a great deal of planning and effort to deploy a new server successfully. It requires just as much planning and effort—if not more—to ensure that you can restore a server when disaster strikes. Why? Because you not only need to plan and implement a backup for each and every server on your network but also need to perform backups regularly and test the backup process and procedures to ensure that when disaster strikes you are prepared.

Disaster-planning strategies

Ask three different people what their idea of a disaster is and you'll probably get three different answers. For most administrators, the term "disaster" probably means any scenario in which one or more essential system services can't operate and the prospects for quick recovery are less than hopeful—that is, a disaster is something a service reset or system reboot won't fix.

To ensure that operations can be restored as quickly as possible in a given situation, every network needs a clear disaster recovery plan. Many of the same concepts go into disaster planning as go into planning for highly available, scalable, and manageable systems. Why? Because, at the end of the day, disaster planning involves implementing plans that ensure the availability of systems and services. Remember that part of disaster planning is applying some level of contingency planning to every essential network service and system. You need to implement problem escalation and response procedures. You also need a standing problem-resolution document that describes in great detail what to do when disaster strikes.

Developing contingency procedures

You should identify the services and systems that are essential to network operations. Typically, this list will include the following components:

- Network infrastructure servers running Active Directory, Domain Name System (DNS), Dynamic Host Configuration Protocol (DHCP), Remote Desktop Services, and Routing and Remote Access Service (RRAS)

- File, database, and application servers, such as servers with essential file shares and those that provide database or email services

- Networking hardware, including switches, routers, and firewalls

Combine your availability, scalability, and manageability plans with plans for contingency procedures in the following areas:

- **Physical security.** Place network hardware and servers in a locked, secure access facility. This could be an office that is kept locked or a server room that requires a passkey to enter. When physical access to network hardware and servers requires special access privileges, you prevent many problems and ensure that only authorized personnel can get access to systems from the console.

- **Data backup.** Implement a regular backup plan that ensures that multiple datasets are available for all essential systems and that these backups are stored in more than one location. For example, if you keep the most current backup sets on site in the server room, you should rotate another backup set to off-site storage. In this way, if disaster strikes, you will be more likely to be able to recover operations.

- **Fault tolerance.** Build redundancy into the network and system architecture. At the server level, you can protect data using a redundant array of independent disks (RAID) and guard against component failure by having spare parts on hand. These precautions protect servers at a very basic level. For essential services such as Active Directory, DNS, and DHCP, you can build in fault tolerance by deploying redundant systems using techniques discussed throughout this book. You can apply these same concepts to network hardware components, such as routers and switches.

- **Recovery.** Every essential server and network device should have a written recovery plan that details step by step what to do to rebuild and recover it. You should be as detailed and explicit as possible, and don't assume that the readers know anything about the system or device they are recovering. Do this even if you are sure that you'll be the one performing the recovery—you'll be thankful for it, trust me. Things can and do go wrong at the worst times, and sometimes, under pressure, you might forget some important detail in the recovery process—not to mention that, for some reason, you might be unavailable to recover the system.

- **Power protection.** Power-protect servers and network hardware using an uninter-ruptible power supply (UPS) system. Power protection will help safeguard servers and network hardware from power surges and dirty power. Power protection will also help prevent data loss and allow you to appropriately shut down servers through manual or automatic shutdown.

Inside OUT

Using and configuring UPS

Putting in a UPS requires a bit of planning because you need to look not only at servers but also at everything in the server room that requires power. If the power goes out, you want to have ample time for systems to shut down in an orderly fashion. You might also have some systems that you don't want to be shut down, such as routers or servers required for security key cards. In most cases, rather than using individual UPS devices, you should install enterprise UPS solutions that can be connected to several servers or components.

After you install a UPS, you can configure servers to take advantage of UPS using the management software included with the UPS. You can then configure the way a server reacts when it switches to battery power. Typically, you'll want servers to start an orderly shutdown within a few minutes of switching to battery power.

In your planning, remember that 90 percent of power outages last less than 5 minutes and 99 percent of power outages last less than 60 minutes. With this in mind, you might want to plan your UPS implementation so that you can maintain 7 to 10 minutes of power for all server and network components and 60 to 70 minutes for critical sys-tems. You would then configure all noncritical systems to shut down automatically after 5 minutes and configure critical systems to shut down after 60 minutes. In some loca-tions you might also want to invest in a generator that delivers clean AC power.

CHAPTER 21

Implementing problem-escalation and response procedures

As part of planning, you need to develop well-defined problem-escalation procedures that document how to handle problems and emergency changes that might be needed. You need to designate an incident response team and an emergency response team. Although the two teams could consist of the same members, the teams differ in fundamental ways:

- **Incident response team.** The incident response team's role is to respond to security incidents, such as the suspected cracking of a database server. This team is concerned with responding to an intrusion, taking immediate action to safeguard the organiza-tion's information, documenting the security issue thoroughly in an after-action report, and then fixing the security problem so that the same type of incident can't recur. Your organization's security administrator or network security expert should have a key role on this team.

- **Emergency response team.** The emergency response team's role is to respond to service and system outages, such as the failure of a database server. This team is concerned with recovering the service or system as quickly as possible and allowing normal operations to resume. Like the incident response team, the emergency response team needs to document the outage thoroughly in an after-action report and then, if applicable, propose changes to improve the recovery process. Your organization's system administrators should have key roles on this team.

Creating a problem-resolution policy document

Over the years I've worked with and consulted for many organizations, and I've often been asked to help implement information technology (IT) policies and procedures. In the area of disaster and recovery planning, there's one policy document that I always use, regardless of the size of the company I am working with. I call it the *problem-resolution policy document*.

The problem-resolution policy document has the following six sections:

- **Responsibilities.** The overall responsibilities of IT and engineering staff during and after normal business hours should be detailed in this section. For an organization with 24/7 operations, such as a company with a public World Wide Web site maintained by internal staff, the after-hours responsibilities section should be very detailed and let individuals know exactly what their responsibilities are. Most organizations with 24/7 operations will designate individuals as being on call 7 days a week, 365 days a year, and, in that case, this section should explain what being on call means and what the general responsibilities are for an individual on call.

- **Phone roster.** Every system and service you identify in your planning as essential should have a point of contact. For some systems you'll have several points of contact. Consider, for example, a database server. You might have a system administrator who is responsible for the server itself, a database administrator who is responsible for the database running on the server, and an integration specialist responsible for any integration components running on the server.

IMPORTANT

The phone roster should include both on-site and off-site contact numbers. Ideally, this means that you'll have the work phone number and cell phone number of each contact. It should be the responsibility of every individual on the phone roster to ensure that contact information is up to date.

- **Key contact information.** In addition to a phone roster, you should have contact numbers for facilities and vendors. The key contacts list should include the main office phone numbers at branch offices and data centers and contact numbers for the various vendors who installed infrastructure at each office, such as the building manager, Internet service provider (ISP), electrician, and network wiring specialist. It should also include the support phone numbers for hardware and software vendors and the information you'll need to give to get service, such as a customer identification number and service contract information.

- **Notification procedures.** The way problems get resolved is through notification. This section should outline the notification procedures and the primary point of contact in case of outage. If many systems and services are involved, notification and primary contacts can be divided into categories. For example, you might have an external systems-notification process for your public Internet servers and an internal systems-notification process for your intranet services.

- **Escalation.** When problems aren't resolved within a specific time, there should be clear escalation procedures that describe whom to contact and when. For example, you might have level 1, level 2, and level 3 points of contact, with level 1 contacts being called immediately, level 2 contacts being called when problems aren't resolved in 30 minutes, and level 3 contacts being called when problems aren't resolved in 60 minutes.

IMPORTANT

You should also have a priority system in place that dictates what types of incidents or outages take precedence over others. For example, you could specify that service-level outages, such as those that involve the complete system, have priority over isolated outages involving a single server or application, but that suspected security incidents have priority over all other concerns.

- **Post-action reporting.** Every individual involved in a major outage or incident should be expected to write a post-action report. This section explains what should be in that report. For example, you would want to track the notification time, the actions taken after notification, the escalation attempts, and other items that are important to improving the process or preventing the problem from recurring. Remember, the purpose of post-action reporting isn't pointing fingers or assigning blame. It's about working to understand the root cause of a problem and improving recovery processes and procedures.

Every IT group should have a general policy with regard to problem-resolution procedures, and this policy should be detailed in a problem-resolution policy document or one like it. The document should be distributed to all relevant personnel throughout the organization so that

CHAPTER 21

every person who has some level of responsibility for ensuring system and service availability knows what to do in the case of an emergency. After you implement the policy, you should test it to help refine it so that the policy will work as expected in an actual disaster.

Disaster preparedness procedures

Just as you need to perform planning before disaster strikes, you need to perform certain pre-disaster preparation procedures. These procedures ensure that you are able to recover systems as quickly as possible when a disaster strikes, and they include the following:

- Backups

- Startup repair

- Recovery disks

- Startup and recovery options

Performing backups

You should perform regular backups of every server. Backups can be performed using several techniques. Most organizations choose a combination of dedicated backup servers and per-server backups. If you use professional backup software, you can use one or more dedicated backup servers to create backups of other servers on the network and then write the backups to media on centralized backup devices. If you use per-server backups, you run backup software on each server that you want to back up and store the backup media on a local backup device. By combining the techniques, you get the best of both worlds.

With dedicated backup servers, you purchase professional backup software, a backup server, and a scalable backup device. The initial costs for purchasing the required equipment and the time required to set up the backup environment can be substantial. However, after the backup environment is configured, it's rather easy to maintain. Centralized backups also offer substantial time savings for administrators because the backup process itself can be fully automated.

With per-server backups, you use a backup utility to perform manual backups of physical servers. If the physical servers are hosts for virtual machines (VMs), backing up the host server with VSS-aware backup software ensures that the virtual machines are also backed up and can be recovered individually. The primary tool for performing per-server backups is the Windows Server Backup utility, which is VSS-aware and is discussed later in this chapter in the section entitled "Backing up and recovering your data." Because this tool is included with Windows Server 2012 R2, there is no initial cost for implementation. However, because the backup options are limited, the process might require more time than using centralized backup servers.

Repairing startup

Like its predecessors, Windows Server 2012 R2 has several automatic repair features. If the boot manager or corrupted system file is preventing startup, the Startup Repair tool is started automatically and will initiate the repair of the server. The Startup Repair tool can be helpful if one or more of the following problems are preventing startup:

- A virus infection in the master boot record

- A missing or corrupt boot manager

- A boot configuration data store with bad entries

- A corrupted system file

Although Startup Repair typically runs automatically, you can manually initiate this feature by completing the following steps:

1. If the computer won't start normally, you'll see a Windows Boot Manager error screen stating that Windows failed to start. Press Enter.

2. On the OS Selection screen, press F8.

3. On the Advanced Boot Options screen, choose an appropriate Safe Mode or other alternate mode to try to start the server so that you can log in to diagnose and resolve the problem.

You also can use the installation disk to initiate recovery. To do so, follow these steps:

1. Insert the Windows Installation disk and then boot from the installation disk by pressing a key when prompted during startup. If the server does not allow you to boot from the installation disk, you might need to change firmware options to allow booting from a CD/DVD-ROM drive.

2. Windows Setup should start automatically. On the Install Windows page, select the language, time, and keyboard layout options that you want to use. Tap or click Next.

3. When prompted, do not tap or click Install Now. Instead, tap or click the Repair Your Computer link in the lower-left corner of the Install Windows page.

4. On the Automatic Repair screen, tap or click Troubleshoot. Then, on the Advanced Options screen, tap or click Command Prompt to access the Windows PE environment. The Windows PE environment gives you access to many command-line tools.

CHAPTER 21

5. Change directories to x:\sources\recovery by typing **cd recovery**.

6. Run the Startup Repair Wizard by typing **startrep**.

You can recover a server's operating system or perform a full system recovery by using a Windows installation disk and a backup that you created earlier with Windows Server Backup. To initiate a recovery, on the Automatic Repair screen, tap or click Troubleshoot. Then, on the Advanced Options screen, tap or click System Image Recovery.

With an operating system recovery, you recover all critical volumes but don't recover nonsystem volumes. If you recover a full system, Windows Server Backup reformats and repartitions all disks that are attached to the server. Because of this, you should use this method only when you want to recover the server data onto separate hardware or when all other attempts to recover the server on the existing hardware have failed.

Setting startup and recovery options

As part of planning for the worst-case scenarios, you need to consider how you want systems to start up and recover if a stop error is encountered. The options you choose can add to the boot time or they can specify that if a system encounters a stop error it does not reboot.

You can configure startup and recovery options by completing the following steps:

1. In the Control Panel, tap or click System And Security\System to start the System utility.

2. Tap or click Advanced System Settings. This opens the System Properties dialog box.

3. In the Advanced tab, tap or click Settings in the Startup And Recovery panel. This displays the dialog box shown in Figure 21-1.

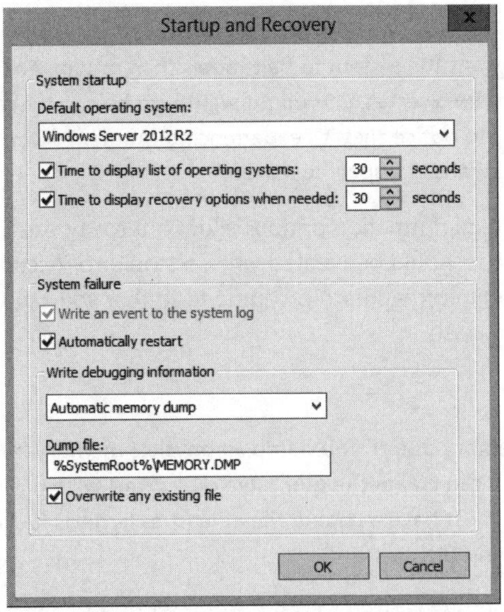

Disaster preparedness procedures   755

Figure 21-1 Configure startup and recovery options.

4. In the Startup And Recovery dialog box, you configure the settings as follows:

   - If a server has multiple operating systems, you can set the default operating system by selecting one of the operating systems in the Default Operating System list. These options are obtained from the boot manager.

   - When multiple operating systems are installed, the Time To Display List Of Operating Systems option controls how long the system waits before booting to the default operating system. In most cases you won't need more than a few seconds to make a choice, so reduce this wait time to perhaps 5 or 10 seconds. Alternatively, you can have the system automatically choose the default operating system by clearing this option.

   - When you want to display recovery options, the operating system uses the Time To Display Recovery Options When Needed setting to determine how long to wait for you to choose a recovery option. The default wait time is 30 seconds. If you don't choose a recovery option in that time, the system boots normally without recovery. As with operating systems, you won't need more than a few seconds to make a choice, so reduce this wait time to perhaps 5 or 10 seconds.

   - Under System Failure, you have several important options for determining what happens when a system experiences a stop error. By default, the Write An Event To The System Log check box is selected so that the system logs an error in the system log. The check box appears dimmed, so it can't normally be changed. The Automatically Restart check box is selected to ensure that the system attempts to reboot when a stop error occurs.

IMPORTANT

In some cases you might want the system to halt rather than reboot. For example, if you are having problems with a server, you might want it to halt so that an administrator will be more likely to notice that it's experiencing problems. Don't, however, prevent automatic reboot without a specific reason.

- The Write Debugging Information options allow you to choose the type of debugging information that should be created when a stop error occurs. In most cases you will want debug information to be dumped so that you can use it to determine the cause of a crash.

IMPORTANT

If you choose a kernel memory dump, you dump all physical memory being used at the time of the failure. You can create the dump file only if the system is properly configured. The system drive must have a paging file at least as large as RAM and adequate disk space to write the dump file.

- By default, dump files are written to the %SystemRoot% folder. If you want to write the dump file to a different location, type the file path in the Dump File box. Select the Overwrite Any Existing File option to ensure that only one dump file is maintained.

5. Tap or click OK twice to close all open dialog boxes.

Developing backup strategies

Backups are insurance plans, plain and simple—and every administrator should see them that way. When disaster strikes, your backup implementation will either leave you out of harm's way or drowning without a life preserver. Trust me: you don't want to be drowning when it should be your moment to shine. After all, if you've implemented a well-thought-out backup plan and practiced the necessary recovery procedures until they are second nature, a server that has stopped working is nothing more than a bump in the road that you can smooth out—even if you have to rebuild a server from scratch to do it.

Creating your backup strategy

So, where do you start? Start by outlining a backup and recovery plan that describes the servers and the data that need to be backed up. Ask yourself the following questions:

- How important is the role that the server is performing?

- How important is the data stored on the server?

- Is the data unique, or are multiple masters available?

- How often does the data change?

- How much data in total is there to back up?

- How long does each backup take?

- How quickly do you need to recover the data?

- How much historical data do you need to store?

- Do you have the equipment needed to perform backups?

- Do you need to store backups off site?

- Who will be responsible for performing backups?

The answers to these questions will help you develop your backup and recovery plan. Often you'll find that your current resources aren't enough and that you need to obtain additional backup equipment. It might be one of the ultimate ironies in administration, but you often need more justification for backup equipment than for any other type of equipment. Fight to get the backup resources you need and do so without reservation. If you have to make incremental purchases over a period of several months to get the backup equipment and supplies, do so without hesitation.

Backup strategy considerations

In most cases your backup strategy should involve performing some type of backup of every server daily and full backups of these servers at least once a week. You should also regularly inspect the backup log files and periodically perform test restores of the data to ensure that data is being properly written to the backup media.

It's all about the data

Much of your backup strategy depends on the importance of the data, the frequency of changes to it, and the total amount of data to back up. Data that is of higher importance or that frequently changes needs to be backed up more often than other types of data. As the amount of data you are backing up increases, you need to be able to scale your backup implementation. If you are starting out with a large amount of data, you need to consider how much time a complete backup of the data set will take. To ensure that backups can be performed quickly, you might have to purchase faster equipment or purchase backup devices with multiple drives.

CHAPTER 21

Plan separate backup strategies for system files and data files.

- System files are used by the operating system and applications. These files change when you install new components, service packs, or patches. They include system state data.

NOTE
For systems that aren't domain controllers, the system state data includes essential boot files, key system files, the COM+ class registration database, and the registry data. For domain controllers, the Active Directory database and System Volume (Sysvol) files are included as well, and this data typically changes on a daily basis.

- Data files are created by applications and users. Application files contain configuration settings and data. User files contain the daily work of users and can include documents, spreadsheets, media files, and so on. These files change every day.

Administrators often back up an entire machine and dump all the data into a single backup. This strategy has several problems. First, on non–domain controllers, system files don't change that often but data files change frequently. Second, you typically need to recover data files more frequently than system files. You recover data files when documents are corrupted, lost, or accidentally deleted and can't be recovered using other means, such as Previous Versions. You recover system files when you have serious problems with a system and typically are trying to restore the whole machine. Sometimes, however, rather than restore a failed server, it might be faster and easier to set up a new server that provides the same services. For example, with a domain controller that doesn't perform any operations master roles, you might be able to set up a new domain controller from media faster than you can restore the original failed domain controller.

Look at the timing of backups as well. With earlier releases of Windows, you are often concerned about the time that backups are performed. You want backups to be performed when the system's usage is low so that more resources are available and few files are locked and in use. With the advances in backup technology made possible by the Shadow Copy API built into Windows Server, the backup time is less of a concern than it previously was. Any backup programs that implement the Shadow Copy API allow you to back up files that are open or locked. This means that you can perform backups when applications are using files and no longer have to worry about backups failing because files are being used.

Selecting the optimal backup techniques

When it comes to backup, there is no such thing as a one-size-fits-all solution. Often you'll implement one backup strategy for one system and a different backup strategy for a different system. It all comes down to the importance of the data, the frequency of changes to it, and how much data there is to back up on each server. But don't overlook the importance of recovery speed. Different backup strategies take longer to recover than others, and there might be differing levels of urgency involved in getting a system or service back online. Because of this, I recommend a multipronged backup strategy that is optimized on a per-server basis.

Key services running on a system have backup functions that are unique. Implement and use those backup mechanisms as your first line of defense against failure. Remember that a backup of the system state includes a full backup of a server's registry and that system configuration includes the configuration of all services running on a system. However, if a specific service fails, it is much easier and faster to recover that specific service than to try to recover the whole server. You'll have fewer problems, and it is less likely that something will go wrong.

Specific backup and recovery techniques for key services are as follows:

- With Dynamic Host Configuration Protocol (DHCP), you should periodically back up the DHCP configuration and the DHCP database, as discussed in the sections entitled "Saving and restoring the DHCP configuration" and "Managing and maintaining the DHCP database" in Chapter 5, "Configuring DHCP Services."

- If you haven't decommissioned Windows Internet Naming Service (WINS), you should periodically back up the WINS database, as discussed in the section entitled "Maintaining the WINS database" in Chapter 9, "Implementing and maintaining WINS."

- With Domain Name System (DNS), your backup strategy depends on whether you are using Active Directory–integrated zones, standard zones, or both. When you are using Active Directory–integrated zones, DNS configuration data is stored in Active Directory. By default, when you are using standard zones, DNS configuration data is stored in the %SystemRoot%\System32\DNS folder and backups of zone data are stored in the %SystemRoot%\System32\DNS\Backup folder.

- With Group Policy, you should periodically back up the Group Policy Object (GPO) configuration as discussed in the section entitled "Maintaining and troubleshooting Group Policy" in Chapter 17, "Managing Group Policy."

- With file servers, you should implement the Volume Shadow Copy Service (VSS) for all network file shares. This makes it easier to restore previous versions of files. In addition, you should regularly back up all user data files on the file server.

Take the time to develop plans and procedures that can help you through everything from a power outage to the worst-case scenario. Don't forget that when you use BitLocker without Network Unlock, protected computers are locked until you provide the necessary recovery password. When a computer is locked, you must use the recovery password from a USB flash drive or use the function keys to enter the recovery password. F1 through F9 represent the digits 1 through 9, and F10 represents 0.

Finally, you also need to perform regular backups of both system and user data. Most backup programs, including Windows Backup, which is included in Windows Server 2012 R2, support several types of backup jobs. The type of backup job determines how much data is backed up and what the backup program does when it performs a backup.

Inside OUT

How backup programs use the archive bit

Most backup operations make use of the archive attribute that can be set on files. The archive attribute, a bit included in the directory entry of each file, can be turned on or off. In most cases a backup program will turn off (clear) the archive attribute when it backs up a file. The archive bit is turned on (set) again when a user or the operating system later modifies a file. When the backup program runs again, it knows that only the files with the archive attribute set must be backed up—because these are the only files that have changed since the last backup.

Understanding backup types

The basic types of backups include the following:

- **Normal.** A normal backup is a full backup of all the files and folders you select, regardless of the archive attribute's setting. When a file is backed up, the archive attribute is turned off.

- **Copy.** A copy backup is a full backup of all files and folders you select, regardless of the archive attribute's setting. Unlike a normal backup, a copy backup doesn't turn off the archive attribute on files. This means that you can use a copy backup to create an additional or supplemental backup of a system without interfering with the existing backup strategy.

- **Incremental.** An incremental backup is used to create a backup of all files that have changed since the last normal or incremental backup. As such, an incremental backup is a partial backup. The backup program uses the archive attribute to determine which files should be backed up and turns off the archive attribute after backing up a file. This means that each incremental backup contains only the most recent changes.

- **Differential.** A differential backup is used to create a backup of all files that have changed since the last normal backup. Like an incremental backup, in a differential backup the backup program uses the archive attribute to determine which files should be backed up. However, the backup program does not change the archive attribute. This means that each differential backup contains all changes.

- **Daily.** A daily backup uses the modification date on a file rather than the archive attribute. If a file has been changed on the day the backup is performed, the file will be backed up. This technique doesn't change the archive attributes of files and is useful when you want to perform an extra backup without interfering with the existing backup strategy.

As part of your backup strategy, you'll probably want to perform normal backups on a weekly basis and supplement this with daily, differential, or incremental backups. The advantage of normal backups is that they are a complete record of the files you select. The disadvantage of normal backups is that they take longer to make and use more storage space than other types of backups. Incremental and differential backups use less space and are faster because they are partial backups. The disadvantage is that the recovery of systems and files using incremental and differential backups is slower than when you only have to perform a recovery from a normal backup. To see why, consider the following backup and recovery examples:

- **Normal backup with daily incremental backups.** You perform a normal backup every Sunday and incremental backups Monday through Saturday. Monday's incremental backup contains changes since Sunday. Tuesday's incremental backup contains changes since Monday, and so on. If a server malfunctions on Thursday and you need to restore the server from backup, you do this by restoring the normal backup from Sunday, the incremental backup from Monday, the incremental backup from Tuesday, and the incremental backup from Wednesday—in that order.

- **Normal backup with daily differential backups.** You perform a normal backup every Sunday and differential backups Monday through Saturday. Monday's differential backup contains changes since Sunday, as does Tuesday's differential backup, Wednesday's differential backup, and so on. If a server malfunctions on Thursday and you need to restore the server from backup, you do this by restoring the normal backup from Sunday and then the differential backup from Wednesday.

Using media rotation and maintaining additional media sets

As part of your backup strategy, you might also want to use copy backups to create extended backup sets for monthly and quarterly use. You might also want to use a media rotation scheme to ensure that you always have a current copy of your data and several previous data sets. Although tapes were traditionally used for backups, many organizations have moved to disk backup instead of tape backup as disk drives have become more affordable. With disks you can use a rotation schedule similar to the one you use with tapes.

The point of a media rotation scheme is to reuse media in a consistent and organized manner. If you use a media rotation scheme, monthly and quarterly media sets can simply be media sets that you are rotating to off-site storage. Consider the following media rotation scenarios:

- **Media rotation with three weekly media sets and one monthly media set.** In a 24/7 environment, you use a total of 14 disk drives as a media set. Seven of those disk drives contain your normal weekly backups for a set of servers. The other seven disk drives contain your daily incremental backups for that set of servers—one tape or disk for each day of the week. Three weekly media sets are maintained on site. Once a month, you rotate the previous week's media set to off-site storage.

- **Media rotation with three weekly media sets, one monthly media set, and one quarterly media set.** In a 9-to-5 environment, you use a total of 14 disk drives as a media set. Nine of those disk drives contain your normal weekly backups for a set of servers. The other five disk drives contain your daily incremental backups for that set of servers—one tape or disk for each workday. Three weekly media sets are maintained on site. Once a month, you rotate the previous week's media set to off-site storage. Once a quarter, you rotate the previous week's media set to off-site storage.

Backing up and recovering your data

Many backup and recovery solutions are available for use with Windows Server 2012 R2. When selecting a backup utility, you need to keep in mind the types of backups you want to perform and the types of data you are backing up.

Windows Server 2012 R2 includes Windows Server Backup and backup command-line tools. Windows Server Backup is a basic and easy-to-use backup and recovery utility. When the related feature is installed on a server, you'll find a related option on the Administrative Tools menu. The utility is also added to Server Manager. A set of backup and recovery commands is accessible through the Wbadmin command-line tool. You run and use Wbadmin from an administrator command prompt. Type **wbadmin /?** for a full list of supported commands.

Windows Server Backup Module for Windows PowerShell provides a set of backup and recovery cmdlets accessible through Windows PowerShell. You run and use these cmdlets from an administrator PowerShell prompt. Enter **get-help *wb*** for a full list of supported cmdlets.

You can use Windows Server Backup to perform full, copy, and incremental backups on the local system. You can't use Windows Server Backup to perform differential backups. Windows Server Backup uses the Volume Shadow Copy Service (VSS) to create fast block-level backups of the operating system, files and folders, and disk volumes. After you create the first full backup, you can configure Windows Server Backup to perform either full or incremental backups on a recurring scheduled basis automatically.

When you use Windows Server Backup, you need separate dedicated media for storing archives of scheduled backups. Although you can't back up to tapes, you can back up to external and internal disks, DVDs, and shared folders. Although you can recover full volumes from

DVD backups, you can't recover individual files, folders, or application data from DVD backups. Windows Server Backup automatically manages backup disks for you. You can run backups to multiple disks in rotation just by adding each disk as a scheduled backup location. After you configure a disk as a scheduled backup location, Windows Server Backup automatically manages the disk storage, ensuring that you no longer need to worry about a disk running out of space. Windows Server Backup automatically reuses the space of older backups when creating newer backups. To help ensure that you can plan for additional storage needs, Windows Server Backup displays the backups that are available and the current disk usage information.

You can use Windows Server Backup for recovery in several ways. Rather than having to manually restore files from multiple backups if the files are stored in incremental backups, you can recover folders and files by choosing the date on which you backed up the version of the item or items you want to restore. You can recover data to the same server hardware or to new server hardware that has no operating system.

Using the backup utility

To perform backup and recovery operations, you must use an account that is a member of the Administrators or Backup Operators group. Only members of these groups have authority to back up and restore files, regardless of ownership and permissions. File owners and those who have been given control over files can also back up files, but only the files that they own or the files that they have permission to access.

The Windows Server backup and recovery tools are available for all editions of Windows Server 2012 R2. Although you can't install the graphical components of these utilities on core installations, you can use the command line or manage backups remotely from another computer.

You install the Windows backup and recovery tools using Server Manager. In Server Manager, select Manage and then tap or click Add Roles And Features. This starts the Add Roles And Features Wizard. After you select the server where these tools should be installed, continue through the wizard pages until you get to the Select Features page. On this page, select Windows Server Backup. Tap or click Next and then tap or click Install.

When the wizard finishes installing the selected backup and recovery tools, tap or click Close. From now on, Windows Server Backup will be available as an option on the Tools menu in Server Manager.

The first time you use Windows Server Backup, you'll see a warning that no backup has been configured for the computer, as shown in Figure 21-2. You clear this warning by creating a backup using the Back Up Once feature or by scheduling backups to run automatically using the Backup Schedule feature.

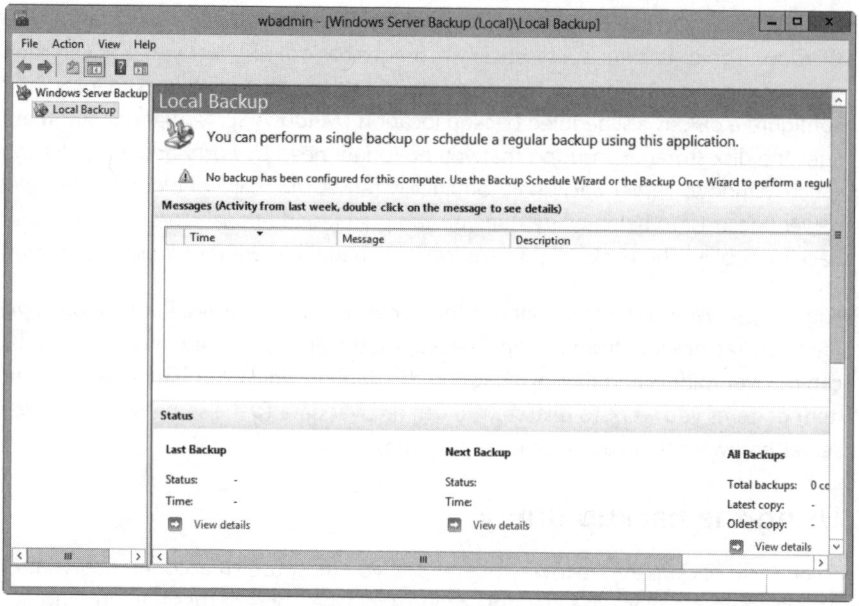

Figure 21-2 Get started with Windows Server Backup.

When you use Windows Server Backup, the first backup of a server is always a full backup. This is because the full backup process clears the archive bits on files so that Windows Server Backup can track which files are updated subsequently. Whether Windows Server Backup performs subsequent full or incremental backups depends on the default performance settings that you configure. When the Local Backup node is selected, you can configure the default performance settings by tapping or clicking Configure Performance Settings in the actions pane. Or on the Action menu you can do one of the following and then tap or click OK:

- Select Normal Backup Performance to perform full backups of all attached drives.

- Select Faster Backup Performance to perform incremental backups of all attached drives.

- Select Custom and then, from the option lists provided, select whether to perform full or incremental backups for individual attached drives.

After you configure the default performance settings, you can start a full or copy backup by choosing Backup Once from the Action menu or in the actions pane. You can configure a backup schedule by tapping or clicking Backup Schedule on the Action menu or in the actions pane. These options are available only when the Local Backup node is selected.

Inside OUT

Performing backups at the command line

Wbadmin is the command-line counterpart to Windows Server Backup. After you install the Backup Command-Line Tools feature as discussed previously, you can use Wbadmin to manage backup and recovery from an administrator command prompt.

Wbadmin is located in the %SystemRoot%\system32\ directory. When you are working with Wbadmin, you can get help on available commands. To view a list of management commands, type **wbadmin /?** at the command prompt. To view the syntax for a specific management command, type **wbadmin CommandName /?**, where *CommandName* is the name of the management command you want to examine, such as **wbadmin enable backup /?**.

Most Wbadmin commands use the *–backupTarget* parameter. The backup target is the storage location you want to work with, and it can be expressed as a local volume name, such as D:, or as a network share path, such as \\BackupServer05\backups \Server24.

CHAPTER 21

Windows Backup has several improvements for Windows Server 2012 R2. Previously, you could not back up volumes larger than 2 terabytes (TBs) and volumes had to have 512-byte sectors. Now you can back up volumes larger than 2 TBs and volumes can use sector sizes other than 512 bytes. Previously, when you backed up virtual machines as part of a volume backup, the virtual machines could not be backed up or restored separately. Now you can select individual virtual machines to include in a backup and restore individual virtual machines from a recovery point. Additionally, when you are backing up a volume, you can specify a deletion policy to determine whether backups should be deleted after a certain number of backups have elapsed or whether they should be deleted only when space is needed for additional backups.

Backing up your data

As part of your planning for each server you plan to back up, you should consider which volumes you want to back up and whether backups will include system-state recovery data, application data, or both. As part of the backup process, you also need to specify a storage location for backups. Keep the following in mind when you are choosing storage locations:

- When you use an internal hard disk for storing backups, you are limited in how you can recover your system. You can recover the data from a volume, but you can't rebuild the entire disk structure.

- When you use an external hard disk for storing backups, the disk will be dedicated for storing your backups and will not be visible in File Explorer. Choosing this option will format the selected disk or disks, removing any existing data.

- When you use a remote shared folder for storing backups, your backup will be overwritten each time you create a new backup. Do not choose this option if you want to store multiple backups for each server.

- When you use removable media or DVDs for storing backups, you can recover only entire volumes, not applications or individual files. The media you use must be at least 1 gigabyte (GB) in size.

When you create or schedule backups, you need to specify the volumes that you want to include, and this will affect the ways you can recover your servers and your data. Back up just critical volumes if you want to be able to recover only the operating system. Back up just individual volumes if you want to be able to recover only files, applications, or data from those volumes.

Back up all volumes with application data if you want to be able to fully recover a server, with its system state and application data. Because you are backing up all files, the system state, and application data, you should be able to fully restore your server using only the Windows backup tools.

Back up all volumes without application data if you want to be able to restore a server and its applications separately. With this technique, you back up the server using the Windows tools and then back up applications using third-party tools or tools built into the applications. You can fully recover a server using the Windows backup utilities and then use a third-party utility to restore backups of application data.

Scheduling backups

To automate the backup process, you can create a scheduled task that runs Windows Server Backup for you. Task creation and scheduling processes are integrated into Windows Server Backup. You can schedule automated backups using Windows Server Backup. Select the Local Backup node and then tap or click Backup Schedule on the Action menu or in the actions pane to start the Backup Schedule Wizard. After scanning the available disks, Windows Server Backup starts the Backup Schedule Wizard. Tap or click Next.

On the Select Backup Configuration page, shown in Figure 21-3, note the backup size listed under the Full Server option. This is the storage space required to back up the server data, applications, and system state. To back up all volumes on the server, choose the Full Server option and then tap or click Next. To back up selected volumes on the server, choose Custom and then tap or click Next.

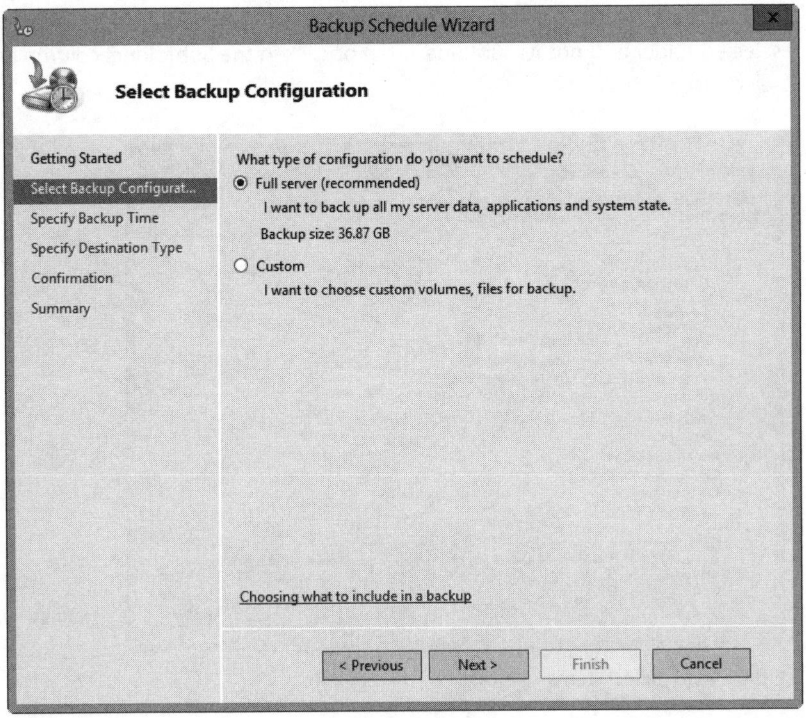

Figure 21-3 Select data to be included in the backup.

If you chose Custom, the Select Items For Backup page is displayed. Tap or click Add Items. As shown in Figure 21-4, select the check boxes for the volumes that you want to back up and clear the check boxes for the volumes that you want to exclude. Only locally attached disks can be included in scheduled backups. Volumes that contain boot files, operating system files, or applications are included in the backup by default and can't be excluded. Choose the Bare Metal Recovery option if you want to be able to fully recover the operating system. If the server is a Hyper-V host, you can select individual virtual servers to back up using their saved state and the host component.

Next, tap or click Advanced Settings to display the Advanced Settings dialog box. You can now do the following:

- Use the options in the Exclusions tab to exclude files by folder and type. To define an exclusion, tap or click Add Exclusion, use the Select Items To Exclude dialog box to select a folder that should be excluded, and then tap or click OK. This adds the folder to the Excluded File Types list in the Advanced Settings dialog box. By default, all files and subfolders in the specified folder are excluded. To exclude specific types of files in the selected folder, tap or click in the File Type column and enter the file types to exclude in a comma-separated list, such as .tmp, .temp, .htm, and .html. To include only the selected folder and not its subfolders, tap or click in the Subfolders column and then select No.

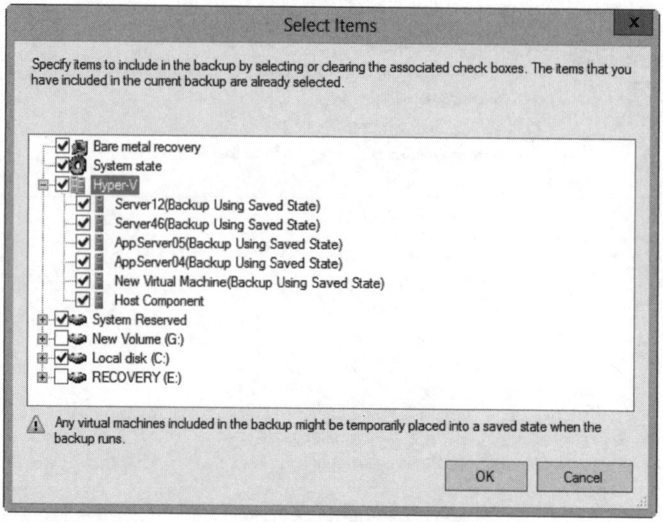

Figure 21-4 Select items to include in the backup.

- Use the options in the VSS Settings tab to specify the type of backup to create. The default backup type is a copy backup, which retains application log files and doesn't clear the archive attribute on files. Copy backup maintains compatibility with other products you might use to back up applications that are on volumes included in the backup. If you don't use other products to back up applications, you can instead use a full backup, which clears the archive attribute and doesn't retain application logs.

On the Specify Backup Time page, shown in Figure 21-5, you can specify how often and when you want to run backups. To perform backups daily at a specific time, choose Once A Day and then select the time to start running the daily backup. To perform backups multiple times each day, choose More Than Once A Day. Next, tap or click a start time under Available Time and then tap or click Add to move the time under Scheduled Time. Repeat for each start time that you want to add. When you are ready to continue, tap or click Next.

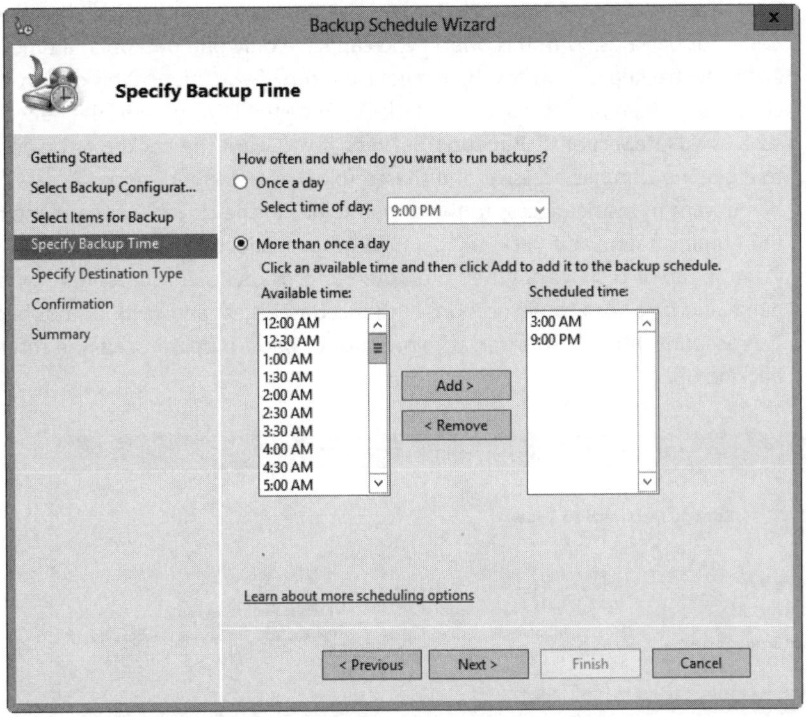

Figure 21-5 Schedule when backups occur.

On the Specify Destination Type page, shown in Figure 21-6, you have these options:

- **Back Up To A Hard Disk That Is Dedicated For Backups.** Use this option to specify a dedicated hard disk for backups. Each external disk can store up to 512 backups, depending on the amount of data contained in each backup. If you select multiple disks, Windows Server Backup will rotate among them. Any selected disks will be formatted and then dedicated only to backups. This option is recommended because you'll get the best performance. If you choose this option, tap or click Next, select the disk or disks to use, and then tap or click Next again.

- **Back Up To A Volume.** Use this option to write backups to individual volumes on a hard disk. Because any volume you select is not dedicated to backups, it can be used for other purposes. However, the performance of any of the selected volumes is reduced while backups are being written. If you choose this option, tap or click Next, use the Add and Remove options to select the volumes to use, and then tap or click Next again.

CHAPTER 21

- **Back Up To A Shared Network Folder.** Use this option to specify a shared network folder for backups. With this option you can have only one backup at a time because each new backup overwrites the previous backup. If you choose this option, tap or click Next. When prompted, tap or click OK. Type the UNC path to the network share, such as **\\DataServer18\Backups\Servers**. If you want the backup to be accessible to everyone who has access to the shared folder, select Inherit under Access Control. If you want to restrict access to the shared folder to the current user and members of the Administrators and Backup Operators groups, select Do Not Inherit under Access Control. Tap or click Next. When prompted to provide access credentials, type the user name and password for an account authorized to access and write to the shared folder. This account should also be an administrator or backup operator on the server you are backing up.

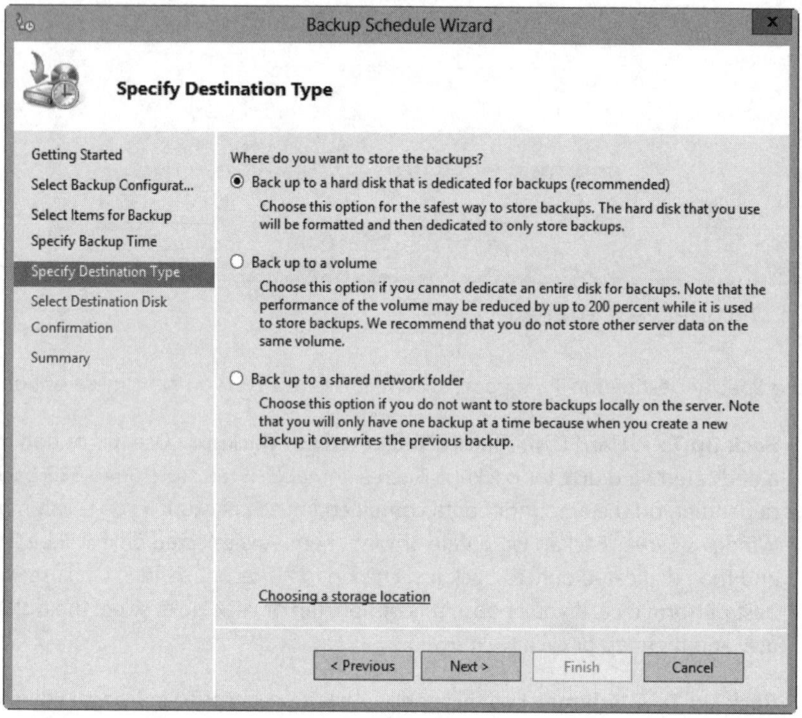

Figure 21-6 Select a backup target.

On the Confirmation page, review the details and then tap or click Finish. With dedicated backup disks, the wizard will then format the disks. The formatting process might take several minutes or considerably longer, depending on the size of the disk. When this process finishes, the Summary page should show that you successfully created the backup schedule. Tap or click Close. Your backups are now scheduled for the selected server. You need to check period-ically to ensure that backups are being performed as expected and that the backup schedule meets current needs.

After you configure scheduled backups on a server, you can modify or stop the scheduled backups using the Backup Schedule Wizard. Choose Backup Schedule from the Action menu or in the actions pane. On the Modify Scheduled Backup Settings page, Modify Backup is selected by default. Use this option if you want to add or remove backup items, times, or targets.

If you want to stop the scheduled backups from running, select Stop Backup instead, tap or click Next, and then tap or click Finish. When prompted to confirm, tap or click Yes and then tap or click Close. Keep in mind that stopping backups releases dedicated backup disks for normal use. Backup archives are not deleted from the backup disks and remain available for use in recovery.

Performing a one-time backup

Regardless of whether you want to back up data using a recurring schedule or perform a manual backup, the techniques are similar. In this section I discuss manual backups so that you know how to perform backups manually. You can perform a manual backup using Windows Server Backup. Tap or click Backup Once on the Action menu or in the actions pane to start the Backup Once Wizard.

After scanning the available disks, Windows Server Backup gives you the backup options shown in Figure 21-7. If you want to back up the server using the same options that you use for the Backup Schedule Wizard, choose Scheduled Backup Options, tap or click Next, and then tap or click Backup to perform the backup. Otherwise, choose Different Options, tap or click Next, and then continue through the wizard pages to perform the backup.

On the Select Backup Configuration page, shown in Figure 21-8, note the backup size listed under the Full Server option. This is the storage space required to back up the server data, applications, and system state. To back up all volumes on the server, choose the Full Server option and then tap or click Next. To back up selected volumes on the server, choose Custom and then tap or click Next.

CHAPTER 21

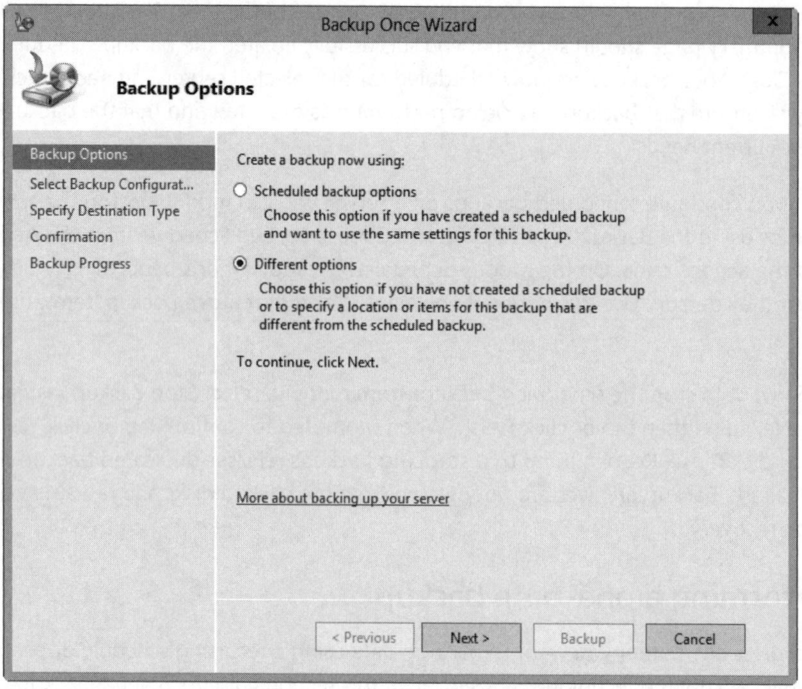

Figure 21-7 Choose Different Options to manually configure volumes to back up.

If you chose Custom, the Select Items For Backup page is displayed. Tap or click Add Items. Select the check boxes for the volumes that you want to back up and clear the check boxes for the volumes that you want to exclude. If you want to be able to fully recover the operating system, choose the Bare Metal Recovery option. If the server is a Hyper-V host, you can select individual virtual servers to back up using their saved state and also back up the host component. Tap or click OK and then tap or click Next.

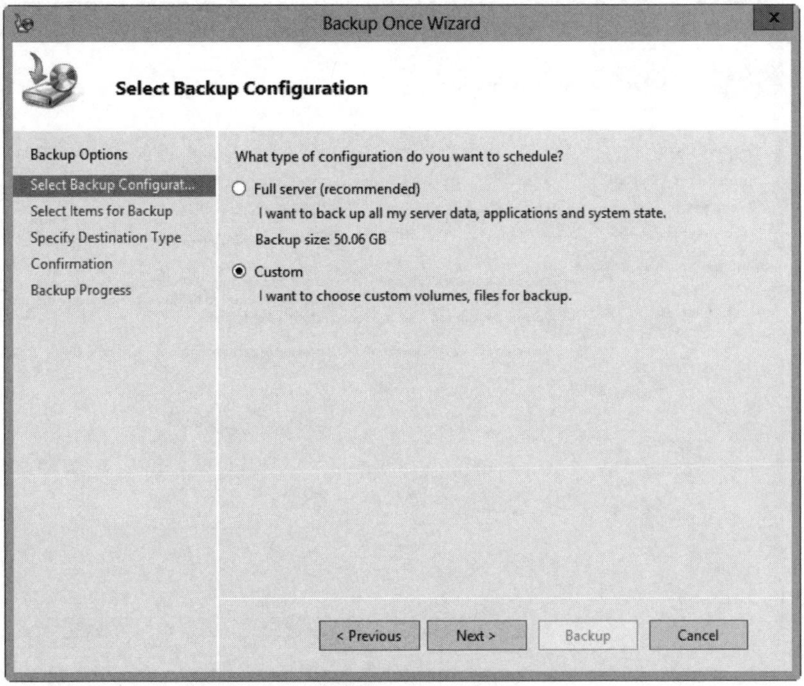

Figure 21-8 Choose the backup configuration.

On the Specify Destination Type page, do either of the following:

- If you want to back up to local drives, select Local Drives and then tap or click Next. On the Select Backup Destination page, shown in Figure 21-9, select the internal or DVD drive to use as the backup target. If you select a volume that is being used for scheduled backups, you can continue only if you used the same settings as you used for scheduled backups. Backups are compressed when stored on a DVD. As a result, the size of the backup on a DVD might be smaller than the volume on the server and you will be able to recover only full volumes. Also, you can't perform a partial backup of volumes or component files to a DVD. Tap or click Next.

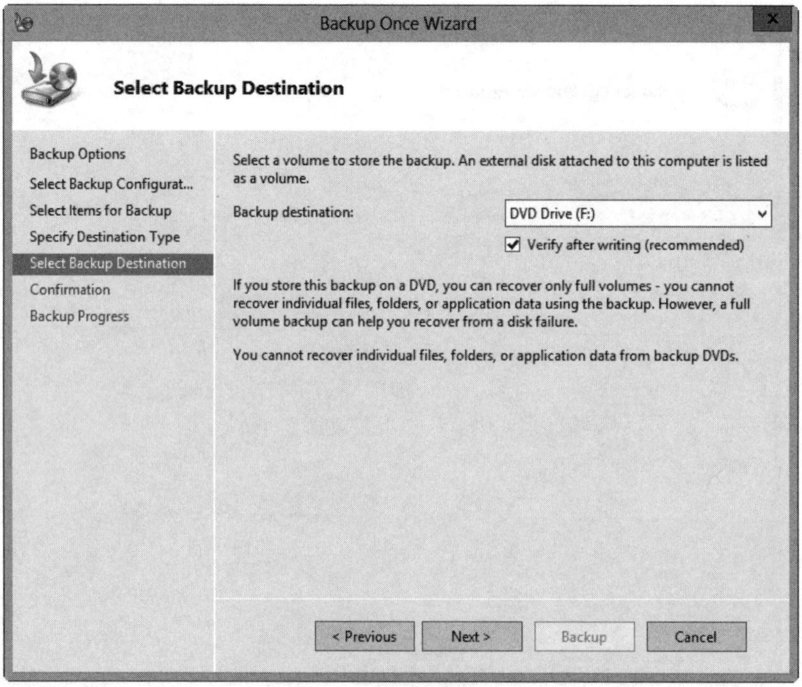

Figure 21-9 Choose a volume to store the backup.

- If you want to back up to a remote shared folder, select Remote Shared Folder and then tap or click Next. On the Specify Remote Folder page, shown in Figure 21-10, type the UNC path to the remote folder, such as **\\BackupServer06\backups\Server21**. If you want the backup to be accessible to everyone who has access to the shared folder, choose Inherit under Access Control. If you want to restrict access to the shared folder to the current user, administrators, and backup operators, choose Do Not Inherit under Access Control. Tap or click Next. When prompted to provide access credentials, type the user name and password for an account authorized to access and write to the shared folder.

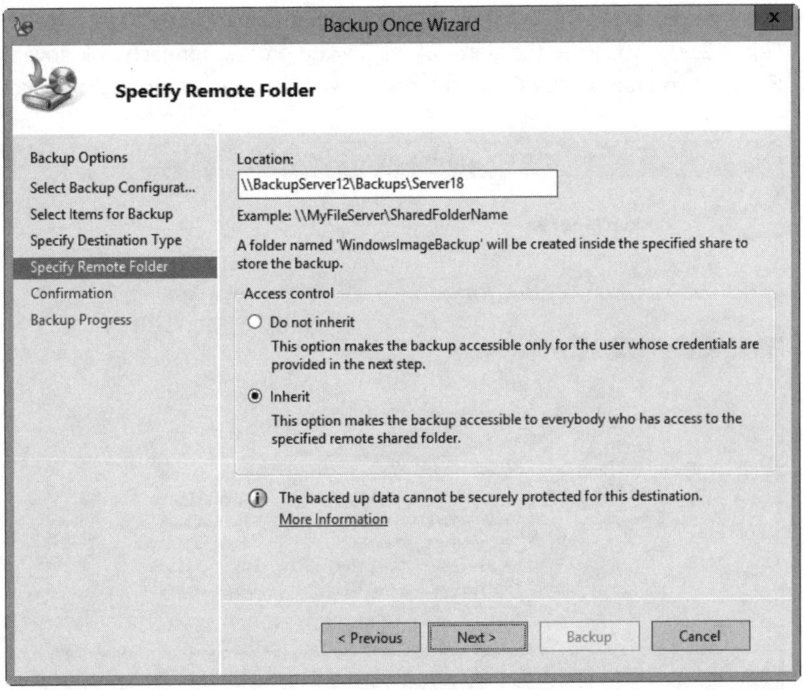

Figure 21-10 Restrict or allow user access using inheriting options.

Afterward, tap or click Next and then tap or click Backup. The wizard starts by creating a shadow copy of the selected volumes. When this process finishes, the wizard tries to write to the media you selected. If you are backing up to DVD, note the disk label in the prompt to insert a disk. As shown in Figure 21-11, the prompt includes a time and date stamp and a unique identifier for each disk in the backup set in sequential order. To help you keep track of your disk, you should write the label on the disk before inserting it in the DVD drive.

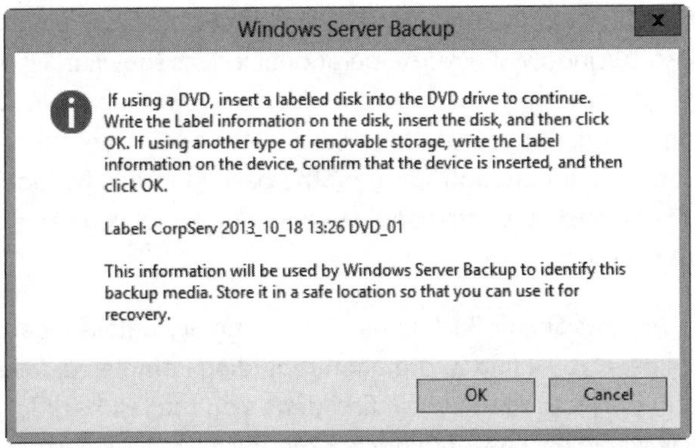

Figure 21-11 Insert a disk into the DVD drive to continue the backup.

The wizard displays the progress of the backup in the Backup Progress dialog box, as shown in Figure 21-12. You'll see the status of the backup process for each disk drive that you are backing up. If you tap or click Close, the backup will continue to run in the background.

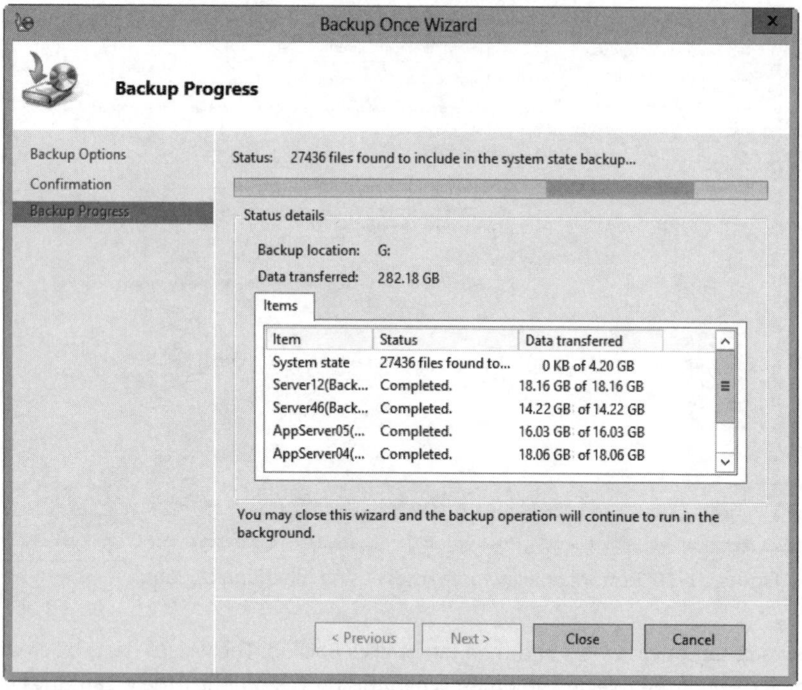

Figure 21-12 The Backup Once Wizard displays the progress of the backup.

Tracking scheduled and manual backups

Whenever Windows Server Backup backs up a server, it writes events related to the Windows event logs. You'll find events related to shadow copies in the Application log and all other backup events in the Microsoft\Windows\Backup\Operational log, as shown in Figure 21-13. By looking through the Operational log, you can quickly determine when backups were started, when they were completed, and reasons for failure, such as when another administrator canceled backups or there was not enough space on the backup target. By looking at the time difference between when a backup started and when it completed, you can also determine how long backups are taking.

As shown in Figure 21-14, Windows Server Backup provides summary details regarding backups as well. In the Messages pane you'll find information regarding completed, failed, and currently running backups. In the Status pane you'll find details on the last backup, the next scheduled backup, and all available backups. Tap or click the View Details links to determine what volumes were backed up, the backup type, and more. In the Details dialog box, you can track errors that occurred during the backup in the Errors tab.

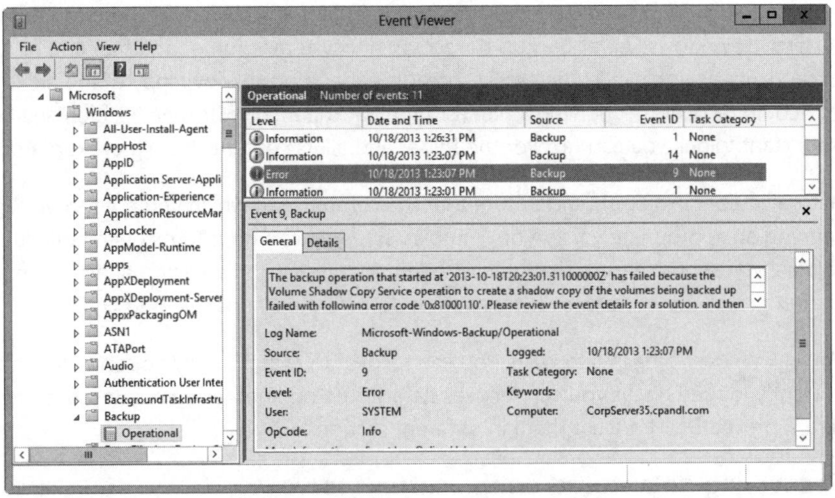

Figure 21-13 Windows Server Backup writes backup events in the event logs.

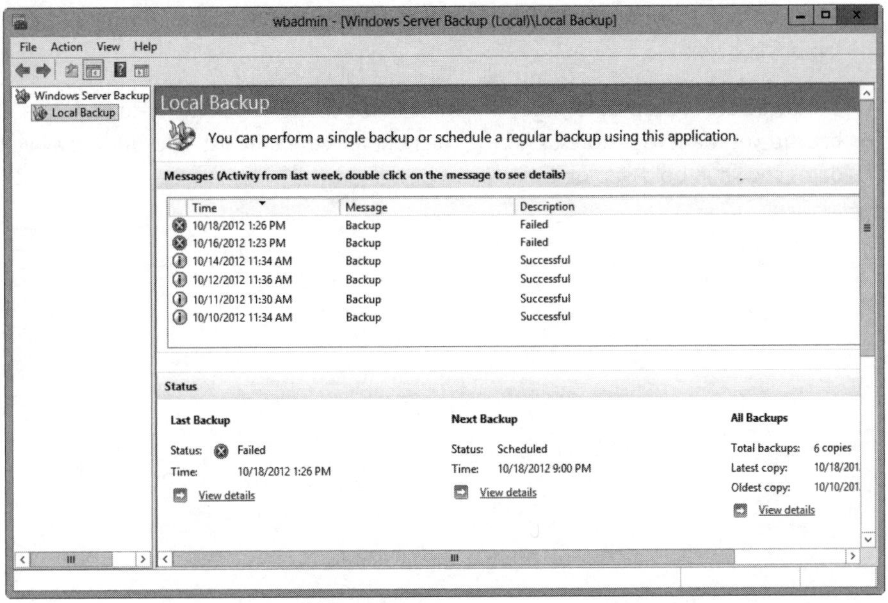

Figure 21-14 Review the backup status in Windows Server Backup.

Recovering your data

Windows Server 2012 R2 provides separate processes for system-state recovery, full-server recovery, and recovery of individual volumes and files and folders. You use the Recovery Wizard in Windows Server Backup to recover nonsystem volumes and files and folders from a backup. For example, if Mary loses a spreadsheet and no shadow copy of the file is available, you could recover the individual file from the backup archive. If John accidentally deletes an important folder, you can recover the folder and all its contents from a backup archive.

Before you begin, you should ensure that the computer to which you are recovering files is running an appropriate version of Windows Server. If you want to recover individual files and folders, you should ensure that at least one backup exists on an external disk or in a remote shared folder. You can't recover files and folders from backups saved to DVDs.

You can recover data in two ways. You can recover data stored on the server to which you are currently logged on, or you can recover data stored on another server. Because these are different procedures, I discuss them in different sections.

Recovering data stored on the current server

To recover nonsystem volumes, files and folders, or application data, start Windows Server Backup. Tap or click Recover in the actions pane or on the Action menu to start the Recovery Wizard. On the Getting Started page, choose This Server, as shown in Figure 21-15, and then tap or click Next.

On the Select Backup Date page, shown in Figure 21-16, select the date and time of the backup you want to restore using the calendar and the time list. Backups are available for dates shown in bold. Tap or click Next.

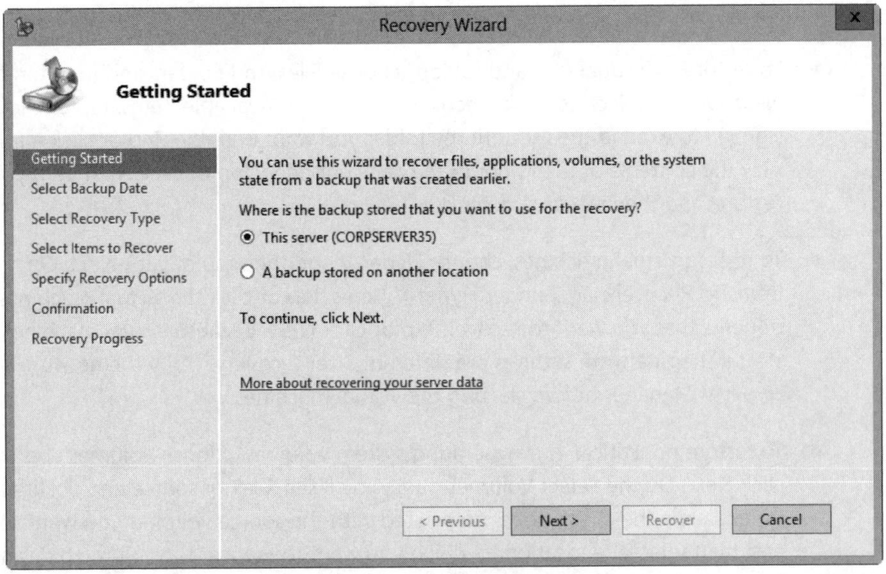

Figure 21-15 Select a server from which to recover data.

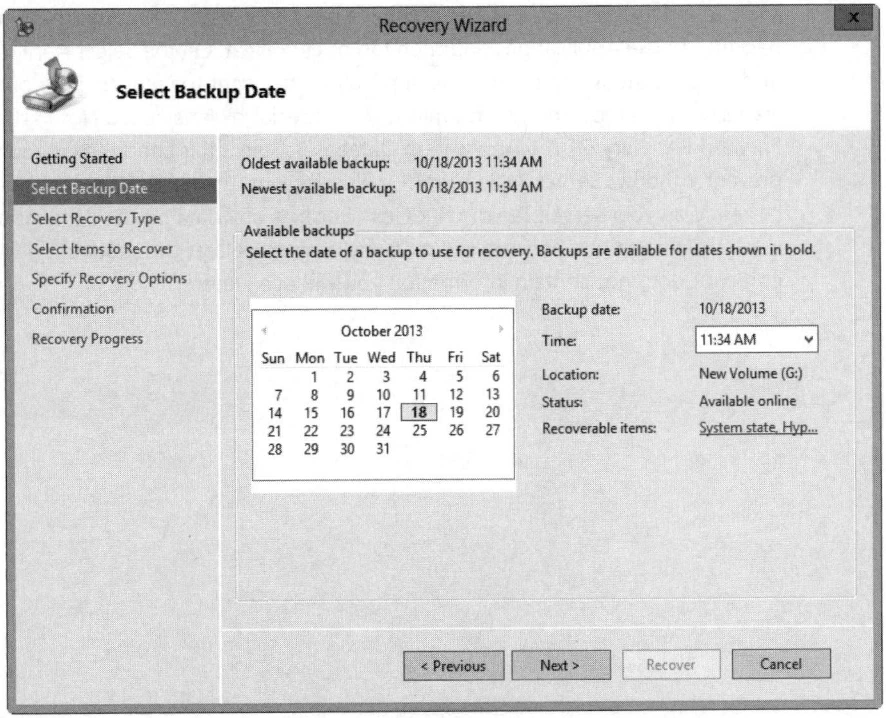

Figure 21-16 Select the date and time of the backup you want to restore.

On the Select Recovery Type page, shown in Figure 21-17, do one of the following:

- To restore individual files and folders, choose Files And Folders and then tap or click Next. On the Select Items To Recover page, under Available Items, tap or click the plus sign (+) to expand the list until the folder you want is visible. Tap or click a folder to display the contents of the folder in the adjacent pane, tap or click each item you want to restore, and then tap or click Next.

- To restore virtual machines, choose Hyper-V and then tap or click Next. On the Select Items To Recover page, under Hyper-V Items, tap or click the virtual machines and components that you want to recover. Tap or click Next. Because virtual machines might not start if their network settings are different after recovery, verify the network settings in Hyper-V Manager before starting the virtual machines.

- To restore noncritical, non–operating system volumes, choose Volumes and then tap or click Next. On the Select Volumes page, you'll see a list of source and destination volumes. Select the check boxes associated with the source volumes you want to recover and then select the location to which you want to recover the volume by using the Destination Volume lists. Tap or click Next. If prompted to confirm the recovery operation, tap or click Yes.

- To restore data from applications that have been registered with Windows Server Backup, choose Applications and then tap or click Next. On the Select Application page, under Applications, tap or click the application you want to recover. If the backup you are using is the most recent, you might see a check box labeled Do Not Perform A Roll-Forward Recovery Of The Application Databases. Select this check box if you want to prevent Windows Server Backup from rolling forward the application database that is currently on your server. Tap or click Next. Because any data on the destination volume will be lost when you perform the recovery, make sure that the destination volume is empty or does not contain information you will need later.

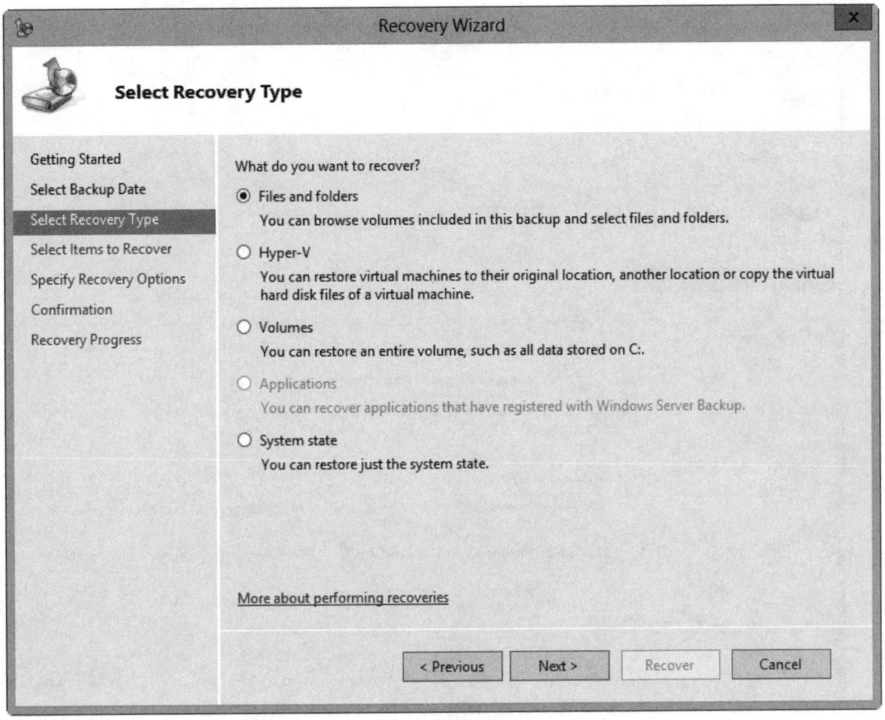

Figure 21-17 Specify the type of data to recover.

On the Specify Recovery Options page, shown in Figure 21-18, specify whether you want to restore data to its original location (nonsystem files only) or an alternate location. For an alternate location, type the path to the location or tap or click Browse to select it. With applications, you can copy application data to an alternate location. You can't, however, recover applications to a different location or computer.

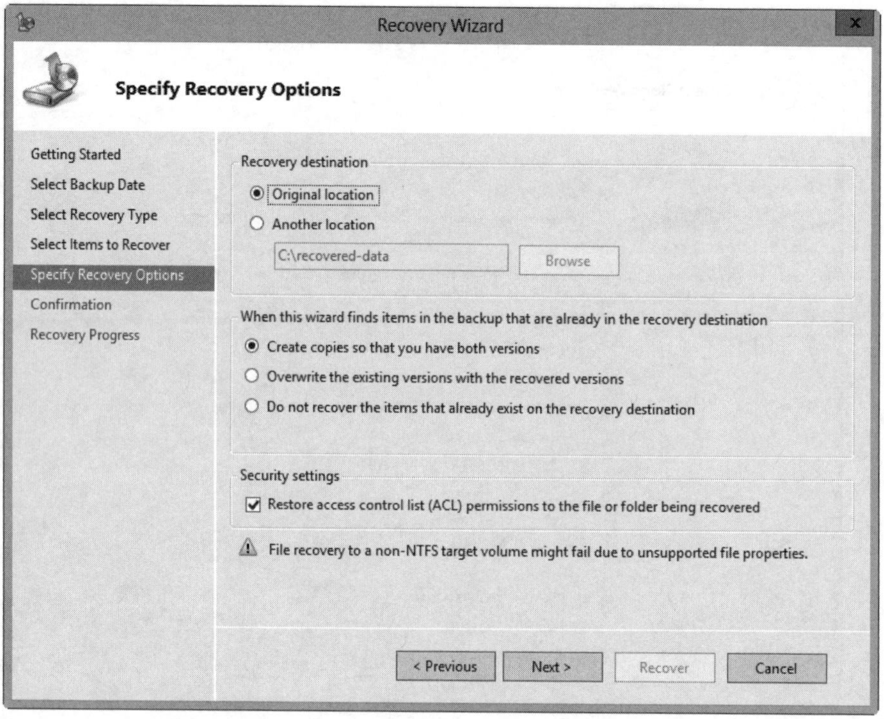

Figure 21-18 Specify the location to which you want to restore the backup.

For file and folder recovery, choose a recovery technique to apply when files and folders already exist in the recovery location. You can create copies so that you have both versions of the file or folder, overwrite existing files with recovered files, or skip duplicate files and folders to preserve existing files. By default, the Recovery Wizard restores the security settings. In most cases you'll want to use this option. When you're ready to continue, tap or click Next.

On the Confirmation page, review the details and then tap or click Recover to restore the specified items. The wizard displays the progress of the recovery in the Recovery Progress dialog box. If you tap or click Close, the recovery will continue to run in the background.

Windows Server Backup provides summary details regarding recovery in the Messages pane. You'll find information regarding completed, failed, and currently running recovery operations. Windows Server Backup also writes recovery events related to the Windows event logs. You'll find events related to shadow copies in the Application log and all other recovery events in the Microsoft\Windows\Backup\Operational log. By looking through the Operational log, you can quickly determine when recovery operations were started, when they were completed, and reasons for failure. By navigating through the recovery-related events, you can also find an event that provides the location of a log file that lists all files restored in the recovery operation. Figure 21-19 shows an example.

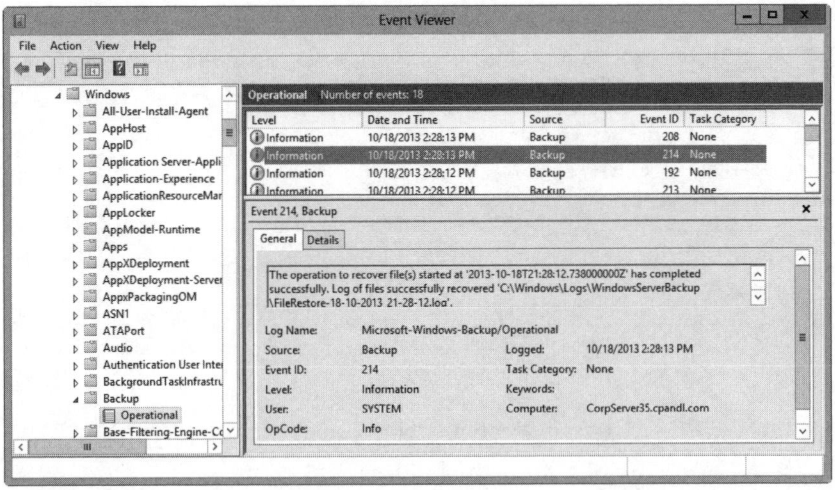

Figure 21-19 Windows Server Backup writes tracking events for recovery in the event logs.

Recovering data stored on another server

To recover nonsystem volumes, files and folders, or application data, start Windows Server Backup. Tap or click Recover in the actions pane or on the Action menu to start the Recovery Wizard. On the Getting Started page, choose A Backup Stored On Another Location, as shown in Figure 21-20, and then tap or click Next.

On the Specify Location Type page, select Remote Shared Folder and then tap or click Next. On the Specify Remote Folder page, type the path to the folder that contains the backup, such as **\\FileServer07\Servers\Server18Backup**. If you are prompted to provide your logon credentials, enter the user name and password for an account with owner or coowner permissions on the shared folder.

The rest of the recovery operation is the same as discussed previously, starting with the Select Backup Date page.

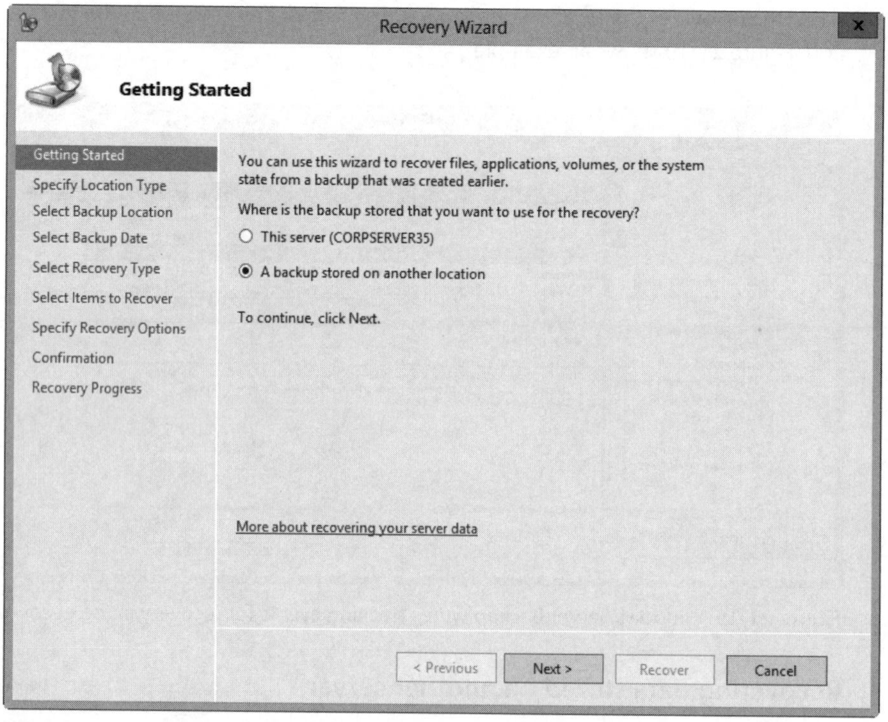

Figure 21-20 Recover data stored on another server.

Recovering the system state

There are over 50,000 system-state files, and these files use 4 to 7 GBs of disk space. The fastest and easiest way to back up and restore a server's system state is to use Wbadmin. With Wbadmin, you can use the Start SystemStateBackup command to create a backup of the system state for a computer and the Start SystemStateRecovery command to restore a computer's system state.

> **NOTE**
>
> When you select a system-state restore on a domain controller, you have to be in the Directory Services Restore mode. To learn how to restore Active Directory, see the section entitled "Backing up and restoring Active Directory" later in this chapter.

You can back up a server's system state by typing the following at an elevated command prompt:

```
wbadmin start systemstatebackup -backupTarget:VolumeName
```

Here, *VolumeName* is the storage location for the backup, such as G:.

You can restore a server's system state by typing the following at an elevated command prompt:

```
wbadmin start systemstaterecovery -backupTarget:VolumeName
```

Here, *VolumeName* is the storage location that contains the backup you want to recover, such as G:.

You can use other parameters for recovery operations as well. Use the *–recoveryTarget* parameter to restore to an alternate location. Use the *–machine* parameter to specify the name of the computer to recover if the original backup location contains backups for multiple computers. Use the *–authorsysvol* parameter to perform an authoritative restore of the Sysvol.

Restoring the operating system and the full system

As discussed previously, Windows Server 2012 R2 includes startup repair features that can recover a server in the case of corrupted or missing system files. These features can also recover from some types of boot failures involving the boot manager. If these processes fail and the boot manager is the reason you can't start the server, you can use the Windows Server 2012 R2 installation disk to restore the boot manager and enable startup.

When the automated recovery features fail to recover normal operations, you can recover a server's operating system or perform a full system recovery by using a Windows installation disk and a backup that you created earlier with Windows Server Backup. These two operations differ in fundamental ways:

- With an operating system recovery, you recover all critical volumes but don't recover nonsystem volumes. A critical volume is a volume that has files that the operating system needs during startup and normal operations. A critical volume also includes both the boot volume and the system volume (which might or might not be the same volume). You should use this method only when you can't recover the operating system using other means.

- With a full system recovery, Windows Server Backup reformats and repartitions all disks that are attached to the server and then sets about recovering the server's volumes. Data that was not included in the original backup will be deleted when you recover the system, including any volumes that are currently used by the server but were not included in the backup. You should use this method only when you want to recover the server data onto separate hardware or when all other attempts to recover the server on the existing hardware have failed.

Before you begin, you should ensure that your backup data is available. You can recover a server's operating system or perform a full system recovery by inserting the Windows installation disk into the DVD drive and turning on the computer. If needed, press the required key to boot from the disk. Windows Setup should start automatically. On the Install Windows page, select the language, time, and keyboard layout options that you want to use. Tap or click Next.

Don't click Install Now. Instead, tap or click Repair Your Computer. On the Automatic Repair screen, tap or click Troubleshoot. On the Advanced Options screen, tap or click System Image Recovery and then tap or click Windows Server 2012 R2 to select it as your target operating system. On the Select A System Image Backup page, tap or click Use The Latest Available System Image (Recommended) and then tap or click Next. Or tap or click Select A System Image and then tap or click Next.

If you select an image to restore, do one of the following on the Select The Location Of The Backup page:

- Tap or click the location that contains the system image you want to use and then tap or click Next. Afterward, tap or click the system image you want to use and then tap or click Next.

- To browse for a system image on the network, tap or click Advanced and then tap or click Search For A System Image On The Network. When you are prompted to confirm that you want to connect to the network, tap or click Yes. In the Network Folder text box, specify the location of the server and shared folder in which the system image is stored, such as \\BackupServer15\Backups, and then tap or click OK.

- To install a driver for a backup device that doesn't show up in the location list, tap or click Advanced and then tap or click Install A Driver. Insert the installation media for the device and then tap or click OK. After Windows installs the device driver, the backup device should be listed in the location list.

On the Choose Additional Restore Options page, complete the following optional tasks and then tap or click Next:

- Select the Format And Repartition Disks check box to delete existing partitions and reformat the destination disks to be the same as the backup.

- Select Only Restore System Drives to restore only the drives from the backup that are required to run Windows: the boot, system, and recovery volumes. If the server has data drives, they will not be restored.

- Tap or click Install Drivers to install device drivers for the hardware you are recovering.

- Tap or click Advanced to specify whether the computer is restarted and the disks are checked for errors immediately after the recovery operation is completed.

On the Confirmation page, review the details for the restoration and then tap or click Finish. The wizard then restores the operating system or the full server as appropriate for the options you selected.

Backing up and restoring Active Directory

Backing up Active Directory is easy. Recovery of Active Directory, however, is different from recovery of other types of network services. A key reason for this involves the way Active Directory data is replicated and restored. Because of this, let's look at backup and recovery strategies for Active Directory and then look at various restore techniques.

Backup and recovery strategies for Active Directory

Domain controllers have replication partners with whom they share information. When you have multiple domain controllers in a domain and one fails, the other domain controllers automatically detect the failure and change their replication topology accordingly. You can repair or replace the failed domain controller from backup. However, the restore doesn't recover Active Directory information stored on the domain controller.

To restore Active Directory on the failed domain controller, you use either a nonauthoritative or authoritative approach. A nonauthoritative restore allows the domain controller to come back online and then get replication updates from other domain controllers. An authoritative restore makes the restored domain controller the authority in the domain, and its data is replicated to other domain controllers.

In most cases you'll have multiple domain controllers in a domain, giving you flexibility in your disaster recovery plan. If one of the domain controllers fails, you can install a new domain controller, clone an existing domain controller, or promote an existing member server to be a domain controller. The directory on the new domain controller is updated automatically through replication. You could also recover the failed domain controller and then perform a nonauthoritative restore. In this case you would restore Active Directory on the domain controller and obtain directory updates from other domain controllers in the domain.

In some cases you might need to perform an authoritative restore of Active Directory. For example, if a large number of objects were deleted from Active Directory and you aren't using Active Directory Recycle Bin as discussed in the "Extensible Storage Engine" section of Chapter 10, "Active Directory architecture," the only way to recover those objects would be to use an authoritative restore. In this case you would restore Active Directory on a domain controller and use the recovered data as the master copy of the directory database. This data is then replicated to all other domain controllers.

The disaster recovery strategy you choose for Active Directory might depend on whether you have dedicated or nondedicated domain controllers, for the following reasons:

- When you have dedicated domain controllers that perform no other domain services, you can implement a very simple disaster recovery procedure for domain controllers. As long as you have multiple domain controllers in each domain, you can restore a failed domain controller by installing a new domain controller or cloning an existing domain controller and then populating the directory on this new domain controller. You can do so through replication or by recovering the domain controller using a nonauthoritative restore. You should always back up one or more of the domain controllers and their system state so that you always have a current snapshot of Active Directory in the backup archives. If you need to recover from a disaster that has caused all your domain controllers to fail or if Active Directory has been corrupted, you can recover using an authoritative restore in the Directory Services Restore mode.

- When you have nondedicated domain controllers, you should back up the system state whenever you perform a full backup of a domain controller. This stores a snapshot of Active Directory with the other pertinent system information that you can use to fully recover the domain controller. If a domain controller fails, you can recover the server the way you recover any server. You then have the option of restoring the system state data and Active Directory to allow the server to resume operating as a domain controller by using a nonauthoritative restore in the Directory Services Restore mode. If you need to recover from a disaster that has caused all your domain controllers to fail or if Active Directory has been corrupted, you also have the option of using an authoritative restore in the Directory Services Restore mode.

When planning backups of Active Directory, you should also remember the tombstone lifetime. In Chapter 10 I discussed how Active Directory doesn't actually delete objects when you remove them from the directory. Instead, objects are either logically deleted or *tombstoned* (marked for deletion) and this state is replicated to all the other domain controllers. By default, the deleted object lifetime and the tombstone lifetime are 60 days, meaning that a deleted object will remain in the directory for at least 60 days. To ensure that you don't accidentally restore objects that have actually been removed from Active Directory, you are prevented from restoring Active Directory if the backup archive is older than the tombstone lifetime. This means that, by default, you can't restore a backup of Active Directory that is older than 60 days.

System information other than Active Directory is contained in the system state. Any restore of Active Directory includes all that information, and that information will also be restored to its previous state. If a server's configuration changed since the backup, the configuration changes will be lost.

Performing a nonauthoritative restore of Active Directory

When a domain controller fails, you can restore it the way you restore any other server, except when it comes to Active Directory. With this in mind, first fix the problem that caused the server to fail. After you restore the server, you can then work to restore Active Directory.

You recover Active Directory by restoring the system state on the domain controller using a special recovery mode called Directory Services Restore mode. If you made changes to Active Directory since the backup, the system-state backup will not contain those changes. However, other domain controllers in the domain will have the most recent changes and the domain controller will be able to obtain those changes through the normal replication process.

When you want to restore Active Directory on a domain controller and have the domain controller get directory updates from other domain controllers, you perform a nonauthoritative restore. A nonauthoritative restore allows the domain controller to come back online and then get replication updates from other domain controllers.

Schedule a full server backup of a domain controller to ensure the recovery of the server operating system and application data in the event of a hardware failure. Schedule a separate backup of critical volumes to ensure timely recovery of Active Directory. To guard against unforeseen problems, schedule backups on at least two domain controllers for each domain and schedule additional backups on any domain controller with a unique application partition.

A full server backup is a backup of every volume on the server. You can use this type of backup to recover a domain controller onto new hardware. On a domain controller, critical volumes include the boot volume and the volumes that contain the following data:

- Operating system files

- The registry

- The Active Directory database and log files

- SYSVOL folders

You can use critical-volume backups to restore Active Directory on a domain controller. Critical-volume backups can also be restored and copied to transferrable media to install a new domain controller in the same domain.

The procedure to perform a full server or critical-volume recovery of a domain controller is the same as for any server. When you do this, you will also be performing a nonauthoritative restore of Active Directory. After the recovery is complete, restart the domain controller in the standard operations mode and then verify the installation. When you restart the domain controller, Active Directory automatically detects that it has been recovered from a backup. Active Directory will then perform an integrity check and reindex the database. From that point on the server can act as a domain controller and it has a directory database that is current as of the date of the backup. The domain controller then connects to its replication partners and begins updating the database so that any changes since the backup are reflected.

After you log on to the server, check Active Directory and verify that all of the objects that were present in the directory at the time of the backup are restored. The easiest way to confirm this is to browse Active Directory Users And Computers, Active Directory Domains And Trusts, and Active Directory Sites And Services.

Performing an authoritative restore of Active Directory

An authoritative restore is used when you need to recover Active Directory to a specific point in time and then replicate the restored data to all other domain controllers. Consider the following example: John accidentally deleted the Marketing organizational unit (OU) and all the objects it contained. Because the changes have already been replicated to all domain controllers in the domain and Recycle Bin is not enabled, the only way to fully restore the OU and the related objects would be to use an authoritative restore. Similarly, if Active Directory were somehow corrupted, the only way to fully recover Active Directory would be to use an authoritative restore.

When performing authoritative restores, you should consider several significant issues. The first and most important issue has to do with passwords used for computers and Windows NT LAN Manager (NTLM) trusts. These passwords are changed automatically every seven days. If you perform an authoritative restore of Active Directory, the restored data will contain the passwords that were in use when the backup archive was made. If you monitor the event logs after the restore, you might see related events or you might hear from users who are experiencing problems accessing resources in the domain.

Computer account passwords allow computers to authenticate themselves in a domain using a computer trust. If a computer password has changed, the computer might not be able to reauthenticate itself in the domain. In this case you might need to reset the computer account password by pressing and holding or right-clicking the computer account in Active Directory Users And Computers and then selecting Reset Account. If the reset of the password doesn't work, you might need to remove the computer account from the domain and then add it back.

Realm trusts are trusts between Active Directory domains and non-Windows Kerberos realms. If a trust password has changed, the trust between the Active Directory domains and the Kerberos realms might fail. In this case you might need to delete the trust and then re-create it, as discussed in the section entitled "Establishing external, shortcut, realm, and cross-forest trusts" in Chapter 11, "Designing and managing the domain environment."

Another significant issue when performing an authoritative restore has to do with group membership. Problems with group membership can occur after an authoritative restore for several reasons.

In the first case, an administrator might have updated a group object's membership on a domain controller that has not yet received the restored data. In this case the domain controller might replicate the changes to other domain controllers, causing a temporary inconsistency. The changes shouldn't be permanent, however, because when you perform an authoritative restore, the update sequence number (USN) of all restored objects is incremented by 100,000. This ensures that the restored data is authoritative and overwrites any existing data.

Another problem with group membership can occur if group objects contain user accounts that don't currently exist in the domain. In this case, if group objects are replicated before these user accounts are, the user accounts that don't currently exist in the domain will be seen as invalid user accounts. As a result, the user accounts will be deleted as group members. When the user accounts are later replicated, the user accounts will not be added back to the groups.

Although there is no way to control which objects are replicated first, there is a way to correct this problem. You must force the domain controller to replicate the group membership list with the group object. You can do this by creating a temporary user account and adding it to each group that contains user accounts that are currently not valid in the domain. Here's how this would work: you authoritatively restore and then restart the domain controller. The domain controller begins replicating its data to other domain controllers. When this initial replication process finishes, you create a temporary user account and add it to the requisite groups. The group membership list will then be replicated. If any domain controller has removed previously invalid user accounts as members of these groups, the domain controller will then return the user accounts to the group.

You can perform an authoritative restore by completing the following steps:

1. Perform a full server or critical-volume recovery of the domain controller. After you repair or rebuild the server, restart the server and access the Advanced Boot Options menu. Typically, to do this you must press F8 before the Windows splash screen appears.

2. From the Advanced Boot Options menu, choose Directory Services Repair Mode. Windows will then restart in Safe Mode without loading Active Directory components.

3. You next need to choose the operating system you want to start.

4. Log on to the server using the Administrator account with the Directory Services Repair Mode password that was configured on the domain controller when Active Directory was installed.

CHAPTER 21

5. The Desktop prompt warns you that you are running in Safe Mode, which allows you to fix problems with the server but makes some of your devices unavailable. Tap or click OK.

6. At an elevated command prompt, type **ntdsutil**. This starts the Directory Services Management Tool.

7. At the Ntdsutil prompt, type **authoritative restore**. You should now be at the Authoritative Restore prompt, where you have the following options:

   - You can authoritatively restore the entire Active Directory database by typing **restore database**. If you restore the entire Active Directory database, a significant amount of replication traffic will be generated throughout the domain and the forest. You should restore the entire database only if Active Directory has been corrupted or there is some other significant reason for doing so.

   - You can authoritatively restore a container and all its related objects (referred to as a *subtree*) by typing **restore subtree ObjectDN**, where *ObjectDN* is the distinguished name of the container to restore. For example, if someone accidentally deleted the Marketing OU in the cpandl.com domain, you could restore the OU and all the objects it contained by typing the command **restore subtree ou=marketing,dc=cpandl,dc=com**.

   - You can authoritatively restore an individual object by typing **restore object ObjectDN**, where *ObjectDN* is the distinguished name of the object to restore. For example, if someone accidentally deleted the Sales group from the default container for users and groups (cn=users) in the cpandl.com domain, you could restore the group by typing the command **restore object cn=sales,cn=users,dc=cpandl,dc=com**.

8. When you type a restore command and press Enter, the Authoritative Restore Confirmation dialog box appears, which prompts you to tap or click Yes if you're sure you want to perform the restore action. Tap or click Yes to perform the restore operation.

9. To exit Ntdsutil and restart the server, type **quit** twice.

NOTE
Every object that is restored will have its USN incremented by 100,000. When you are restoring the entire database, you can't override this behavior, which is necessary to

ensure that the data is properly replicated. For subtree and object restores, you can override this behavior by setting a different version increment value using the Verinc option. For example, if you want to restore the Sales group in the cpandl.com domain and increment the USN by 500 rather than 100,000, you could do this by typing the command **restore object cn=sales,cn=users,dc=cpandl,dc=comverinc 500**.

Restoring Sysvol data

The Sysvol folder is backed up as part of the system-state information and contains critical domain information, including GPOs, Group Policy templates, and scripts used for startup, shutdown, logging on, and logging off. If you restore a domain controller, the Sysvol data will be replicated from other domain controllers. Unlike Active Directory data, Sysvol data is replicated using the File Replication Service (FRS).

When you perform a nonauthoritative restore of a domain controller, the domain controller's Sysvol data is not set as the primary data. This means that the restored Sysvol would not be replicated and could instead be overwritten by Sysvol data from other domain controllers.

When you perform an authoritative restore of a domain controller, the domain controller's Sysvol data is set as the primary data for the domain. This means that the restored Sysvol would be replicated to all other domain controllers. For example, if someone deleted several scripts used for startup or logon and there were no backups of these scripts, you could restore these by performing an authoritative restore and allowing the restored authoritative domain controller's Sysvol data to be replicated.

You can prevent a restored authoritative domain controller's Sysvol data from overwriting the Sysvol on other domain controllers. To do this, you should back up the Sysvol in the desired state on another domain controller before performing the authoritative restore. After you complete the authoritative restore, you can then restore the Sysvol in the desired state to the authoritative domain controller.

Restoring a failed domain controller by installing a new domain controller

Sometimes you won't be able to—or won't want to—repair a failed domain controller and might instead elect to install a new domain controller. You can install a new domain controller by promoting an existing member server so that it's a domain controller or by installing a new computer and then promoting it. Either way, the domain controller will get its directory information from another domain controller.

Installing a new domain controller is the easy part. When you've done that, you need to clean up references to the old domain controller so that other computers in the domain don't try to connect to it anymore. You need to remove references to the server in DNS, and you need to examine any roles that the failed server played. If the failed server was a global catalog server, you should designate another domain controller as a global catalog server. If the failed server held an operations master role, you need to seize the role and give it to another domain controller. Let's start with DNS and roles:

- To clean up DNS, you need to remove all records for the server in DNS. This includes SRV records that designate the computer as a domain controller and any additional records that designate the computer as a global catalog server or PDC emulator if applicable.

- To designate another server as a global catalog server, see the section entitled "Designating global catalog servers" in Chapter 11.

- To transfer operations master roles, see the section entitled "Design considerations for Active Directory operations masters" in Chapter 11.

To clean up references to the failed domain controller in Active Directory, you need to use Ntdsutil. You must use an account with Administrator privileges in the domain, and you should run Ntdsutil on your Windows Server. The cleanup process is as follows:

1. At an elevated command prompt, type **ntdsutil**. This starts the Directory Services Management Tool.

2. At the Ntdsutil prompt, type **metadata cleanup**. You should now be at the Metadata Cleanup prompt.

3. Access the Server Connections prompt so that you can connect to a domain controller. To do this, type **connections** and then type **connect to server *DCName***, where *DCName* is the name of a working domain controller in the same domain as the failed domain controller.

4. Exit the Server Connections prompt by typing **quit**. You should now be back at the Metadata Cleanup prompt.

5. Access the Select Operation Target prompt so that you can work your way through Active Directory from a target domain to a target site to the actual domain controller you want to remove. Type **select operation target**.

6. List all the sites in the forest by typing **list sites** and then type **select site *Number***, where *Number* is the number of the site containing the failed domain controller.

7. List all the domains in the site by typing **list domains in site** and then type **select domain *Number***, where *Number* is the number of the domain containing the failed domain controller.

8. List all the domain controllers in the selected domain and site by typing **list servers in site** and then type **select server *Number***, where *Number* is the number of the server that failed.

9. Exit the Select Operation Target prompt by typing **quit**. You should now be back at the Metadata Cleanup prompt.

10. Remove the selected server from the directory by typing **remove selected server**. When prompted, confirm that you want to remove the selected server.

11. Type **quit** twice to exit Ntdsutil. Next, remove the related computer object from the Domain Controllers OU in Active Directory Users And Computers. Finally, remove the computer object from the Servers container for the site in which the domain controller was located by using Active Directory Sites And Services.

Troubleshooting startup and shutdown

Troubleshooting startup and shutdown are also part of system recovery. When problems occur, you need to be able to resolve them, and the key techniques are discussed in this part of the chapter. As part of your troubleshooting, you might need to refer to the extensive startup troubleshooting techniques discussed in *Windows Server 2012 R2 Inside Out: Configuration, Storage, & Essentials* (Microsoft Press 2014). See Chapter 3, "Boot configuration" and the "Troubleshooting hardware" section of Chapter 7, "Managing and troubleshooting hardware."

Resolving startup issues

When you have problems starting a system, think about what has changed recently. If you and other administrators keep a change log, access the log to see what has changed on the system recently. A new device driver might have been installed, or an application might have been installed that incorrectly modified the system configuration.

Often you can resolve startup issues using Safe Mode to recover or troubleshoot system problems. In Safe Mode, Windows Server loads only basic files, services, and drivers. Because Safe Mode loads a limited set of configuration information, it can help you troubleshoot problems. You start a system in Safe Mode by completing the following steps:

1. If the system is currently running and you want to troubleshoot startup, shut down the server and then start it again. If the system is already shut down or has previously failed to start, start the server again.

2. If you see a Windows Boot Manager error screen stating that Windows failed to start, press Enter to continue.

3. Press F8 during startup to access the Windows Advanced Options menu. You must press F8 before the Windows splash screen appears.

4. From the Windows Advanced Options menu, choose a startup mode. The key options are as follows:

- **Safe Mode.** Starts the computer and loads only basic files, services, and drivers during the initialization sequence. The drivers loaded include the mouse, monitor, keyboard, mass storage, and base video. No networking services or drivers are started.

- **Safe Mode With Command Prompt.** Starts the computer and loads only basic files, services, and drivers and then starts a command prompt instead of the graphical interface. No networking services or drivers are started.

- **Safe Mode With Networking.** Starts the computer and loads only basic files, services, drivers, and the services and drivers needed to start networking.

- **Enable Boot Logging.** Starts the computer with boot logging enabled, which enables you to create a record of all startup events in a boot log.

- **Enable Low Resolution Video.** Starts the computer in low-resolution 640 x 480 display mode, which is useful if the system display is set to a mode that can't be used with the current monitor.

- **Last Known Good Configuration.** Starts the computer normally using registry information that the operating system saved at the last working configuration. Generally, you'll want to try using the last known good configuration before you try other options.

- **Debugging Mode.** Starts the system in debugging mode, which is useful only for troubleshooting operating system bugs.

- **Directory Services Recovery Mode.** Starts the system in Safe Mode and allows you to restore the directory service. This option is available on domain controllers.

- **Disable Automatic Restart On System Failure.** Prevents the operating system from automatically restarting after an operating system crash.

- **Disable Driver Signature Enforcement.** Starts the computer in Safe Mode without enforcing digital signature policy settings for drivers. If a driver with an invalid or missing digital signature is causing startup failure, this will resolve the problem temporarily so that you can start the computer and resolve the problem by either getting a new driver or changing the driver signature enforcement settings.

- **Disable Early Launch Anti-Malware Driver.** Starts the computer in Safe Mode without initiating an anti-malware driver. This prevents an anti-malware driver from blocking a critical driver that might be needed for startup.

5. If a problem doesn't reappear when you start in Safe Mode, you can eliminate the default settings and basic device drivers as possible causes. If a newly added device or updated driver is causing problems, you can use Safe Mode to remove the device or roll back the update.

6. Make other changes as necessary to resolve startup problems. If you are still having a problem starting the system, you might need to uninstall recently installed applications or devices to try to correct the problem.

Repairing missing or corrupted system files

If Windows fails to start, Windows Server 2012 R2 enters Windows Error Recovery mode automatically. In this mode you have options similar to those you have when working with the Advanced Boot menu. For troubleshooting, you can choose from the following options to boot the system: Safe Mode, Safe Mode With Networking, or Safe Mode With Command Prompt. You can also choose to use the Last Known Good Configuration or to start Windows normally.

If you can't start or recover a system in Safe Mode, you can manually run Startup Repair to try to force Windows Server 2012 R2 to resolve the problem. To do this, complete the following steps:

1. Insert the Windows installation or Windows Recovery disk for the hardware architecture and then boot from the installation disk by pressing a key when prompted. If the server doesn't allow you to boot from the installation disk, you might need to change firmware options to allow booting from a CD/DVD-ROM drive.

2. With a Windows Recovery disk, choose Windows Setup (EMS Enabled) from the Windows Boot Manager menu to start Windows Setup. With a Windows installation disk, Windows Setup should start automatically.

3. On the Install Windows page, select the language, time, and keyboard layout options that you want to use. Tap or click Next.

4. When prompted, do not tap or click Install Now. Instead, tap or click the Repair Your Computer link in the lower-left corner of the Install Windows page.

5. On the Automatic Repair screen, tap or click Troubleshoot. Then, on the Advanced Options screen, tap or click Command Prompt to access the Windows PE environment. The Windows PE environment gives you access to the command-line tools.

6. At the command prompt, change directories to x:\sources\recovery by typing **cd recovery**.

7. Run the Startup Repair Wizard by typing **startrep**.

Resolving restart or shutdown issues

Normally, you can shut down or restart Windows Server 2012 R2 by tapping or clicking the Power button on the Settings panel and then selecting Shut Down or Restart as appropriate. Sometimes, however, Windows Server 2012 R2 won't shut down or restart normally and you are forced to take additional actions, such as stopping programs that have stopped responding when prompted. Telling Windows Server to stop programs that aren't responding to the shutdown event won't always resolve your problem, however. In these cases, follow these steps:

1. Press Ctrl+Alt+Delete. The Windows Security screen should be displayed. If the Windows Security screen doesn't appear, skip to step 4.

2. Tap or click Task Manager and then look for an application that is not responding. If all programs appear to be running normally, skip to step 4.

3. Select the application that is not responding and then tap or click End Task. If the application fails to respond to the request, you'll see a prompt that you can use to end the application immediately or cancel the End Task request. Tap or click End Now.

4. Try shutting down or restarting the computer. Press Ctrl+Alt+Delete, tap or click the Power button on the Settings panel, and then tap or click Shut Down. As a last resort, you might be forced to perform a hard shutdown by holding down the physical power button or unplugging the computer. If you do this, run Check Disk the next time you start the computer to check for errors and problems that might have been caused by the hard shutdown.

Index

About the author

William R. Stanek (*http://www.williamstanek.com/*) has more than 20 years of hands-on experience with advanced programming and development. He is a leading technology expert, an award-winning author, and a pretty-darn-good instructional trainer. Over the years, his practical advice has helped millions of programmers, developers, and network engineers all over the world. William's 150th book was published in 2013, and more than 7.5 million people have read his many works.

William has been involved in the commercial Internet community since 1991. His core business and technology experience comes from more than 11 years of military service. He has substantial experience in developing server technology, encryption, and Internet solutions. He has written many technical white papers and training courses on a wide variety of topics. He frequently serves as a subject matter expert and consultant.

William has an MS with distinction in information systems and a BS in computer science, magna cum laude. He is proud to have served in the Persian Gulf War as a combat crewmember on an electronic warfare aircraft. He flew on numerous combat missions into Iraq and was awarded nine medals for his wartime service, including one of the United States of America's highest-flying honors, the Air Force Distinguished Flying Cross. Currently, he resides in the Pacific Northwest with his wife and children.

William recently rediscovered his love of the great outdoors. When he's not writing, he can be found hiking, biking, backpacking, traveling, or trekking in search of adventure with his family! In his spare time, William writes books for children, including *The Bugville Critters Explore the Solar System* and *The Bugville Critters Go on Vacation*.

Find William on Twitter at *www.twitter.com/WilliamStanek* and on Facebook at *www.facebook .com/William.Stanek.Author*.

Now that you've read the book...

Tell us what you think!

Was it useful?
Did it teach you what you wanted to learn?
Was there room for improvement?

Let us know at http://aka.ms/tellpress

Your feedback goes directly to the staff at Microsoft Press,
and we read every one of your responses. Thanks in advance!